THE SPACE-AGE PRESIDENCY OF JOHN F. KENNEDY

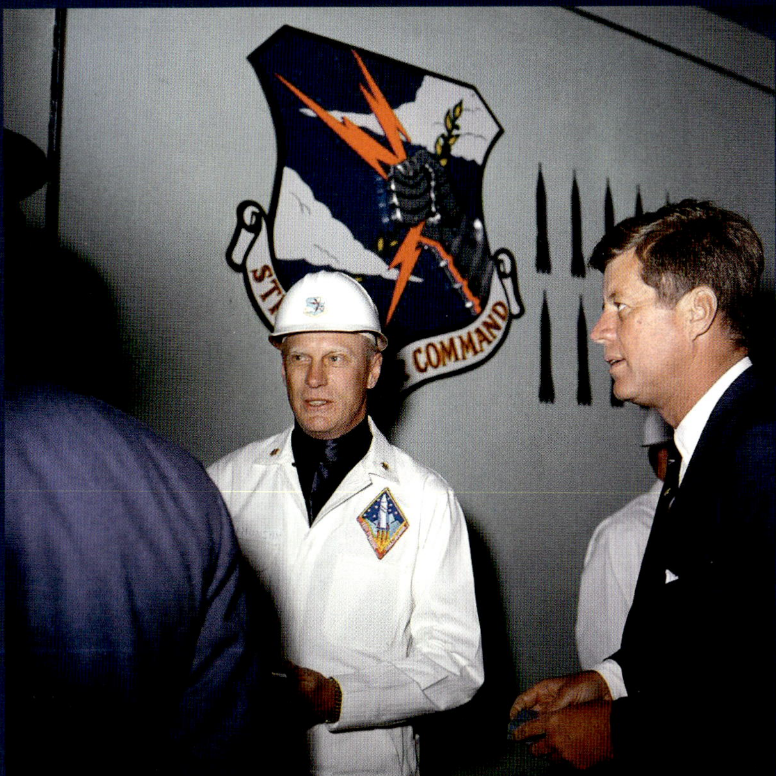

THE SPACE-AGE PRESIDENCY

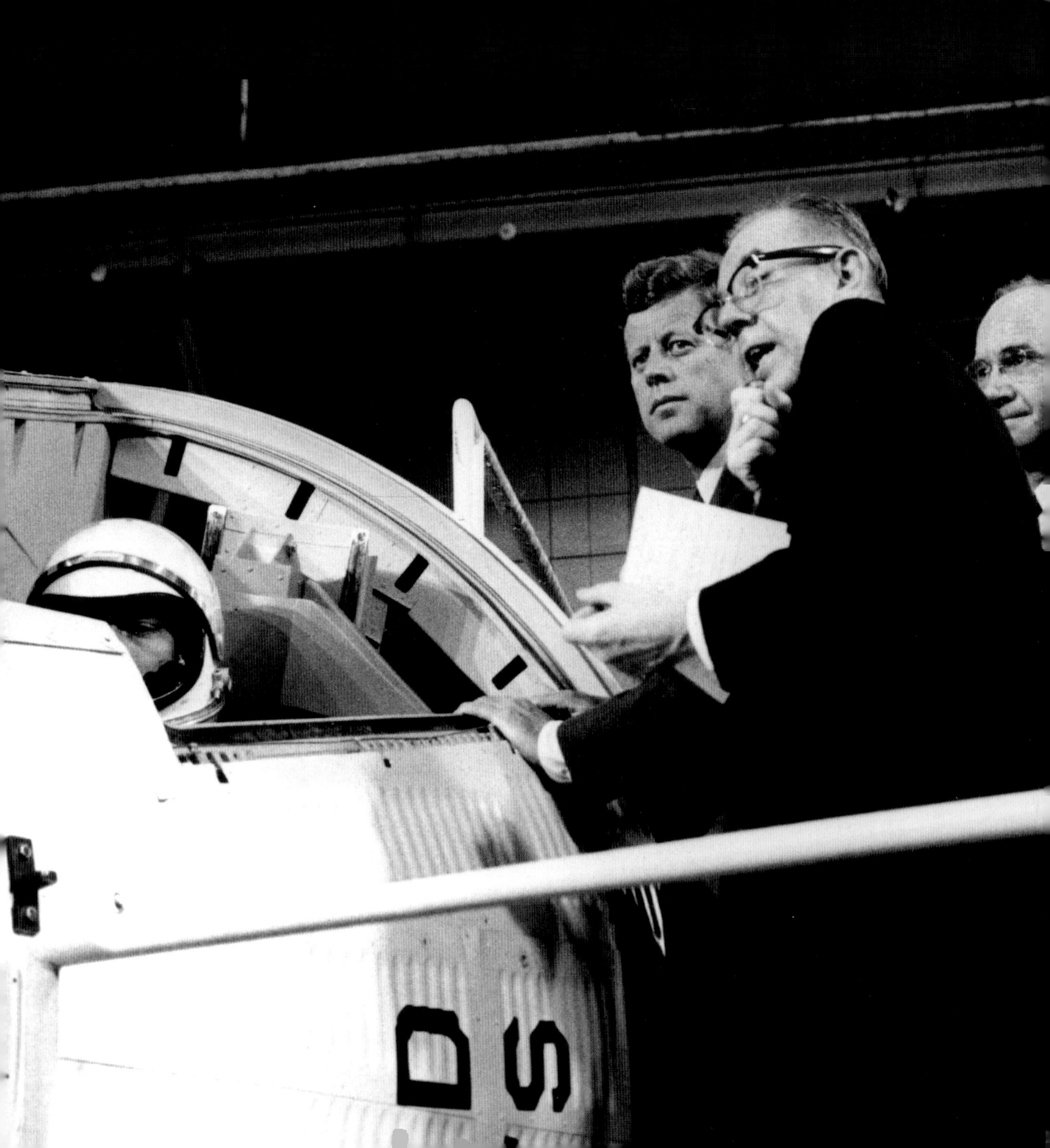

OF JOHN F. KENNEDY

A Rare Photographic History

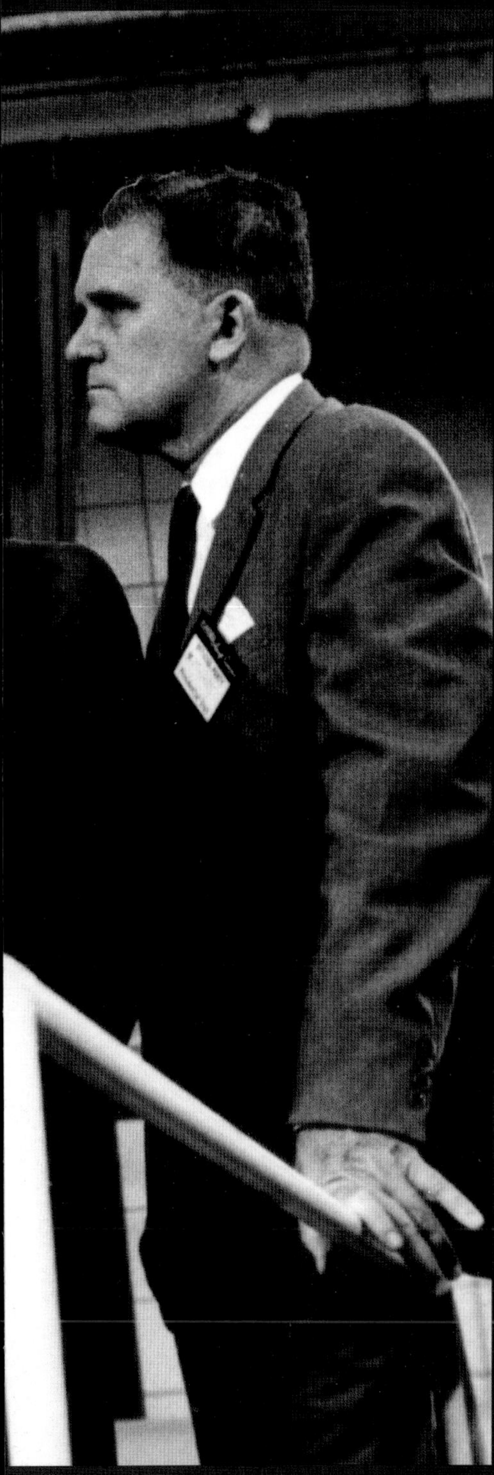

JOHN BISNEY AND J. L. PICKERING

Foreword by Christopher C. Kraft Jr.

University of New Mexico Press · Albuquerque

Printed in Korea

ISBN 978-0-8263-5809-7 (CLOTH)
ISBN 978-0-8263-5810-3 (E-BOOK)

Library of Congress Cataloging-in-Publication data is on file with the Library of Congress

Cover illustration courtesy of the John F. Kennedy Presidential Library and Museum

DESIGNED BY **TERESA W. WINGFIELD**
Composed in Scala Pro and Scala Sans Pro

CONTENTS

FOREWORD

AT THE TIME OF ALAN SHEPARD'S first US manned space flight in May 1961, there was great interest in the country regarding the launch and the subsequent results. The worldwide response, however, was overwhelming and unexpected. It was this reaction that prompted the Kennedy White House to ask NASA's leadership to brief the president on its present status and what the agency might be considering beyond the coming first orbital flight of Project Mercury. In this meeting, the president stated that he had been very impressed with the tremendous response throughout the world. It was obvious that he was considering how this might be used as an exhibition of the preeminence of the United States.

The NASA leaders were somewhat taken aback by the president's query but told him that they had been giving some thought to a manned flight around the moon and that with a large increase in their budget, it might be possible to perform such a difficult mission in maybe ten years. It was obvious that the president liked this idea, and he asked immediately, "Why just fly around the moon? Why not land?" That question spawned the eventual goal for Project Apollo. It took a while to arrive at that point, but the president made two speeches committing the nation to a lunar landing program—one before Congress and one at Rice University in Houston. These two speeches are part of one of the greatest decisions made in US history.

Another great aspect about President Kennedy was the inspiration he provided to Apollo, not only to those directly involved in the program but to the American people in general—surely this made him one of the greatest leaders of all time. (I was honored to receive the John F. Kennedy Astronautics Award for 1996.)

This book is a chronicle of the president's visits throughout the United States to several locations where the work toward Apollo was taking place. Many directly involved with NASA and the aerospace industry are seen briefing the president on their activities. This was no small task because of the thousands of people involved. There was hardly a state in the country where Apollo was not represented (an indication of the large economic and scientific impact of the program). At the peak of the Apollo program, approximately four hundred thousand people were involved. It was my privilege to serve as the flight director during all six of the manned Mercury missions, and subsequently first as the director of Flight Operations at the Manned Spacecraft Center and later as the center director.

From a personal point of view, I considered President Kennedy one of the finest leaders I have known. At the time I thought he was divinely inspired, and his assassination was a terrible blow to all of us. For that reason I give President Lyndon Johnson high praise for continuing the Apollo program.

DR. CHRISTOPHER C. KRAFT JR.
Houston, Texas

ACKNOWLEDGMENTS

WE WOULD LIKE TO EXTEND a special thanks to Laurie Austin, Maryrose Grossman, and Heather Joines of the John F. Kennedy Presidential Library and Museum for their wonderful hospitality, cooperation, and knowledge. Our appreciation also to Jill McLaughlin and Tris DeRoma at the *Los Alamos Monitor* for their help with locating retired Los Alamos Labs workers, and to Mahlon T. Wilson for reviewing that chapter. Thanks as well to Alan Brady Carr for providing a wealth of photos from the Los Alamos National Laboratory Archives. Others who helped make this book possible include:

Zamir Ahmed
Darren Court
Joel Dahlby
Sid Davis
Jim Eckles
Harold Finger
Harold P. Gerrish Jr.
Ed Hengeveld
Clint Hill
Christopher C. Kraft Jr.
Alan Lawrie
H. H. "Luge" Luetjen
Roger McCormick
Doyle Piland
Lutisha Piland
Donald J. Prichard
James Ragusa
Morgan Raines
Bob Sieck
Reece Schonfeld
Stephen C. Smith
Kris Stoever
Jeffrey Thomas
Mark Usciak
Tom Usciak
Jonathan Ward

INTRODUCTION

JOHN F. KENNEDY'S political life was unavoidably shaped by the geopolitical struggle between the United States and the Union of Soviet Socialist Republics (USSR) following World War II. When he first ran for office in 1946, however, he could never have envisioned himself as the driving force behind putting the first man on the moon. Yet fifteen years later, it became a major goal during his presidency in a dramatic space race pitting the two former war allies against each other.

At stake was perhaps world dominance, or at least influence, through advanced military weapons systems that would exploit the next great unexplored frontier: outer space. During the late 1940s and '50s, both nations had developed long-range missiles and aircraft that could reach targets around the globe carrying nuclear warheads, creating a new, uneasy standoff, dubbed the "Cold War."

By the time he is the Democratic nominee for president in 1960, a perceived "missile gap" (a term first coined by Kennedy in 1958 and repeated during his Senate reelection campaign that year) between the two superpowers is a major national issue. In campaign speeches in September, Kennedy says, "I am not satisfied as an American to be second to the Soviet Union in sending a missile to the moon or sending Sputnik around the globe" and "We are in a strategic space race with the Russians, and we have been losing . . . if a man orbits the earth this year, his name will be Ivan."

During his third debate with Republican nominee and Vice President Richard Nixon in October, Kennedy portrays the competition as critical to US leadership:

> If we are on the mount, if we are rising, if our influence is spreading, if our prestige is spreading, then those who stand now on the razor edge of decision between us or between the communist system, wondering whether they should use the system of freedom to develop their countries or the system of Communism, they'll be persuaded to follow our example. There have been several indications that our prestige is not as high as it once was. Mr. George Allen, the head of our information service, said that a result of our being second in space, in the Sputnik in 1957, and I quote him, I believe I paraphrase him accurately. He said that many of these countries equate space developments with scientific productivity and scientific advancement. And therefore, he said, many of these countries now feel that the Soviet Union, which was once so backward, is now on a par with the United States.

Once in office, Soviet capabilities continue to surprise the young administration; the most significant of these is Moscow's accomplishment to quickly put the first human in space. It presents Kennedy with a dilemma: he recognizes what a valuable Cold War propaganda tool such stunning achievements represent, yet he had not been planning on an expensive space program and, in fact, favored cooperation in space and its demilitarization. The president would make repeated overtures to the USSR during his administration for joint space exploration, which would be met with a contradictory series of tantalizing yes, no, or maybe responses from Moscow that would never bear fruit. Consequently, Kennedy is revered today as the impetus behind a landmark achievement in American and human history: the Apollo 11 manned lunar landing in 1969.

Indeed, the genesis for this book was the universal interest and enthusiasm I received when I happened to show several fellow baby boomers some of the beautiful color photos of White House ceremonies involving Kennedy and the Mercury astronauts that my coauthor, J. L. Pickering, already had in his archives. That led us to wonder what else might be available from the John F. Kennedy Presidential Library and Museum. Once we realized we had plenty of unpublished or rarely seen material to work with, our goal became to follow the template of our previous two space history photo books, complete with detailed captions. Unattributed photos are either from NASA or from the John F. Kennedy Presidential Library and Museum, taken by White House photographers. I must repeat here what I have asked so many times before: How is it possible that no one has done this book before us during the last fifty-five years? The result is an unprecedented look at the early US space program through the eyes of the young and bold president, who saw it as a weapon in the Cold War for global superiority. *The Space-Age Presidency of John F. Kennedy* presents a broader view of his experiences beyond Project Mercury, however, encompassing the new age of satellites, space probes, and nuclear missiles. We take you behind the scenes at the White House and on field trips to military and space facilities around the country as Kennedy explores his nation's growing capabilities.

We also try to make connections among the people, places, and organizations, both at the time and into the future. We occasionally provide details about news media coverage—a key part of the public's view of JFK and space. And in all cases we have done our best, as in our prior books, to identify as many of the people in each photo as possible (the hardest to track down were the Los Alamos National Laboratory staff). We also intersperse images of various items from the John F. Kennedy Presidential Library and our own collections to provide texture.

In the news business, a minute-by-minute account is known as a "tick-tock," and the captions often do include the local time to provide an on-the-spot sense of Kennedy's activities and to show how much he accomplished in short trips. Also of interest to us are the logistics of moving the president and his party from place to place—usually involving his Boeing 707 aircraft, a fleet of military helicopters, and a number of new convertibles obtained from the closest Lincoln-Mercury dealer.

We have included relevant sections from Kennedy's speeches, news conferences, and public comments, as well as excerpts from his once secret Oval Office recordings to provide the reader with more context through the president's spoken words.

Our research turned up a few surprises. At the Marshall Space Flight Center, for example, the president was escorted right up to a Saturn rocket test stand minutes after a firing, and at Cape Canaveral he entered an altitude chamber—small details, to be sure, but these moments are absent from all written accounts and motion pictures, demonstrating the value still photography can add to the historical record. A truly surprising discovery was how a photo of Kennedy from his first State of the Union address in January 1961 has become widely identified (even by NASA) and accepted as taken during his "moon speech" four months later (we show you the right one).

In that January speech, just ten days after taking office, the president acknowledged the lead the Soviet Union had over the United States in "lift capability," which in astronautics refers to how much weight a rocket can place into orbit. Throughout his term it was a competition he returned to frequently in public remarks, always promising America would soon catch up. Three years later he finally had the satisfaction of knowing he'd been right, thrilled to have seen the first two-stage Saturn I booster on the pad weeks before its record-setting flight.

Kennedy would not live to see that launch, nor the triumph of Apollo; and although history has shown his commitment to the program to have been largely politically motivated, his space legacy lives on in many ways. J. L. and I hope this book will bring it into a sharper visual focus.

JOHN BISNEY
Seminole, Florida

ABBREVIATIONS

AEC	Atomic Energy Commission
AFB	air force base
CM	command module
CMR	Chemistry and Metallurgy Research
FAA	Federal Aviation Agency
FCC	Federal Communications Commission
HAFB	Holloman Air Force Base
ICBM	intercontinental ballistic missile
JPL	Jet Propulsion Laboratory
KSC	Kennedy Space Center
LASL	Los Alamos Scientific Laboratory
LC	launch complex
MCC	Mercury Control Center, Mission Control Center
MSC	Manned Spacecraft Center
MSFC	Marshall Space Flight Center
MSS	Mobile Service Structure
NACA	National Advisory Committee for Aeronautics
NASA	National Aeronautics and Space Administration
NATO	North Atlantic Treaty Organization
NERVA	Nuclear Engine for Rocket Vehicle Application
RCA	Radio Corporation of America
R-MAD	Reactor Maintenance, Assembly and Disassembly
SAC	Strategic Air Command
SAM	Special Air Mission
SLBM	submarine launched ballistic missile
TEL	transporter-erector-loader
USAF	United States Air Force
USSR	Union of Soviet Socialist Republics
VAB	Vehicle Assembly Building
WSMR	White Sands Missile Range

THE SPACE-AGE PRESIDENCY OF JOHN F. KENNEDY

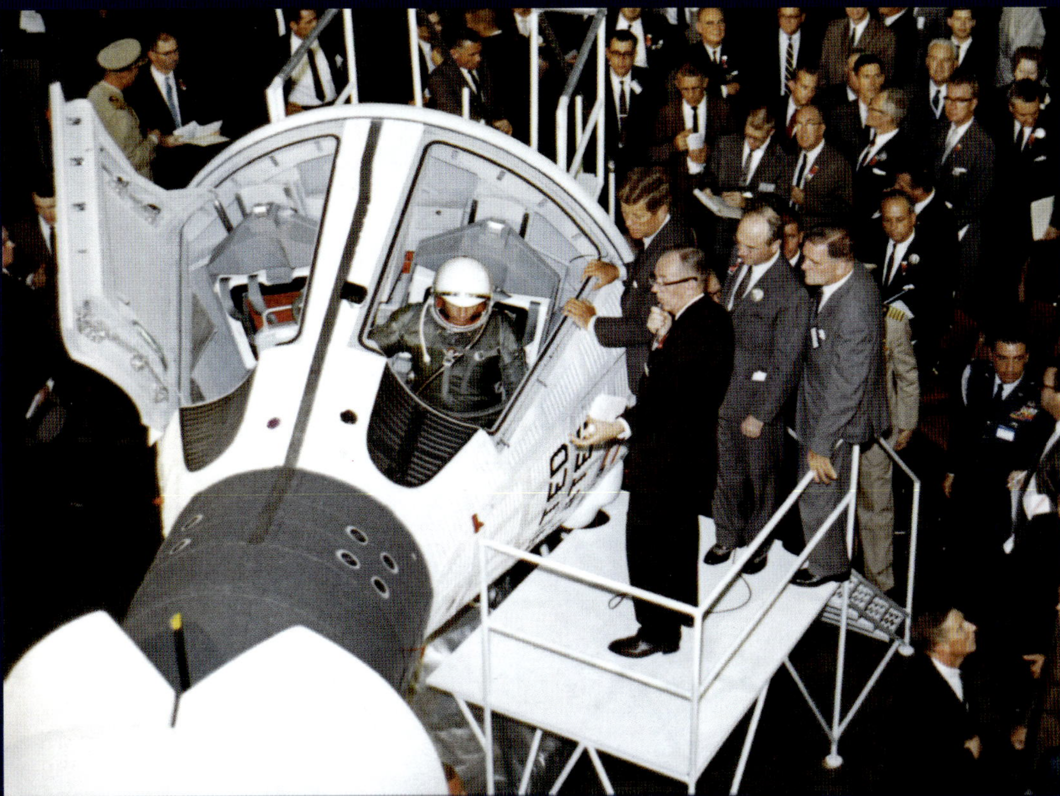

:01

1961

"Here we are behind"

WHEN JOHN KENNEDY, forty-three, takes office as the youngest elected president of the United States in January 1961, the Cold War with the Soviet Union is the central foreign policy issue he faces. Each nation deploys powerful missiles to threaten the other with nuclear strikes, and plans for a peaceful civilian space program take a back seat.

As a US senator, Kennedy did not support a manned space program. The new president and his advisors still consider it too expensive, but they are jolted into action when, less than twelve weeks after Kennedy's inauguration, the Soviets launch the first person, cosmonaut Yuri Gagarin, into orbit. Less than a week later, the failed US-backed invasion of Cuba at the Bay of Pigs adds to the administration's woes, and Kennedy asks what impressive space goals might be accomplished to help counter the Soviets on the world stage.

Vice President Lyndon Johnson's resulting memo concludes that a manned lunar landing is far enough in the future that the United States could likely achieve it first. Kennedy announces the eight-year goal to a joint session of Congress on May 25, just three weeks after the first American had been put into space: Alan Shepard had made a short, fifteen-minute suborbital flight.

The only other manned American flight during 1961 is another brief suborbital mission by Gus Grissom in July that almost ends tragically when his spacecraft sinks in the Atlantic Ocean. The Soviets also conduct a second manned mission, sending cosmonaut Gherman Titov on a seventeen-orbit flight in August. One week later, construction of the Berlin Wall begins.

In October the United States successfully launches the first of the Saturn family of large boosters being developed for the Apollo moon landing program. The Soviets that month detonate the most powerful nuclear weapon in history, albeit too heavy for delivery by a missile.

▼ Kennedy delivers his first State of the Union address at 12:30 p.m. EST on January 30, 1961, in the US House chamber.

> I now invite all nations, including the Soviet Union, to join with us in developing a weather

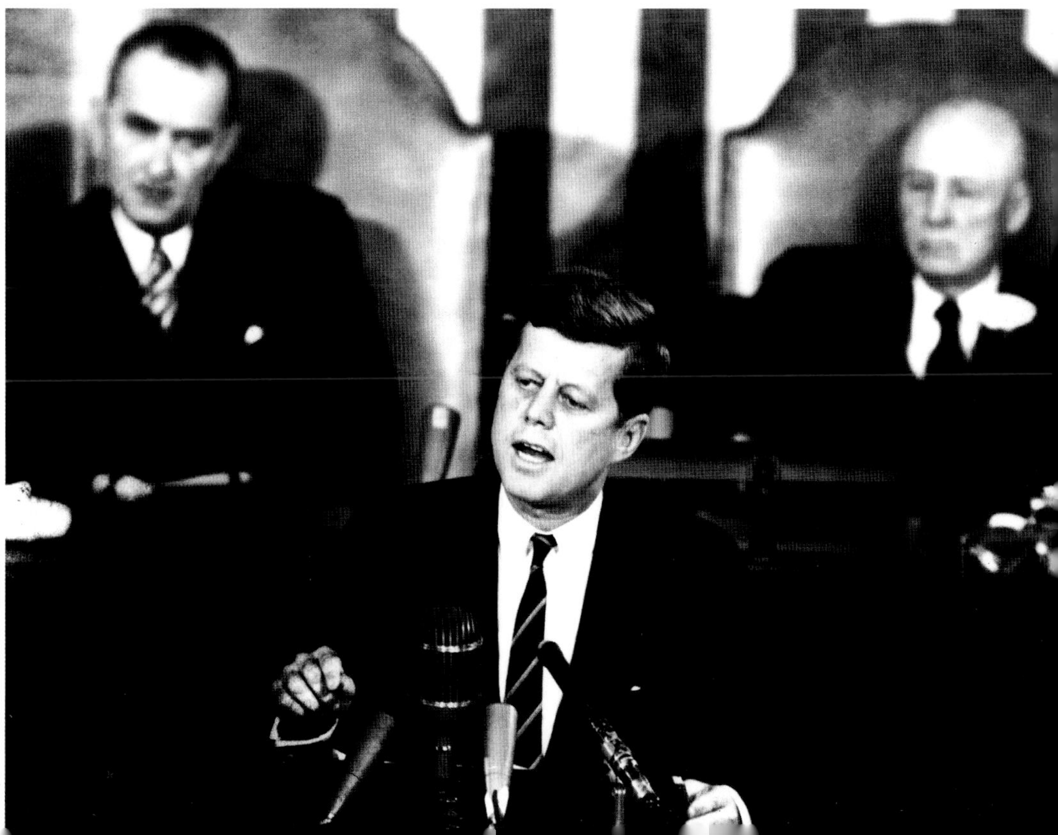

prediction program, in a new communications satellite program and in preparation for probing the distant planets of Mars and Venus, probes which may someday unlock the deepest secrets of the universe.

Today this country is ahead in the science and technology of space, while the Soviet Union is ahead in the capacity to lift large vehicles into orbit. Both nations would help themselves as well as other nations by removing these endeavors from the bitter and wasteful competition of the Cold War. The United States would be willing to join with the Soviet Union and the scientists of all nations in a greater effort to make the fruits of this new knowledge available to all.

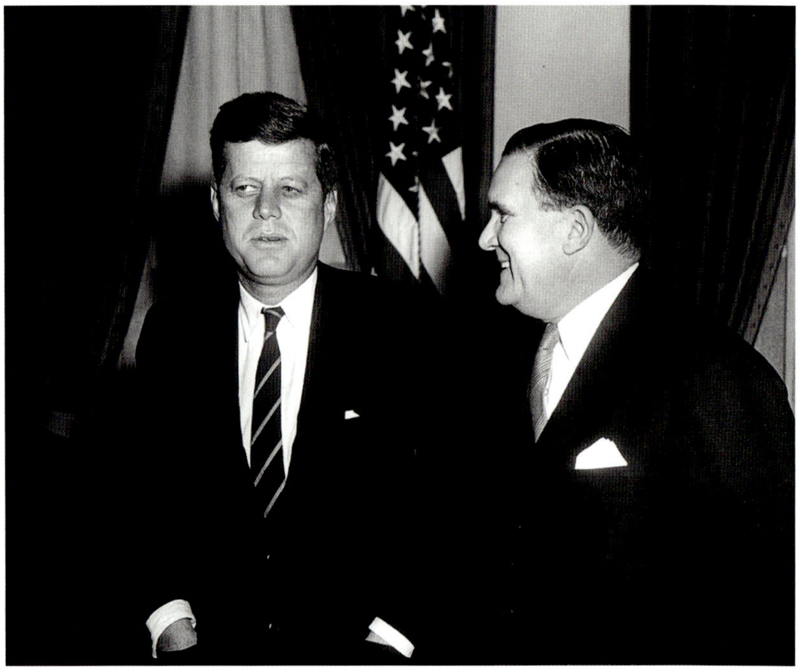

▲ That afternoon, the president meets with James E. Webb in the Oval Office and nominates him to become the second administrator of the National Aeronautics and Space Administration (NASA); he is confirmed by the Senate ten days later. Several other candidates had turned down the job, aware space was not a priority in the new White House. Webb, a former budget director and State Department official in the Truman administration, is an effective leader during the early years of the space program, but as a Democrat, he resigns in 1968 when Republican Richard Nixon takes the presidency.

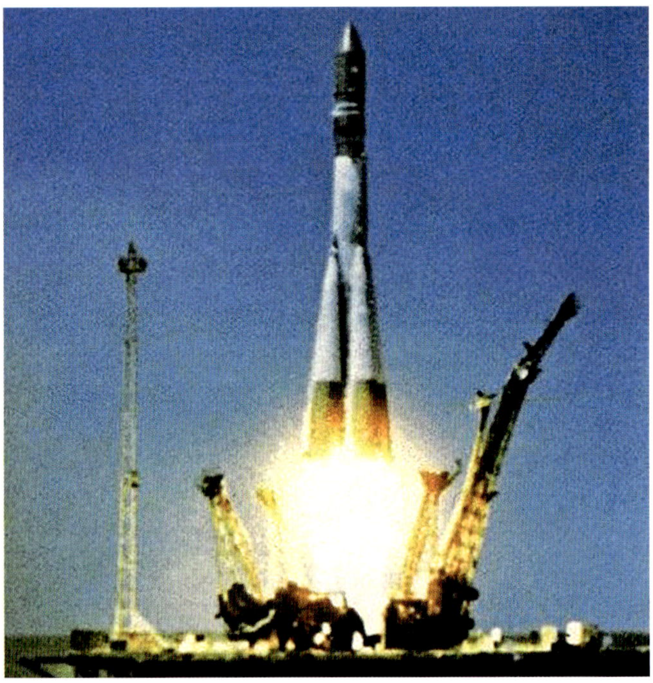

▲ On April 12, 1961, the Soviets score a major propaganda victory launching cosmonaut Yuri Gagarin, the first human in space, on a full orbit of the earth using a Vostok-K booster from the USSR's Baikonur Cosmodrome in the Kazakh Republic. It's the same launch site used in 1957 for Sputnik 1, the first Earth satellite, which shocked the West.

The previous week, US intelligence notified the president that the Soviets were likely within days of orbiting a man and recovering him, and rumors had been circulating publicly. Kennedy Science Advisor Jerome Wiesner calls Press Secretary Pierre Salinger with news of the launch at 1:35 a.m., and Salinger informs the president at 8:00 a.m., who approves a prepared congratulatory statement for the press. "The news from Moscow was thus anything but unexpected," writes Time Life correspondent Hugh Sidey. "Yet there was dismay and disappointment at most levels of the US government. . . . Now, even if everything goes off on schedule and an [American] astronaut is launched late this month or early next, the achievement will seem pallid."

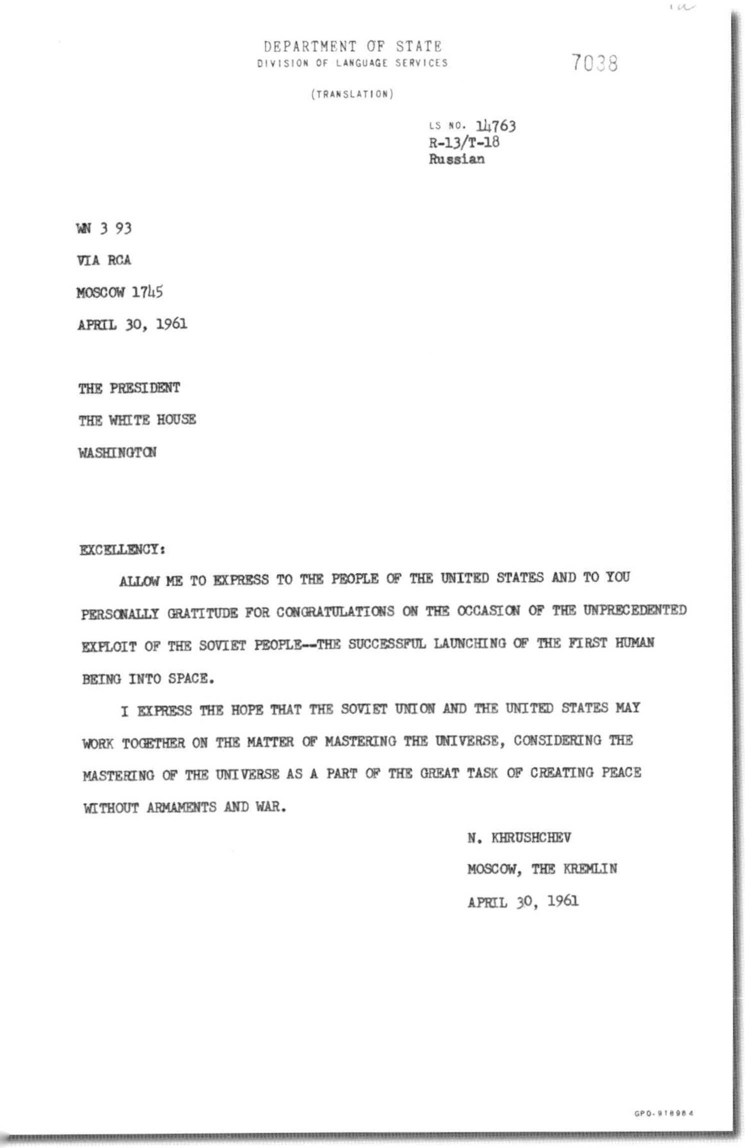

DEPARTMENT OF STATE
DIVISION OF LANGUAGE SERVICES

7038

(TRANSLATION)

LS NO. 14763
R-13/T-18
Russian

WN 3 93
VIA RCA
MOSCOW 1745
APRIL 30, 1961

THE PRESIDENT
THE WHITE HOUSE
WASHINGTON

EXCELLENCY:

ALLOW ME TO EXPRESS TO THE PEOPLE OF THE UNITED STATES AND TO YOU PERSONALLY GRATITUDE FOR CONGRATULATIONS ON THE OCCASION OF THE UNPRECEDENTED EXPLOIT OF THE SOVIET PEOPLE--THE SUCCESSFUL LAUNCHING OF THE FIRST HUMAN BEING INTO SPACE.

I EXPRESS THE HOPE THAT THE SOVIET UNION AND THE UNITED STATES MAY WORK TOGETHER ON THE MATTER OF MASTERING THE UNIVERSE, CONSIDERING THE MASTERING OF THE UNIVERSE AS A PART OF THE GREAT TASK OF CREATING PEACE WITHOUT ARMAMENTS AND WAR.

N. KHRUSHCHEV
MOSCOW, THE KREMLIN
APRIL 30, 1961

GPO-918984

◀ State Department translation of a telegram from Khrushchev to Kennedy, responding to US congratulations on Gagarin's flight and proposing peaceful cooperation in space.

▼ At a 4:00 p.m. news conference in the State Department auditorium on April 12, Kennedy is asked about Gagarin's flight that morning, to which he responds:

> Well, it is a most impressive scientific accomplishment, and also I think that we, all of us as members of the race, have the greatest admiration for the Russian who participated in this extraordinary feat. I have already sent congratulations to Mr. Khrushchev, and I send congratulations to the man who was involved.
>
> I indicated that the task force which we set up on space way back last January,

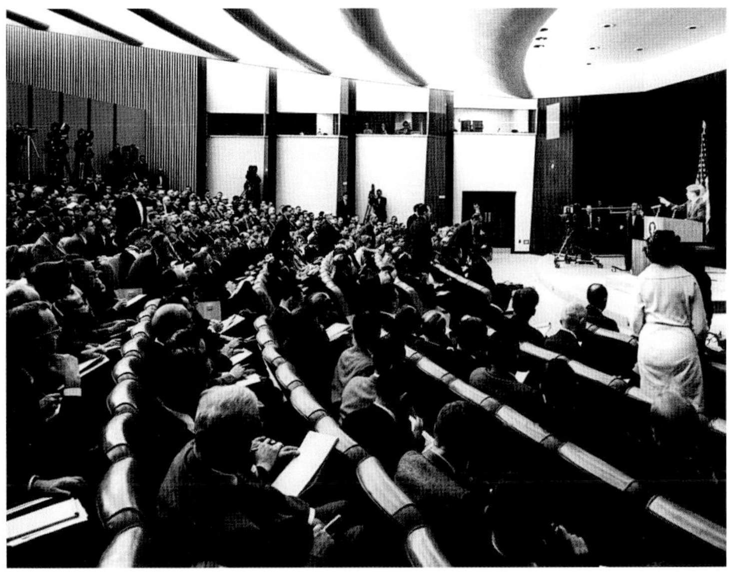

▼ Soviet Premier Nikita Khrushchev salutes the crowd gathered in Moscow's Red Square on May 1, 1961, with Gagarin and Leonid Brezhnev, chairman of the Presidium of the Supreme Soviet.

Khrushchev would meet Kennedy only once, at their Vienna summit a month later.

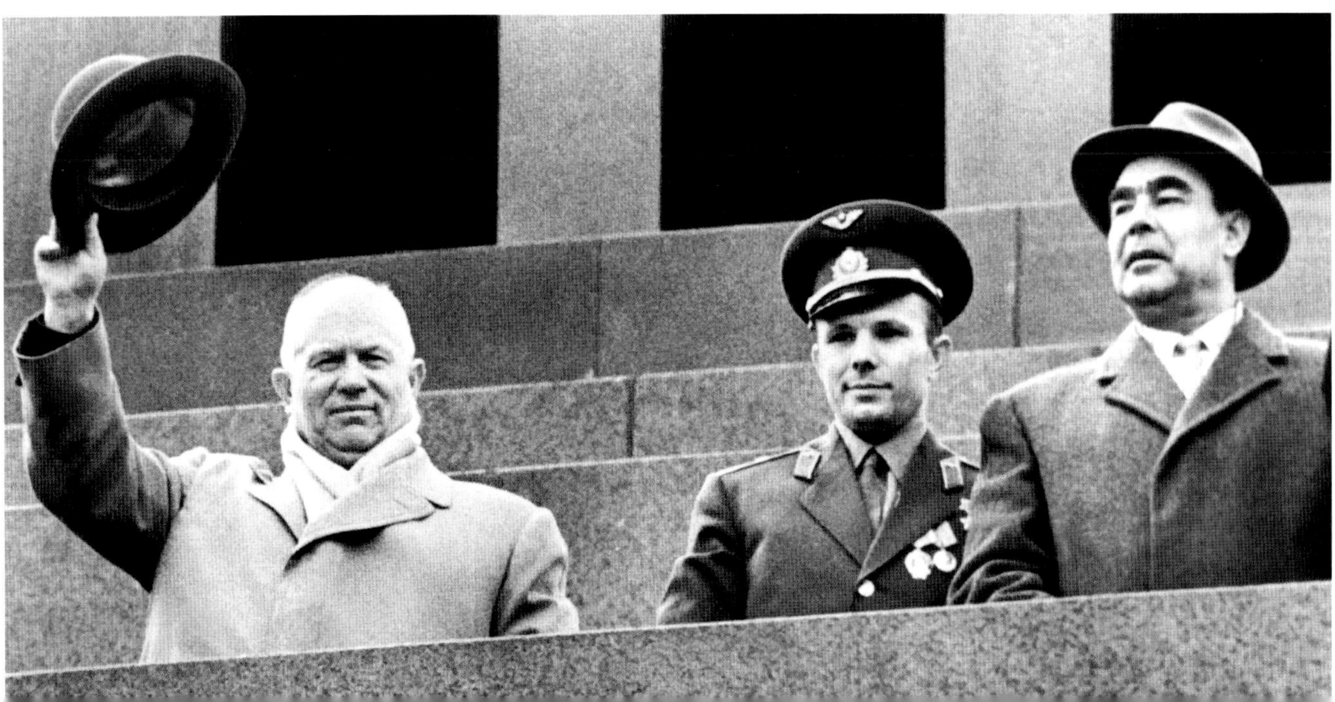

January 12th, indicated that because of the Soviet progress in the field of boosters, where they have been ahead of us, that we expected that they would be first in space, in orbiting a man in space. And, of course, that has taken place. We are carrying out our program and we expect to—hope to—make progress in this area this year ourselves.

▶ Q: "Mr. President, a member of Congress said today that he was tired of seeing the United States second to Russia in the space field. . . . Now, you have asked Congress for more money to speed up our space program. What is the prospect that we will catch up with Russia and perhaps surpass Russia in this field?"

A: "Well, the Soviet Union gained an important advantage by securing these large boosters which were able to put up greater weights, and that advantage is going to be with them for some time. However tired anybody may be, and no one is more tired than I am, it is a fact that it is going to take some time and I think we have to recognize it.

"They secured large boosters which have led to their being first in Sputnik and led to their first putting their man in space. We are, I hope, going to be able to carry out our efforts with due regard to the problem of the life of the man involved this year. But we are behind and I am sure that they are making a concentrated effort to stay ahead. We have provided additional emphasis on [the] Saturn [booster]; we have provided additional emphasis on [the] Rover [nuclear rocket engine]; we are attempting to improve other systems which will give us a stronger position—all of which are very expensive, and all of which involve billions of dollars.

"So that in answer to your question, as I said in my State of the Union Message, the news will be worse before it is better, and it will be some time before we catch up. We are, I hope, going to go in other areas where we can be first and which will bring perhaps more long-range benefits to mankind. But here we are behind."

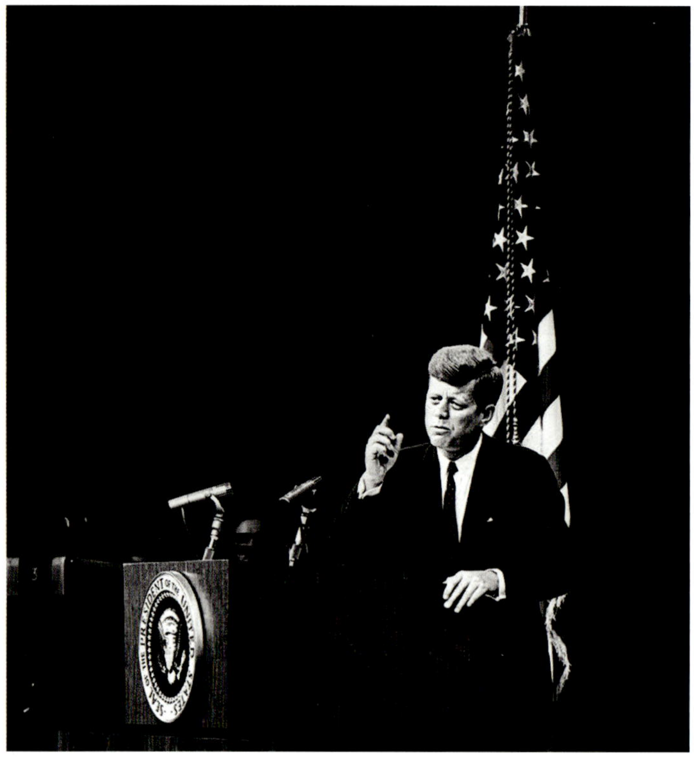

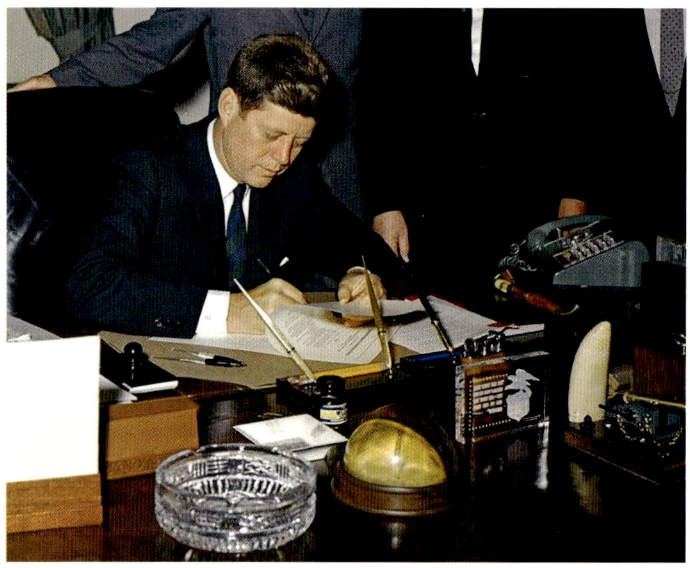

▲ Kennedy signs legislation in the Oval Office at 9:52 a.m. on April 25, 1961, to amend the National Aeronautics and Space Act and make the vice president the head of the National Aeronautics and Space Council. In practice, however, the council's role is more one of coordination than setting policy.

▶ "Enactment of this measure," the president says, "is symbolic of our government's intention to translate leadership and determination into action. I congratulate the Congress—all the members—and particularly the Space Committees of both houses, for their speed and understanding in passing this bill. HR 6169 is a key step toward moving the United States into its proper place in the space race. Prior to this, I have sent to the Congress a request for additional funds to accelerate the large booster development, which is essential to our moving ahead in space."

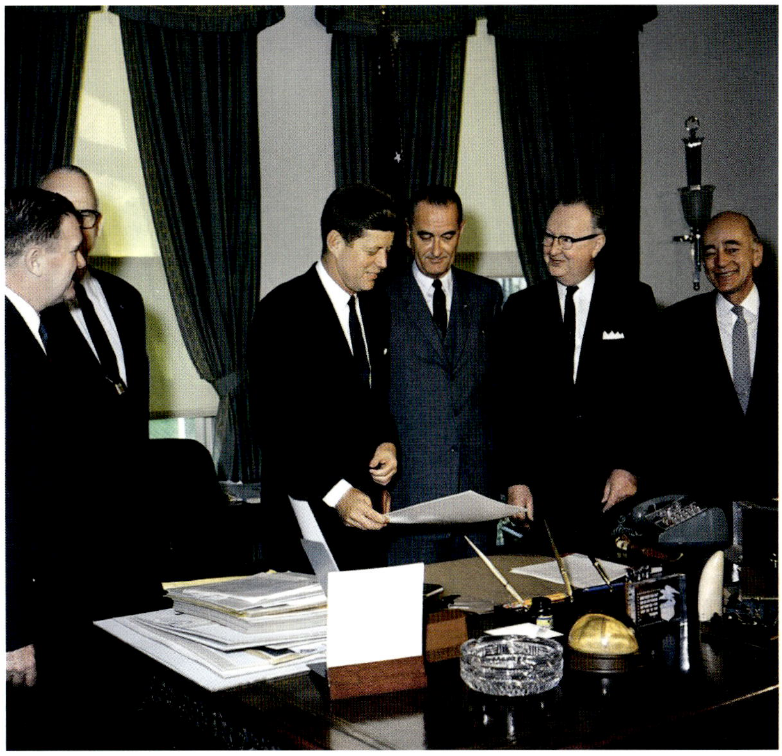

L-R: NASA Administrator Webb; Sen. Robert Kerr (D-Okla.); Kennedy; Johnson; Rep. Overton Brooks (D-La.); and the council's executive secretary, Edward Welsh.

▶ On May 5, 1961, the president's National Security Council meeting is interrupted so he can watch the launch of America's first astronaut, Navy Cmdr. Alan Shepard, at 9:34 a.m. EDT on a local TV station.

Some in the White House worried about the prospect of an overpublicized fiasco. On March 9, Kennedy Science Advisor Jerome Wiesner sent a memo to National Security Advisor McGeorge Bundy expressing concerns for safety reasons. He feared that live television coverage would become "a Hollywood production" and urged the astronaut be debriefed after landing before meeting the media. In the days before the flight, presidential Press Secretary Pierre Salinger called NASA seeking reassurance that the Mercury spacecraft's escape tower would reliably perform in a launch emergency.

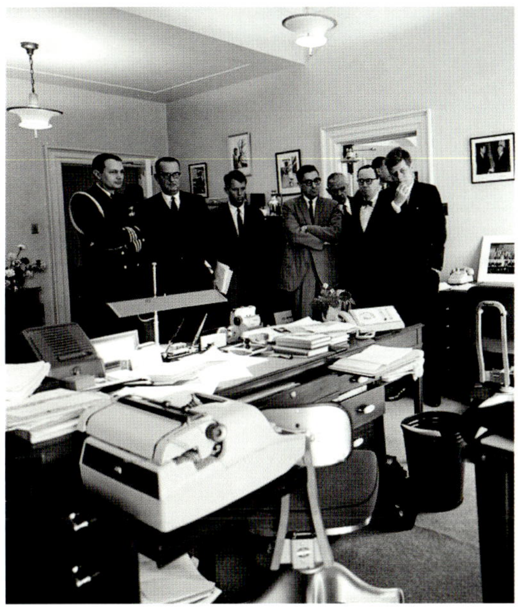

L-R, in the office of Kennedy's secretary: naval aide Cmdr. Tazewell Shepard Jr.; Vice President Johnson; Attorney General Robert Kennedy; Assistant Special Counsel to the President Richard Goodwin; Assistant Defense Secretary for International Security Affairs Paul Nitze; Special Assistant to the President Arthur Schlesinger Jr.; Director of the Bureau of the Budget David Bell (in doorway, facing away); and Kennedy.

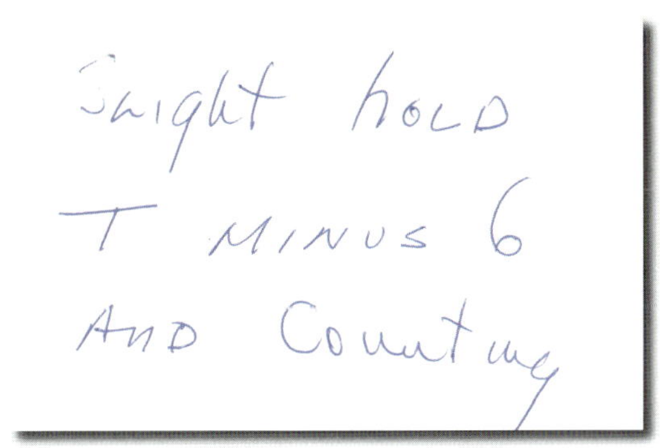

Flight hold
T minus 6
And Counting

▲ Note handed to Kennedy during the meeting.

▶ Johnson poses with the black-and-white TV set. The live televised launch stands in deliberate contrast to the Soviets' secrecy.

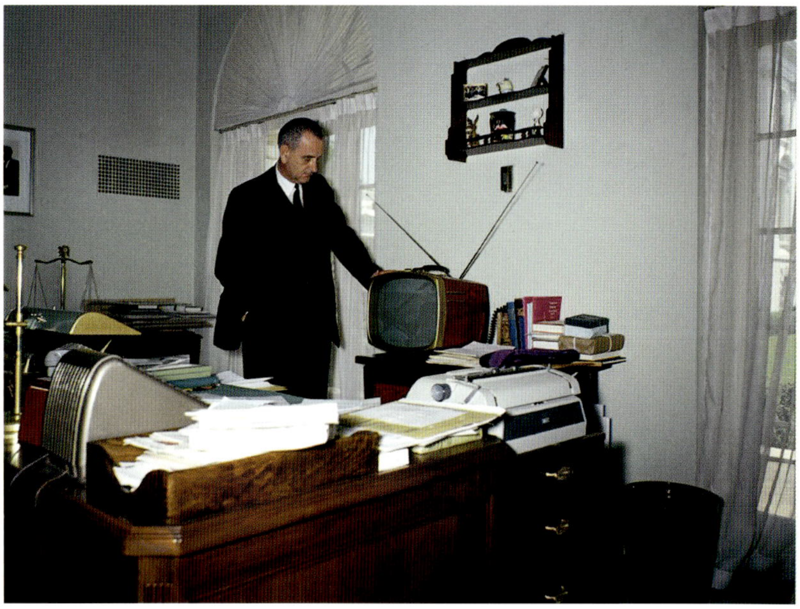

▼ First Lady Jacqueline Kennedy joins the group when she comes by the office. "As an American, I am, of course, proud of the effort that a great many scientists and engineers and technicians have made, of all of the astronauts, and, of course, particularly of Commander Shepard and his family," Kennedy tells a news conference that afternoon. "We have a long way to go in the field of space. We are behind. But we are working hard and we are going to increase our effort."

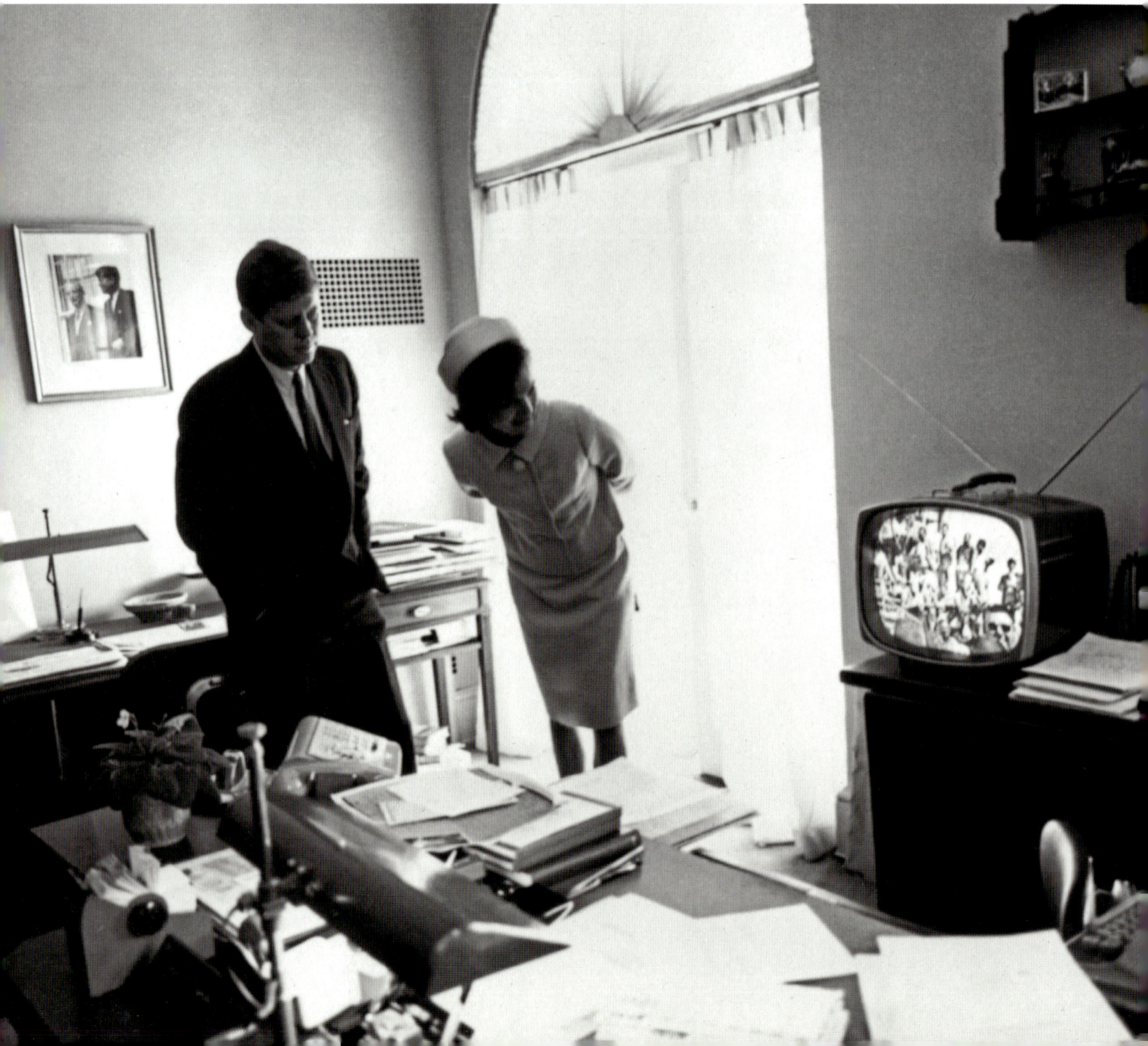

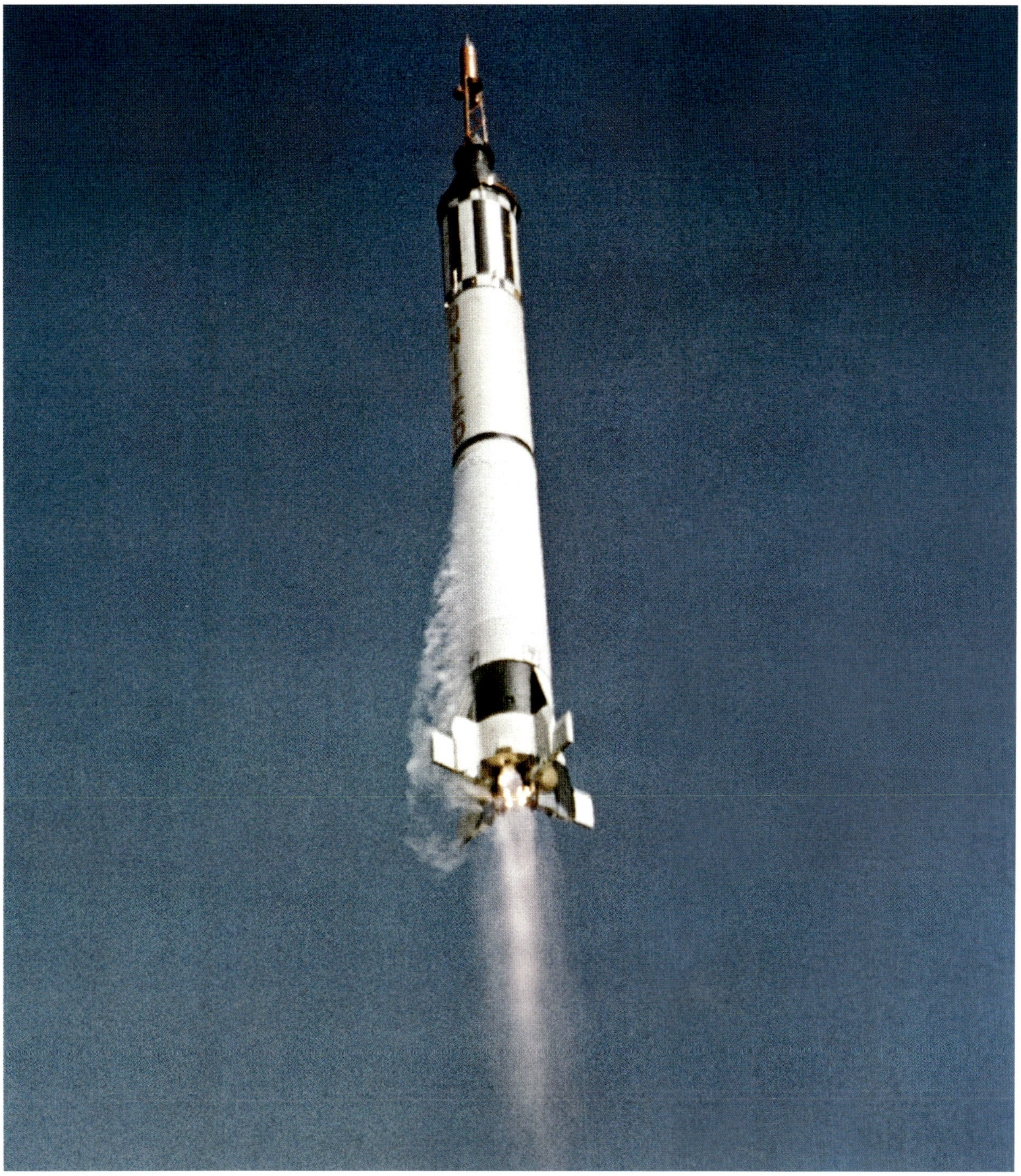

▲ Shepard, thirty-seven, is launched aboard *Freedom 7* on a fifteen-minute suborbital flight from Launch Complex (LC) 5 at Florida's Cape Canaveral Missile Test Annex out over the Atlantic Ocean atop a modified Redstone ballistic missile.

Chrysler-built Redstones with nuclear warheads had been in operation by two US Army battalions in West Germany since 1958 as part of NATO's Cold War deterrent against the USSR.

▶ Aboard his recovery ship, the aircraft carrier USS *Lake Champlain*, Shepard speaks to the president for the first time. He had been called to the flag bridge unexpectedly. "I was surprised when the phone call came through," Shepard said in 1964. "I talked first to Captain Taz Shepard, the president's naval aide, who is a personal friend of mine."

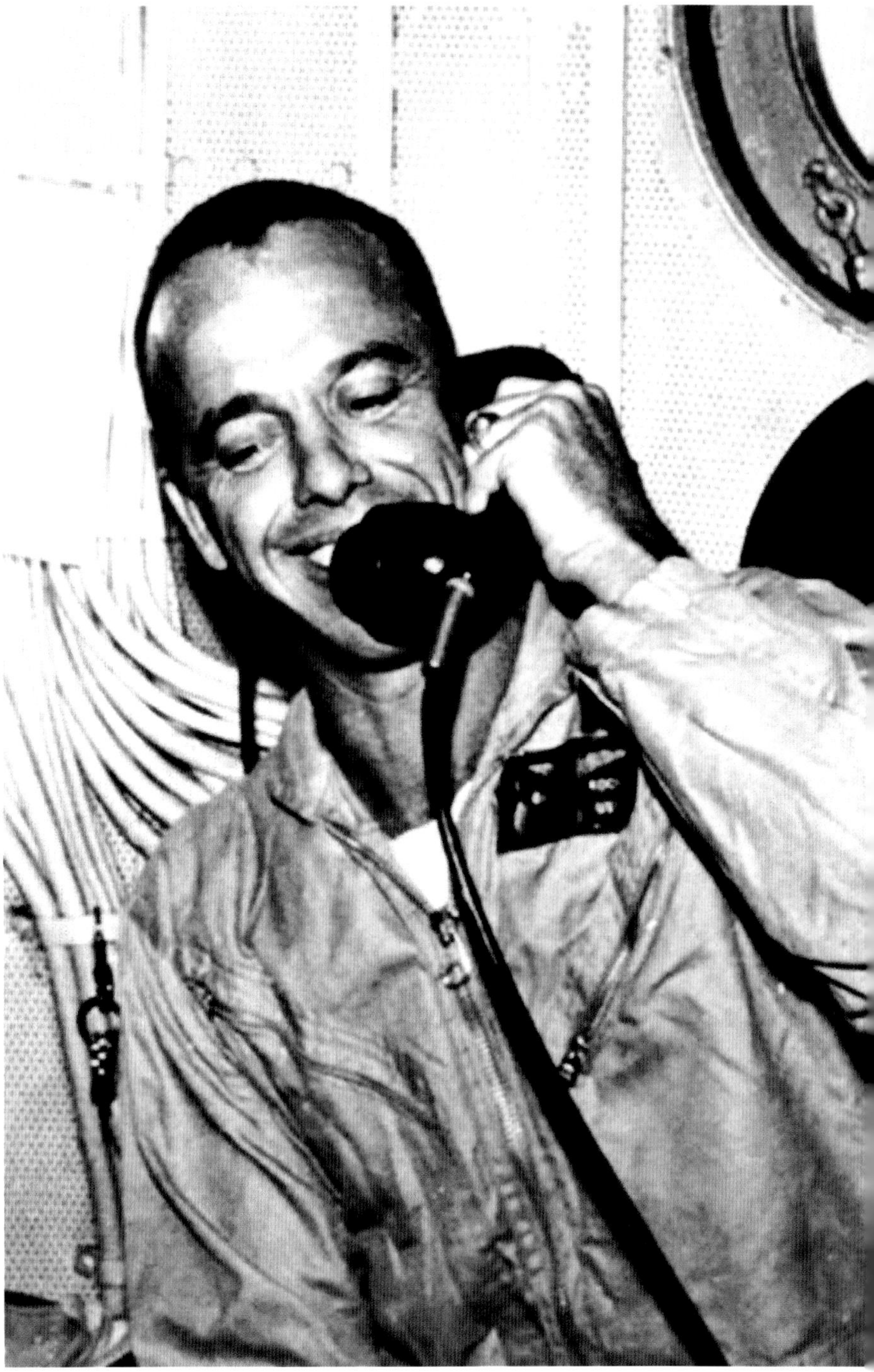

Kennedy: "Hello, commander."
Shepard: "Yes sir."
Kennedy: "I want to congratulate you very much."
Shepard: "Thank you very much Mr. President."
Kennedy: "We watched you on TV of course and we are awfully pleased and proud of what you did."
Shepard: "Well thank you sir. As you know by now, everything worked just about perfectly and it was a very rewarding experience for me and the people who made it possible."
Kennedy: "We are looking forward to seeing you up here, commander."
Shepard: "Thank you very much. I am looking forward to it I assure you."
Kennedy: "The members of the National Security Council are meeting on another matter this morning and they all want me to give you their congratulations."
Shepard: "Thank you very much, sir, and I'm looking forward to meeting you in the near future."
Kennedy: "Thank you commander and good luck."

In a 1964 interview, Shepard recalled, "The connection was very good. And then the President came on, and, I must say, I was even more thrilled at that moment in talking to him than I had been after the flight. . . . I actually had been on board the carrier for about an hour and the first flush of success had worn off to some degree, but it certainly was reactivated when I talked to him."

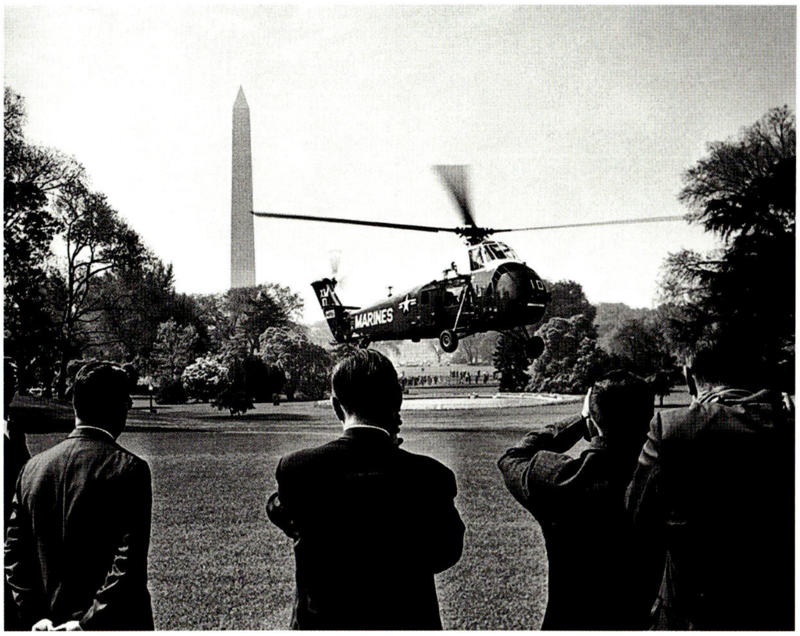

▲ On May 8, 1961, the first of three Marine Corps Sikorsky HUS-1Z *Seahorse* helicopters ferrying the seven Mercury astronauts, their wives, and other guests of the White House from Andrews AFB, Maryland, lands on the South Lawn of the White House just after 10:00 a.m. EDT, where Shepard will receive NASA's highest award, the Distinguished Service Medal.

The astronauts had arrived at Andrews earlier that morning from Grand Bahama Island, where Shepard had undergone medical tests after his mission.

▼ Three-year-old Caroline Kennedy watches the arrivals from the Truman Balcony on the second floor with the First Lady's secretary, Mary Gallagher. "Hi, mommy!" she shouts to her mother below.

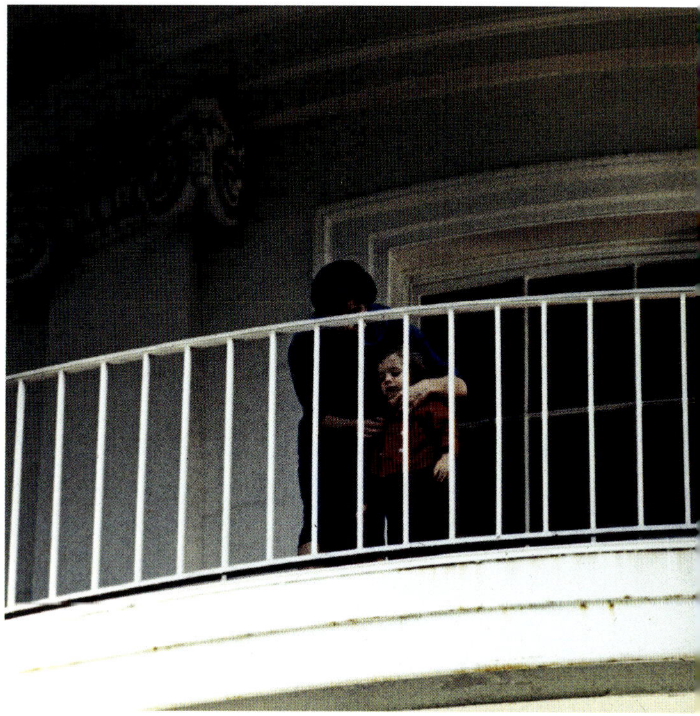

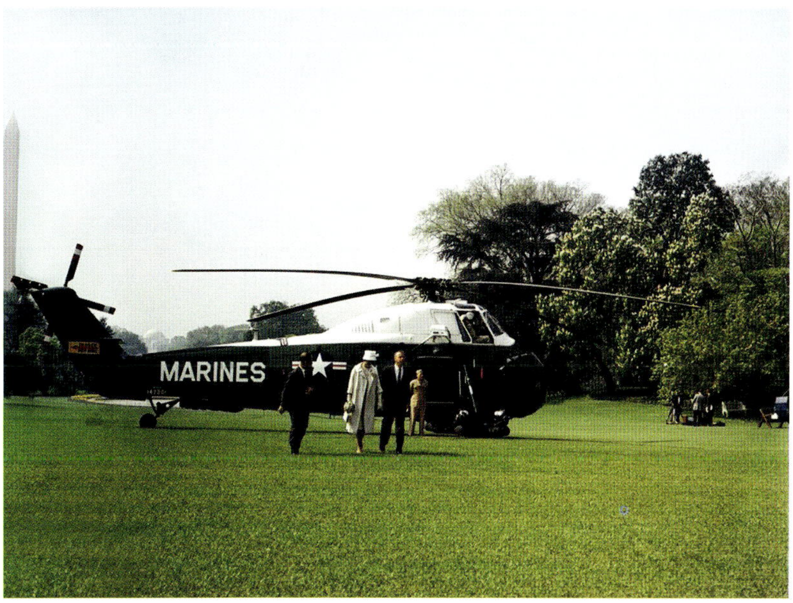

◀ The third chopper, which serves Kennedy as Marine One, brings NASA public affairs officer John "Shorty" Powers (left) and Shepard and his wife, Louise. A network TV crew is set up at right; the ceremony is carried live by the national radio and TV networks.

▶ As astronaut John Glenn crosses behind them, the Kennedys and Johnson greet the Shepards at the South Portico. Powers is at far left. About five hundred guests gather on the South Lawn; the White House decides against having a larger ceremony with a band, preferring to focus on the accomplishment itself. It's the first time Kennedy meets the seven Mercury astronauts.

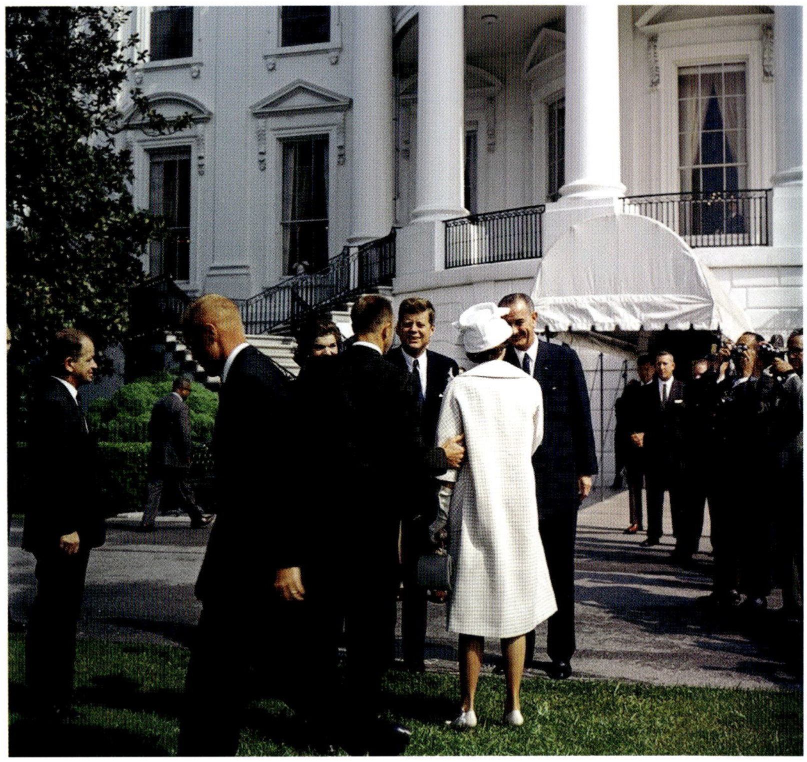

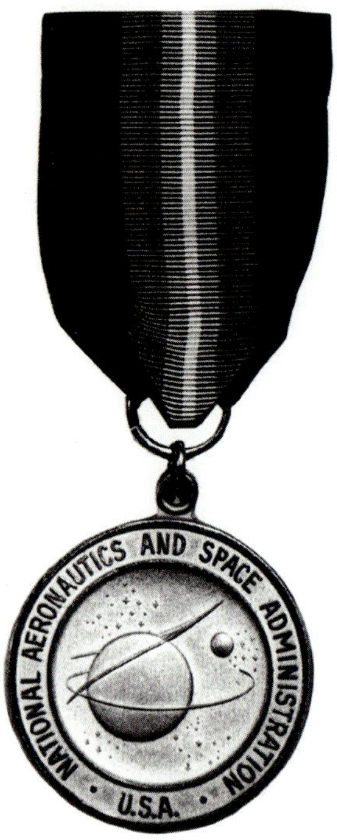

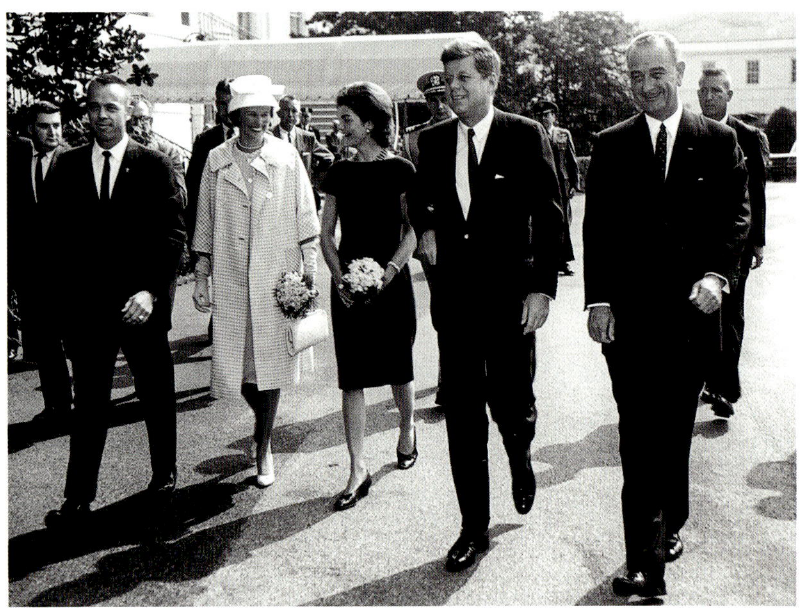

▲ The Shepards and the Kennedys, accompanied by Johnson at right, walk to the Rose Garden for the medal ceremony. The president's press secretary, Pierre Salinger, is at far left.

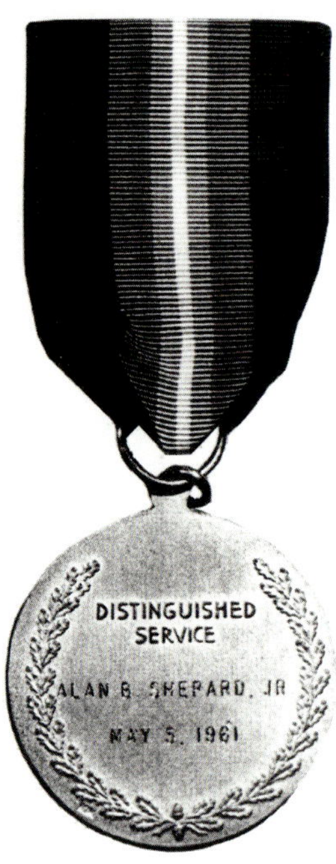

◀ Shepard receives this first version of the medal—as would the other Mercury astronauts—issued from 1959 until 1963, when the design becomes more elaborate.

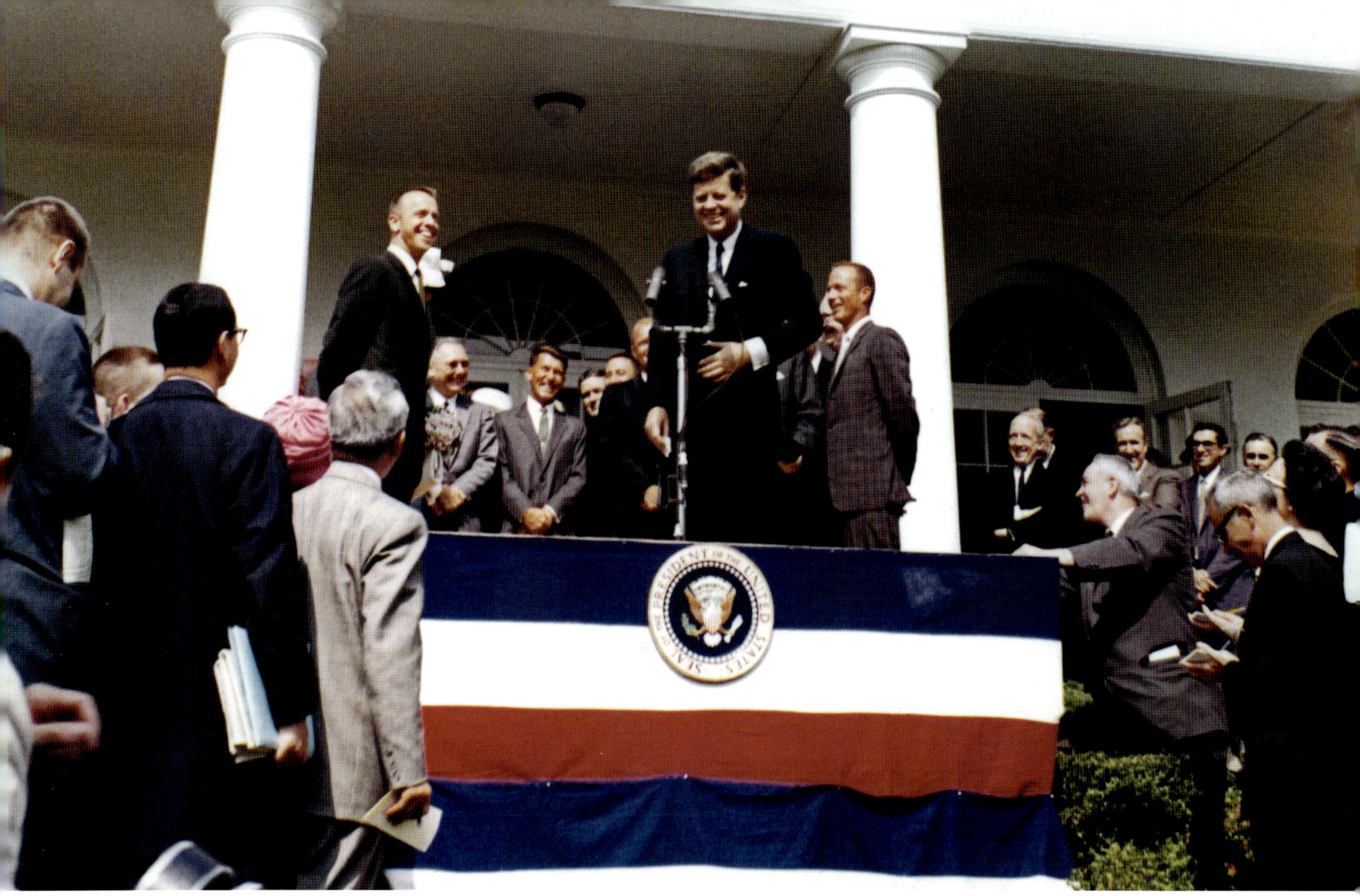

▲ The astronauts "are the tanned and healthy ones," Kennedy jokes as he begins. "The others are Washington employees." Between Shepard and Kennedy are NASA Deputy Administrator Hugh Dryden, astronaut Wally Schirra, Navy Secretary John Connally, and astronauts Gus Grissom and John Glenn. Astronaut Scott Carpenter is to Kennedy's left. Members of the White House press corps surround the platform, including Carroll Kilpatrick of the *Washington Post*, looking at his notes at right.

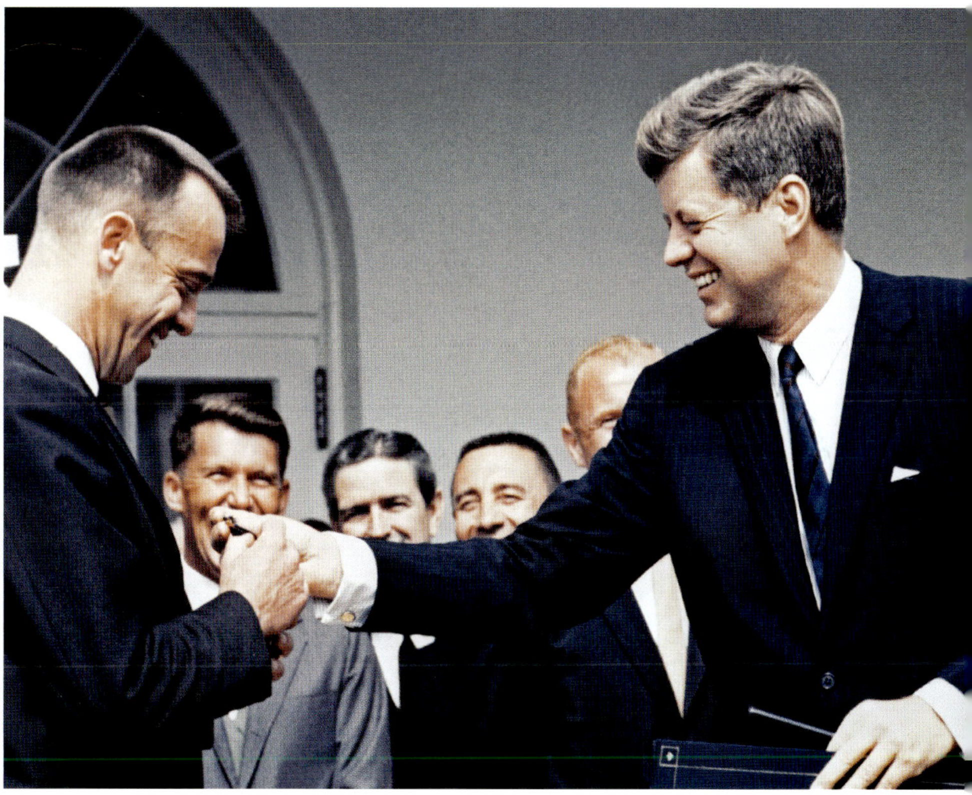

▶ Kennedy hands Shepard the NASA Distinguished Service Medal, "which has gone from the ground up," after it slips out of his hand and falls to the wooden platform's floor. "I . . . want to take cognizance of the fact that this flight was made out in the open with all the possibilities of failure, which would have been damaging to our country's prestige," the president says. "Because great risks were taken in that regard, it seems to me that we have some right to claim that this open society of ours, which risked much, gained much."

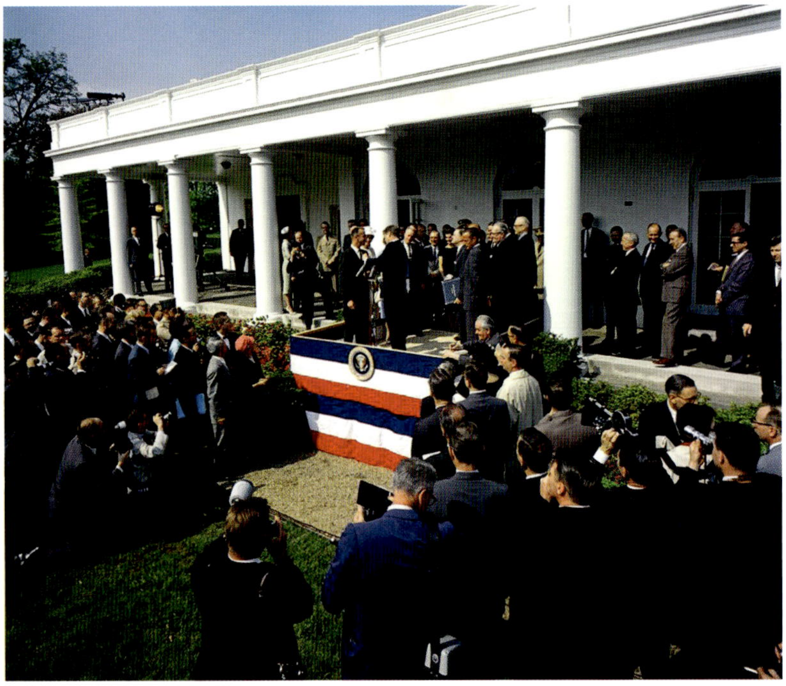

◀ Kennedy finally pins the medal to Shepard's coat only after the First Lady reminds him he has not yet done so.

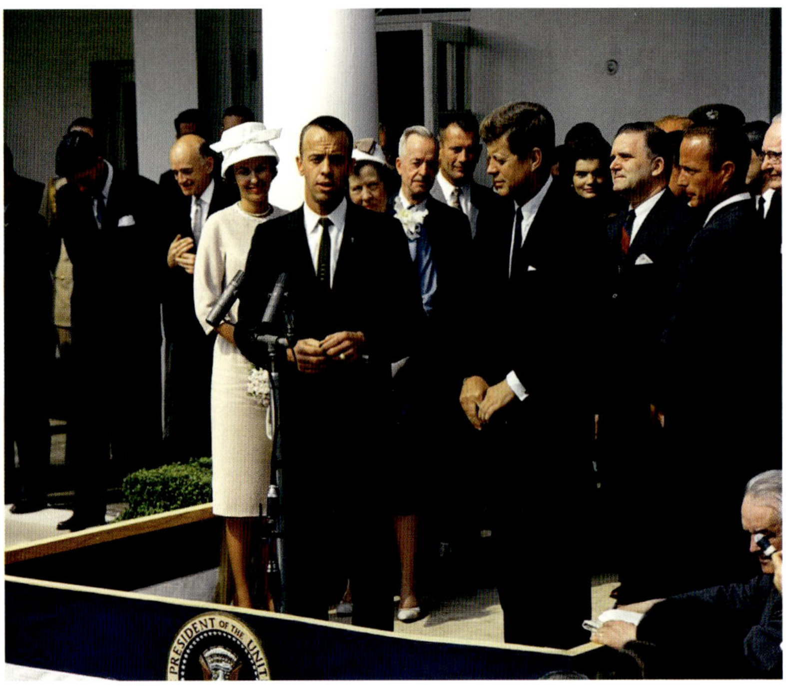

◣ "I thought that last Friday was a thrilling day," Shepard begins his speech.

> Today surpasses even last Friday, and as a matter of fact, I got far less sleep last night than I did before the flight.
>
> I am very . . . very mindful at this moment of the honor which has been bestowed upon me, an honor which is really one which should go to the hundreds of people who made my flight possible. We have been working approximately two years as you know, because of the press coverage which we've had, on a devoted effort to put a man in space. And it is really to these hundreds of people that the accolades of today should go.
>
> We are most anxious to talk with the president here in a few minutes to tell him about our flight, and I understand we have a chance later on today to tell you all and to tell the world about it. Thank you very much.

L–R: Federal Aviation Agency (FAA) Administrator Najeeb Halaby; Executive Secretary of the National Aeronautics and Space Council Edward Welsh; Shepard's wife, Louise; Shepard; Shepard's parents, Renza Shepard and Lt. Col. Alan B. Shepard Sr.; astronaut Deke Slayton; Kennedy; the First Lady; NASA Administrator James Webb; astronaut Scott Carpenter; and Rep. Overton Brooks (D-La.).

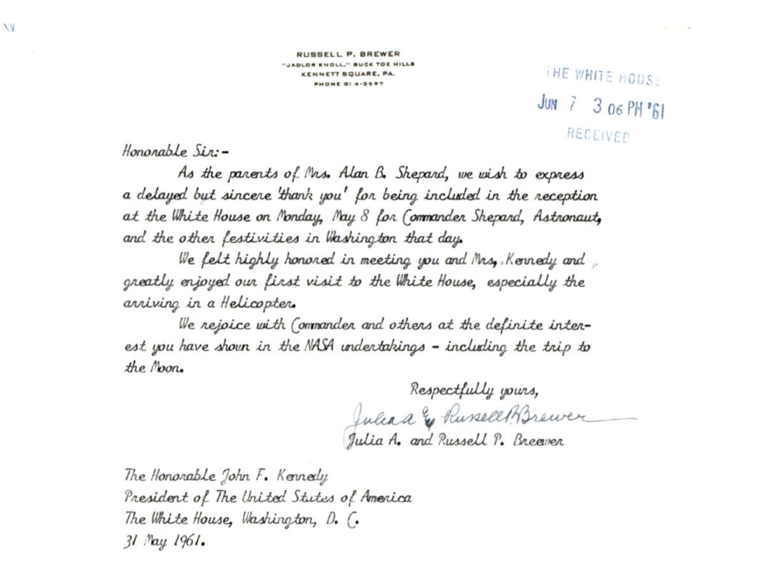

RUSSELL P. BREWER
"JADLOR KNOLL," BUCK TOE HILLS
KENNETT SQUARE, PA.
PHONE 91 4-3597

THE WHITE HOUSE
JUN 7 3 06 PM '61
RECEIVED

Honorable Sir:-

As the parents of Mrs. Alan B. Shepard, we wish to express a delayed but sincere 'thank you' for being included in the reception at the White House on Monday, May 8 for Commander Shepard, Astronaut, and the other festivities in Washington that day.

We felt highly honored in meeting you and Mrs. Kennedy and greatly enjoyed our first visit to the White House, especially the arriving in a Helicopter.

We rejoice with Commander and others at the definite interest you have shown in the NASA undertakings - including the trip to the Moon.

Respectfully yours,

Julia A. & Russell P. Brewer

Julia A. and Russell P. Breewer

The Honorable John F. Kennedy
President of The United States of America
The White House, Washington, D. C.
31 May 1961.

▶ After the ceremony the women and children gather in the Green Room for a reception. Louise Shepard accepts a bouquet as Mrs. Kennedy looks on at right.

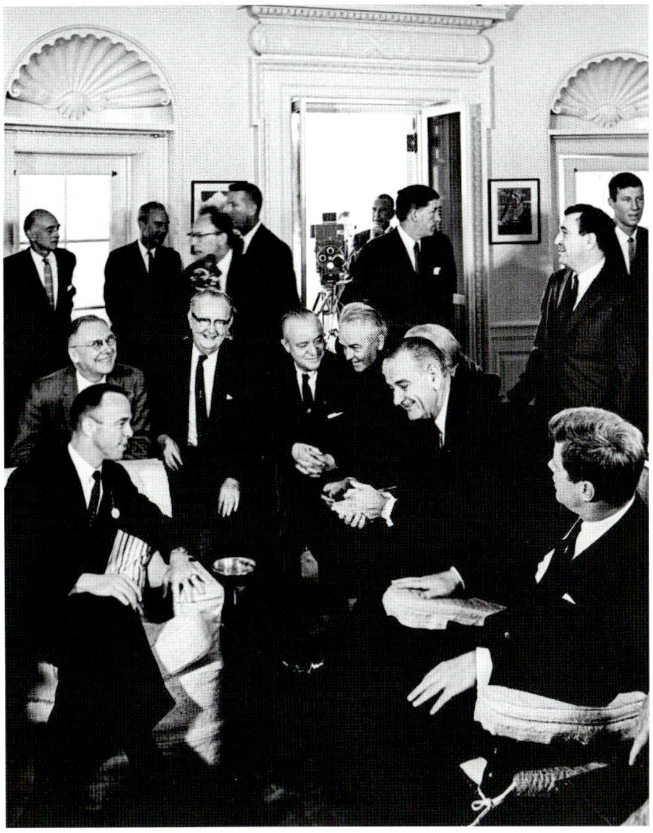

◀ The men meet in the Oval Office after the ceremony at 10:25 a.m. Much of the discussion centers on how the flight overcame concerns that a human would not be able to perform effectively in a weightless environment.

Seated (L-R): Shepard; Dryden (behind Shepard); Rep. Overton Brooks (D-La.), chairman of the House Science and Astronautics Committee; Sen. Styles Bridges (R-N.H.), top Republican on the Senate Aeronautical and Space Sciences Committee; unidentified; Johnson; and Kennedy. Also pictured: Welsh (standing, far left); Halaby (in front of doorway with head turned); Kennedy Science Advisor Jerome Weisner (standing, second from right); Secret Service Director U. E. Baughman; and Secret Service agents Arthur Godfrey and Jim Johnson.

The vice president and Bridges cosponsored the 1958 Senate bill creating NASA. A network TV pool camera is in the hallway, although audio is not permitted.

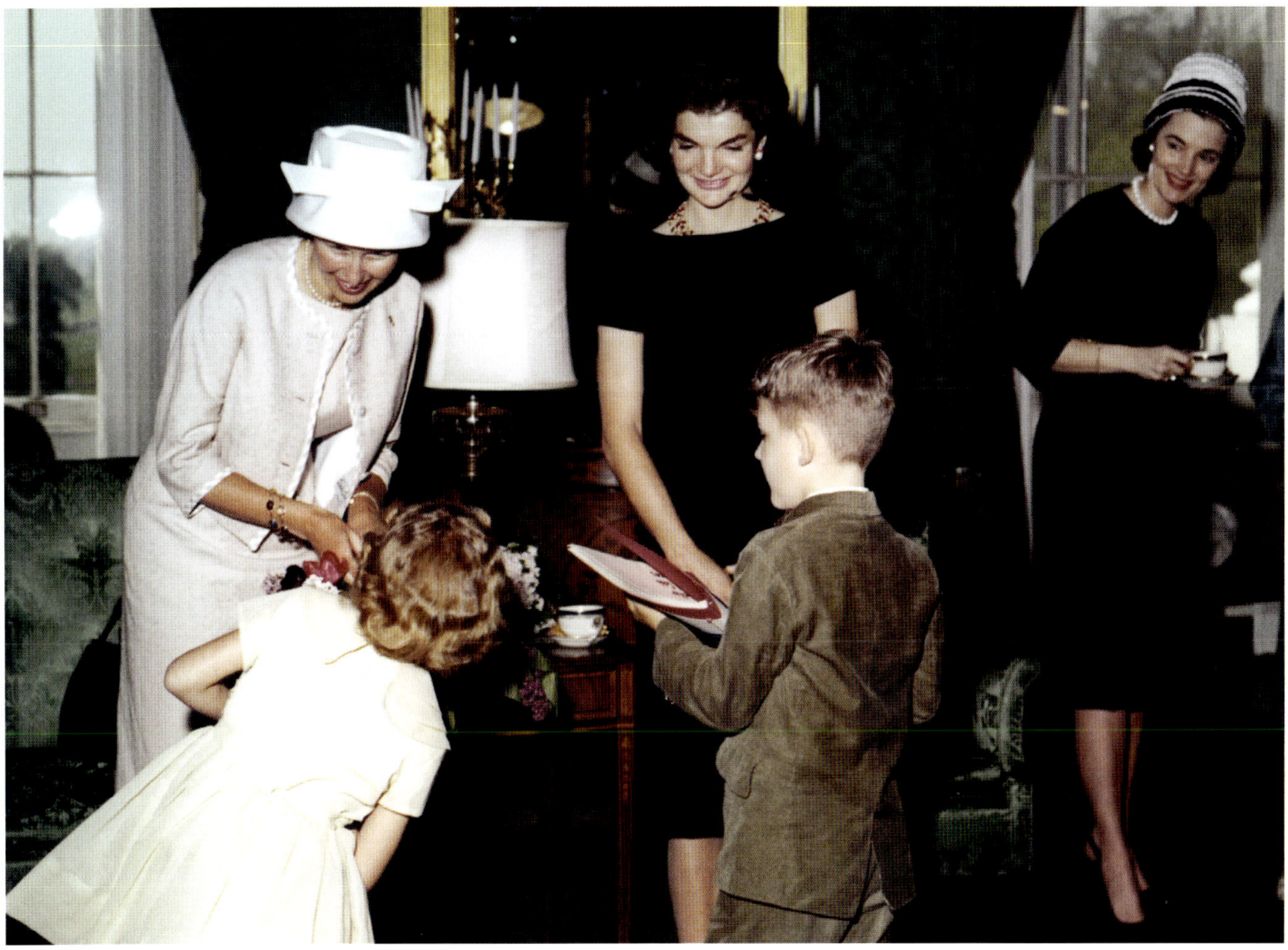

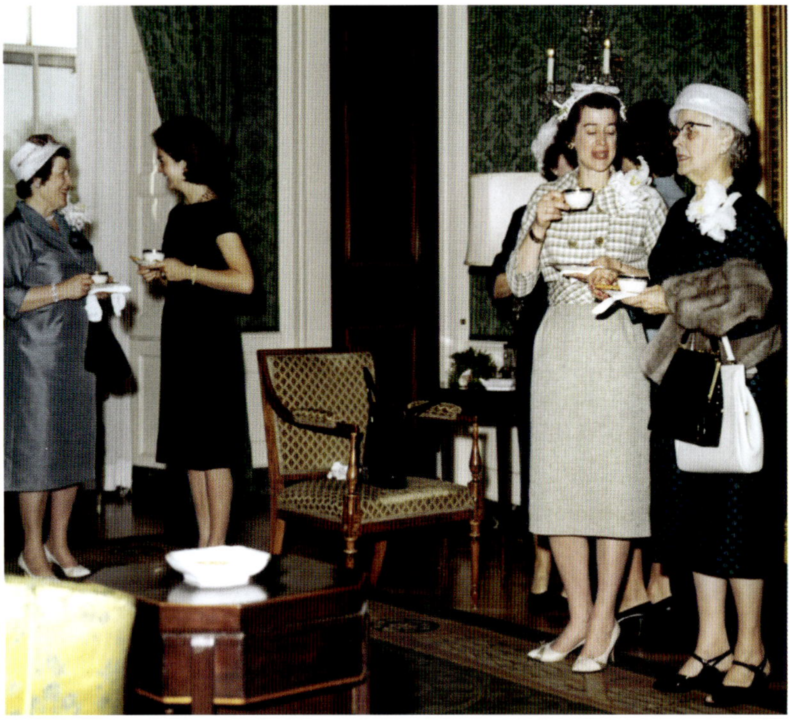

◀ Shepard's mother, Renza, enjoys tea with Mrs. Kennedy at left as Shepard's sister, Pauline Sherman, and his maternal grandmother, Julia Brewer, visit at right.

▼ The Green Room is one of three state parlors on the first floor of the White House. Mrs. Kennedy was to oversee a restoration of the room and its furnishings beginning later that year as part of a more comprehensive refurbishment of the mansion, although the Green Room changes will not be finished before her husband's death in 1963.

L–R: Shepard's mother; his wife; the First Lady; the president's sister-in-law, Ethel Kennedy; Pauline Sherman; and Julia Brewer.

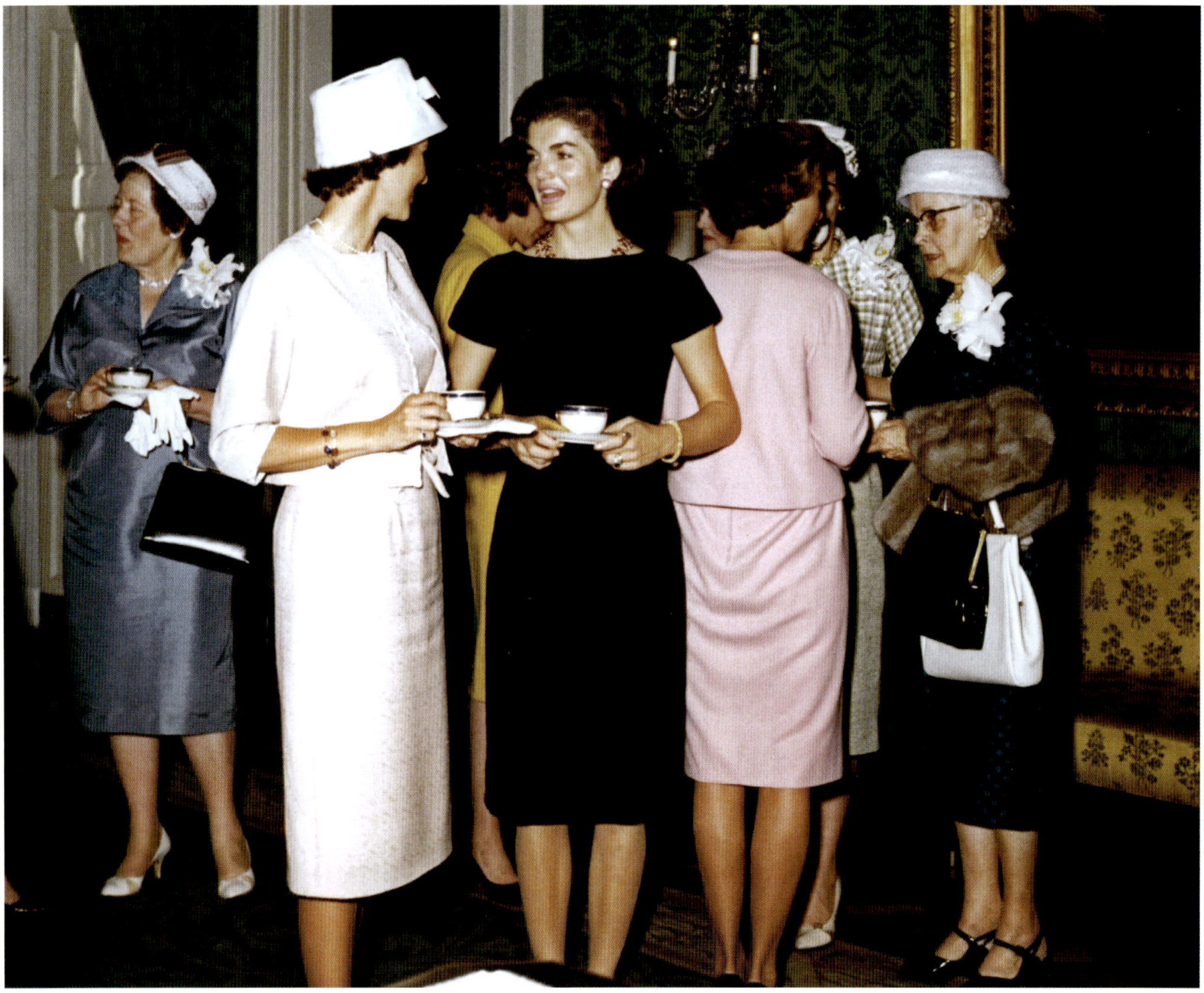

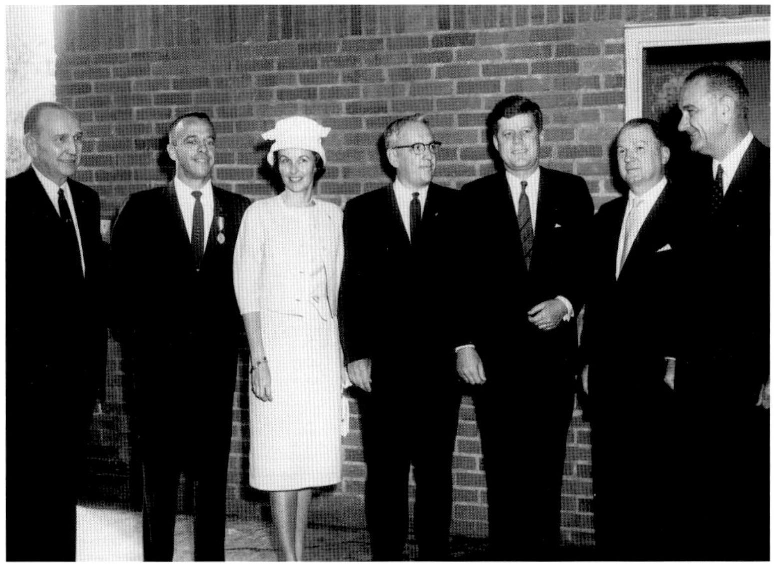

▶ In a last-minute decision, Kennedy brings the Shepards with him to the opening session of the 39th annual meeting of the National Association of Broadcasters at the nearby Sheraton Park hotel, where he would deliver a speech.

L–R: Hotel manager George D. Johnson; the Shepards; Dwight W. Martin, co-chairman of the NAB convention committee; Kennedy; Clair McCollough, chairman of the NAB Board of Directors; and Johnson.

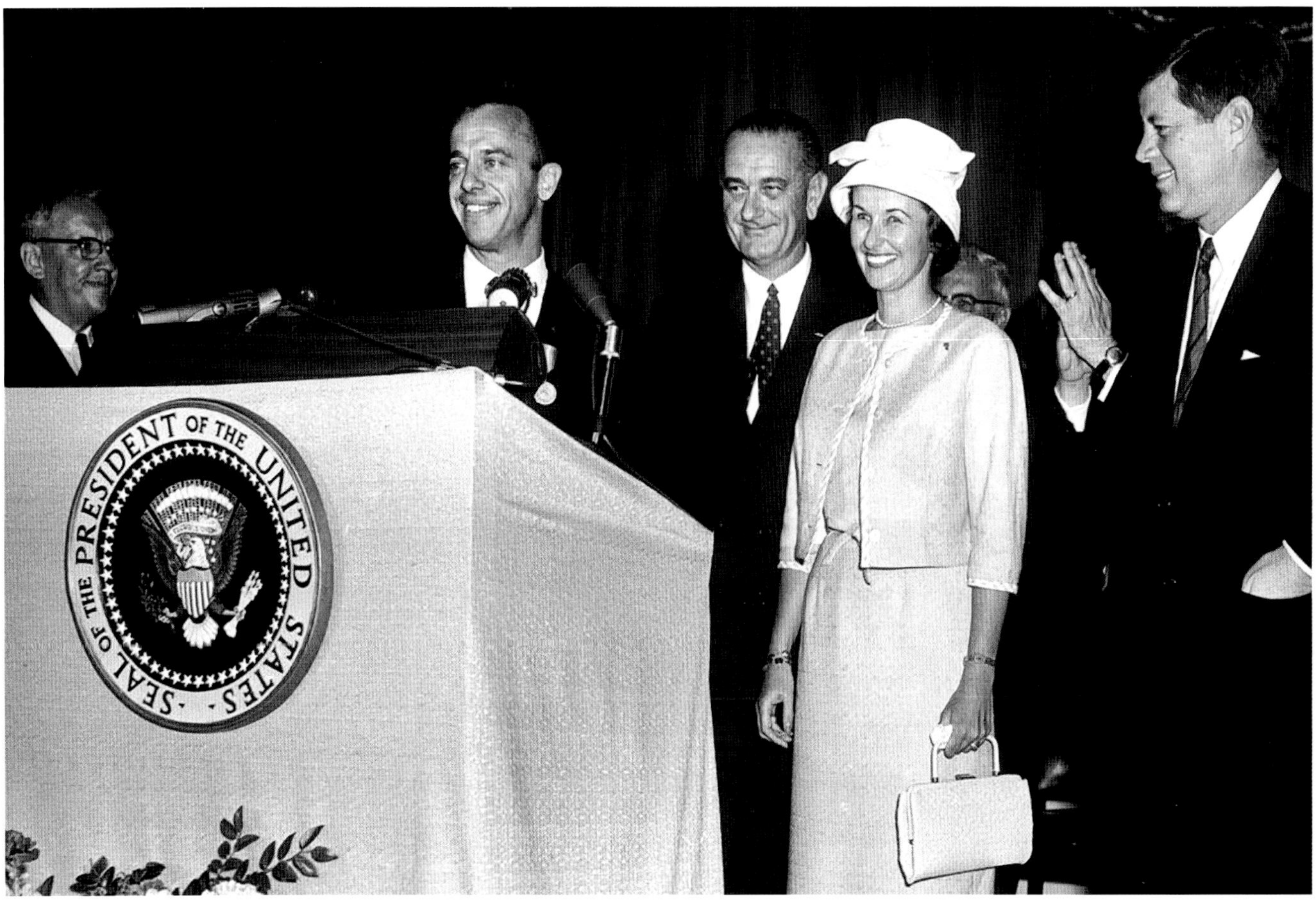

▲ "We have with us today the nation's number one television performer," Kennedy tells the convention at 11:00 a.m., "who, I think, on last Friday morning secured the largest rating of any morning show in recent history." Shepard's only comment is, "We only have time for a few words here, because I understand we have a rather busy day ahead of us. I just want to say, thank you very much for the warm welcome." Shepard wrote in 1994 that he "disliked, intensely, being used. Walking in on the broadcasters' convention with the president would be showing off a war trophy named Shepard, and it smelled."

The Shepards and Johnson then leave by motorcade for a Capitol Hill reception.

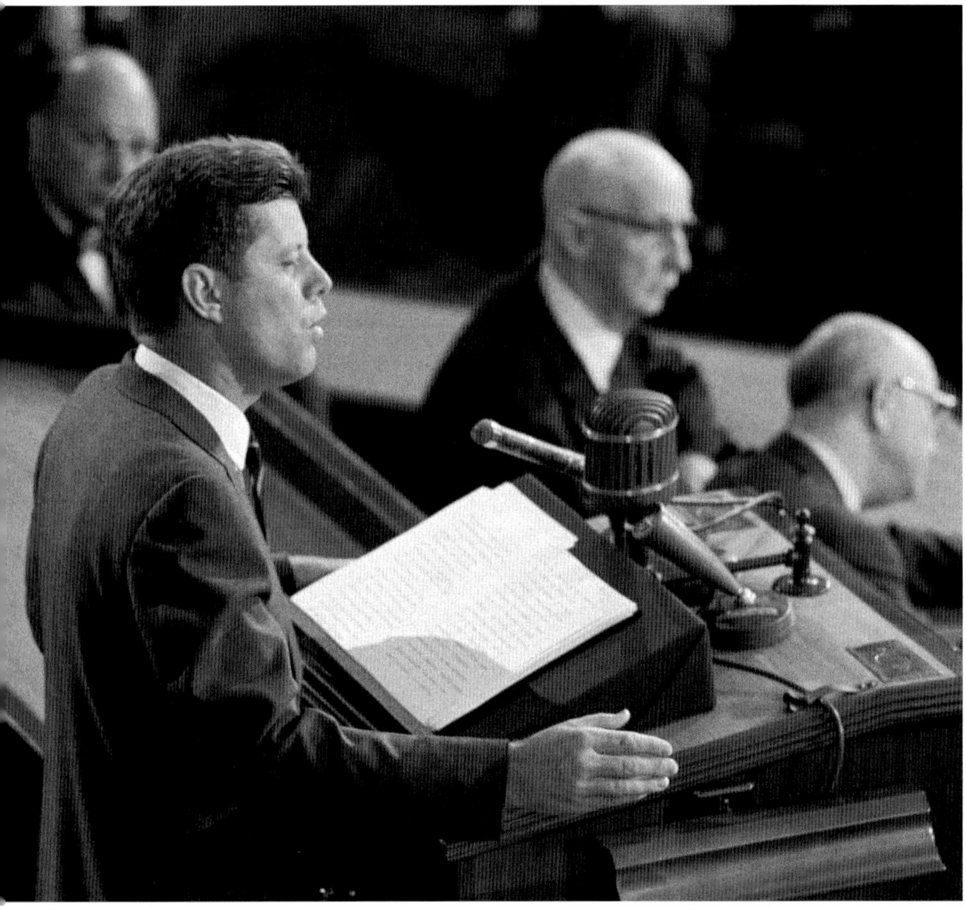

◀ On May 25, 1961, the president delivers his "Special Message to Congress on Urgent National Needs" in the US House chamber. The 12:30 p.m. speech, televised live by the networks, is perceived as a "second State of the Union" address.

▼ Johnson (left) and House Speaker Sam Rayburn (D-Tex.) sit behind Kennedy. The two, along with Rep. Albert Thomas (D-Tex.), lobby to locate NASA's Manned Spacecraft Center (MSC) and its new Mission Control Center in Houston. The decision would be announced in September.

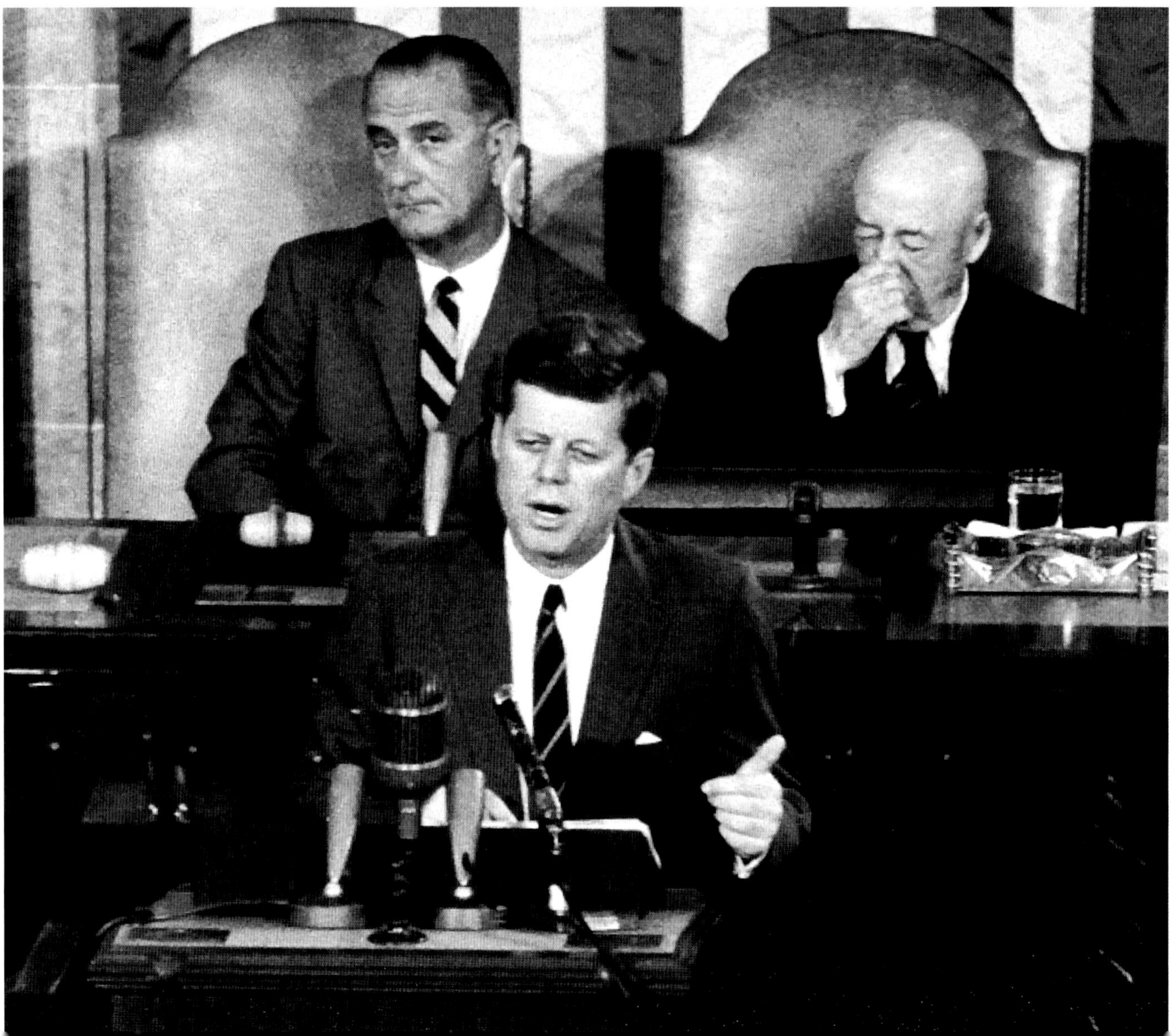

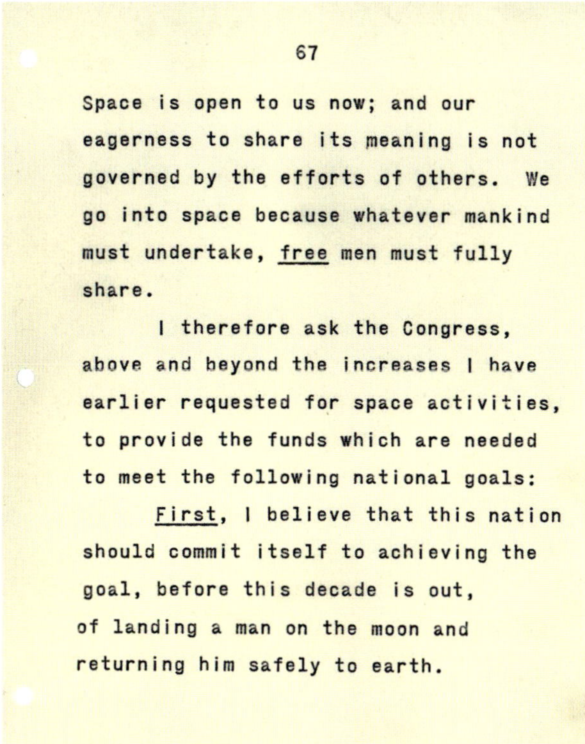

67

Space is open to us now; and our eagerness to share its meaning is not governed by the efforts of others. We go into space because whatever mankind must undertake, free men must fully share.

I therefore ask the Congress, above and beyond the increases I have earlier requested for space activities, to provide the funds which are needed to meet the following national goals:

First, I believe that this nation should commit itself to achieving the goal, before this decade is out, of landing a man on the moon and returning him safely to earth.

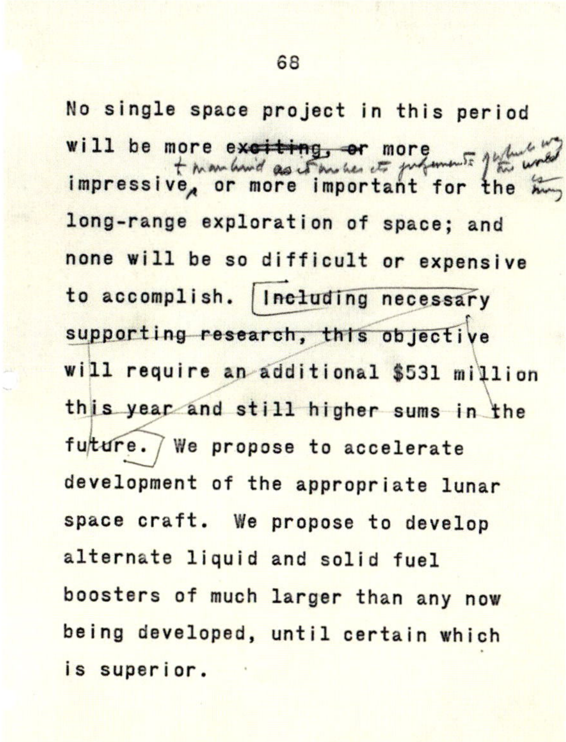

68

No single space project in this period will be more ~~exciting, or~~ more impressive, or more important for the long-range exploration of space; and none will be so difficult or expensive to accomplish. ~~Including necessary supporting research, this objective will require an additional $531 million this year and still higher sums in the future.~~ We propose to accelerate development of the appropriate lunar space craft. We propose to develop alternate liquid and solid fuel boosters of much larger than any now being developed, until certain which is superior.

▲ Pages from the reading copy of the president's speech with his hand-written changes. (Courtesy of the John F. Kennedy Presidential Library and Museum.)

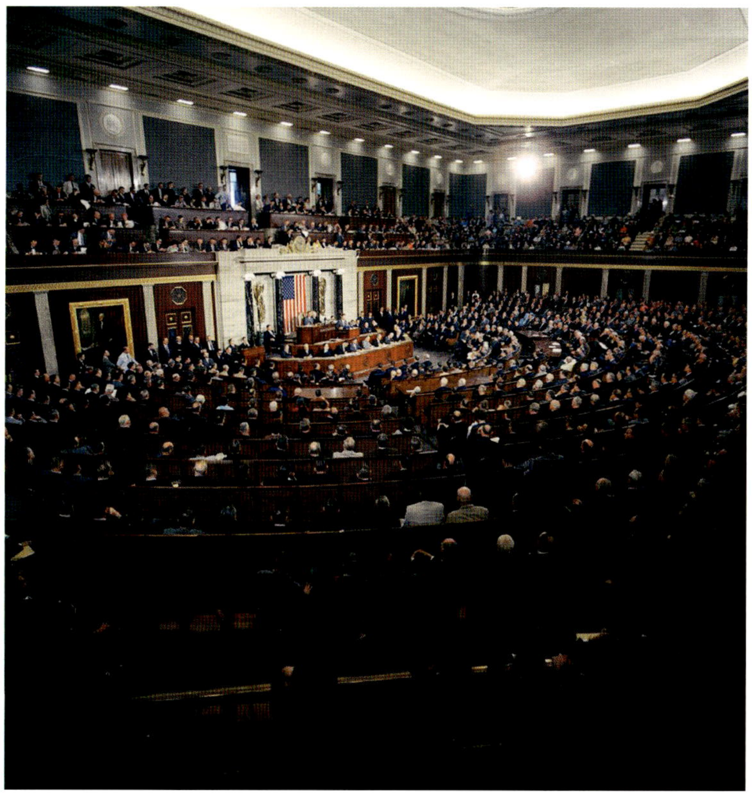

▶ In his "Special Message to Congress" Kennedy continues,

> Recognizing the head start obtained by the Soviets with their large rocket engines, which gives them many months of lead-time, and recognizing the likelihood that they will exploit this lead for some time to come in still more impressive successes, we nevertheless are required to make new efforts on our own. For while we cannot guarantee that we shall one day be first, we can guarantee that any failure to make this effort will make us last.
>
> We take an additional risk by making it in full view of the world, but as shown by the feat of astronaut Shepard, this very risk enhances our stature when we are successful. But this is not merely a race. Space is open to us now; and our eagerness to share its meaning is not governed by the efforts of others. We go into space because whatever mankind must undertake, free men must fully share.
>
> I therefore ask the Congress, above and beyond the increases I have earlier requested for space activities, to provide the funds which are needed to meet the following national goals:

> First, I believe that this nation should commit itself to achieving the goal, before this decade is out, of landing a man on the moon, and returning him safely to the Earth. No single space project in this period will be more impressive to mankind, or more important for the long-range exploration of space; and none will be so difficult or expensive to accomplish. We propose to accelerate the development of the appropriate lunar spacecraft. We propose to develop alternate liquid and solid fuel boosters, much larger than any now being developed, until certain which is superior. We propose additional funds for other engine development and for unmanned explorations—explorations which are particularly important for one purpose which this nation will never overlook: the survival of the man who first makes this daring flight.
>
> But in a very real sense, it will not be one man going to the moon—if we make this judgment affirmatively, it will be an entire nation. For all of us must work to put him there.

June 21, 1961

Dear Mr. Chairman:

I want to express to you my very great appreciation for your thoughtfulness in sending to me the model of an American whaler, which we discussed while in Vienna. It now rests in my office here at the White House.

Mrs. Kennedy and I were particularly pleased to receive "Pushinka". Her flight from the Soviet Union to the United States was not as dramatic as the flight of her mother, nevertheless, it was a long voyage and she stood it well. We both appreciate your remembering these matters in your busy life.

We send to you, your wife and your family our very best wishes.

Sincerely yours,

His Excellency
Nikita S. Khrushchev
Chairman of the Council of Ministers of the
Union of Soviet Socialist Republics
Moscow

Just ten days after the speech, Kennedy raises the prospect of a joint lunar mission with Khrushchev at a summit in Vienna, but the Soviet leader is noncommittal.

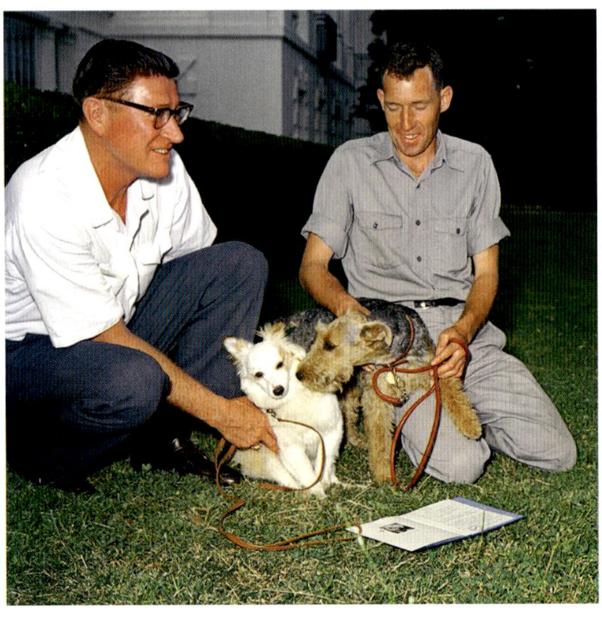

◀ After the June summit in Vienna, Soviet Premier Khrushchev sends a surprise gift: Pushinka, a mutt whose mother is Strelka, one of the first two dogs sent into orbit to be recovered alive (aboard *Korabl-Sputnik 2* on August 19, 1960). Pushinka is examined at Walter Reed Army Medical Center in Washington, DC, to be certain the dog is not bugged with any listening devices before she is permitted to settle into her new home.

L–R: Groundskeeper Hassel Adams; Pushinka; the Kennedys' family dog, Charlie, a Welsh terrier; and Robert Redmond, White House chief gardener, on the South Lawn on June 20, 1961.

▶ In June 1963 Pushinka and Charlie produce four puppies, which the president dubs *pupniks*. When they are two months old, the White House announces two would be given up for adoption based on a letter-writing contest. The First Lady's staff chooses ten finalists from among the five thousand letters received; Mrs. Kennedy then selects the two winning children, who adopt Butterfly and Streaker (on display on August 19, 1963, on the South Lawn). The other puppies, White Tips and Blackie, are adopted by family friends.

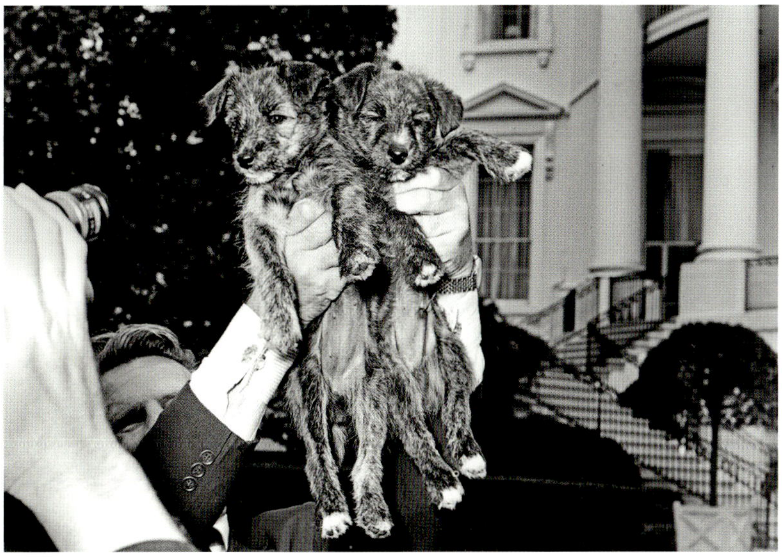

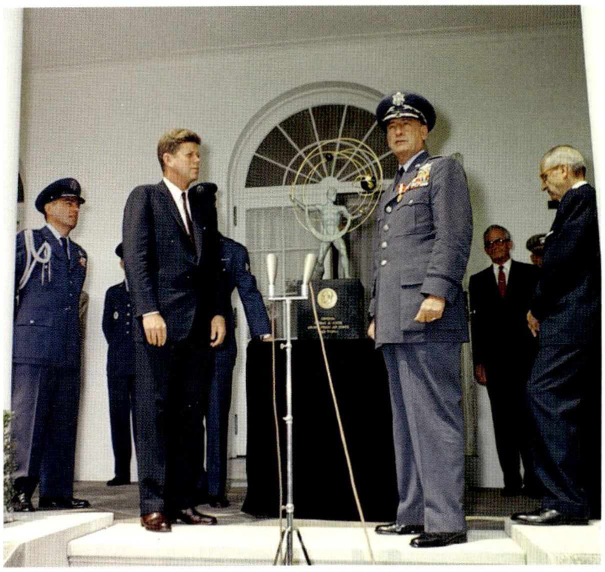

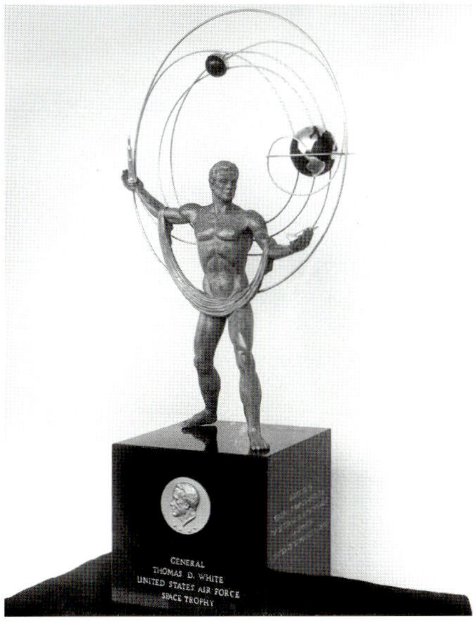

▲ On June 28, 1961, Kennedy poses outside the Cabinet Room with the new USAF Space Trophy, displayed for the first time, named in honor of Gen. Thomas D. White, center. White, the retiring USAF chief of staff, has just received the Distinguished Service Medal (the Army award) from the president in a Rose Garden ceremony.

After White announced his retirement, his friend, National Geographic Society Vice President Thomas McKnew (right), established the annual award and commissioned a trophy. The bronze figure holds in his right hand a Saturn C-1, originally intended to be a military booster, and in his other hand he holds a Dyna-Soar X-20 space plane. The award was to be given to a military or civilian person for outstanding contribution to American aerospace progress. Its first recipients would be Mercury astronaut Gus Grissom (1961), X-15 pilot Robert White (1962), and astronaut Gordon Cooper (1963).

"General White discharged with great distinction the tremendous responsibility of assuring strong, effective deterrent forces in being while simultaneously integrating into the Air Force the new military systems which are the product of modern technology," his medal citation reads. White was succeeded as USAF chief of staff by Gen. Curtis LeMay.

L–R: USAF presidential aide Col. Godfrey McHugh; Kennedy; White; Sen. Barry Goldwater (R-Ariz.); and McKnew. Goldwater, a brigadier general in the USAF Reserve and a friend of Kennedy's, will emerge as one of Kennedy's top Republican opponents in his run for a second term as president in 1964.

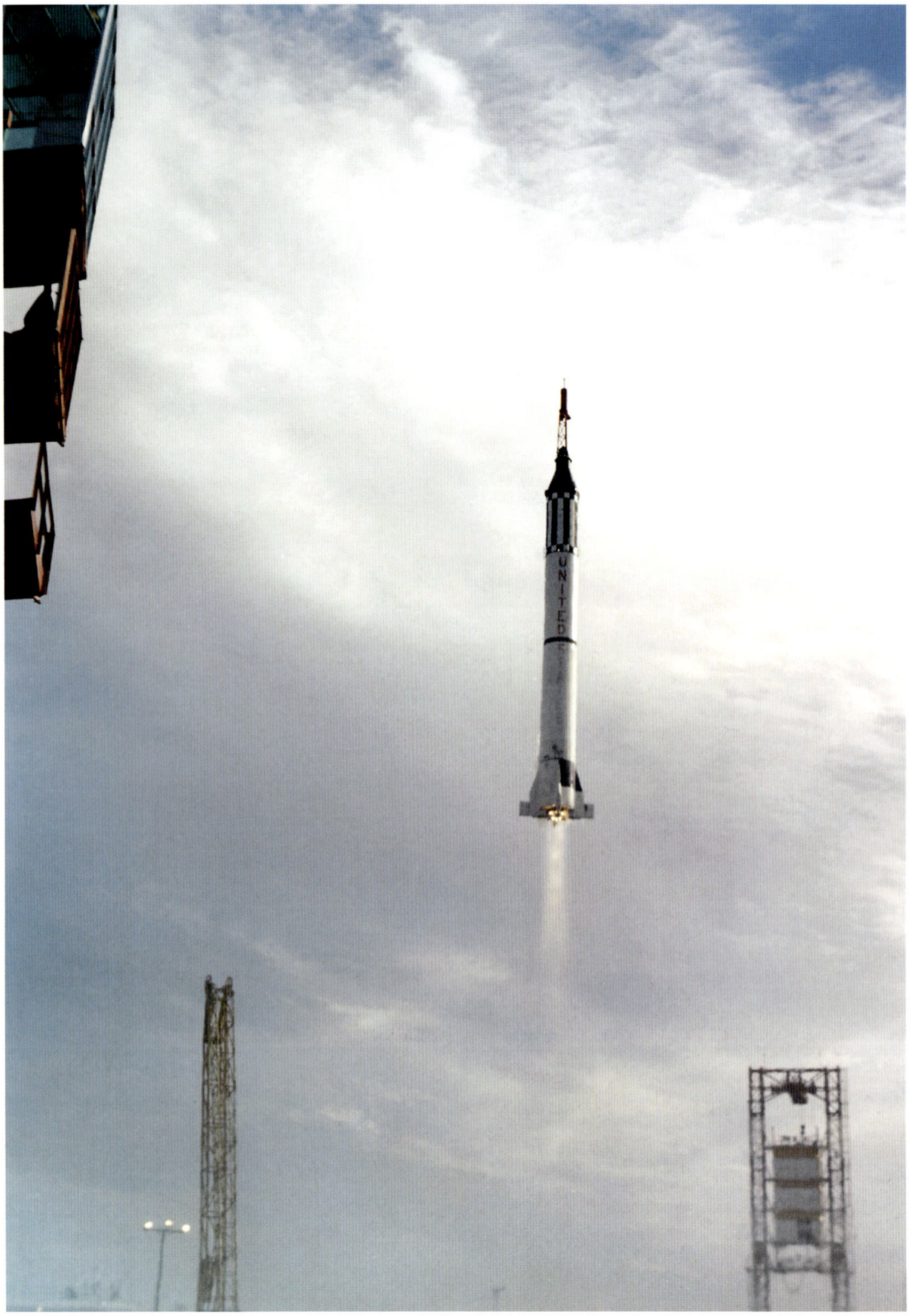

▲ At 7:30 a.m. on July 21, 1961, USAF Capt. Gus Grissom, thirty-five, is launched from LC-5 to become America's second astronaut. A Redstone booster, also used in Shepard's flight, sends him aboard *Liberty Bell 7* some 118 miles high and 302 miles out over the Atlantic—fifteen minutes from launch to splashdown. The president watched the launch on his bedroom TV.

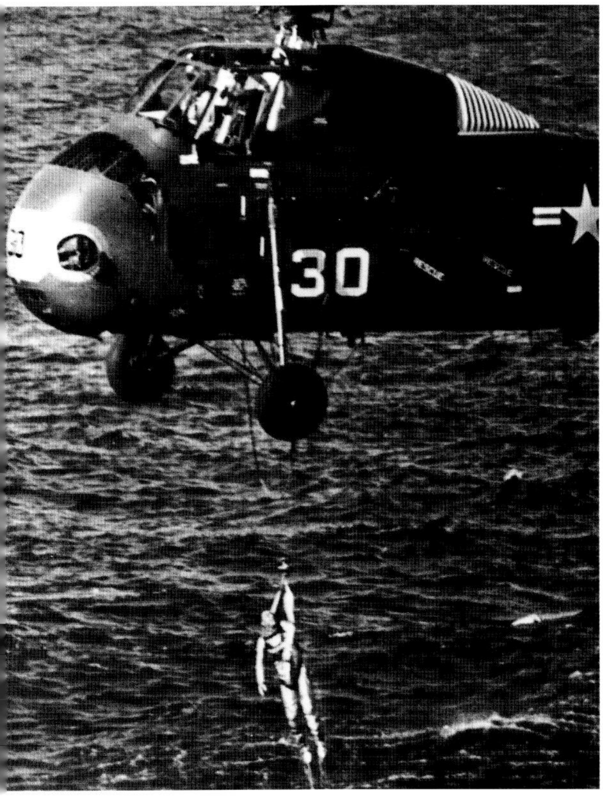

▲ The flight is successful, but the spacecraft is lost after the explosively actuated egress hatch blows prematurely. *Liberty Bell 7* sinks in fifteen thousand feet of water; Grissom is retrieved from the ocean after about four minutes.

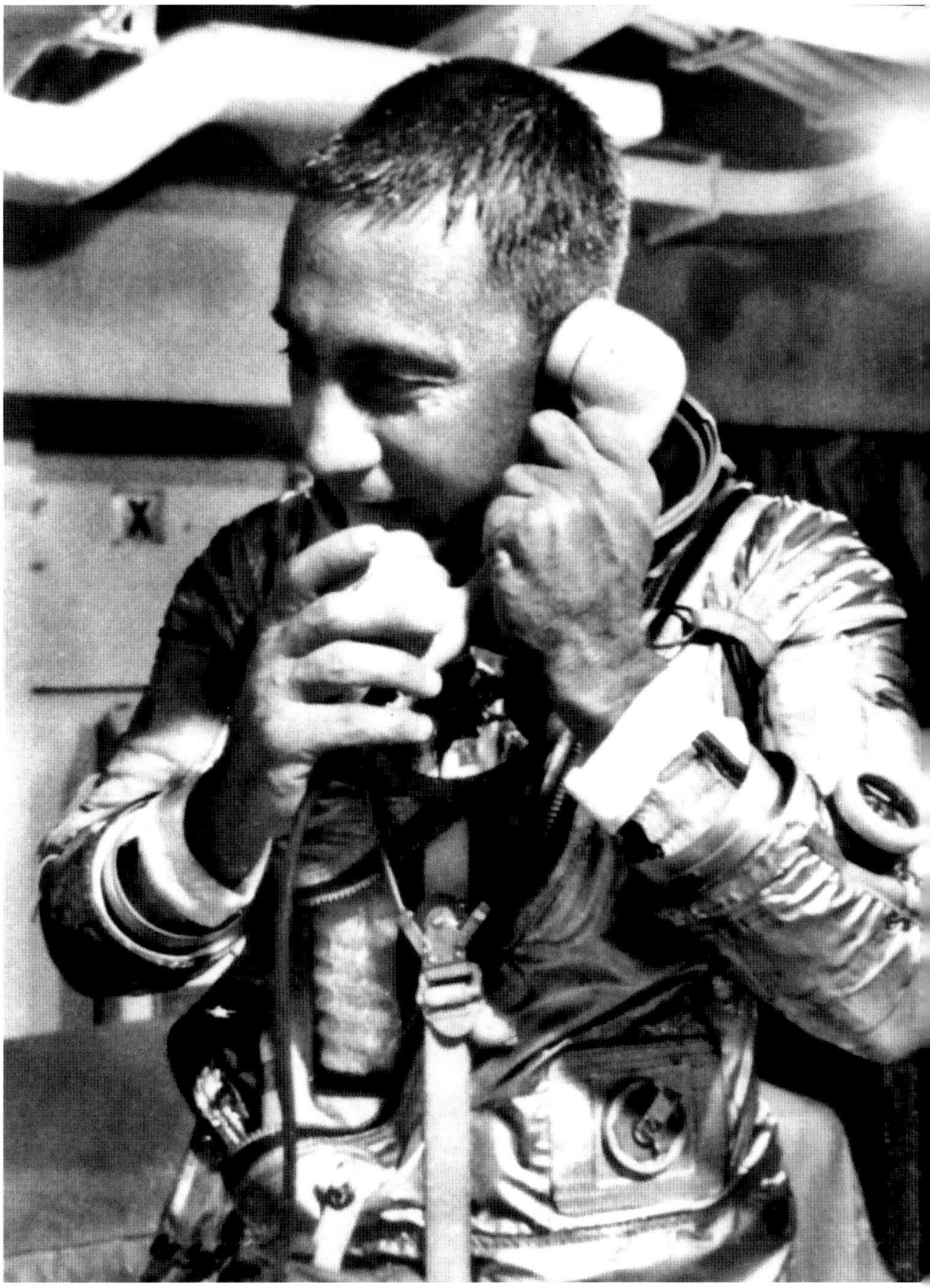

▶ Grissom speaks with Kennedy from the aircraft carrier USS *Randolph.*

Kennedy: "Captain, I wanted to congratulate you. Hello?"

Grissom: "Hello."

Kennedy: "Oh, captain, I wanted to congratulate you. I've been watching your flight on TV here, and I'm delighted that you got through all right."

Grissom: "Yes sir, I got through all right. They just informed me that we lost the capsule. I am shattered at this."

Kennedy: "Yeah, but it was a wonderful job and we really are delighted that it worked out well for you."

Grissom: "Well, thank you very much, sir. I hope it does something for you like Commander Shepard's did."

Kennedy: "Oh, well it's a big help, I'll tell you that, so we look forward to seeing you sometime soon."

Grissom: "Thank you very much, sir. It has been very nice talking with you again."

Kennedy: "Well, good luck, captain."

Grissom: "Thank you, sir."

Kennedy: "Bye-bye."

Grissom receives his Distinguished Service Medal from Webb the next day at the Cape.

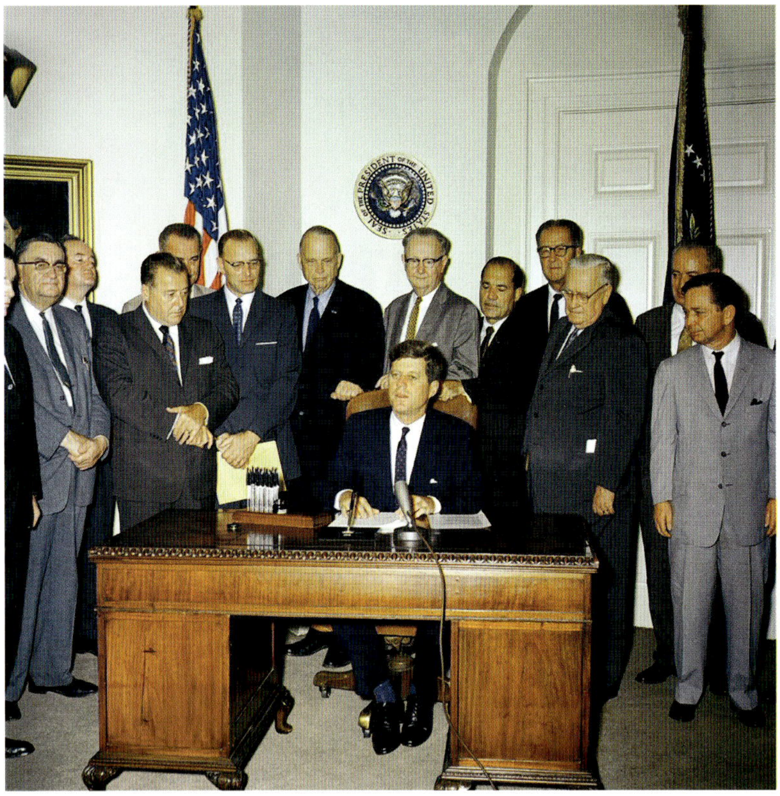

◀ That afternoon, Kennedy signs the NASA funding authorization bill for 1962—$1.78 billion, or almost double the $964 million in fiscal year 1961. He says the timing is significant with Grissom's launch "before the eyes of the watching world and with all the hazard it entails."

In the Fish Room (today known as the Roosevelt Room) at the White House are (L–R) Rep. James Fulton (D-Penn.) (mostly out of frame), Rep. J. Edgar Chenoweth (R-Colo.), Sen. Hubert Humphrey (D-Minn.) (Senate majority whip), Sen. Warren Magnuson (D-Wash.), Johnson, Rep. Joseph Karth (D-Minn.), Sen. Robert Kerr (D-Okla.), Rep. Overton Brooks (D-La.), Rep. Victor Anfuso (D-N.Y.), Sen. Clinton Anderson (D-N.Mex.), Sen. Alexander Wiley (R-Wisc.), Sen. Styles Bridges (R-N.H.) (partially hidden), and Rep. Carl Albert (D-Okla.) (House majority whip). Brooks is the first chairman of the House Science and Astronautics Committee, created in 1959; Karth, Anfuso, Chenowith, and Fulton are members. Kerr chairs the Senate Aeronautical and Space Sciences Committee, created in 1958, with members Anderson, Wiley, and Bridges.

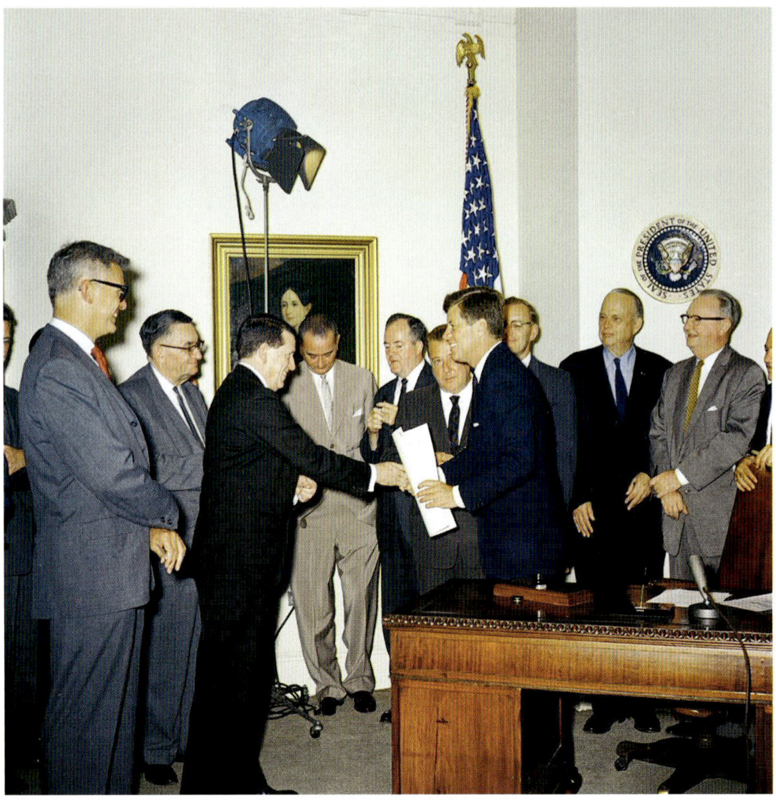

◀ Kennedy shakes hands with Rep. Fulton as he hands out ceremonial pens following the bill signing. In 1970 Fulton, as the senior Republican on the House Committee on Science and Astronautics, will broker a key compromise that preserves early funding for the Space Shuttle program. At left is Robert Seamans Jr., NASA associate administrator.

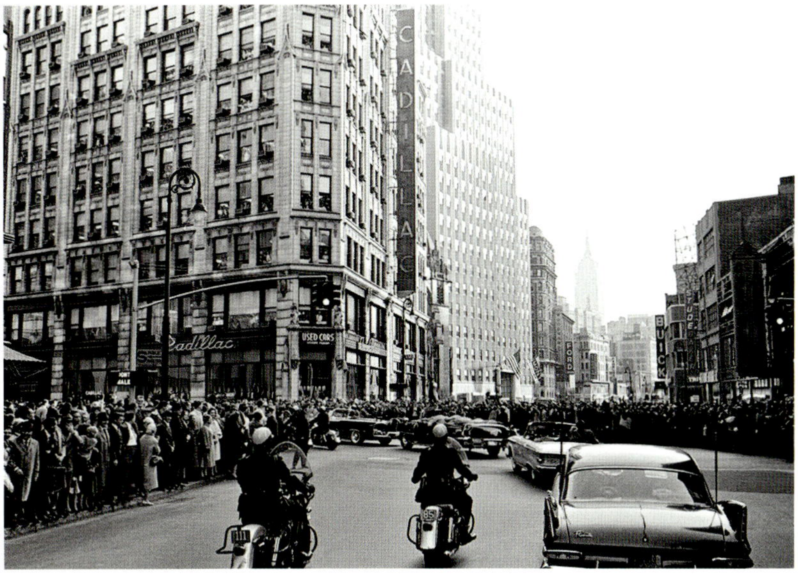

◀ On September 25, 1961, sidewalks and windows are filled as the president's motorcade turns onto West 57th Street from Broadway in New York at about 11:15 a.m., where he will address the 16th General Assembly at the United Nations.

His limousine is passing the Argonaut Building, owned by General Motors, which houses a Cadillac showroom. Other dealerships on Automobile Row are seen looking south along Broadway with the Empire State Building at center in the distance.

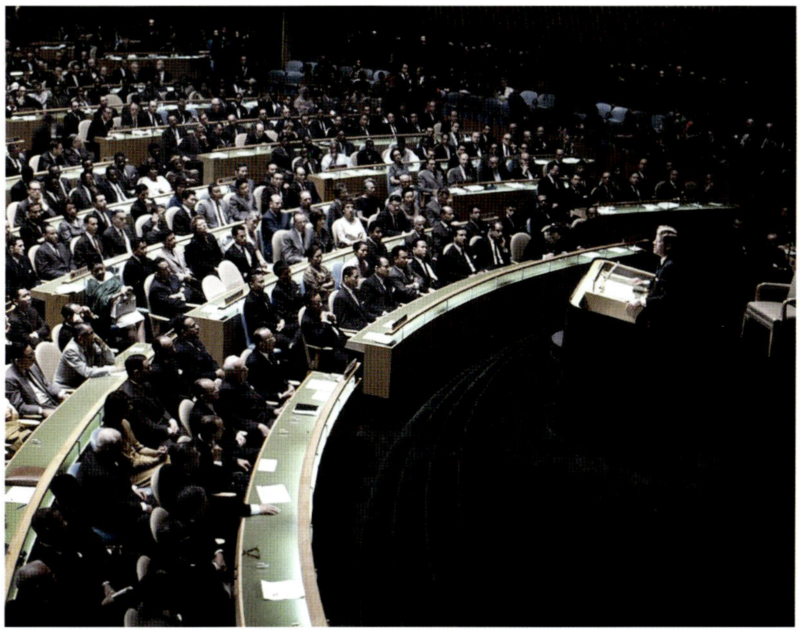

▶ "As we extend the rule of law on earth," Kennedy tells the delegates, "so must we also extend it to man's new domain—outer space. All of us salute the brave cosmonauts of the Soviet Union. The new horizons of outer space must not be driven by the old bitter concepts of imperialism and sovereign claims. The cold reaches of the universe must not become the new arena of an even colder war." He continues,

> To this end, we shall urge proposals extending the United Nations Charter to the limits of man's exploration in the universe, reserving outer space for peaceful use, prohibiting weapons of mass destruction in space or on celestial bodies, and opening the mysteries and benefits of space to every nation.
>
> We shall propose further cooperative efforts between all nations in weather prediction and eventually in weather control. We shall propose, finally, a global system of communications satellites linking the whole world in telegraph and telephone and radio and television. The day need not be far away when such a system will televise the proceedings of this body to every corner of the world for the benefit of peace.

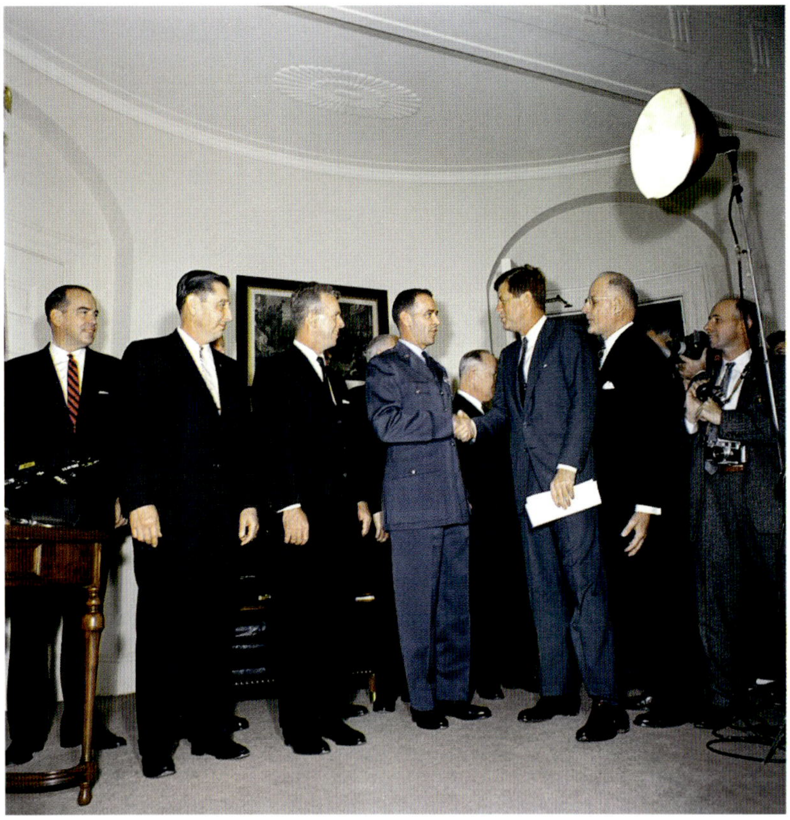

On November 28, 1961, the president greets the three winners of the 1960 Harmon International Trophy for Aviators in the Fish Room at 12:00 p.m. They all piloted the rocket-powered, record-setting X-15 research aircraft, a joint NASA-USAF project from 1957 to 1968.

"I think that this award is particularly gratifying," the president says in presenting it, "because it is a very exact combination of technical development, engineering skill by the companies involved in manufacturing this plane, by the Air Force, and by the three men, who demonstrate that even though we may be able to make the most advanced contributions in the field of scientific development, the men are required—particularly those that are highly trained and with unusual courage and skill."

L–R: Harmon trustee Col. Ansel Talbert; North American pilot Scott Crossfield; NASA pilot Joe Walker; USAF pilot Maj. Robert White; Kennedy; and Harmon trustee William Schramek.

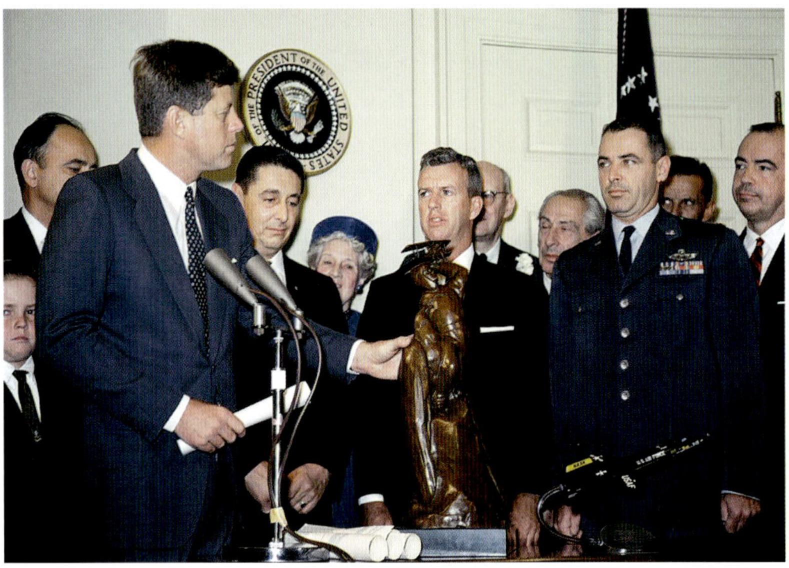

"Your achievements," he says, "give us the greatest possible satisfaction and a sense of pride in knowing that Americans have made this tremendous contribution—and that we produced you three."

L–R: Thomas Crossfield; Joseph Charyk, the first director of the National Reconaissance Office; Kennedy; Scott Crossfield; unidentified woman; Walker; unidentified man; aviation pioneer Maj. Alexander de Seversky (the 1939 winner); White; unidentified man; and Schramek.

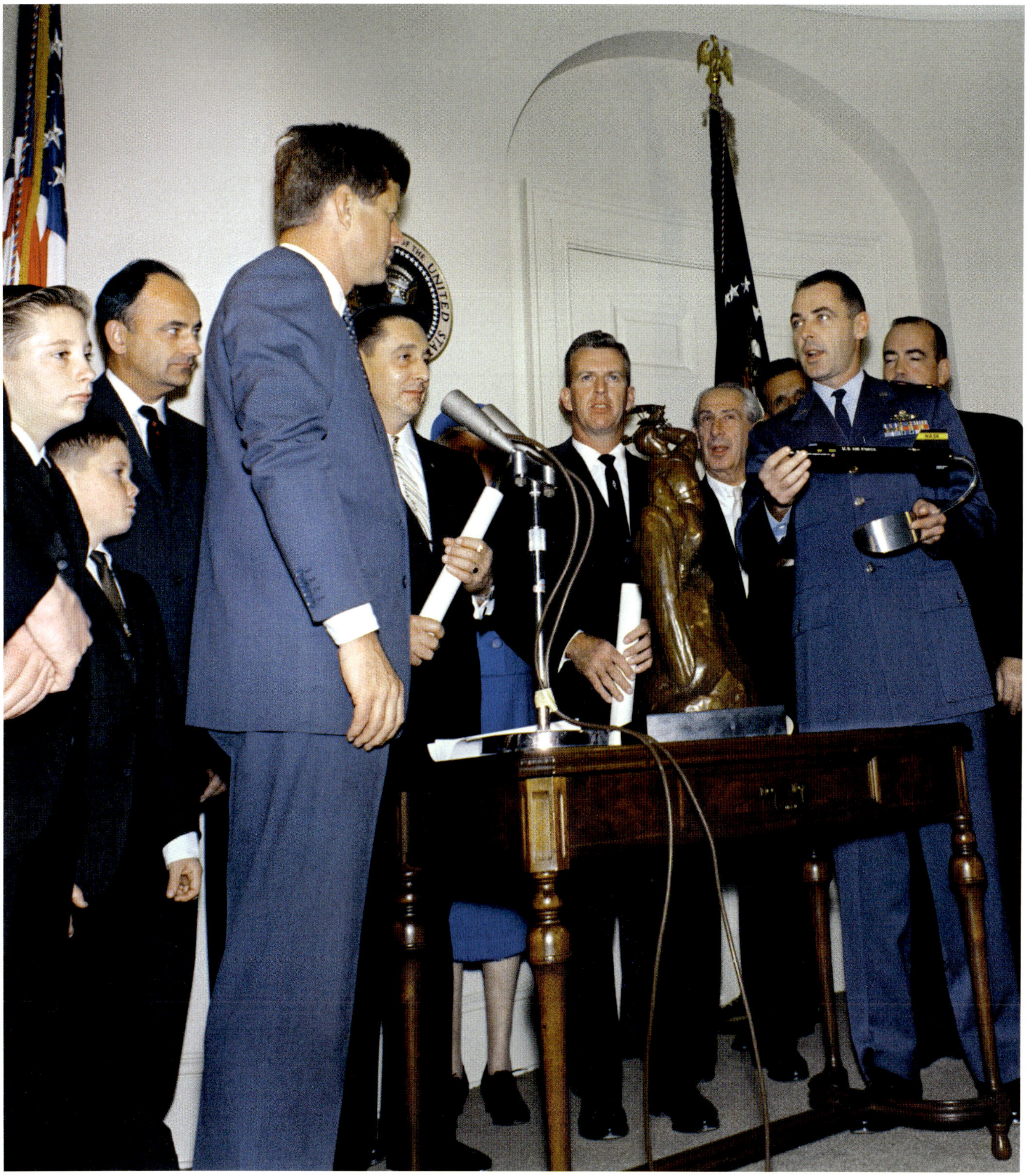

▲ White shows the president an X-15 scale model brought for the ceremony. The president would receive a different X-15 model (see next page) as a gift a few minutes later in the Oval Office. The world's first hypersonic aircraft, the X-15 is capable of suborbital space flights of more than sixty miles in altitude; in 1967 an X-15 will set an unchallenged world speed record for a manned rocket plane of Mach 6.7. Three were built by North American Aviation.

L–R: Thomas and Paul Crossfield (sons of Scott Crossfield); Charyk; Kennedy; Crossfield; Walker; de Seversky; and White.

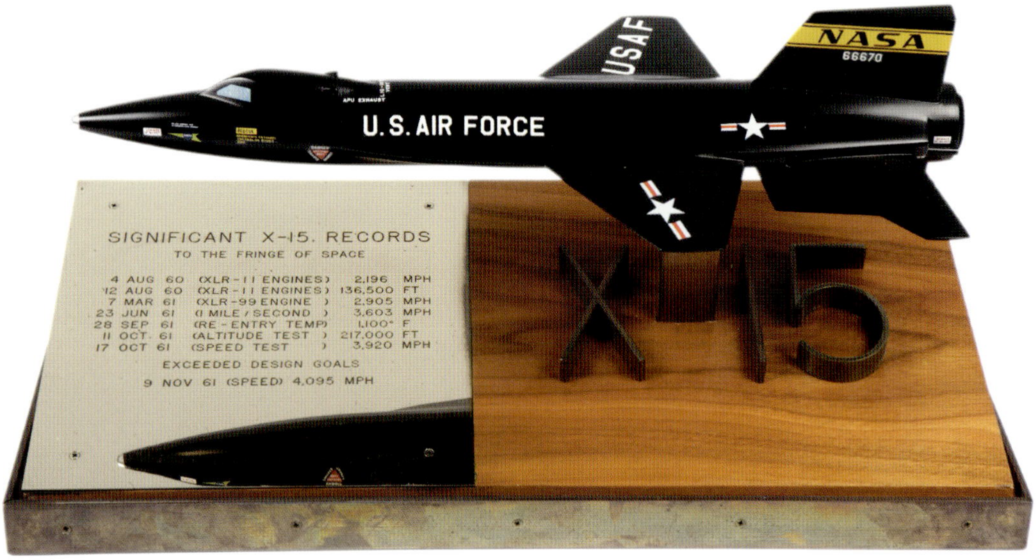

▲ This model now resides in the John F. Kennedy Presidential Library and Museum collection.

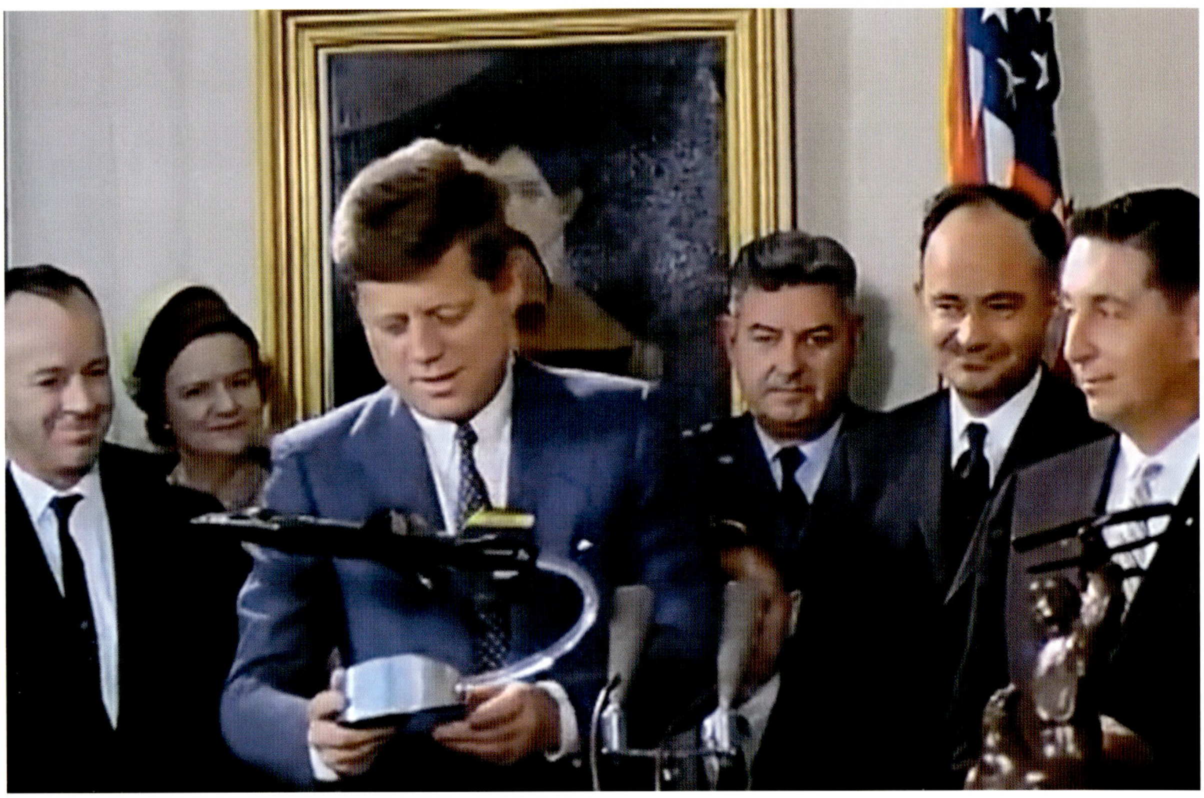

▲ Gen. Curtis LeMay (right of Kennedy) won the Harmon International Trophy for Aviators in 1957 for setting a distance and speed record for transport jets in a KC-135.

L–R: Harrison Storms Jr., president of North American Aviation's Space and Information Systems (Storms was previously the chief engineer at NAA for the X-15 and later managed NAA's work on the Apollo spacecraft, but he was fired after the Apollo 1 fire in 1967); unidentified woman; Kennedy; Paul Crossfield (hidden); LeMay; Charyk; and Crossfield. (USAF film still frame)

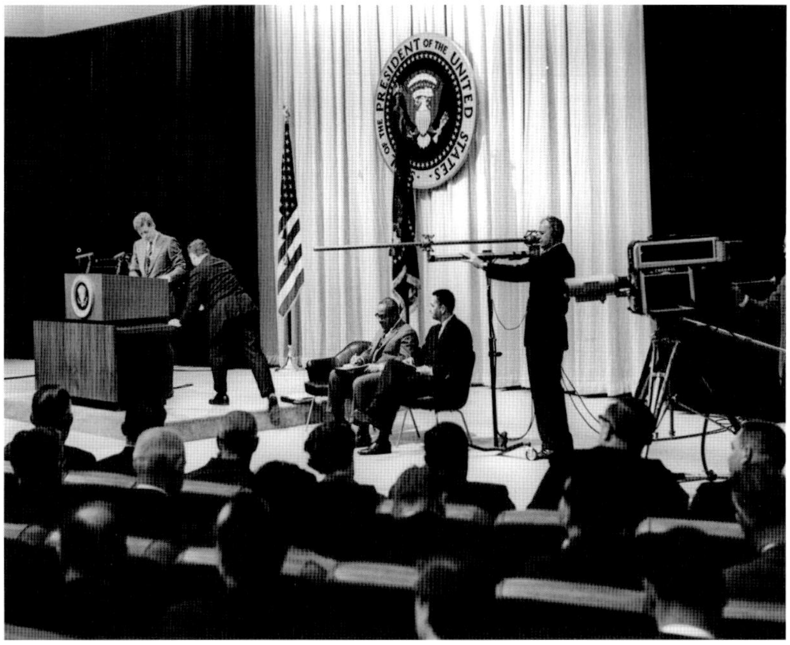

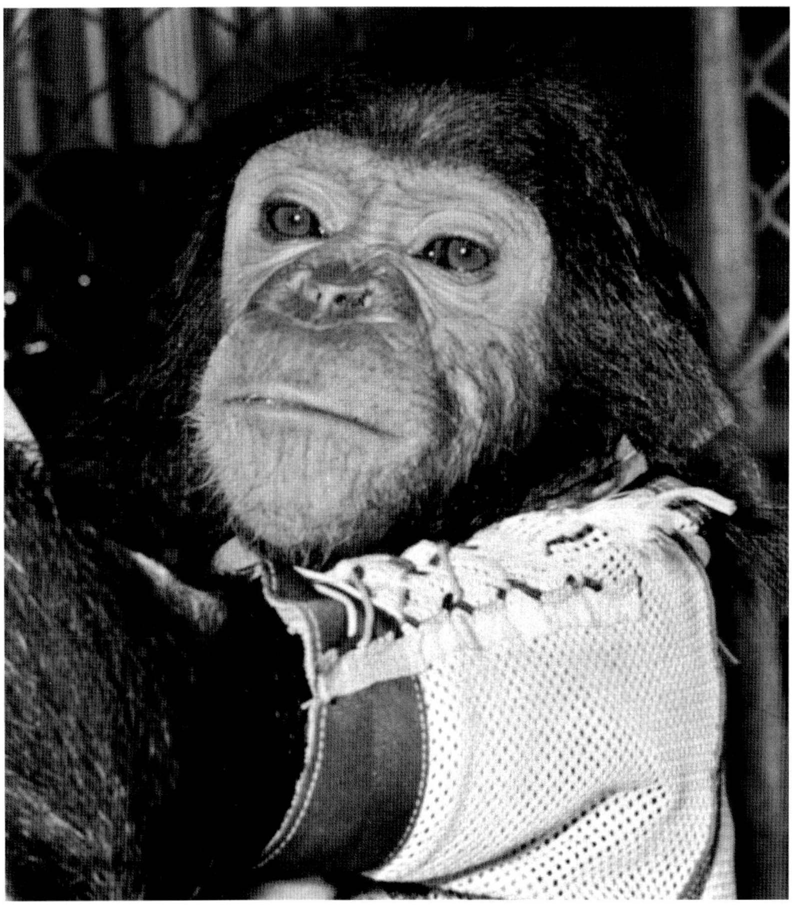

On November 29, 1961, Press Secretary Pierre Salinger hands the president a note during a morning news conference at the State Department. After reading it, Kennedy looks up and tells reporters, "This chimpanzee who was flying in space took off at 10:08. He reports that everything is perfect and working well." Much laughter ensues.

NEXT PAGE: The launch at Cape Canaveral is of Enos, (pictured at left), a specially trained chimp who orbits the earth twice before a successful splashdown. It helps qualify the Mercury spacecraft for manned orbital flights and provides another test of its booster, a man-rated version of the first US intercontinental ballistic missile (ICBM). Atlas ICBMs with nuclear warheads are deployed at eleven sites across the country from 1959 to 1965.

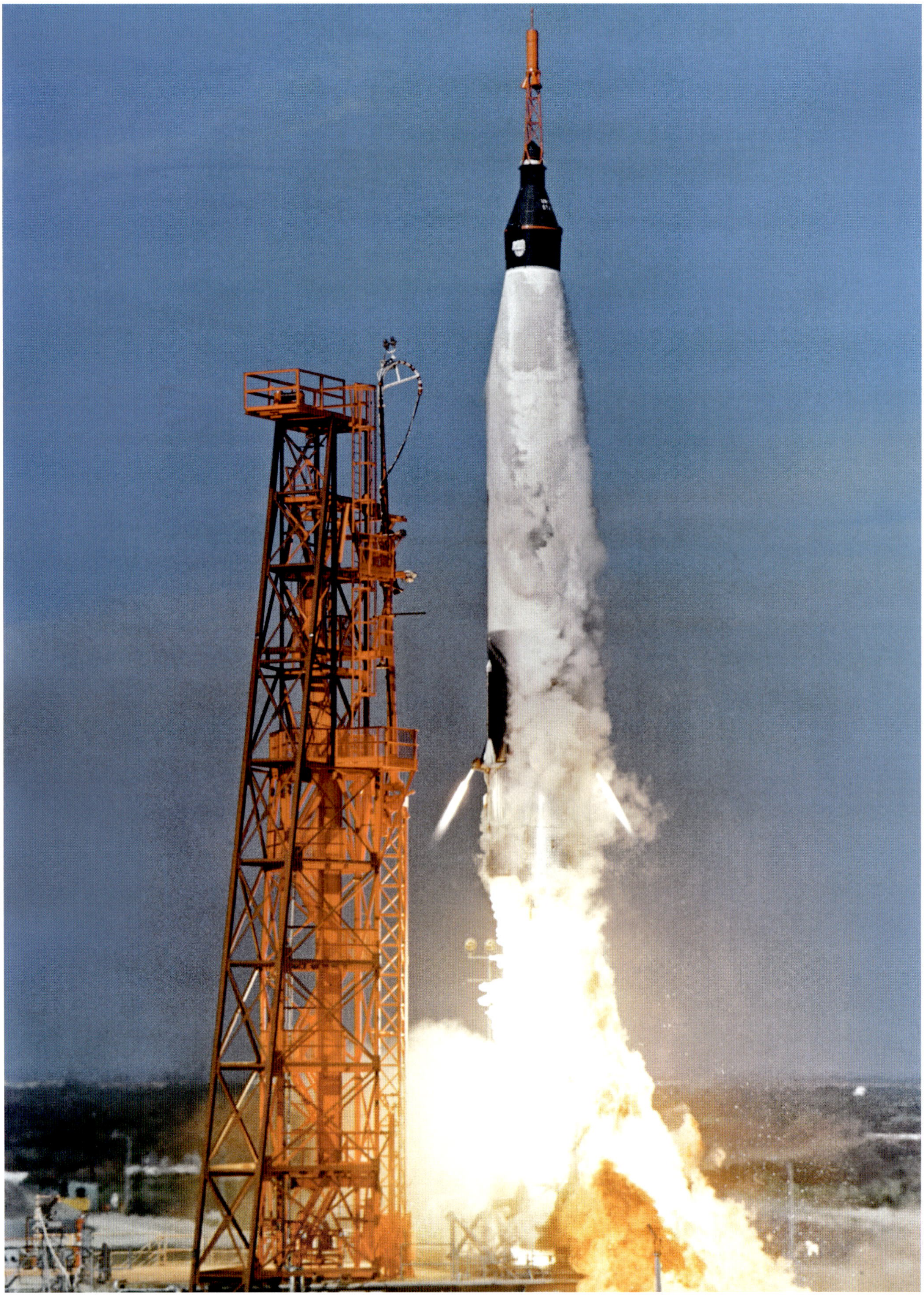

:02

FEBRUARY 1962

"The kind of American of whom we are the most proud"

AS 1962 BEGINS, the Kennedy administration badly needs a boost. The first year of the president's term had been tough—the Bay of Pigs fiasco, an awkward summit with Khrushchev, and the construction of the Berlin Wall. None of his domestic priorities had moved in Congress. America has also not yet put an astronaut into orbit, while the Soviet Union has already accomplished two such flights. But the United States is about to join the club, thanks to Marine Lt. Col. John H. Glenn Jr. On February 20, he completes three Earth orbits and becomes the nation's newest hero.

At a news conference the next day, President Kennedy announces that Khrushchev has suggested a cooperative space program in his congratulatory telegram after Glenn's flight and that he'll be responding that day. Asked by a reporter if he has seen any other signs, the president replies, "No, we have seen no evidence that we would be able to confidently expect in the last 12 months that this kind of cooperation would take place. But we, I might say, now have more chips on the table than we did some time ago. So perhaps the prospects are improving."

Just three days after Glenn's mission, Kennedy flies to Cape Canaveral for a medal ceremony and a tour of the facilities; it is his first of three visits to the Florida launch site. Two more successful Mercury flights follow in 1962. And during the year, the United States racks up fifty orbital launches compared to the twenty-two by the USSR. America is also busy trying to lay the groundwork for a manned lunar landing, attempting to send three in its Ranger series of unmanned spacecraft to the moon during the same year, primarily to photograph the surface of the moon, although all three missions are failures, including two at launch.

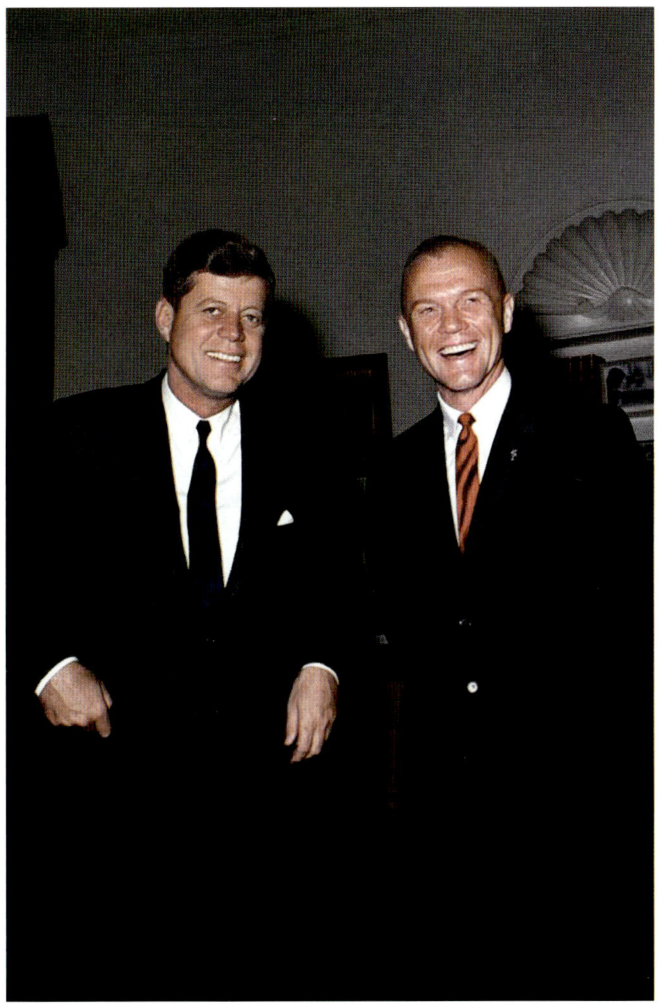

▲ Kennedy poses with Glenn, forty, in the Oval Office after the two meet at 9:40 a.m. on February 5, 1962, just more than two weeks before Glenn's space flight. At the time, Glenn's launch is expected eight days later.

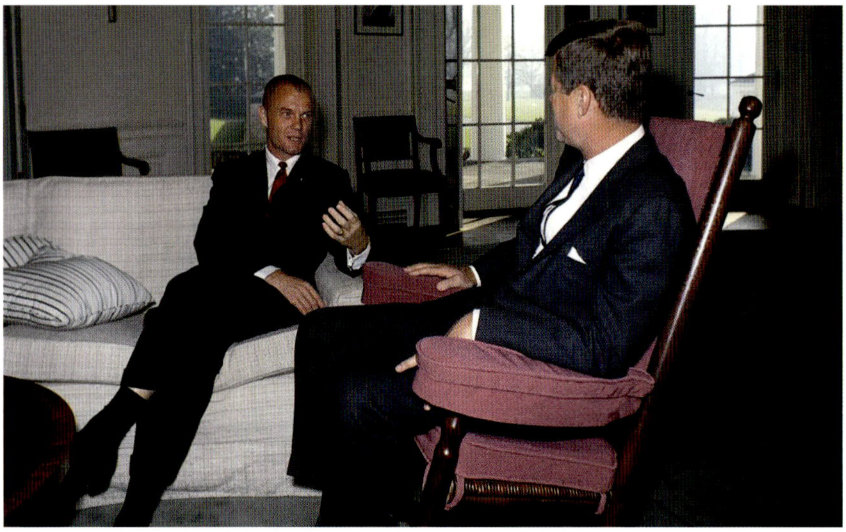

▲ Glenn discusses plans for his upcoming orbital mission. The astronaut had spent the weekend with his family at their home in nearby Arlington, Virginia, after his mission was postponed on January 30 because of problems with the rocket's Atlas booster.

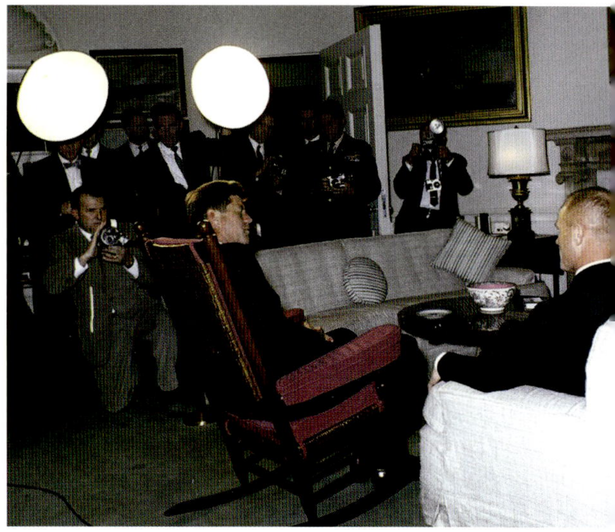

▲ Reporters and photographers are admitted at the end of the ten-minute meeting, prompting the president to comment that Glenn must be used to such media attention. "I don't mind," Glenn replies, "but I think our emphasis is on the wrong point sometimes. There is a great deal of personal publicity but not enough emphasis on the scientific aspects of Mercury." The media, he says, seem to be more interested in topics such as "how [his wife] Annie is getting her hair fixed." He had been besieged by reporters and photographers two days earlier at his home.

In a 1964 interview, Glenn said he was impressed by the president's detailed questions during the meeting, including the amount of g-forces he'd experience and what control he'd have over the Atlas booster.

Kennedy had used a rocking chair since 1955 at his doctor's suggestion to help ease chronic back pain aggravated by a World War II injury as a Navy torpedo boat commander.

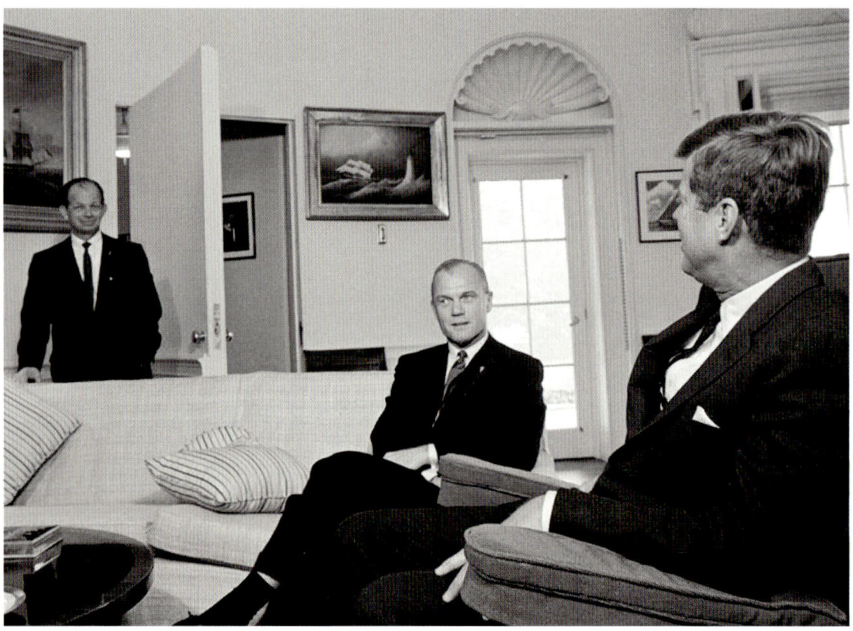

▲ The media's view of the Oval Office meeting. At left is NASA public affairs officer Shorty Powers. Upon departure, Glenn walks unrecognized past a group of protesters in front of the White House demonstrating against nuclear weapons.

◥ On February 20, 1962, Glenn's Atlas booster carries his *Friendship 7* spacecraft toward orbit at 9:47 a.m. from LC-14. This view looks north along ICBM Row at the Cape, with the service towers for LC-12 and LC-13 at right. About fifty-five thousand people gather in Cocoa Beach to the south to watch while an estimated one hundred

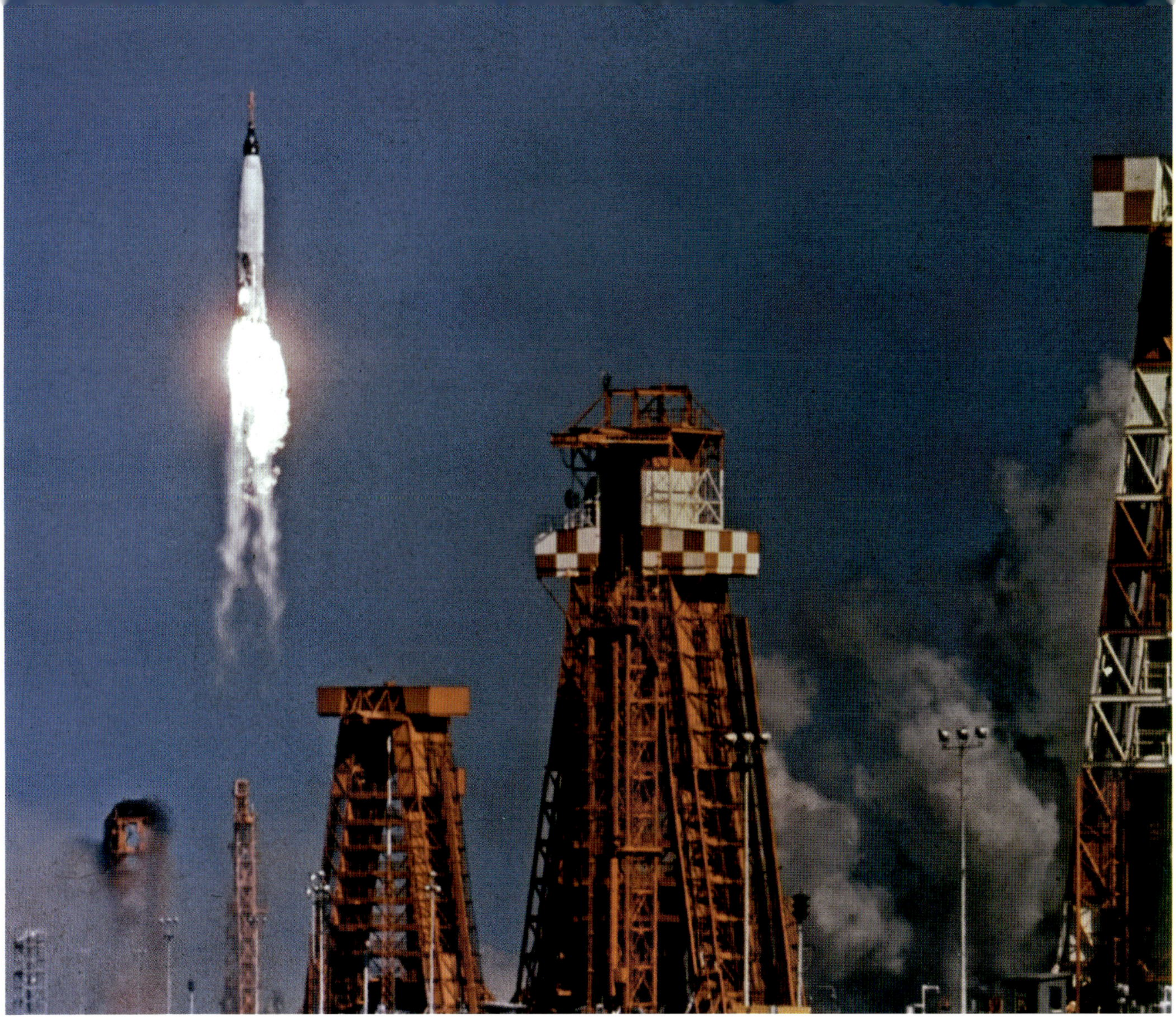

million Americans tune in on television. Five minutes and twenty seconds later, Glenn is in orbit. During his three revolutions around the earth, he sees sunrises and sunsets as well as geographical features, and he carries out tests of the spacecraft and his abilities in weightlessness.

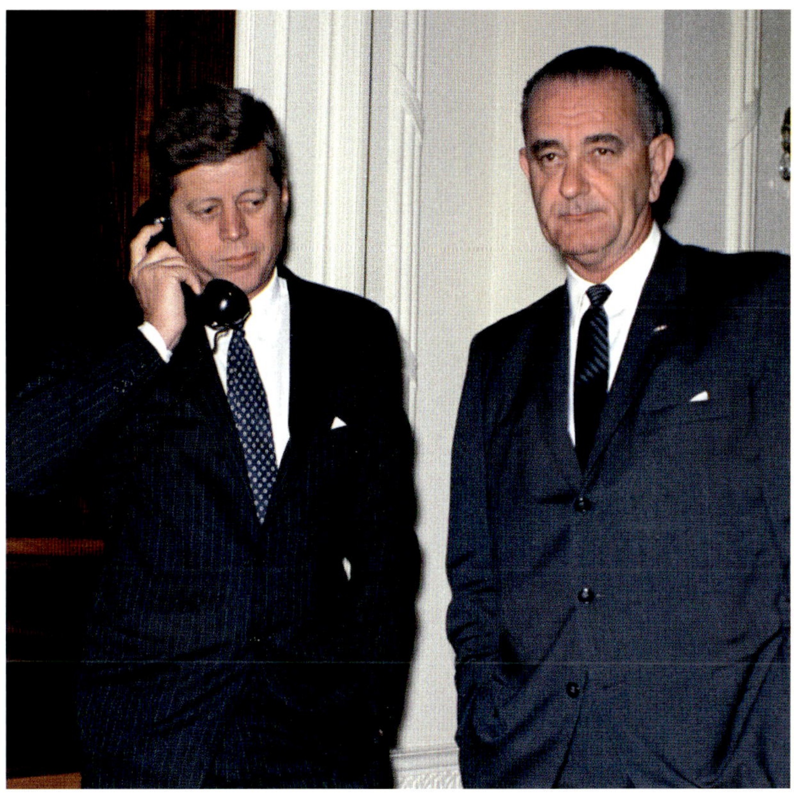

▶ Kennedy and Johnson receive an update on the launch from Cape Canaveral on a special open phone line.

As the five-hour flight proceeds, the president follows TV coverage of Glenn's mission. He also holds a series of meetings in the Oval Office, including with the lieutenant governor of Minnesota, members of Congress, his staff, military aides, and the new Philippine ambassador to the United States.

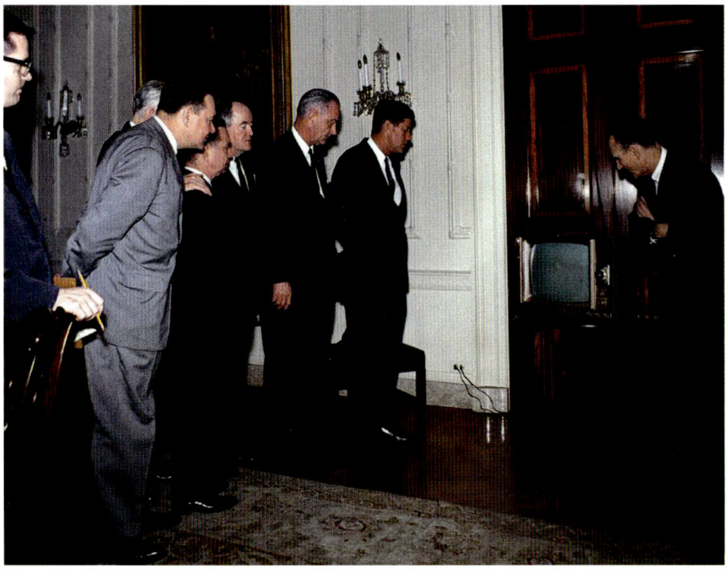

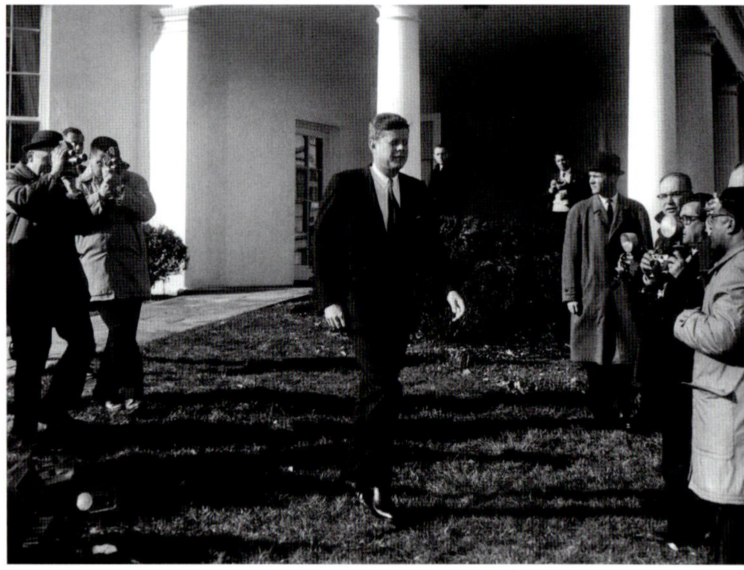

▲ The president watches broadcast TV coverage of Glenn's launch after a regular breakfast with Democratic congressional leaders in the Family Dining Room. House Speaker John McCormack (D-Mass.) later admits to reporters that not much was accomplished at the breakfast.

L-R: Special Counsel to the President Ted Sorensen; Rep. Hale Boggs (D-La.); McCormack (mostly hidden, with hand on Albert's shoulder); Rep. Carl Albert (D-Okla.); Sen. Hubert Humphrey (D-Minn.); Johnson; Kennedy; and Sen. Mike Mansfield (D-Mont.), the Senate majority leader, at far right.

▲ Kennedy receives word of the astronaut's safe Atlantic recovery about a minute before the news is flashed to the public. At 3:30 p.m. he emerges from the Oval Office to make a statement to reporters on the West Wing lawn. "A few days ago, Colonel Glenn came to the White House and visited me," the president says. "And he was, as are the other astronauts, the kind of American of whom we are the most proud. Some years ago, as a Marine pilot, he raced the sun across this country and lost. And today, he won." The president refers to Glenn having made the first supersonic transcontinental flight, from California to New York, in 1957.

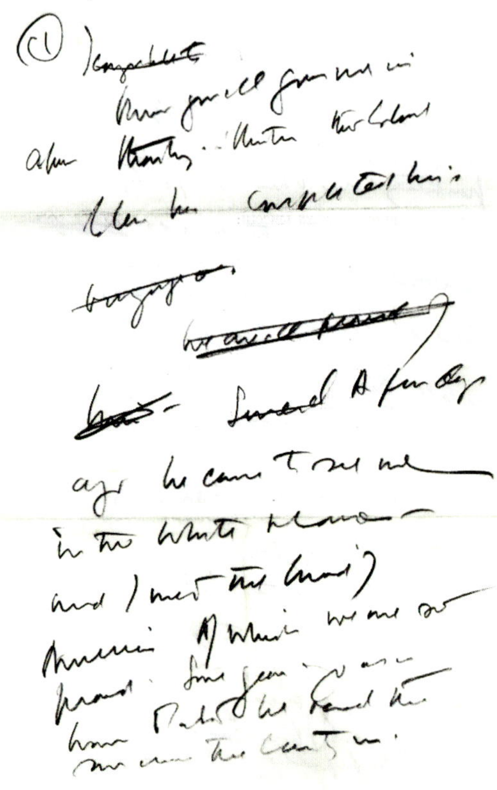

◀ The first page of the president's notes for his remarks with Evelyn Lincoln's "translation." (Courtesy of the John F. Kennedy Presidential Library.)

~~Congratulate~~
I know you will join me in
offering thanks nation [?] that Colonel
Glenn has completed the
~~voyage~~
~~We are all proud of~~
~~him~~ -
~~Several~~ A few days
ago he came to see me
in the White House -
and I met the kind of
American of which we are so
proud. Some years ago as a
Marine pilot he raced the
sun across the country in

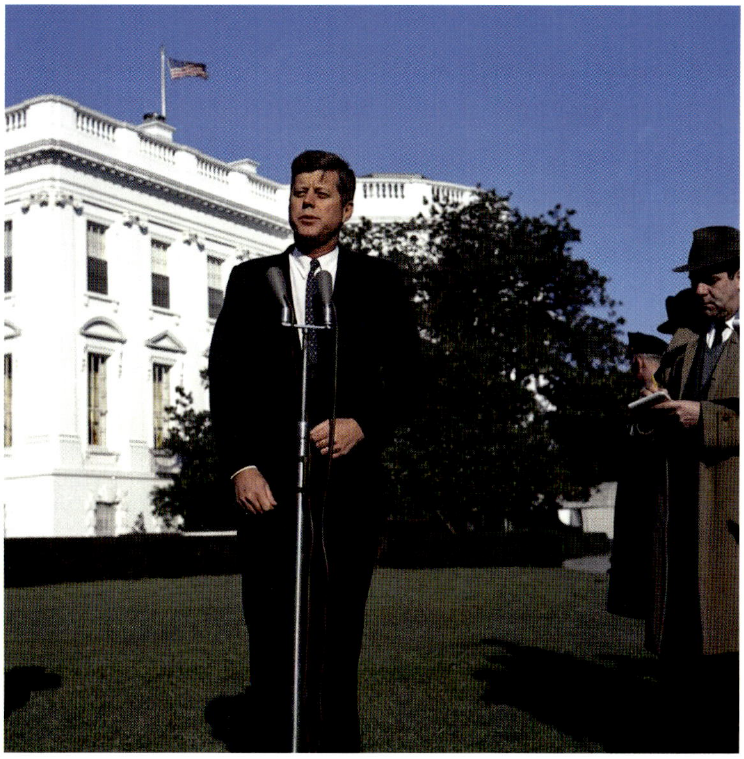

▼ Reporters at right include Tom Wicker of the *New York Times*, Robert Thompson of the *New York Daily News*, Douglas Kiker of the *New York Herald Tribune*, and Sid Davis of Westinghouse Broadcasting.

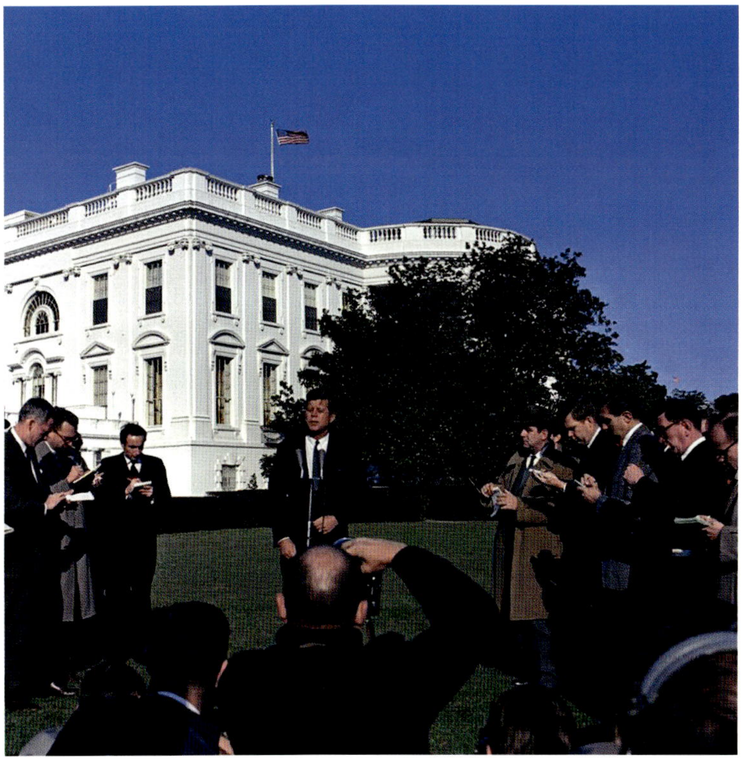

▲ "I also want to say a word for all those who participated with Colonel Glenn at Canaveral. They faced many disappointments and delays; the burdens upon them were great, but they kept their heads and they made a judgment, and I think their judgment's been vindicated."

"We have a long way to go in the space race," Kennedy concludes. "We started late. But this is the new ocean, and I believe the United States must sail on it and be in a position second to none. Some months ago, I said that I hoped that every American would serve his country, today Colonel Glenn served his, and we all express our thanks to him."

▶ The White House called Mercury Control and asked for the president to speak to Glenn during his final orbit. This card was prepared for Kennedy to use, but the plan was scrapped as flight controllers instead wrestled with concerns about Glenn's reentry.

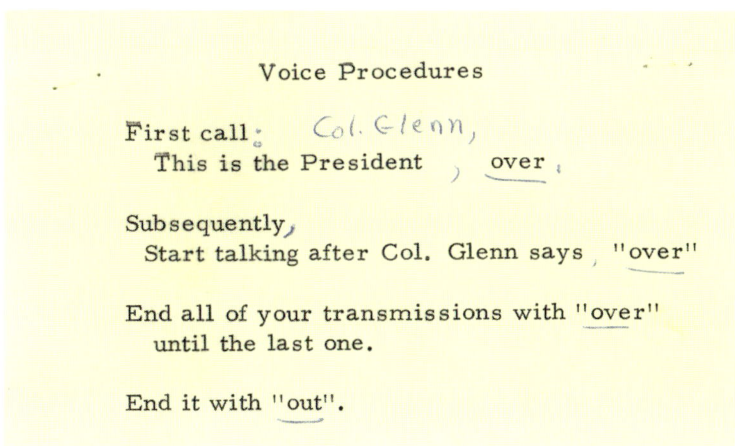

Voice Procedures

First call: Col. Glenn,
This is the President, over.

Subsequently,
Start talking after Col. Glenn says, "over"

End all of your transmissions with "over" until the last one.

End it with "out".

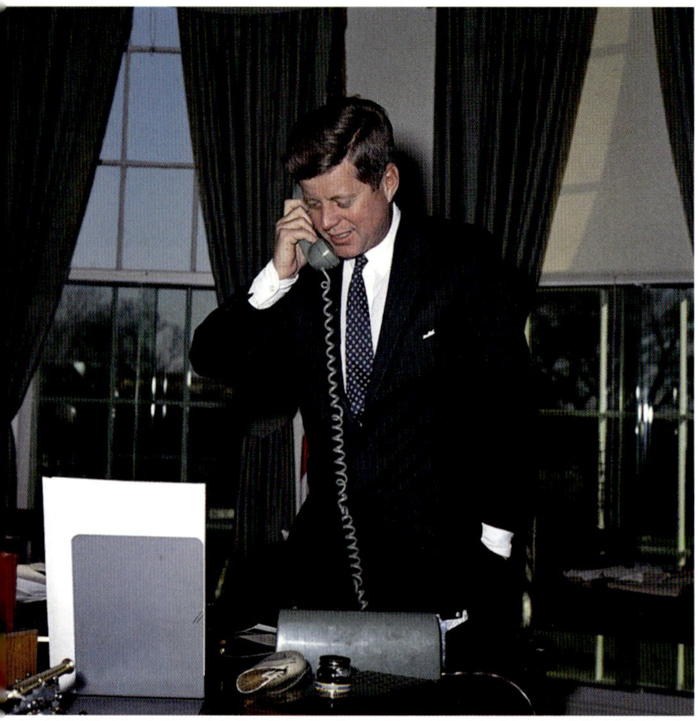

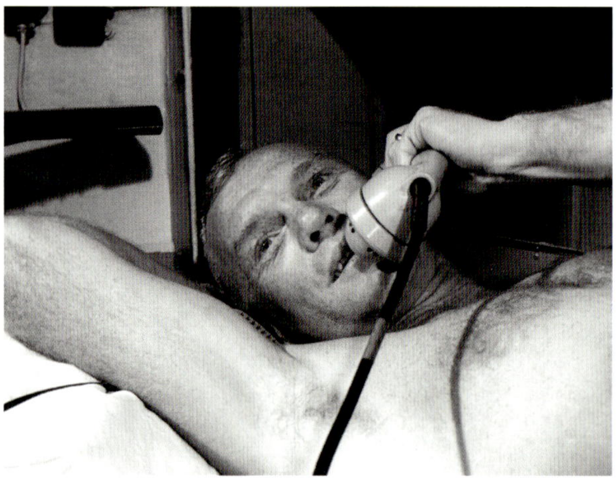

▲ The president calls Glenn aboard the destroyer USS *Noa* from the Oval Office at 4:10 p.m. "Listen, colonel, we are really proud of you and I must say you did a wonderful job. We are glad you got down in good shape. I have just been watching your mother and father on television, and they seem very happy." "It was a wonderful trip," Glenn replies. "Almost unbelievable, thinking back on it right now. But it was tremendous." "Well, I am coming down to Canaveral on Friday," says the president, "and hope you will come up to Washington on Monday or Tuesday, and I will be looking forward to seeing you there." Kennedy also calls Glenn's wife and two children at their Arlington, Virginia, home to offer his congratulations.

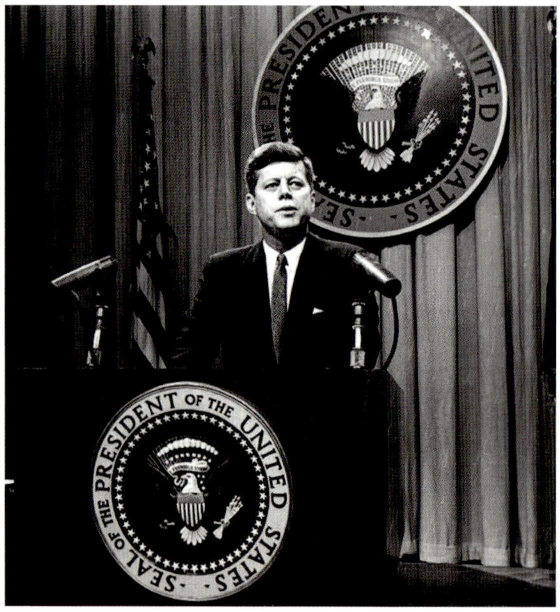

▲ At his 4:00 p.m. news conference the next day at the State Department, Kennedy begins by saying, "It is increasingly clear that the impact of Colonel Glenn's magnificent achievement yesterday goes far beyond our own time and our own country. The success of this flight, the new knowledge it will give us, and the new steps which can now be undertaken, will affect life on this planet for many years to come." He continues,

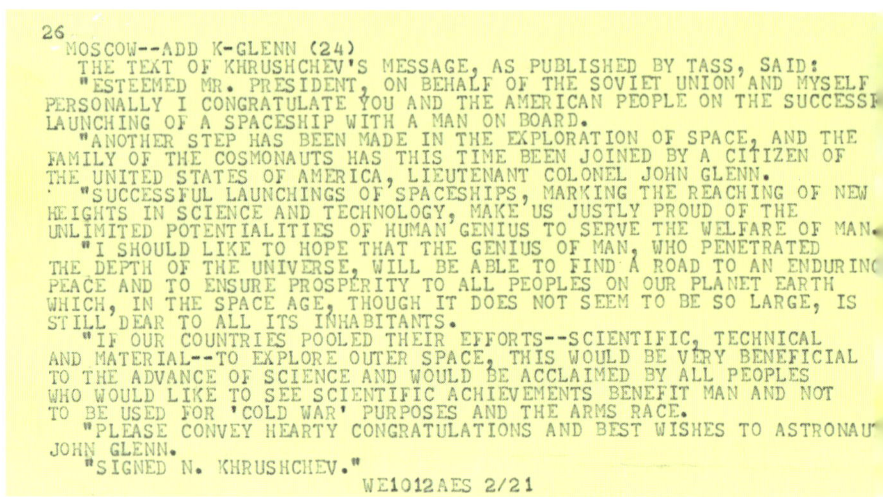

26
MOSCOW--ADD K-GLENN (24)
THE TEXT OF KHRUSHCHEV'S MESSAGE, AS PUBLISHED BY TASS, SAID:
"ESTEEMED MR. PRESIDENT, ON BEHALF OF THE SOVIET UNION AND MYSELF PERSONALLY I CONGRATULATE YOU AND THE AMERICAN PEOPLE ON THE SUCCESSF LAUNCHING OF A SPACESHIP WITH A MAN ON BOARD.
"ANOTHER STEP HAS BEEN MADE IN THE EXPLORATION OF SPACE, AND THE FAMILY OF THE COSMONAUTS HAS THIS TIME BEEN JOINED BY A CITIZEN OF THE UNITED STATES OF AMERICA, LIEUTENANT COLONEL JOHN GLENN.
"SUCCESSFUL LAUNCHINGS OF SPACESHIPS, MARKING THE REACHING OF NEW HEIGHTS IN SCIENCE AND TECHNOLOGY, MAKE US JUSTLY PROUD OF THE UNLIMITED POTENTIALITIES OF HUMAN GENIUS TO SERVE THE WELFARE OF MAN.
"I SHOULD LIKE TO HOPE THAT THE GENIUS OF MAN, WHO PENETRATED THE DEPTH OF THE UNIVERSE, WILL BE ABLE TO FIND A ROAD TO AN ENDURING PEACE AND TO ENSURE PROSPERITY TO ALL PEOPLES ON OUR PLANET EARTH WHICH, IN THE SPACE AGE, THOUGH IT DOES NOT SEEM TO BE SO LARGE, IS STILL DEAR TO ALL ITS INHABITANTS.
"IF OUR COUNTRIES POOLED THEIR EFFORTS--SCIENTIFIC, TECHNICAL AND MATERIAL--TO EXPLORE OUTER SPACE, THIS WOULD BE VERY BENEFICIAL TO THE ADVANCE OF SCIENCE AND WOULD BE ACCLAIMED BY ALL PEOPLES WHO WOULD LIKE TO SEE SCIENTIFIC ACHIEVEMENTS BENEFIT MAN AND NOT TO BE USED FOR 'COLD WAR' PURPOSES AND THE ARMS RACE.
"PLEASE CONVEY HEARTY CONGRATULATIONS AND BEST WISHES TO ASTRONAUT JOHN GLENN.
"SIGNED N. KHRUSHCHEV."
WE1012AES 2/21

This country has received more than thirty messages of congratulations from other heads of state. . . . One of the messages that I received was from Chairman Khrushchev in the Soviet Union, suggesting that it would be beneficial to the advance of science if our countries could work together in the exploration of space.

I am replying to his message today, and I regard it as most encouraging, this proposal for international cooperation in space exploration, including specifically Soviet-American cooperation, which I spelled out in my State of the Union Message of last year, and in my address to the United Nations. . . .

We believe that when men reach beyond this planet, they should leave their national differences behind them. All men will benefit, if we can invoke the wonders of science instead of its terrors. We look forward to visiting with Colonel Glenn on Friday and welcoming him to Washington next Monday.

It has been said that peace has her victories as well as war, and I think all of us can take pride and satisfaction in this victory of technology and the human spirit.

Q: Mr. President, if we could go back to the space question, we have been talking about a race in space, for example a race between the United States and Russia to get to the moon. Suppose now we should get this international cooperation that you've been talking about. What form would it take? Would it go so far, for example, as a joint United States–Russia mission to the moon? Would it go that far? Or just how would it work?

A: Well, I think it would be premature to attempt to suggest, because all we have now, so far, is an indication of interest, and we know from long experience that it's more difficult to transform these general expressions into specific agreements. So I think that we should wait until we see what response we get from the Soviets to our answer to Mr. Khrushchev and then decide what it is we can do.

We are spending billions of dollars in space, and if it's possible to ensure that space is peaceful and that it can be used for the benefit of everyone, then the United States must respond to any opportunity we have to ensure that it's peaceful. But I can't give you an answer until we see whether the rain follows the warm wind in this case.

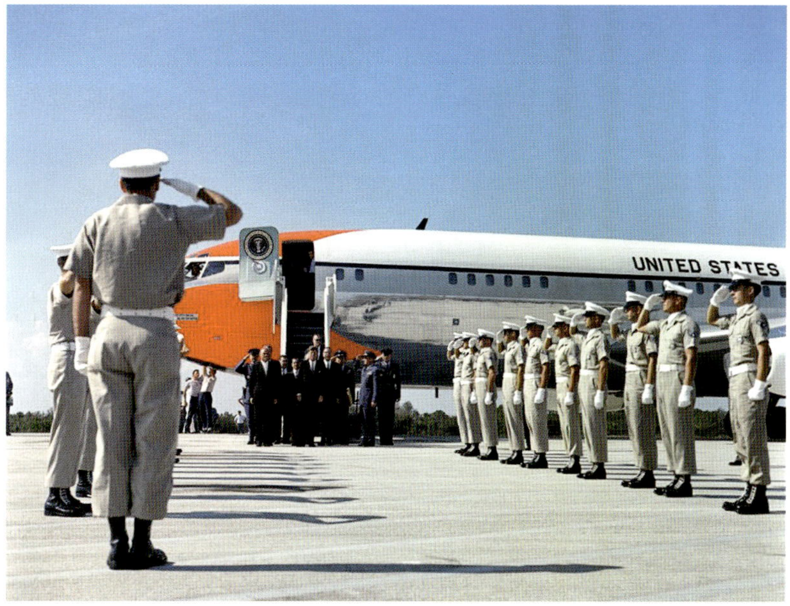

▲ On February 23, 1962, the president and his guests pause in front of Air Force One at the Cape Canaveral Skid Strip after Kennedy lands at 10:35 a.m.

This aircraft is a Boeing 707–153, one of three purchased by the Eisenhower administration for VIP transport. It retains the USAF's highly visible international orange paint scheme. Kennedy would implement the familiar blue-and-white livery for his new presidential aircraft, which would be delivered in October.

L-R: Assistant to the Air Force Aide to the President Maj. Frank Evans; Glenn; Vice President Johnson; Press Secretary Pierre Salinger; Rep. Dante Fascell (D-Fla.); Kennedy; Rep. Paul Rogers (D-Fla.); USAF Aide to the President Brig. Gen. Godfrey McHugh; and Commander of the Air Force Missile Test Center Maj. Gen. Leighton Davis. Secret Service Agent Floyd Boring (in back) stands on the airplane stairs with a USAF honor guard at attention in the foreground.

▼ Glenn and Kennedy head toward the guests and the motorcade with Rep. Fascell behind them. Press Secretary Pierre Salinger is at far left.

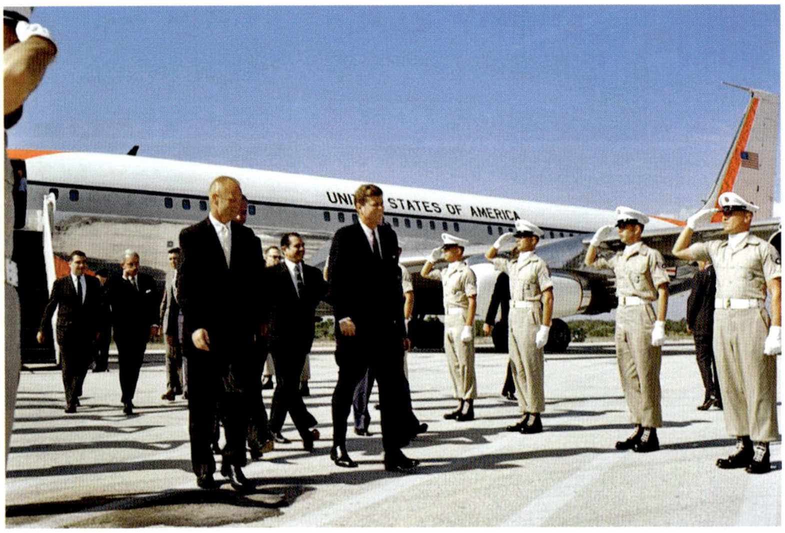

▼ The president greets Glenn's mother, Clara, who says she hopes to meet CBS newsman Walter Cronkite. During the medal ceremony Kennedy introduces the astronaut's parents as "Mr. and Mrs. Glenn, who launched Colonel Glenn originally."

The three TV networks cover the morning's events live, beginning with Glenn's arrival at Patrick at 8:45 a.m. and the parade to the Cape.

To the displeasure of the Secret Service, the crowd rushes past the security line, and the VIPs are briefly surrounded by reporters and others.

L-R: Glenn; Kennedy; Sen. Warren Magnuson (D-Wash.); Rep. Edward Boland (D-Mass.); Mrs. Glenn; unidentified; and Glenn's father, John H. Glenn Sr.

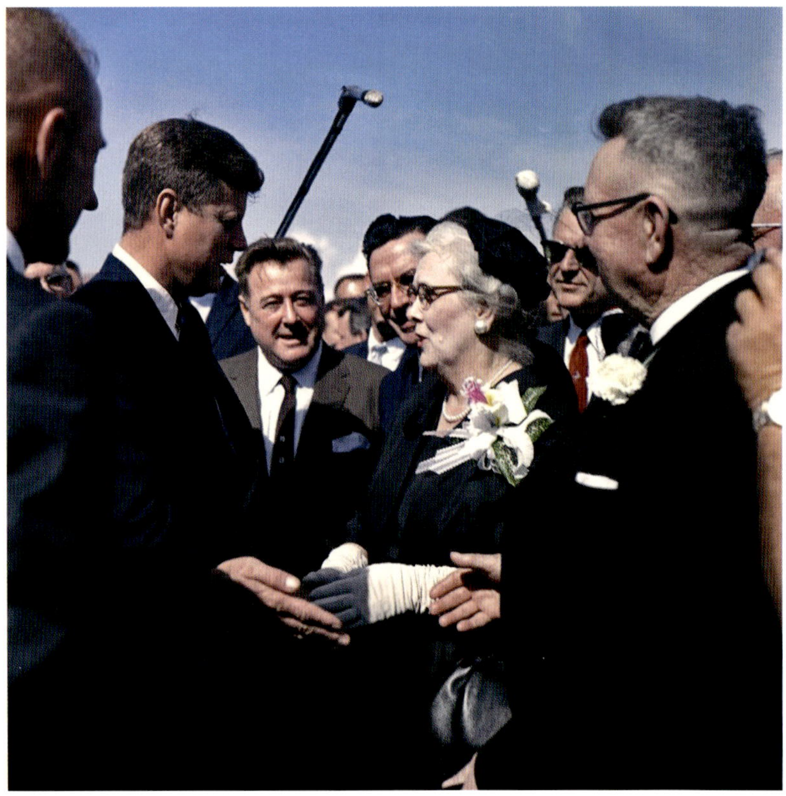

The president had flown to Palm Beach AFB, Florida, the previous afternoon from Washington with Glenn's family so he could visit his ailing father, Joseph P. Kennedy Sr., at the family estate during the weekend. The senior Kennedy had suffered a disabling stroke two months earlier.

Glenn and Johnson had flown from Grand Turk Island to Patrick AFB south of the Cape earlier this morning, where Glenn was first reunited with his family. The group then rode in a motorcade north through Cocoa Beach to Cape Canaveral to await the president. Although residents are disappointed that Kennedy isn't with them, about a hundred thousand people line the eighteen-mile route—almost twice as many as had turned out for Glenn's launch.

Built in 1952, the Skid Strip is a ten-thousand-foot runway at Cape Canaveral Air Force Station (known as Cape Canaveral Missile Test Annex in 1962) for cargo aircraft delivering rocket stages and spacecraft for NASA and the military.

▶ Badge and button as worn by Mary Bubb on next page.

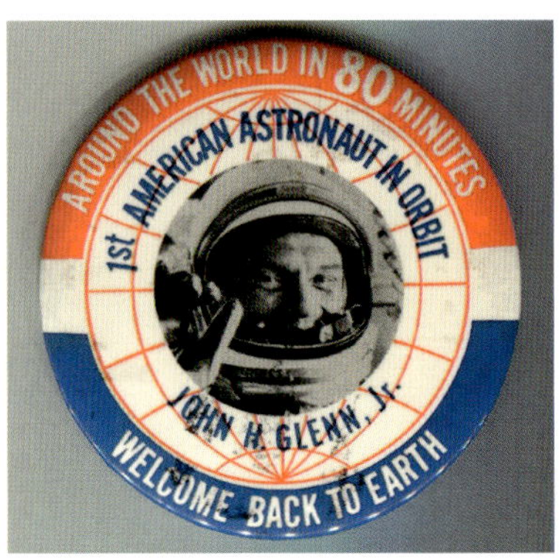

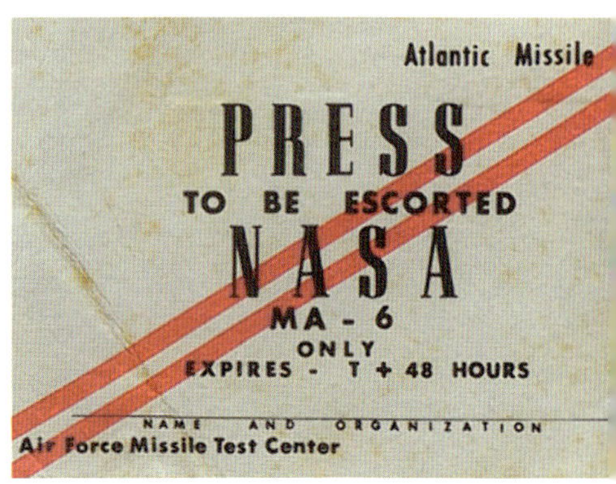

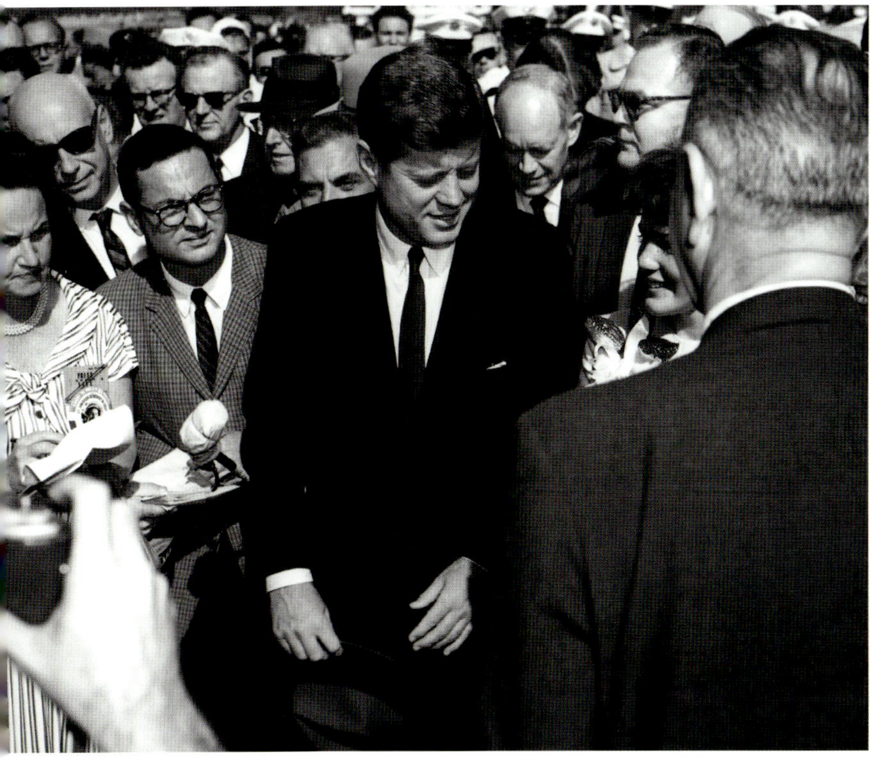

▼ News photographers snap away as Glenn and Kennedy climb into a 1962 Lincoln Continental for a tour of Mercury launch facilities.

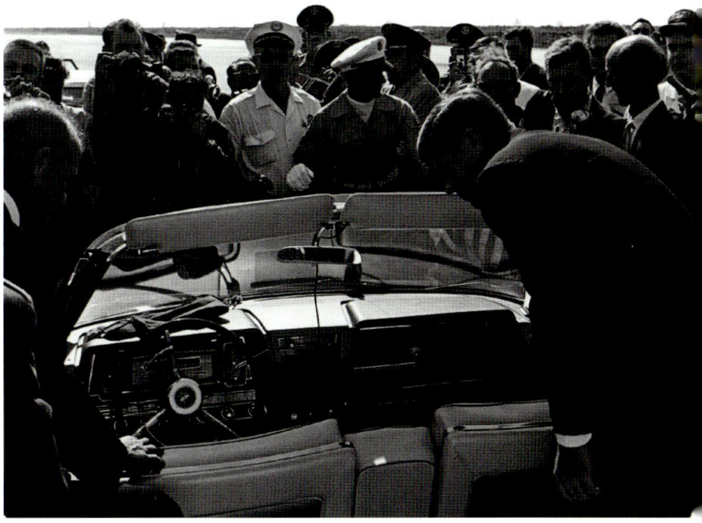

▲ Kennedy carries his Cavanaugh snap-brim fedora, with Lyn Glenn and Johnson at right. At left is Mary Bubb of Reuters, a pioneering woman space reporter. MSC Director Robert Gilruth is behind her.

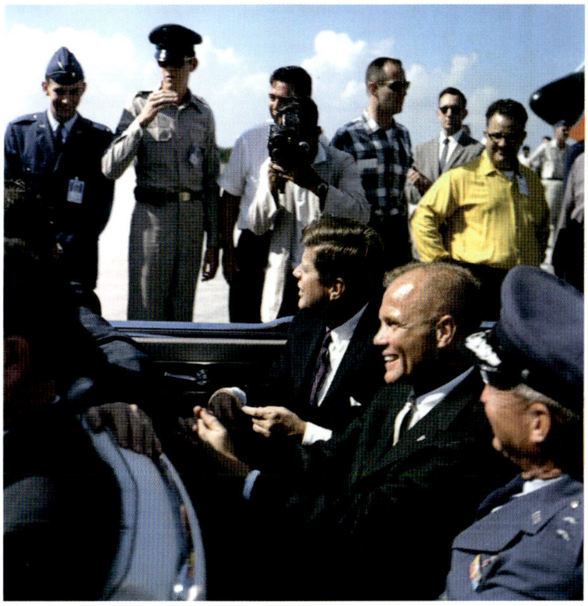

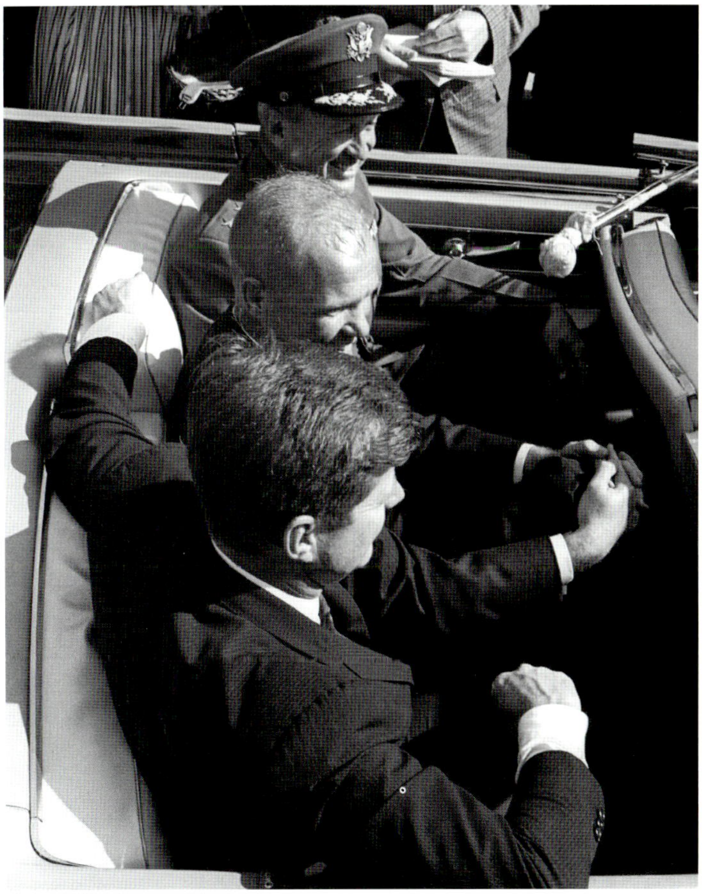

▲ Joining them in the back seat is Maj. Gen. Davis.

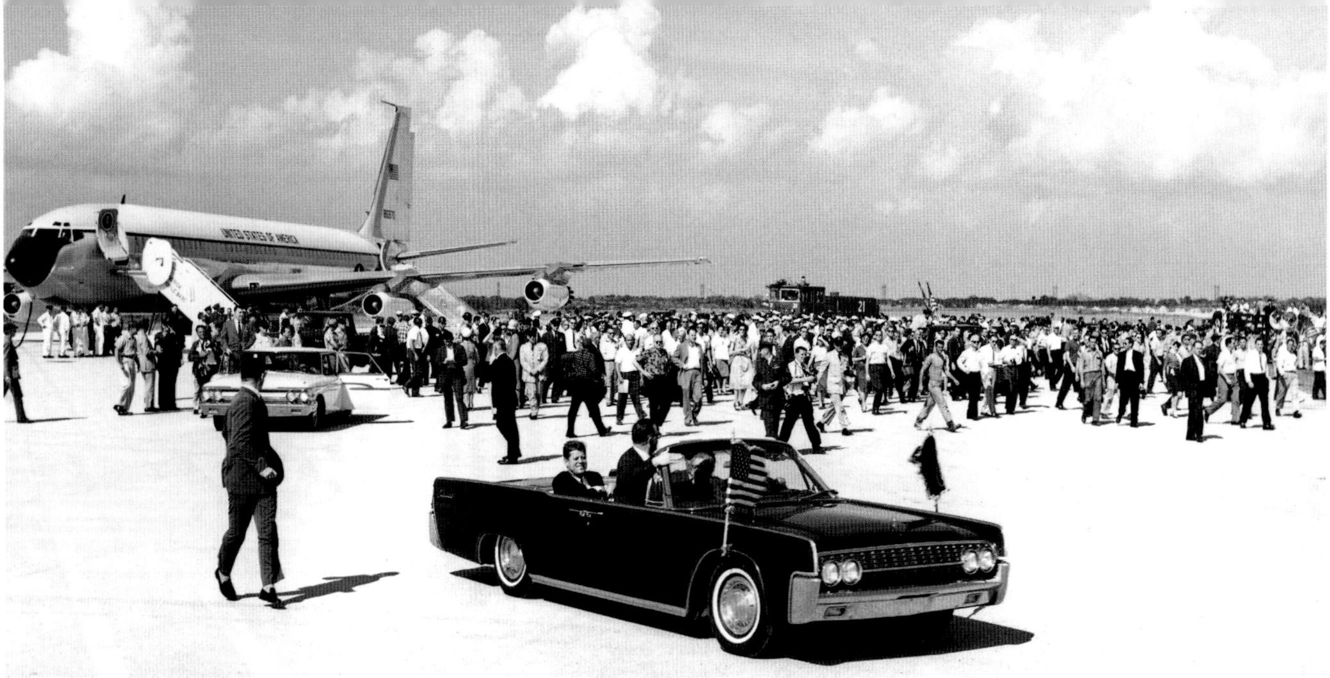

▶ The president, Glenn, and Maj. Gen. Davis leave the Skid Strip at 10:40 a.m. Glenn's mother sits between two Secret Service agents in the front seat; Agent Bill Greer is at the wheel.

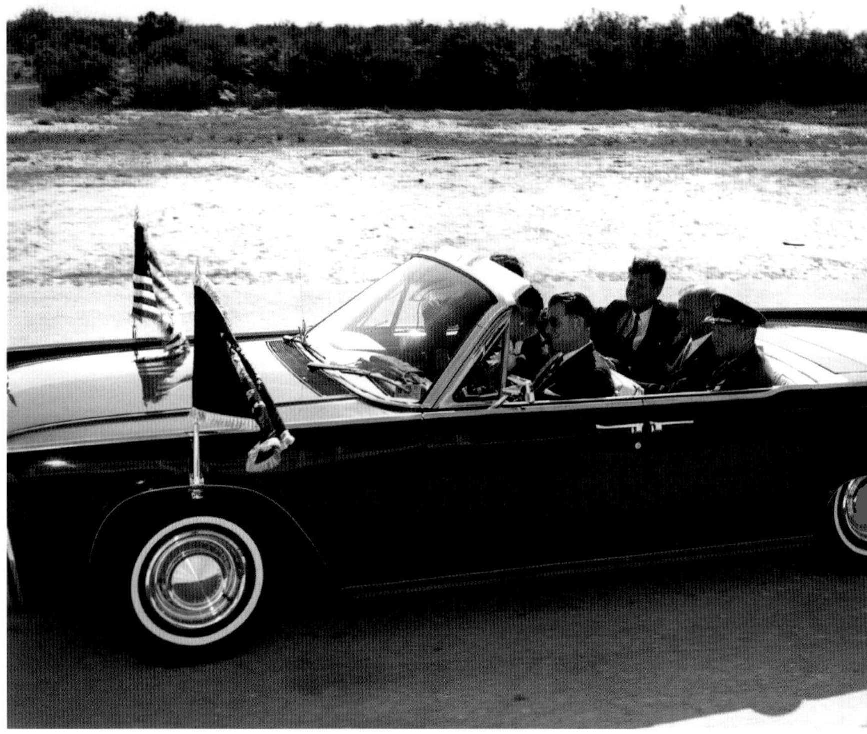

▼ At 10:47 a.m., the president's tour stops first at the Mercury Control Center (MCC) in the Engineering Support Building, less than one mile south of the Skid Strip. The Cape tracking and communications antenna for the Manned Space Flight Network looms behind the facility.

The building, later placed on the National Register of Historic Places, is demolished in 2010 because of concerns about asbestos and the estimated $5 million cost of repairs after forty years of exposure to salt air with almost no maintenance.

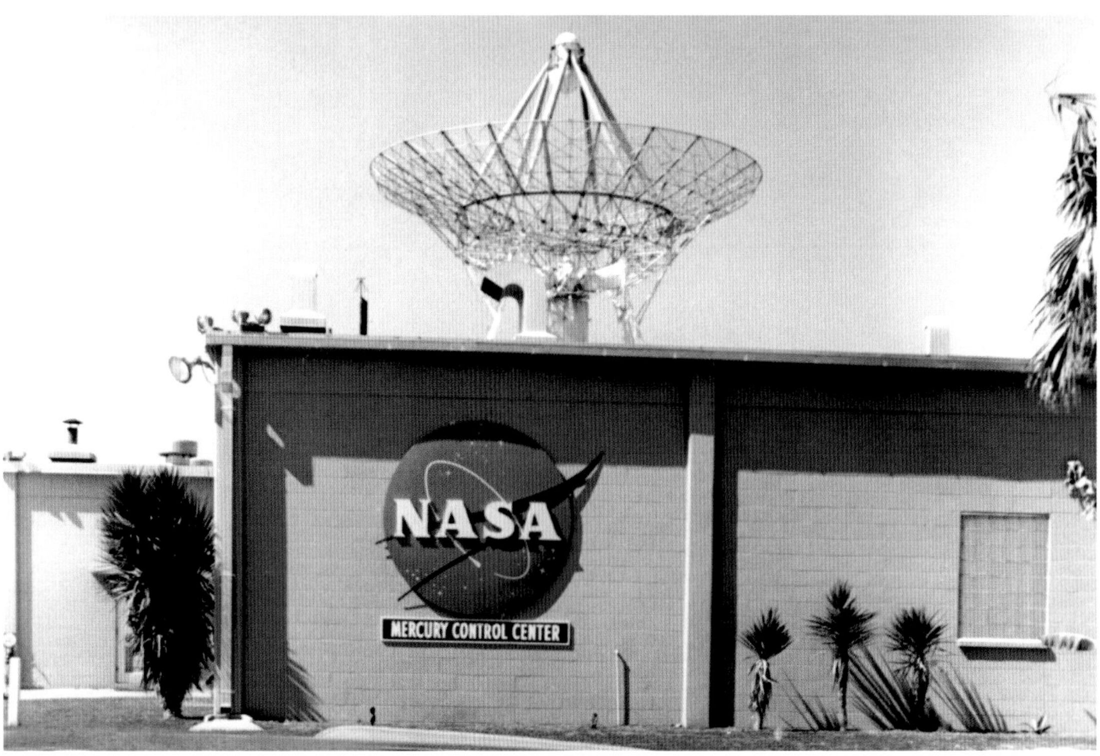

▶ Kennedy chats with Glenn and Alan Shepard near the capsule communicator console in the MCC. The glassed-in area behind them is the visitors' viewing gallery.

"He seemed, as he always seemed when we discussed the program, to be extremely interested in it," Shepard recalled in 1964, "and even in some of the details of how flight controllers reacted, how they responded, what their jobs were, and so on."

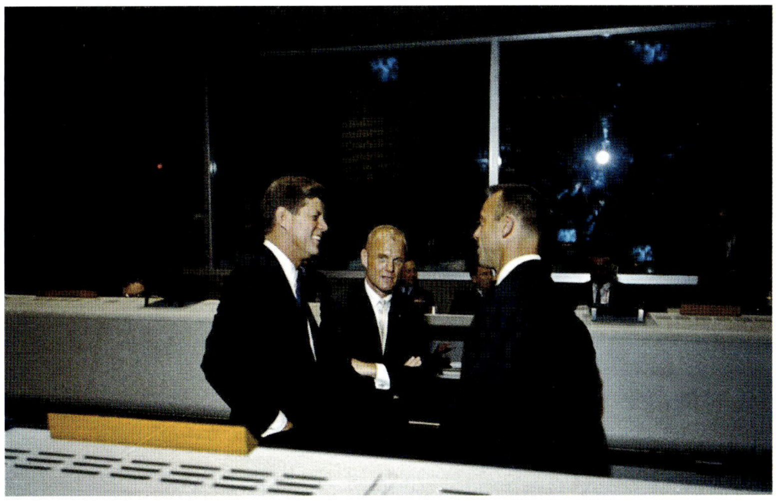

▶ Tecwyn Roberts, Mercury's first flight dynamics officer who monitors the booster's trajectory during launch, explains a chart plotter to the president, with Kraft at right. His console is in the foreground. Roberts would soon manage development of the new Mission Control Center in Houston.

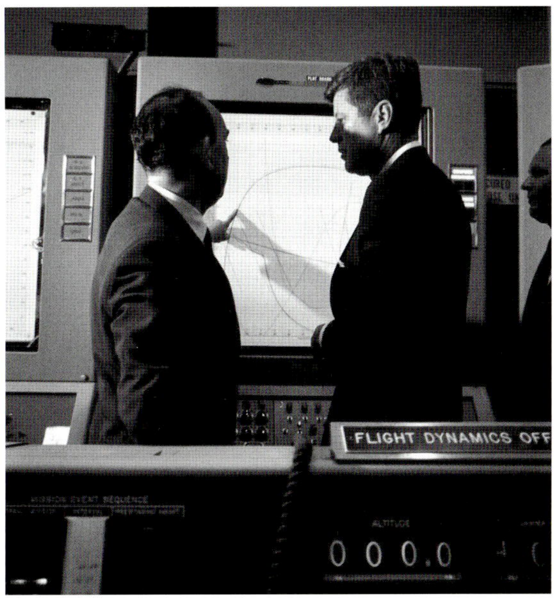

▼ The president huddles with Glenn and Mercury Flight Director Chris Kraft at the retrofire console. They are likely discussing the period during Glenn's reentry when a faulty light indicated his heat shield might be loose. NASA photographer Bill Taub, holding his camera near his nose, stands across from the trio.

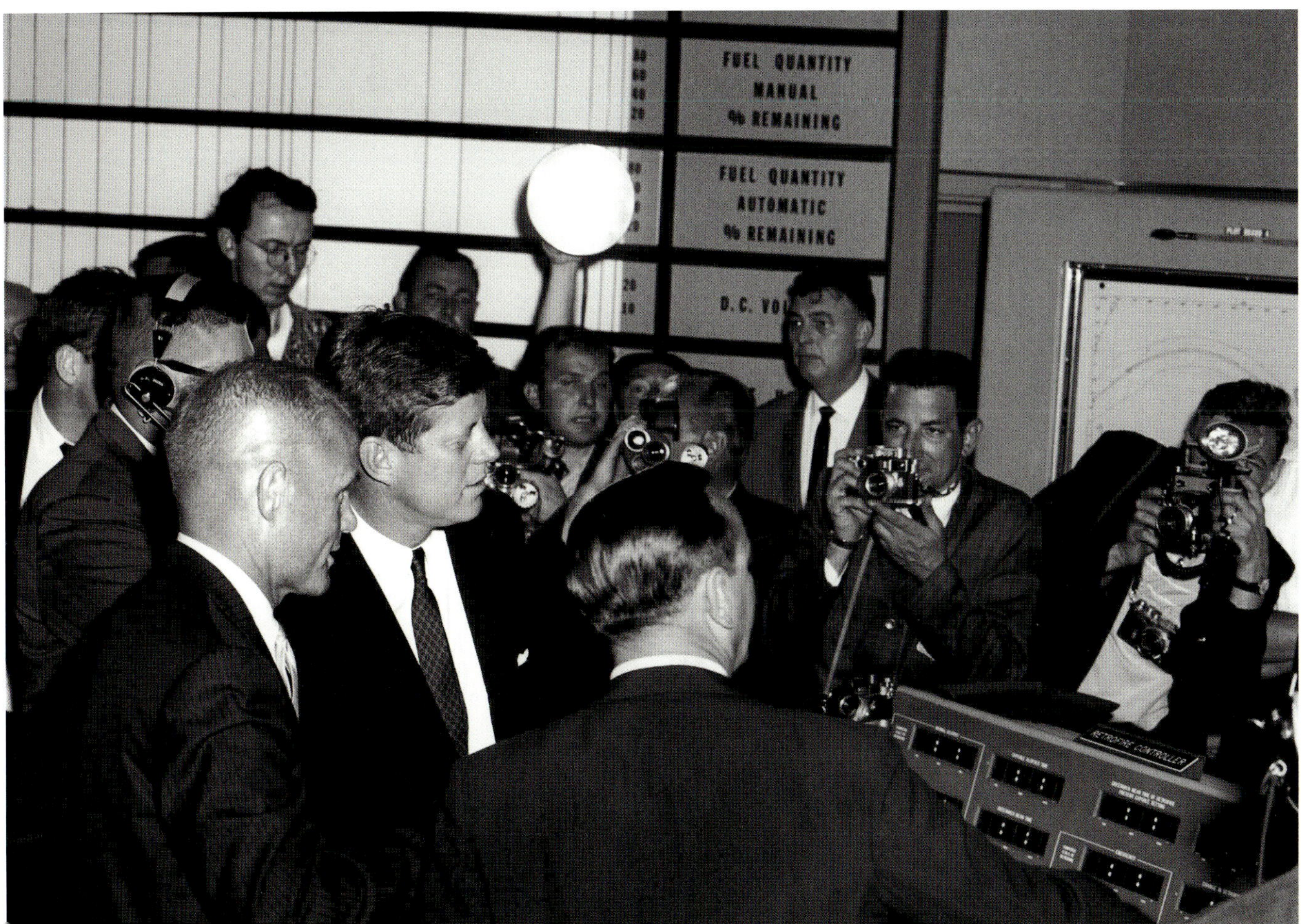

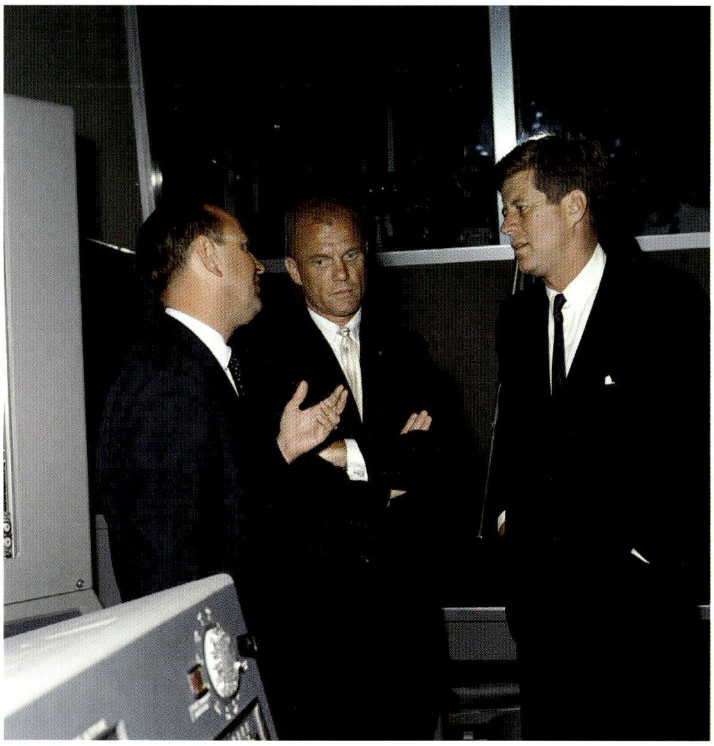

▲ Kraft speaks with Glenn and Kennedy near a chart plotter in the MCC. On first meeting them, he recalled, both men extended their hands simultaneously, forcing Kraft to make a decision. He chose to shake Glenn's hand first, prompting a grin from the president. Kraft serves as flight director for all six manned Mercury missions and succeeds Gilruth as director of MSC in Houston in 1972.

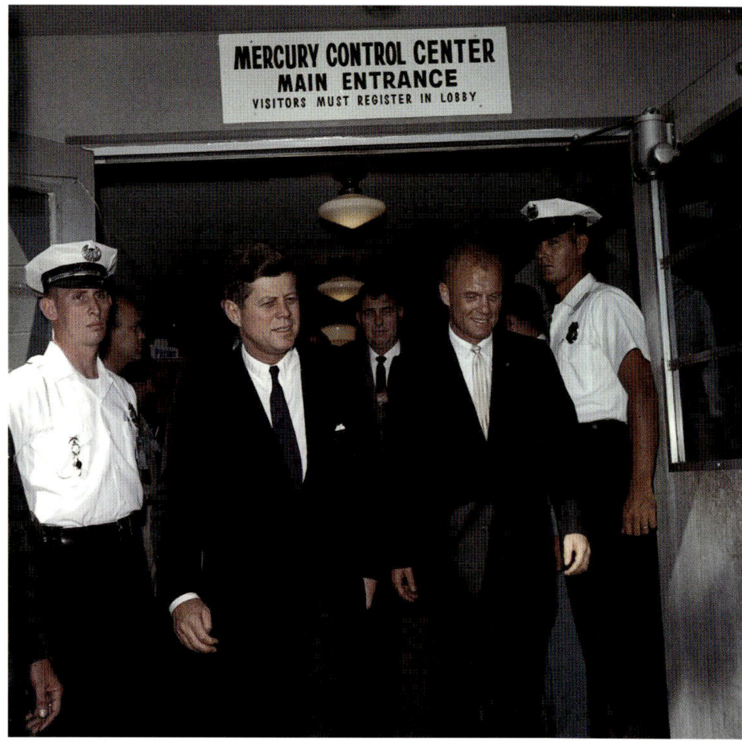

▲ Kennedy and Glenn leave the MCC after about twenty minutes. The police officers are employed by the Aeronautical Systems Division of Pan American World Airways, which holds the base services contract for Cape Canaveral.

▼ The president and Glenn return to the Lincoln to head to Glenn's launch site. A NASA TV pool camera at left used for Glenn's launch transmits the scene; a news media microphone is temporarily mounted above the entrance.

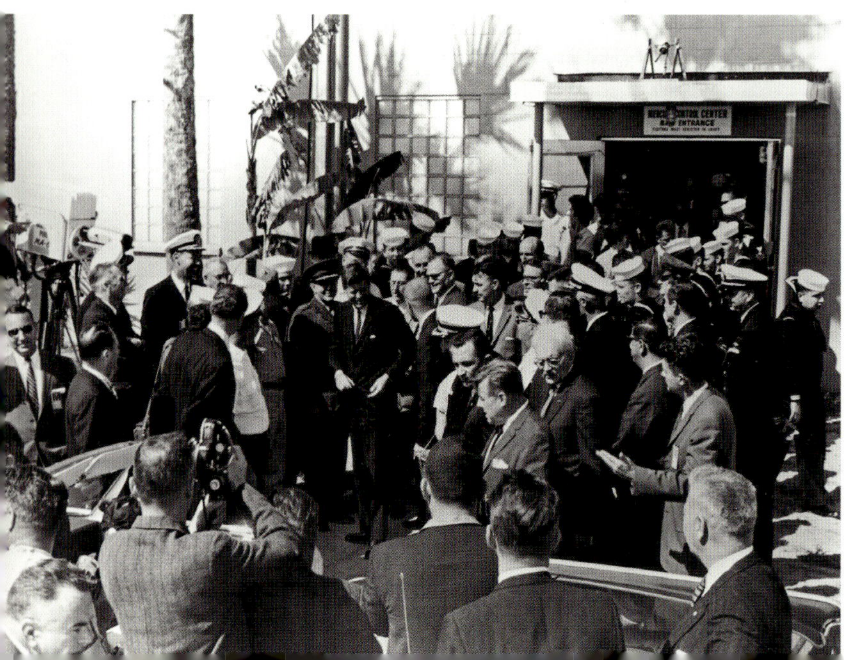

▼ With NASA, USAF, and contractor personnel watching at left, Glenn shakes hands with Paul Donnelly, a key NASA test conductor at the Cape who would be named launch operations manager for the Kennedy Space Center (KSC) in 1964. Between Glenn and Donnelly is H. H. "Luge" Luetjen, manager of the McDonnell Aircraft team at the Cape, contractor for the Mercury spacecraft.

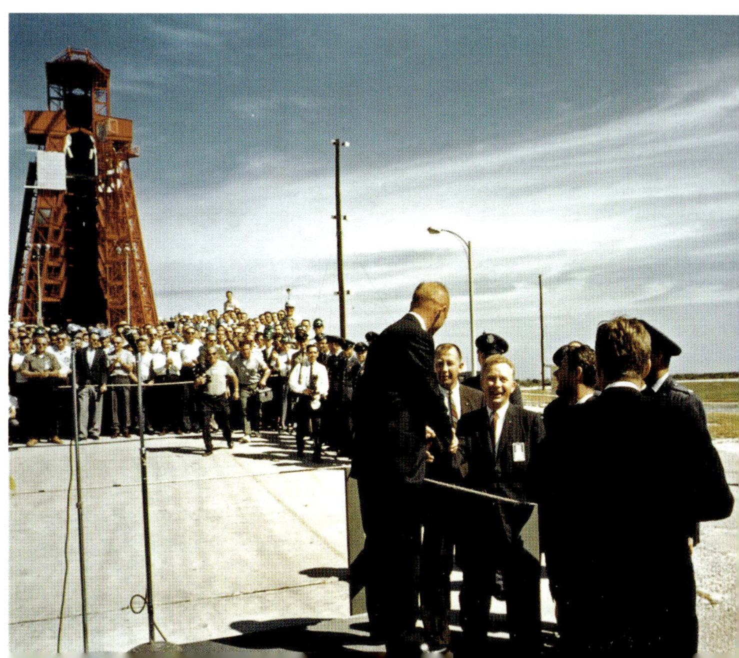

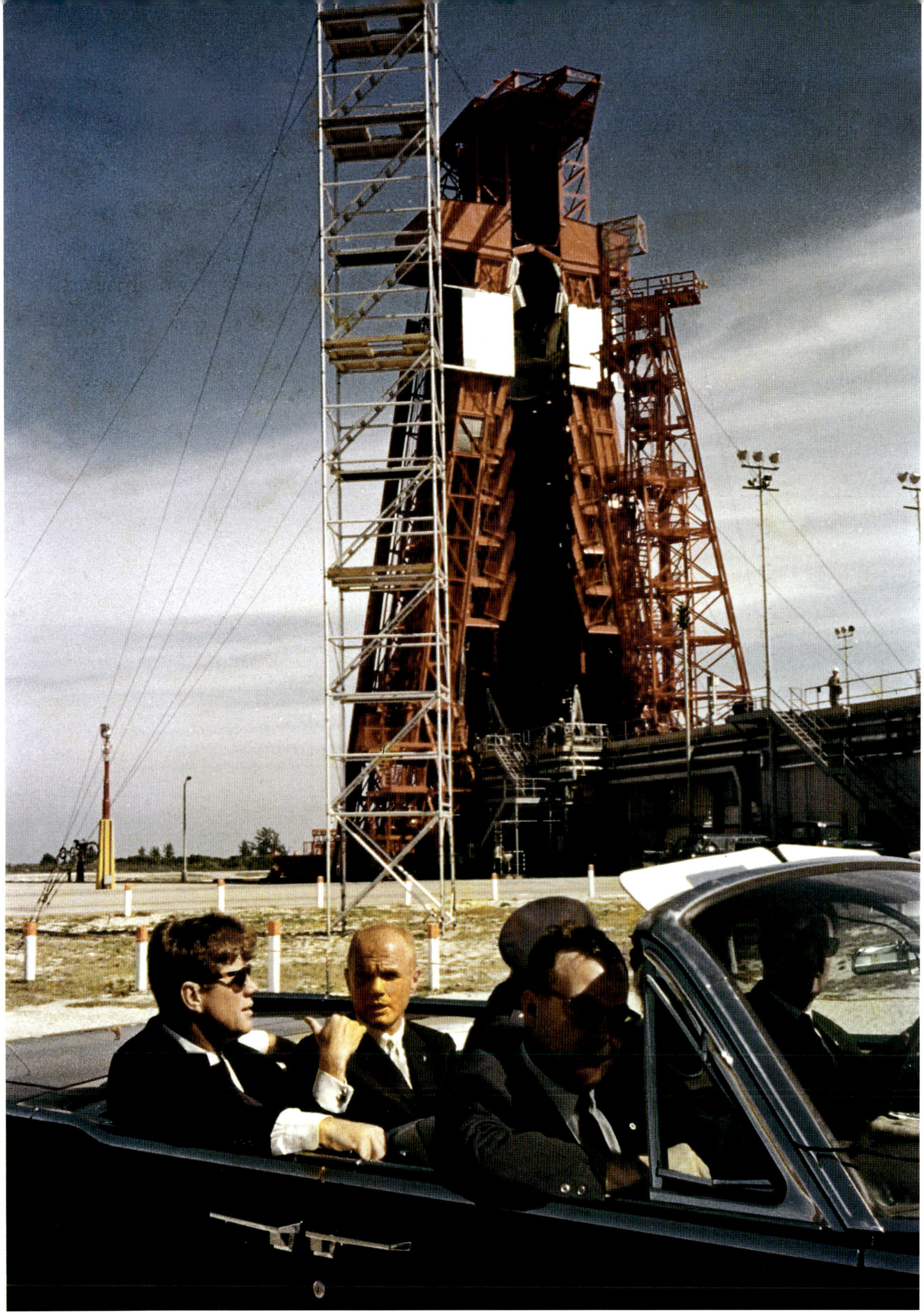

▲ The tour arrives at LC-14 (about three miles northeast of the MCC) at 11:10 a.m., where Glenn was launched into orbit just three days earlier. At center is the red service tower that provides access to the Atlas booster, with its shorter umbilical tower to the right.

▼ Glenn presents the president with a McDonnell hard hat, which is to make Kennedy "an honorary member of the launch crew." Kennedy tells the assembled workers that Glenn "wants to come back and thank you, I think!"

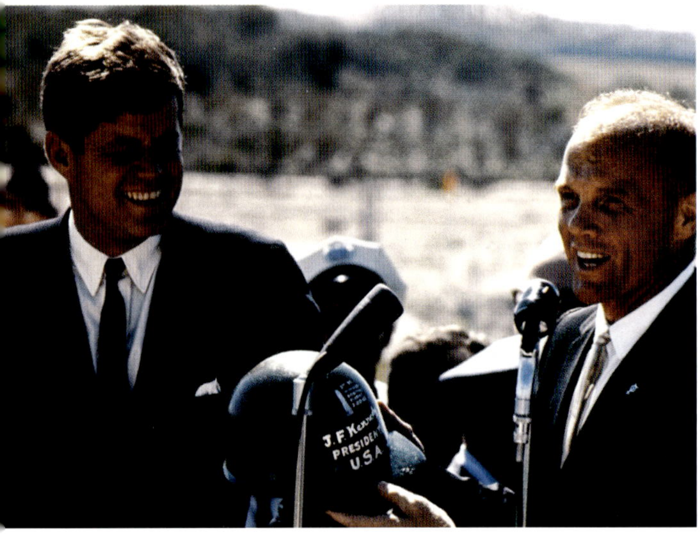

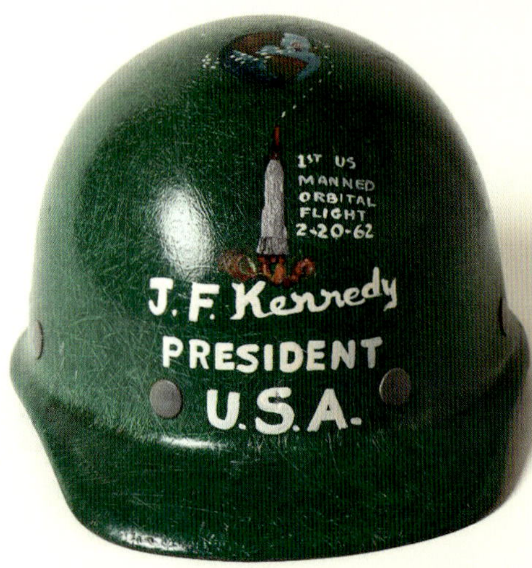

▲ Hard hat in the John F. Kennedy Presidential Library and Museum collection.

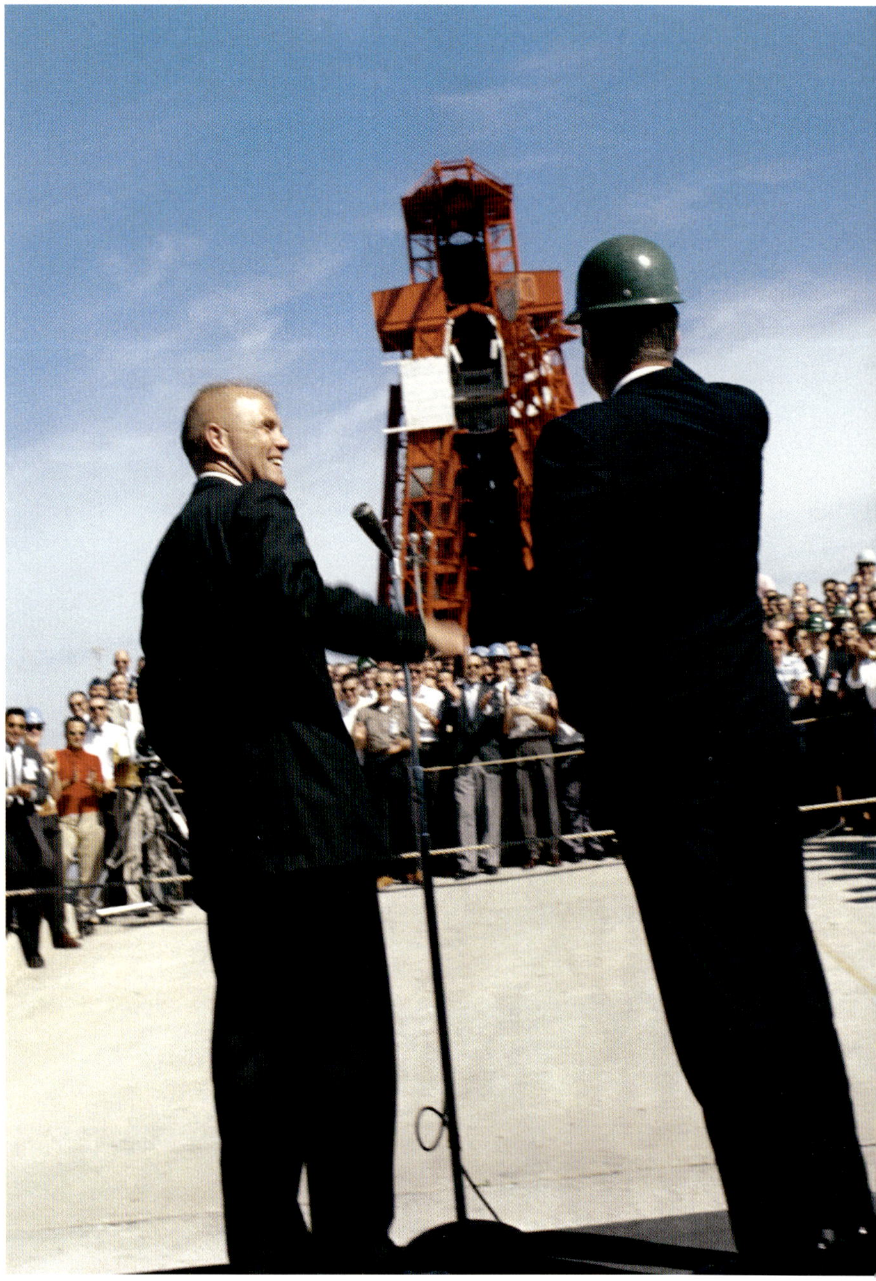

▲ Kennedy briefly dons the hard hat to the delight of the crowd after Glenn reached out to put it on his head. Like most presidents, Kennedy is reluctant to wear headgear of any sort; he rarely wears his fedora.

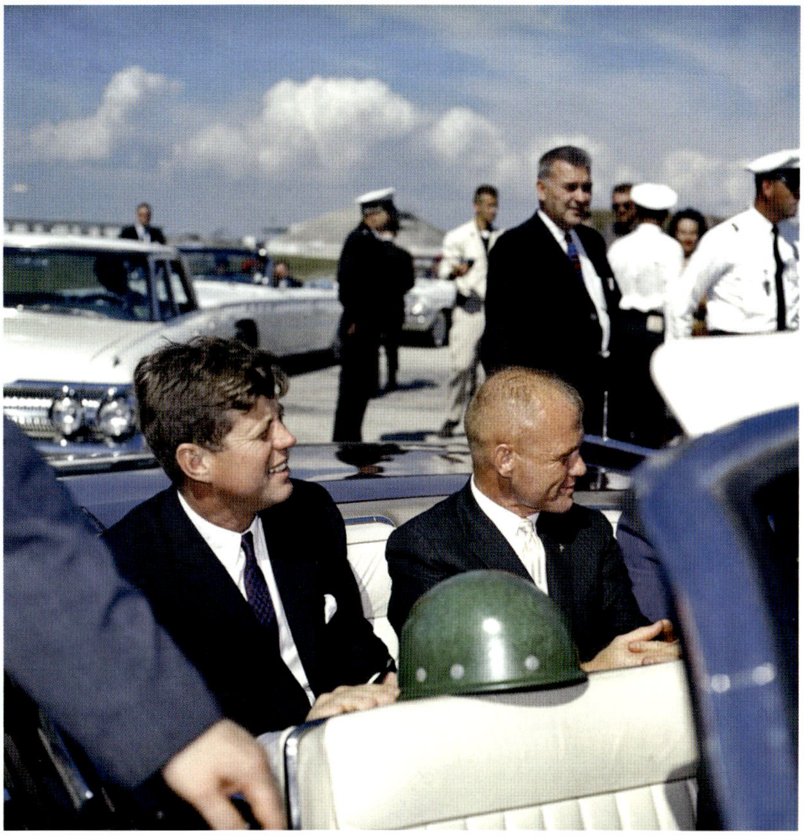

▲ The motorcade prepares to depart LC-14, heading for Hanger S, after about twenty-five minutes. The blockhouse for the complex where the launch team was based is the igloo-like structure in the distance at center.

▼ NASA Administrator James Webb speaks first at the medal ceremony at 11:30 a.m. at Hangar S in the Industrial Area, a short drive from LC-14. The building, owned by the USAF, is the home of the Pre-Flight Operations Division of the Space Task Group (which becomes MSC) from 1959 to 1963. Mercury spacecraft are received, tested, and prepared for flight in the hangar, which also houses the astronauts' training and preflight preparation facilities, including their living quarters, on the second floor.

Shepard and Grissom are seated far left; Glenn's spacecraft, *Friendship 7*, is at right. Much of the president's visit is carried live on all three national television networks, NBC, ABC, and CBS.

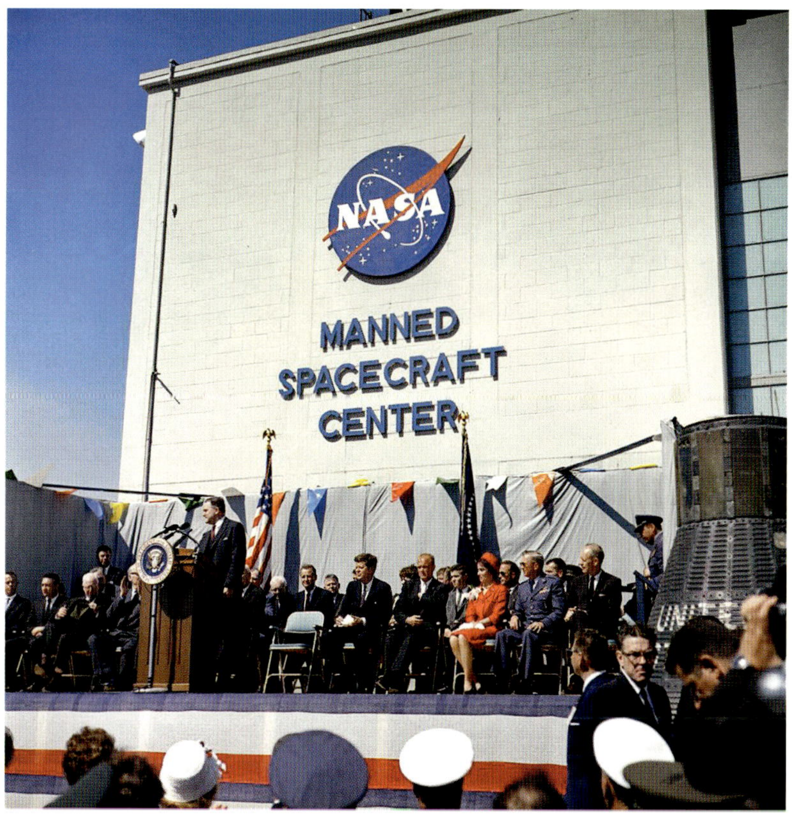

▼ With her family at left, Annie Glenn speaks with the president at the bottom of the pad ramp.

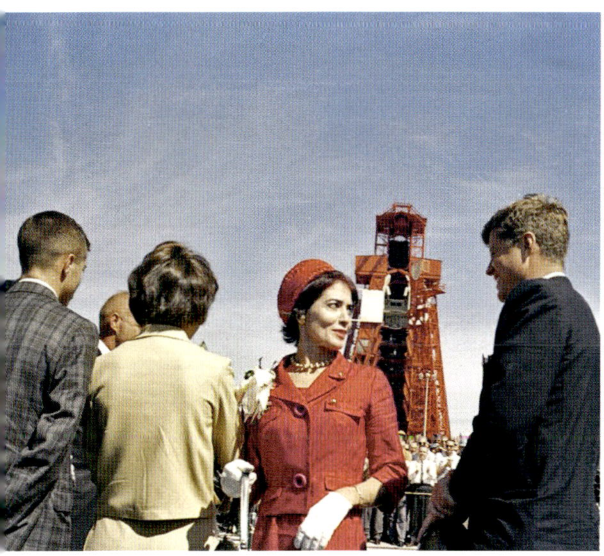

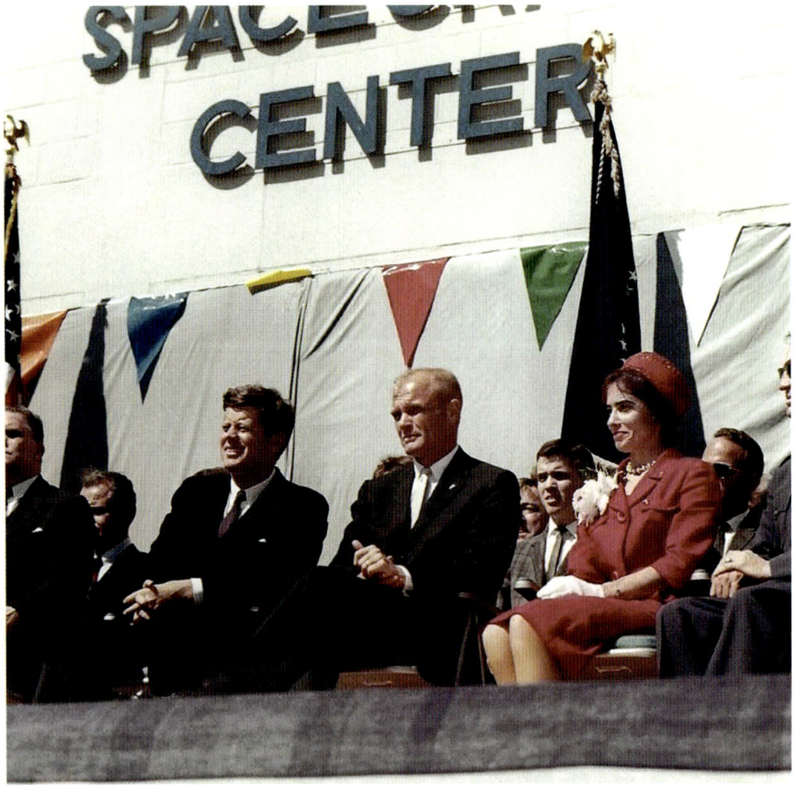

▶ Webb, Kennedy, and the Glenns listen as Vice President Johnson introduces the president.

Astronaut Scott Carpenter, who would make the next Mercury flight, sits behind Mrs. Glenn; his spacecraft is also on display.

▼ The president and Glenn before the ceremony begins.

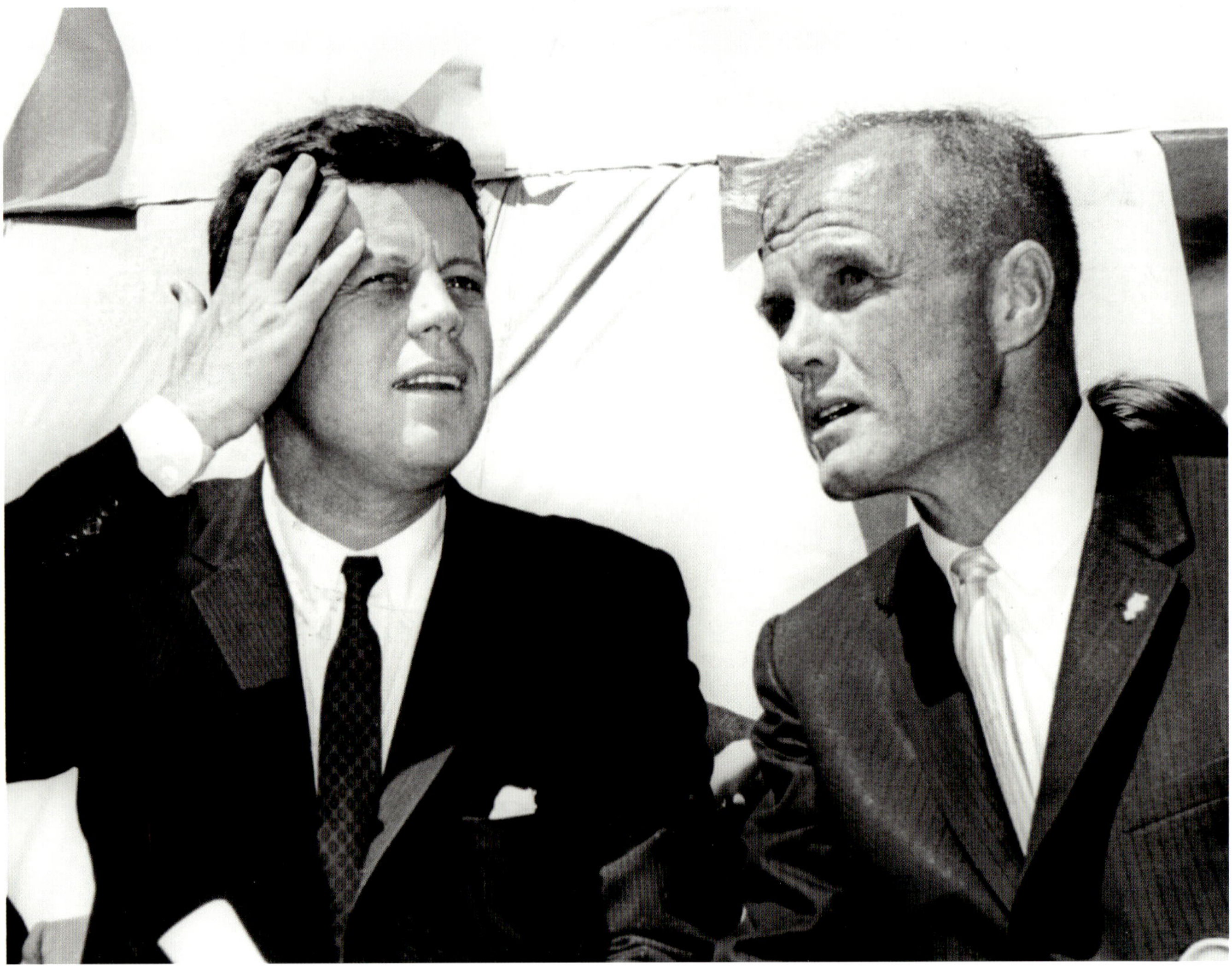

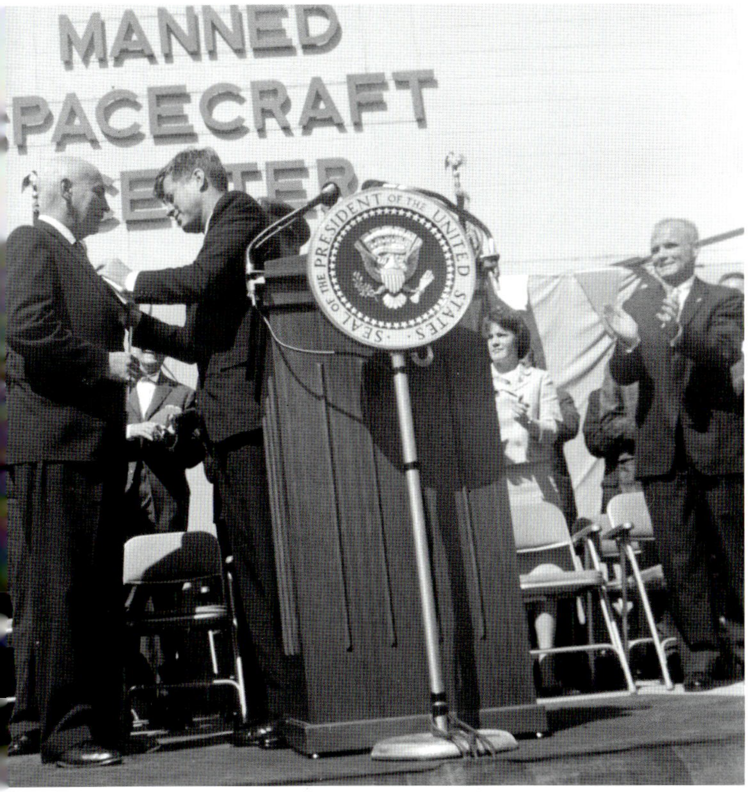

▲ Kennedy first awards the NASA Distinguished Service Medal to MSC and Project Mercury Director Robert Gilruth, who can say little beyond, "I'm very, very proud."

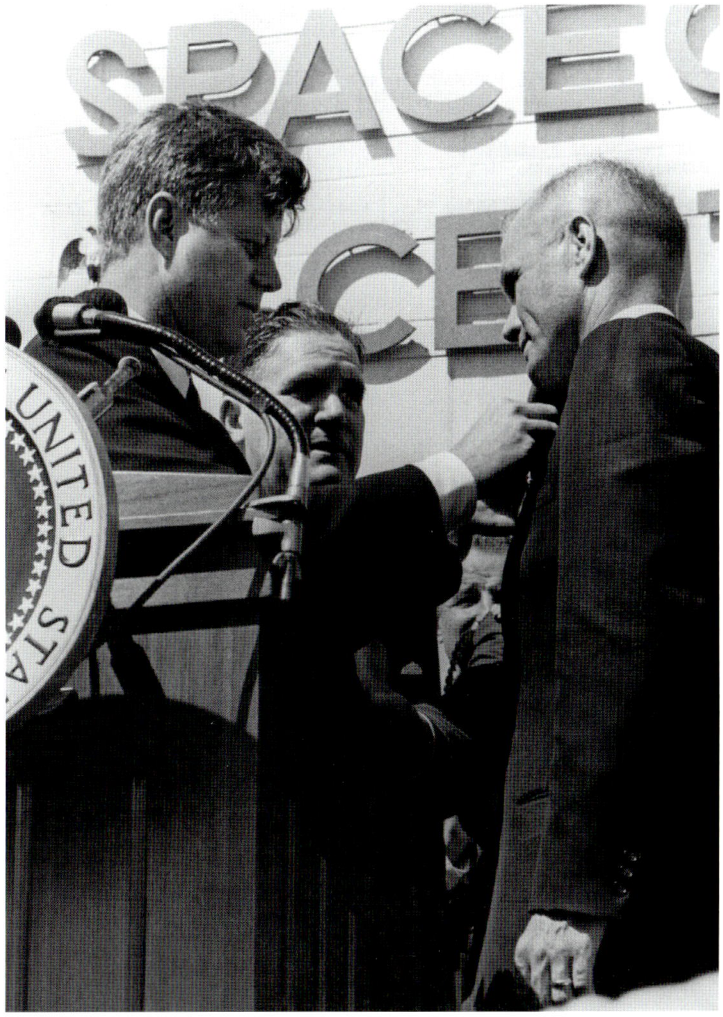

▲ The president then pins the same decoration on Glenn.

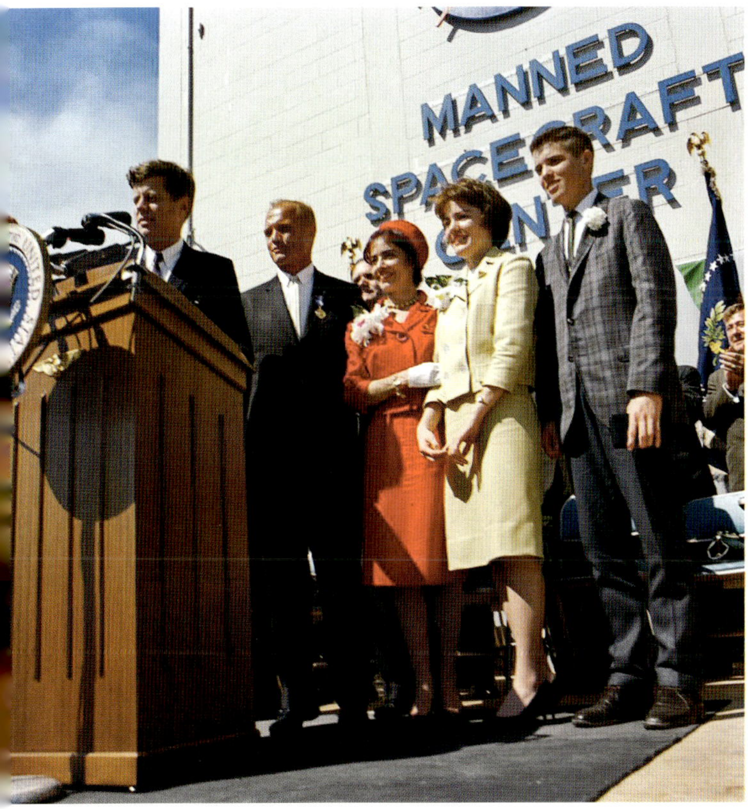

◄ "Seventeen years ago, the Marines planted the American flag on Mt. Suribachi [Iwo Jima]," the president says. "So it's very appropriate that today we decorate Colonel Glenn of the United States Marine Corps. And we also realize that in the not too distant future a Marine or a naval man or an air force man will put the American flag on the moon. Our boosters may not be as large as others, but our men and women are."

Kennedy then reads Glenn's medal citation, "His performance in fulfillment of this most dangerous assignment reflects the highest credit upon himself and the United States."

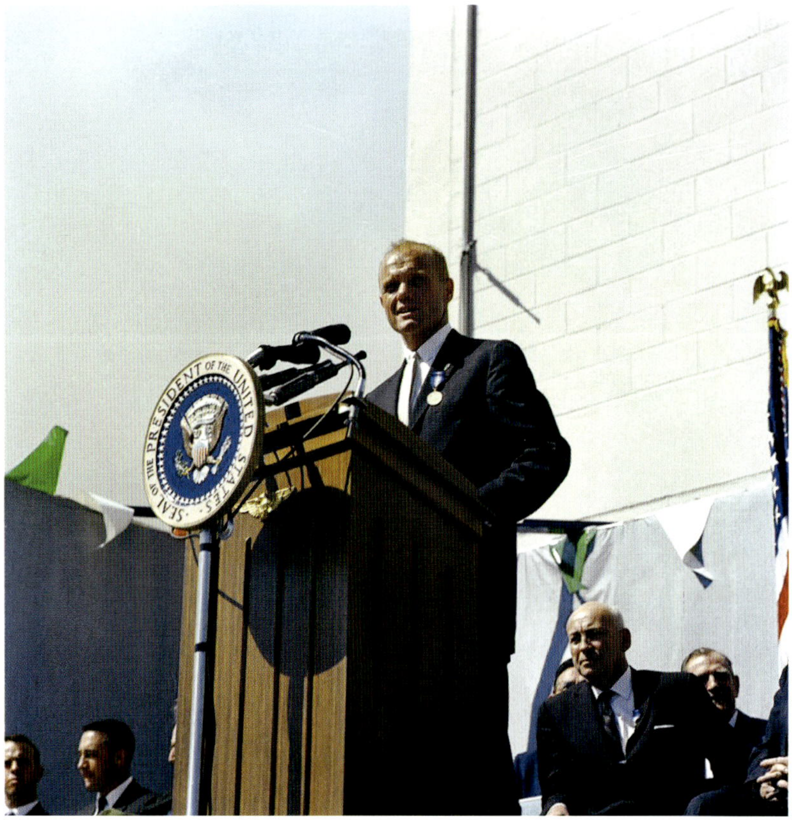

▶ "I can't express my appreciation adequately to be here accepting this," Glenn tells the crowd, "when I know how many thousands of people all over the country were involved in helping accomplish what we did last Tuesday and knowing how particularly this group at the Cape and many of the group here on the platform and our own group of astronauts who were scattered all around the world and who performed their functions here at the Cape also." He continues,

> We all acted literally and figuratively as a team and it was a real team effort all the way. We have stressed the team effort in Project Mercury. It goes across the board, I think—sort of a crosscut of Americans, of industry and military and civil service, government work, contractors, the . . . it's almost a crosscut of American effort in the technical field, I think. It wasn't specialized by any one particular group. It was headed up by NASA, of course, but thousands and thousands of people have contributed as certainly as much or more than I have to the project.
>
> I would like to consider that I was sort of the figurehead for this whole big tremendous effort and I'm very proud of this medal I have on my lapel here for all of us—you included—because I think it represents all of our efforts—not just mine. Thank you very much and thank you, Mr. President.

Mercury's first two astronauts, Shepard and Grissom, are seated at left; Gilruth is at right with Rep. Thomas behind him.

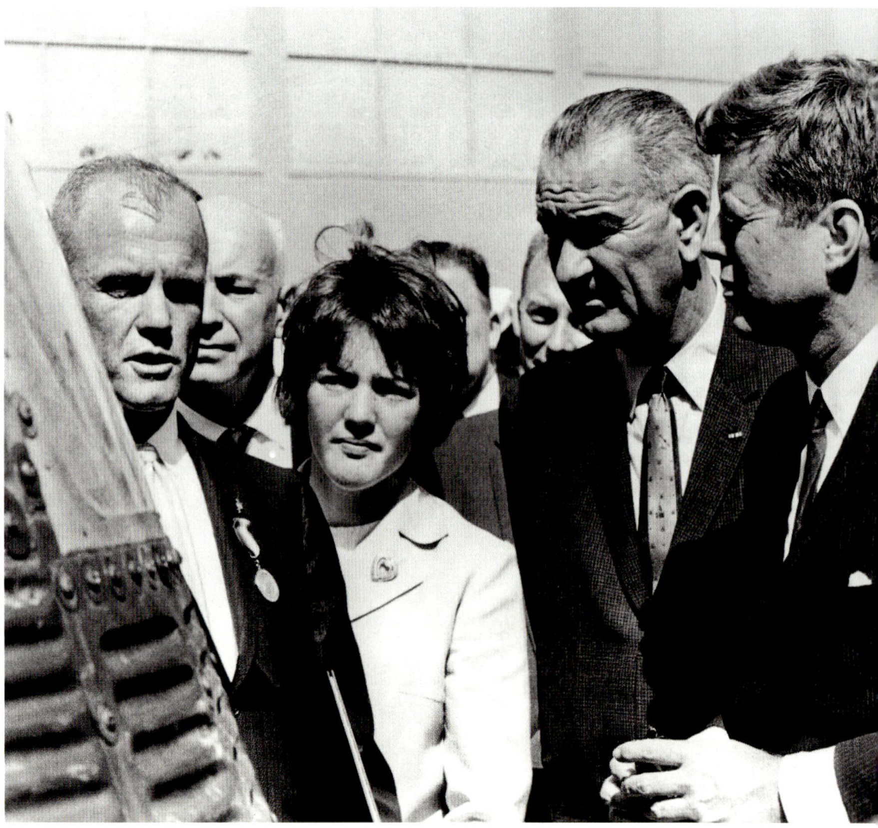

▶ During a brief inspection of *Friendship 7*, Glenn discusses his flight with Gilruth, daughter Lyn, Johnson, and the president. Johnson prompts him to describe his "most harrowing moment" to Kennedy (his reentry): "It was an interesting return," he tells the vice president.

▶ Kennedy peers into the cabin through the hatch. At right are David Glenn, Sen. George Smathers (D-Fla.), and Gilruth.

The motorcade leaves Hangar S at noon to return to the Skid Strip, from where the president flies back to Palm Beach at 12:10 p.m. to spend the weekend with his father and family. The following Monday, Kennedy, the Glenns, and other NASA astronauts and officials fly to Washington on Air Force One for ceremonies there.

During the flight, according to Shepard, the astronauts discuss with Kennedy how they could personally "help sell the space program" and still have enough time for training and other duties.

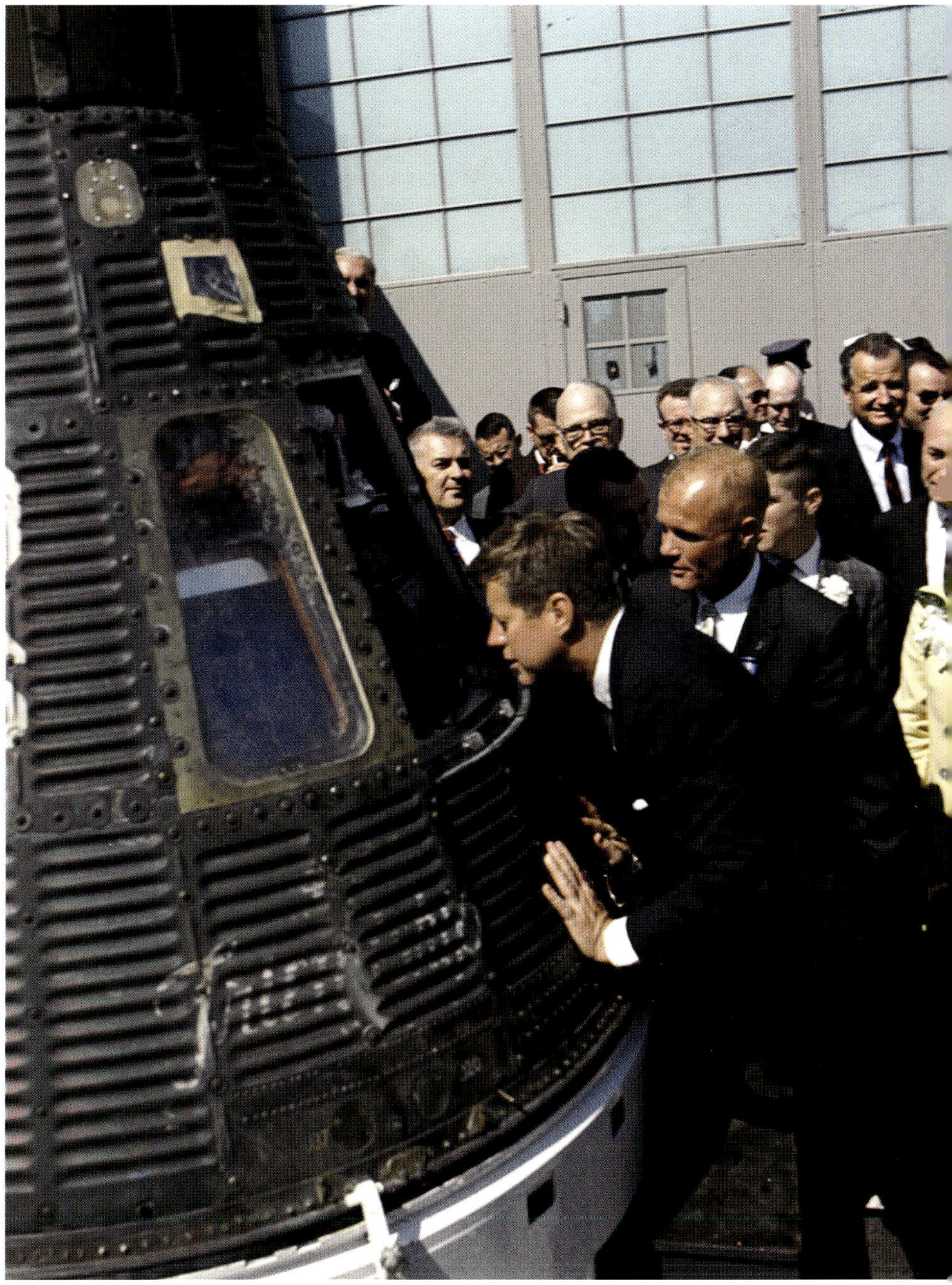

▼ The president and Glenn arrive at the West Wing Colonnade just before noon on February 26, 1962, with Johnson at left. They had landed at Andrews AFB that morning to take part in a brief red-carpet ceremony, which had been moved into a hangar because of rain.

During his speech to Congress that afternoon, Glenn relates a story from the flight from Florida aboard Air Force One: "We had the opportunity to meet Mrs. Kennedy and Caroline before we took off. I think Caroline really cut us down to size and put us back in our proper position, though, when after being introduced, she looked up and said, 'Where is the monkey?'" The House chamber erupts.

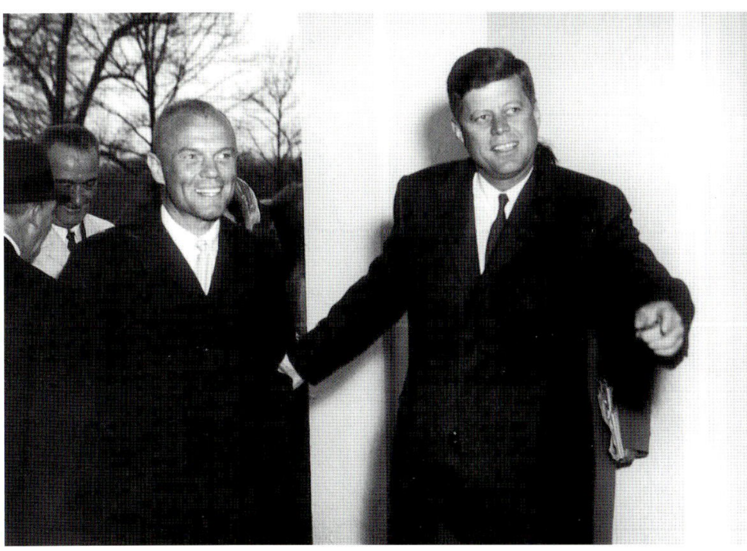

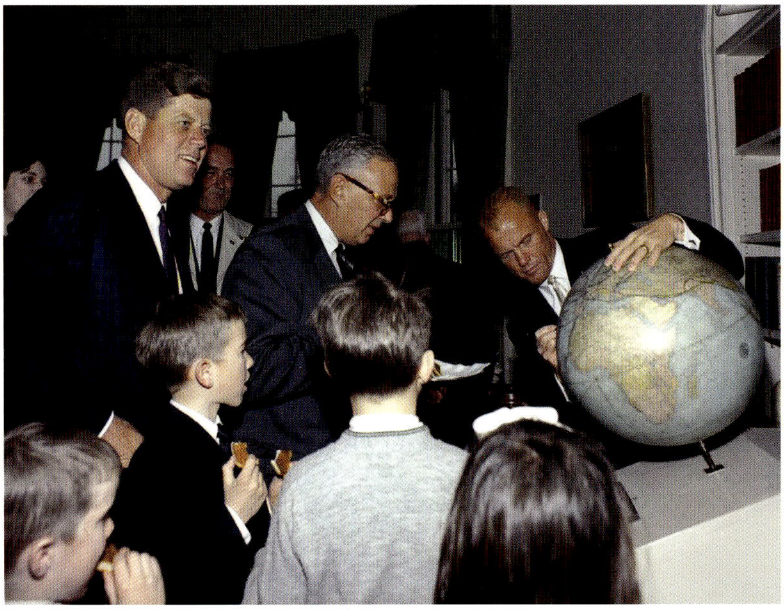

◀ In the Oval Office, Glenn adds his signature to the Flyers & Explorers Globe, an eighteen-inch Rand McNally Terrestrial Globe owned by the American Geographical Society. Some fifty-six previous explorers had already signed it.

Society Director Charles Hitchcock (in profile, wearing glasses) and several children, including Kennedy's nephew Robert F. Kennedy Jr. (in foreground, second from left) and his niece Maria Shriver (right), look on.

Astronauts Shepard, Grissom, Carpenter, Schirra, and Slayton are also present; Cooper has just returned from duty at the Woomera, Australia, tracking station.

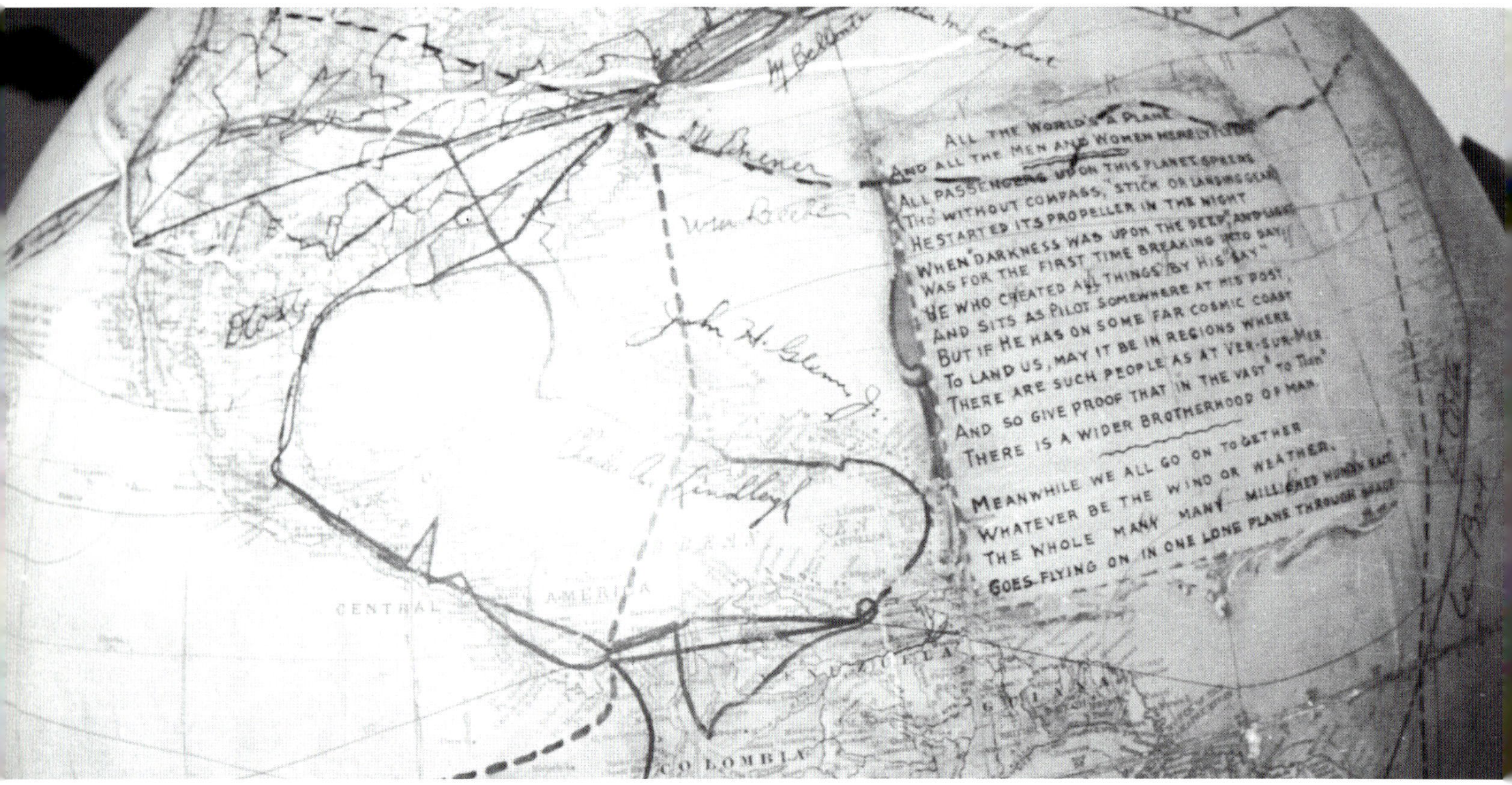

▲ Glenn signed the globe along the Atlantic Missile Range, above aviator Charles Lindbergh's signature.

▶ L-R: Kennedy; Johnson; Glenn; and Webb on the North Portico at 12:15 p.m.

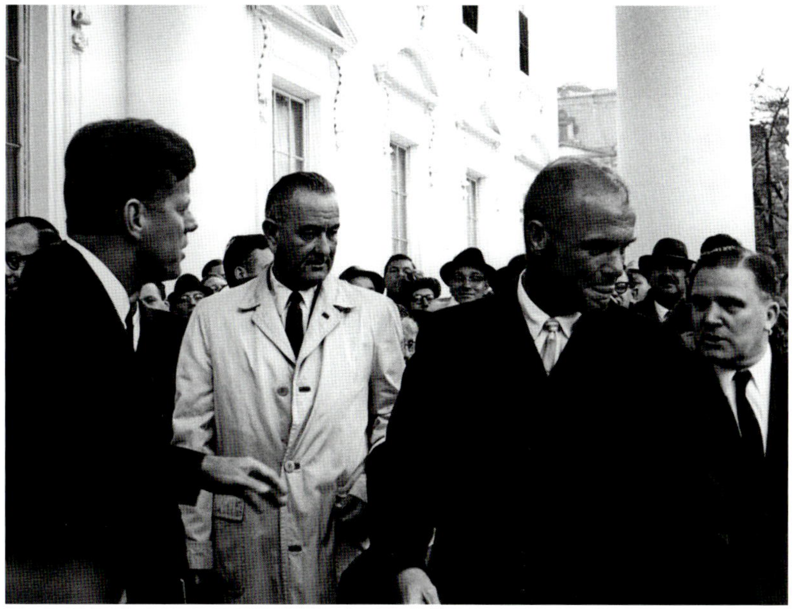

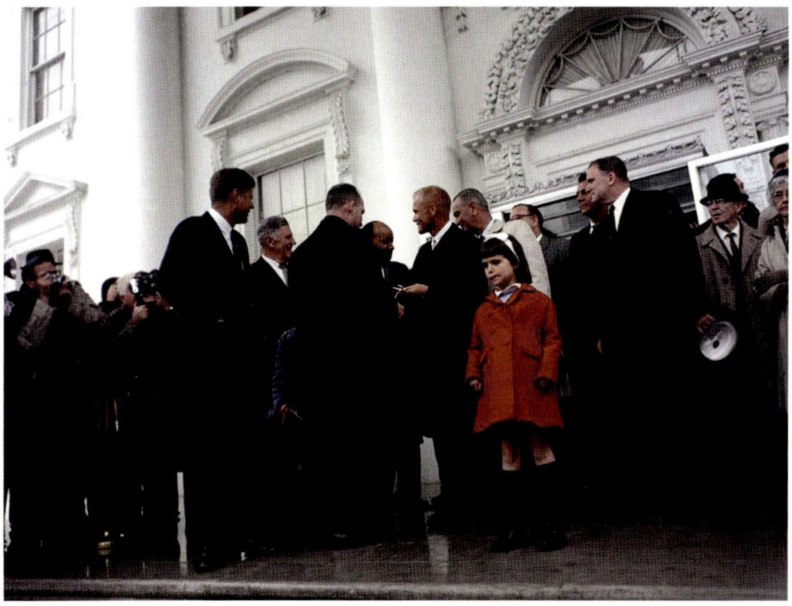

◀ Before departing, Glenn receives a key to the city of Washington, presented by District of Columbia Engineer Commissioner Brig. Gen. Frederick Clarke (second from left). Maria Shriver is at center.

▶ With a network pool TV camera and other members of the media behind them, Mrs. Glenn and Johnson get into the back seat of the presidential limousine that takes them to the US Capitol for Glenn's address before a joint meeting of Congress. Kennedy smiles at Glenn's daughter Lyn. The modified 1961 Lincoln Continental limousine, code-named SS-100-X by the Secret Service, is the same one Kennedy will use in Dallas on Nov. 22, 1963.

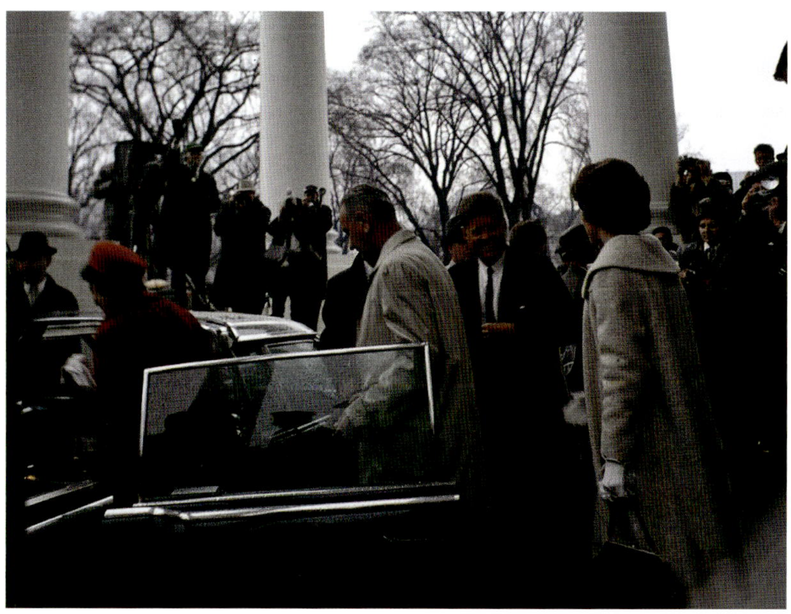

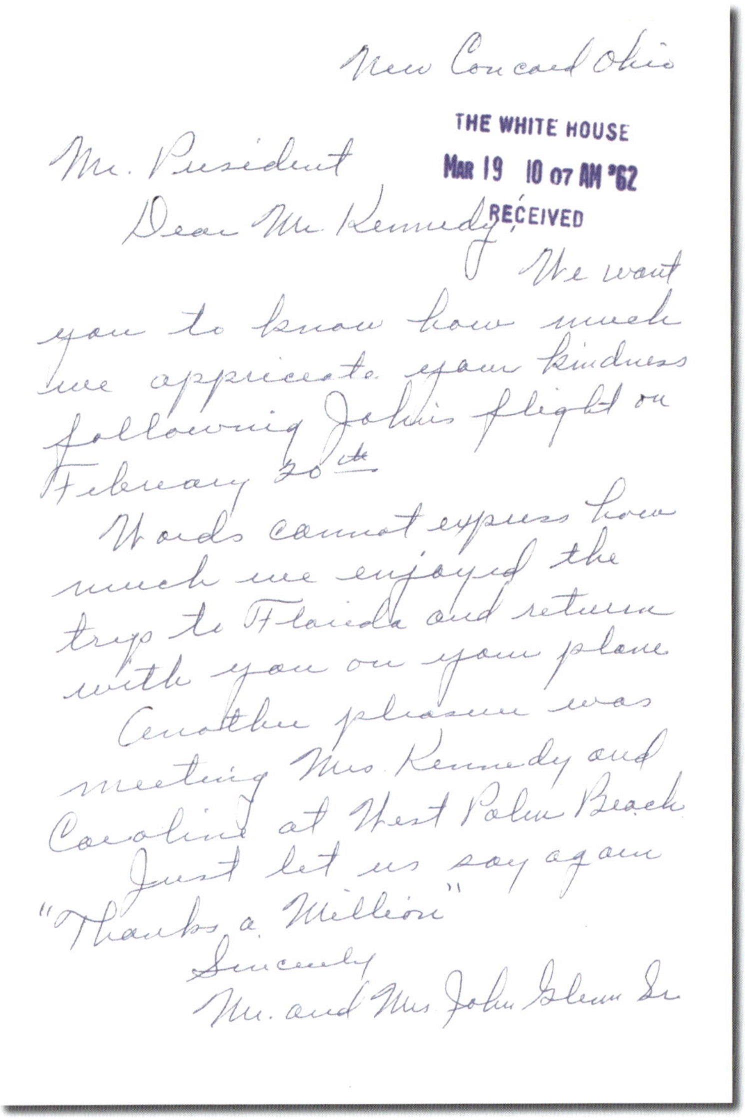

New Concord Ohio

THE WHITE HOUSE
MAR 19 10 07 AM '62
RECEIVED

Mr. President

Dear Mr. Kennedy,

We want you to know how much we appreciate your kindness following John's flight on February 20th.

Words cannot express how much we enjoyed the trip to Florida and return with you on your plane.

Another pleasure was meeting Mrs. Kennedy and Caroline at West Palm Beach.

Just let us say again "Thanks a Million"

Sincerely

Mr. and Mrs John Glenn Sr

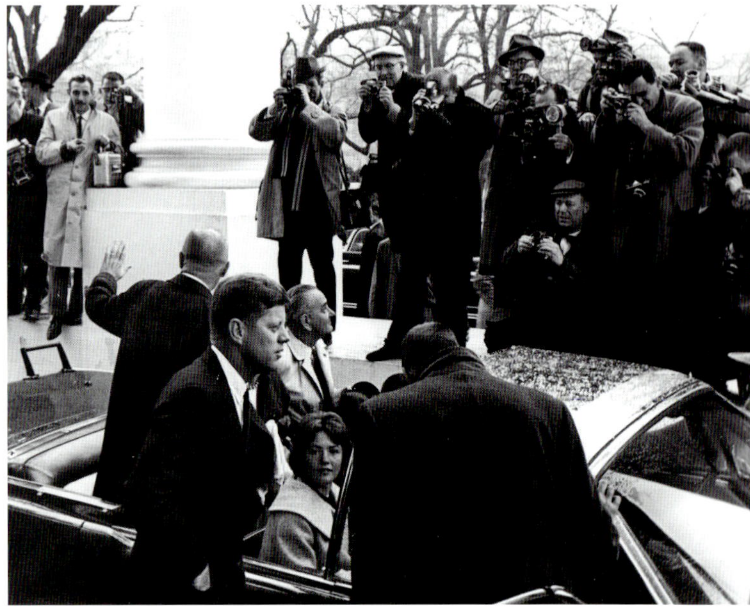

▲ Glenn waves as the motorcade is ready to depart at 12:20 p.m. *New York Times* photographer George Tames (kneeling at center) is the photographer of the iconic 1961 "The Loneliest Job" Oval Office image of Kennedy.

◀ Letter of thanks to the president from Mr. and Mrs. John Glenn Sr.

:03

MARCH–AUGUST 1962

"We are glad to see you again"

NASA'S ONLY MANNED spaceflight during the spring and summer of 1962 sends Navy Lt. Cmdr. Scott Carpenter on a three-orbit mission. His flight ends on an unplanned note—a combination of a tight timeline just before reentry and problems with his maneuvering jets results in Carpenter overshooting his planned landing site in the Atlantic Ocean by 250 miles.

Kennedy flies to the West Coast and becomes the first president to see an ICBM launch. Back at the White House, he receives a variety of guests and gifts in connection with the space program.

Most of the remaining US launches during that year are various military missile tests, although on April 26, NASA's Ranger 4 probe strikes the far side of the moon. It becomes the first US spacecraft to reach another celestial body, albeit its photo mission is a failure. (In 1959 the Soviets had already undertaken a photo mission to the far side of the moon. They first crashed Luna 2 onto the moon that year; a month later, however, Luna 3 succeeded in sending back the first photos of the moon's far side).

NASA also launches its second Saturn C-1 booster on April 25, a predecessor to the much larger, three-stage Saturn for the Apollo missions that will achieve Kennedy's moon-landing goal.

▼ On March 23, 1962, the president and Gen. Thomas Power (center), commander of the Strategic Air Command (SAC), arrive at Vandenberg AFB, California, at 4:05 p.m. PST. Power had briefed Kennedy aboard Air Force One on the flight from Alameda Naval Air Station. They are greeted by the Fifteenth Air Force Band from March AFB, California, and the SAC Guard Squadron from Offutt AFB, Nebraska. The USAF's code name for the visit is Project Sky Rocket. Kennedy views a display near the flight line of Atlas D, Thor-Agena, Titan I, and Minuteman I missiles before taking a thirty-mile, two-and-a-half-hour tour of base missile facilities. His brother Robert coincidentally had taken in the same runway display earlier in the day, passing through on his way to a crime conference in Los Angeles in his role as attorney general.

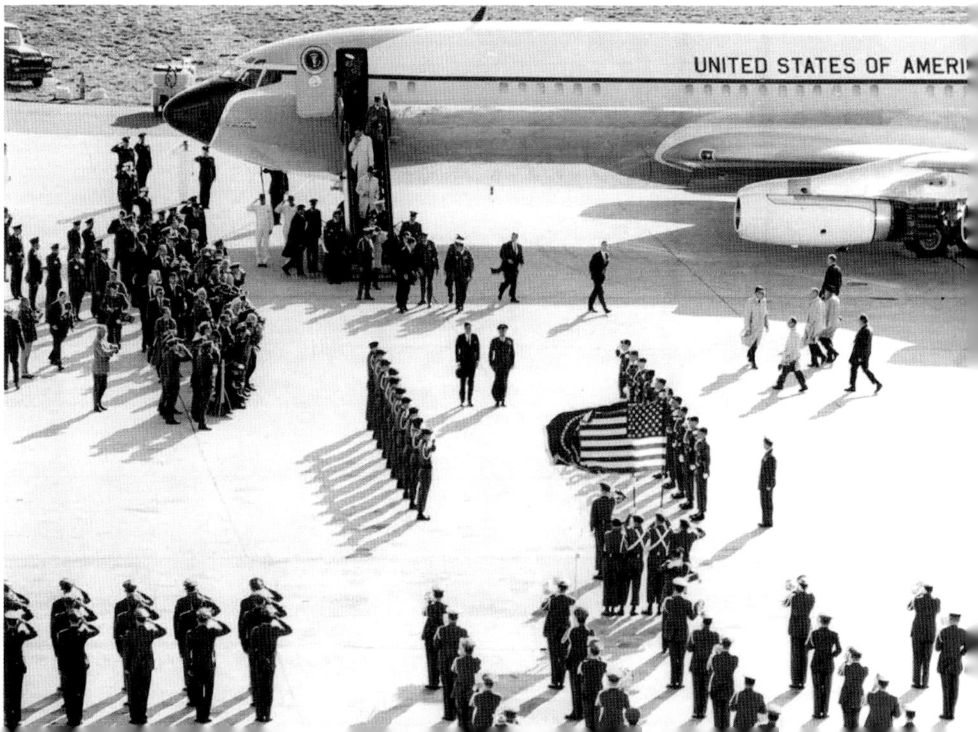

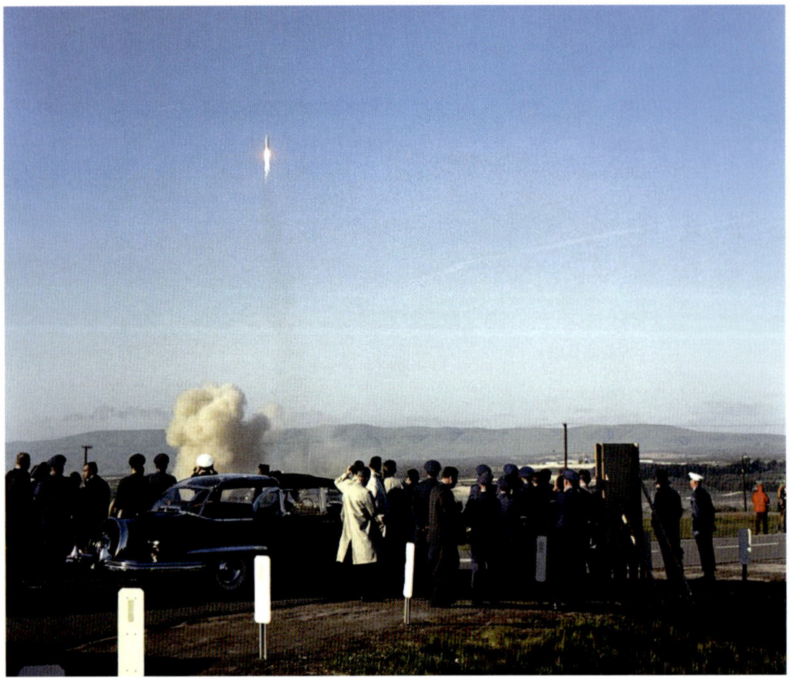

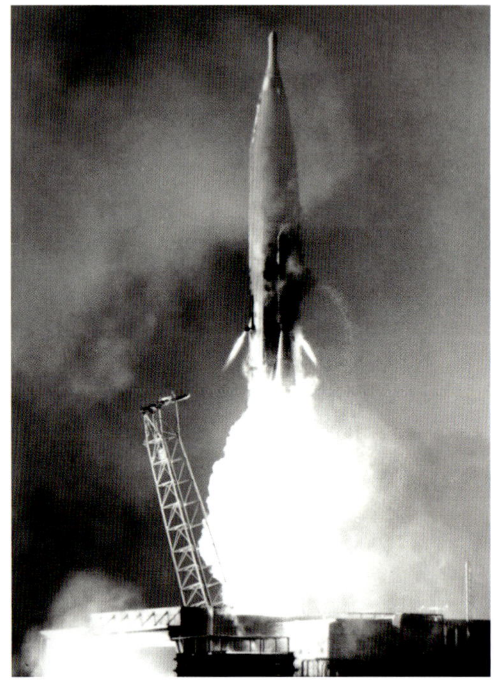

▲ The first stop is LC-576A on a bluff about one thousand yards from LC-576B. At 4:39 p.m.,Atlas 134D is launched from an above-ground emplacement westward down the Pacific Missile Range, and Kennedy becomes the first commander-in-chief to witness a missile launch.

A small Atlas ICBM squadron, the nation's first, is on alert at this launch complex from 1959 to 1964. Atlas is made by the Convair Division of General Dynamics.

In 1959 a train carrying Soviet Premier Nikita Khrushchev had passed by the complex, where two Atlas Ds were purposefully displayed. Khrushchev looked away. "I'm not interested in your missiles," he says. "We have more than you do and ours are better."

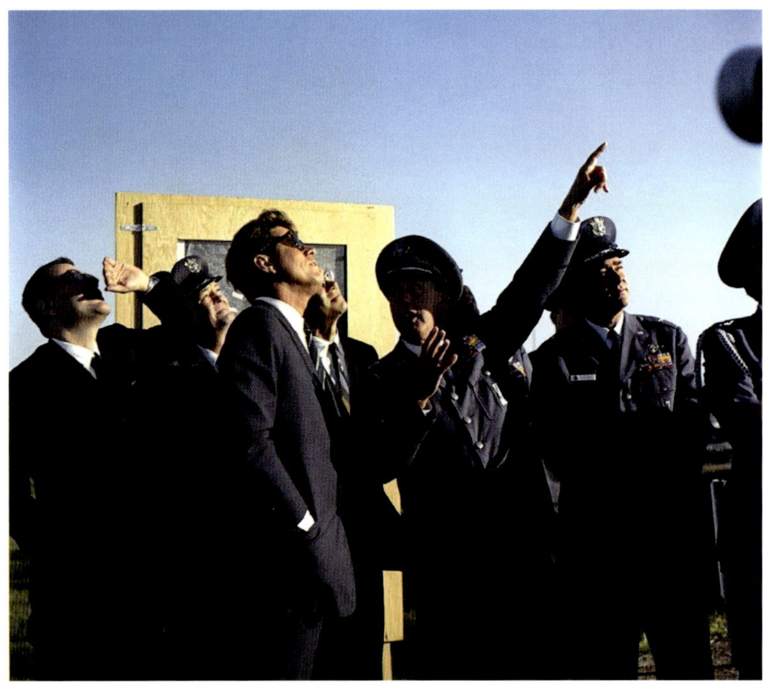

▲ Kennedy watches the launch, code-named Curry Comb I, with Gen. Power and Harold Brown (left), director of Defense Research and Engineering. Defense Secretary Robert McNamara stands behind the president with Brig. Gen. Seth McKee, SAC planning director, at right. Presidential USAF aide Brig. Gen. Godfrey McHugh has been such an advocate for the Atlas that Kennedy tells him, "If this thing doesn't go off, McHugh, you'll be managing a PX on Monday." The president had promoted him in January.

▶ The president watches the Atlas head skyward as Gen. Power provides commentary.

"McHugh is saved," Kennedy quips after the launch. Brown would serve as USAF secretary in the Johnson administration and as defense secretary under President Carter. No previous or subsequent missile launch has or will be attended by as many high-ranking US officials as this one.

The ICBM's unarmed Mark 3 reentry vehicle misses its bull's-eye in the Eniwetok Atoll lagoon by only 8/10th of a mile—a 4,385 mile flight in 26 minutes. Eniwetok, in the Marshall Islands, is the site of 43 US nuclear tests from 1948 to 1958.

L–R: Military policeman; Secret Service Agent Bob Lilley; Kennedy; Brown; Power; and McHugh. An unidentified photographer crouches in the foreground.

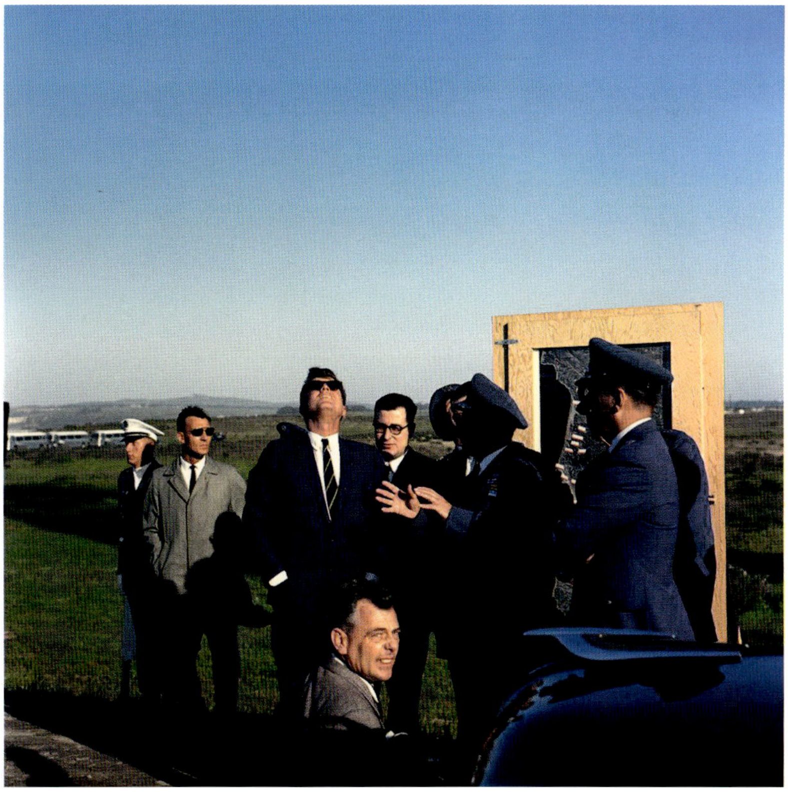

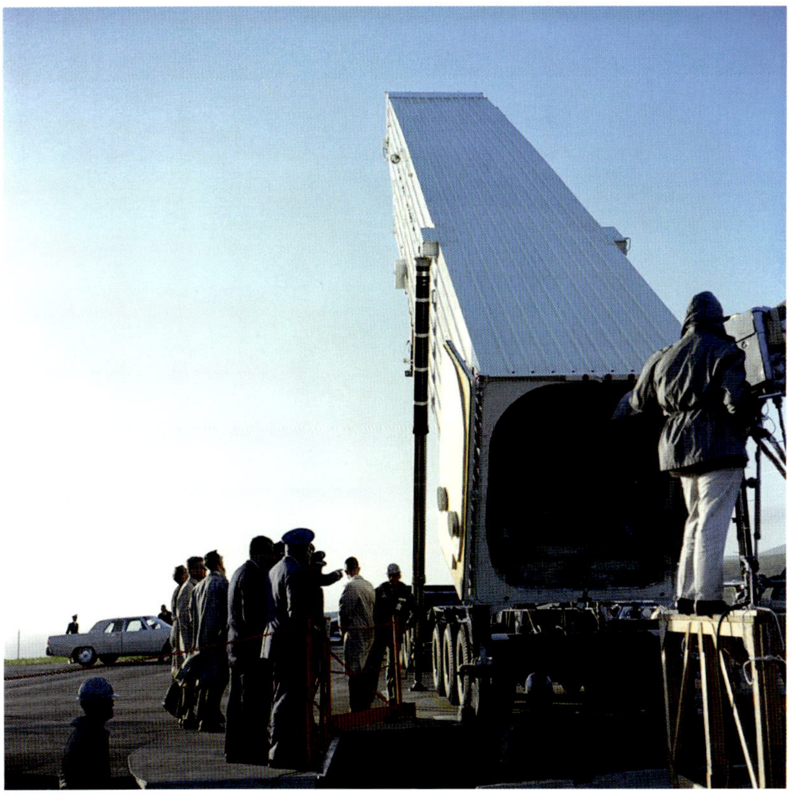

◀ Kennedy's tour next stops at the Minuteman launch control center at 5:05 p.m., where the president goes underground for twelve minutes. He then sees an empty Minuteman transporter-erector-loader (TEL) semi-trailer. A network pool TV camera is at right.

The sixty-five-foot-long TEL, specially built by Boeing, GMC, and Cessna, is used to transport the missile and lower it into its silo with a winch.

The Vandenberg facilities at complex 394 are for training only; its first Minuteman test launch is six months away, with nuclear-armed deployments in Montana, the Dakotas, Wyoming, and Missouri soon following.

Subsequent versions of Minuteman make up the backbone of the US ICBM force into the first decades of the 2000s.

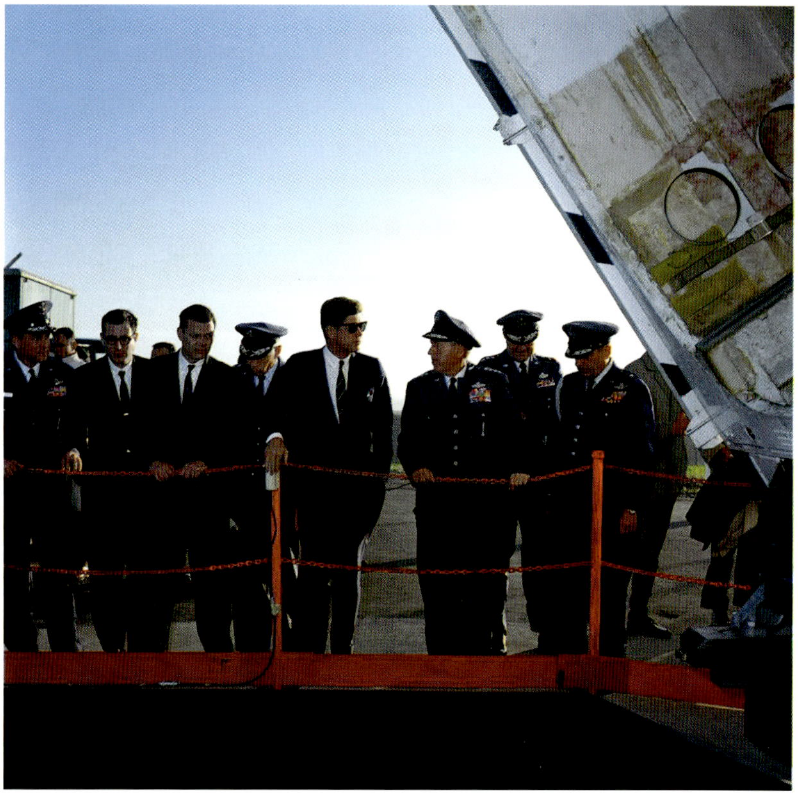

◢ A Minuteman is on display in the eighty-foot-deep silo.

Minuteman I is tasked primarily with deterrence—threatening Soviet cities with a nuclear counterattack if the United States were attacked. Because it uses solid fuel, Minuteman can stand ready for extended periods of time with little maintenance and launch quickly in contrast to liquid-fueled Atlas and Titan I missiles. The system also has cheaper production costs, attractive to McNamara for a large deployment (eventually numbering one thousand). Atlas and Titan I squadrons will be deactivated by 1965 as a result.

L–R: Brig. Gen. McKee; Brown; McNamara; Maj. Gen. Joseph Preston, commander of SAC's 1st Strategic Aerospace Division at Vandenberg; Kennedy; Gen. Power; Lt. Gen. Howell Estes Jr., deputy commander of Aerospace Systems for USAF Systems Command; and Brig. Gen. McHugh.

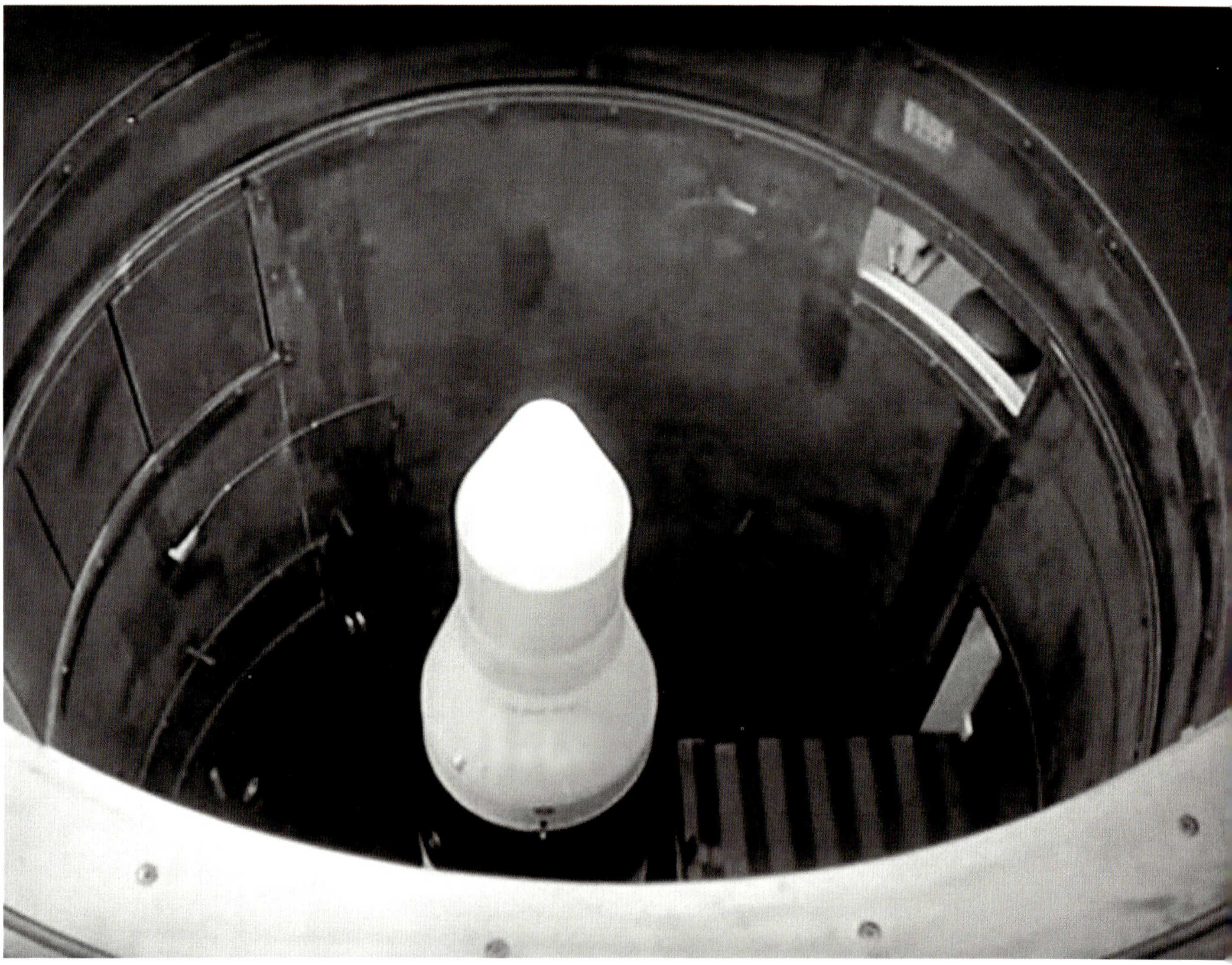

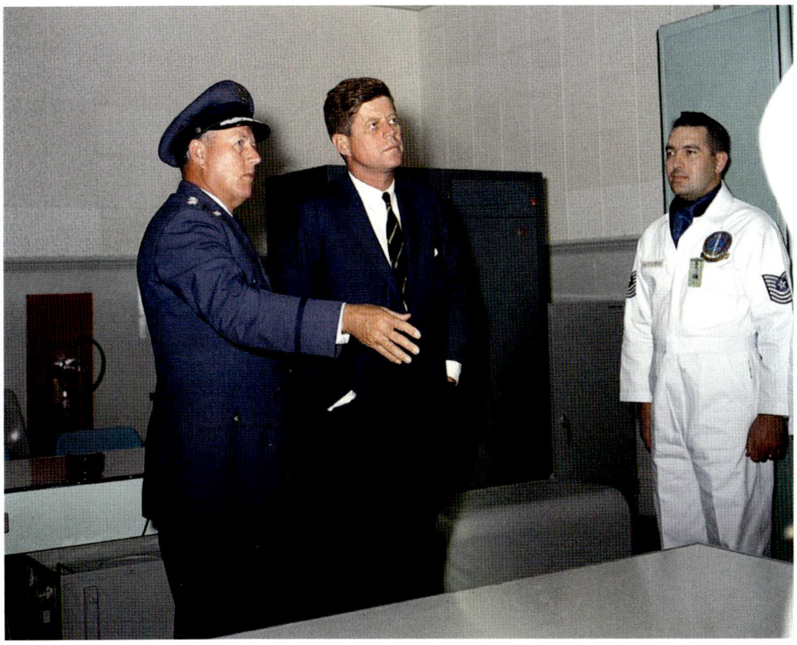

◀ Next stop is the Titan I launch control center for LC-395A at 5:24 p.m. After a short briefing on the missile and the facility, a 395th Strategic Missile Squadron crew conducts a simulated countdown. Two Titans are elevated from their silos so Kennedy can see them, one after he pushes the button. Titan I, the first US multistage ICBM, uses liquid oxygen and RP-1 kerosene as propellants. Titan is made by the Martin Company, which has just merged with the American Marietta Corporation.

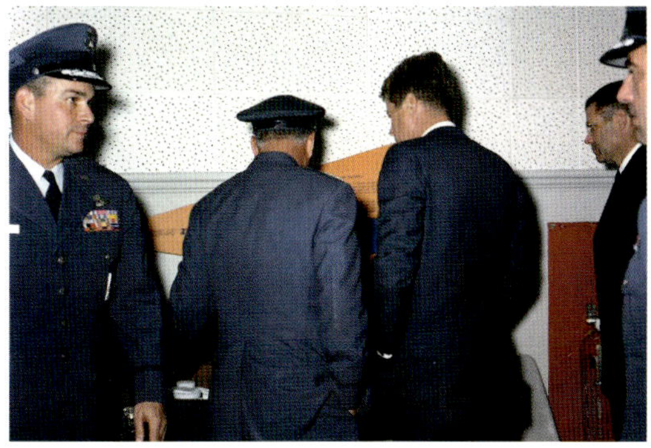

▲ L–R: Brig. Gen. McKee; Gen. Power; Kennedy; McNamara; and Brig. Gen. McHugh.

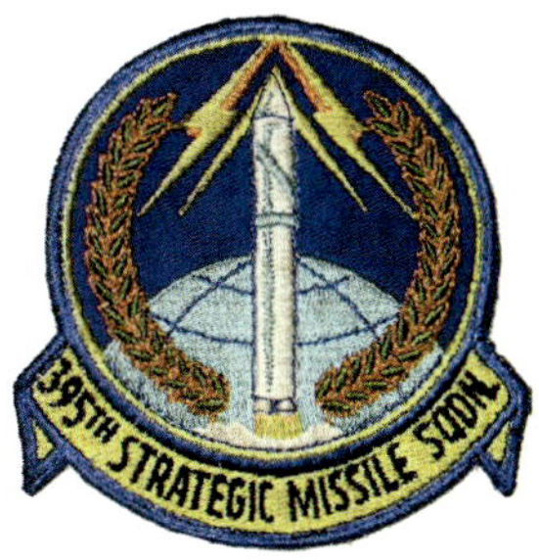

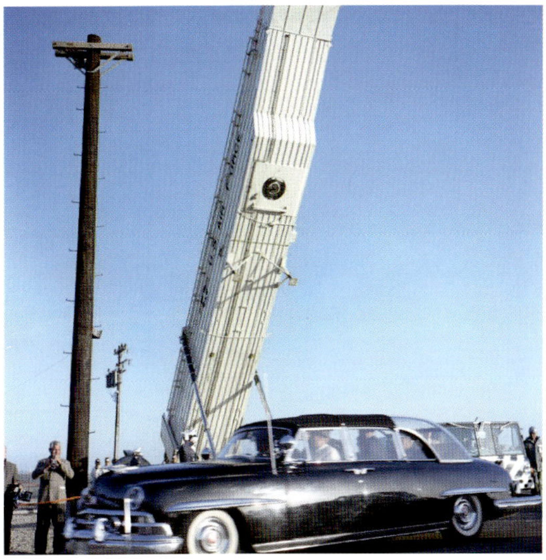

▲ Kennedy departs in a modified 1950 Lincoln Cosmopolitan; he rode in the same car for his January 1961 inaugural parade. The car is the only convertible among ten Cosmopolitans purchased by the Truman administration. President Dwight Eisenhower requested the clear Plexiglas "bubble top" roof section be added. Known as SS-4B by the Secret Service and retired in 1967, it is on display at the Henry Ford Museum in Dearborn, Michigan, as is Kennedy's modified Lincoln Continental limousine.

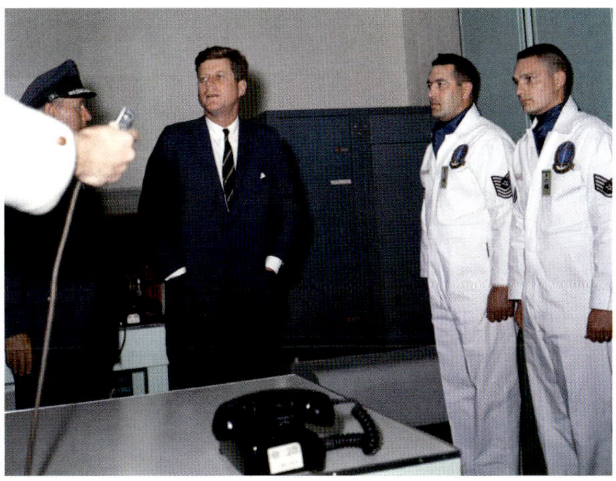

▲ The president takes a question from a pool TV reporter, with two launch crew members at right. About fifty members of the news media cover the visit.

As with Minuteman, Vandenberg is only used as a training and testing launch site; sixty Titan Is with thermonuclear warheads are stationed in Colorado, Idaho, South Dakota, California, and Washington state at the time.

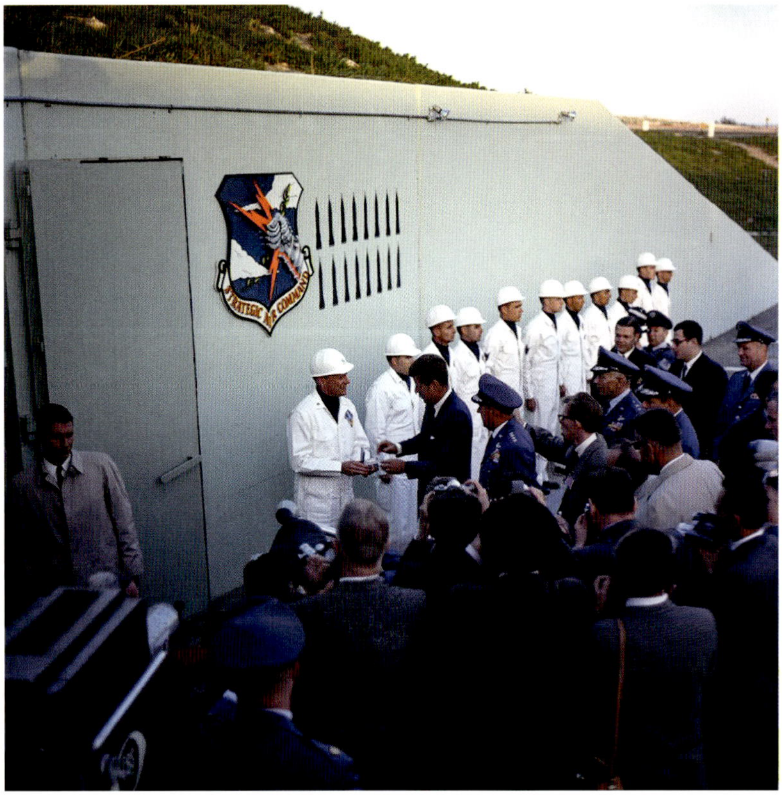

◀ At LC-576B, the president meets Launch Crew R-07 from the 565th Strategic Missile Squadron detailed from Warren AFB, Wyoming, which had launched the Atlas earlier that afternoon.

Newsmen are in the foreground with a CBS-TV pool camera at left.

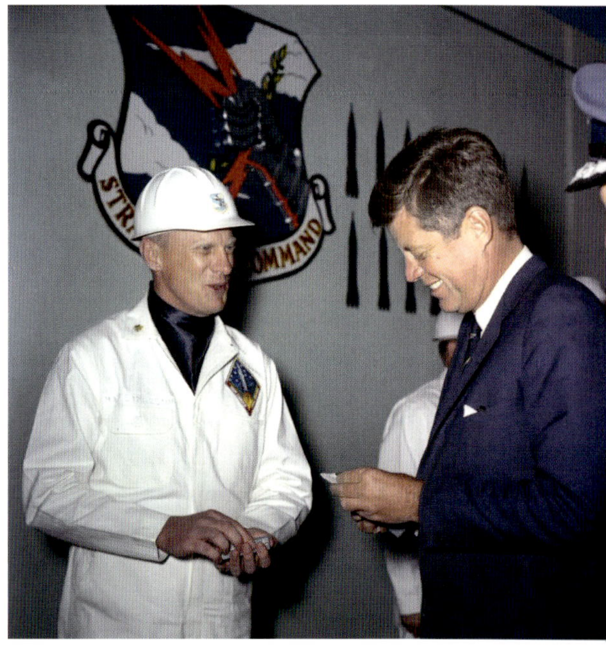

▲ Maj. Clifford Simonson, forty-one, commander of the missile combat crew, presents the commander-in-chief with a silver missileman badge engraved with the date (at left) to make him an honorary member of the crew. (Courtesy of the John F. Kennedy Presidential Library and Museum.)

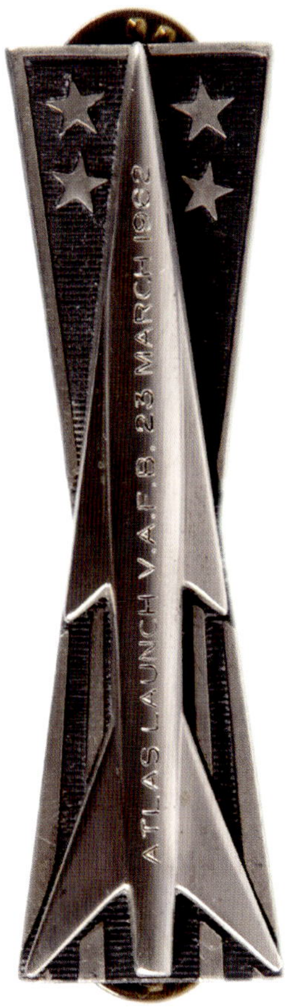

▲ (Courtesy of the John F. Kennedy Presidential Library and Museum.)

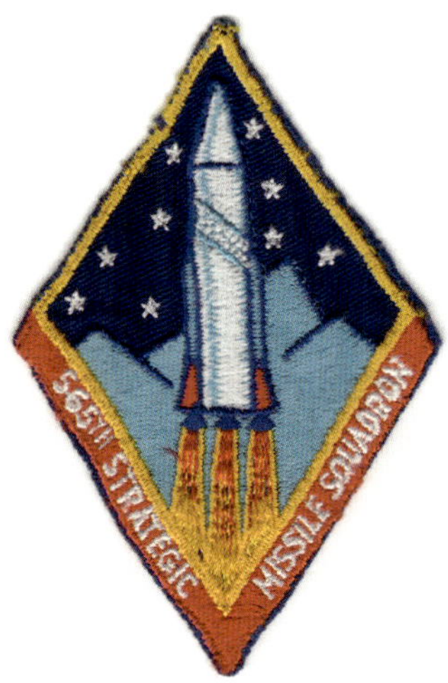

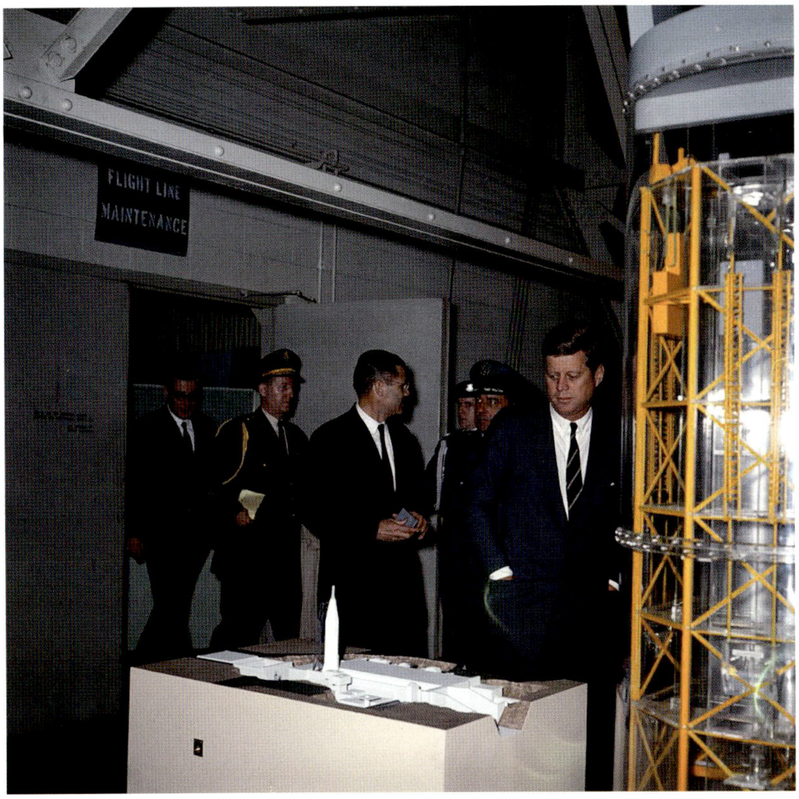

◀ The president's party enters a display area in a hangar about 6:00 p.m. as Kennedy looks at a model of an above-ground Atlas launch facility. Army Maj. Gen. Chester "Ted" Clifton Jr., who is part of this party, is responsible for the president's daily intelligence briefings.

After touring the displays, the president receives a classified presentation on Project Orion, a Pentagon plan to launch huge military spacecraft using a series of small nuclear explosions for propulsion. Kennedy, McNamara, and NASA are not supporters and funding is cut. The group also sees a movie that depicts an armed fleet of the USAF's proposed X-20 manned space planes, an over-the-top prospect that, according to Brown, both appalls and amuses Kennedy. X-15 test pilot Neil Armstrong trains as an X-20 pilot from March until he joins NASA in September.

Flash photography in this series of White House images makes the hangar interior appear much darker than it is.

L–R: Brown; Clifton Jr.; McNamara; and McHugh.

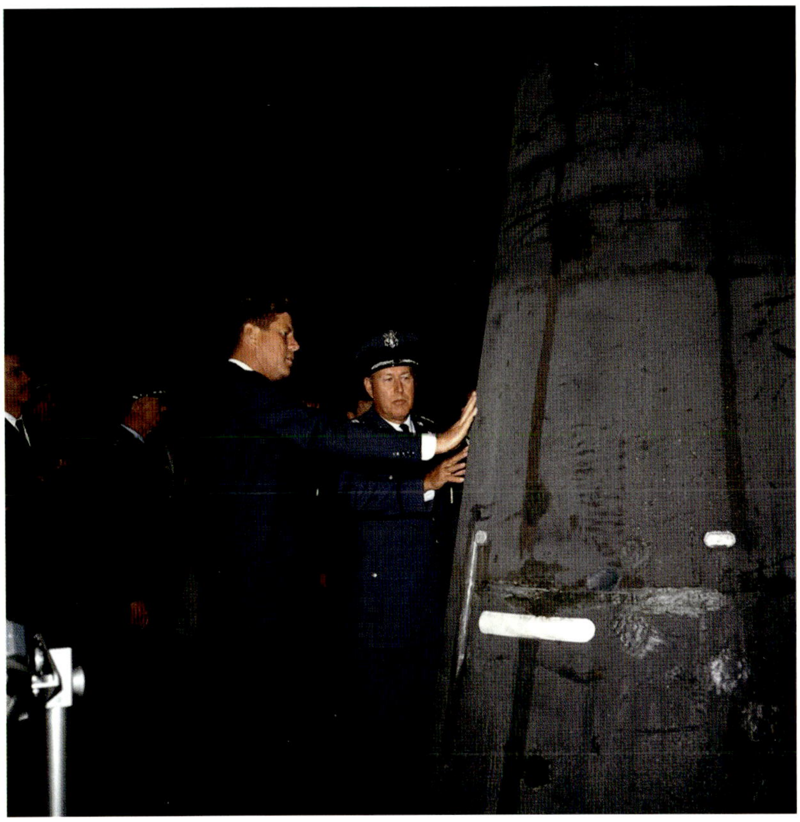

◀ The president examines an ablative nose cone, scorched by the heat of reentry, launched from Cape Canaveral by Atlas 8C on July 21, 1959. The RVX-2 reentry vehicle, which would have protected a nuclear warhead, is the first ablative nose cone adapted to Atlas and the first to be recovered, after traveling 2,724 miles down the Atlantic Missile Range. The test also gives Project Mercury engineers additional confidence in using ablation for their spacecraft's heat shield.

L–R: McNamara; Brig. Gen. McHugh; Maj. Gen. Preston; Kennedy; and Gen. Power.

▶ Kennedy views a display on the Minuteman guidance and control system with Gen. Power and Brown. Minuteman incorporates several major advances in its guidance system, including using an onboard general purpose computer, which allows its targeting information to be quickly updated. It also required developing more reliable transistors, an enormous benefit to the electronics industry.

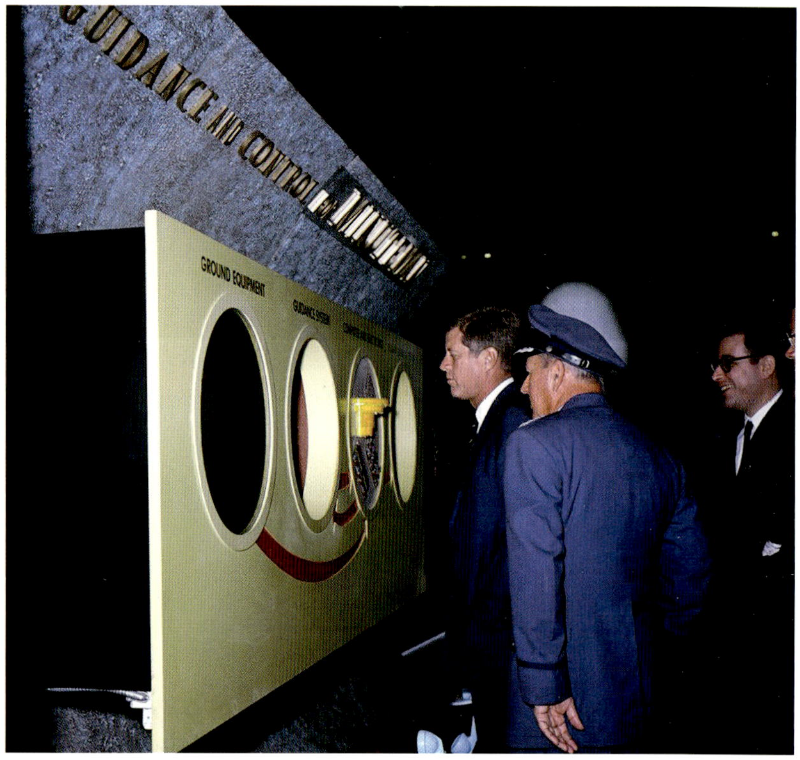

▼ Power points out a revolving model of Pioneer 5, a joint NASA-USAF spin-stabilized probe that investigates interplanetary space between the orbits of Earth and Venus. Launched on March 11, 1960, from Cape Canaveral, it establishes a communications link with the earth from a then-record distance of 22.5 million miles on June 26, 1960, the last day of contact.

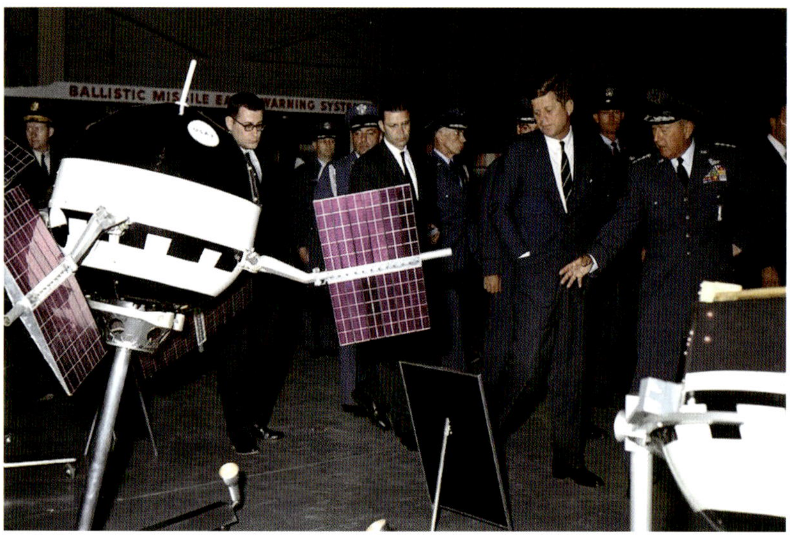

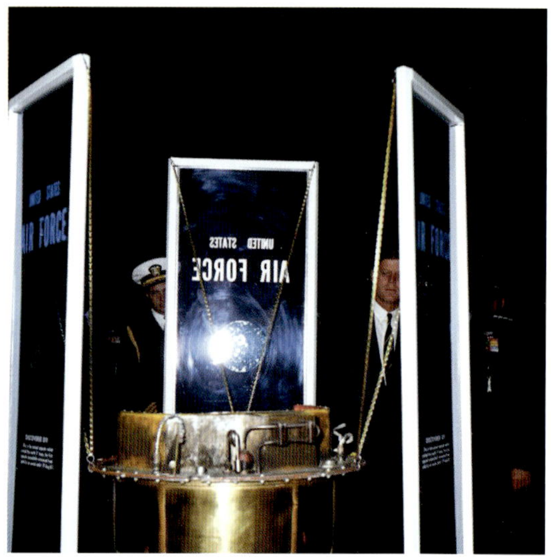

The display on the far wall concerns the Missile Defense Alarm System (MIDAS), a classified system of pioneering early-warning satellites that provide limited notice of Soviet ICBM launches between 1963 and 1966.

L–R: Maj. Gen. Clifton (left of satellite); Brown; unidentified officer in background; Brig. Gen. McHugh (behind McNamara); McNamara; Maj. Gen. Preston, Kennedy; unidentified officer in background; and Gen. Power.

◥ The president sees the reentry capsule of Discoverer 14, a CIA Corona program satellite, which is the first successful photo surveillance spacecraft. It was launched into a polar orbit by a Thor booster from Vandenberg AFB on August 18, 1960, and photographed targets in the Soviet Union. The capsule separated from the satellite and was snagged by an aircraft over the Pacific Ocean on August 20. It was the first successful recovery of film from a satellite and the first mid-air retrieval of a reentering object. Though reported to be a spy satellite, its exact mission was not disclosed at the time. The program will end in 1972 and will remain classified until 1992. Presidential aide Capt. Tazewell Shepard Jr.—he had been promoted on September 8, 1961—is at left.

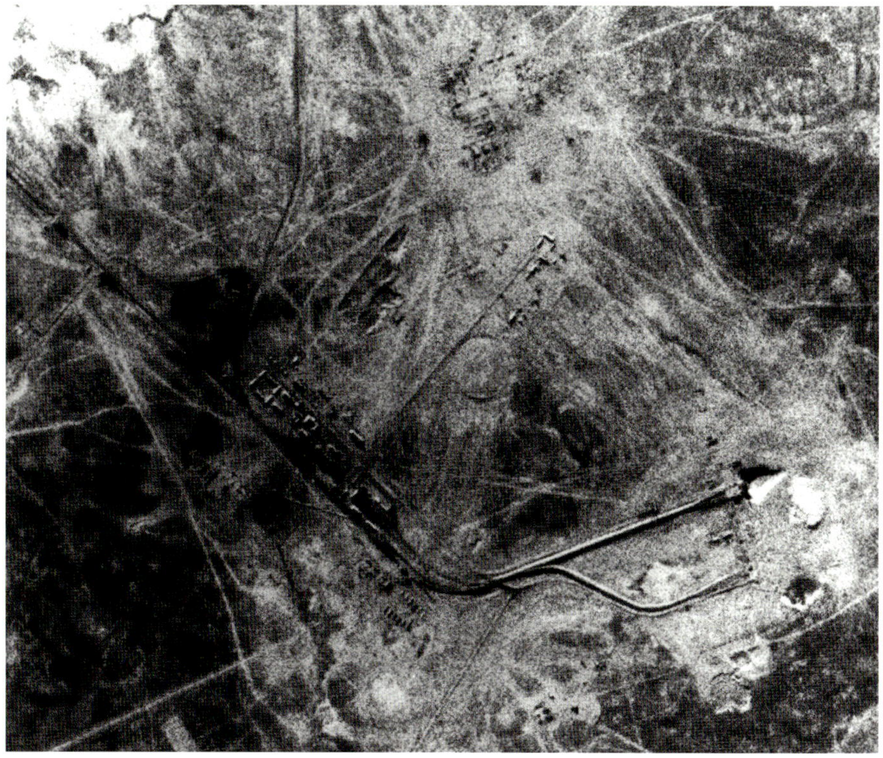

▶ Discoverer 14 photo of the Baikonur Cosmodrome, the Soviets' launch site.

▼ Kennedy enters a domed mockup of an envisioned lunar hut. "Five years ago people would have thought we were crazy to think of such a thing," he says upon exiting.

The mockup is likely related to the USAF's Project Lunex begun in 1958 to build a manned lunar base by 1968. The display, Brown recalled in an interview in 1964, did not impress the president.

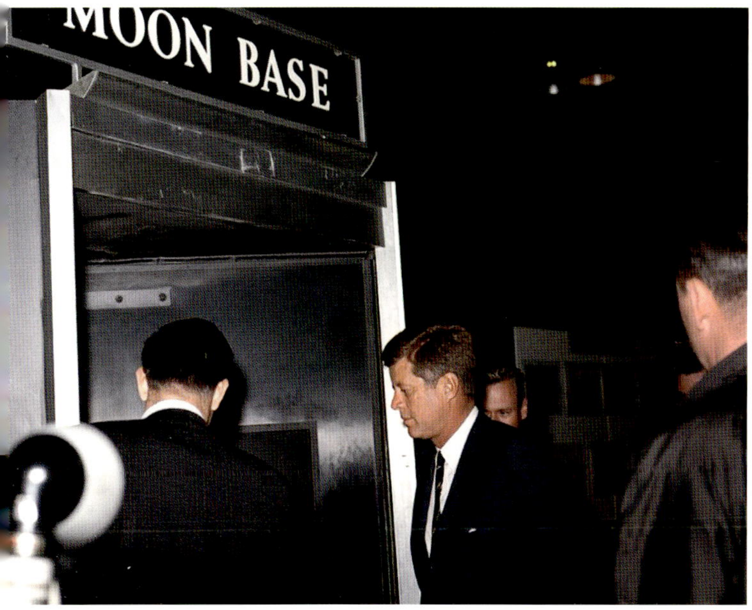

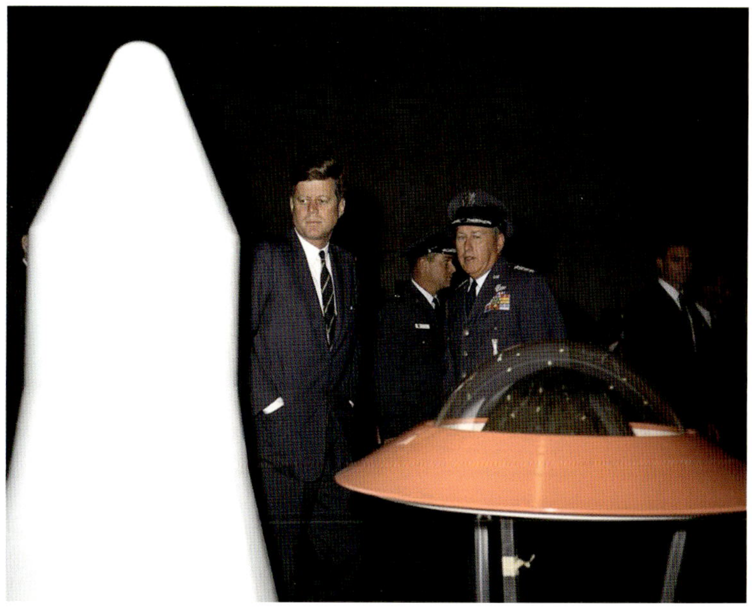

◥ The president with a Minuteman Mark 5 reentry vehicle (left) and, in a protective display, an ablated nose cap (right) of an RVX 1–5 reentry vehicle. It is the first reentry vehicle recovered by the United States after an intercontinental-range flight. Launched on April 8, 1959, on a Thor-Able rocket from Cape Canaveral, it was recovered in the South Atlantic after a flight of 6,325 miles, reaching temperatures above 12,000° Fahrenheit.

During October of that year, Gen. Power had made a controversial decision to broadcast the heightened US military alert status during the Cuban Missile Crisis on an unscrambled radio channel the Soviets could monitor, although the reason may have been strategic as he urged his subordinates to "use calm judgment during this tense period."

The presidential party departs Vandenberg AFB at 6:30 p.m. and Air Force One flies to Palm Springs Municipal Airport. Kennedy spends the weekend at the estate of entertainer Bing Crosby, where actress Marilyn Monroe is also a guest. He also visits former president Eisenhower in nearby Palm Desert.

L–R: Kennedy; Brig. Gen. McKee; and Power.

▶ On May 3, 1962, the fourth man in space comes calling at the White House. Cosmonaut Maj. Gherman Titov is in Washington as a Soviet delegate to an international space conference. After a tour of the city by John Glenn, they stop by at 12:47 p.m. EDT to visit President Kennedy for about fifteen minutes. Titov had completed seventeen orbits the previous August.

Titov and Glenn arrive, with Assistant Appointments Secretary Dave Powers and interpreter Ivan Shklyar at right.

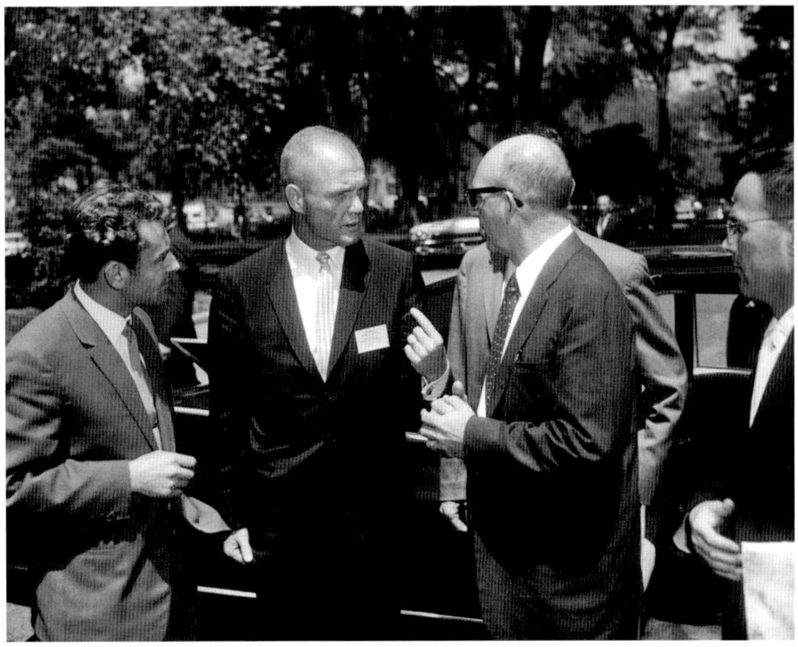

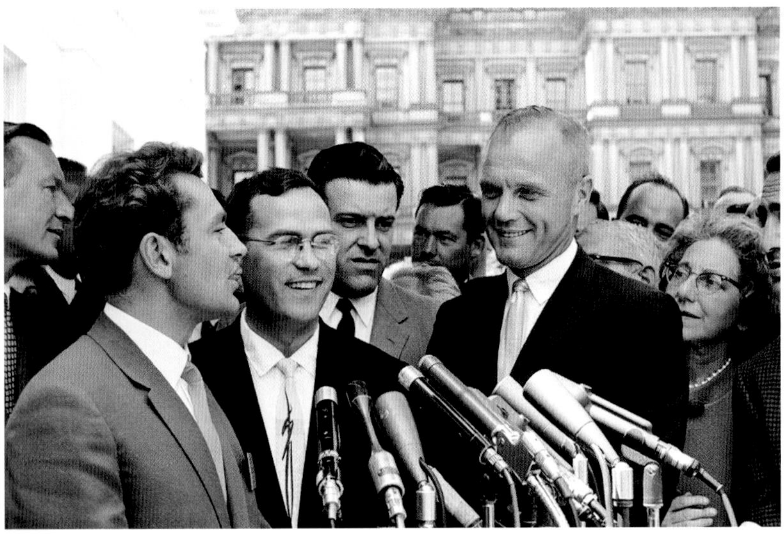

◀ Titov and Glenn take reporters' questions outside the West Wing entrance. Interpreters Shklyar and Walter Skuby are to Titov's left. *Newsweek* correspondent Charles Roberts is far left; Jeanette Rudellat of the US Information Agency is at right behind Glenn. At far right, almost out of frame, is NBC News correspondent Herb Kaplow, the first American reporter to interview Cuban president Fidel Castro after the failed Bay of Pigs invasion.

▶ Glenn, Kennedy, and Titov chat on the West Wing Colonnade after meeting in the Oval Office. Soviet Ambassador to the United States Anatoly Dobrynin is at left.

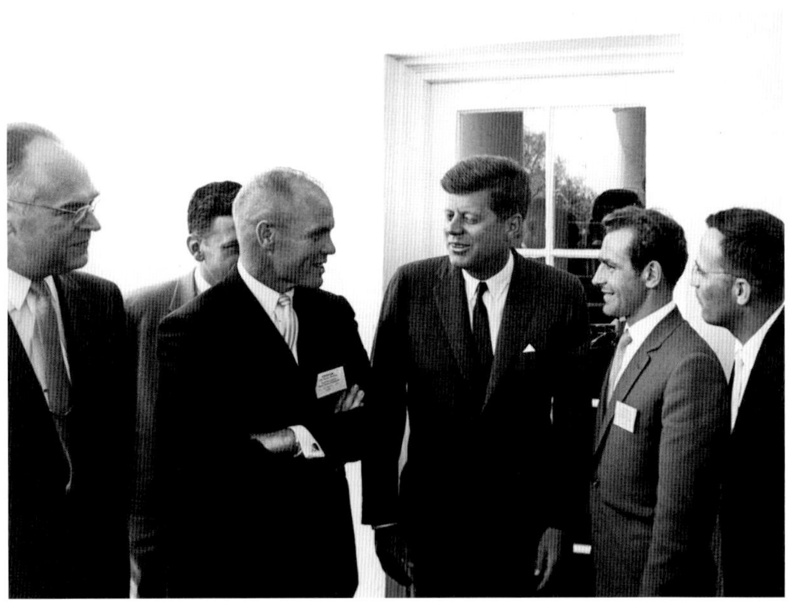

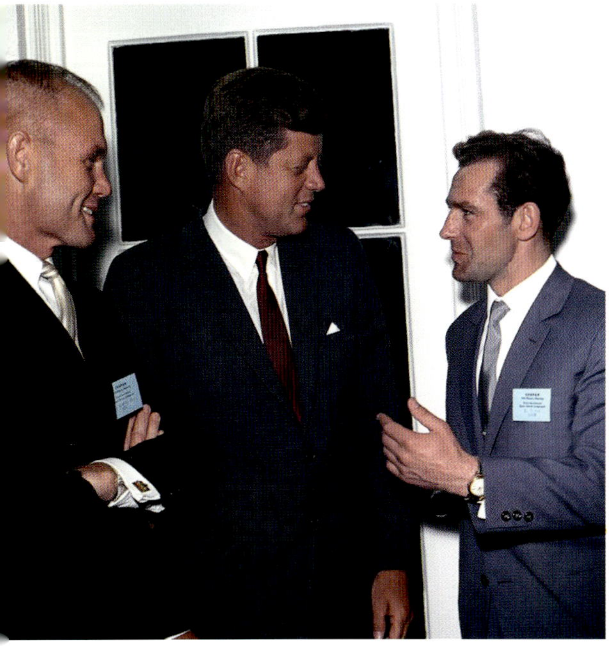

▲ The previous September in East Berlin, Titov had said the Soviet Union was prepared to "crush and destroy once and for all" any imperialists who tried to interfere with the partition of the city. Nonetheless, Kennedy here tells the cosmonaut, "I'm very happy to welcome you, as are the American people. I admire what you did very much."

Titov tells Kennedy, "Colonel Glenn wanted to show me the city from the top of the Washington monument, but it was too misty."

Titov and Glenn speak that afternoon to the third annual space symposium of the Committee on Space Research of the International Council of Scientific Unions at the National Academy of Sciences. At a news conference later the two spar over Soviet secrecy about its space program but agree the glowing particles each had seen outside his craft in orbit were probably residual fuel.

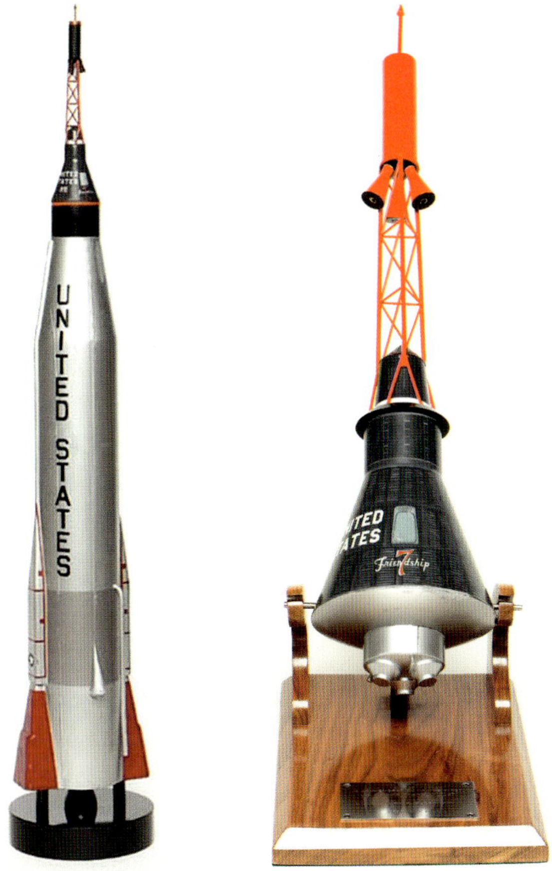

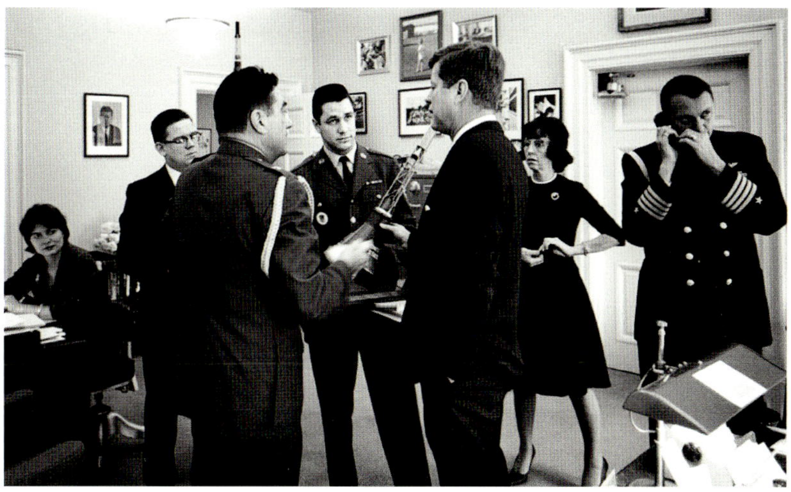

▲ The president receives two models as gifts from John Glenn in May 1962 in the office of his secretary, Evelyn Lincoln.

L–R: Priscilla Wear, staff member in the secretary's office; Presidential Assistant John McNally, holding a Mercury/Atlas booster model (hidden); USAF aide Brig. Gen. McHugh; unidentified military aide with the *Friendship 7* model; Kennedy; Mrs. Lincoln; and naval aide to the president Capt. Tazewell Shepard Jr. (Models in John F. Kennedy Presidential Library and Museum.)

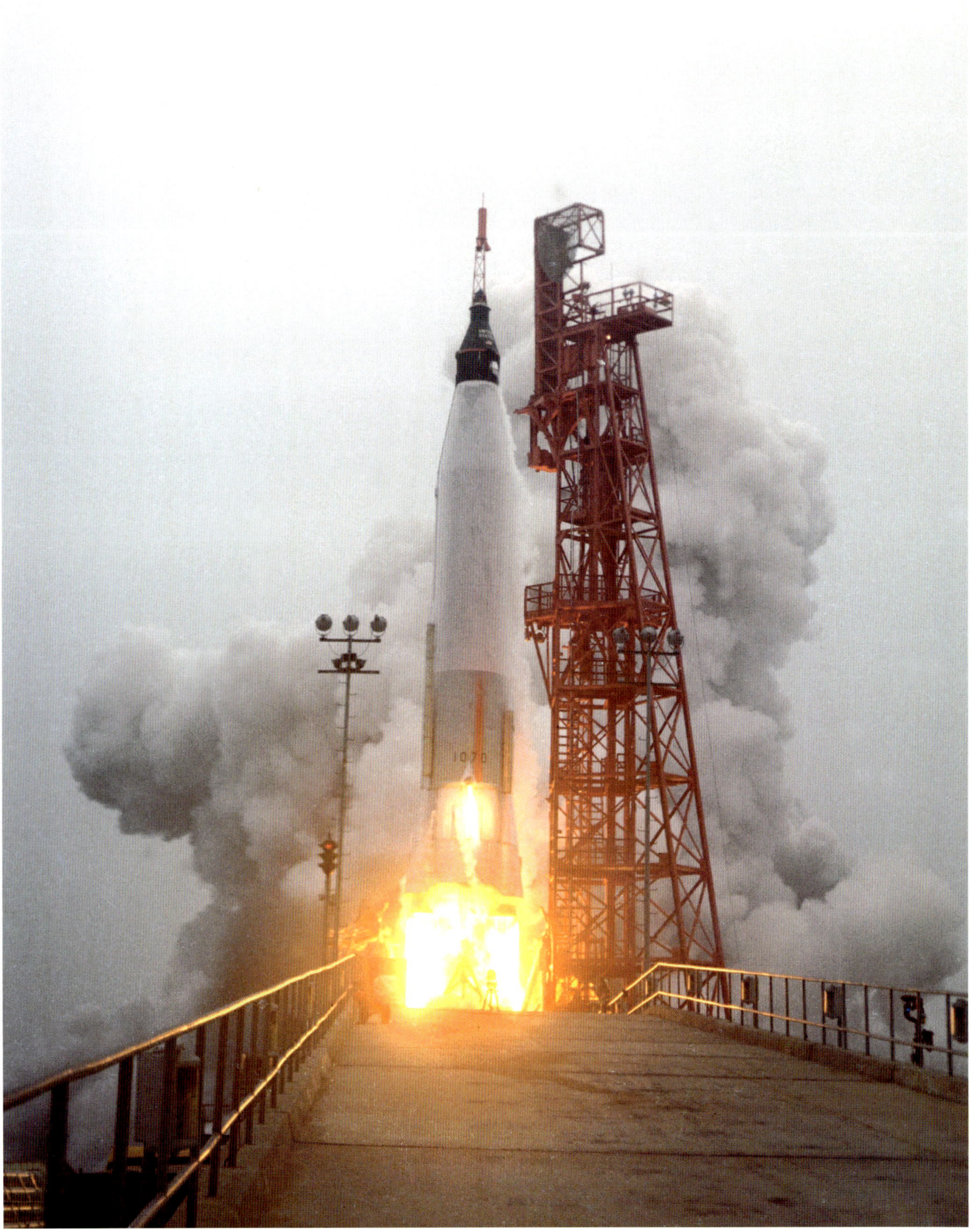

◀ The second Mercury orbital flight, carrying Navy Lt. Cmdr. Scott Carpenter, thirty-seven, lifts off from LC-14 at 8:46 a.m. EDT on May 24, 1962. Kennedy again watched on his bedroom TV. Like Glenn, Carpenter completes three Earth orbits in his spacecraft, *Aurora 7*.

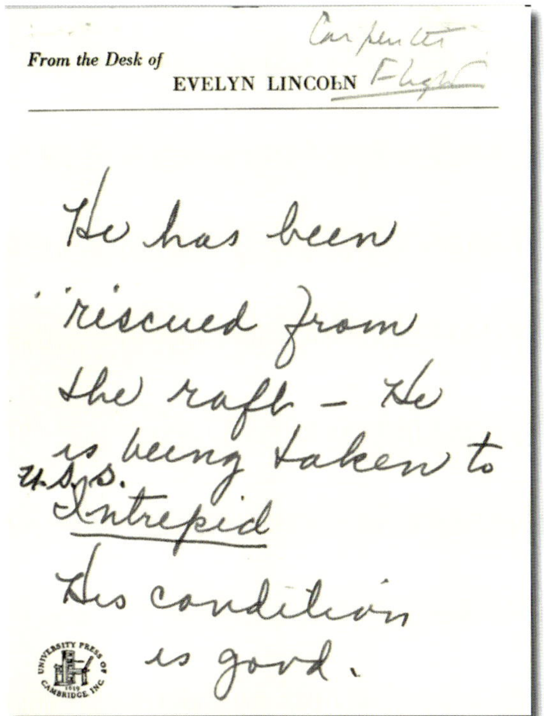

From the Desk of
EVELYN LINCOLN Carpenter Flight

He has been rescued from the raft – He is being taken to U.S.S. Intrepid
His condition is good.

▶ Note handed to the president from his secretary during a meeting on Laos in the Cabinet Room that afternoon. Carpenter missed his splashdown target by 250 miles and his status was unknown for more than an hour.

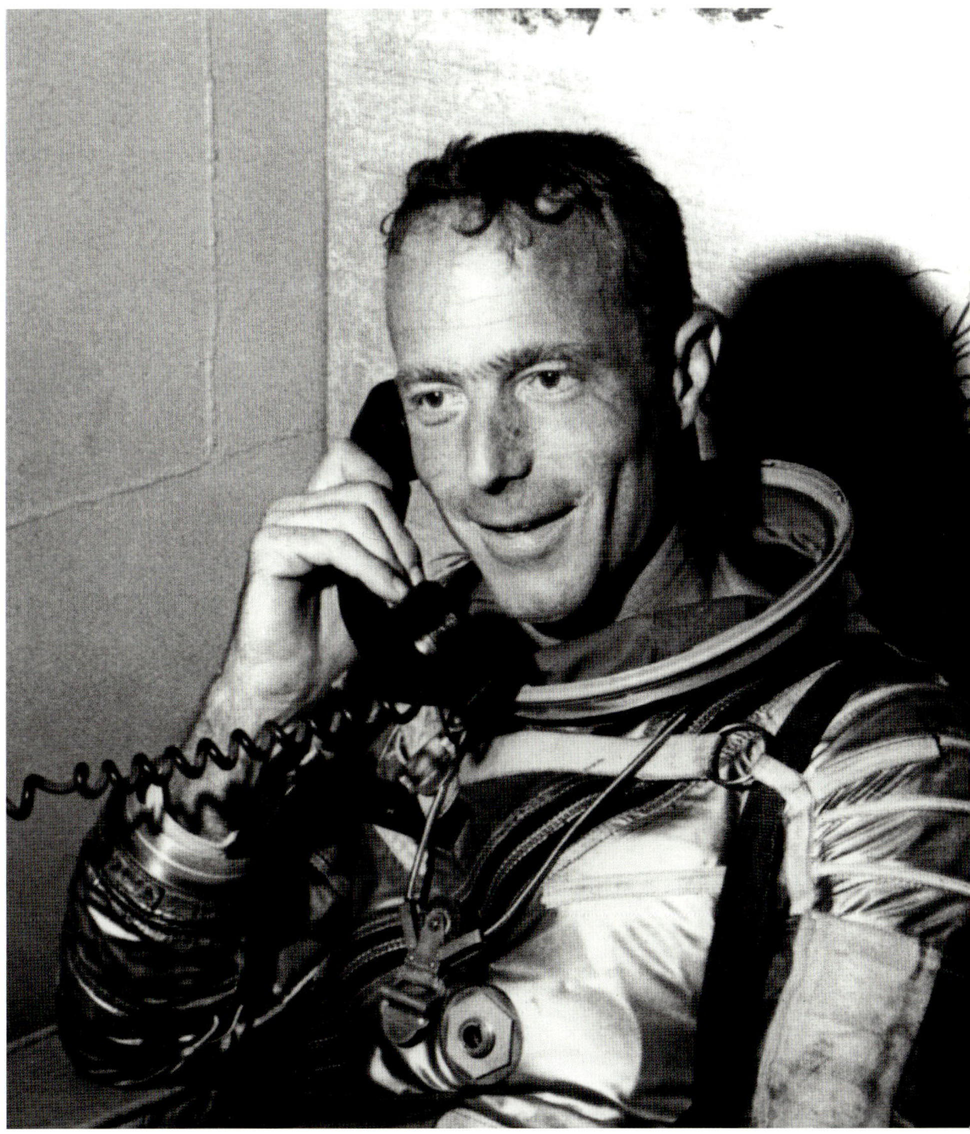

◢ Carpenter's post-flight medical exam aboard the aircraft carrier USS *Intrepid* is delayed by a call from Kennedy at about 5:15 p.m.

Kennedy: "Hello . . . hello. Hello, Scott. Come in—are we talking to Scott Carpenter?"

Carpenter: "Mr. President, I'm . . . I hear you, sir."

Kennedy: "Oh, well, I wanted to tell you that we are relieved, and very proud of your trip. I am glad that you got picked up in good shape, and we want to tell you that we are all for you and send you the very best luck to you and your wife."

Carpenter: "My apologies for not having aimed a little bit better on reentry."

Kennedy: "Oh, fine and good. Well, we want to congratulate you and I look forward to seeing you in Washington some time soon."

Carpenter: "I look forward to that, sir."

Kennedy: "Very good. Good luck now, Scott. Bye-bye."

Carpenter: "Thank you very much, sir."

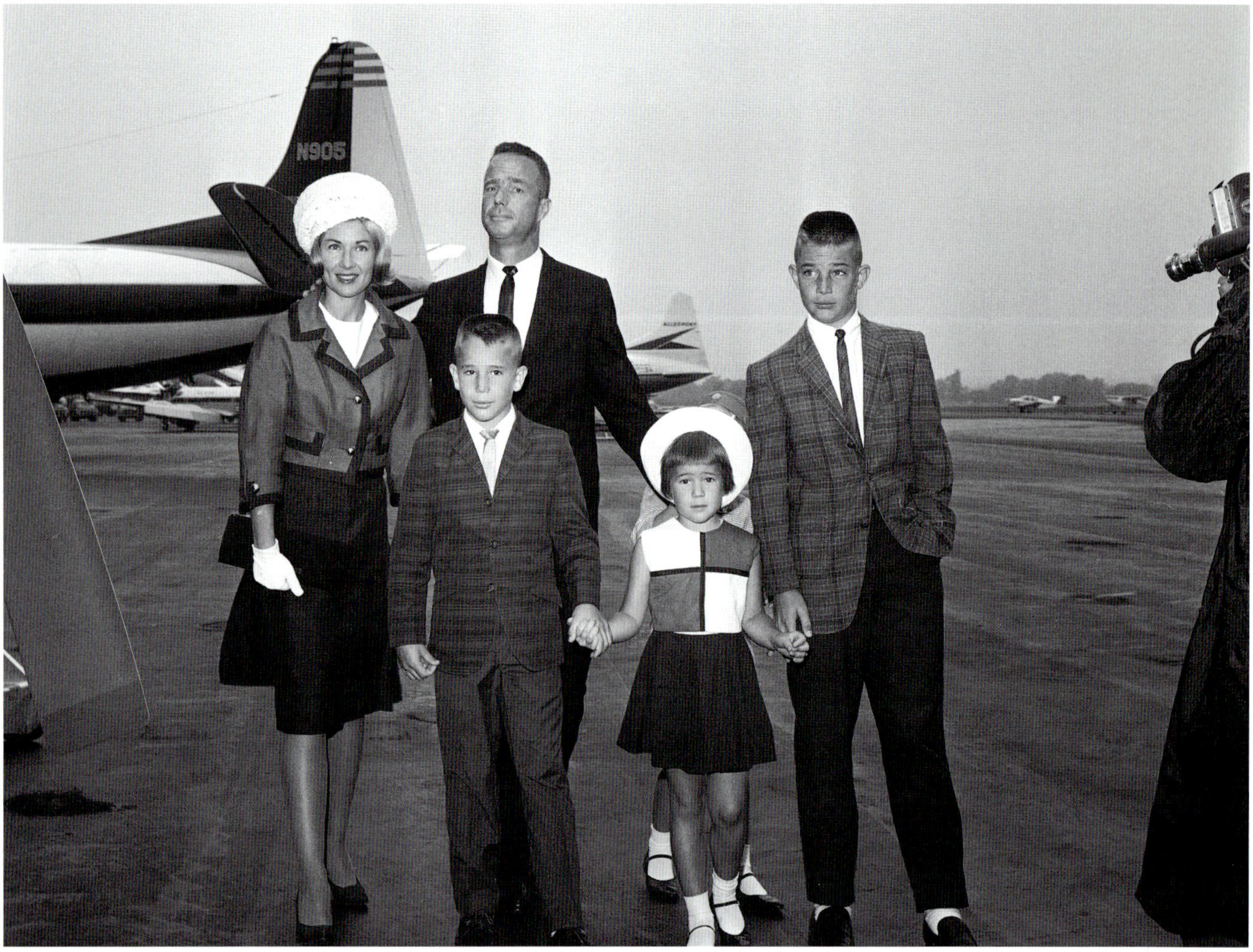

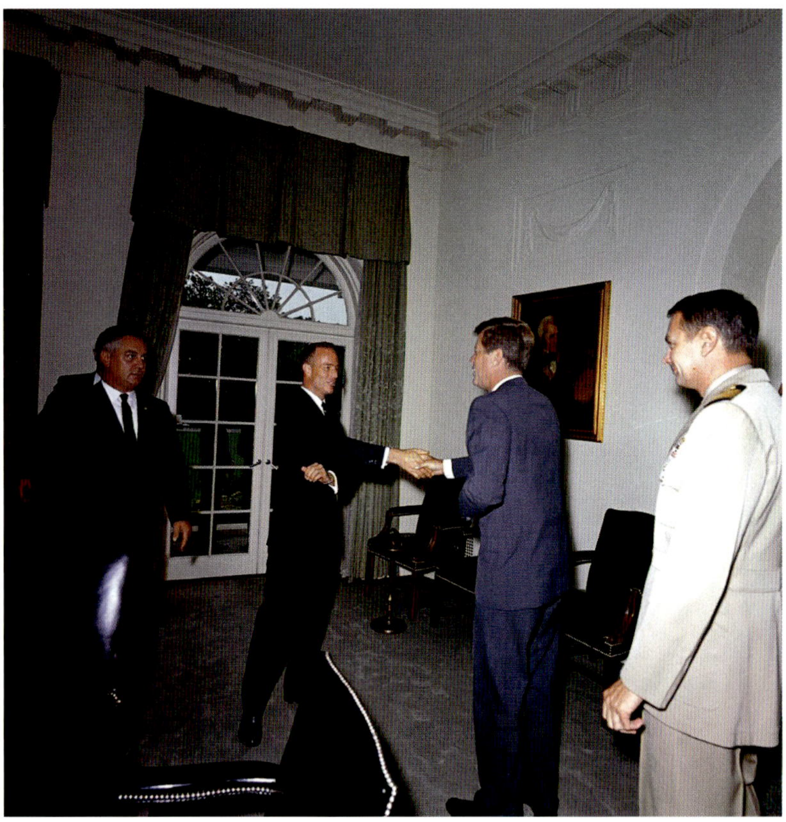

▲ The Carpenter family arrives at Washington National Airport on June 5, 1962, after flying in from Langley AFB, Virginia. That same day, Kennedy receives an eight-page letter from Webb detailing the "increasing participation by business concerns in practically all sections of the country" in NASA procurement and stressing how many contractors were benefiting from NASA spending.

L–R: Wife Rene; Carpenter; Robyn (ten); Candice (five); and Marc (twelve). Six-year-old Kristen is hidden behind Candice.

◀ Kennedy welcomes Carpenter to the White House in the Cabinet Room at 10:00 a.m. along with Mercury Operations Director Walter Williams (left). At right is the president's naval aide, Capt. Tazewell Shepard Jr., who received the Navy Cross, the highest naval award for heroism after the Medal of Honor, for bravery during the Battle of Guadalcanal in 1942. He would retire as a rear admiral in 1973.

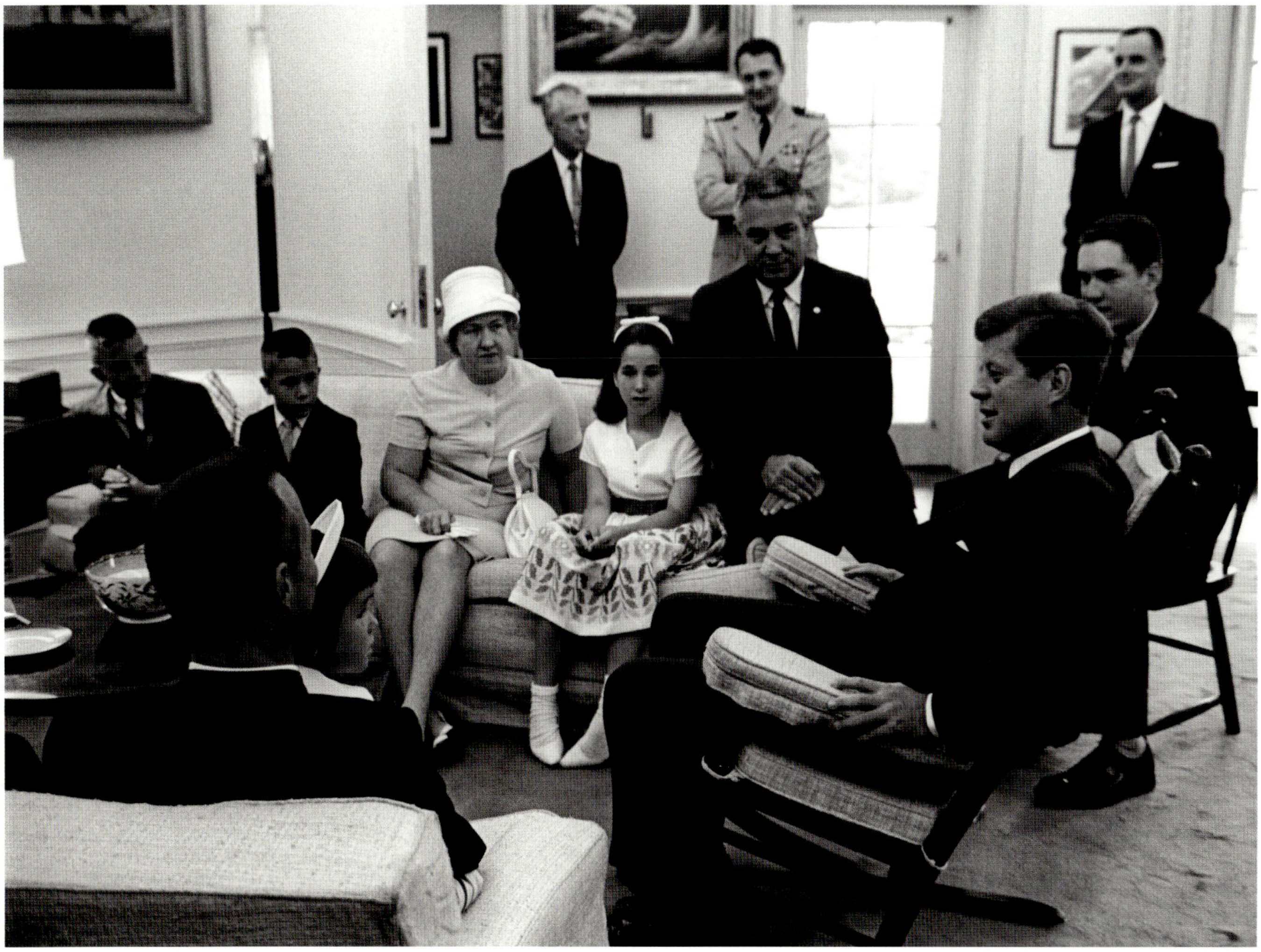

▲ Kennedy chats with his guests in the Oval Office.

L–R: Marc and Robyn Carpenter; Mrs. Helen Williams; daughter Elizabeth; Williams; Kennedy; and son Howard Williams. Carpenter and daughter Kristen are seated to the president's left.

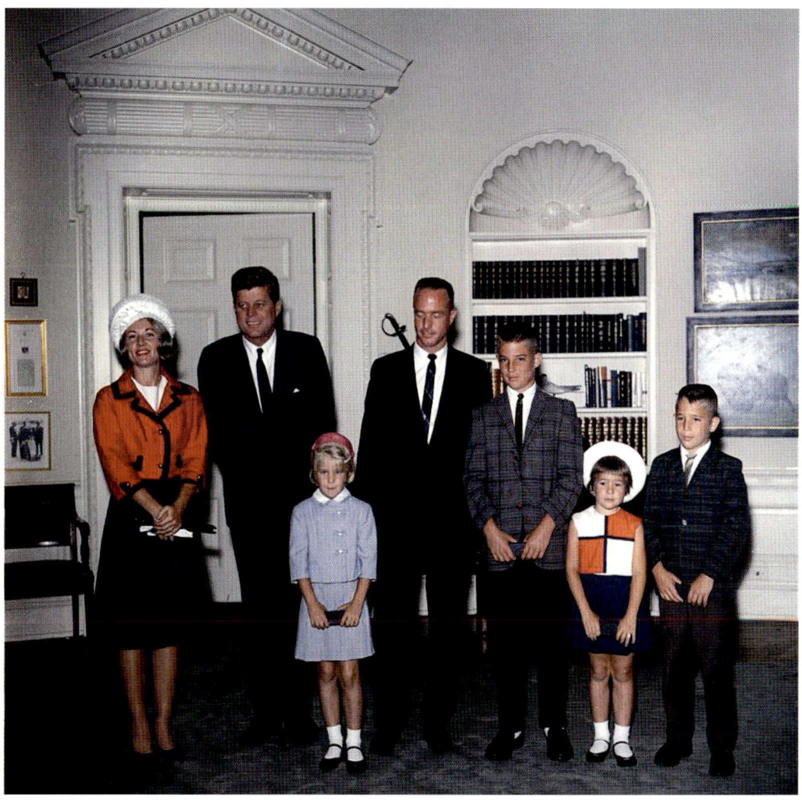

▶ The president poses with the Carpenter family. The astronaut had received his NASA Distinguished Service Medal from NASA Administrator Webb at Cape Canaveral on May 27.

L–R: Carpenter's wife, Rene; Kennedy; Kristen; Carpenter; Marc; Candace; and Robyn. The children hold boxes with presidential tie clips (boys) and bracelets (girls).

▶ After about twenty minutes, Kennedy and his guests move to the Fish Room for comments to the media. Kennedy also introduced Carpenter to a group of White House secretaries, and he invited into the room six high school students from West Virginia who had won an essay contest and happened to be visiting that day.

Between the president and Carpenter, UPI photographer Tommy Craven Sr. checks his light meter. Second from right (glasses) is Sid Davis of Westinghouse Broadcasting.

"Oh my," Mrs. Carpenter comments, "[my children] are much better behaved here."

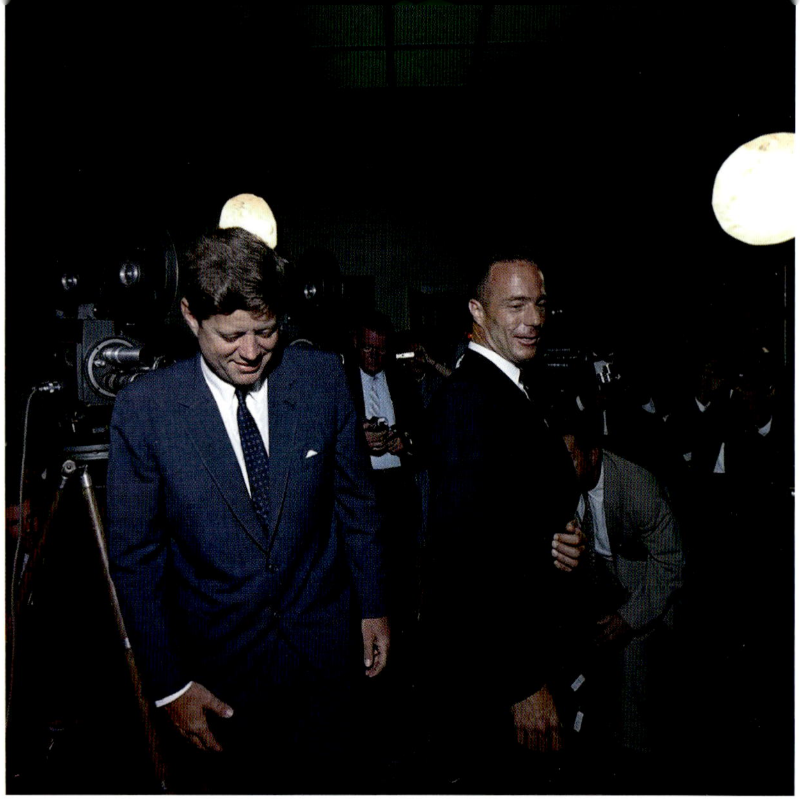

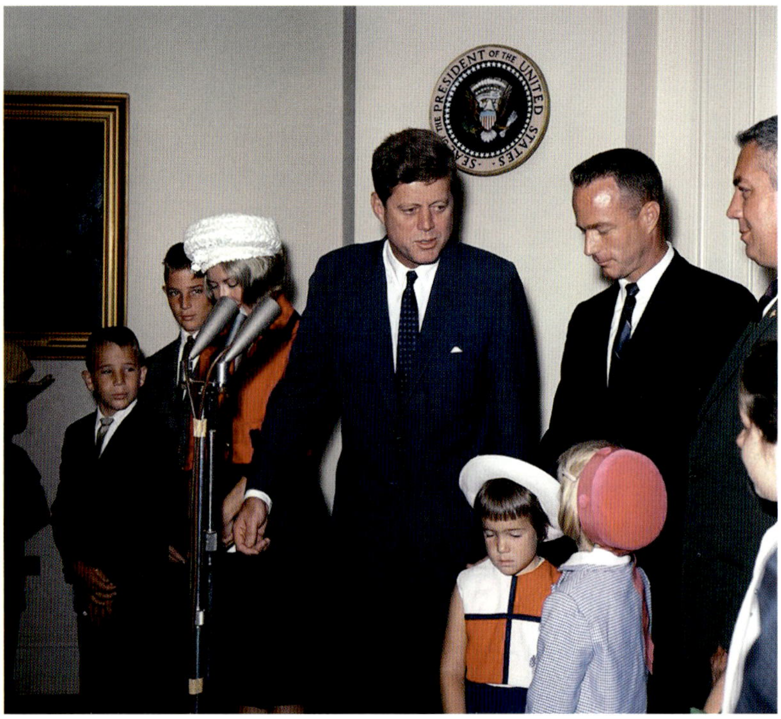

◀ "I think that all of us, as Americans, take the greatest pride and satisfaction in the tremendous technical accomplishments which have made the flights of the astronauts possible," the president says. "And we take the greatest pride in them and their families." He goes on,

> I cannot imagine better representatives of what we like to think our country stands for than the four men who have taken part in the flights. It is a source of great satisfaction to me as president at this time in our history to have these Americans who are so conspicuous on the world stage and who symbolize our country. . . . They have served our country, all of them, in a way which I am sure for the rest of their lives will be a source of satisfaction to them. So we want you to know that we are glad to see you again.

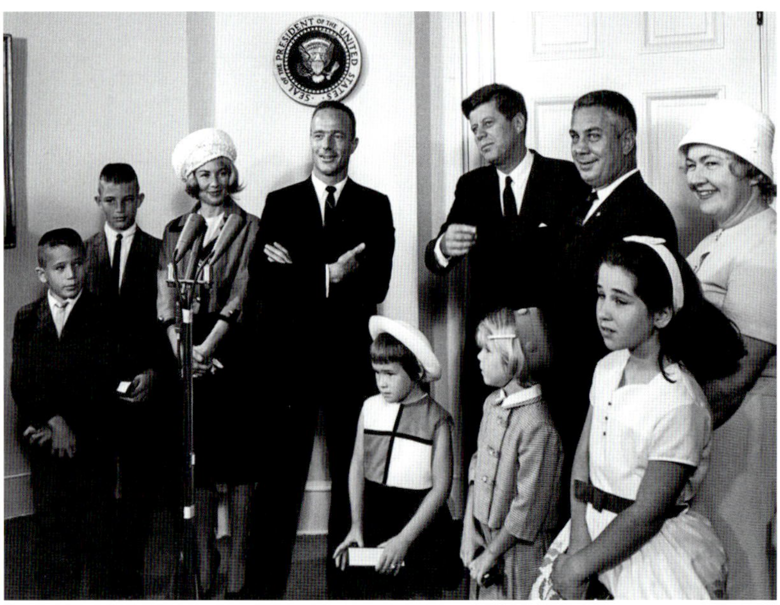

◀ The president also congratulates Williams, with his wife and daughter at right. An aerospace pioneer, Williams had been instrumental in developing the X-15 research aircraft.

Both families then fly to New York, where Carpenter addresses a luncheon at the Waldorf-Astoria hotel, attended by former US presidents Herbert Hoover and Harry Truman.

▶ "The main feeling I came back with was one of awe and inspiration," Carpenter says.

> The feeling I have now in the aftermath of the flight is one of humility, because although I happen to be the person who was the passenger, we are doing this for something more than just to provide the human experience. The support that we have received from all of you, from the whole country, in Project Mercury, has been invaluable. Continued support is necessary because we all feel in the project . . . that we stand to gain more not only as Americans, but as representatives of all mankind—we stand to gain more from what we will learn as a result of space flight than any other undertaking that men have made.

Taking notes below the painting at left is Naomi Nover, columnist for the Denver Post.

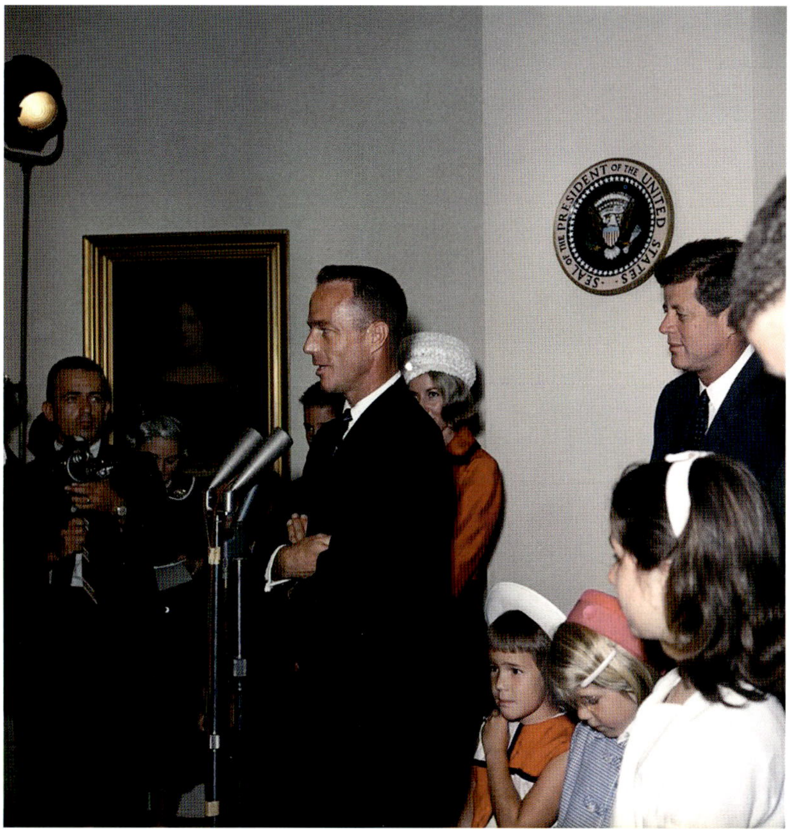

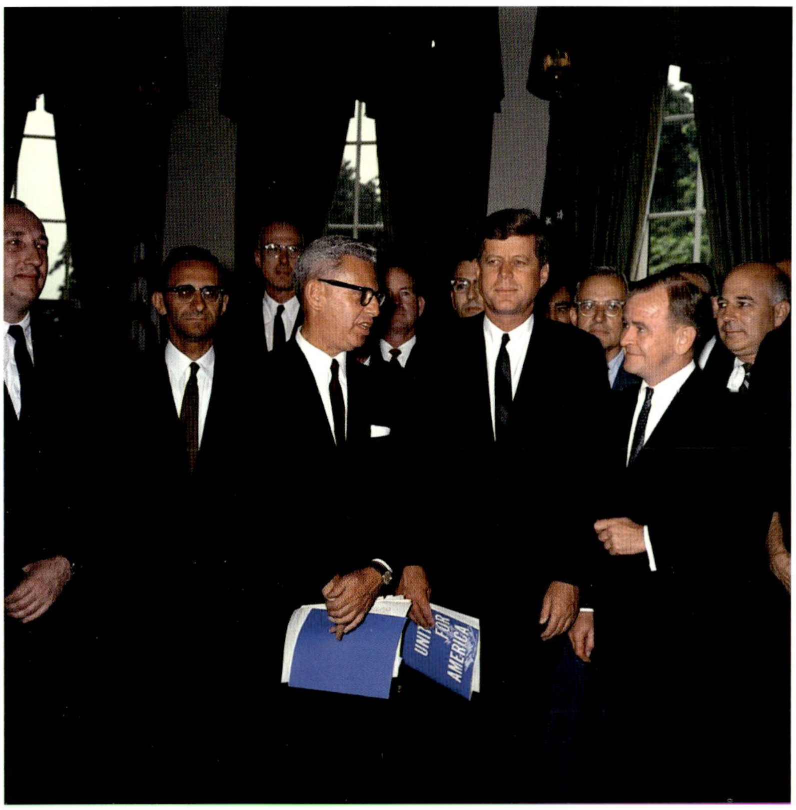

◀ The space program isn't all a blaze of glory. On June 14, 1962, Kennedy receives the first report from the President's Missile Sites Labor Commission at 12:40 p.m. in the Oval Office. He establishes it in May 1961 as a way to try to settle labor disputes at the government's twenty-two missile bases under construction, including Cape Canaveral. Senate hearings that April conclude that the US manned space effort has been set back six months by strikes. Although the work of the committee, and other factors, lead to a marked decrease in man-days lost at the Cape, strikes plague the space center into 1965. The eleven-member panel includes representatives of labor, management, and the government. It would be abolished in 1967.

L–R (in foreground): Assistant Defense Secretary for Manpower Carlisle Runge, Samuel Silver (of Runge's staff), Commission Chairman and Labor Secretary Arthur Goldberg, Kennedy, and Assistant USAF Secretary Joseph Imirie.

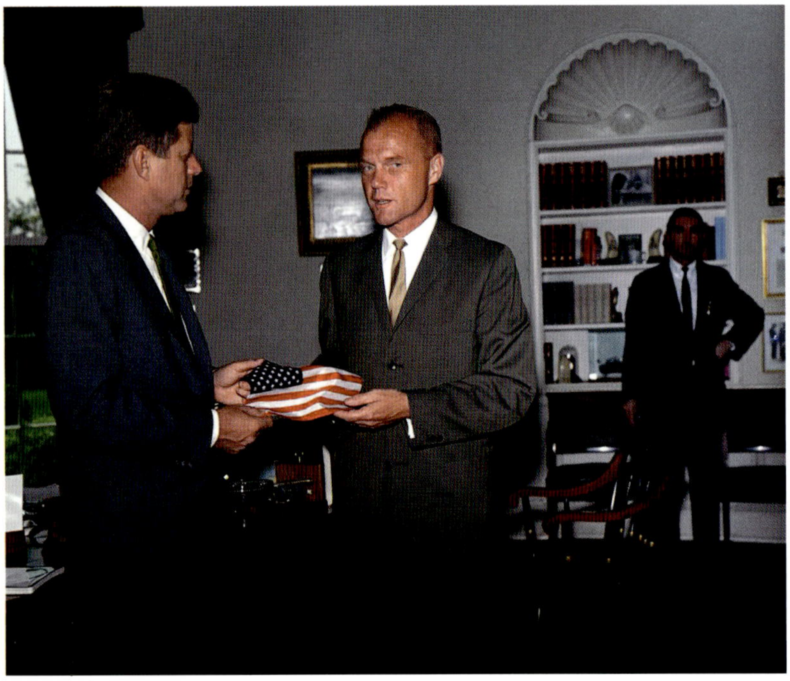

▼ On July 18, 1962, the president greets relatives of four X-15 pilots outside the Oval Office before presenting the flyers with the 1961 Robert J. Collier Trophy at 11:30 a.m.

The trophy has been presented since 1912 for the greatest American achievement in aeronautics or astronautics.

▲ On June 27, 1962, Kennedy receives a gift of an American flag from John Glenn. The astronaut had carried the nylon flag aboard *Friendship 7* during his February flight. Special Assistant to the President Kenneth P. O'Donnell is at right in the Oval Office. O'Donnell, who serves as Kennedy's appointments secretary, is a close friend of both the president and his brother Robert, who had also been a long-time campaign aide.

The president encourages Glenn to pursue his interest in politics, but an injury will force him to drop out of a campaign for the US Senate from Ohio less than two years later. He remains close to the Kennedy family, however, and is with Robert when he is assassinated in 1968. Glenn will be elected senator in 1974, serving for twenty-four years. He will run for the Democratic presidential nomination in 1984. In 1998 he will fly again—this time aboard the space shuttle *Discovery*.

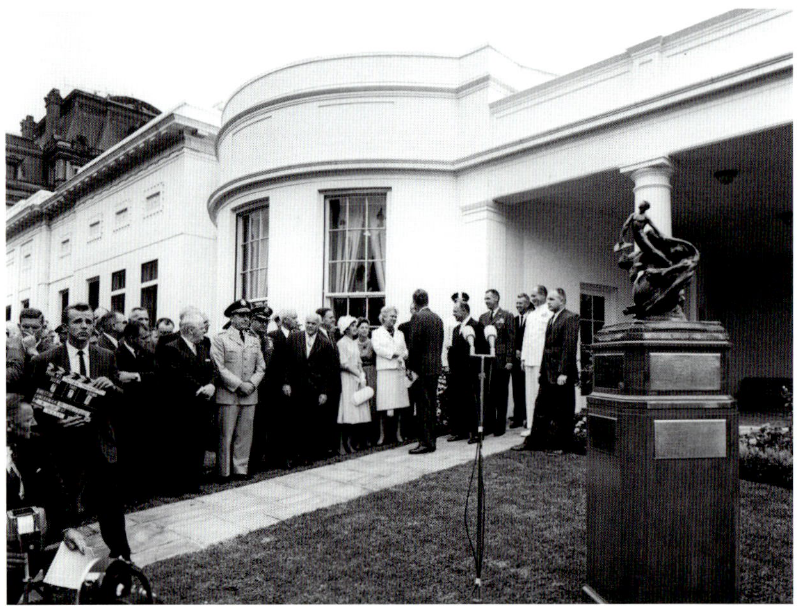

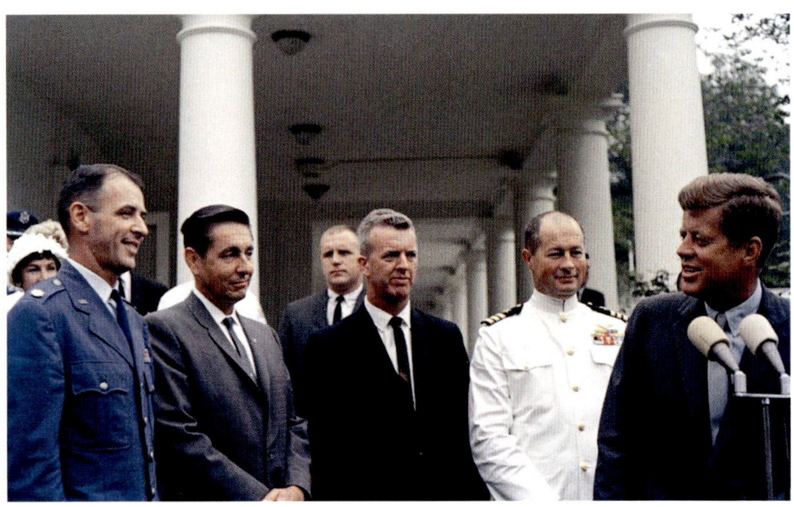

▶ In 1953, North American's pilot Scott Crossfield had become the first pilot to fly at twice the speed of sound.

L–R: USAF Maj. Robert White; Crossfield; NASA's Joe Walker; Navy Cmdr. Forrest Petersen; and Kennedy.

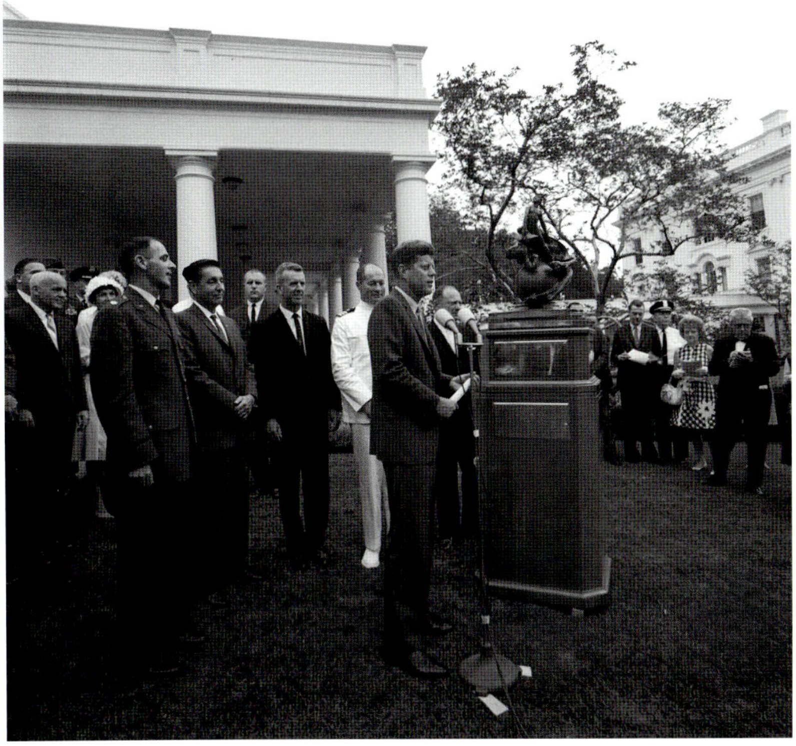

▼ White accepts the award for his colleagues. Twelve hours earlier, he had set a new altitude record for manned aircraft of 59.6 miles in an X-15, qualifying him for his USAF astronaut wings. Dropped from a B-52 over the Nevada desert, his ten-minute flight ends at Edwards AFB, California. Walker will reach 67 miles high in 1963.

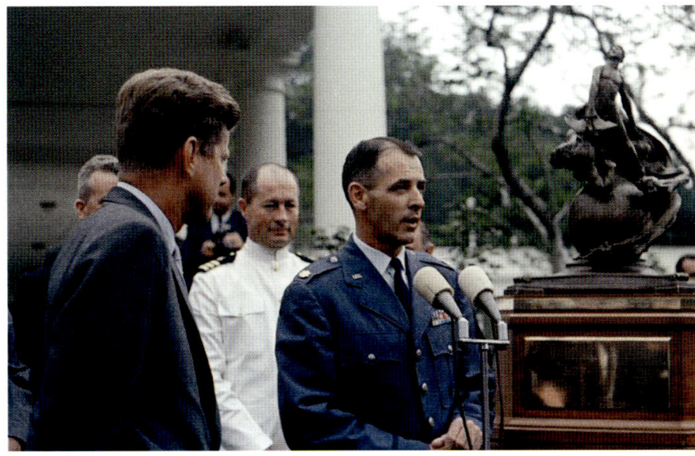

▲ "We are very proud of these four young men who are among the finest that we have," the president says. "We have welcomed the astronauts who also occupy the same domain, and now these flyers who take a manned aircraft into space."

Crossfield had flown the first eight test flights; Walker, Petersen, and White had all taken an X-15 to beyond Mach 5.

That afternoon the pilots receive the NASA Distinguished Service Medal from Johnson at NASA Headquarters, except for Crossfield, who had not flown NASA missions.

That same day, NASA announces that another X-15 pilot, Neil Armstrong, has a seventy-five percent chance of joining the astronaut corps to which he'd applied.

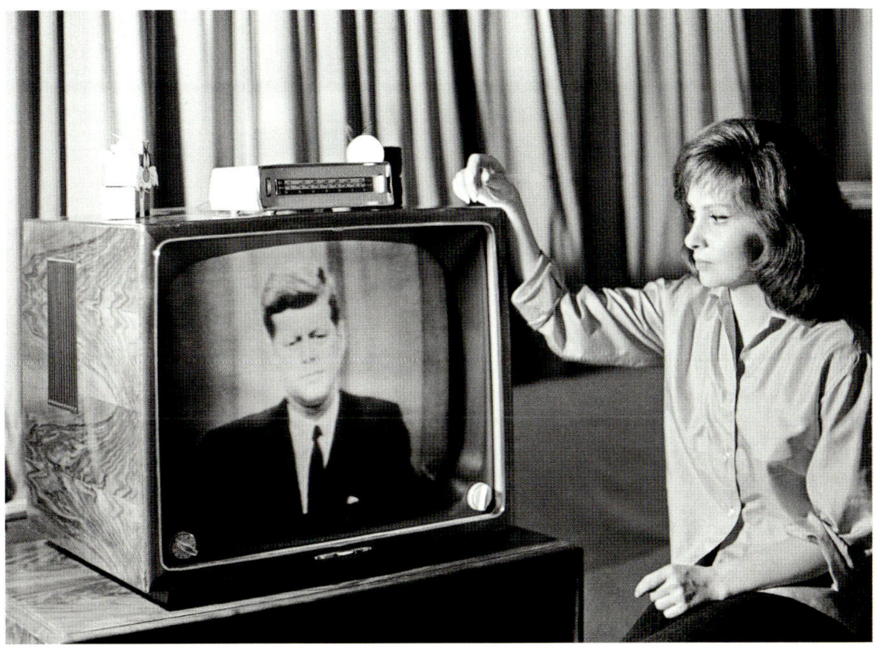

▲ At her Rome villa, Italian actress Gina Lolobridgida watches the first few minutes of the president's 3:00 p.m. EDT news conference on July 23, 1962, part of the first scheduled live transatlantic television transmission, relayed to Europe by the Telstar I satellite launched 13 days earlier from Cape Canaveral.

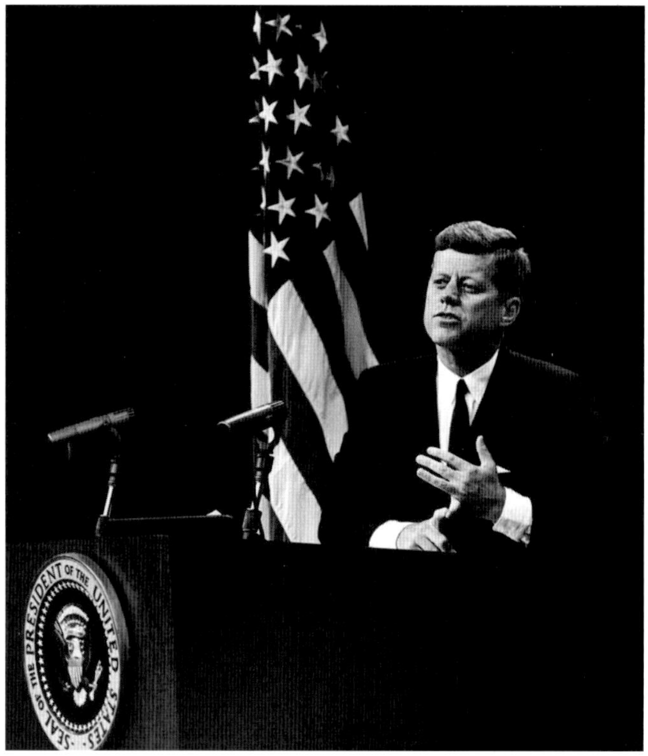

▶ Kennedy opens the conference at the State Department Auditorium by noting, "This is another indication of the extraordinary world in which we live. This satellite must be high enough to carry messages from both sides of the world, which is of course a very essential requirement for peace, and I think this understanding which will inevitably come from the speedier communications is bound to increase the well-being and security of all people, here, and those across the oceans. So we are glad to participate in this operation developed by private industry, launched by government, in admirable cooperation."

The first questions, however, focus on the Berlin standoff and Soviet nuclear weapons testing.

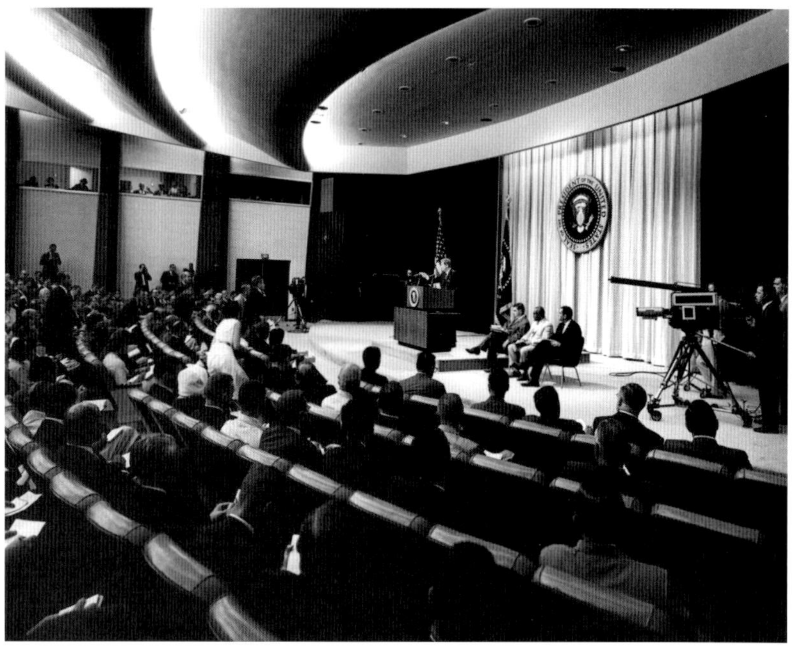

▶ Seated on stage are (L-R) Press Secretary Pierre Salinger, Associate Press Secretary Andrew Hatcher, and Assistant Press Secretary Malcolm Kilduff.

Earlier that afternoon, Alan Shepard and his wife attended a White House luncheon for the president of Ecuador. Shepard's presence at this event was to make up for his missing an earlier invitation to a May dinner for the French culture minister that included aviator Charles Lindbergh. Shepard was at NASA's California tracking station preparing for Carpenter's upcoming mission, but his regrets did not make it to Kennedy.

"It's my understanding that on the morning of that particular affair," he said, "the president was reviewing the guest list and wanted to know where my name was. You can imagine the confusion that created over at NASA Headquarters when they received the call from the president wanting to know where Shepard was. They immediately contacted me, just at the end of an all-night session at the tracking station, and I wasn't too happy about it. Anyway, I was able to explain the situation to them."

Glenn had been photographed waterskiing the day before with the First Lady at the Kennedy compound at Hyannis Port, Massachusetts, wearing a T-shirt. In 1964 Shepard recalled that at the luncheon he and the president "agreed it was rather sorry-looking to be skiing around with a T-shirt on in front of all the cameras."

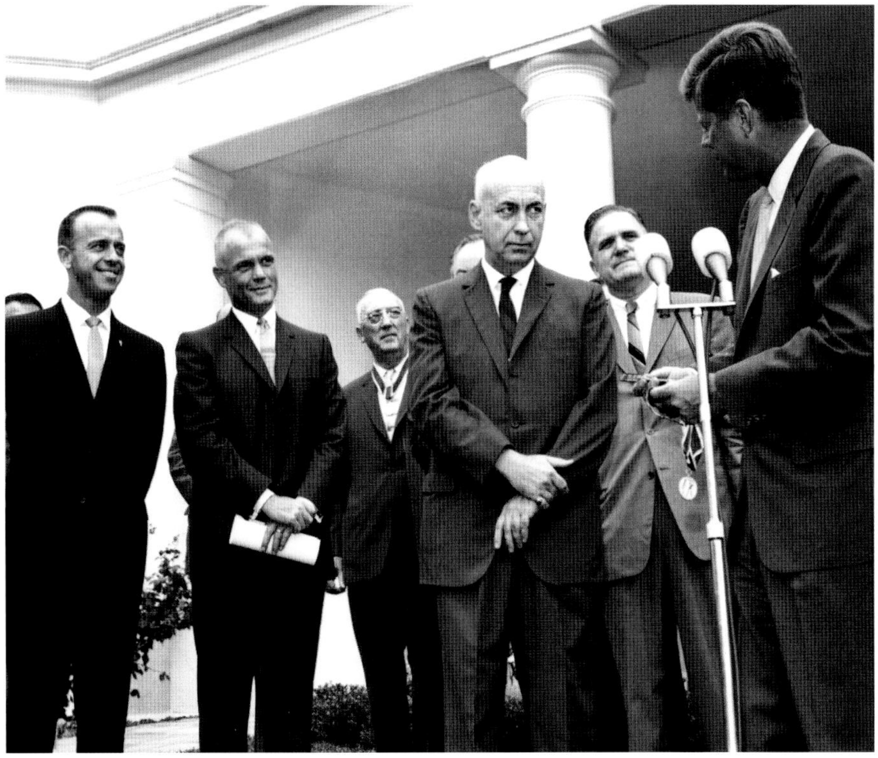

▶ Kennedy presents MSC Director Robert Gilruth with the President's Award for Distinguished Federal Civilian Service outside the Oval Office on August 7, 1962.

The president asks Shepard and Glenn to step forward "as objects of [Gilruth's] experiments."

"His management of this very sophisticated and sensitive [Mercury] program involves a great national commitment and also the lives of some of our best citizens," the president says. "The fact that it has been done with such distinction, I know, heartens him and encourages all of us, and it has also been of the greatest possible benefit to our country and around the world."

NASA chief Webb, between Gilruth and Kennedy, is also chairman of the Distinguished Civilian Service Awards Board.

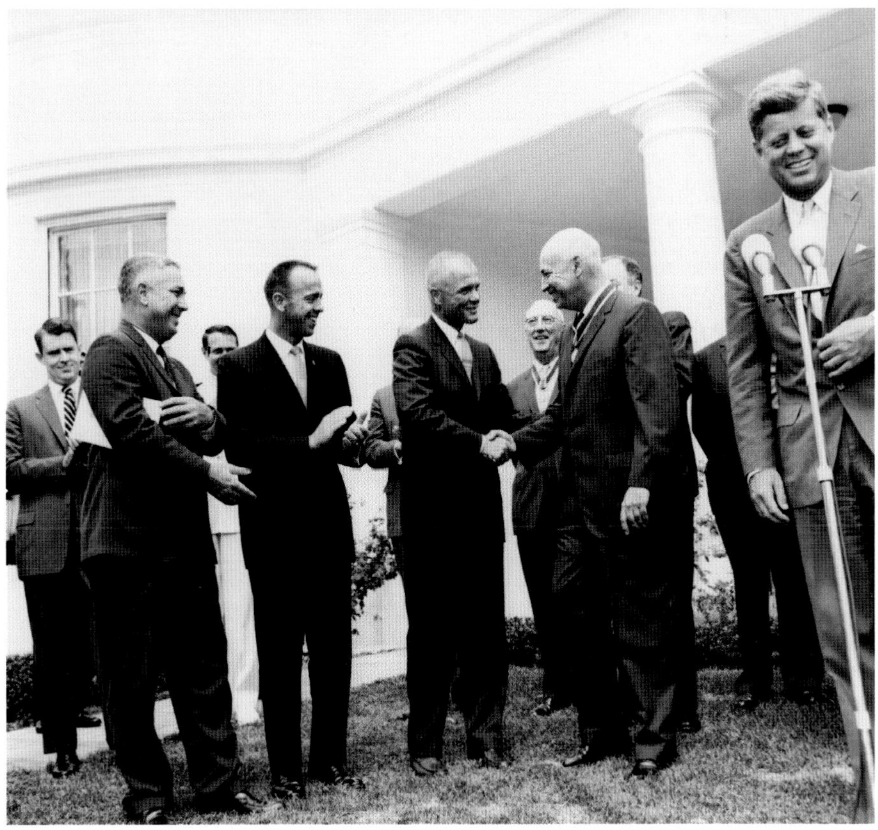

▶ Gilruth is named director of the Space Task Group at Langley Research Center, Virginia, the nucleus for the manned space program, in 1958. He oversees development of the Mercury spacecraft, makes the flight assignments for its astronauts, and serves as MSC director through the Gemini and Apollo programs.

Gilruth updates the president on the progress of moving the Space Task Group to the new installation in Houston, and how contracting is coming along for the Apollo spacecraft.

L–R: Army Secretary Cyrus Vance; Mercury Operations Director Walter Williams; Capt. Tazewell Shepard Jr. (in back); Shepard; Glenn; award recipient and President of the Federal National Mortgage Association J. Stanley Baughman; Sen. Hubert Humphrey (D-Minn.) (hidden); and Kennedy.

▶ Kennedy hands a pen he used to sign the Communications Satellite Act of 1962 to Rep. Samuel Friedel (D-Md.) in the Oval Office on August 31, 1962, at 9:45 a.m. The measure outlines how private communication companies will utilize the tiny but growing number of communication satellites the United States is putting in orbit.

The major player is the American Telephone and Telegraph Co., which owns Telstar I, launched the previous month, but competitors argue it should not have a dominant role in the burgeoning field. That, plus other anti-trust concerns, leads Congress to approve the act. The compromise regulates the industry but gives all companies registered by the Federal Communications Commission (FCC) nondiscriminatory access to satellite systems.

"The benefits which a satellite system should make possible within a few years," the president says, "will stem largely from a vastly increased capacity to exchange information cheaply and reliably with all parts of the world by telephone, telegraph, radio, and television."

Kennedy was part of Telstar I's first scheduled transatlantic television (see pages 69–70); news of his death will be included in the first transpacific television transmission (to Japan) on Nov. 22, 1963, by Relay 1.

L–R: Sen. Everett Dirksen (R-Ill.); Rep. J. Arthur Younger (R-Calif.) (turned away from camera); Rep. John Bennett (R-Mich.); Rep. Friedel; Rep. Oren Harris (D-Ark.) (mostly hidden behind hand); Sen. Warren Magnuson (D-Wash.); Speaker of the House John McCormack (D-Mass.); Sen. Robert Kerr (D-Okla.); Sen. Richard Russell (D-Ga.); Sen. Humphrey; Sen. John Sparkman (D-Ala.); Joseph Beirne, vice president of the American Federation of Labor and Congress of Industrial Organizations (AFL-CIO); Rep. William Springer (R-Ill.); unidentified (partially hidden behind Springer); Sen. John Pastore (D-R.I.); Newton Minow, FCC chairman; and Executive Secretary of National Aeronautics and Space Council Edward Welsh.

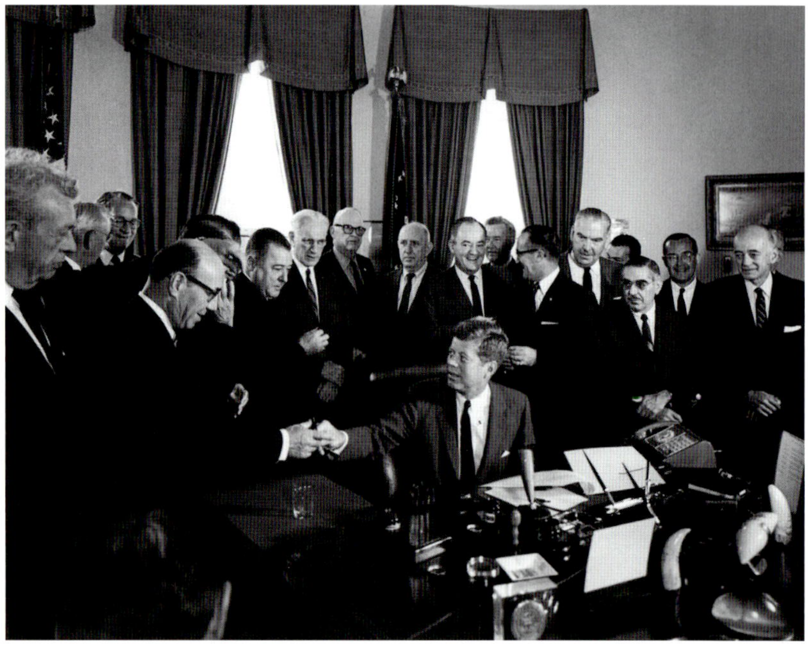

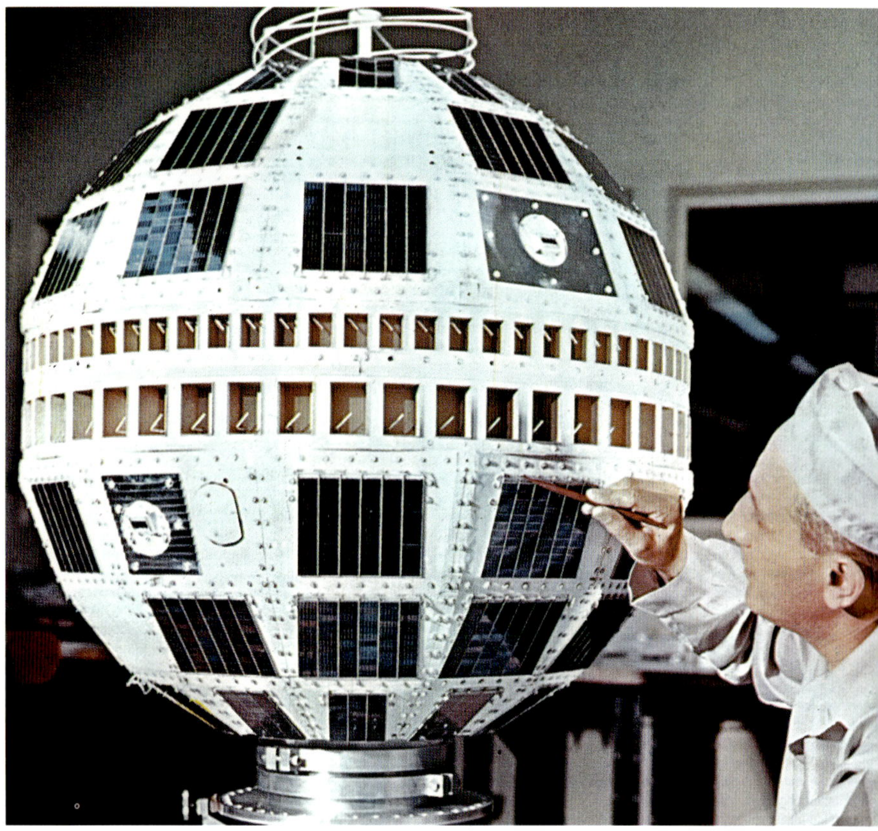

▲ Telstar I undergoes checks at Bell Labs. Its transistors are done in after just eighteen months by radiation from high-altitude US and Soviet nuclear tests.

:04

SEPTEMBER 11, 1962

"Do you think we have bitten off more than we can chew?"

IN SEPTEMBER 1962, President Kennedy embarks on a two-day whirlwind tour of NASA's three major space centers in Alabama, Florida, and Texas, with a final stop in Missouri at the agency's biggest manned spacecraft contractor at the time.

The outing is intended to give him background for the fiscal year 1963 space budget he would submit to Congress in January. Spending had been steadily growing—from $744 million in 1961 to $1.3 billion in 1962 to an expected $2.4 billion in 1963.

Just a month before his trip, the Soviets had launched Vostok 3 and Vostok 4 one day apart on trajectories that brought them within about four miles of each other. It was the first time that more than one manned spacecraft—and person—were in orbit at the same time. During the Florida leg of his trip, the president asks Launch Operations Center Director Kurt Debus what the Soviets are up to. Debus responds that their Vostok maneuvers are likely the first step toward a rendezvous and possible docking in orbit—a capability critical for a manned moon landing.

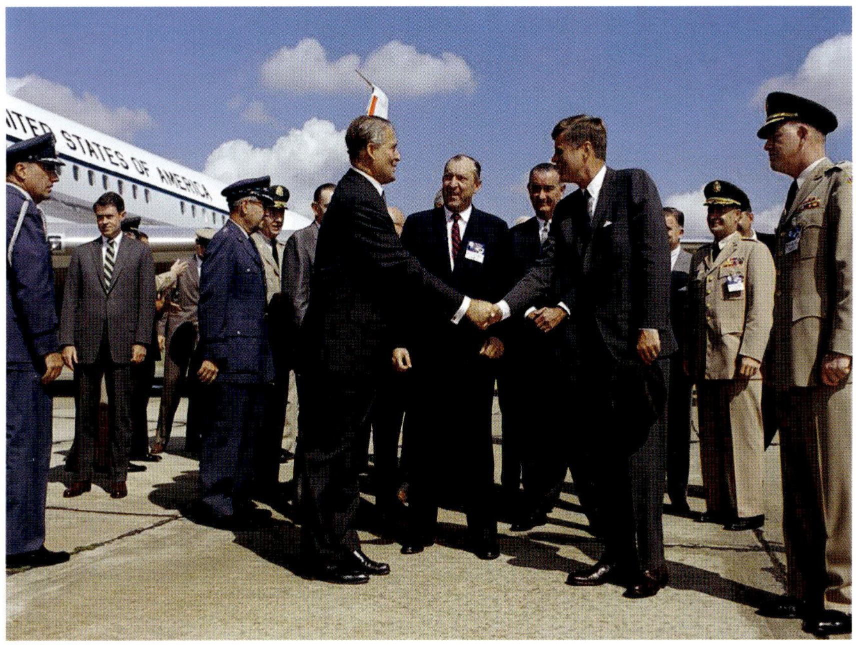

◥ George C. Marshall Space Flight Center (MSFC) Director Wernher von Braun greets the president at 9:40 a.m. CDT on September 11, 1962. NASA's MSFC is located adjacent to the airfield and within Redstone Arsenal, a US Army installation.

L–R: Aide to the president Brig. Gen. Godfrey McHugh; Secretary of the Army Cyrus Vance; USAF Chief of Staff Gen. Curtis LeMay; Maj. Gen. Clifton; Rep. Albert Thomas (mostly hidden); von Braun; Rep. Robert E. Jones (D-Ala.); Johnson; Kennedy; Webb (partially hidden); Commander of the US Army Materiel Command Lt. Gen. Frank Besson Jr.; and Commanding General of the US Army Missile Command Maj. Gen. Francis McMorrow.

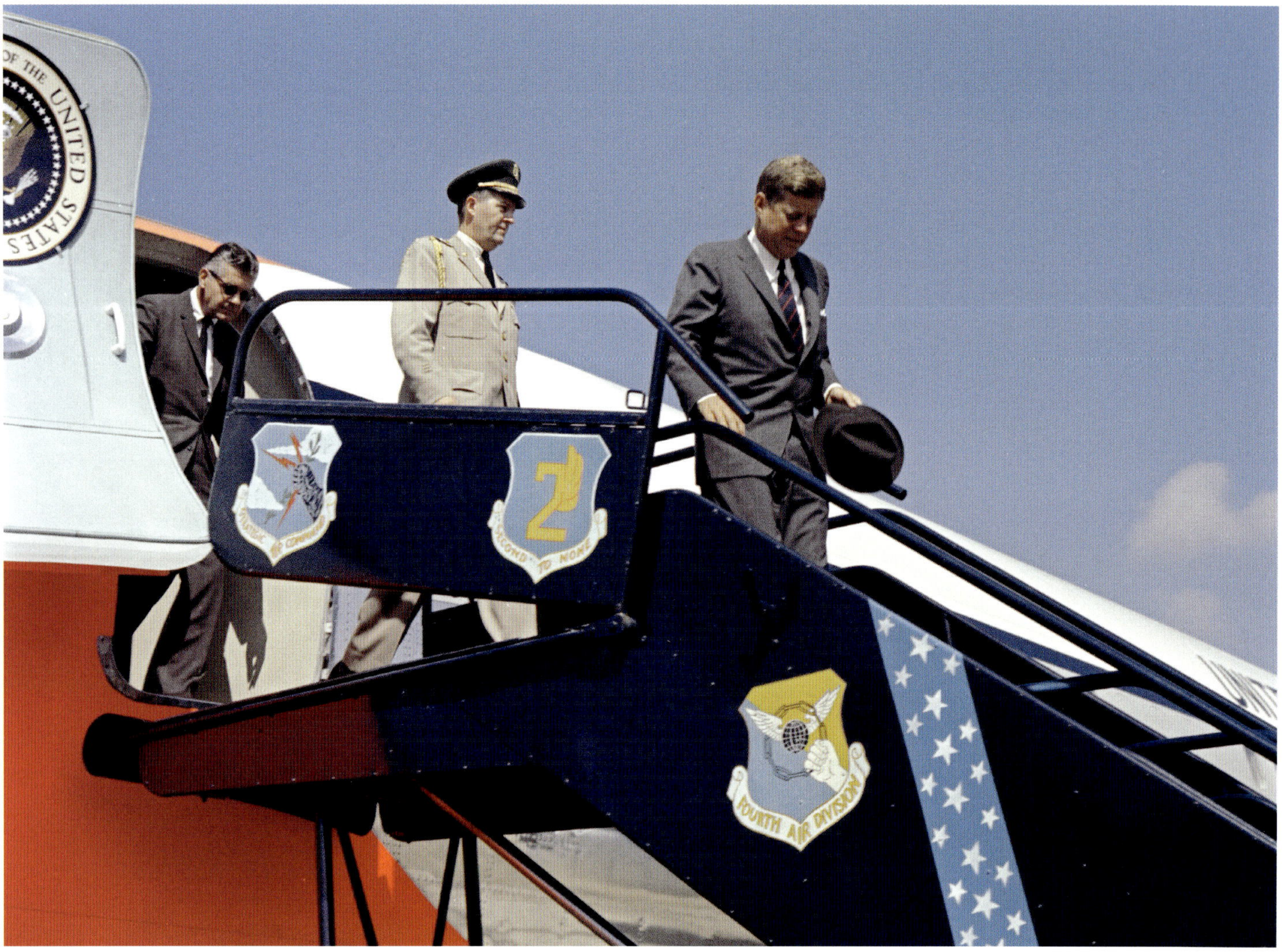

▲ The president arrives at Redstone Army Airfield in Huntsville, Alabama, at 9:35 a.m. aboard Air Force One. Disembarking behind Kennedy are Maj. Gen. Clifton and Secret Service Agent Jerry Behn.

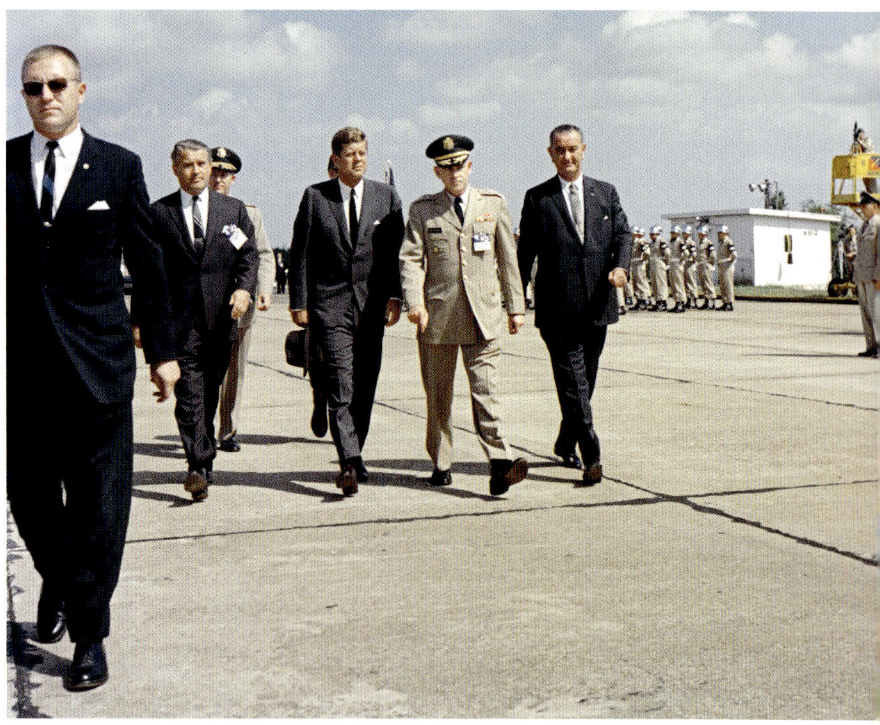

▶ The president heads toward a platform to make brief remarks to 470 troops from thirteen nations visiting Redstone Arsenal for a missile operation and maintenance training program at the Army Ordinance Guided Missile School.

L–R: Secret Service Agent Frank Yeager; von Braun, Maj. Gen. Clifton (in back); Kennedy; Maj. Gen. McMorrow; and Johnson. The vice president had arrived aboard Air Force Two.

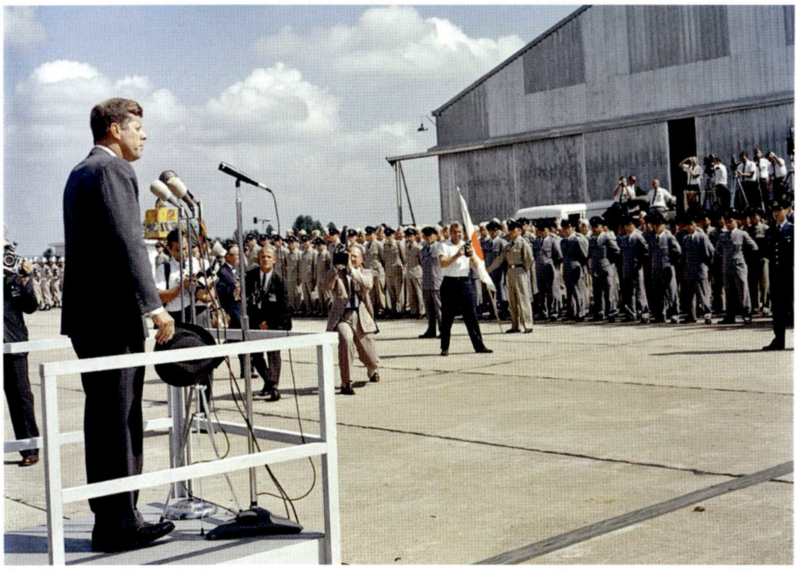

◀ "This kind of joint community effort, the community of free nations, would have been regarded as impossible two decades ago, but now we take it very much for granted," Kennedy tells the troops. "We are glad you're here. The effort that we and you are making in common is to defend our countries, defend our peace, defend the vital interests of the free world in the strong belief that in time the disease of liberty, as Thomas Jefferson called it, will be catching in all parts of the world."

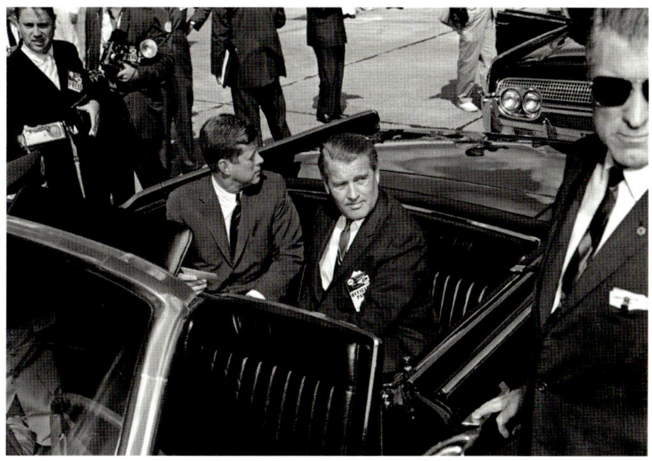

▶ Kennedy prepares to depart the airfield with von Braun at 9:55 a.m. for a series of briefings. Von Braun, who had overseen development of the V-2 missile used against England, is a pioneering German rocket scientist who was brought to the United States after World War II. This Lincoln Continental is loaned by Ray Pearman Lincoln-Mercury in Huntsville.

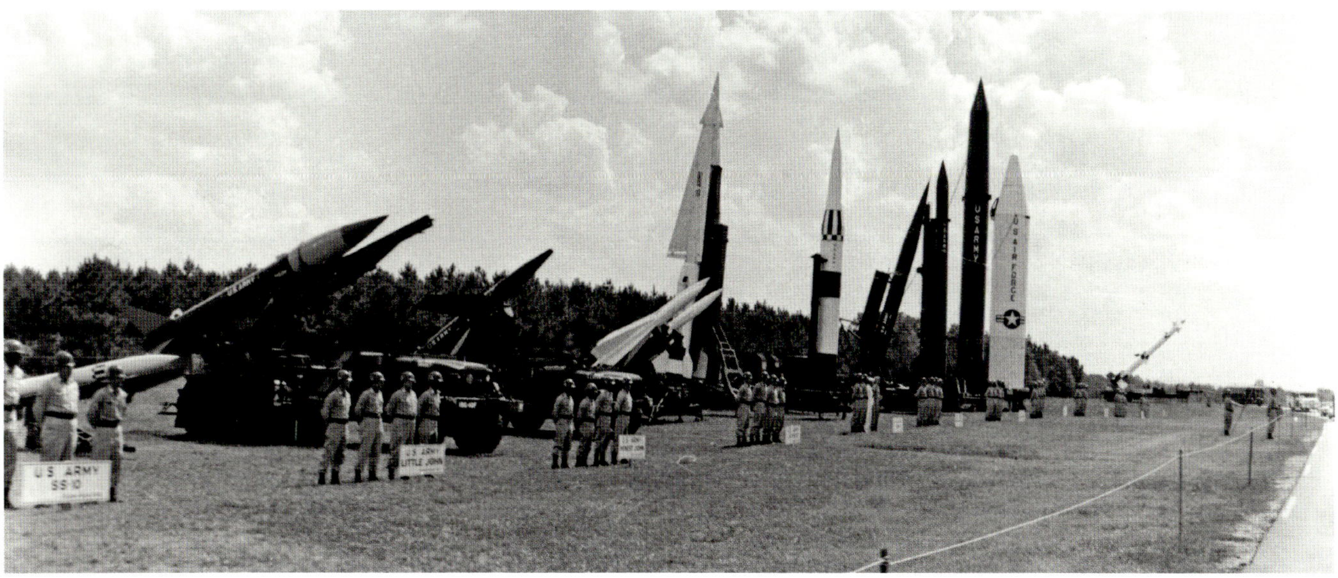

▲ The president's motorcade approaches a display of thirteen missile systems, including the French SS-10, Little John, Honest John, Hawk, Nike Hercules, Sergeant, Pershing, and Thor. All programs except for the USAF's Thor are managed by the Army Materiel Command at the arsenal. The new command is part of a Kennedy administration Army reorganization and had just been activated in May.

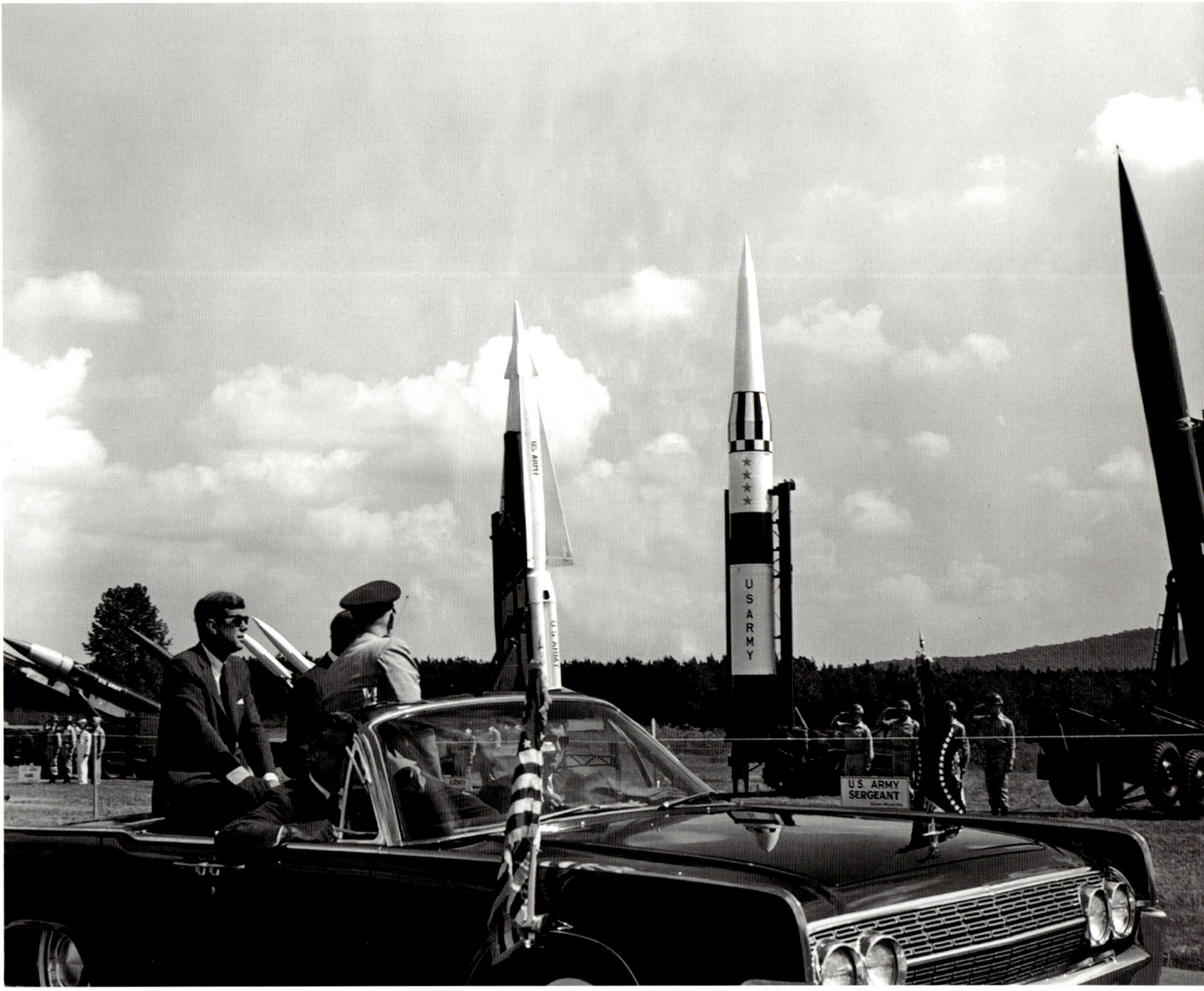

▲ Maj. Gen. McMorrow briefs the president as the motorcade pauses at the missile display. Left to right are Nike Hercules, Sergeant, and Pershing missiles, all capable of carrying nuclear warheads. A Pershing and other missiles were part of Kennedy's inaugural parade in 1961.

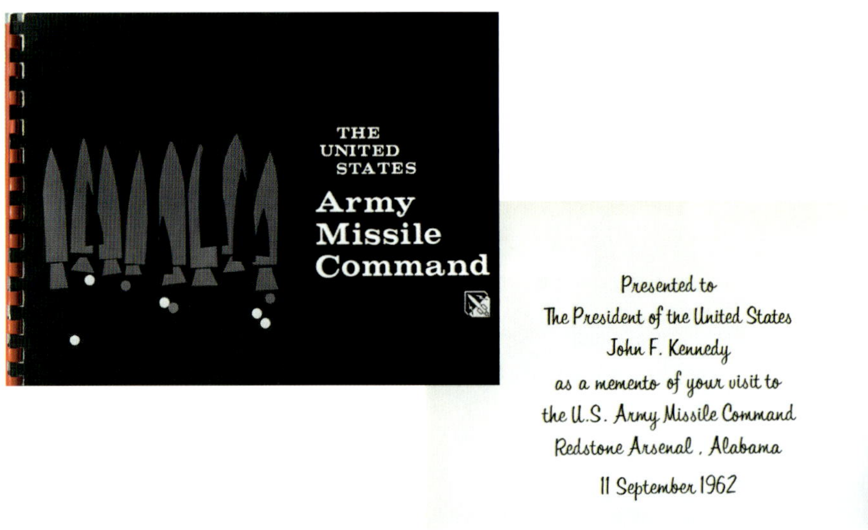

▶ Photo booklet given to the president. (Courtesy of the John F. Kennedy Presidential Library and Museum.)

▶ The president and Maj. Gen. McMorrow depart Building 4722 at 10:15 a.m. following a classified briefing on missile guidance control hardware and inertial guidance systems. Defense Secretary McNamara is at center. Kennedy is also briefed on the Army's work on military applications of lasers, including laser-guided bombs.

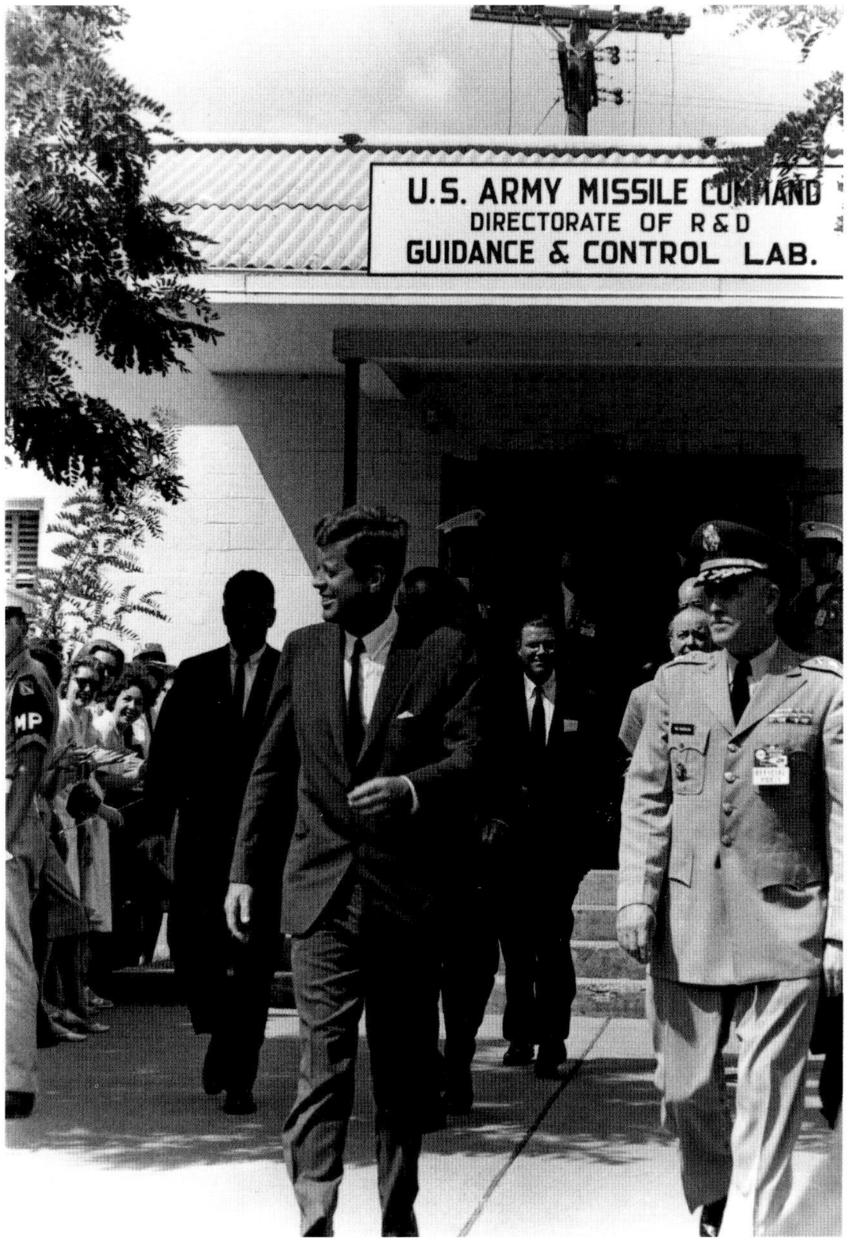

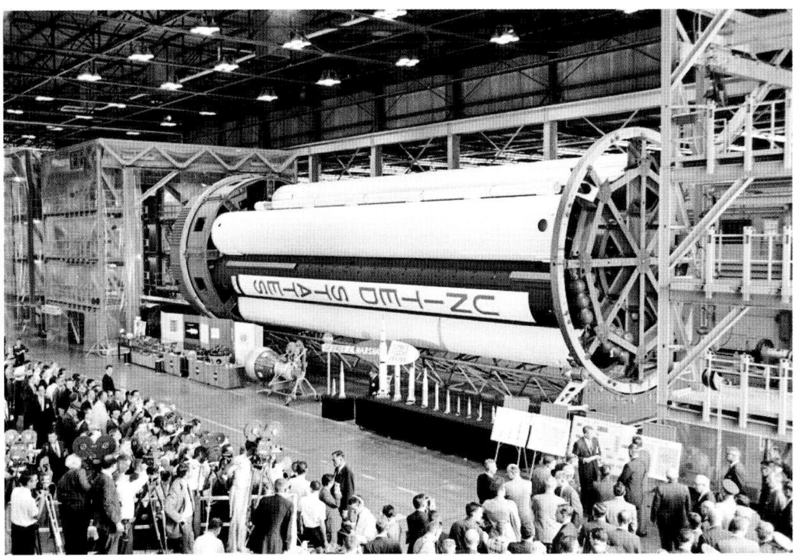

◀ Von Braun begins his briefing at 10:20 a.m. after he arrives with the president at Building 4705, where Saturn boosters are assembled by Marshall's Fabrication and Assembly Engineering Division. This is S-I-D, the first stage of SA-D, a dummy Saturn C-1 dynamic test vehicle that would be subjected to simulated launch vibration. It is now on display at Marshall's Rocket Garden.

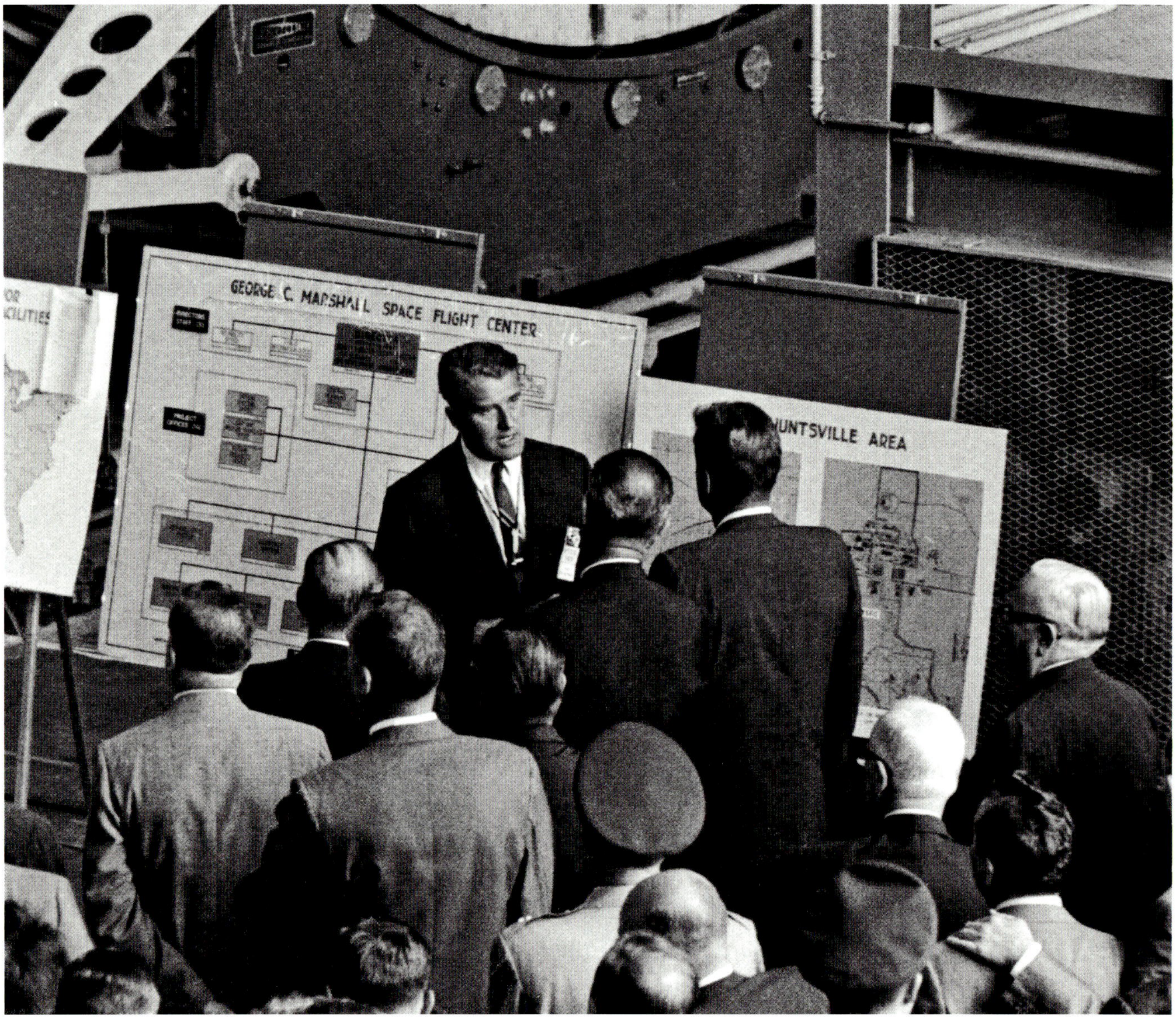

▲ Von Braun goes over the role of Marshall as the rocket development and production center for the Apollo program, its organization, and the locations of its prime contractors. “He was intensely interested in seeing things—in understanding for himself how complex things were,” von Braun recalled in 1964. “He got a little restless with too much detail during briefings; he suspected a snow job behind too much paper displays.”

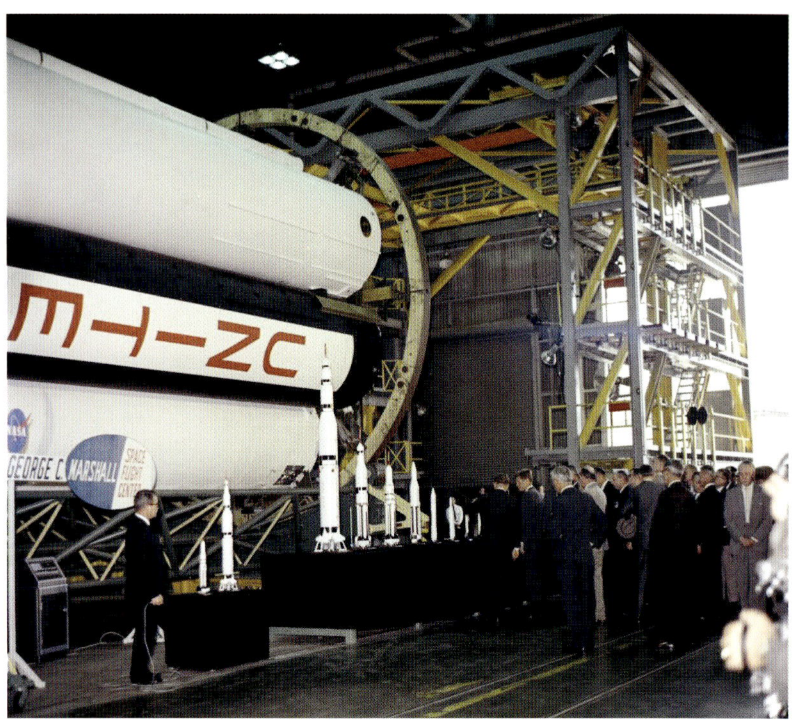

▶ Von Braun uses MSFC-built scale models to discuss the evolution of US booster rockets, including the Saturn family at center.

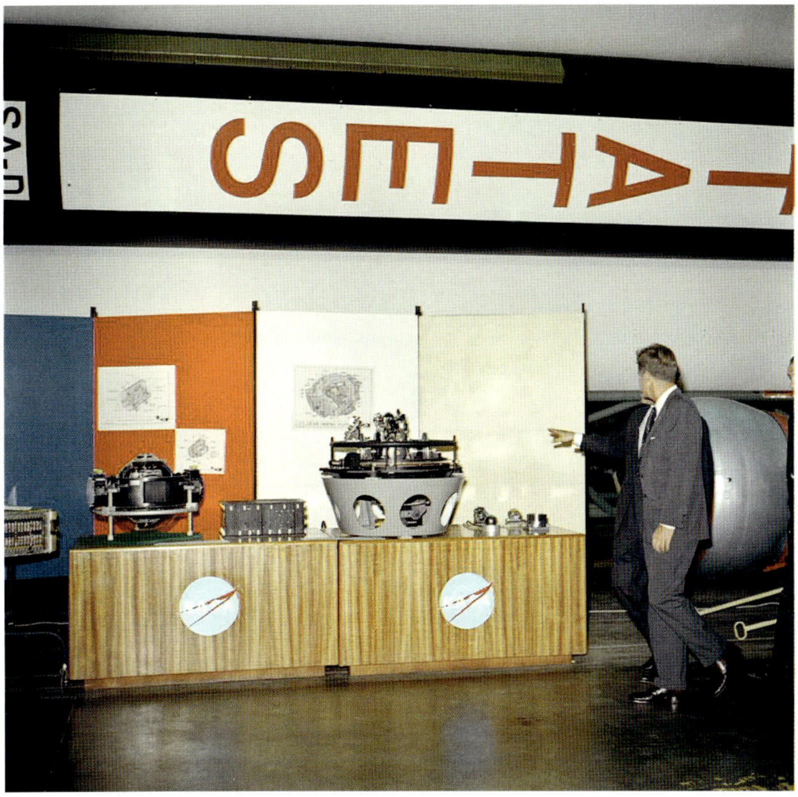

◀ The president sees a display of components that make up the ST-124, an improved inertial guidance platform, which measures the Saturn's acceleration and attitude during flight. It would first fly as a complete system on SA-5.

▼ Von Braun leads the way as the president's party walks toward a mockup of an assembled Saturn C-1. Seamans, Johnson, and Webb follow.

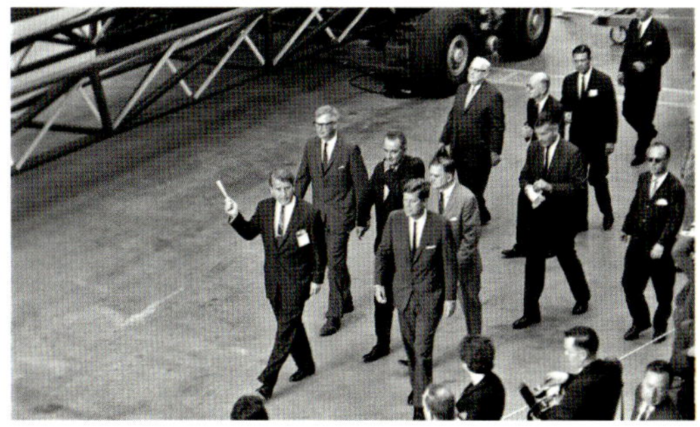

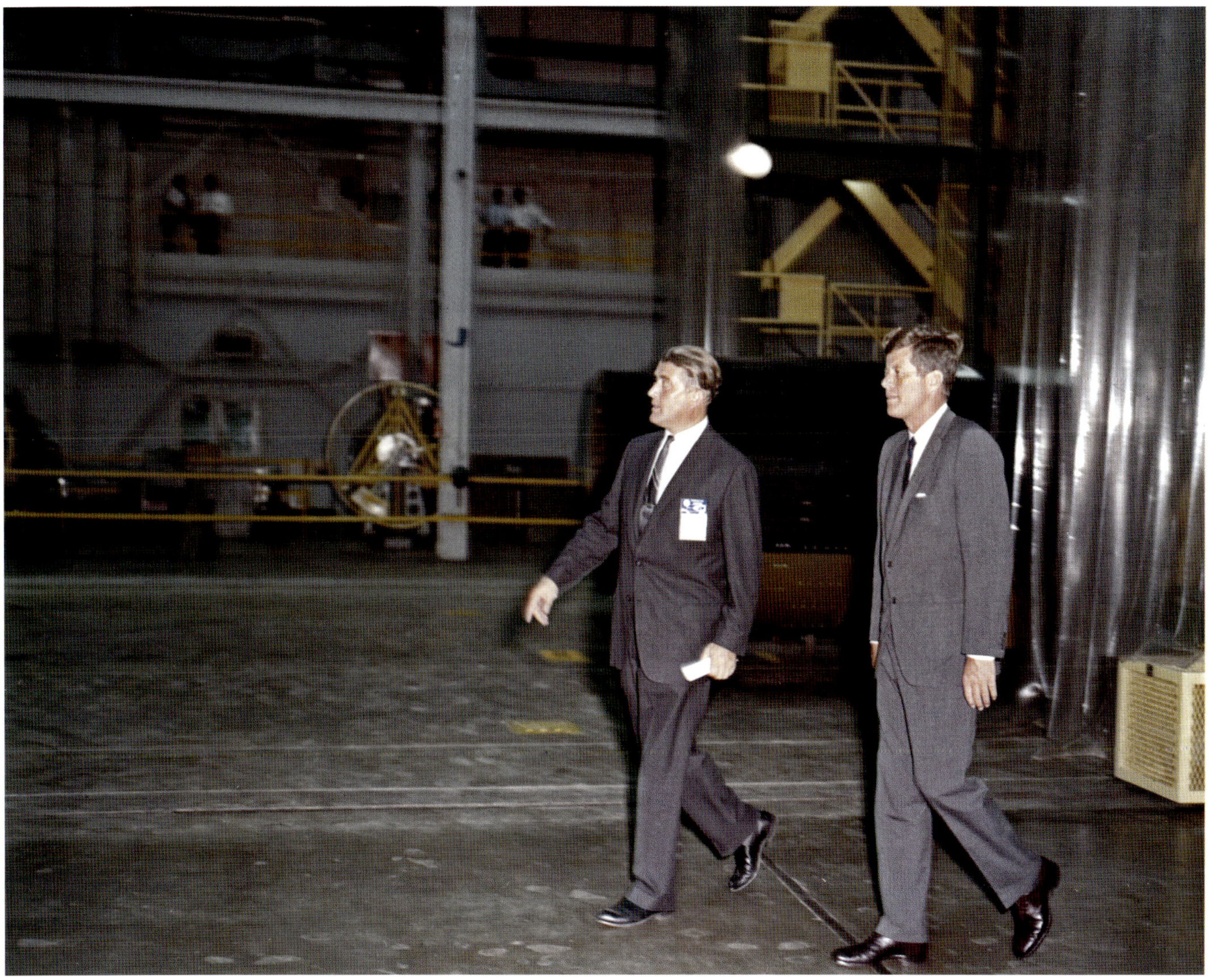

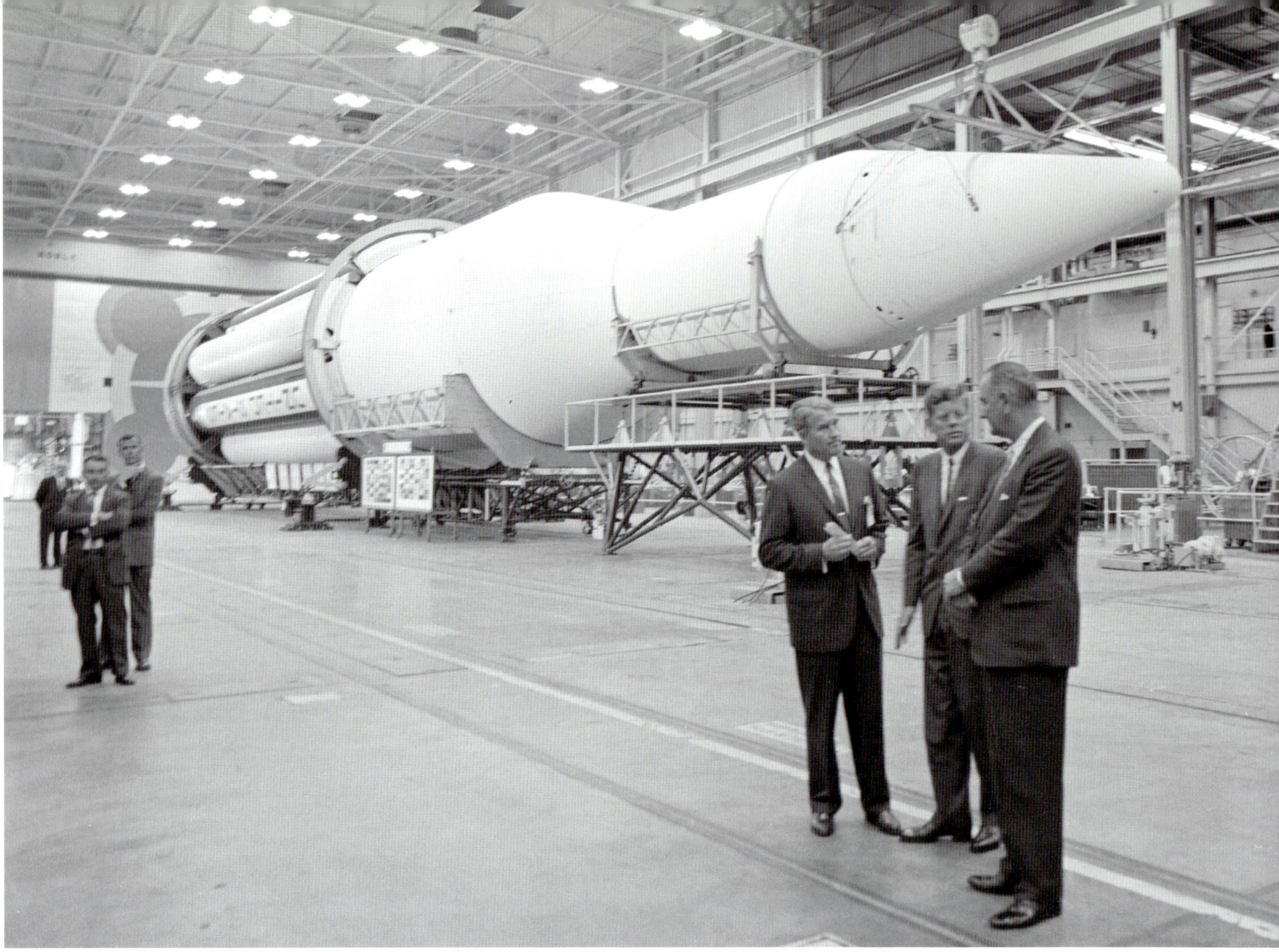

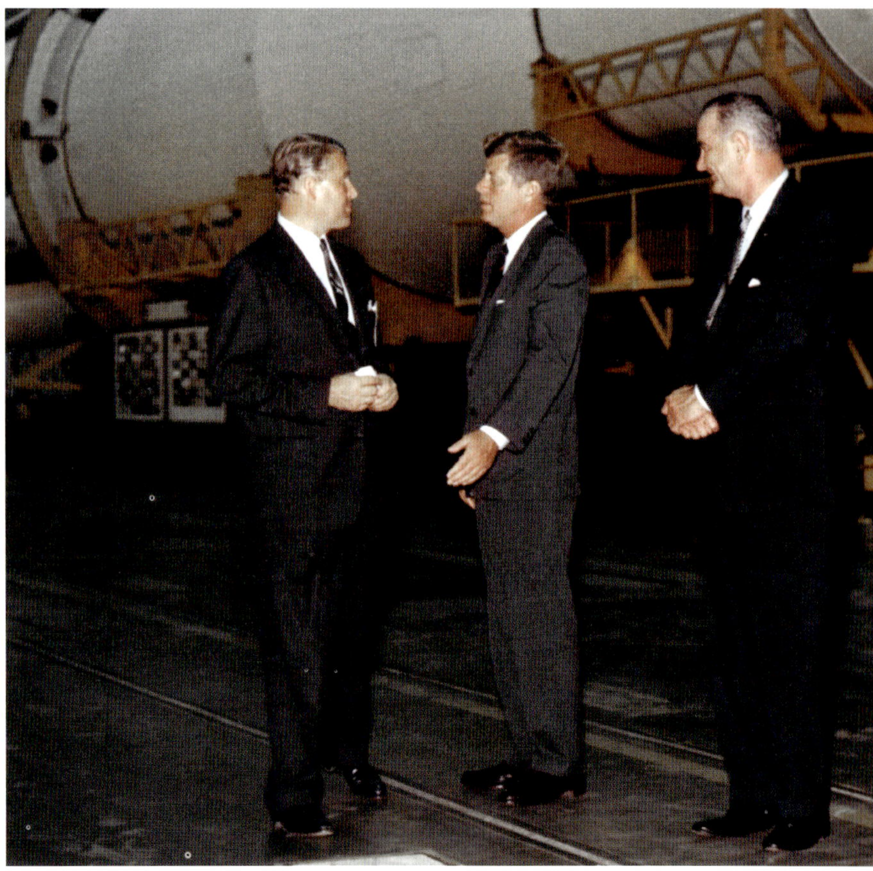

Von Braun, Kennedy, and Johnson stop in front of a Saturn C-1 (renamed Saturn I four months later) mockup at the request of news photographers. Some two hundred media are accredited. The display consists of S-1–5 (which would become the first stage of SA-5), an inert S-IV second stage, and a dummy nosecone. Kennedy would see SA-5 at LC-34 thirteen months later.

Two C-1s have been successfully launched from LC-34, and a third would arrive within days at Cape Canaveral by barge to be launched on November 16.

During the visit, according to von Braun, Kennedy asks, "Well, do you think we have bitten off more than we can chew?"

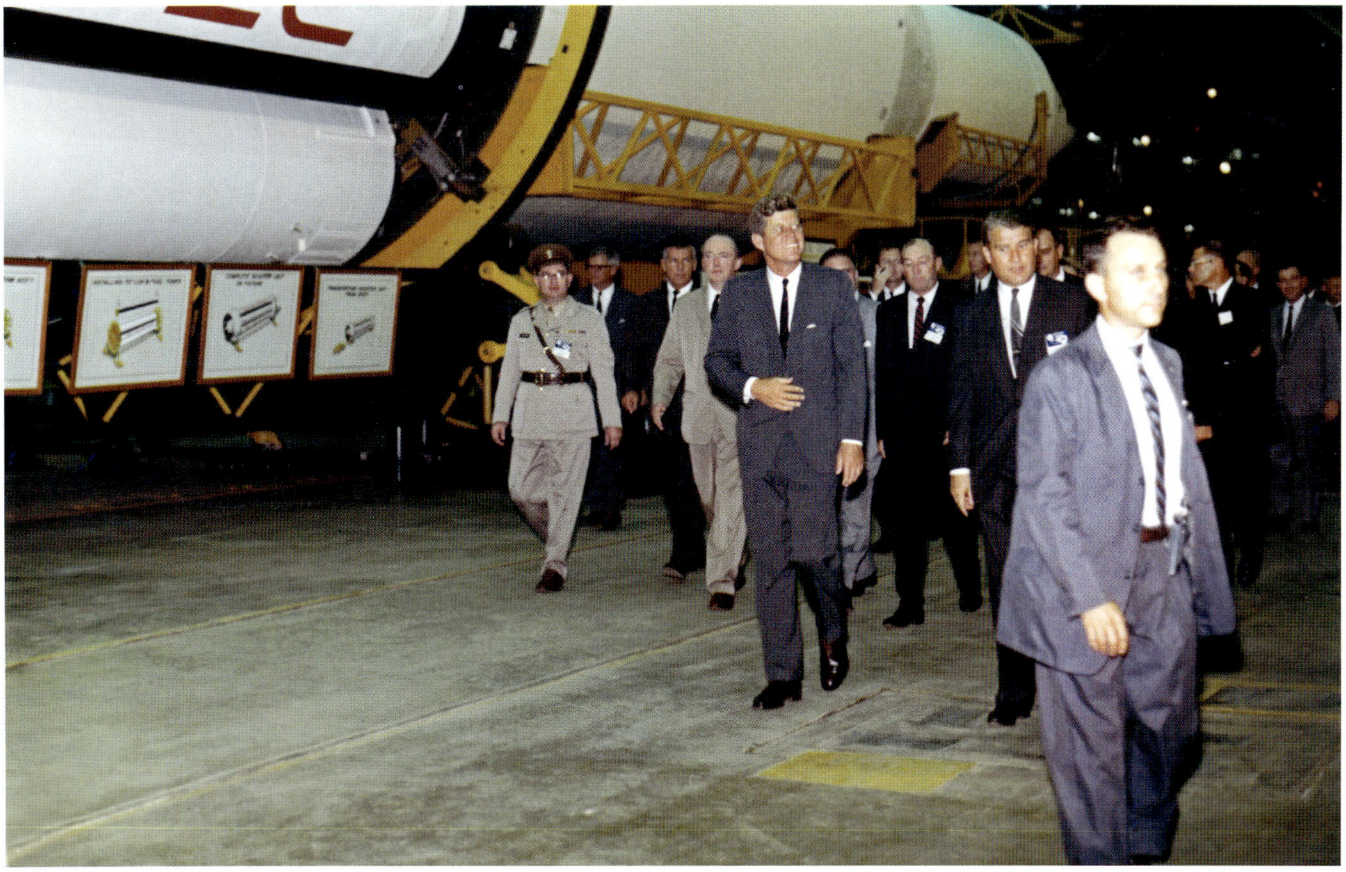

▲ The president's party moves to another area of the building for a display of Saturn engines and other hardware. The drawings at left detail first-stage assembly, which consists of a central Jupiter rocket fuel tank surrounded by a cluster of eight Redstone tanks, all manufactured by Chrysler.

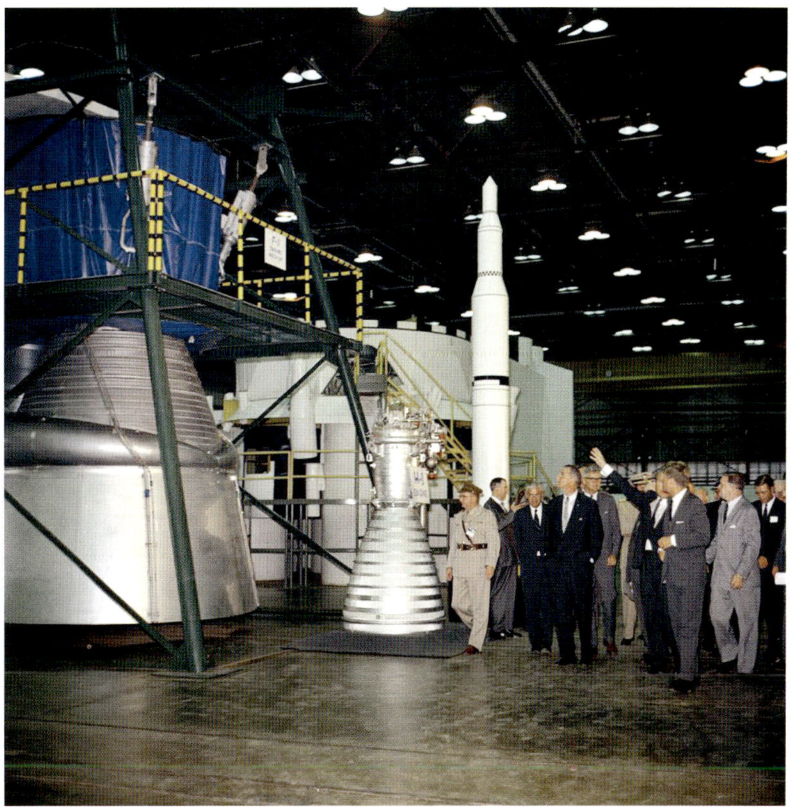

▶ The mockup Saturn engine displays include an F-1 (left), five of which would power the first stage of the Saturn V; an H-1 (center), eight of which are used in the Saturn C-1's first stage; and an RL-10 (see next page), six of which will be used in the Saturn I's eventual second stage, the S-IV. Gesturing toward the towering Saturn C-5 model, von Braun tells Kennedy, "This is the big one. It will fulfill your promise to put a man on the moon in this decade. By God, we'll do it."

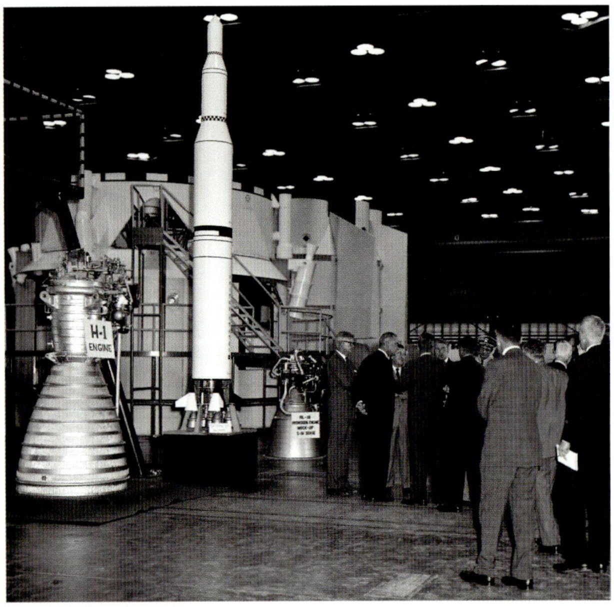

▲ Von Braun and the president's science advisor, Jerome Wiesner (third from left), briefly debate NASA's plan to use a two-stage manned lunar spacecraft, which would require only one Saturn launch instead of two. Kennedy interrupts von Braun, "I understand Dr. Wiesner doesn't agree with this," and turns around to search the entourage. "Where is Jerry?" Kennedy demands. Wiesner outlines his objections, and some lively dialogue ensues, just out of the earshot of reporters. "They obviously knew we were discussing something other than golf scores," Seamans recalled later. It is a pivotal decision, won by von Braun and NASA, in how Apollo would proceed.

▼ Von Braun, the president, and Webb pass partially assembled gore sections of a Saturn C-5 fuel tank bulkhead. Von Braun believed his designers should have hands-on participation in building and testing hardware, and MSFC had impressive fabrication facilities. One or more prototypes of every type of Saturn booster were fabricated in MSFC shops.

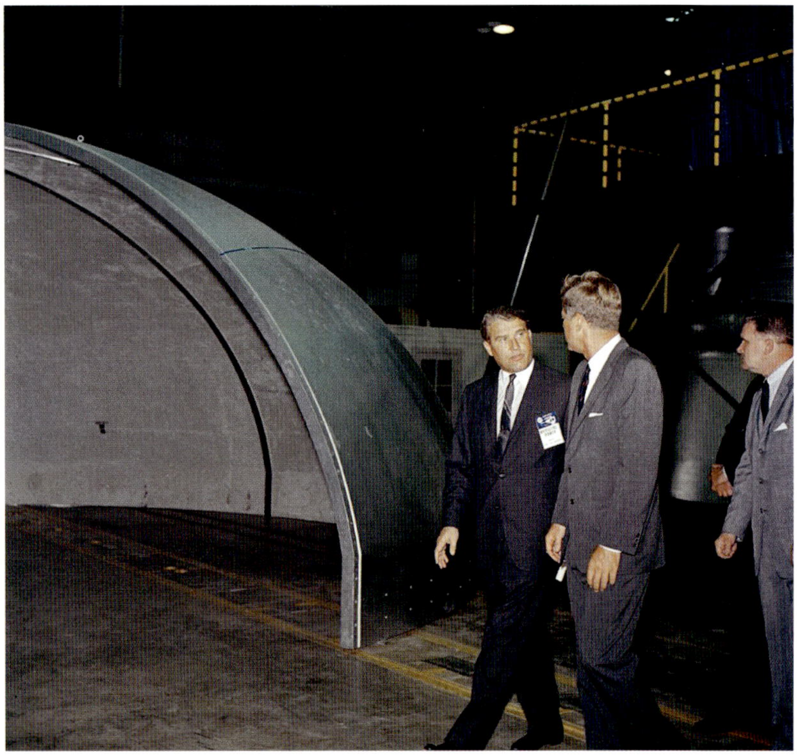

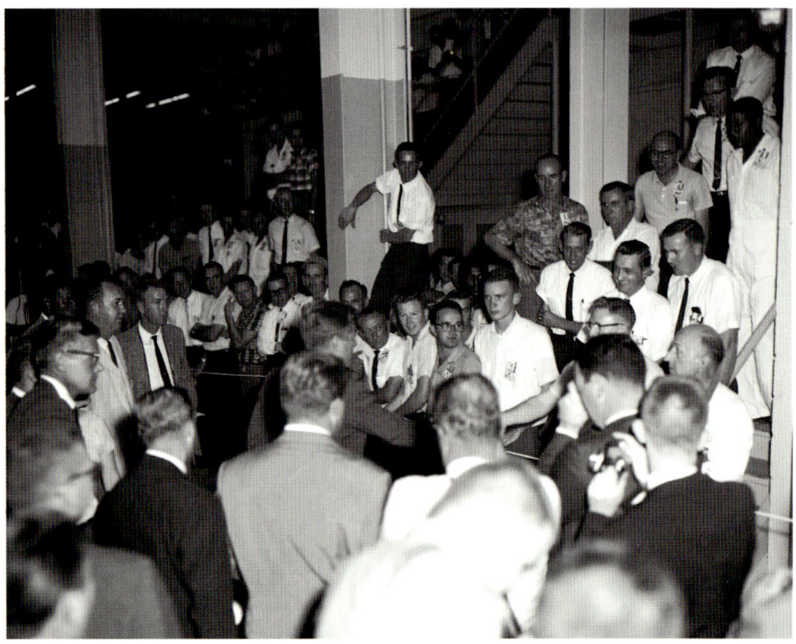

▶ "Many of our hopes and aspirations for the conquest of space ride on your work," the president tells Marshall workers. "I am particularly appreciative of the many dedicated scientists and engineers who have selflessly continued this work, often despite personal sacrifices."

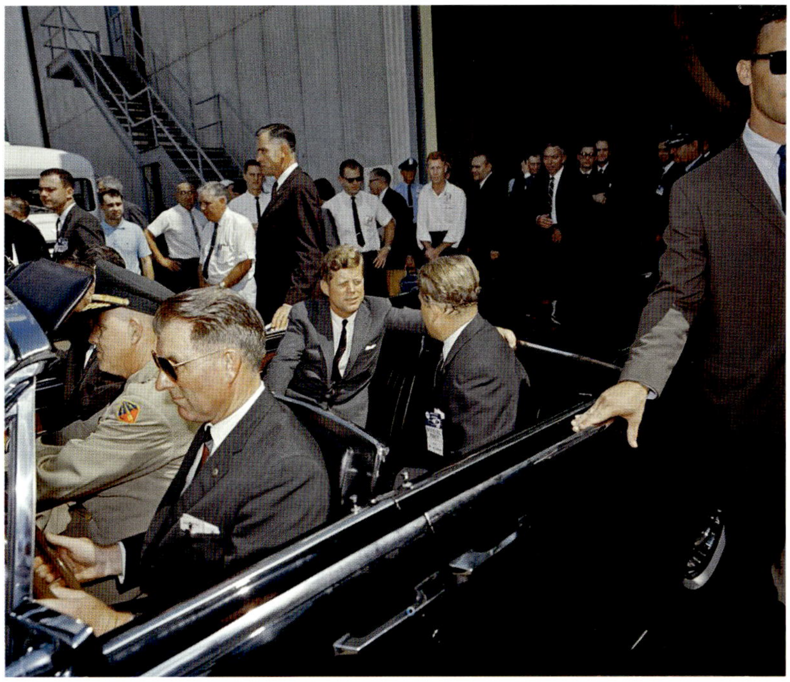

▶ With Agent Bill Greer at the wheel, next to Maj. Gen. McMorrow, the president and von Braun depart Building 4705 at 10:55 a.m., heading for the Static Test Center.

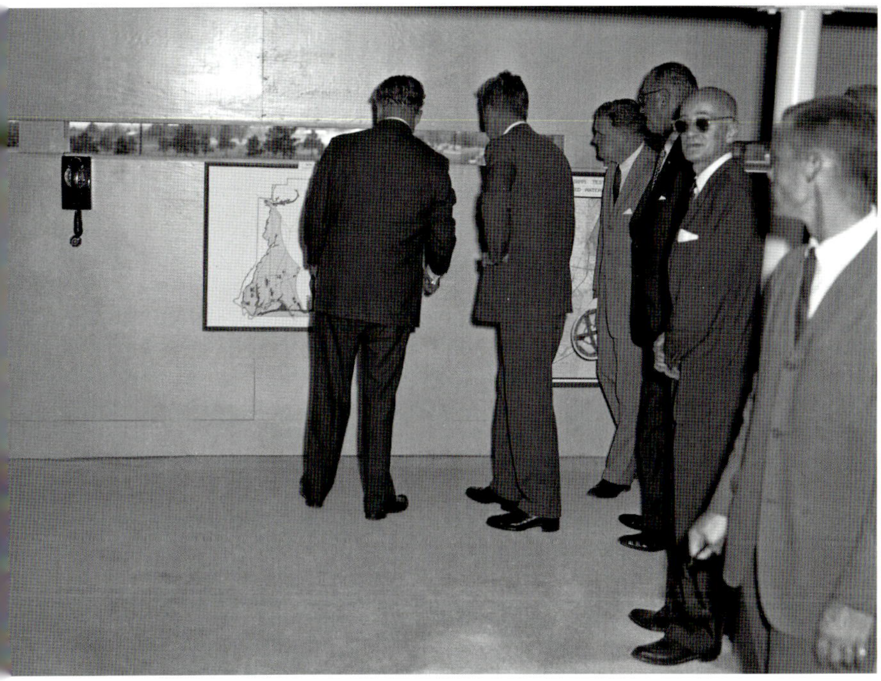

◀ The president arrives at an observation bunker at the Propulsion and Structural Test Facility at 11:00 a.m. to watch a Saturn stage test-firing. Von Braun briefs Kennedy on the test.

L–R: Von Braun; Kennedy; Webb; Johnson; and National Aeronautics and Space Council Executive Secretary Edward Welsh.

▼ The firing as seen from the motorcade parked nearby.

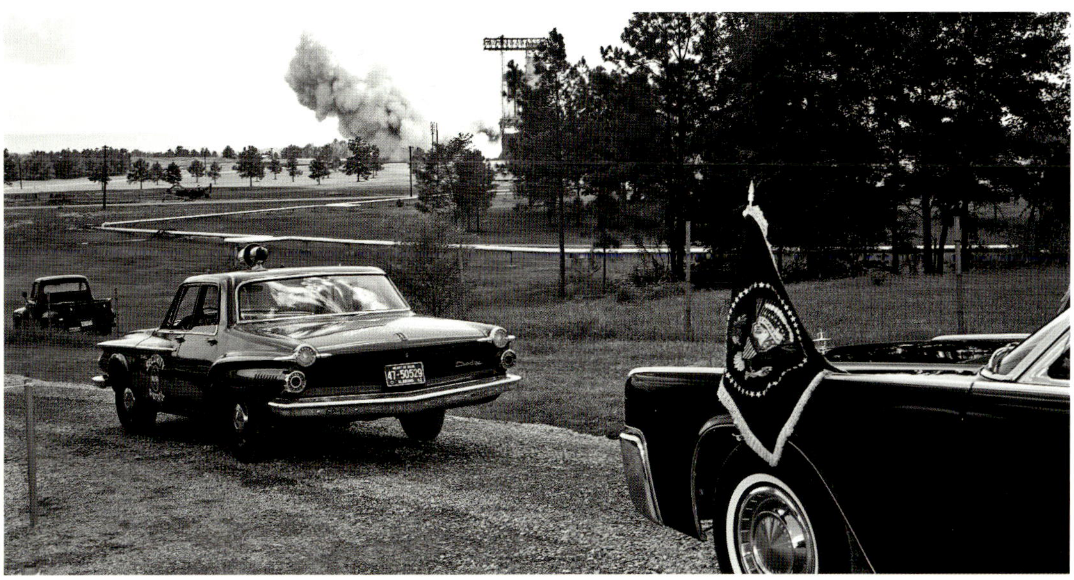

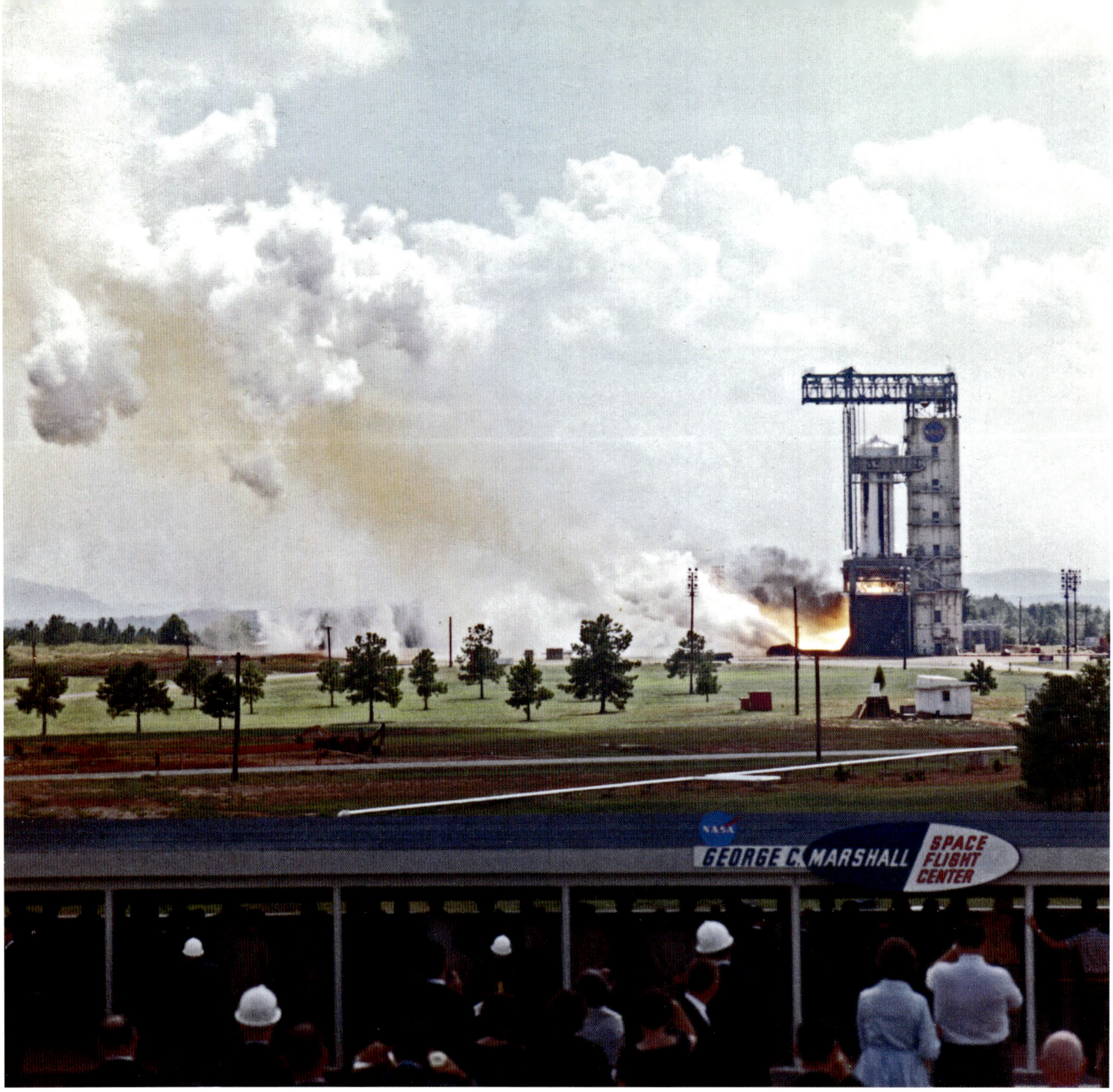

▲ The presidential party and other guests witness a thirty-second static test firing of S-I-4, the first stage of the Saturn C-I booster that would be launched six months later as SA-4. The bunker is about two thousand feet from the test stand. "That's just wonderful," Kennedy tells von Braun. "If only I could show all this to the people in Congress." *The Marshall Star*, the center's newspaper, calls it "the world's largest known rocket stage."

▶ Water continues to cool the test stand and flame deflector as von Braun gives the president a close-up look at the structure after the firing. The system's capacity is forty thousand gallons of water a minute.

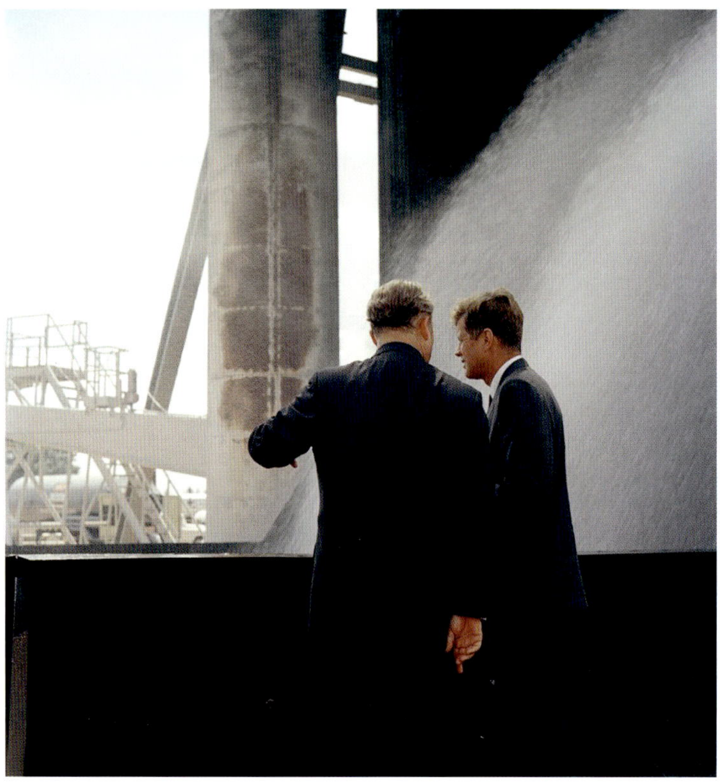

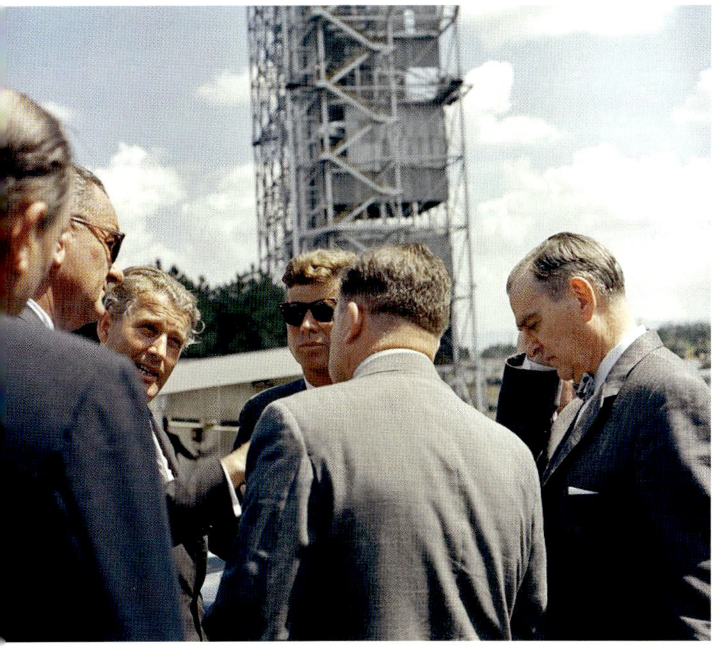

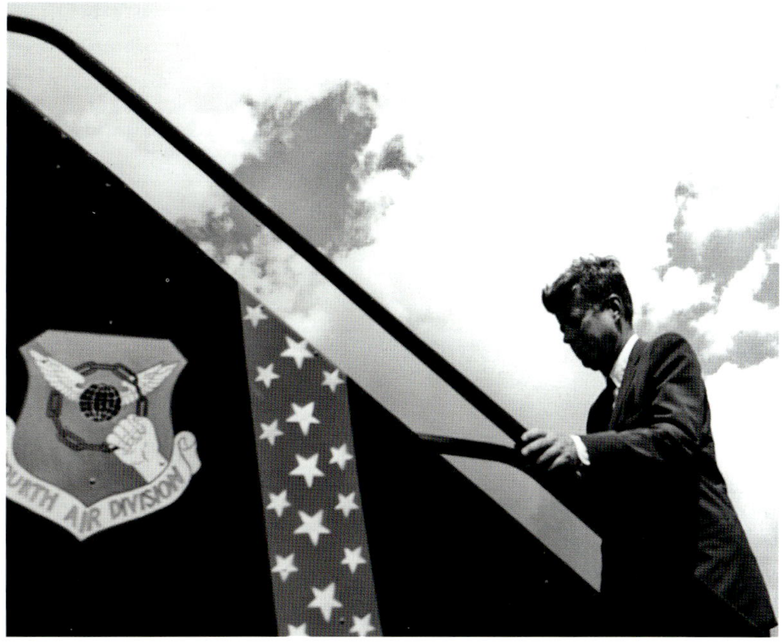

▲ Von Braun speaks to Webb with the test stand in the background. According to Webb, Kennedy asks von Braun how he could best help. "Give us the money, and the complete freedom to spend it any way we want to," von Braun replies. Webb quickly reminds him of congressional oversight of NASA.

L–R: Johnson; von Braun; Kennedy; Webb; and Rep. Thomas.

◥ Air Force One departs Redstone Army Airfield at noon for Cape Canaveral. Joining the trip are USAF Chief of Staff Gen. Curtis LeMay and Eugene Zuckert, USAF secretary.

▼ The president and NASA Launch Operations Directorate Chief Kurt Debus pause during a USAF color guard ceremony after Kennedy arrives at the Cape Canaveral Missile Test Annex Skid Strip at 2:30 p.m. EDT.

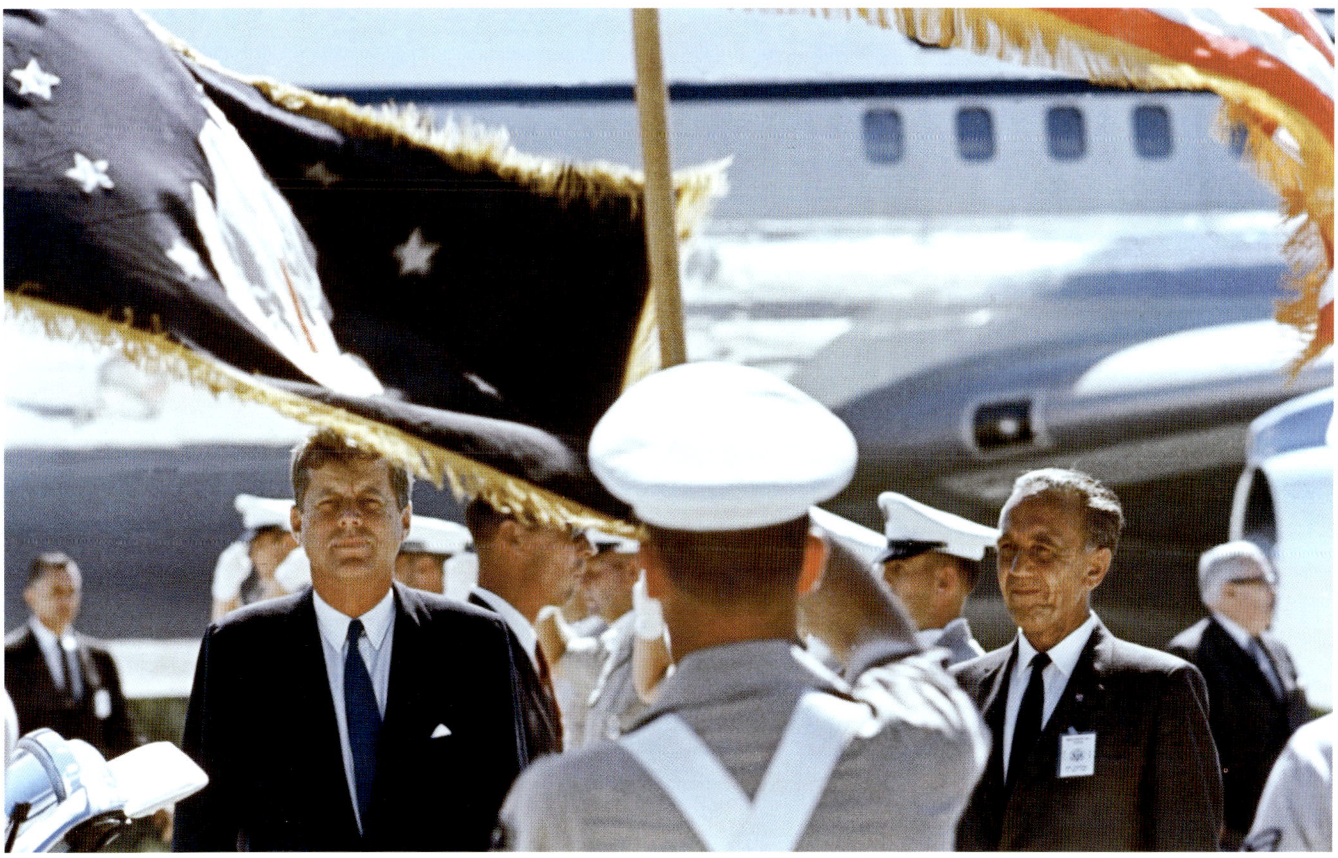

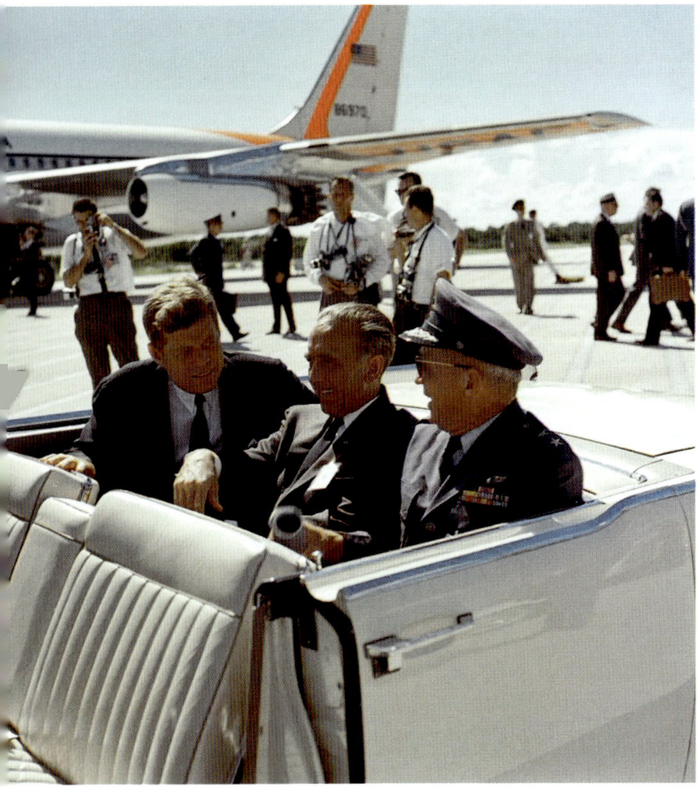

▲ The president chats with Maj. Gen. Leighton Davis, commander of the USAF Missile Test Center, and Debus. Behind and to Kennedy's left is NASA photographer Bill Taub. Debus, like von Braun, is a leading German rocket scientist who had been brought to the United States after World War II. He will remain director of the NASA installation, known as the Kennedy Space Center following the president's death, until he retires in 1974.

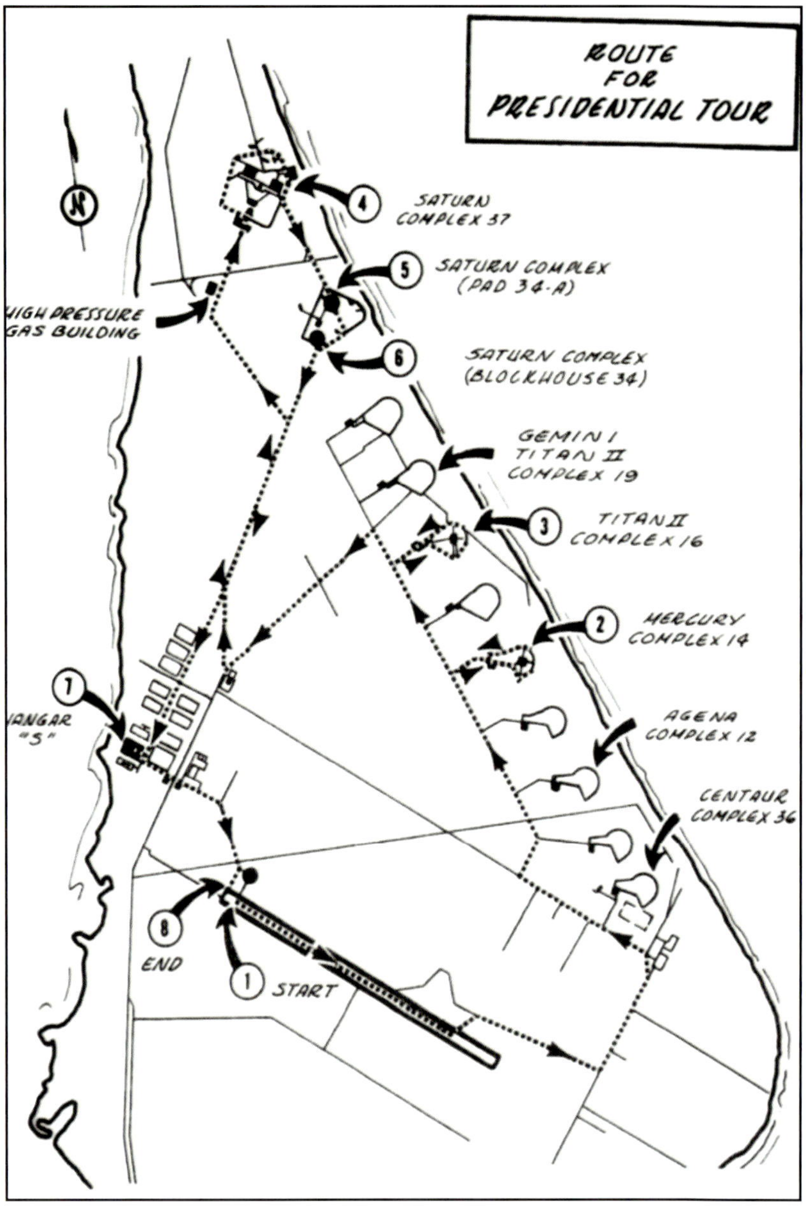

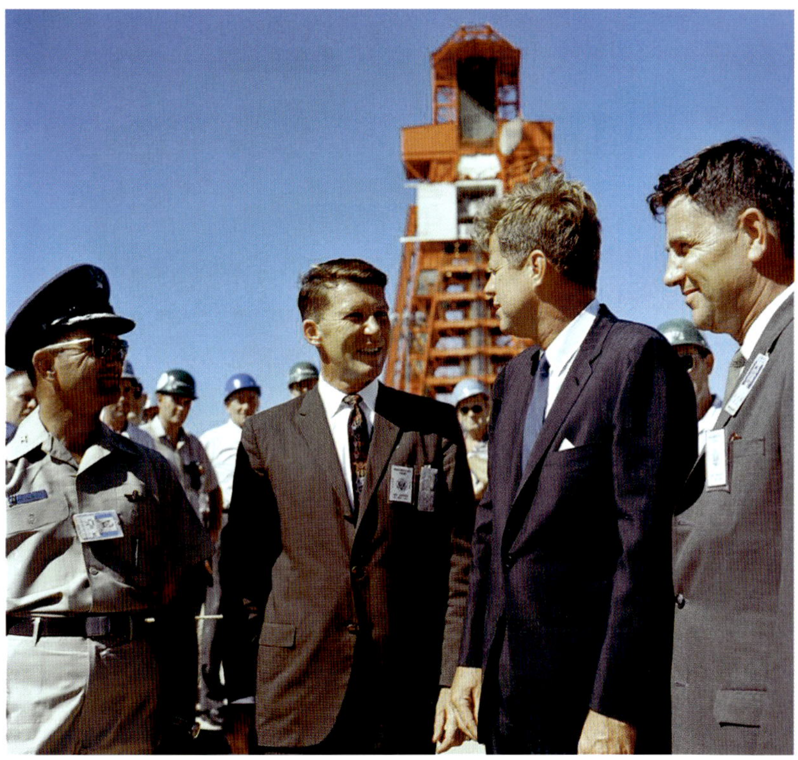

▶ First stop is LC-14, where astronaut Wally Schirra Jr. briefs the president on his upcoming mission, then expected within seventeen days. Kennedy is also briefed by USAF Maj. John Mullady, the Atlas project officer.

L–R: Commander of the 6555th Aerospace Test Wing at Patrick AFB Col. Paul Wignall; Schirra; Kennedy; and G. Merritt Preston, manager of MSC pre-flight operations at the Cape.

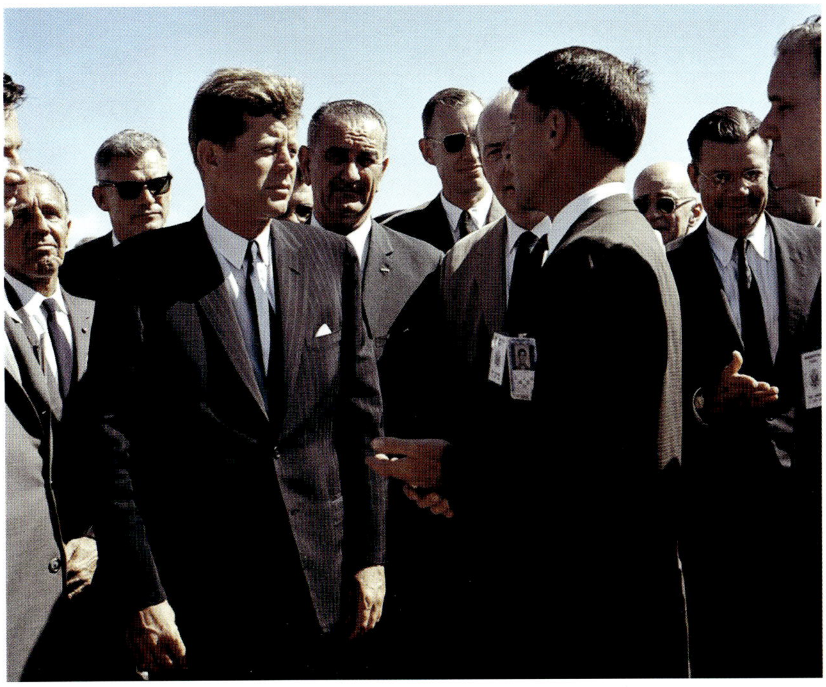

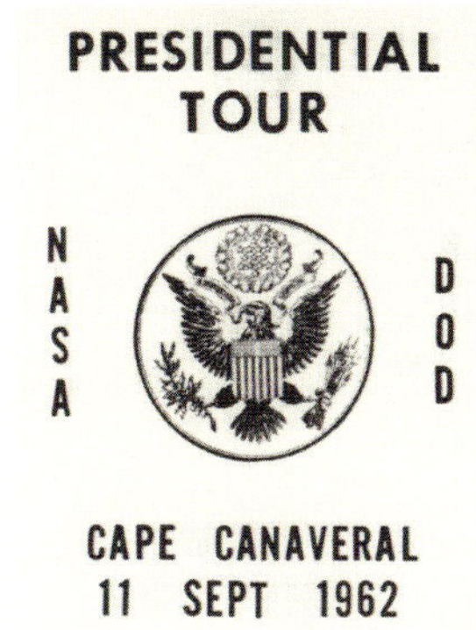

▲ L–R: Preston; Debus; Seamans; Kennedy; Johnson; Budget Director David Bell; British Defence Minister Peter Thorneycroft (partially hidden); Schirra; Welsh; McNamara; and Webb. McNamara has brought Thorneycroft along as part of his first visit to the United States.

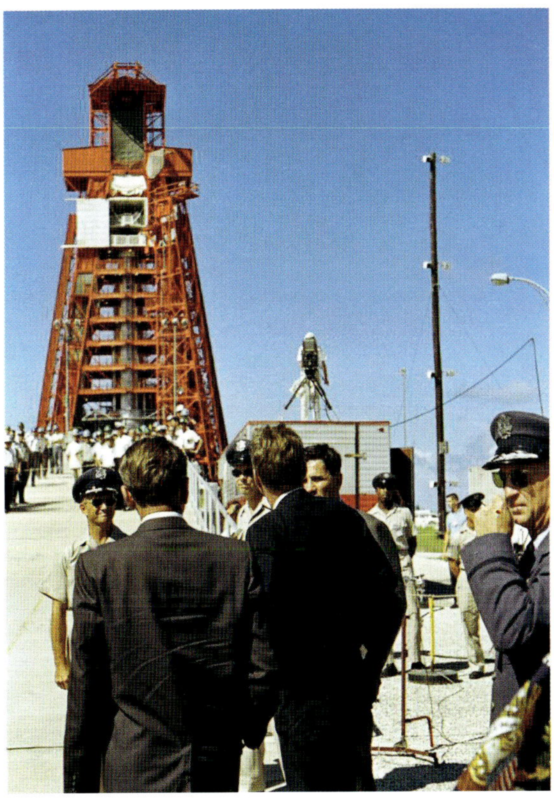

◀ Debus and Kennedy with Schirra's Mercury-Atlas 8 in the service structure at left. Pad crews had just mated his spacecraft to its booster the day before. G. Merritt Preston is to Kennedy's right; Maj. Gen. Davis is at far right.

▶ Photographers jockey as Kennedy and Schirra approach the pad. Complexes 12 and 13 are in the distance at upper left.

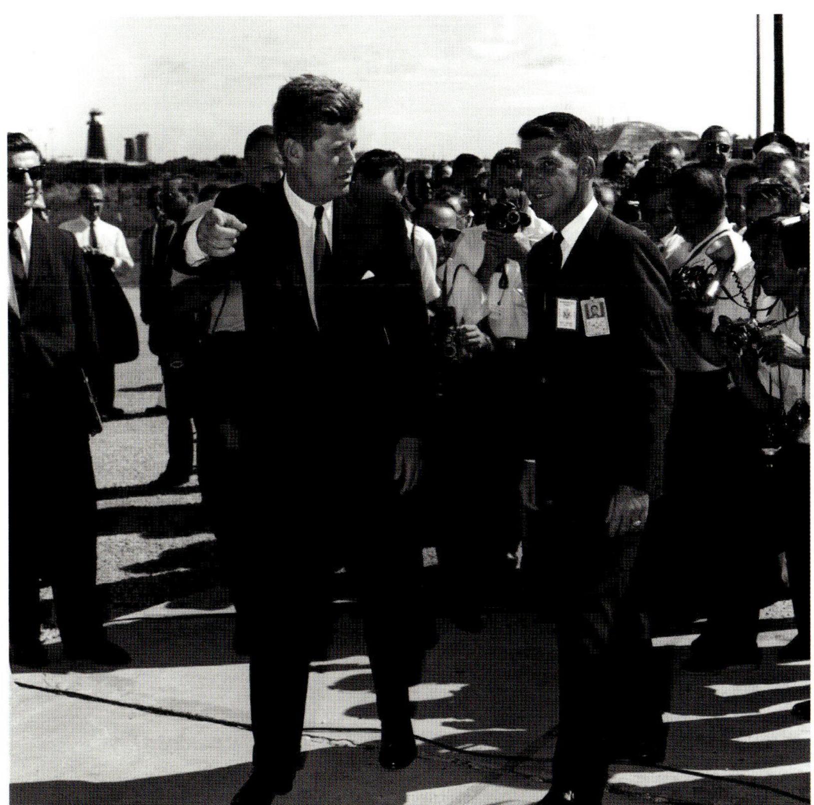

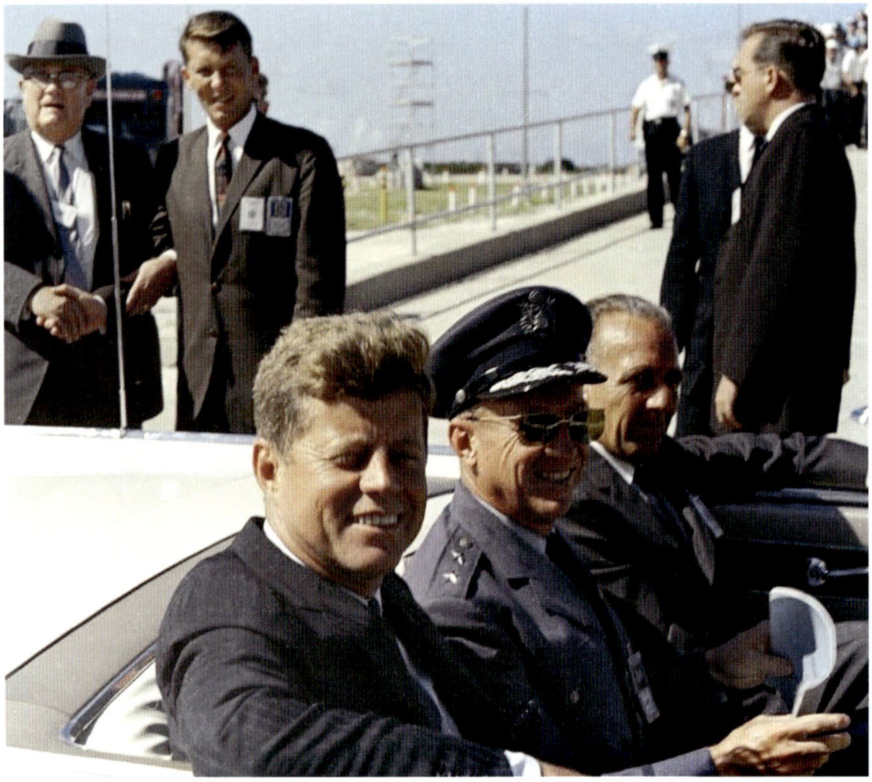

◀ Kennedy, Maj. Gen. Davis, and Debus depart LC-14. Sen. Alexander Wiley (R-Wisc.), the top Republican on the Aeronautical and Space Sciences Committee, and Schirra are at left; Secret Service Agent Dave Grant is at right.

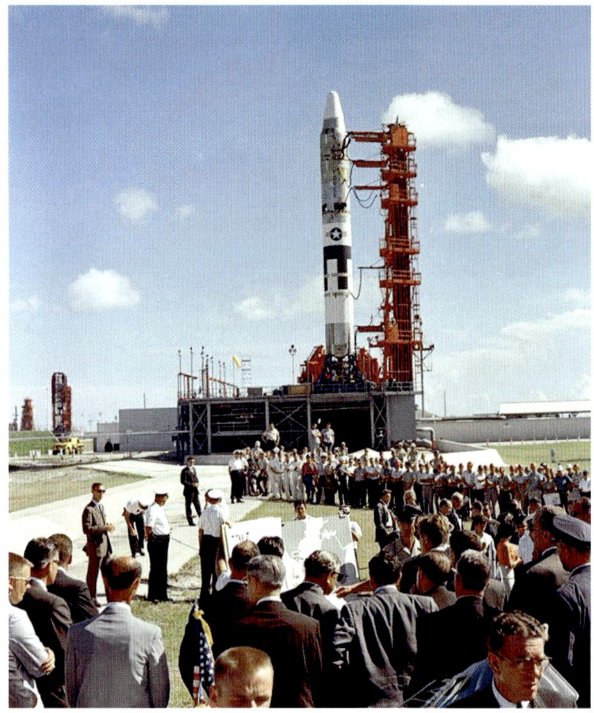

▲ At 3:00 p.m. at LC-16, the president receives a fifteen-minute briefing on the Titan II, the most powerful US missile, from USAF Col. Dan Thompson, deputy chief of staff for the Air Force Missile Test Center. The chart shows the Atlantic Missile Range, a chain of shore and sea-based tracking sites extending to the Indian Ocean. Another Titan II, in the service structure at LC-15 to the south at left, will be launched the next day; Titan launches have proven problematic enough that the USAF is reluctant to schedule one during the president's visit. This missile, N-9, is not fueled and will be successfully launched in October.

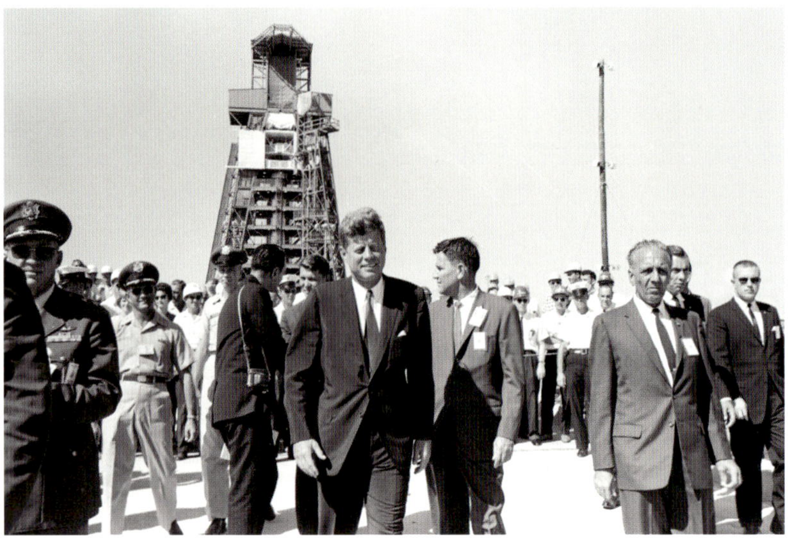

▲ Kennedy returns to his motorcade, with Schirra and Preston behind him; Debus is at right.

◢ Thompson goes over the Titan rocket family variants, including (L–R) HGM-25A Titan I and LGM-25C Titan II, the ballistic missile versions; Titan II GLV, the Gemini launch vehicle; and Titan IIIC, a USAF heavy-lift version with two solid-fuel boosters. It is the first time a Titan IIIC model is shown publicly.

The Titan II GLV would launch ten two-man Gemini flights from 1965 to 1966. Like the Atlas booster used for Mercury, Titan was first developed as an ICBM capable of carrying a nuclear warhead. Like California's Vandenberg AFB, the Cape is a test launch site. Fifty-six Titan II SAC missiles, however, would be operational by the end of 1963, based in California, Arkansas, Arizona, and Kansas.

The motorcade then drives past the entrance to LC-19, where all Gemini missions would be launched.

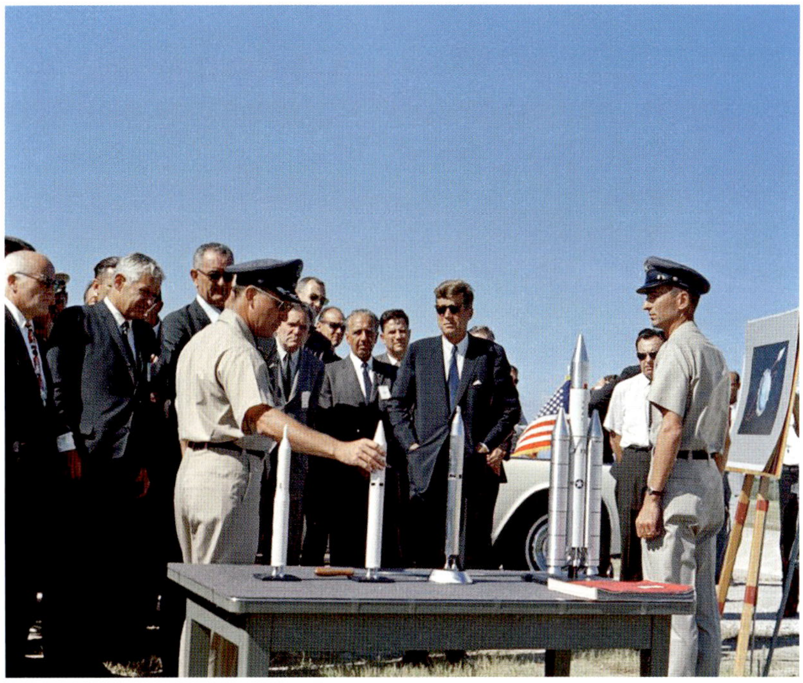

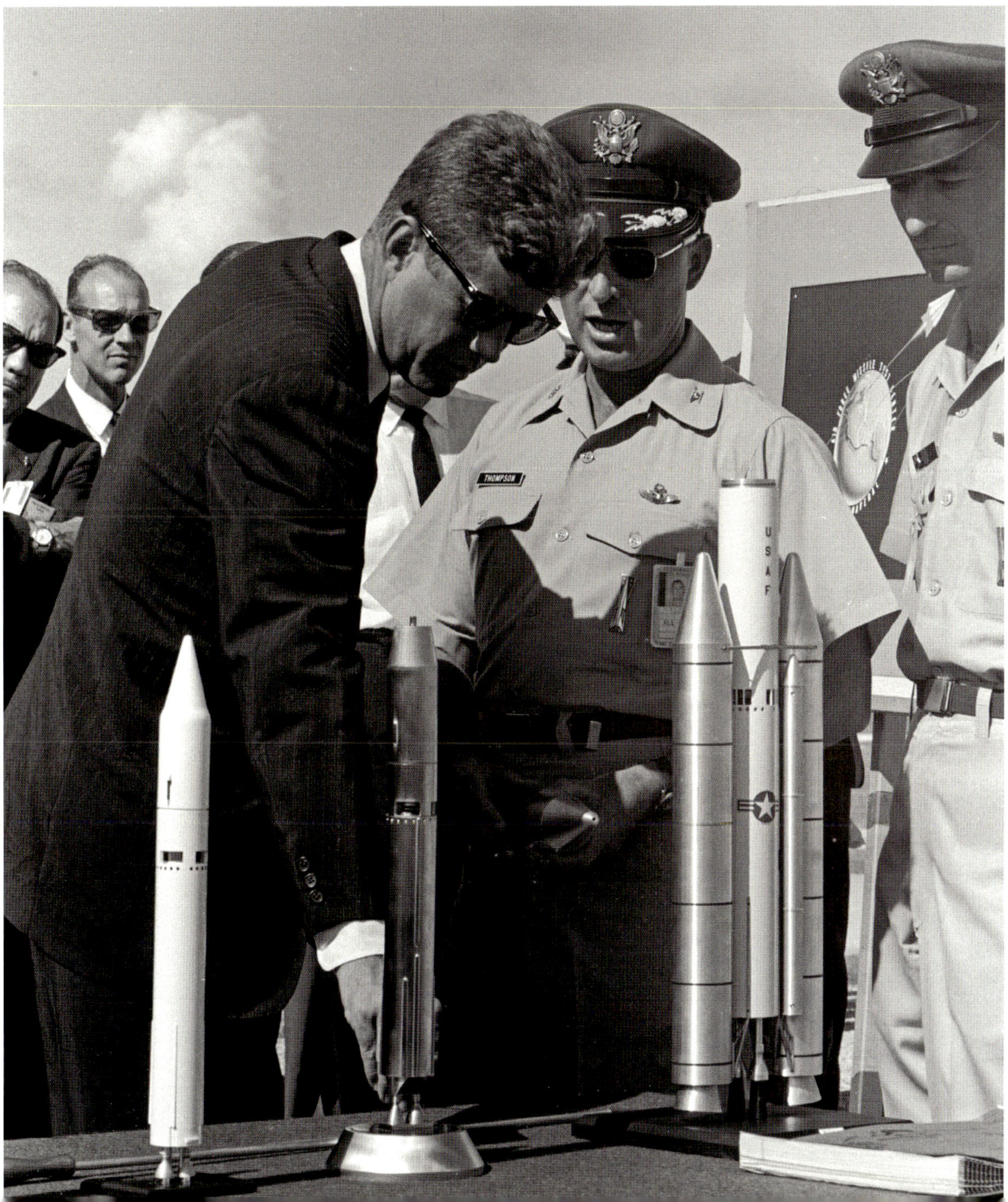

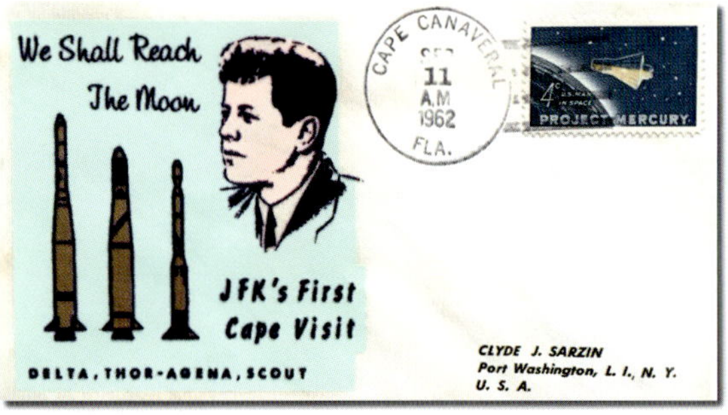

◀ Commemorative postal cover of Kennedy's first visit to Cape Canaveral.

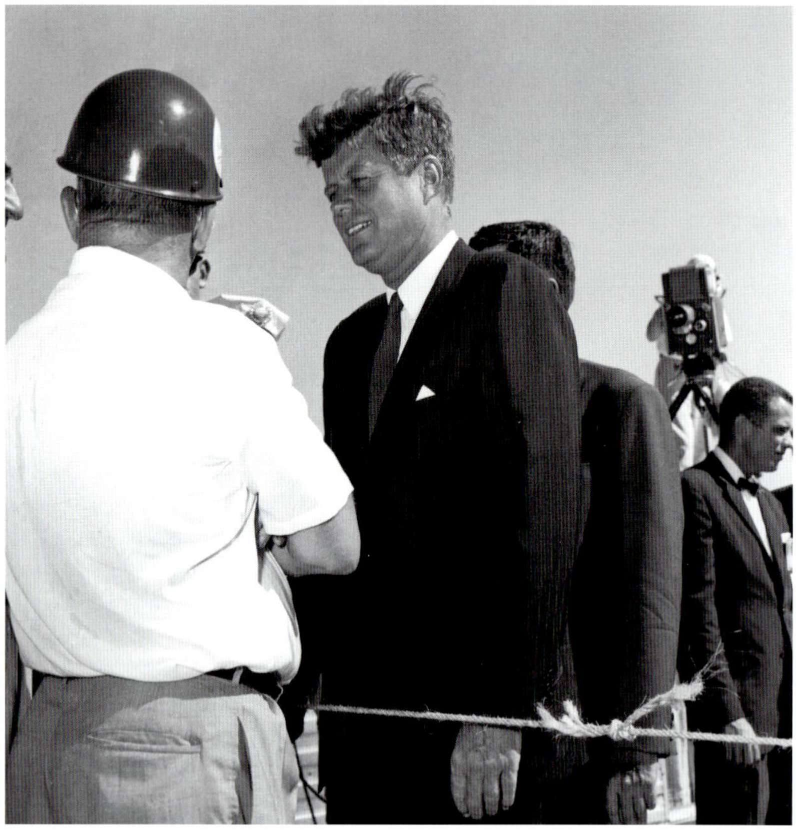

◢ During his tour, the president chats with managers (at LC-14, right) and a Martin Marietta worker (below), identified by his blue hard hat.

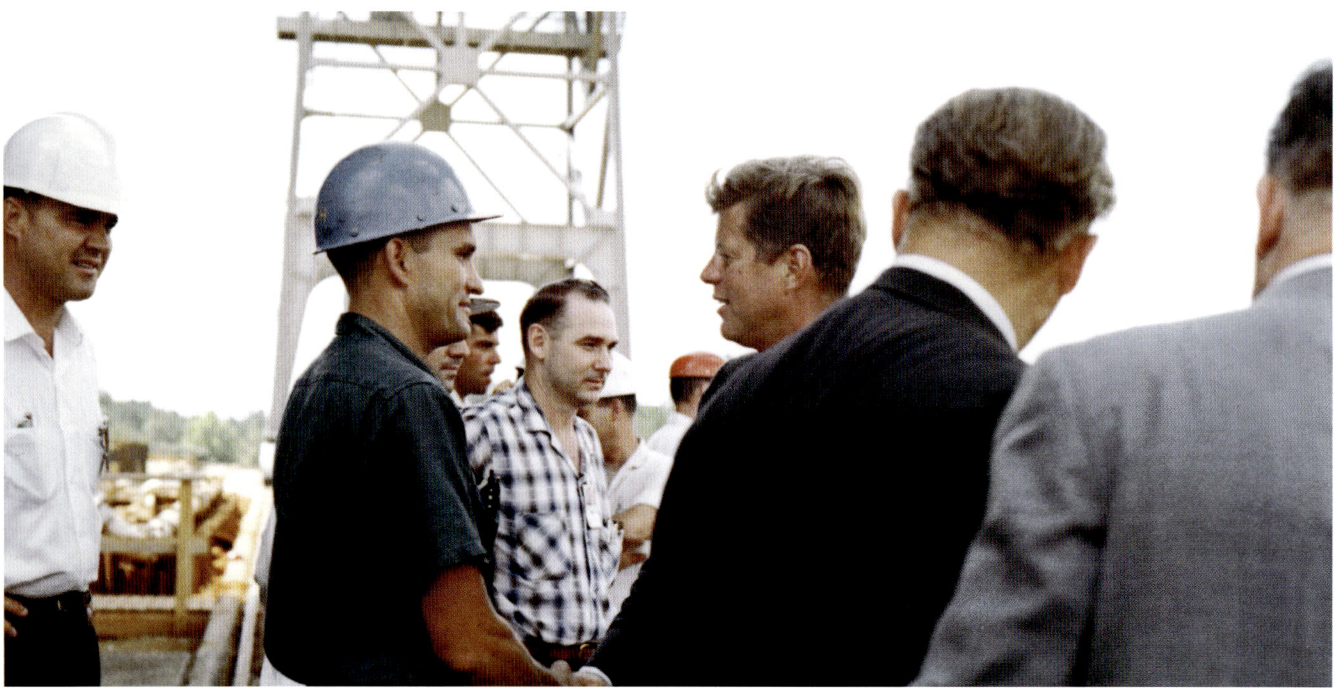

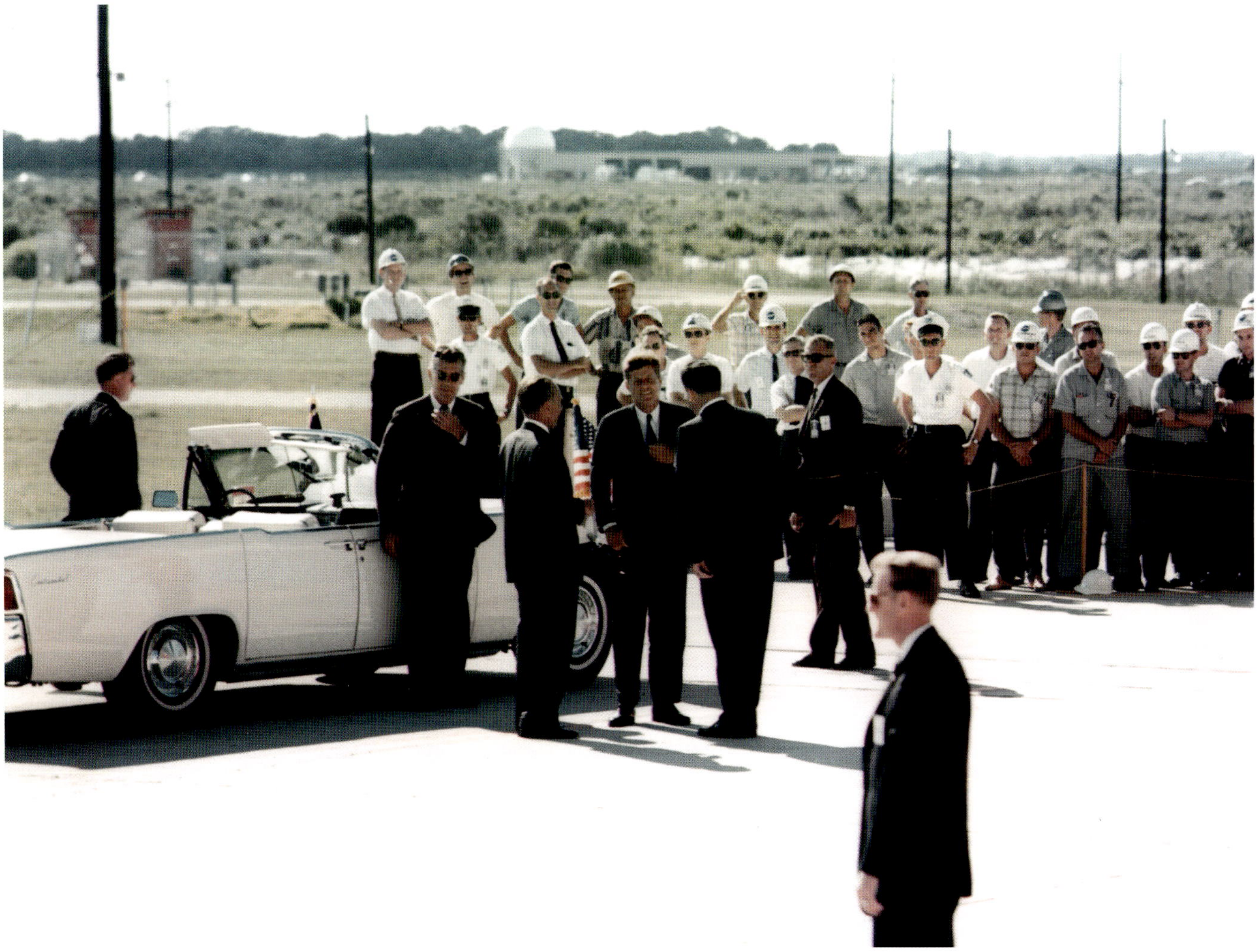

▲ After driving around the perimeter of LC-37, a Saturn complex under construction, the president next arrives at LC-34 at 3:30 p.m., where he and Debus are greeted by Army Lt. Col. Rocco Petrone, Saturn project officer.

▶ Johnson, Webb, Kennedy, Debus, and Assistant Defense Secretary Paul Nitze listen to Petrone's fifteen-minute briefing on launch operations with a Block II Saturn C-1 model and its umbilical tower on a display table.

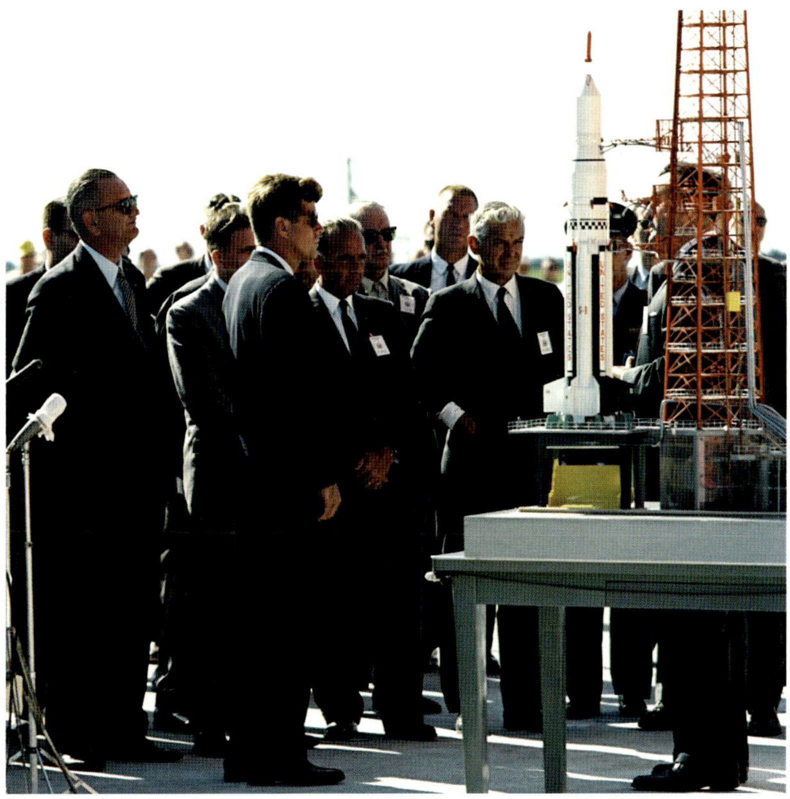

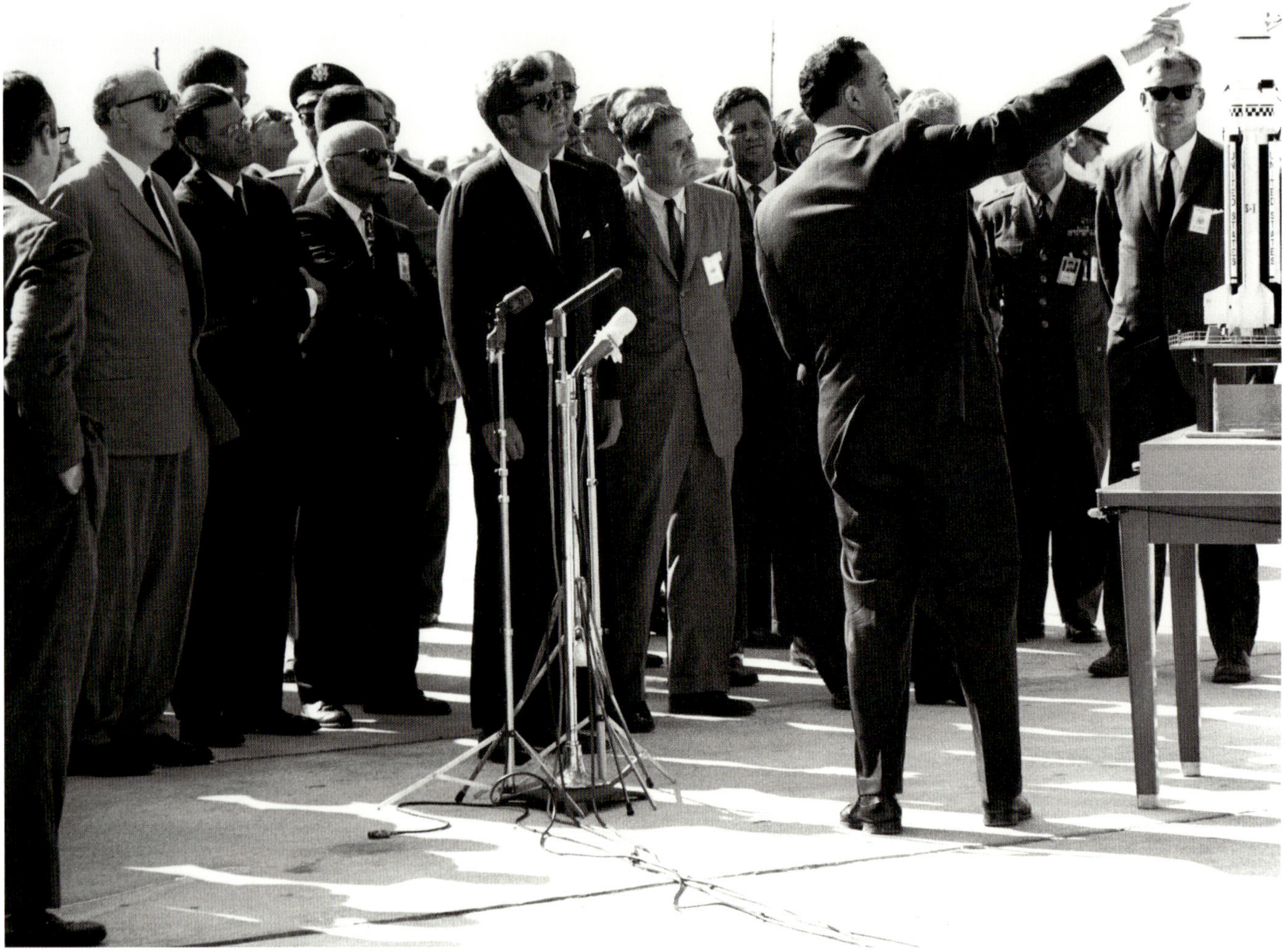

▲ Two Saturn C-1s have already been launched from the pad; a third would go less than a month later.

The complex is where Apollo 1 astronauts Gus Grissom, Ed White, and Roger Chaffee would lose their lives in a spacecraft fire in 1967 but also where the first manned Apollo mission, Apollo 7, would put the program back on track in 1968.

▶ This view from behind the briefing shows the complex's mobile service structure (MSS) on either side of the launch stand, with the pad's umbilical tower at center. Yellow hold-down arms are on the launch stand, with a yellow flame deflector in place below.

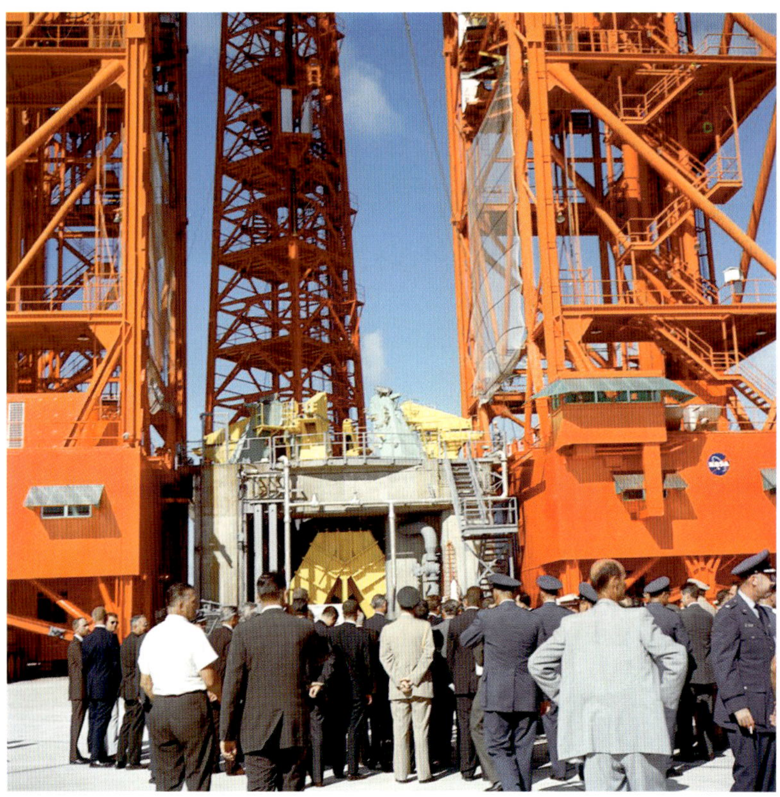

▶ Agent Jerry Behn climbs into the front seat as Kennedy, Debus, and Maj. Gen. Davis prepare for a very short drive to the LC-34 blockhouse, about seven hundred feet away from the pad.

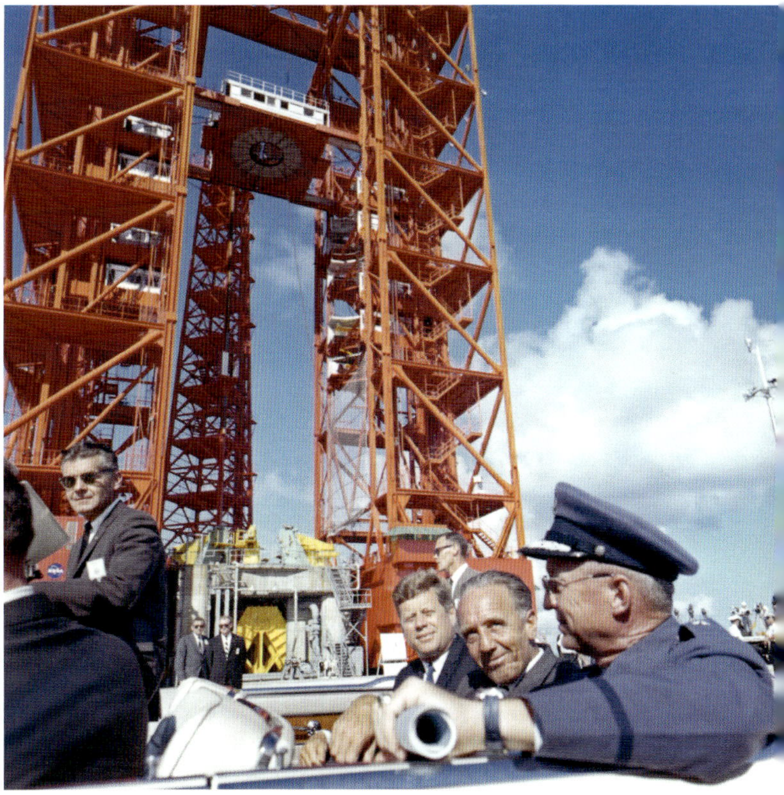

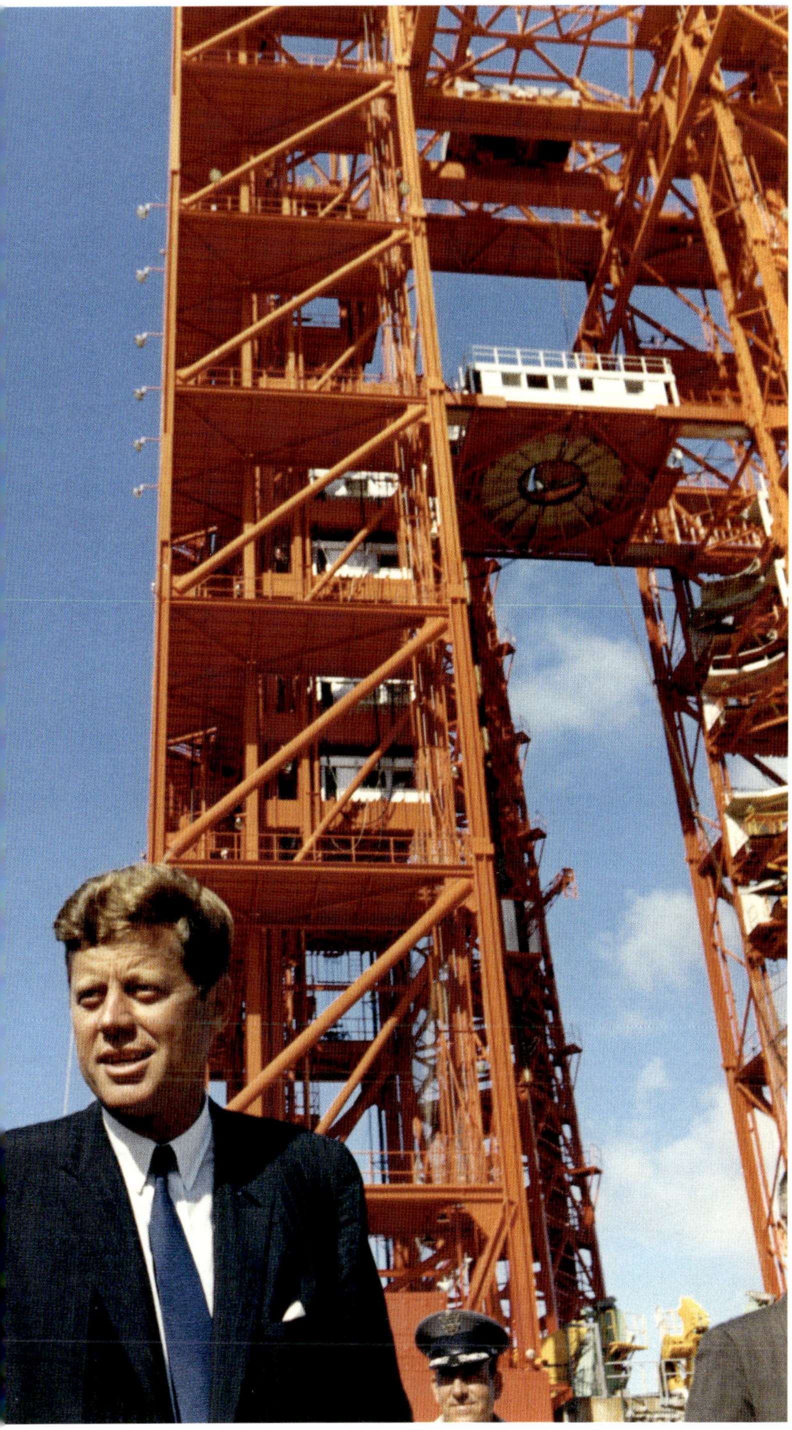

▲ The red MSS looms behind the president. The self-propelled structure, 310 feet high, is mounted on rails and is moved 600 feet west of the pad before a launch.

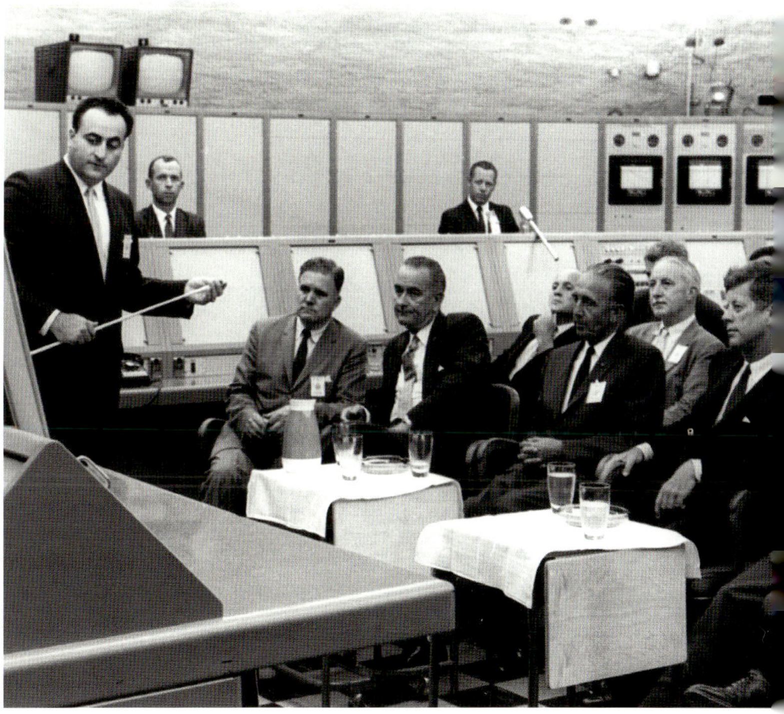

▲ Inside the LC-34 blockhouse, the guests receive a thirty-minute classified briefing on the manned lunar landing program from Petrone.

Behind the consoles at center is NASA Public Affairs Officer Jack King, who would become the "voice of Apollo launch control."

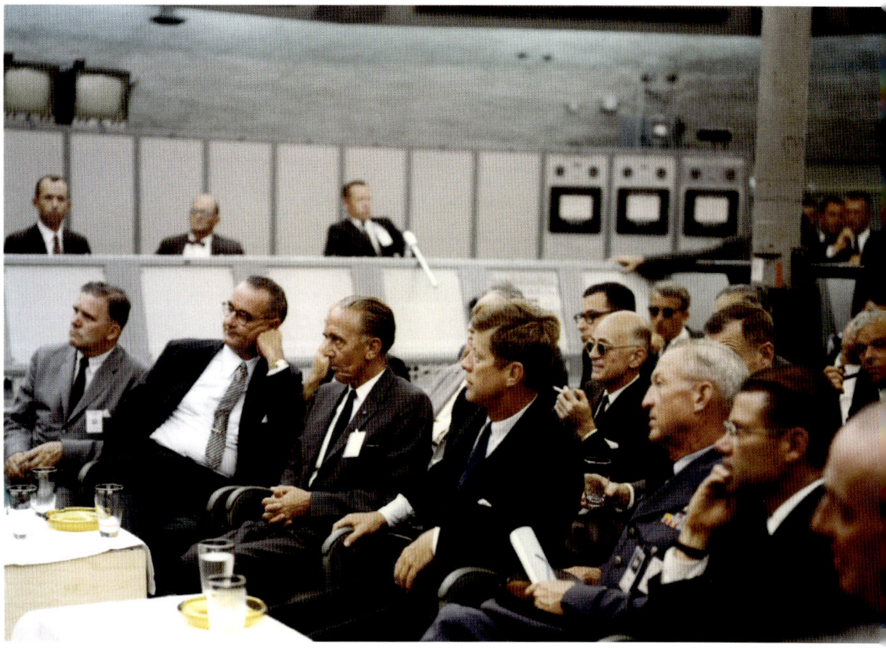

▶ Front row, L–R: Webb; Johnson; Debus; Kennedy; Maj. Gen. Davis; McNamara; and Thorneycroft. Ed Welsh (smoking); von Braun and Nitze (pipe) are also visible. A periscope extends down from the roof at right.

▼ In his conversations with the president during the visit, Debus stresses that launch flexibility for the nation is a goal at the center, not just the moon landing.

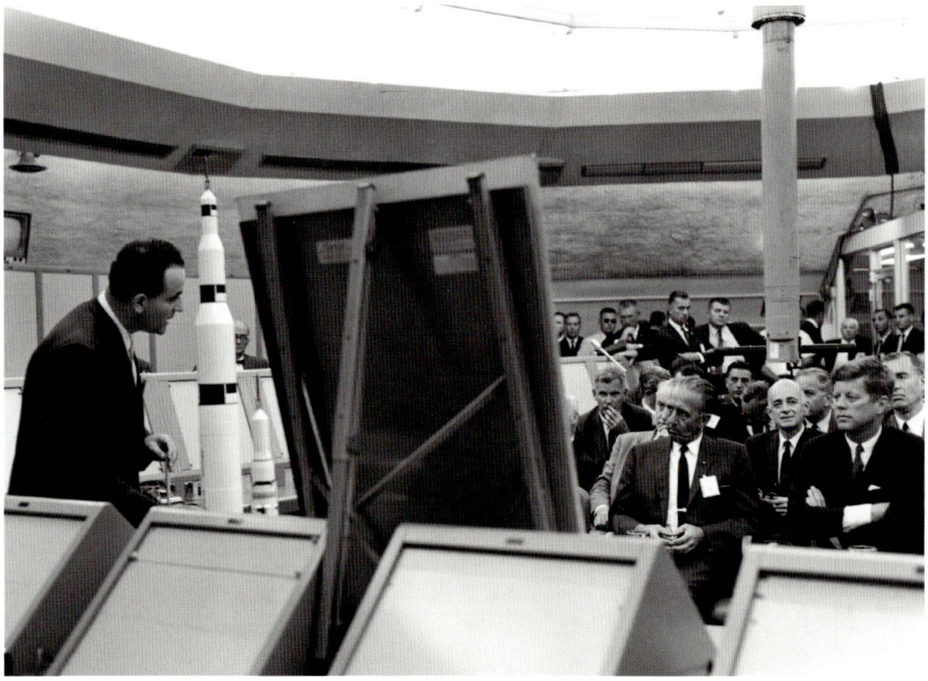

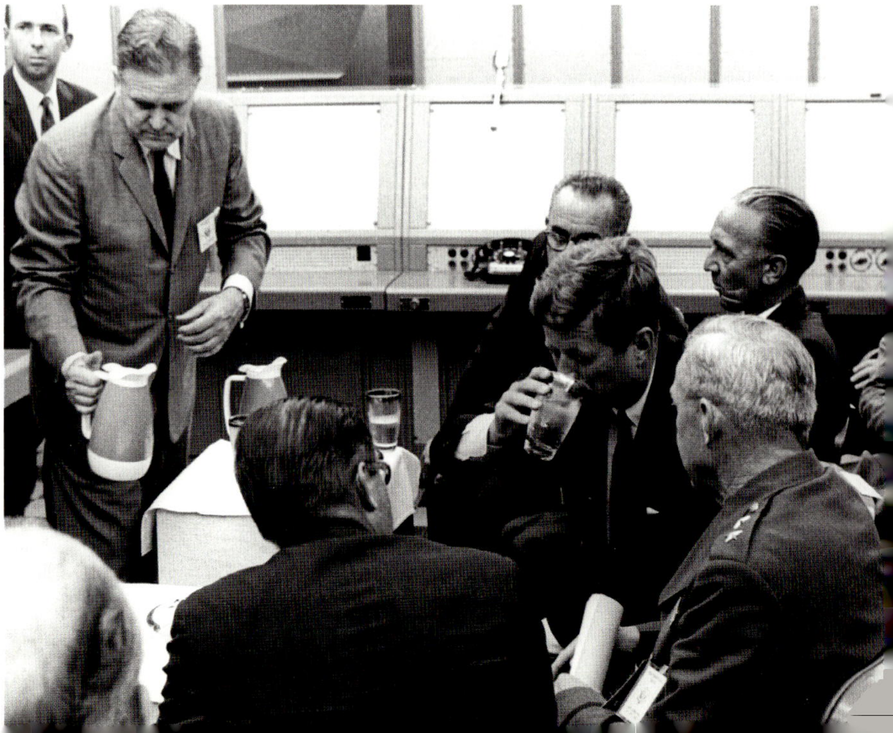

▶ Webb handles the water as the president takes a break.

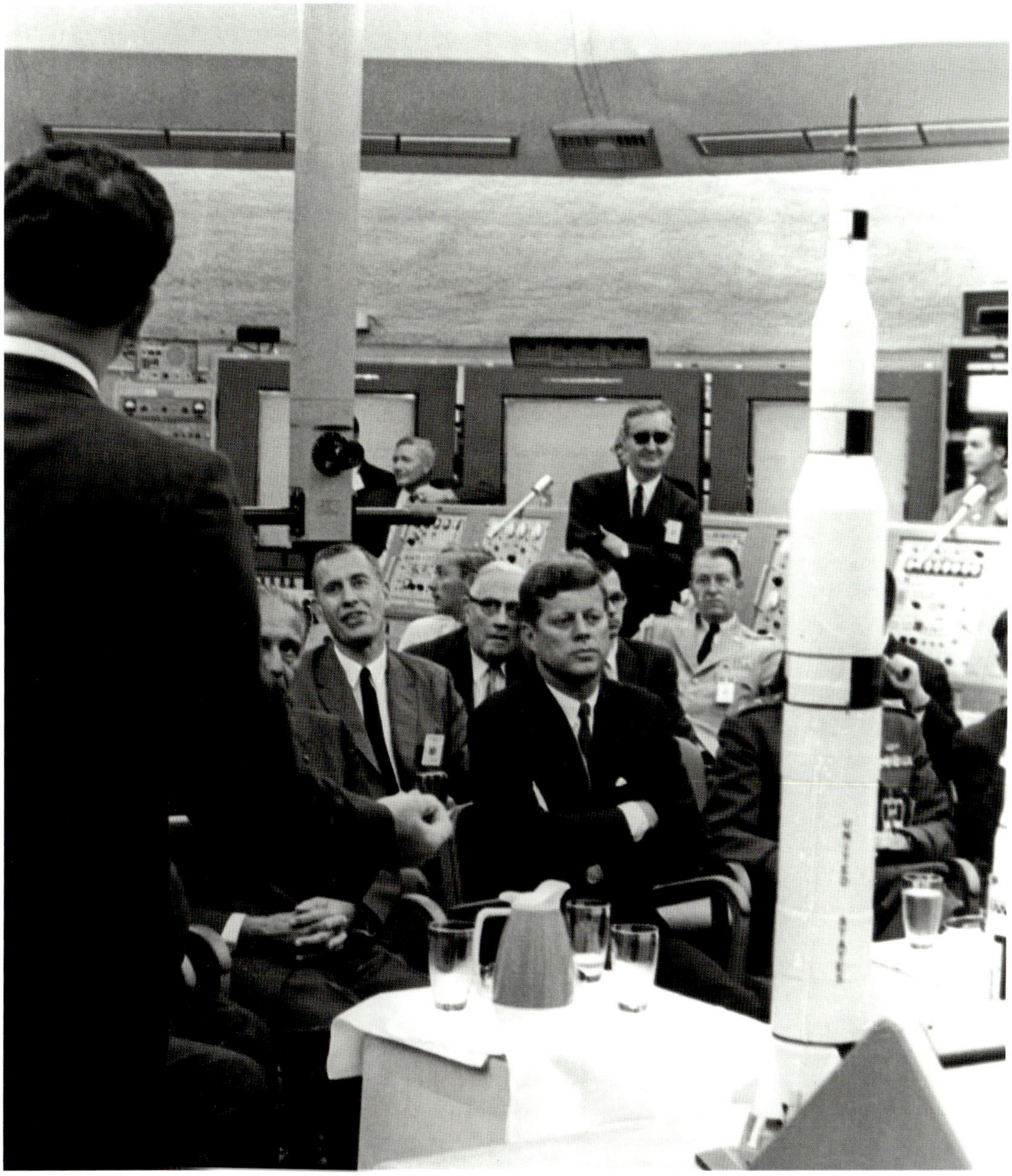

▲ Petrone's briefing includes the Saturn C-5 model at right (renamed Saturn V in 1963). The Army's heavy space vehicle officer at the time, he would become director of launch operations at KSC in 1966, Apollo program director in 1969, and director of MSFC in 1973. Budget Director David Bell, leaning back, is behind the president.

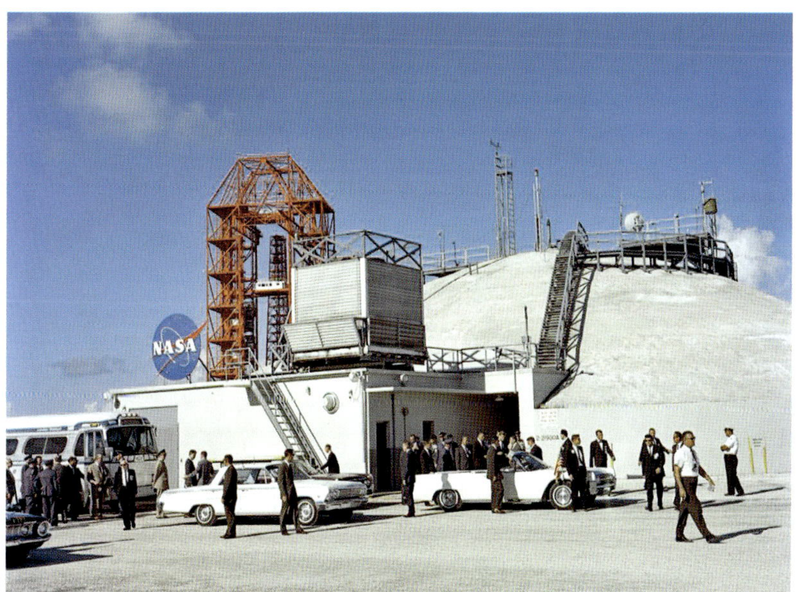

▶ The presidential party departs the LC-34 blockhouse at 4:17 p.m.

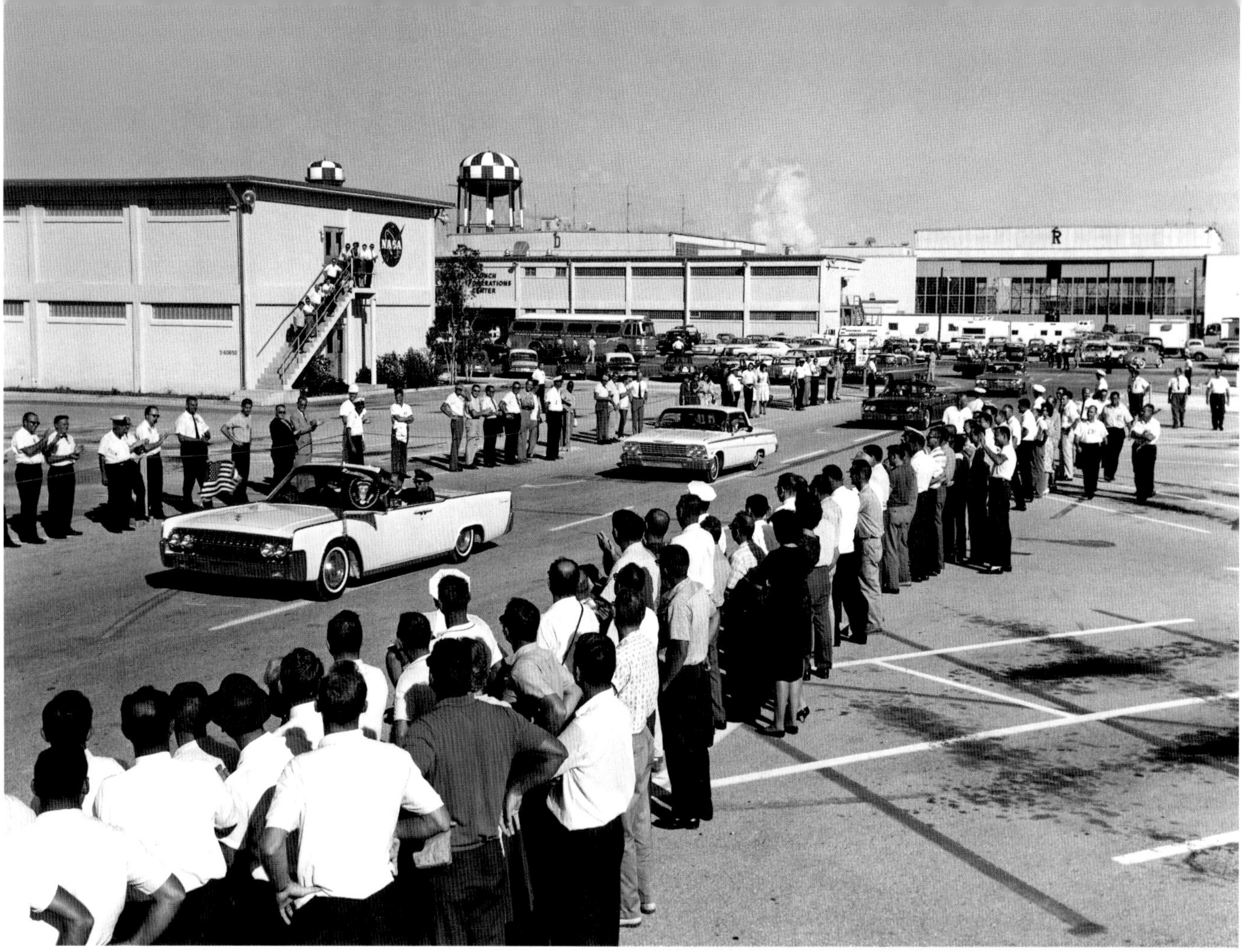

▲ The president's motorcade heads toward Hangar S on Skid Strip Road in the Industrial Area, arriving at 4:20 p.m.

▶ Astronaut Gordon Cooper briefs the president on Mercury spacecraft components in Hangar S as USAF Secretary Zuckert looks on at right. Cooper would make the final flight of Project Mercury in 1963.

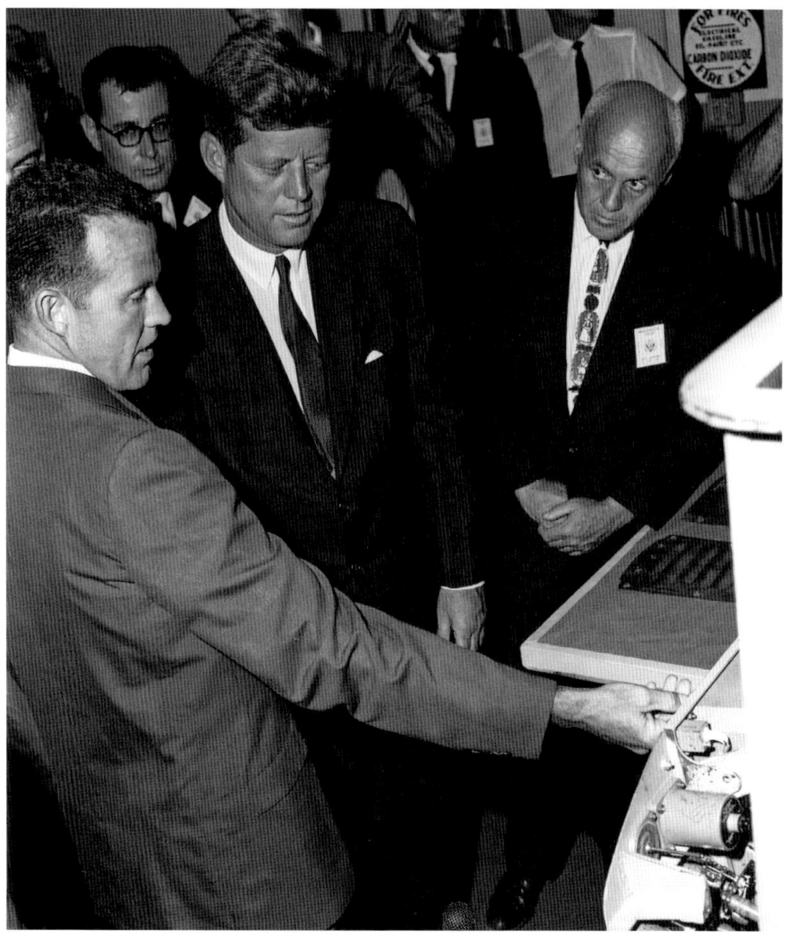

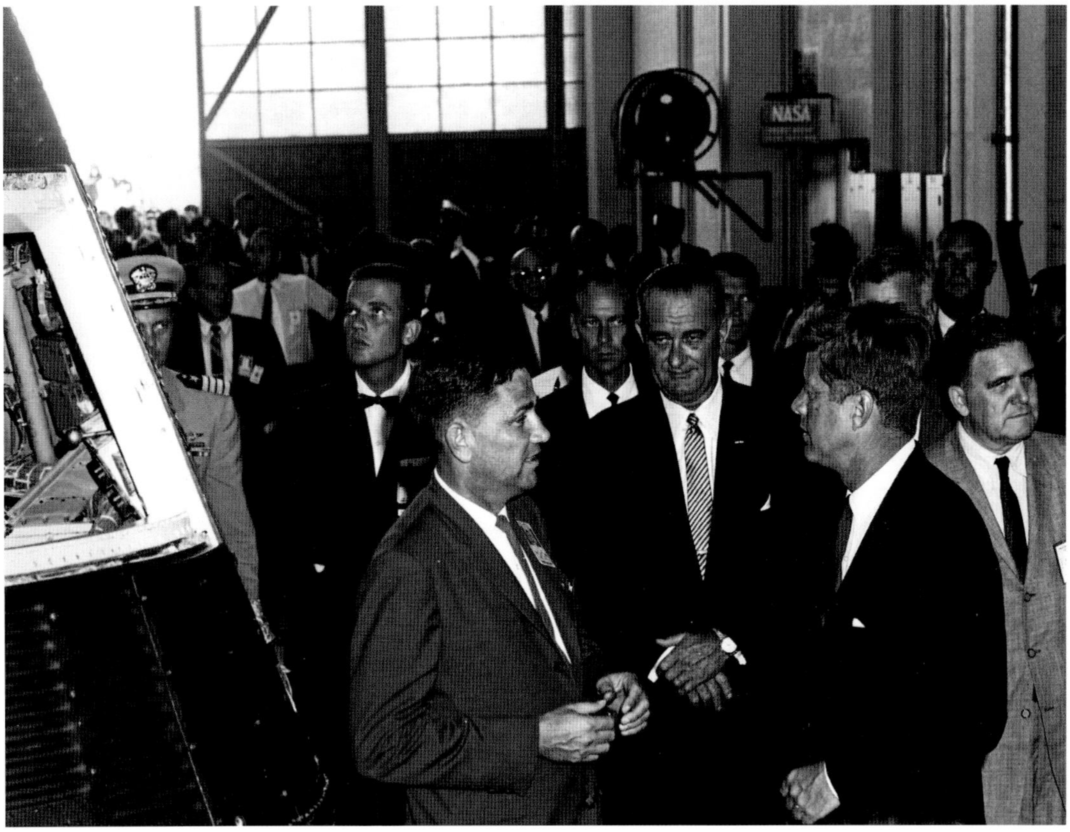

▲ G. Merritt Preston chats with Johnson and Kennedy, with Mercury spacecraft No. 19 at left. Webb is at right. The backup for Schirra's flight, the spacecraft is now on display at the St. Louis Science Center.

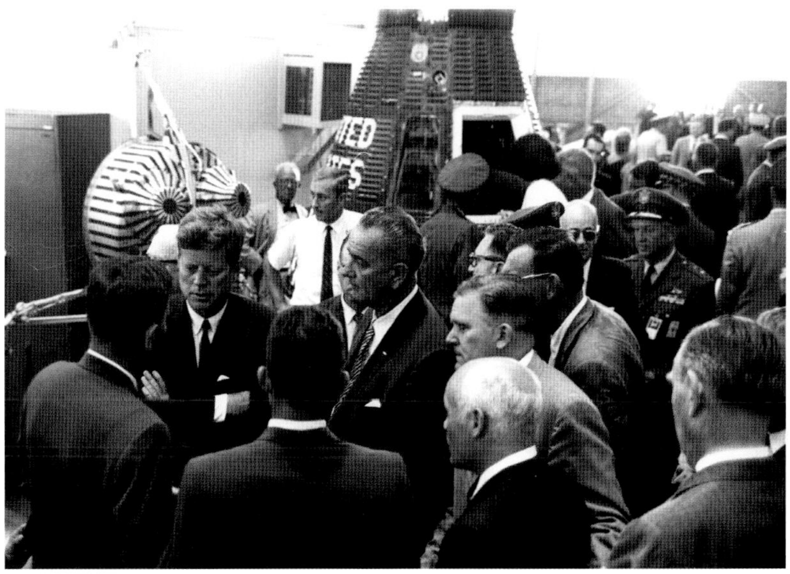

◢ Kennedy listens to Schirra, Preston, and Cooper, with a Mercury spacecraft retro-rocket pack on display at left. Johnson, Webb, and Zuckert listen in.

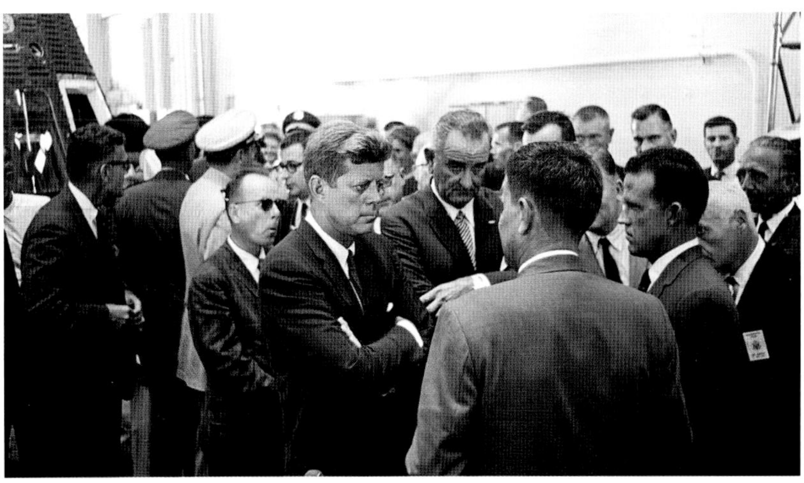

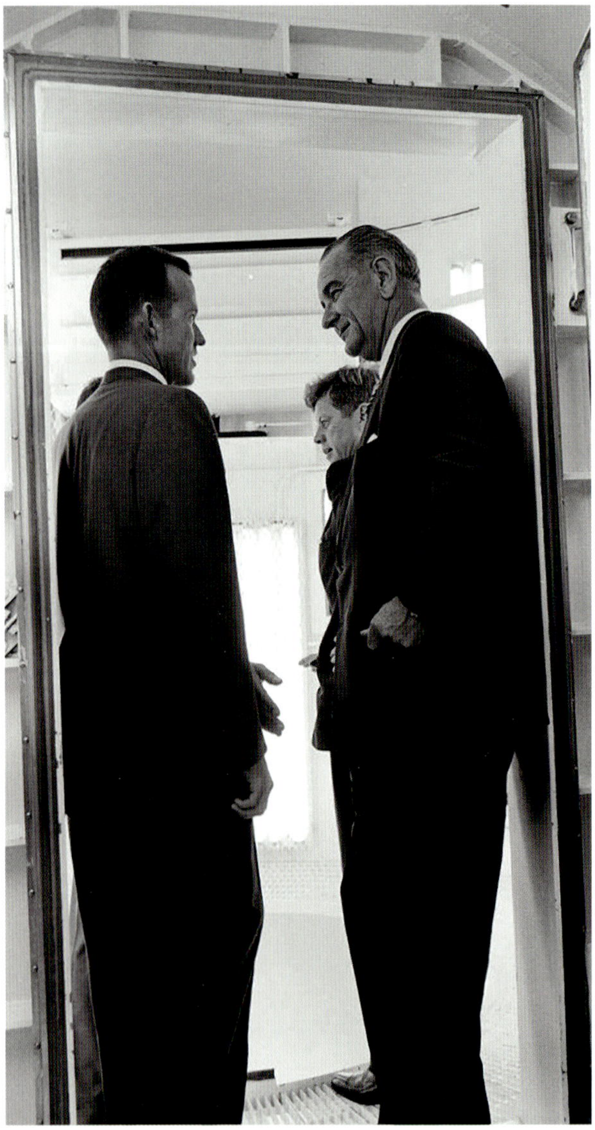

▲ Cooper, Kennedy, and Johnson in the door to the altitude chamber in Hangar S. The chamber is used to test spacecraft and pressure suits for leaks and other operational capability in a near-space atmosphere.

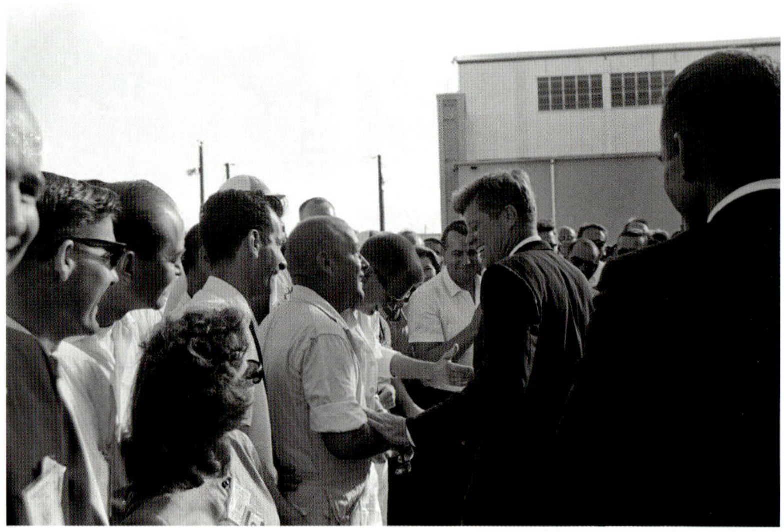

▲ The president greets workers outside Hangar S. About 4:40 p.m. he delivers remarks to some fifteen hundred workers gathered there. Russia's head start, he says, gave "prestige to their system . . . force to their argument that they were an advancing society and that we were on the decline."

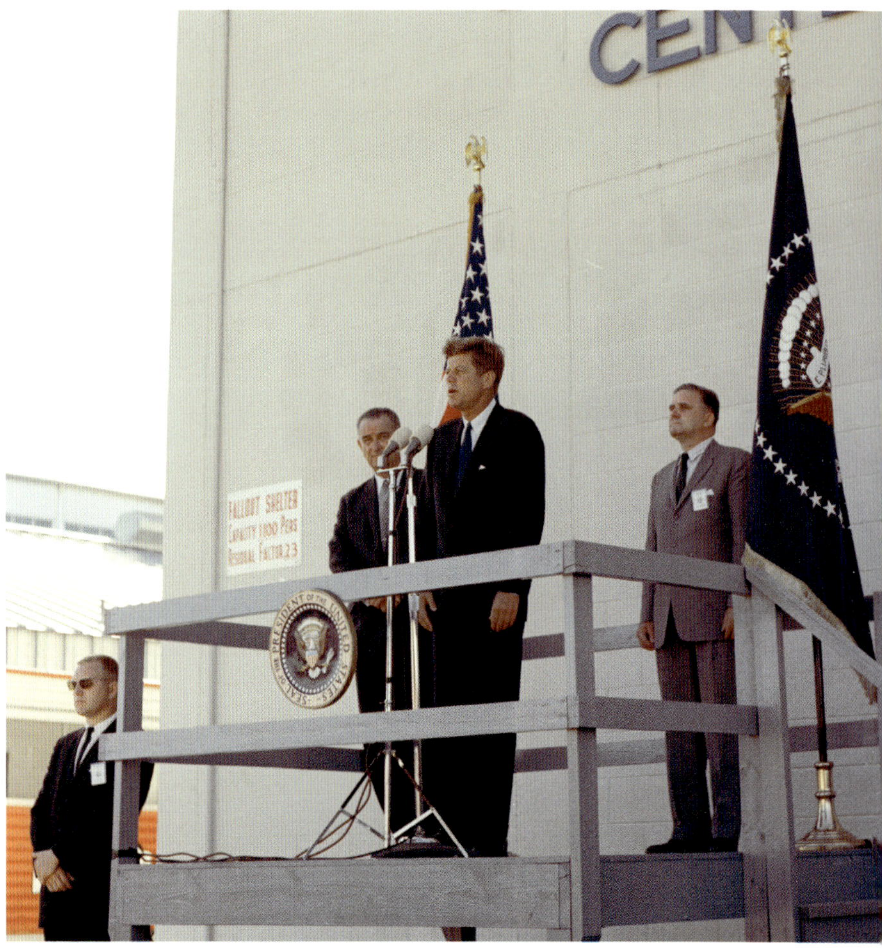

▶ Kennedy adds that the Russians had gained an advantage in space in the 1950s. "But," he assures attendees, "I believe that we're on the rise. With your efforts and with the effort of all others involved in the space program, we shall not be behind." His party leaves for the Skid Strip at 4:50 p.m. for the flight to Houston at 5:00 p.m.

:05

SEPTEMBER 12, 1962

"But why, some say, the moon?"

▼ **CONTINUING HIS** two-day tour, President Kennedy arrives at Houston International Airport (renamed William P. Hobby Airport in 1967) at 5:15 p.m. CDT on September 11. He is followed from Air Force One by Rep. Thomas, Brig. Gen. Godfrey McHugh, and Secret Service Agent Jerry Behn.

"I don't know whether the people of the Southwest realize what a profound effect this whole space program is going to have on this most progressive city and state," Kennedy tells the crowd. "The scientists and engineers and technicians who are going to be attracted to this great space center can really remake the industrial life of the Southwest United States as we reach towards the moon. I think it is most appropriate that this space center should be located here in Houston, here at Rice University—a city which has been identified with progress in this state and country."

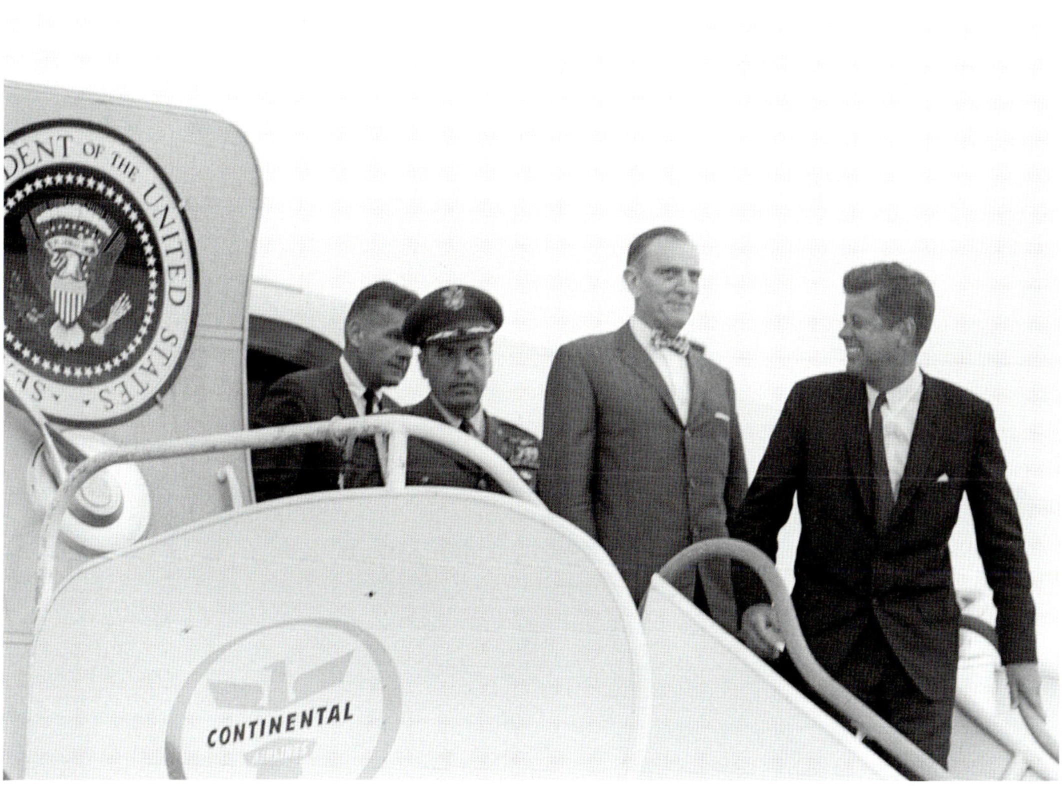

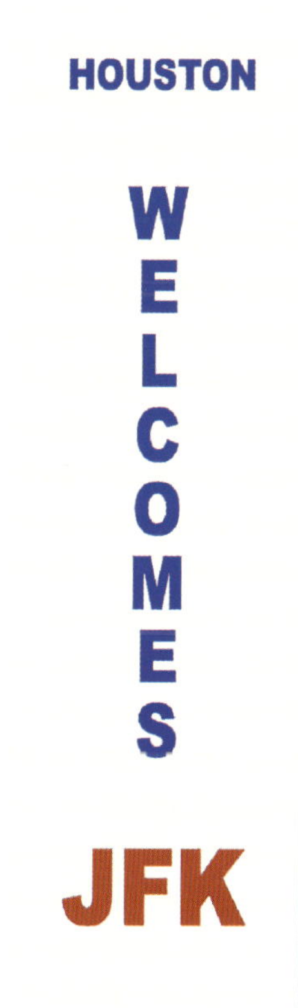

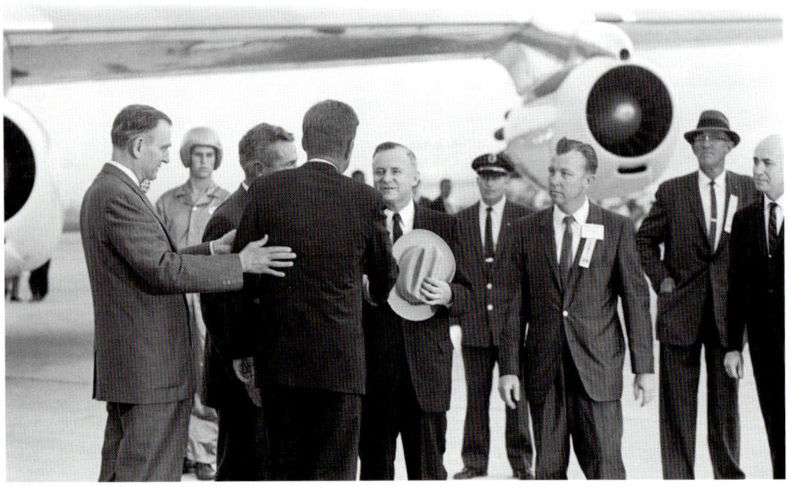

◀ Kennedy is greeted by Texas Gov. Price Daniel.

L–R: Rep. Thomas; Houston Mayor Lewis Cutrer; Kennedy; Daniel; Harris County Judge Bill Elliott; unidentified; and Gilruth.

▶ Mayor Cutrer (left) welcomes the president and his party. To Kennedy's left are Rep. Thomas, Director of NASA's Office of Manned Space Flight D. Brainerd Holmes, and Seamans. Holmes joined NASA in 1961 from RCA, where he had helped oversee development of the Ballistic Missile Early Warning System for the USAF.

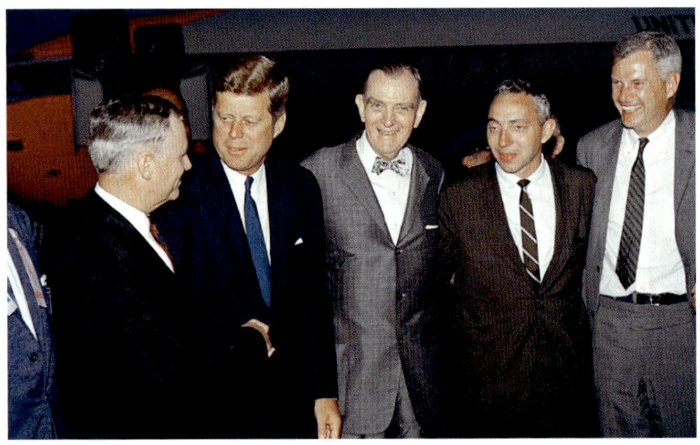

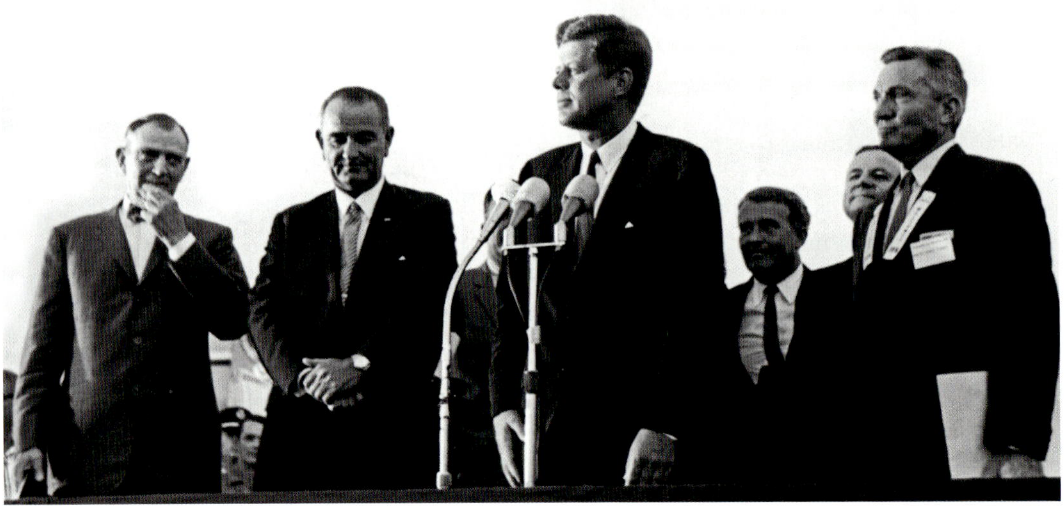

▲ The president speaks to a crowd estimated at more than ten thousand. "So we come here today," he concludes, "to see what is being planned for the future, because from this place in America are going to be laid the plans and designs which will reach out in this decade and put Americans on the moon and bring them back again."

L–R: Rep. Thomas; Johnson; Webb (hidden); Kennedy; von Braun; Gov. Daniel; and Mayor Cutrer, who presents keys to the city to Kennedy and Johnson. An estimated 175,000 spectators line the motorcade route to the downtown Rice Hotel, where Kennedy spends the night.

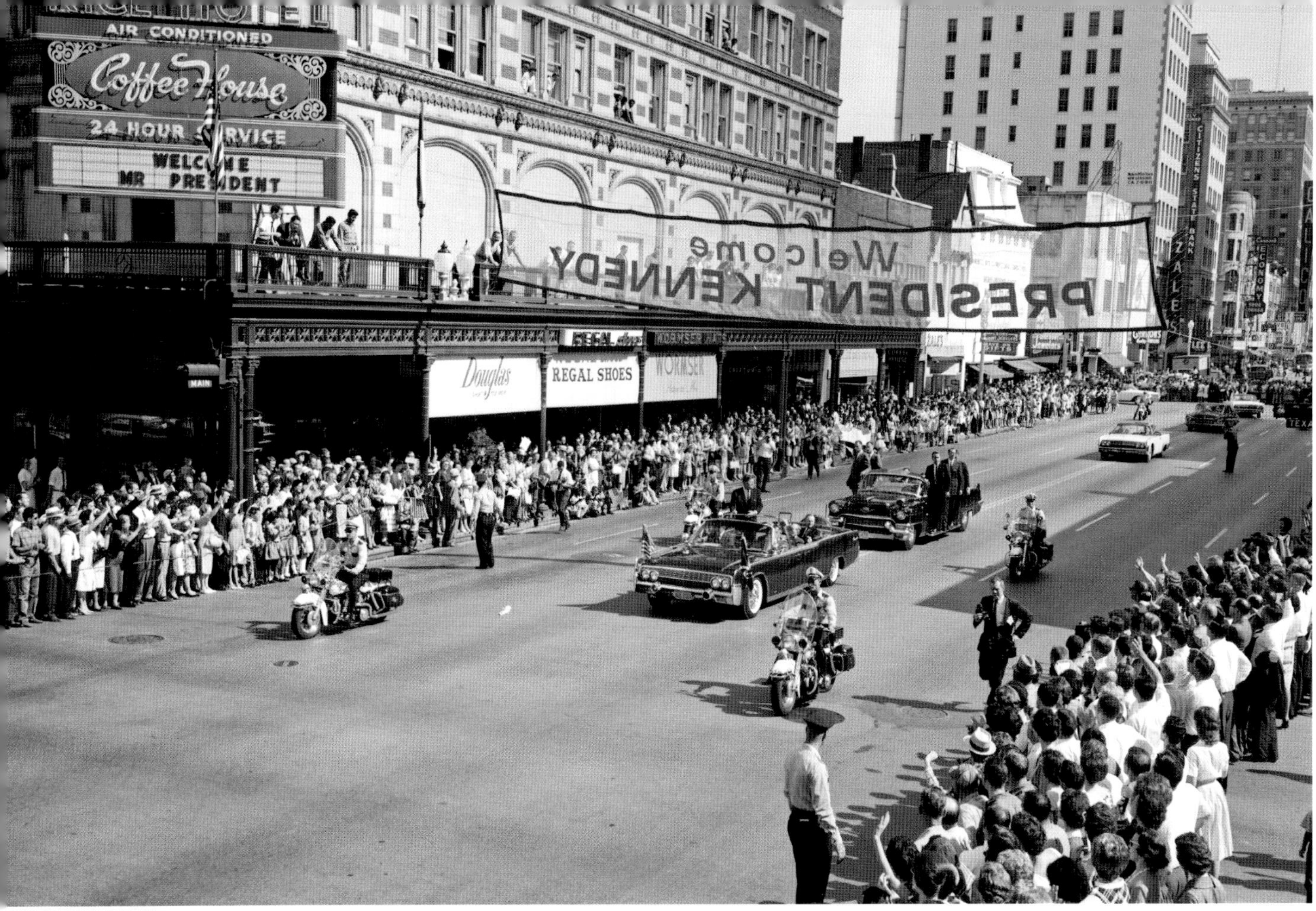

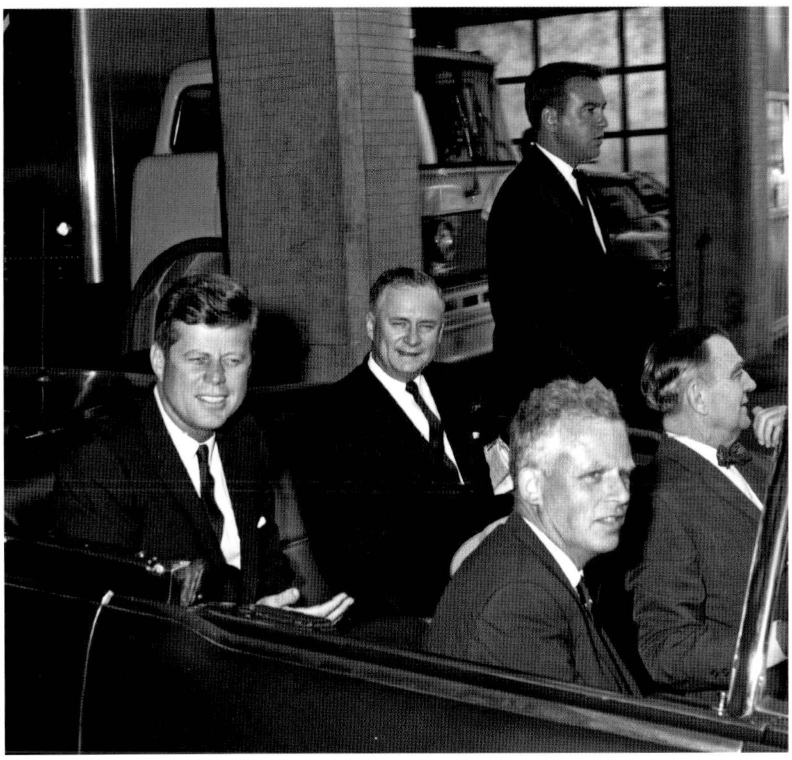

▲ At about 8:40 the next morning, Kennedy's motorcade travels southwest down Main Street from the Rice Hotel to Rice University. The president rides in SS-100-X, which arrives by cargo plane, as does SS-4B behind it. Kennedy's limousine is owned by the Ford Motor Co. and leased to the Secret Service; other Lincolns in the motorcade are from a local dealer.

▲ The president arrives at Rice University Stadium at 9:00 a.m. The university's president, Ken Pitzer, is third from left, next to Rep. Thomas, who is an alumnus of Rice University, at right. Gov. Daniel sits next to Kennedy.

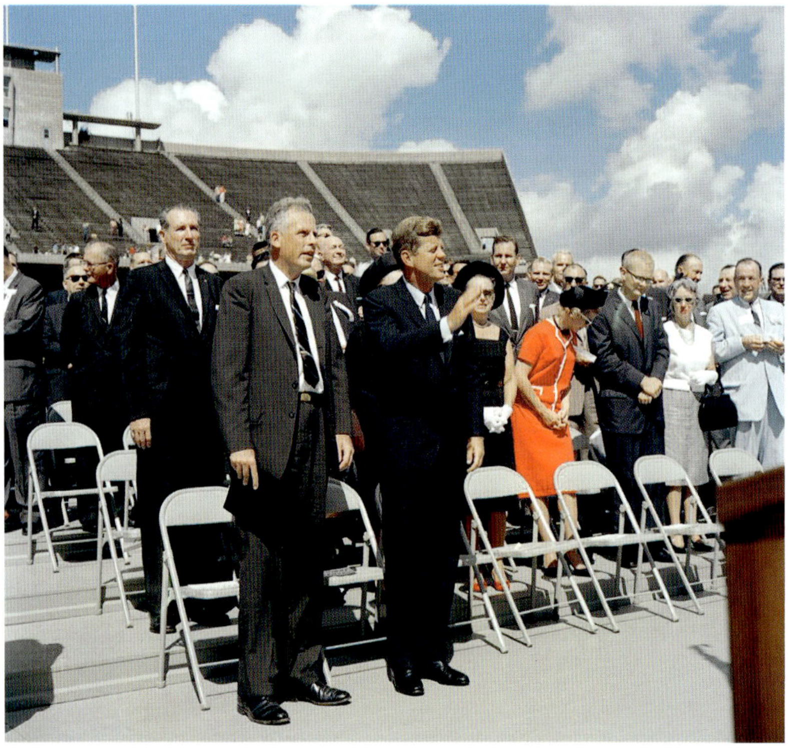

◀ The president acknowledges the crowd as he and Pitzer arrive on stage. Only a portion of the upper deck of the seventy-three-thousand-seat stadium is open, with about half of the estimated crowd of fifty thousand made up of local high school students. It's also freshman orientation week at Rice.

In 1961 the university had "sold" the land where the new space center is under construction to the federal government for $20 after the university received the property as a donation from the Humble Oil Co. on the condition it be offered to the government to lure NASA to the area.

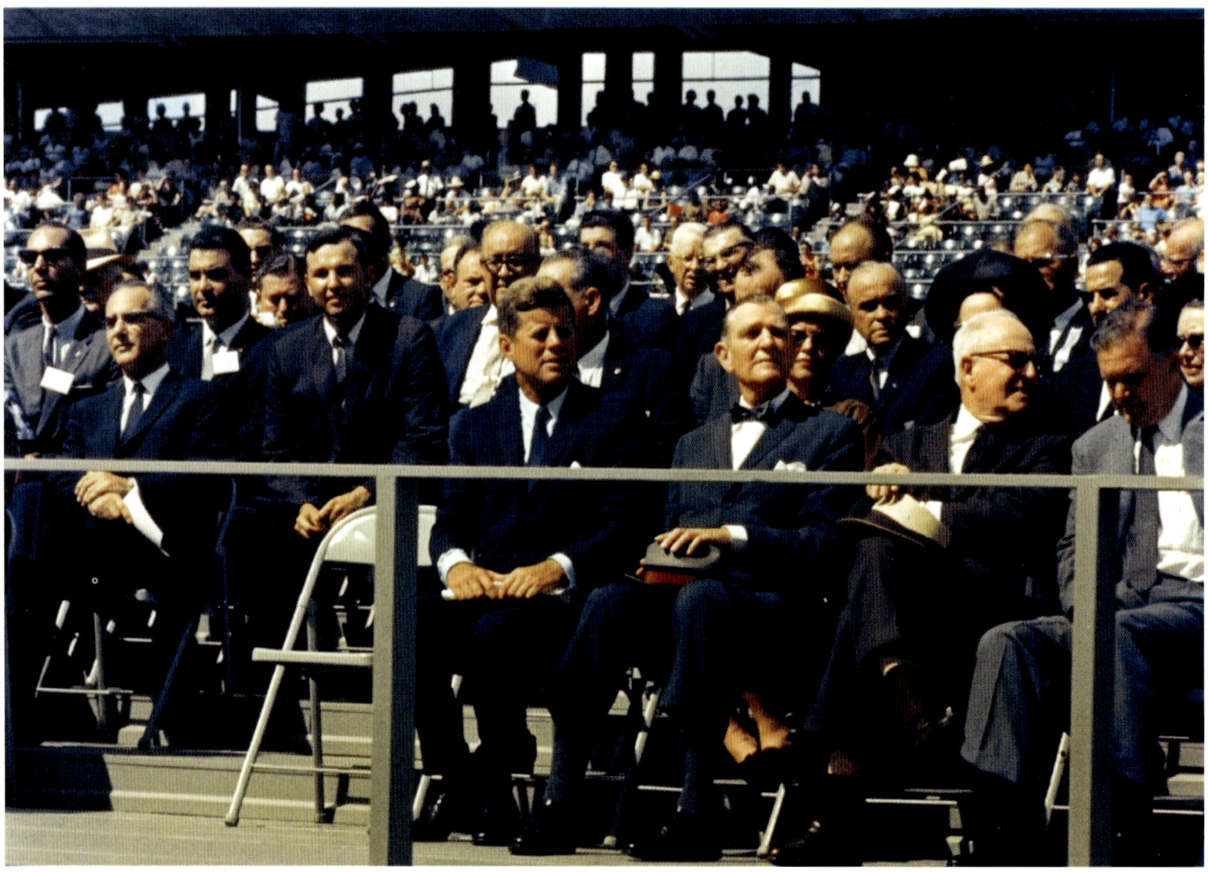

▲ The president, holding his speech, awaits his introduction from Pitzer. To Kennedy's left are Rep. Thomas, Rep. George P. Miller (D-Calif.), and Webb.

▶ "This generation does not intend to founder in the backwash of the coming age of space," Kennedy says.

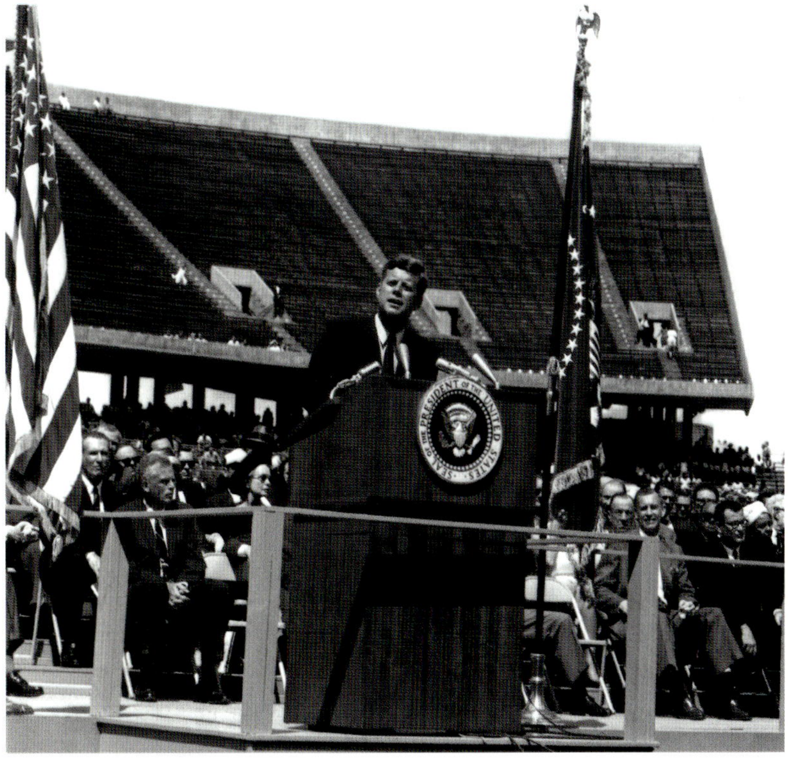

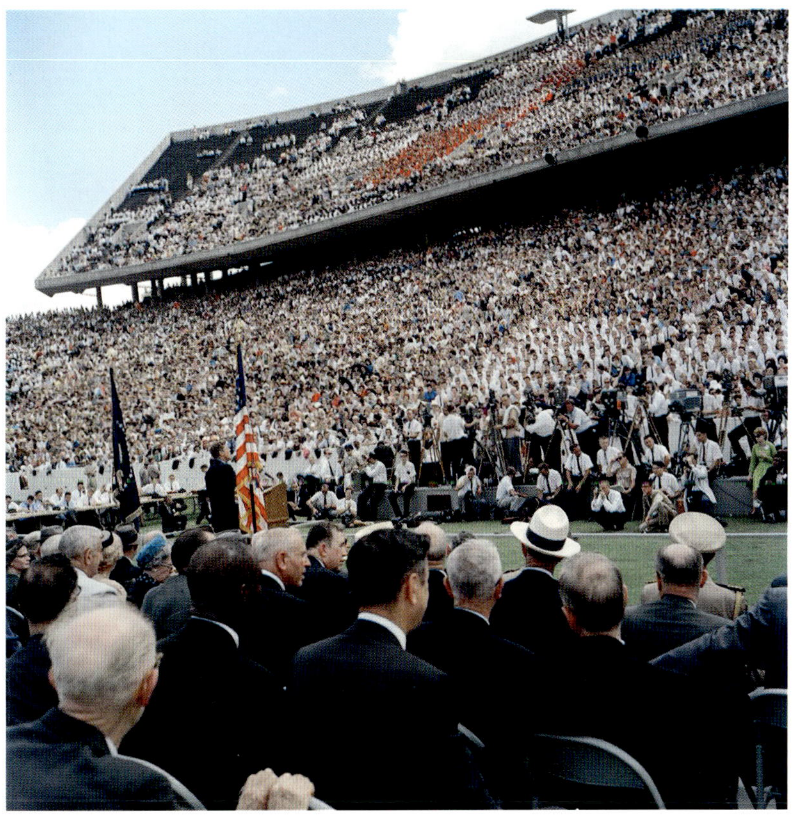

◢ We mean to be a part of it—we mean to lead it. For the eyes of the world now look into space, to the moon and to the planets beyond, and we have vowed that we shall not see it governed by a hostile flag of conquest, but by a banner of freedom and peace. We have vowed that we shall not see space filled with weapons of mass destruction, but with instruments of knowledge and understanding.

Yet the vows of this nation can only be fulfilled if we in this Nation are first, and, therefore, we intend to be first. . . .

We set sail on this new sea because there is new knowledge to be gained, and new rights to be won, and they must be won and used for the progress of all people. For space science, like nuclear science and all technology, has no conscience of its own. Whether it will become a force for good or ill depends on man, and only if the United States occupies a position of pre-eminence can we help decide whether this new ocean will be a sea of peace or a new terrifying theater of war. . . .

. . . But why, some say, the moon? Why choose this as our goal? And they may well ask why climb the highest mountain? Why, 35 years ago, fly the Atlantic? Why does Rice play Texas? [The crowd cheers.]

. . . We choose to go to the moon in this decade and do the other things, not because they are easy, but because they are hard, because that goal will serve to organize and measure the best of our energies and skills, because that challenge is one that we are willing to accept, one we are unwilling to postpone, and one which we intend to win, and the others, too.

▶ Kennedy has added "Why does Rice play Texas?" by hand on this page from the reading copy of his speech. He rarely used a teleprompter and did not use one on this day. (Courtesy of the John F. Kennedy Presidential Library.)

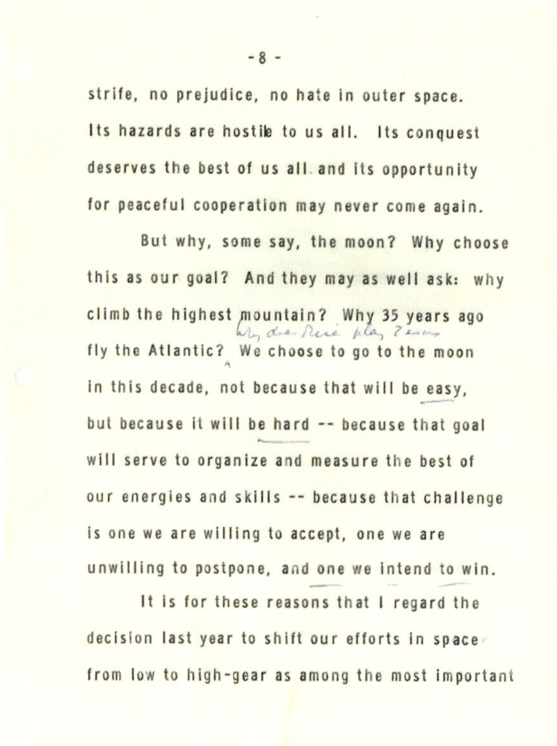
- 8 -

strife, no prejudice, no hate in outer space.
Its hazards are hostile to us all. Its conquest deserves the best of us all and its opportunity for peaceful cooperation may never come again.

But why, some say, the moon? Why choose this as our goal? And they may as well ask: why climb the highest mountain? Why 35 years ago fly the Atlantic? Why does Rice play Texas? We choose to go to the moon in this decade, not because that will be easy, but because it will be hard -- because that goal will serve to organize and measure the best of our energies and skills -- because that challenge is one we are willing to accept, one we are unwilling to postpone, and one we intend to win.

It is for these reasons that I regard the decision last year to shift our efforts in space from low to high-gear as among the most important

▼ In the last 24 hours we have seen facilities now being created for the greatest and most complex exploration in man's history. We have felt the ground shake and the air shattered by the testing of a Saturn C-1 booster rocket, many times as powerful as the Atlas which launched John Glenn. . . .

. . . We have seen the site where five F-1 rocket engines, each one as powerful as all eight engines of the Saturn combined, will be clustered together to make the advanced Saturn missile, assembled in a new building to be built at Cape Canaveral as tall as a 48-story structure, as wide as a city block, and as long as two lengths of this field.

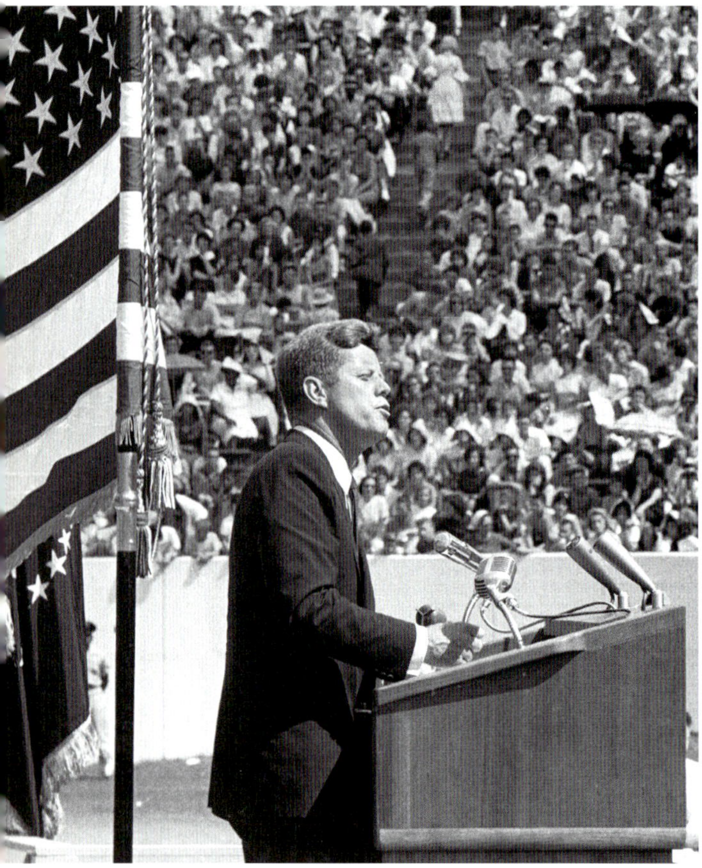

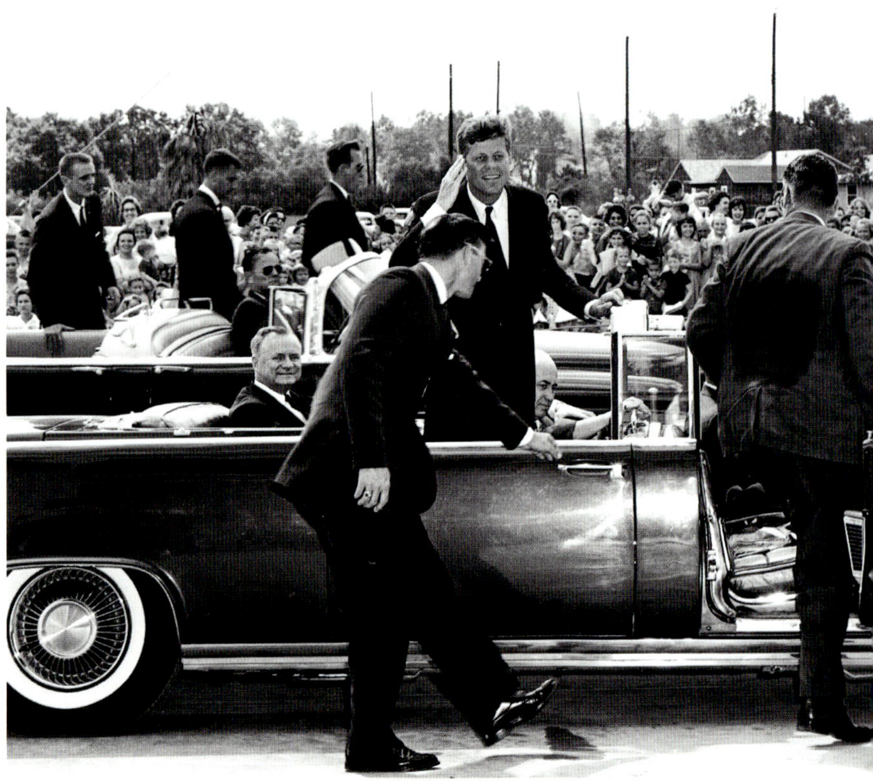

▶ The president arrives at the Rich Building, a temporary MSC location known as Site 3 in southeast Houston, at 10:00 a.m. with Gov. Daniel and MSC Director Robert Gilruth.

▶ The Mariner spacecraft now on its way to Venus is the most intricate instrument in the history of space science. The accuracy of that shot is comparable to firing a missile from Cape Canaveral and dropping it in this stadium between the 40-yard lines. . . .

We have had our failures, but so have others, even if they do not admit them. And they may be less public.

To be sure, we are behind, and will be behind for some time in manned flight. But we do not intend to stay behind, and in this decade, we shall make up and move ahead. . . .

But if I were to say, my fellow citizens, that we shall send to the moon, 240,000 miles away from the control station in Houston, a giant rocket more than 300 feet tall, . . . and then return it safely to earth, re-entering the atmosphere at speeds of over 25,000 miles per hour, causing heat about half that of the temperature of the sun—almost as hot as it is here today—and do all this, and do it right, and do it first before this decade is out—then we must be bold.

I'm the one who is doing all the work, so we just want you to stay cool for a minute. [laughter] . . .

Many years ago the great British explorer George Mallory, who was to die on Mount Everest, was asked why did he want to climb it. He said, "Because it is there."

Well, space is there, and we're going to climb it, and the moon and the planets are there, and new hopes for knowledge and peace are there. And, therefore, as we set sail we ask God's blessing on the most hazardous and dangerous and greatest adventure on which man has ever embarked.

The president's motorcade departs at 9:42 a.m.

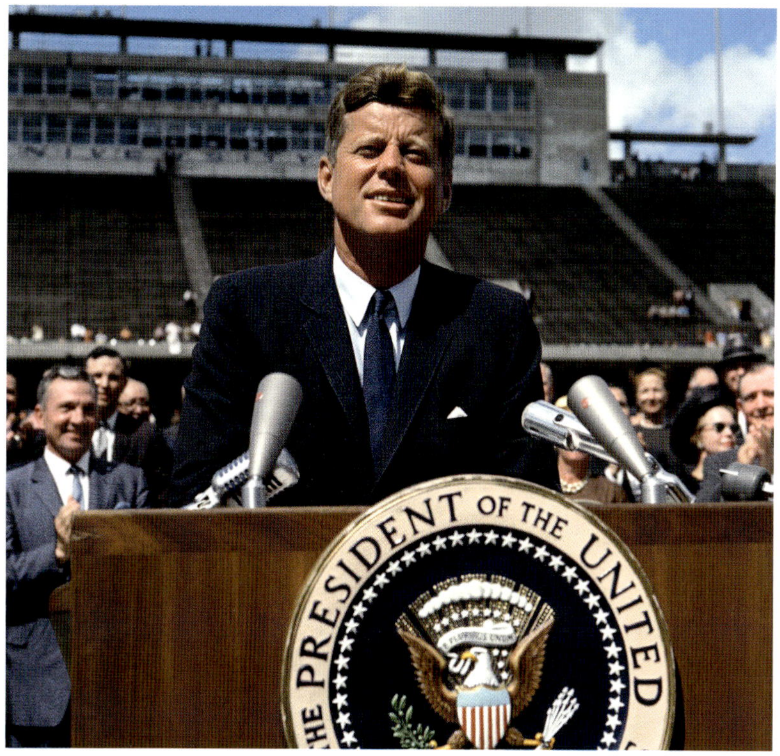

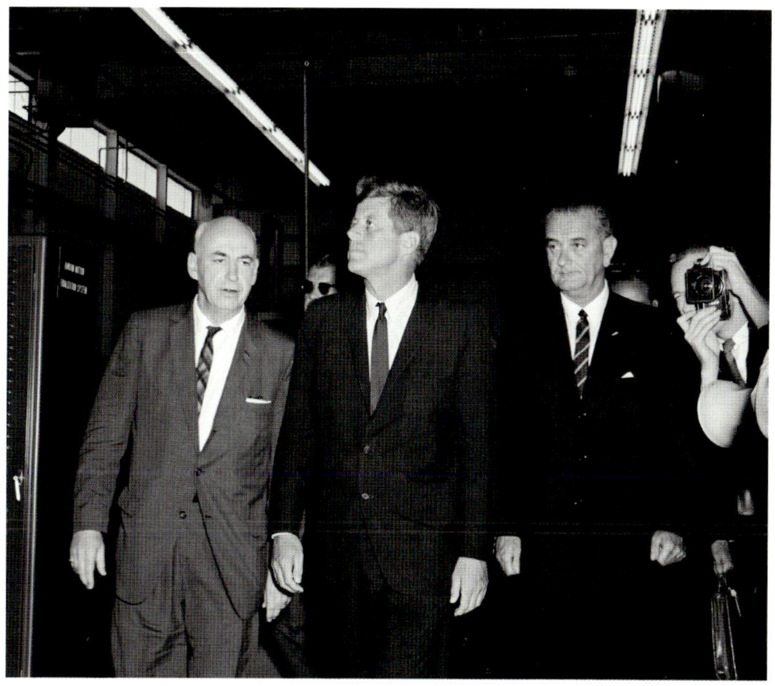

▲ Kennedy first receives a forty-five-minute classified briefing by Gilruth (left). The facility, built to be a fan factory, is being leased by NASA about fifteen miles west of where MSC is starting to rise. It houses the Space Flight Office, the Spacecraft Research Division, and the Systems Evaluation and Development Division.

▶ The president then hears a series of short talks by astronauts on a dozen displays. Astronaut Gus Grissom shows Johnson and Kennedy a food packet at a mockup of the two-man Gemini spacecraft. Grissom would command the first manned Gemini mission in 1965.

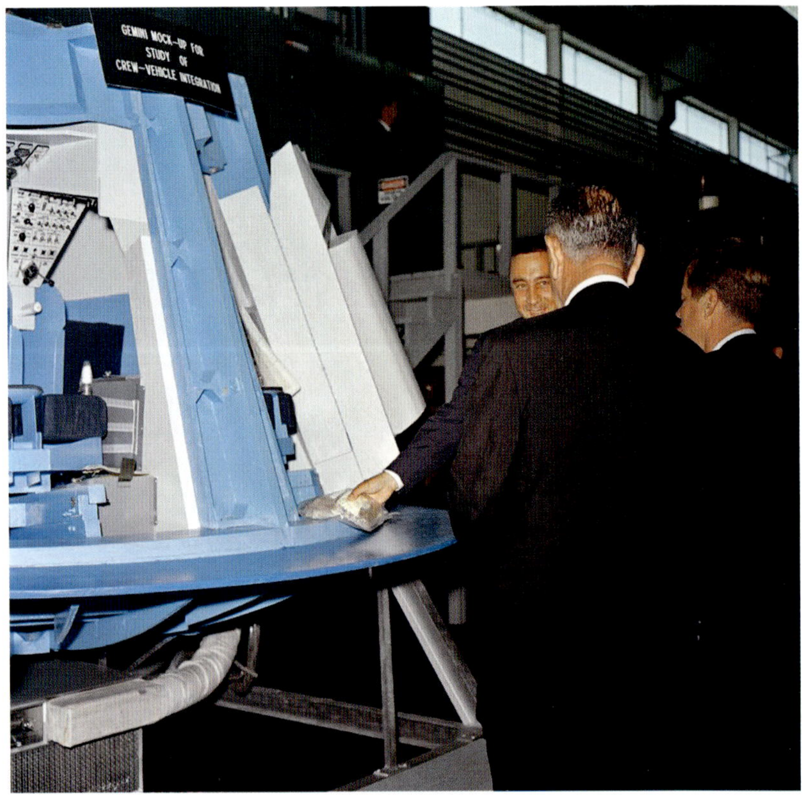

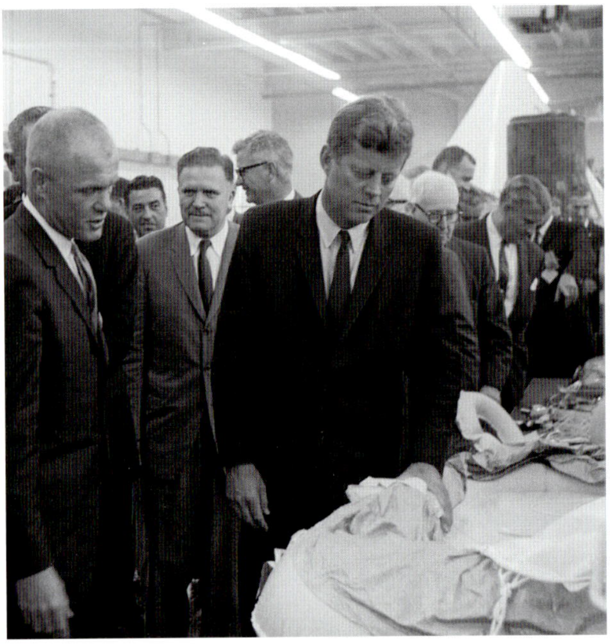

▲ Glenn discusses astronaut survival gear with the president.

L–R: Glenn; Johnson (hidden); Brig. Gen. McHugh; Webb; Seamans; Kennedy; Rep. Miller; David Bell; and von Braun. (At the Cape, Kennedy had spontaneously invited von Braun along on this leg of the trip.)

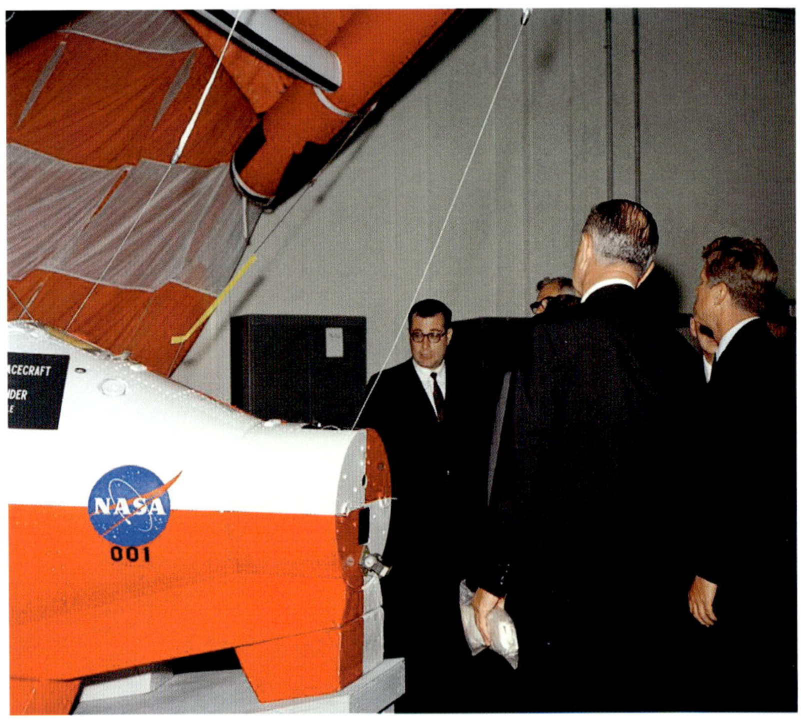

▲ Brown, Seamans (hidden), Johnson, and Kennedy view a half-scale Gemini spacecraft mockup.

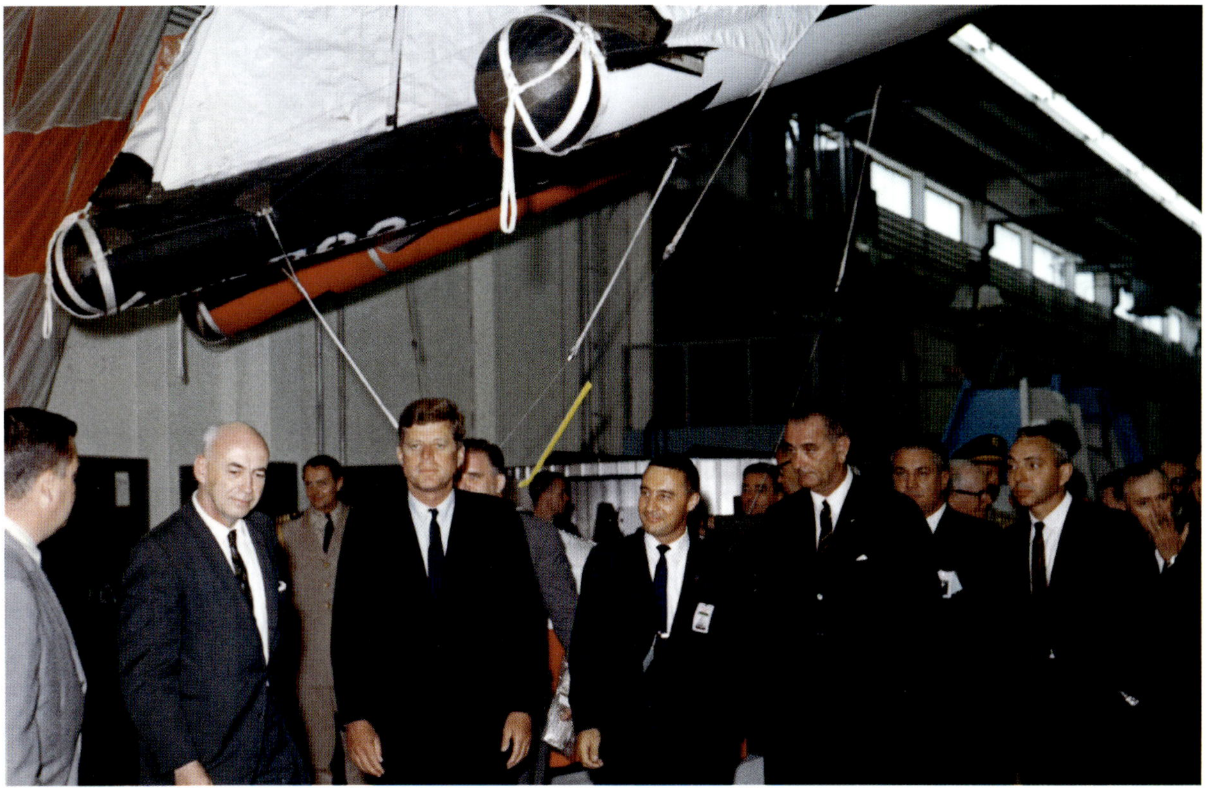

▲ The Gemini spacecraft mockup is rigged to its inflatable "Rogallo Wing" in the display area. A runway landing for Gemini astronauts using a paraglider is studied from 1961 to 1964 but eventually abandoned over its complexity and cost.

L–R: Gilruth; Capt. Tazewell Shepard Jr.; Kennedy; Grissom; Johnson; Walt Williams; Rep. Miller; Holmes; and Gov. Price.

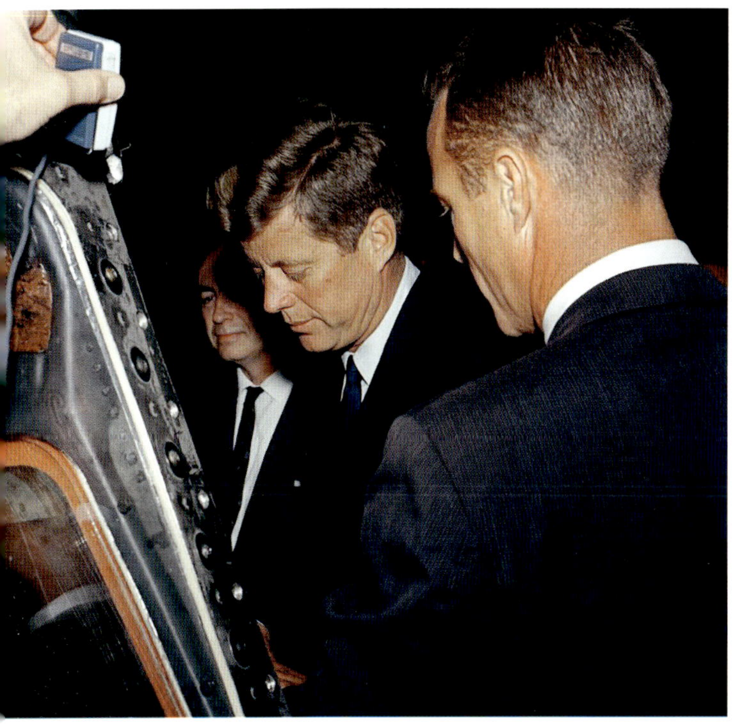

▲ Gilruth and Kennedy listen to Scott Carpenter discuss his *Aurora 7* Mercury spacecraft.

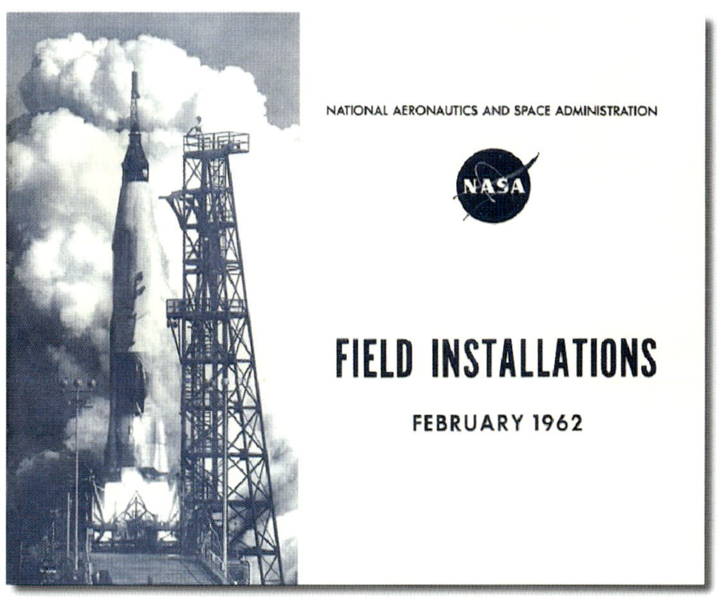

▶ NASA provided these summary booklets to Kennedy's staff for the visit. Booklet in the John F. Kennedy Presidential Library.

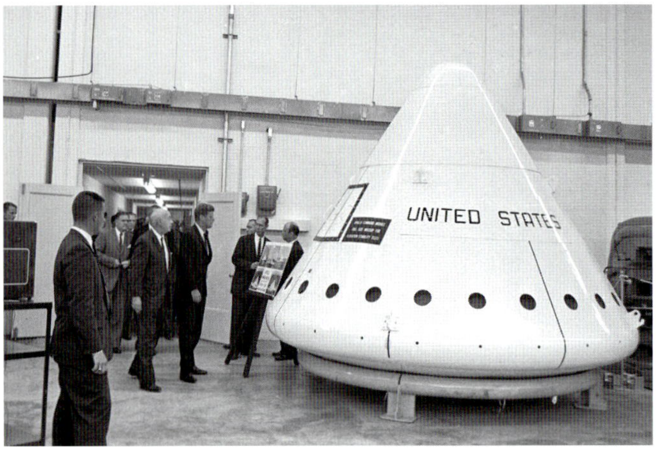

◀ The president sees an Apollo command module (CM) mockup that has been used for floatation stability tests. Gilruth, Johnson (hidden), and Webb follow. This first boilerplate mockup, built by CM prime contractor North American Aviation, has undergone preliminary drop tests on water. It would be subjected to further water and ground tests at MSC, including developing ocean recovery procedures. This mockup has the same center of gravity as an actual CM but no interior.

▼ The president is briefed on a seventeen-foot tall, full-scale mockup of a manned lunar landing craft, the first time it is shown to the media. It was built by North American Aviation; Grumman Aircraft, however, is awarded the lunar lander contract two months later.

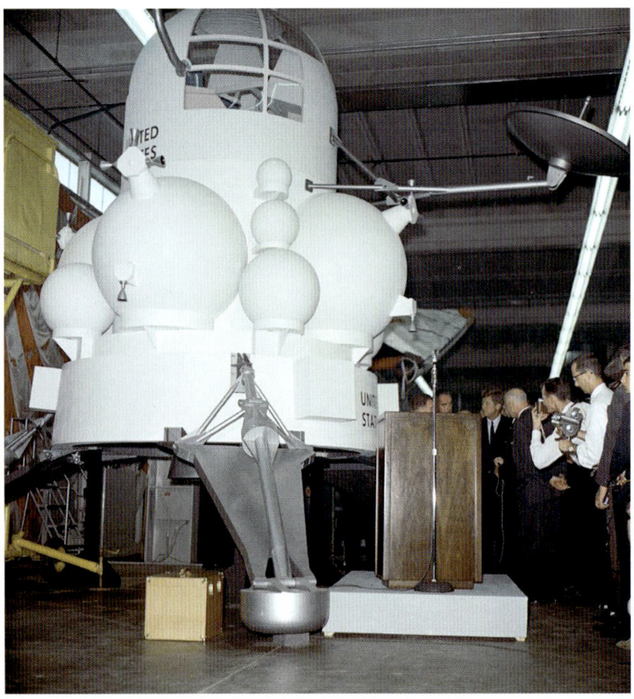

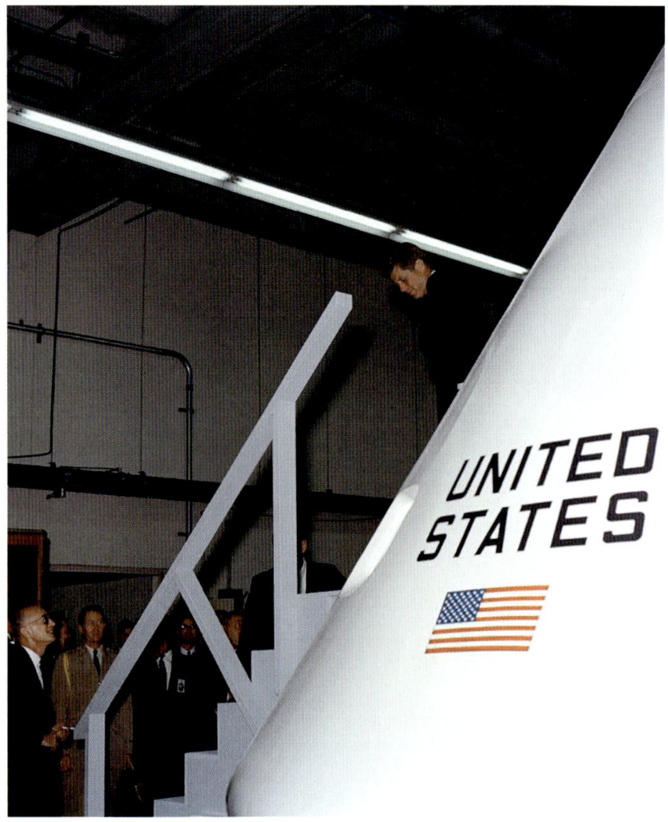

▲ Kennedy exits a different mockup of an Apollo CM, with Ed Welsh and Maj. Gen. Clifton at left. The president briefly climbs in, with astronaut Deke Slayton providing the briefing. This first wooden-and-aluminum mockup, with an interior, was built by the MSC Technical Services shop in the Rich Building for the Communications Branch. The first manned Apollo flight is still more than six years away.

▶ Astronaut Alan Shepard (hidden by Gilruth, back to camera) goes over plans for two astronauts to take a two-stage craft to the lunar surface as Webb, Kennedy, and Gilruth listen.

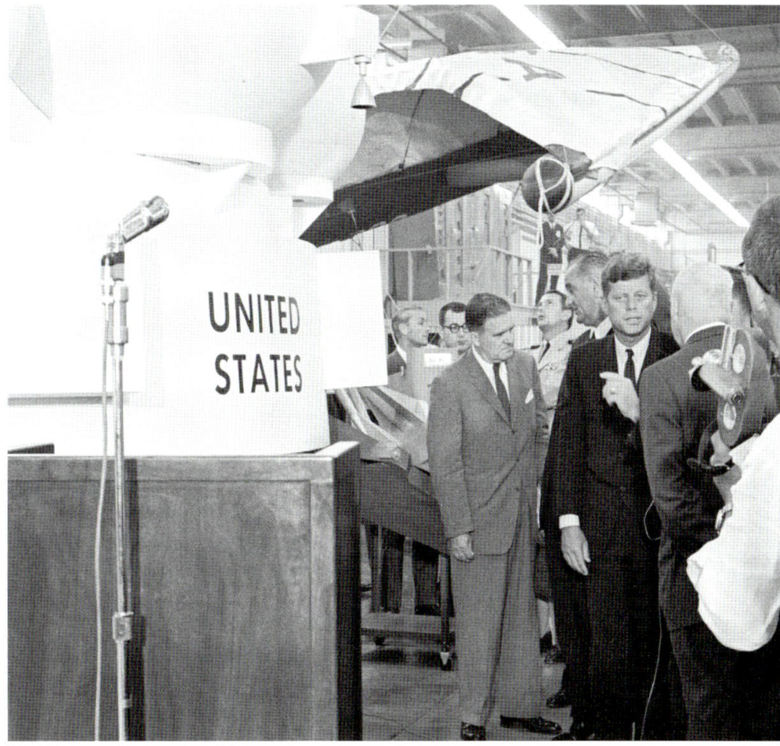

▼ Shepard, Kennedy, and Johnson. Shepard would become the fifth person to walk on the moon as commander of the Apollo 14 mission in 1971.

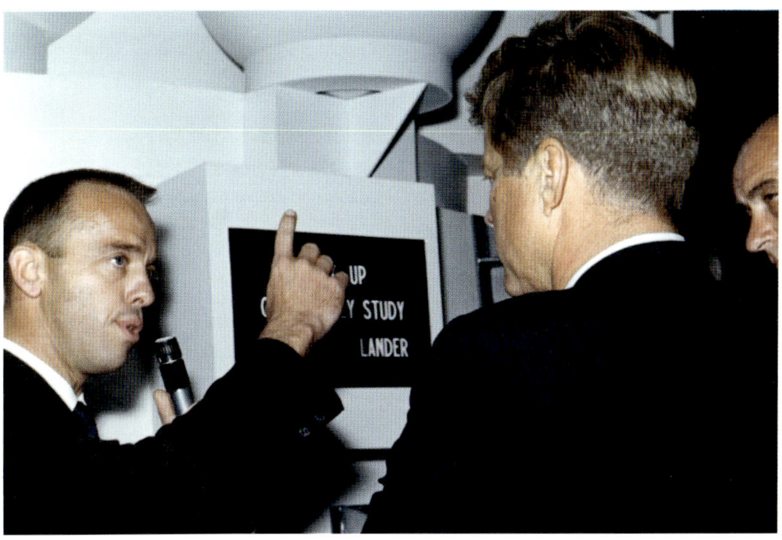

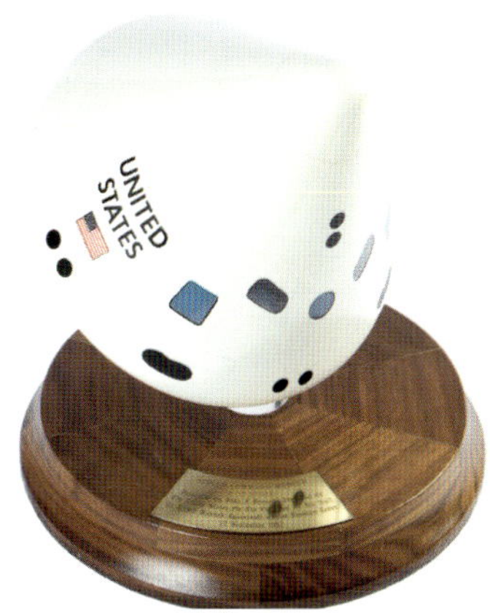

▲ Model in the John F. Kennedy Presidential Library and Museum.

▶ Gilruth presents the president with a 1/15th scale model of an Apollo CM before his remarks. "This model . . . will remind us of this most extraordinary effort which is being made by all the men here and their companions scattered across the country in NASA, in private industry, in universities, all of whom are united in this extraordinary enterprise," Kennedy says.

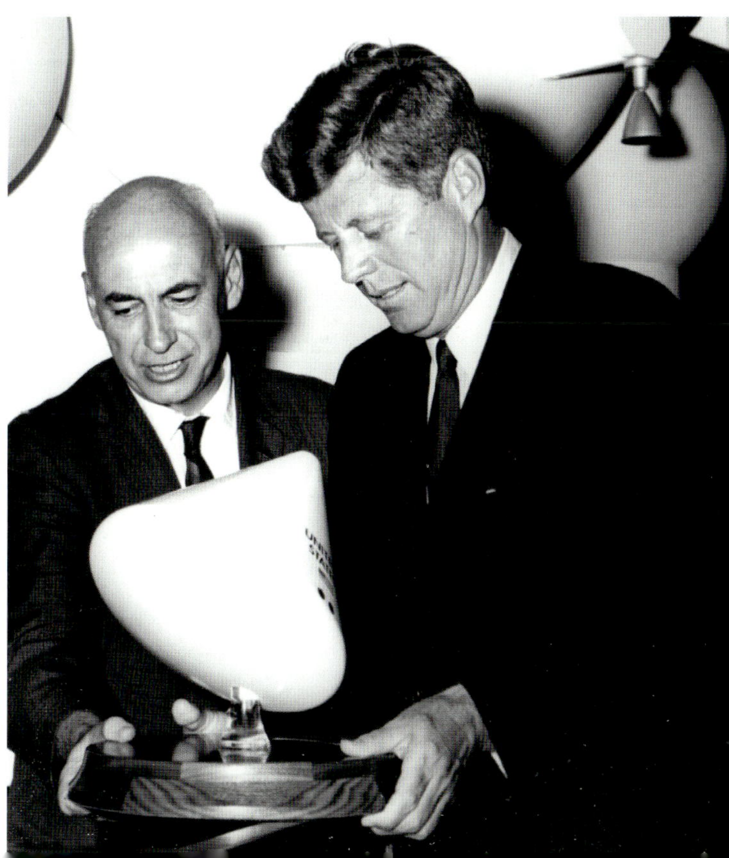

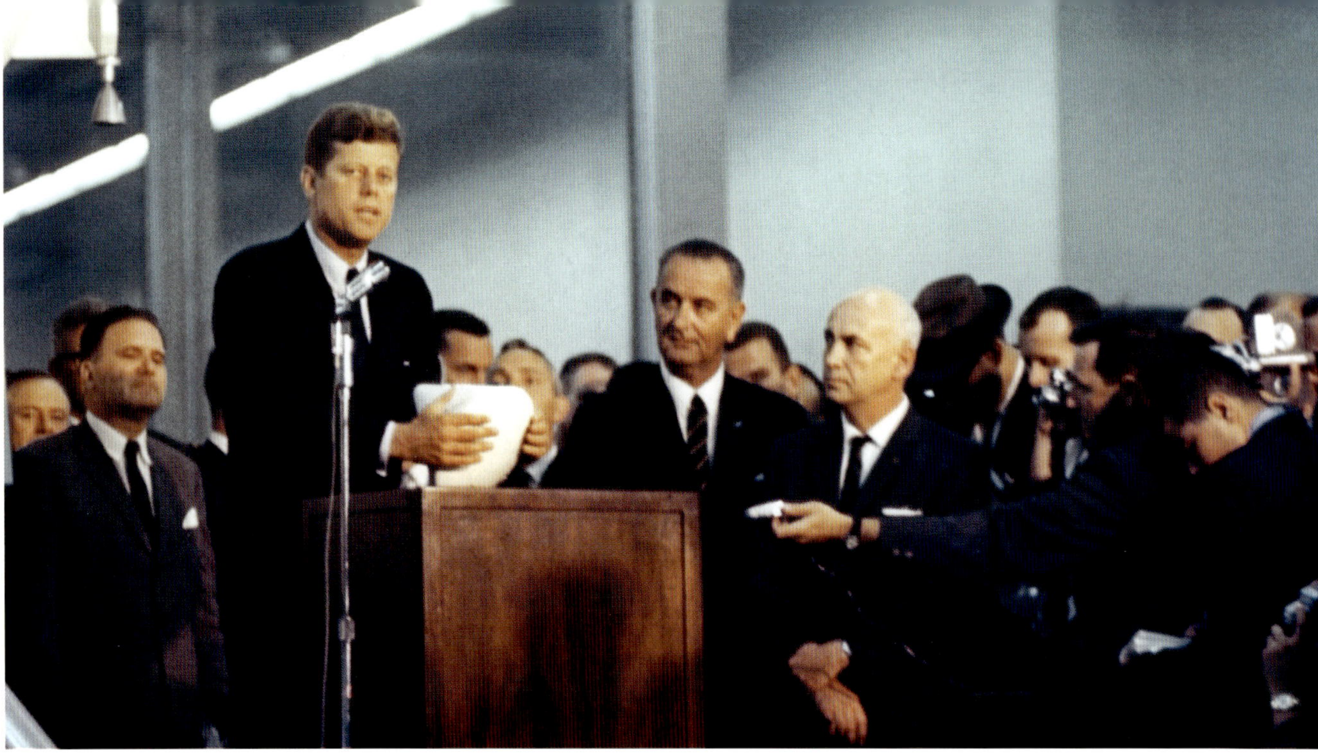

▲ "To talk of placing a tremendous rocket outside the orbit of the Earth, to send it to the moon to rendezvous, go to the moon's surface, to put men on the moon, to take them off, to rendezvous again and bring them back to Earth safely," Kennedy tells MSC staff, "and to talk about doing that in the next six to seven years, indicates how far and how fast we have come and how far and fast we must go . . ."

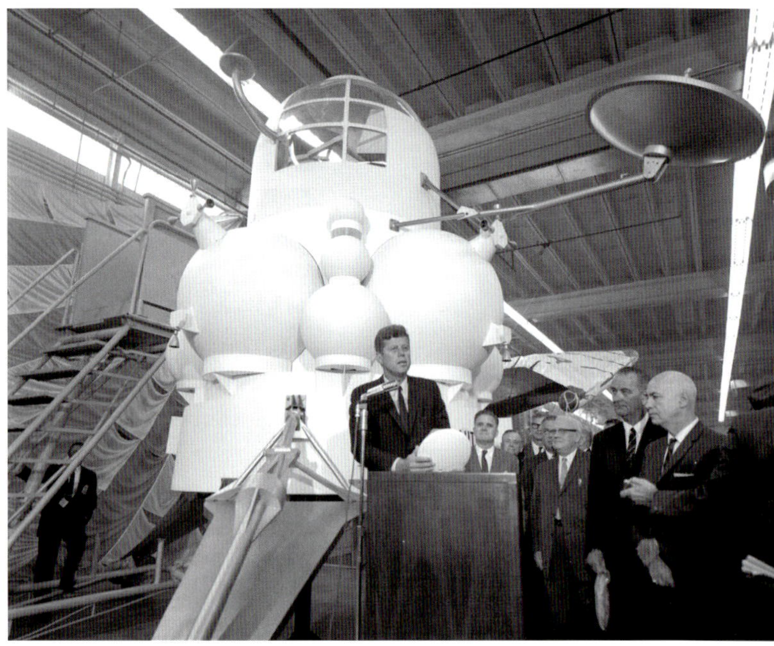

▶ ". . . and in back of all the extraordinary scientific and technical accomplishments which must be made to make this possible, of course, are the men who are involved, and particularly those who are at the point of the sphere, those who must fly this mission into the most unknown sea. So we commend them and all who are associated in putting them there," the president concludes.

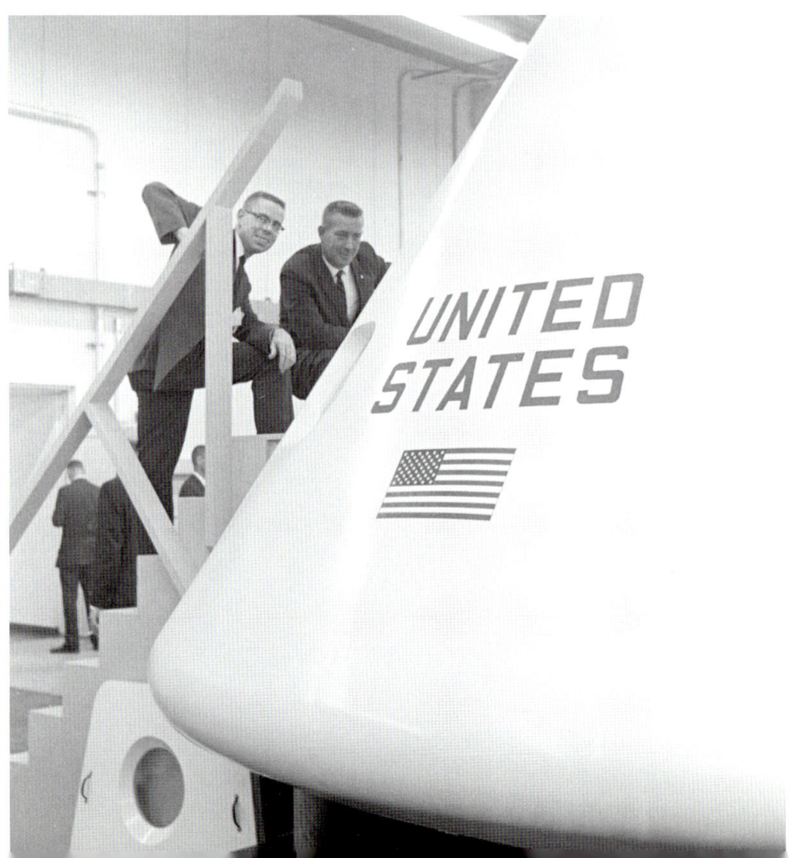

▶ Members of the president's Secret Service detail are not immune from a good photo opportunity. Agent Arthur Godfrey (right) poses with an unidentified NASA employee at the Apollo CM mockup Kennedy had entered.

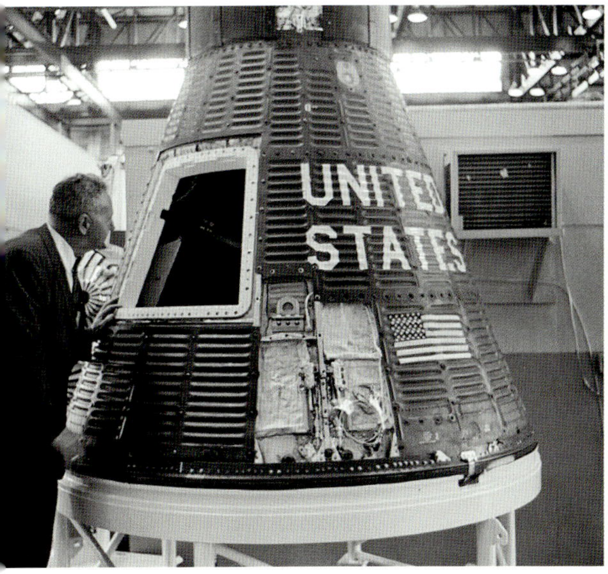

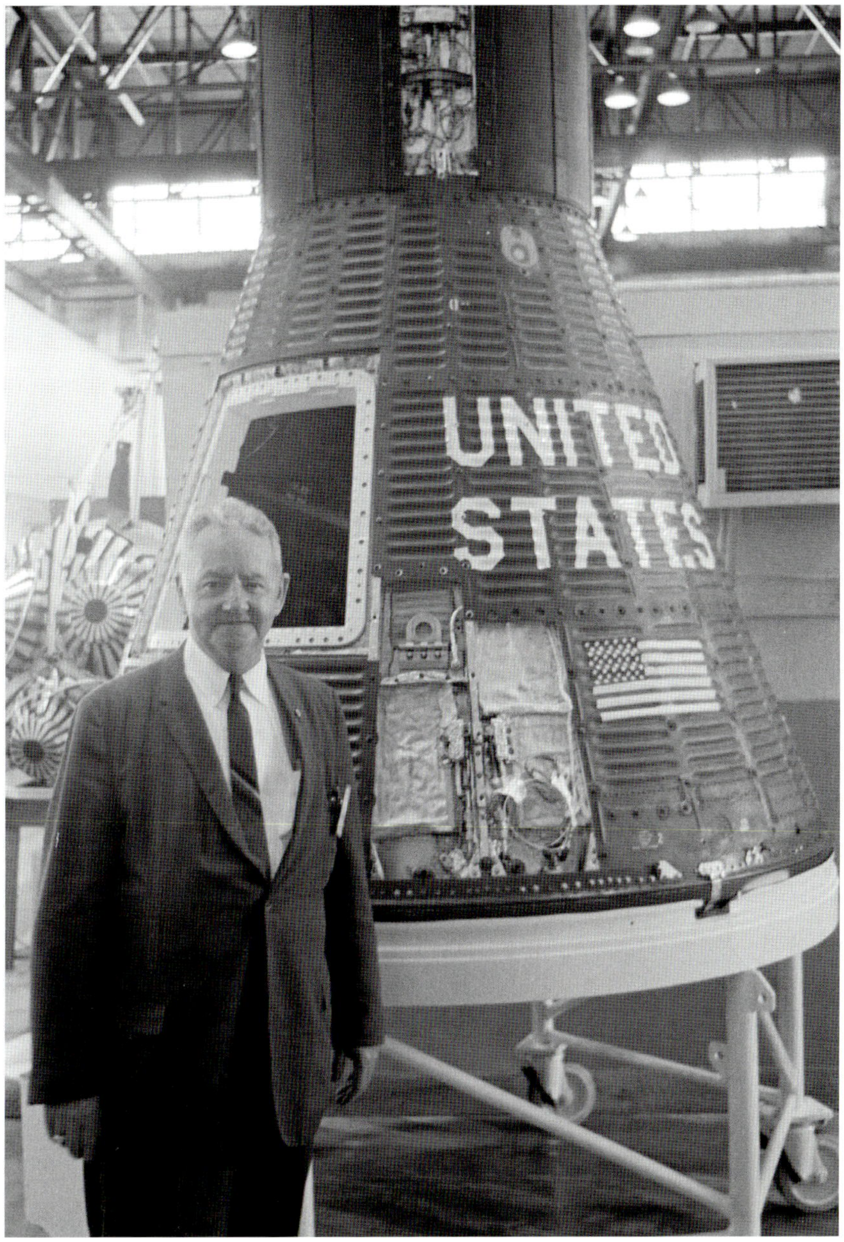

Agent John "Muggsy" O'Leary with Mercury spacecraft No. 19 the previous day in Hangar S at the Cape.

The president leaves the Rich Building at 11:40 a.m. Air Force One is to depart Houston International Airport for St. Louis, Missouri, at 11:51 a.m.

L–R: Kennedy; Gov. Daniel; Rep. Thomas; and Gilruth in the car. Also pictured: Secret Service Agents Ron Pontius and Dave Grant.

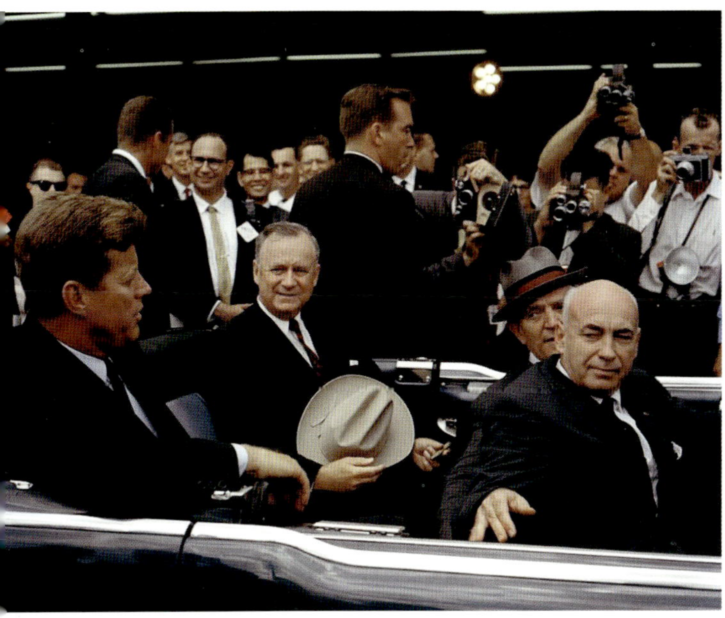

▶ The president debarks Air Force One at Lambert Field in St. Louis at 2:30 p.m. CDT. The final stop on his tour is McDonnell Aircraft Corp., the prime contractor for both the Mercury and Gemini manned spacecraft. The company was formed at Lambert in 1939 and is the largest employer in the St. Louis area.

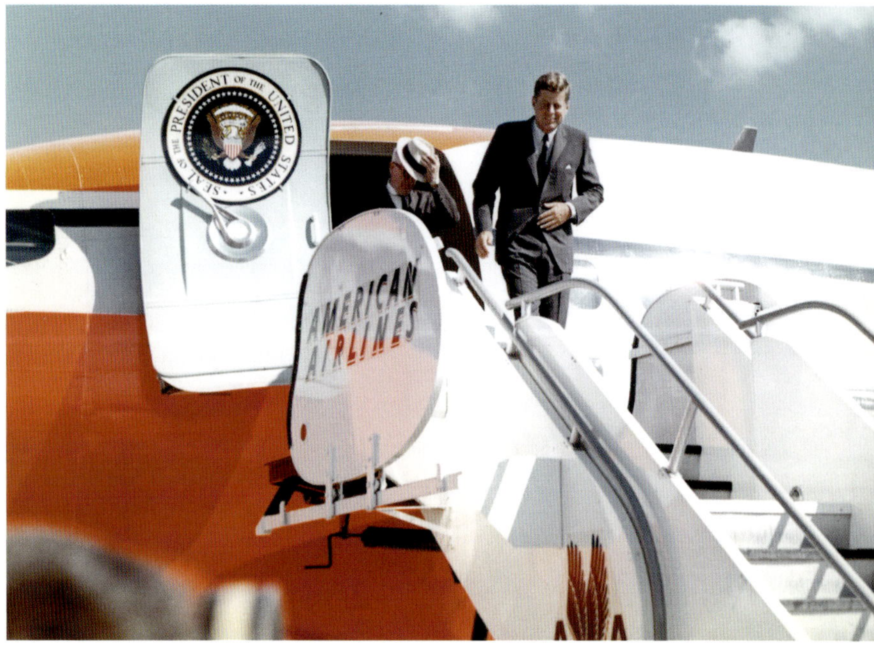

▼ Kennedy is greeted by McDonnell Chairman and CEO James McDonnell, with Webb at right.

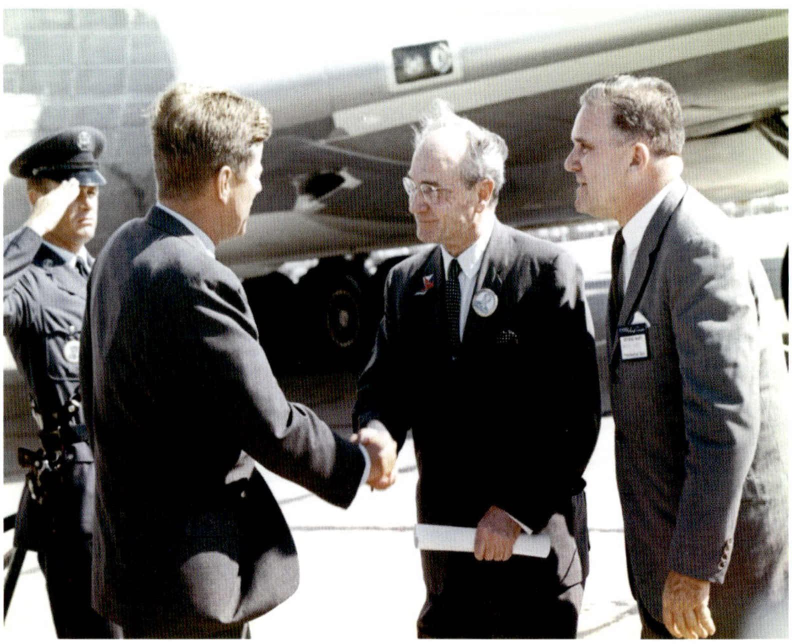

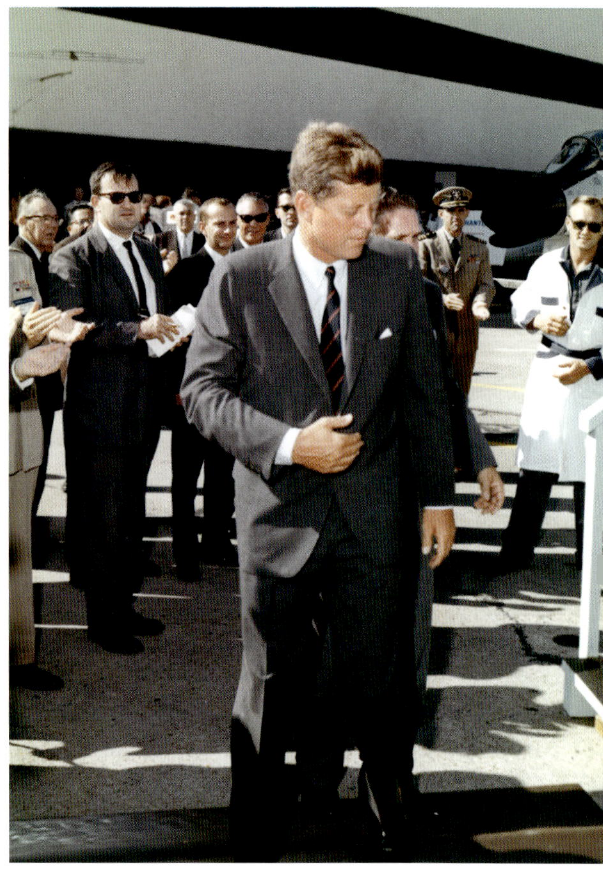

▲ The president heads to a platform for an address to assembled McDonnell workers.

▶ Kennedy speaks to about ten thousand workers, with several F-4H Phantom II fighter-bombers on display; another flies overhead.

> Every citizen of this country has a stake, and is participating in this effort, but it all comes to you, to those in Houston, to those in Cape Canaveral, to those at MIT, to those on the West Coast, who perform the vital functions which make it possible to put one man or two men first in orbit around the Earth, and then in orbit around the moon, and then on the moon, and then come back. And you are part of that great effort.
>
> I can imagine no action, no adventure which is more essential and more exciting than to be involved in the most important and significant adventure that any man has been able to participate in the history of the world.

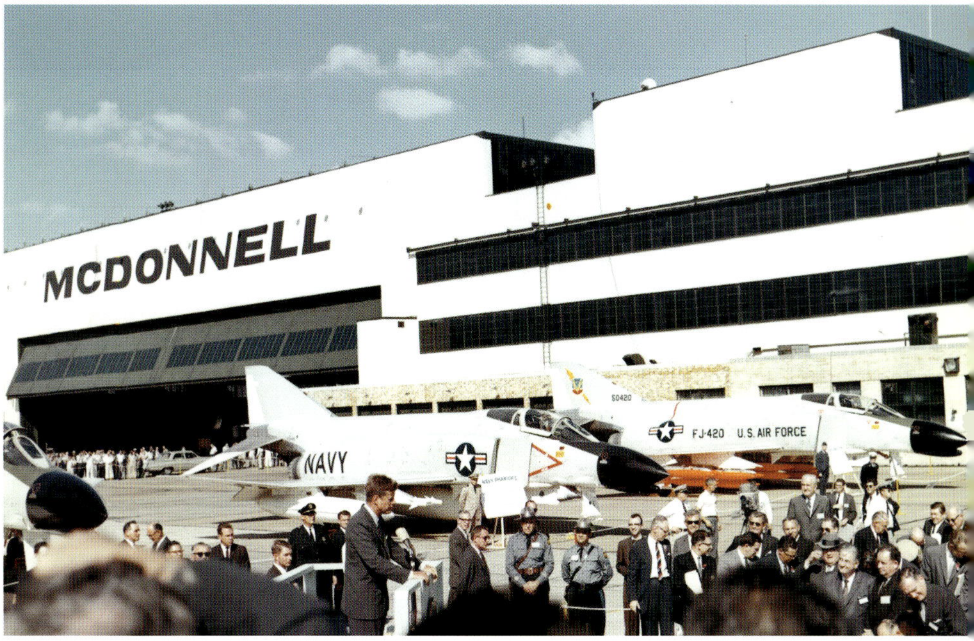

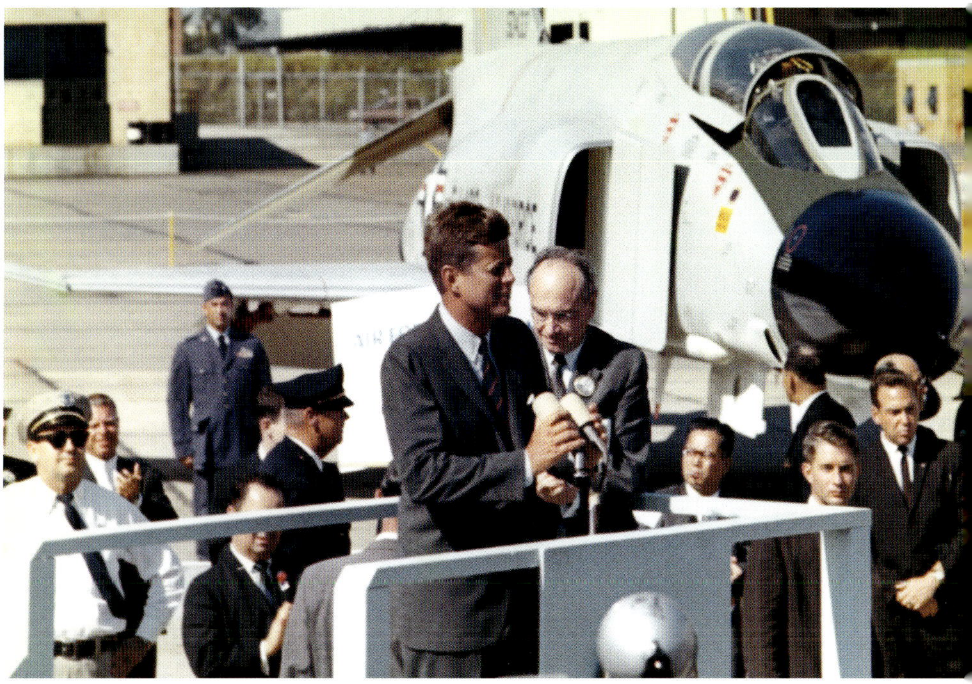

◢ James McDonnell uses an electric factory cart to take the president around the company's plant, acquired from the Curtiss-Wright Corp. in 1951. Sanford McDonnell is seated behind his father; Webb is behind Kennedy. The president inspects Gordon Cooper's spacecraft just before it is shipped to Florida for the final Mercury launch the following May, sees a Gemini spacecraft mockup, and tours the Gemini and F-4 H production lines.

During the visit, Kennedy asks FCC Chairman Newton Minow why he's such an advocate for communication satellites. He replies, "Mr. President, communication satellites are more important than sending a man into space because they will send ideas, and ideas last a lot longer than people." Minow later tells Congress that this is one area where the US is significantly ahead of the Soviets.

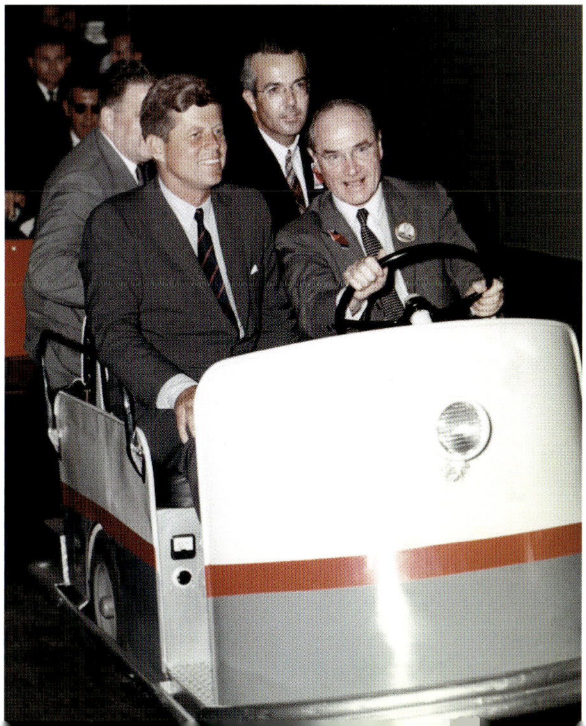

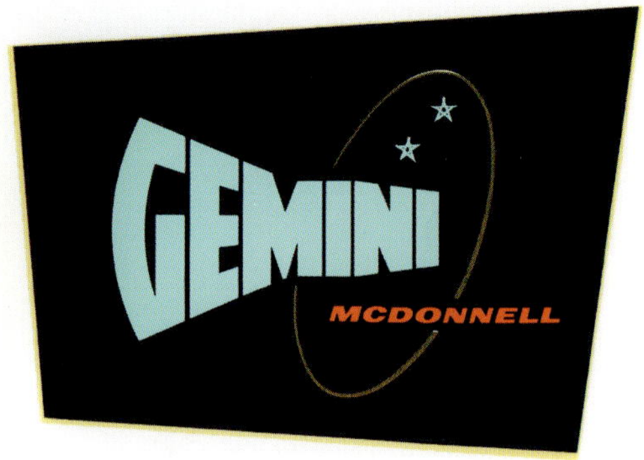

▼ McDonnell Vice President Walter Burke shows Kennedy the company's first two-man Gemini spacecraft engineering mockup, with McDonnell and Webb at right. It is the first time the mockup is exhibited.

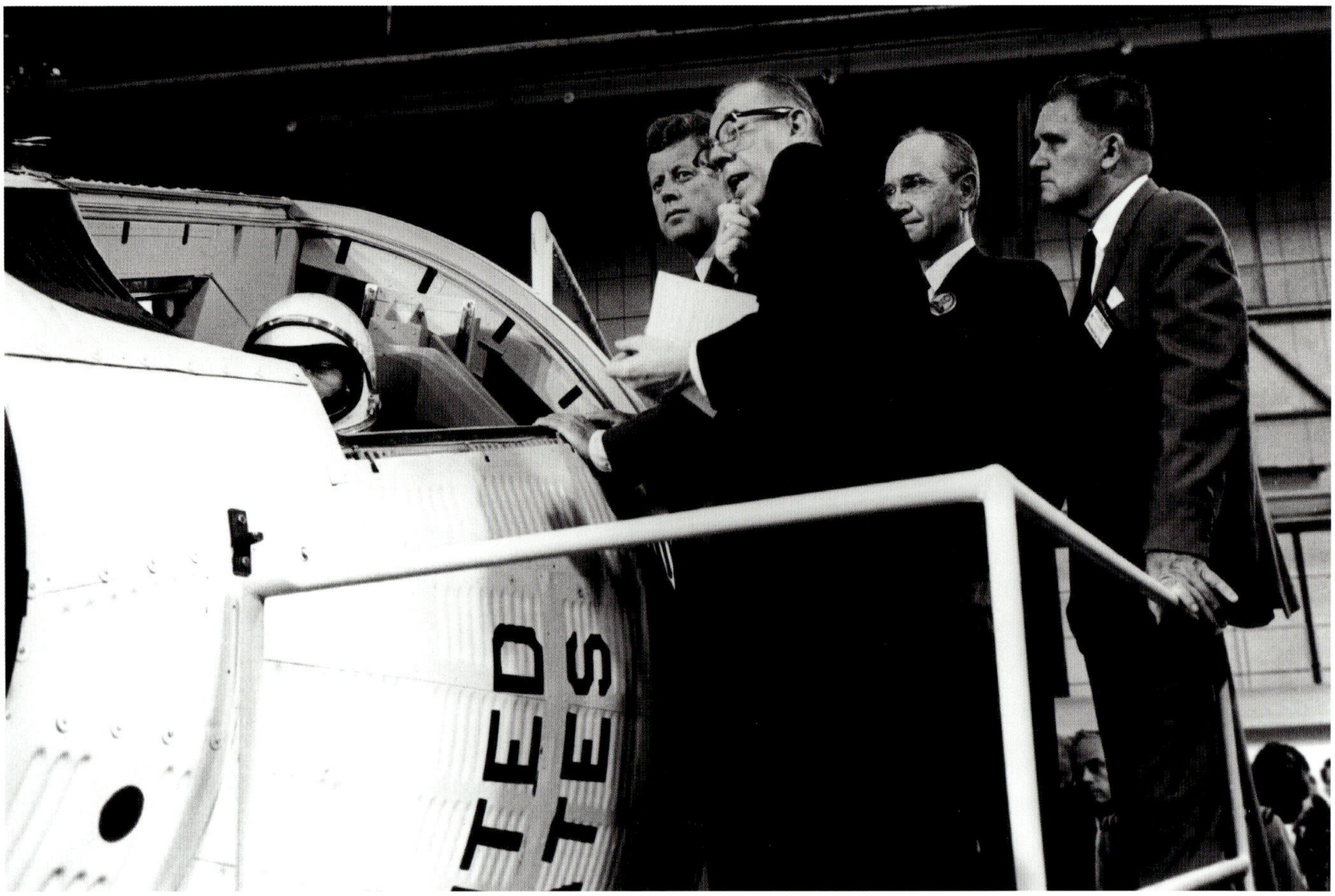

▶ Kennedy and Burke go over the Gemini with McDonnell and Webb at right. McDonnell engineer Elbert Wiegand is in the cockpit. The first manned Gemini flight is still more than two years away.

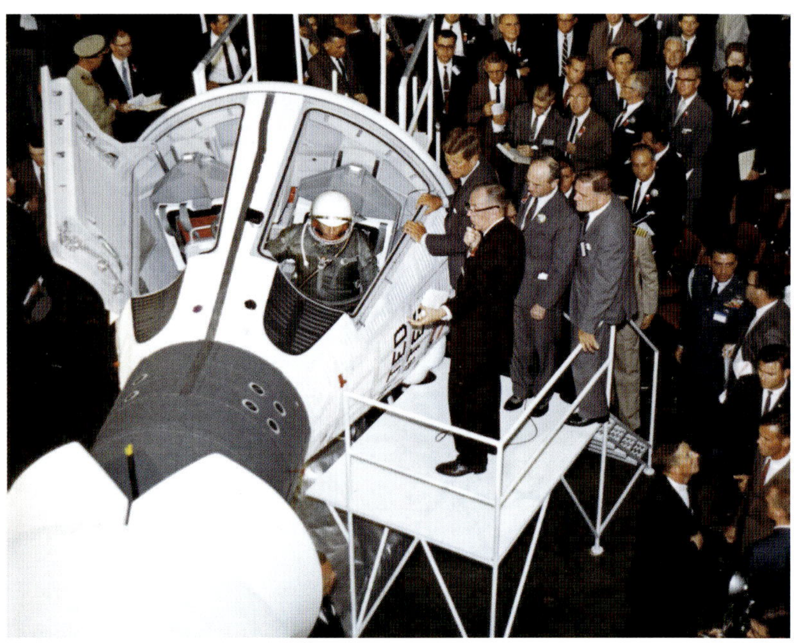

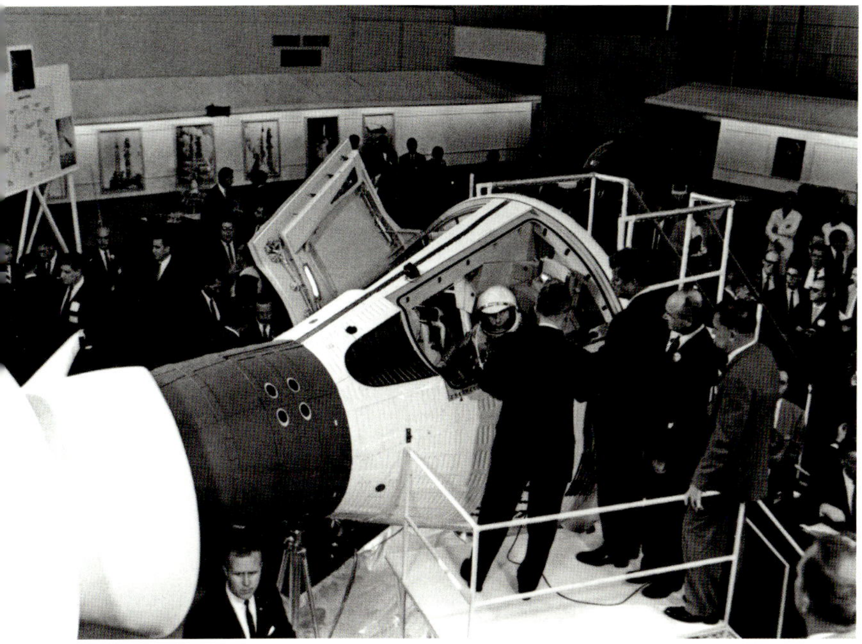

▲ The Gemini command module is docked to a mockup Agena upper stage at left. Rendezvous and docking with another spacecraft, critical to the success of Apollo, is a key objective of Gemini.

After almost two hours inside the facility, Kennedy and his party leave Lambert Field at 5:05 p.m. to fly back to Andrews AFB.

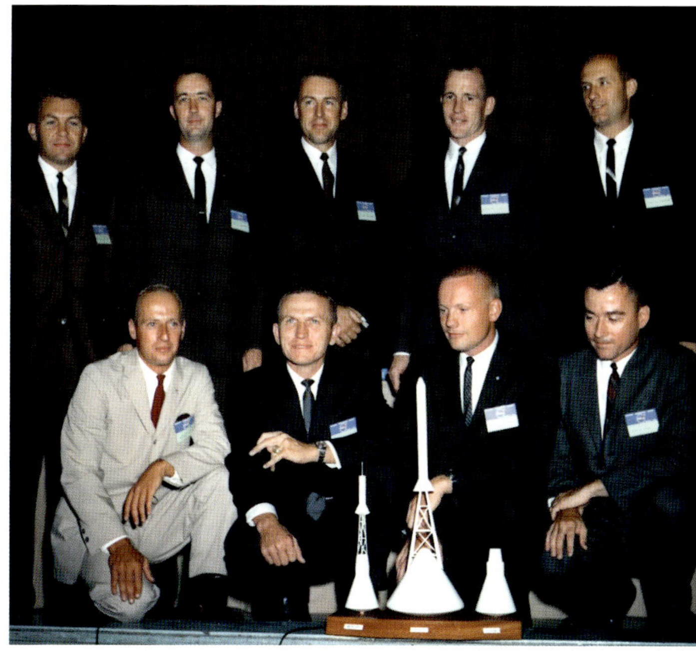

◥ NASA's second group of astronauts poses at the University of Houston's Cullen Auditorium following a news conference announcing their selection on September 17, 1962.

L–R: (back row): Elliott See; James McDivitt; James Lovell; Edward White; and Thomas Stafford. L-R (front row): Charles Conrad; Frank Borman; Neil Armstrong; and John Young. See would die in a NASA aircraft crash in 1966; White would perish in the Apollo 1 launch pad fire in 1967. Lovell, Borman, and Stafford would orbit the moon; Armstrong, Conrad, and Young would walk on it. Kennedy would not meet any of the Group 2 astronauts.

▼ Less than seven years later, Armstrong, seen here at McDonnell Aircraft in late 1962, would fulfill the president's goal of an American on the moon by 1970.

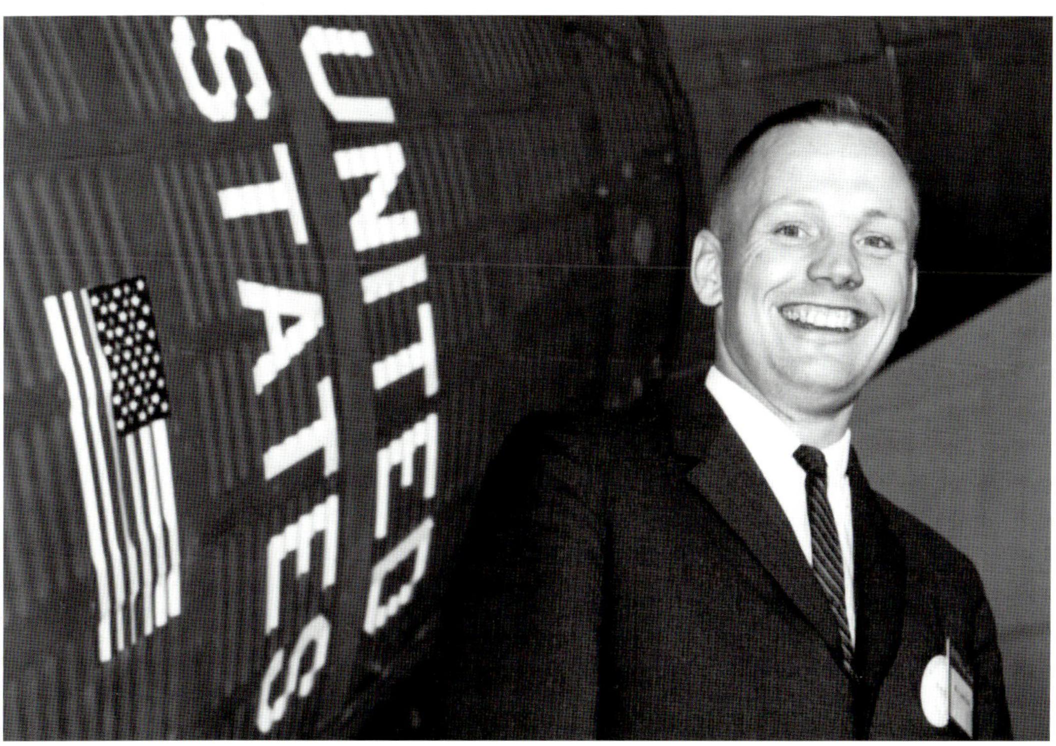

:06

OCTOBER–DECEMBER 1962

"I'm not that interested in space"

THE SPACE HIGHLIGHT FOR the United States during the last quarter of 1962 is the highly successful flight of Mercury astronaut Walter Schirra Jr. on October 3. At nine hours, it is the longest American flight yet but well behind the nearly four-day record set by the Soviets' *Vostok 3* in August.

Also in October the president negotiates the withdrawal of Soviet missiles from Cuba, a much-needed foreign policy victory. The following month, in a White House tape recording, he privately makes clear his interest in the space program is limited to its usefulness as a Cold War weapon against the Soviets.

Kennedy wraps up his second year in office with a tour of the country's most secret nuclear weapons facilities in New Mexico and Nevada for an update on nuclear rocket engine technology.

In addition, the United States is making steady progress toward its moon-landing goal. In November NASA launches its third Saturn C-1, paving the way for the Saturn V moon rocket. In December the American Mariner II probe, launched in August, makes the first successful flyby of a planet (Venus). A previous American Venus mission—as well as four attempts by the Soviets since 1961—had all been failures.

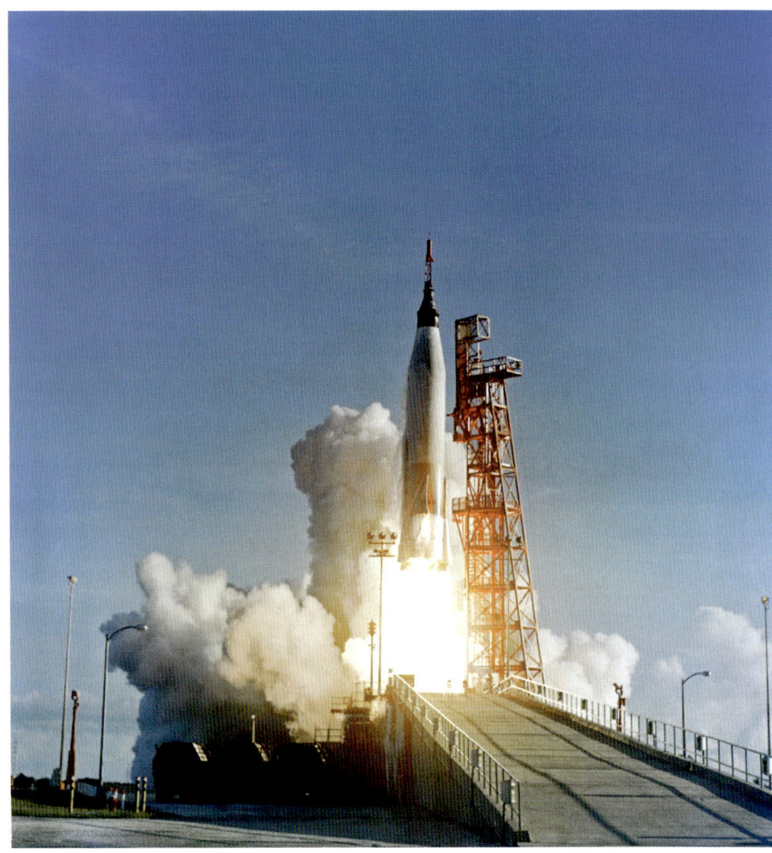

▲ Navy Lt. Cmdr. Walter Schirra Jr., thirty-nine, heads into orbit from the LC-14 launch stand at 7:46 a.m. EST on October 3, 1962, after a near-perfect countdown. He circles the earth six times aboard *Sigma 7*.

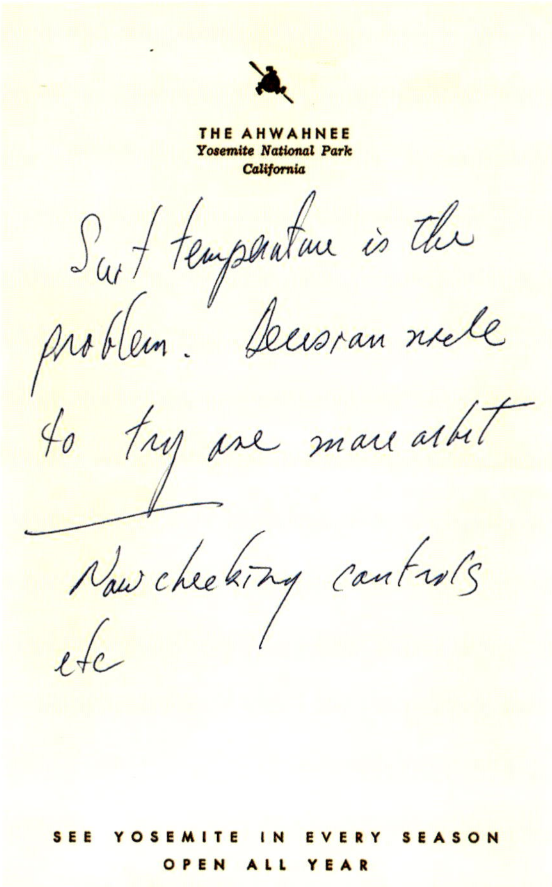

THE AHWAHNEE
Yosemite National Park
California

Suit temperature is the problem. Decision made to try one more orbit

Now checking controls etc

SEE YOSEMITE IN EVERY SEASON
OPEN ALL YEAR

▲ Note handed to the president shortly after he arrived in the Oval Office. Schirra's space suit had begun to overheat after his first orbit, but it was resolved. (The president had visited Yosemite in August.)

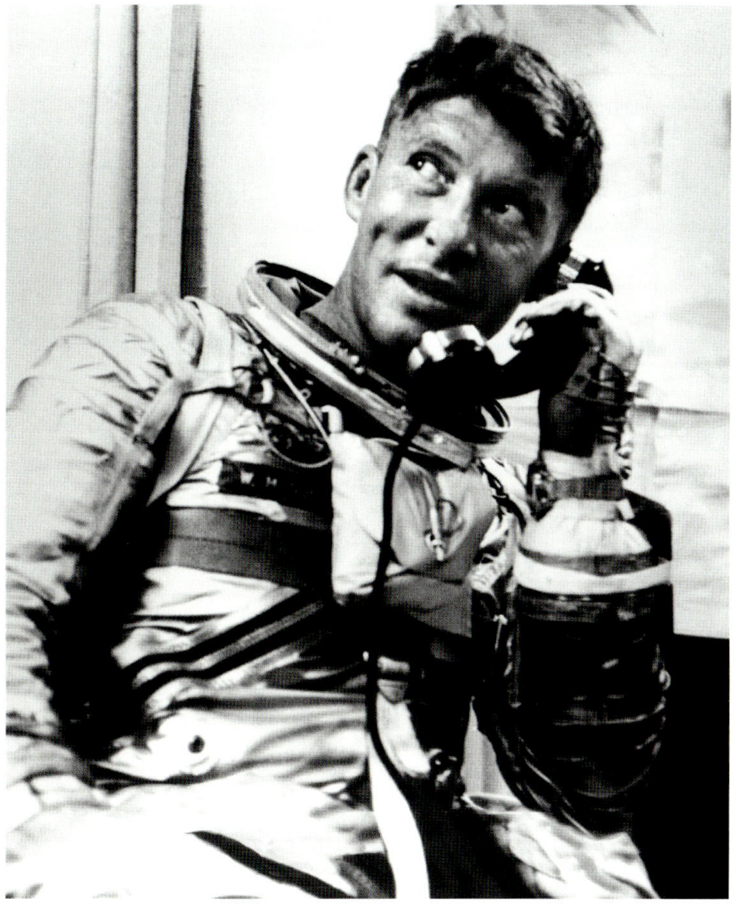

▲ After his six-orbit flight aboard *Sigma 7*, Schirra receives congratulations from Kennedy at 6:17 p.m. in the officer's sickroom aboard the aircraft carrier USS *Kearsarge*.

"I appreciate your coming down [the previous month] and giving our booster a blessing," Schirra tells the president. "It seemed to help."

Schirra would become the only astronaut to fly aboard Mercury, Gemini, and Apollo spacecraft.

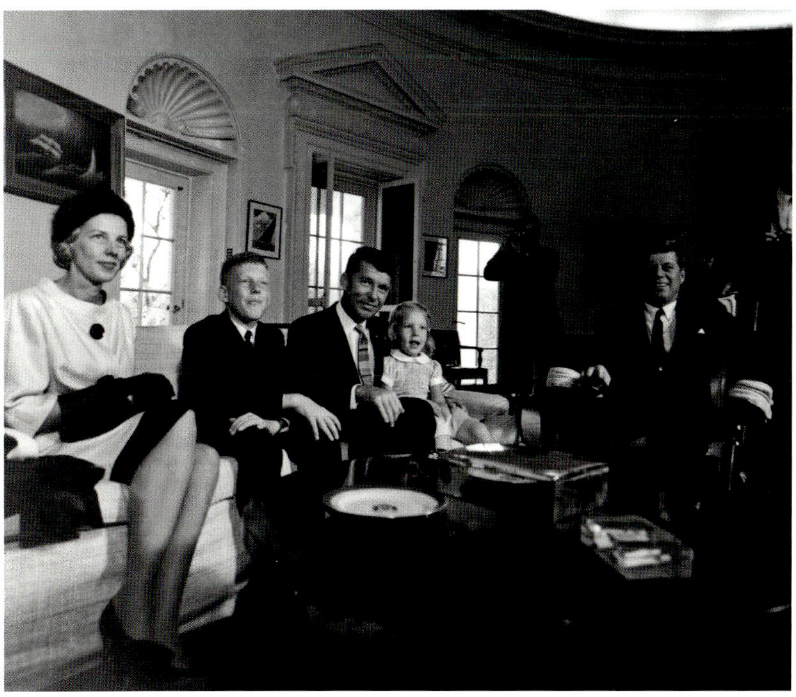

◀ The Schirra family—wife Jo, Walter III, twelve, Schirra, and Suzanne, five—visits with the president in the Oval Office for about twenty minutes on October 16 at 9:30 a.m. EST. Kennedy asks Schirra how zero-gravity felt during his longer flight. The president later takes the family to see the Kennedy children's two ponies on the South Lawn.

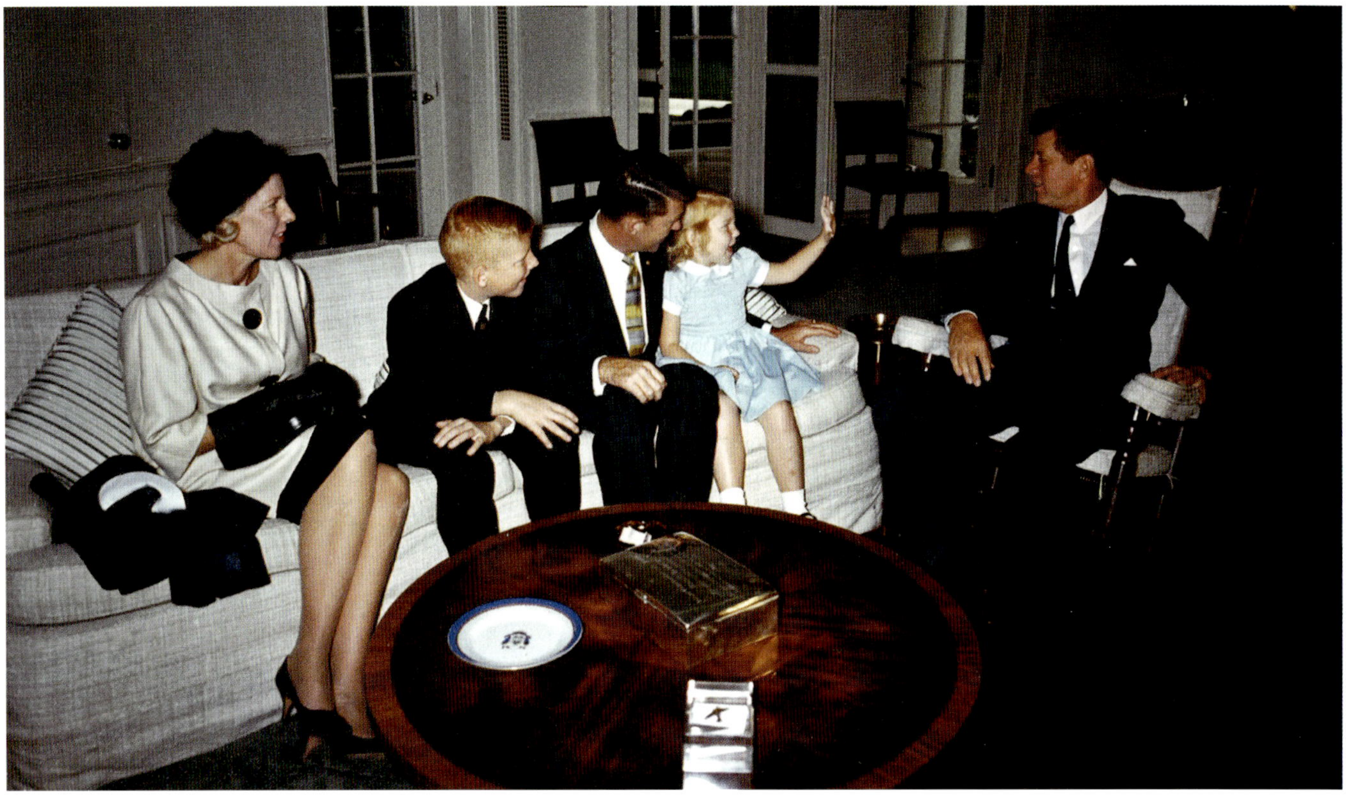

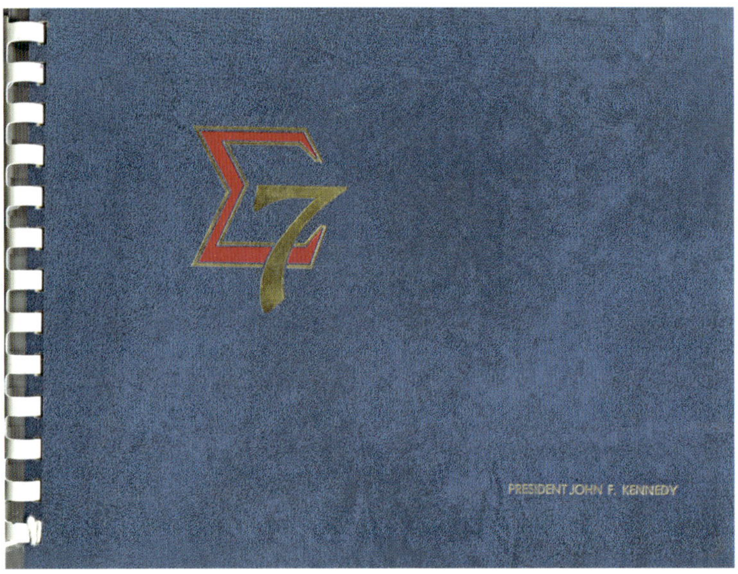

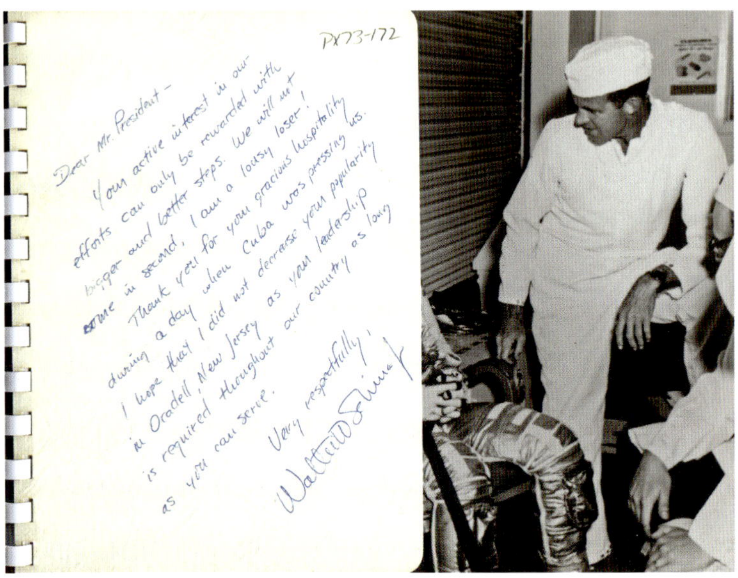

▲ Suzanne shyly tells Kennedy, "I know who you are." Asked her age by the president, she holds up five fingers.

◀ Commemorative photo album Schirra later sends to the president, which bears the *Sigma 7* insignia painted on his spacecraft. (Courtesy of the John F. Kennedy Presidential Library.)

◀ About an hour before the Schirras arrive, National Security Advisor McGeorge Bundy told Kennedy that the CIA has concluded a Soviet missile base is under construction near San Cristobal, Cuba, ninety miles from Florida. Schirra later references the development in his note to the president inside the album.

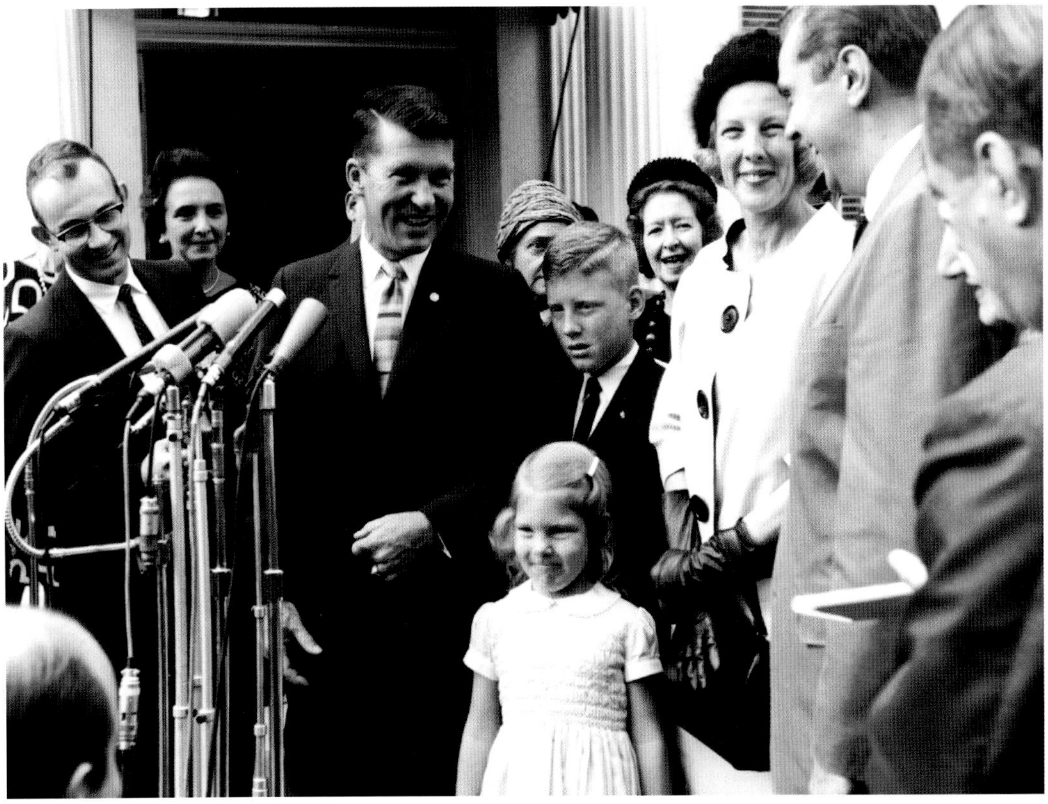

▲ After meeting with the president, Schirra tells reporters outside the White House that Kennedy seems very informed. "It's obvious from his questions that he does a lot of homework," he says. The astronaut had received the NASA Distinguished Service Medal the previous day from Webb in his hometown of Oradell, New Jersey, following a parade from his birthplace, Hackensack. At far left is Westinghouse Broadcasting chief engineer Charles Brailer; May Craig of the *Portland Press-Herald* is between Schirra and his son. UPI's Helen Thomas, second from right, is mostly hidden.

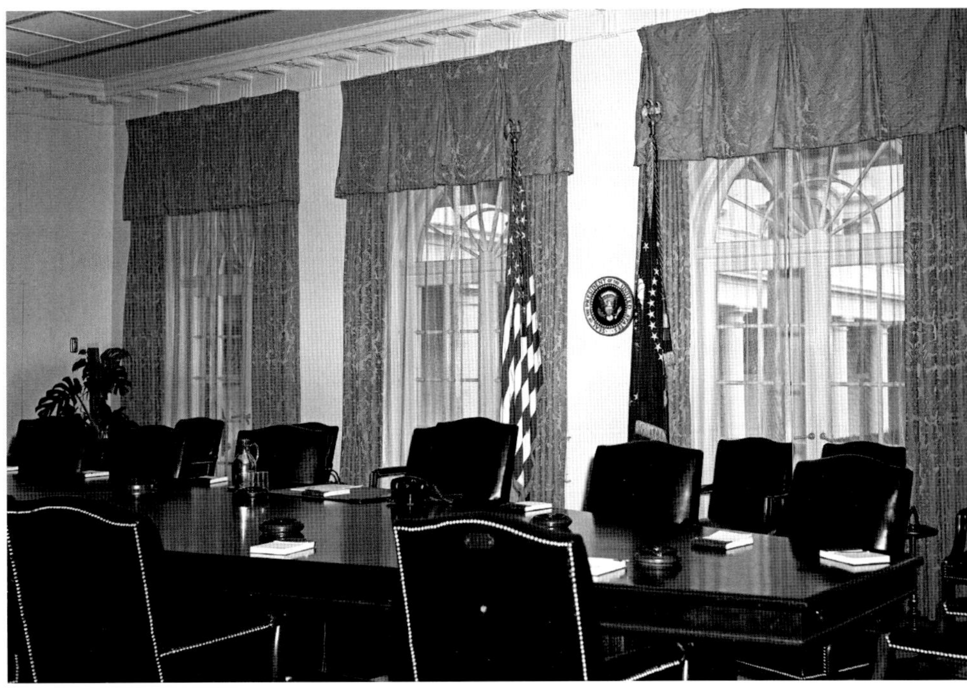

▶ On November 21, 1962, the president meets in the Cabinet Room at 10:00 a.m. with several advisors and NASA officials. The conversation is secretly captured by Kennedy's taping system, installed in July (the tapes will be revealed in 1973).

The subject is whether the administration should ask Congress for more money for NASA. Kennedy wants to make clear he backs the lunar landing program to win the space race with the Soviets, but he is not prepared to spend more on a broad space program.

The White House is represented by Budget Director David Bell and Science Advisor Jerome Wiesner. Webb leads the NASA contingent, made up of Seamans, Holmes, and Hugh Dryden. Below are excerpts of the seventy-three-minute meeting.

Kennedy: "So it's your view that with the 440 million [dollars] . . . you'd probably . . . your judgment is you won't really save any time, is that correct?"

Webb: "In the lunar landing I doubt very much if we'd save much time."

Kennedy: "Now, let me just get back to this, what is your . . . uh, your view is we oughta spend this 440 million?"

Holmes: "My view is that if [we] can strictly spend, it would accelerate the Apollo schedule, yes, sir. Let me say I was very . . . I oughta add that I'm very sorry about this . . . I have no disagreement with Mr. Webb . . . he says with the policy, oh, I think my job is to say how fast I think we can go for what dollars."

Kennedy: "Do you put this program . . . Do you think this program is the top-priority program of the agency?"

Webb: "No, sir, I do not. I think it is one of the top-priority programs, but I think it's very important to recognize here . . . and that you have found what you could do with a rocket as you could find how you could get out beyond the earth's atmosphere and into space and make measurements. Several scientific disciplines that are the very powerful and begin to converge on this area."

Kennedy: "Jim, I think it is the top priority. I think we ought to have that very clear. Some of these other programs can slip six months, or nine months, and nothing strategic is gonna happen, it's gonna . . . But this is important for political reasons, international political reasons. This is, whether we like it or not, in a sense a race. If we get second to the moon, it's nice, but it's like being second any time. So that if we're second by six months, because we didn't give it the kind of priority, then of course that would be very serious. So I think we have to take the view that this is the top priority with us."

Webb: "But the environment of space is where you are going to operate the Apollo and where you are going to do the landing."

Kennedy: "Look, I know all these other things and the satellite and the communications and weather and all, they're all desirable, but they can wait."

Webb: "I'm not putting those . . . I am talking now about the scientific program to understand the space environment within which you got to fly Apollo and make a landing on the moon."

Kennedy: "Wait a minute—is that saying that the lunar program to land the man on the moon is the top priority of the agency, is it?"

Unknown speaker: "And the science that goes with it . . ."

Seamans: "Well, yes, if you add that, the science that is necessary . . ."

Kennedy: "The science . . . Going to the moon is the top-priority project. Now, there are a lot of related scientific information and developments that will come from that which are important. But the whole thrust of the agency, in my opinion, is the lunar program. The rest of it can wait six or nine months."

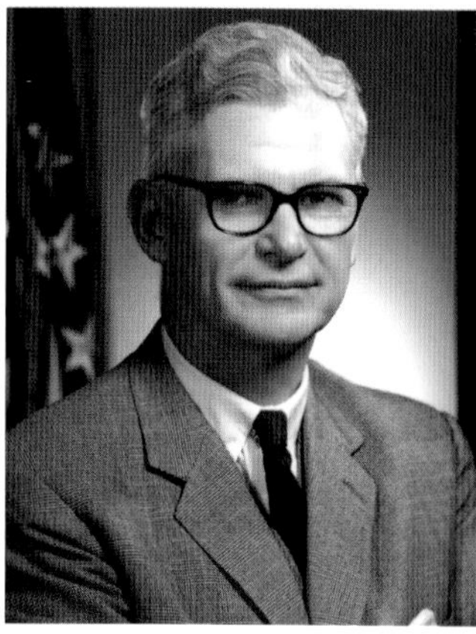

Seamans

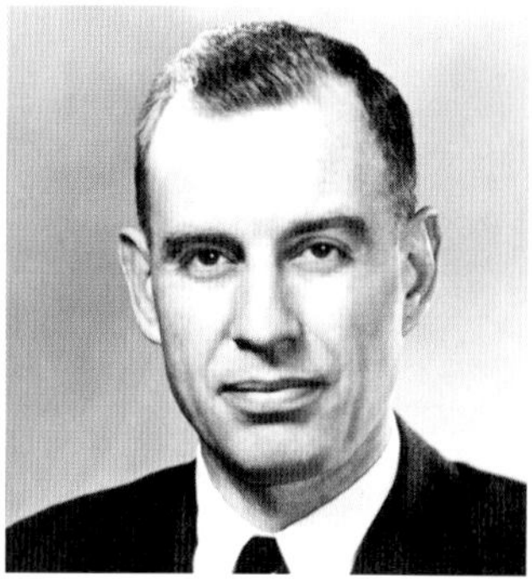

Bell

▶ Wiesner: "Mr. President, I don't think Jim understands some of the scientific problems that are associated with landing on the moon and this is what Dave Bell was trying to say and what I'm trying to say. We don't know a damn thing about the surface of the moon. And we're making the wildest guesses about how we're going to land on the moon, and we could get a terrible disaster from putting something down on the surface of the moon that's very different than we think it is.

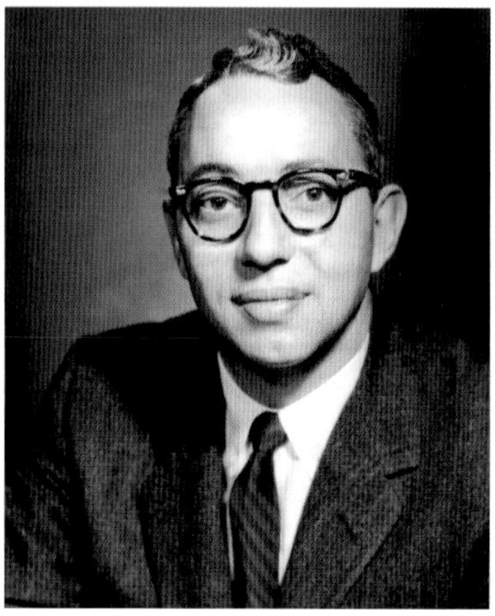

Holmes

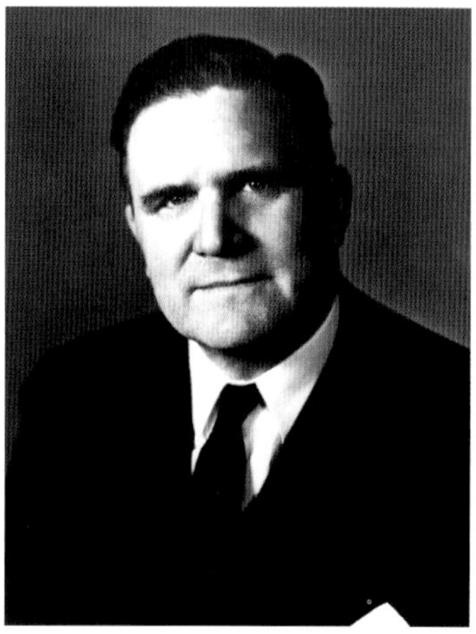

Webb

"And the scientific programs that find us that information have to have the highest priority. But they are associated with the lunar program. The scientific programs that aren't associated with the lunar program can have any priority we please to give 'em."

Kennedy: "Everything that we do ought to really be tied into getting onto the moon ahead of the Russians."

Webb: "Why can't it be tied to preeminence in space, which are your own . . ."

Kennedy: "Because, by God, we keep . . . we've been telling everybody we're preeminent in space for five years and nobody believes it because they have the booster and the satellite. We know all about the number of satellites we put up, two or three times the number of the Soviet Union . . . we're ahead scientifically. It's like that instrument you got up at Stanford which is costing us 125 million dollars and everybody tells me that we're the number one in the world. And what is it? I can't think what it is."

Multiple speakers: "The linear accelerator."

Kennedy: "I'm sorry, that's wonderful, but nobody knows anything about it!"

"We're not going to settle the 400 million this morning. I want to take a look closely at what Dave Bell . . . But I do think we ought to get it, you know, really clear that the policy ought to be that this is the top-priority program of the agency, and one of the two things, except for defense, the top priority of the United States government. I think that that is the position we ought to take.

"Now, this may not change anything about that schedule, but at least we ought to be clear, otherwise we shouldn't be spending this kind of money because I'm not that interested in space. I think it's good; I think we ought to know about it; we're ready to spend reasonable amounts of money.

"But we're talking about these fantastic expenditures which wreck our budget and all these other domestic programs and the only justification for it, in my opinion, to do it in this time or fashion, is because we hope to beat them and demonstrate that starting behind, as we did by a couple years, by God, we passed them."

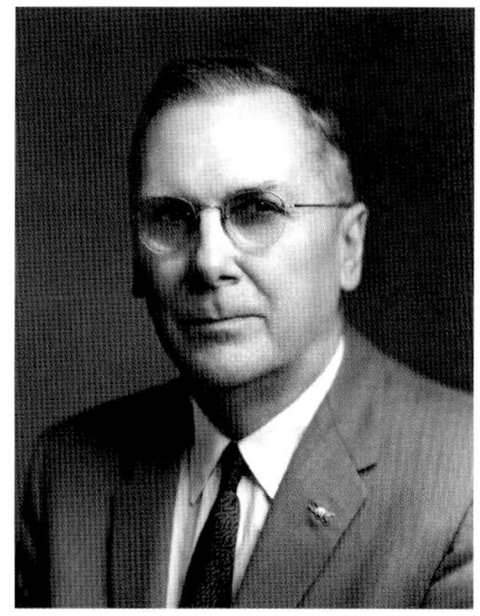

Dryden

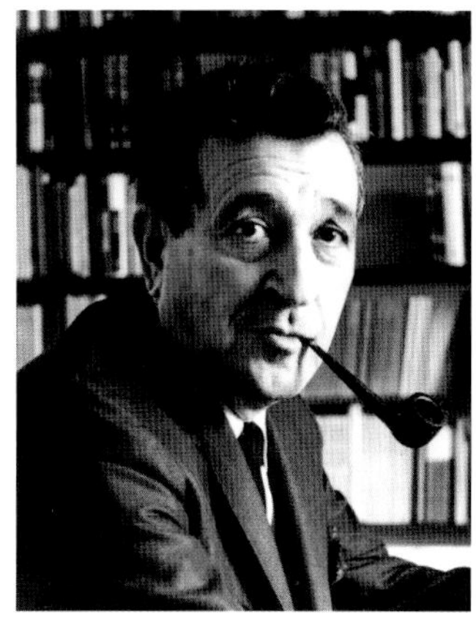

Wiesner

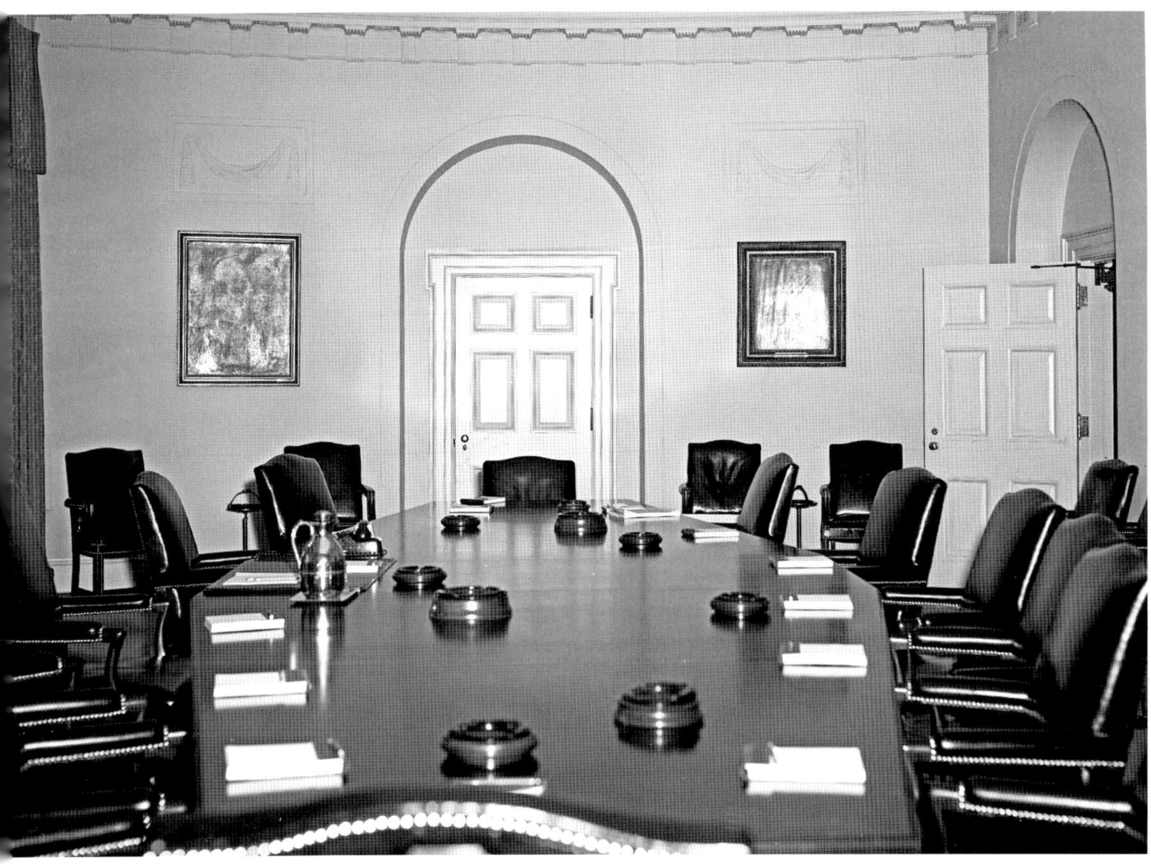

▶ On December 7, 1962, the president visits the Los Alamos Scientific Laboratory (LASL) in Los Alamos, New Mexico, arriving from Santa Fe Municipal Airport at 2:40 p.m. MST for a briefing on Project Rover. The lab's goal is to develop a rocket engine that would use a small nuclear reactor to heat the propellant. Advocates hope the technology might provide power for the third stage of the Saturn C-5 moon rocket among other applications.

The president and Sen. Clinton Anderson (D-N.Mex.) are greeted by Los Alamos Director Norris Bradbury, Rep. Albert Thomas, and Atomic Energy Commission (AEC) Commissioner James Ramey.

After a practice run kicks up too much dust, the helipad is expanded to accommodate the six helicopters carrying some thirty guests in the president's party. Kennedy had flown that morning from Andrews AFB to visit the USAF's SAC headquarters at Offutt AFB in Omaha, Nebraska, before landing in Santa Fe at 2:00 p.m. and choppering to Los Alamos aboard Marine One.

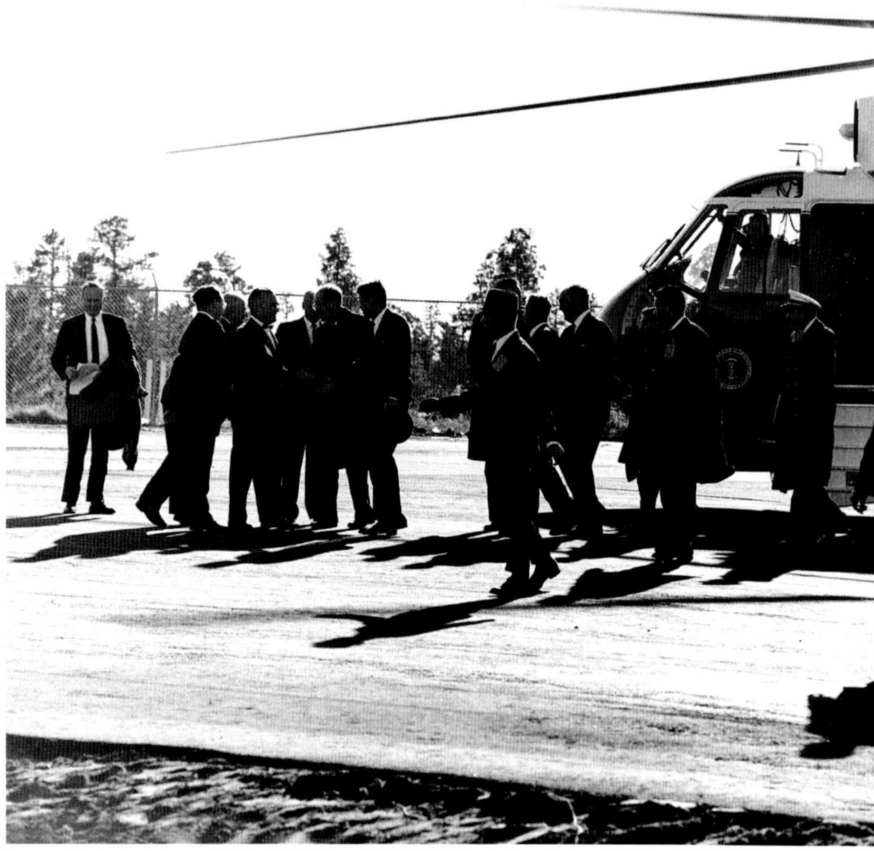

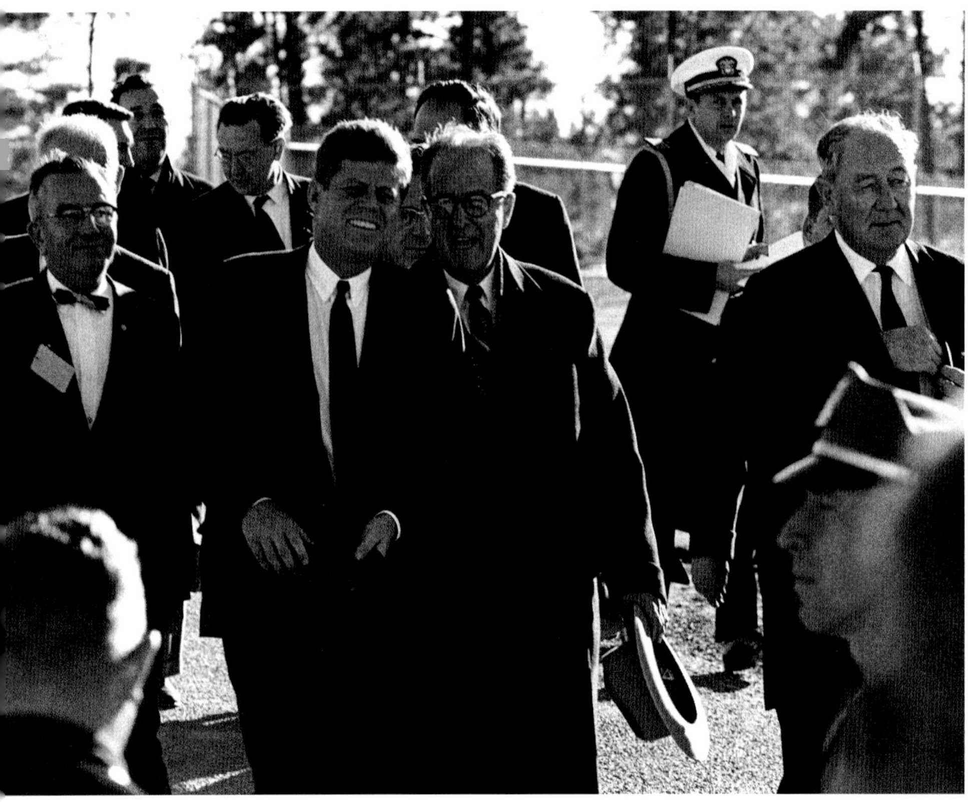

◀ The president walks toward the Chemistry and Metallurgy Research (CMR) Building, flanked by Rep. Thomas (left) and Sen. Anderson. LASL was founded to coordinate the Manhattan Project's nuclear weapons research during World War II and was key in the development of many nuclear weapons including the hydrogen bomb. (Courtesy of Los Alamos National Laboratory Archives.)

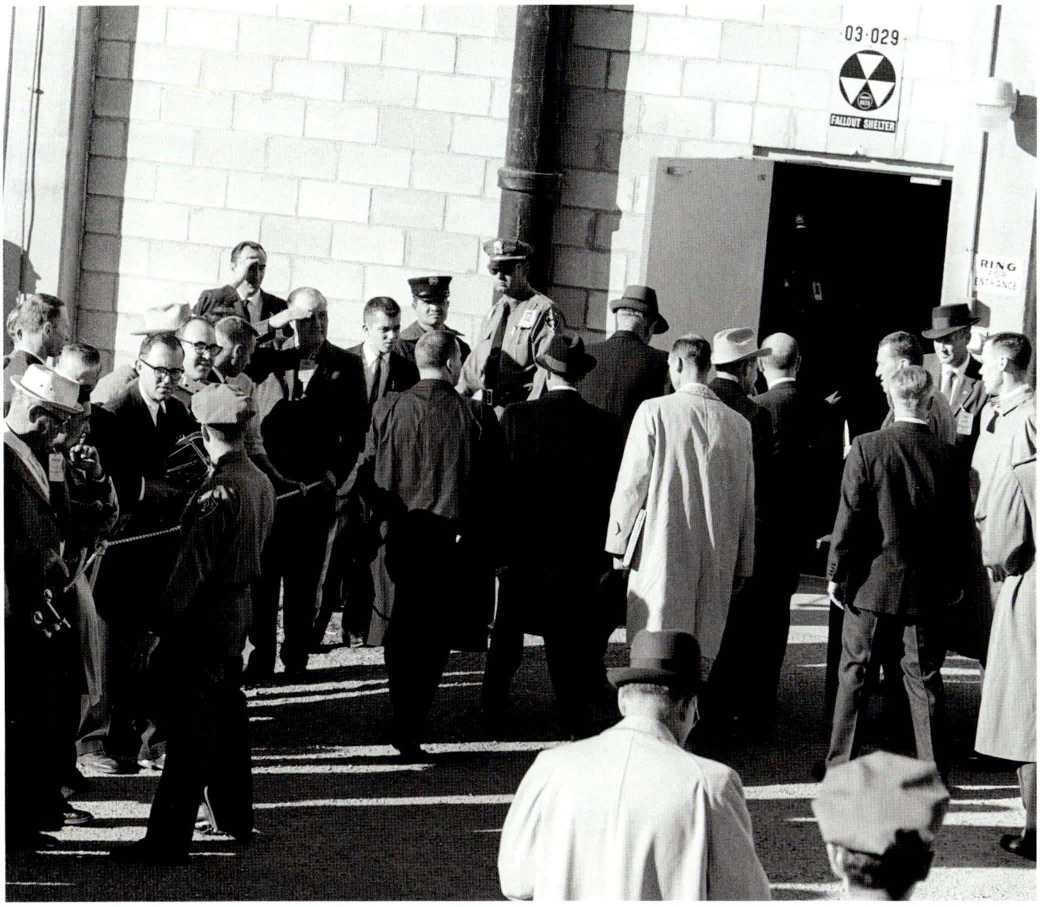

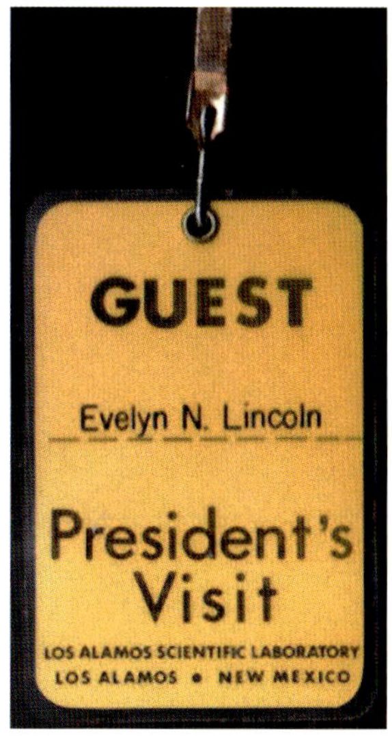

▲ Vice President Johnson, who has arrived first, leads a group into Wing 9 of the CMR Building with reporters at left. The CMR is LASL's largest analytical chemistry laboratory, performing metallurgical research on radioactive materials in support of nuclear weapons programs. Wing 9 has just been completed.

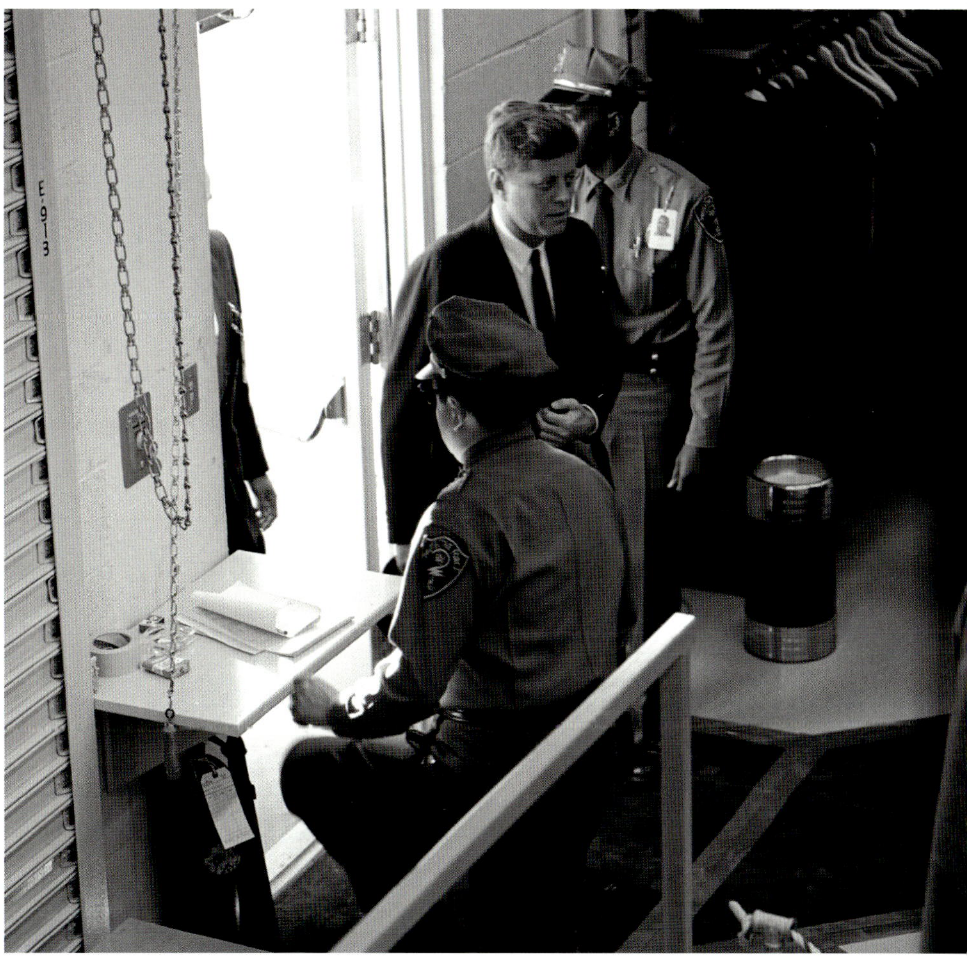

▶ The president enters the CMR Building at 2:45 p.m. (Courtesy of Los Alamos National Laboratory Archives.)

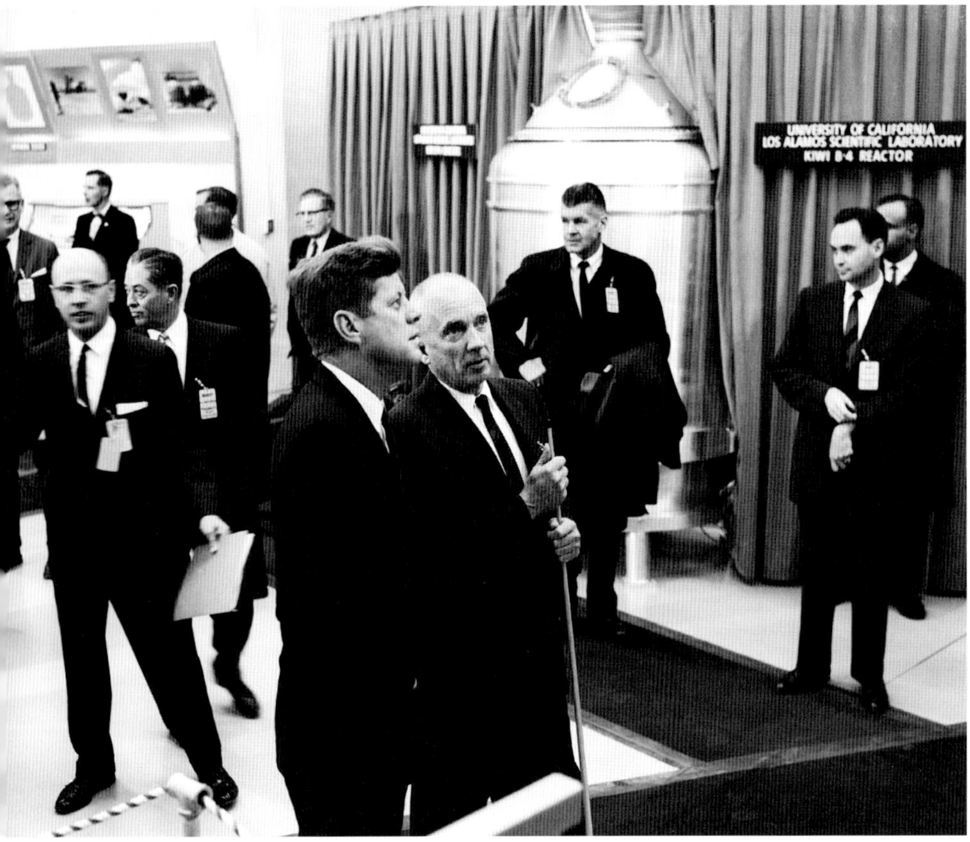

◀ In an exhibit area set up for the visit, Bradbury explains the research under way to develop nuclear propulsion reactors, with a full-scale mockup of a Kiwi B4 reactor at center. Kiwi B4A had failed during testing a week earlier; the president would visit its test site in Nevada the next day. NASA's Robert Seamans is at far left. AEC manager Dwight Ink (glasses) is second from left with Rep. Joseph Montoya (D-N.Mex.) behind him (looking away). Second from right is Harold Finger, manager of the Space Nuclear Propulsion Office, which serves as a liaison with MSFC. Agent Jerry Behn holds the president's hat and coat.

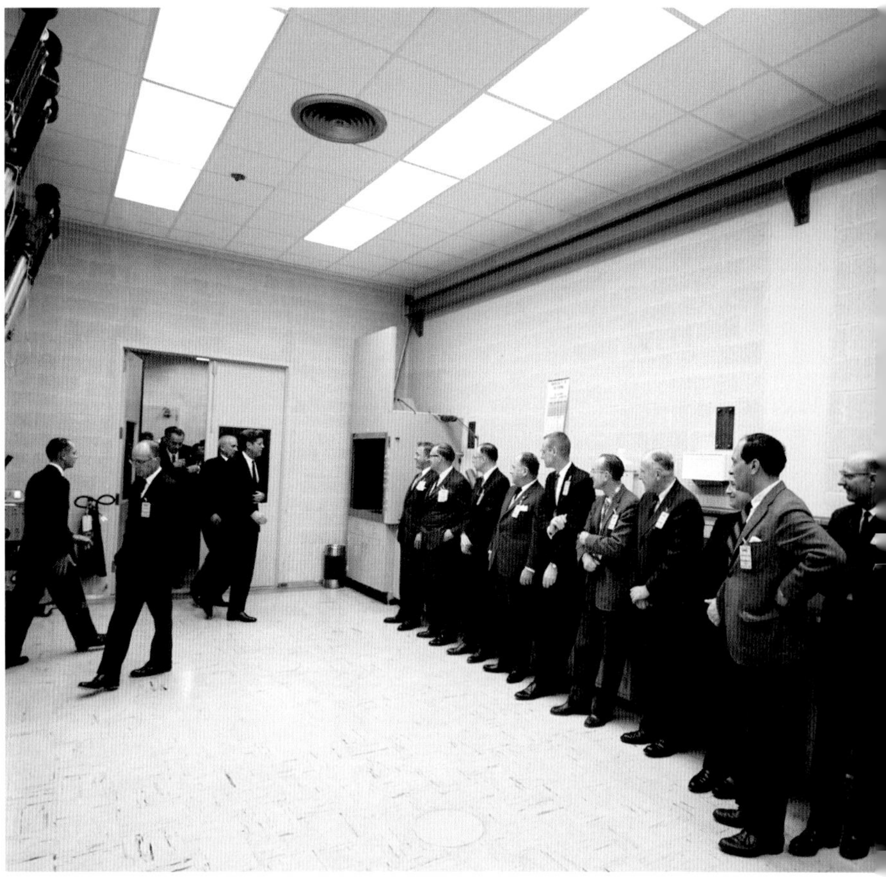

▶ After a forty-minute classified briefing on Rover, Kennedy and his party meet LASL's leading scientists and members of the Rover team at a reception at 3:25 p.m. The room has remote manipulators (at upper left) to safely handle radioactive material in "hot cells," but no such material has been brought into the new wing yet. (Courtesy of Los Alamos National Laboratory Archives.)

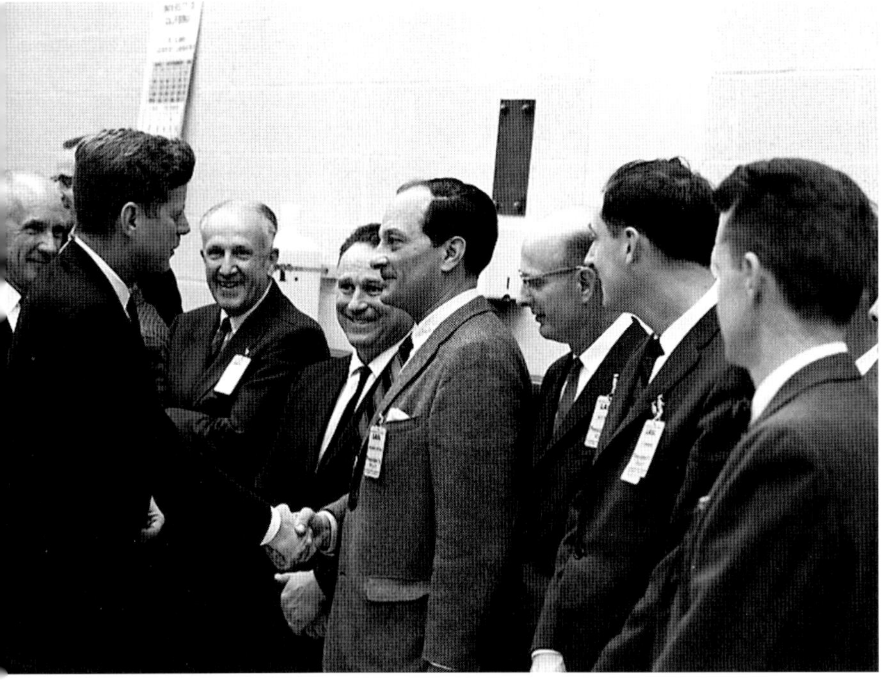

◀ Kennedy shakes hands with Stanislaw Ulam, a Polish American mathematician and a key figure in developing the first atomic bombs. In 1951 Ulam and Edward Teller had developed the modern design of all US thermonuclear weapons.

L–R: Bradbury; Kennedy; Robert Fowler, CMF division leader; Melvin Bowman, CMB group leader; Ulm; unidentified; Fred Edeskuty, assistant cryogenics group leader; and Frank Durham, division leader.

▼ The president by a display of nuclear engine components and materials, with Bradbury at his right, and LASL Deputy Director Darol Froman next to him. (Courtesy of Los Alamos National Laboratory Archives.)

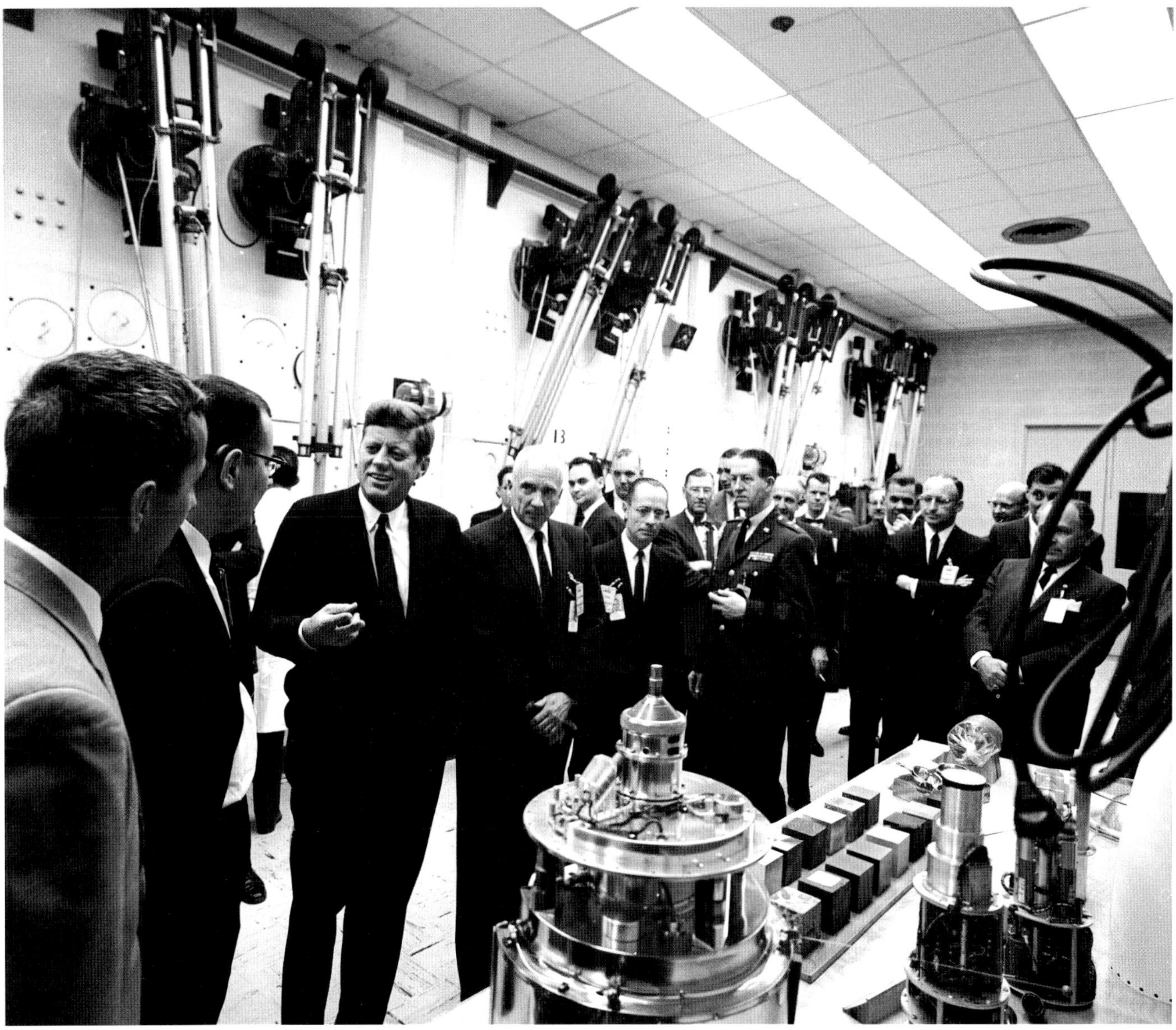

▶ Coffee, tea, and pastries await the guests. L–R: David S. Schaffer, hot cell tech; Mahlon T. Wilson, staff; F. Joseph Fitzgibbon, chief hot cell tech; Ethan "Swede" Eckberg, hot cell tech; Calvin Burwell, staff; Virginia Lyon, food services supervisor; Glenn Mottaz, hot cell tech; and Mildred J. Frentzel, dietician.

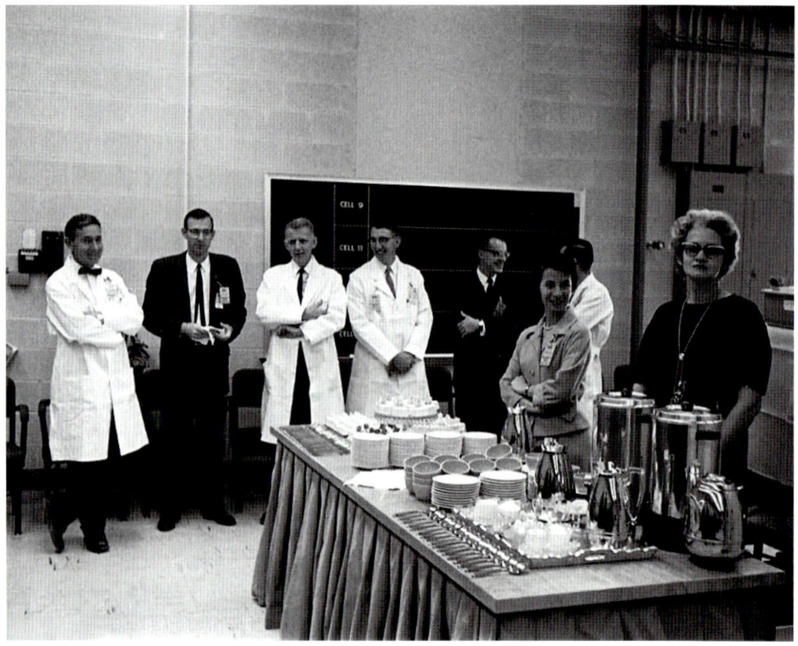

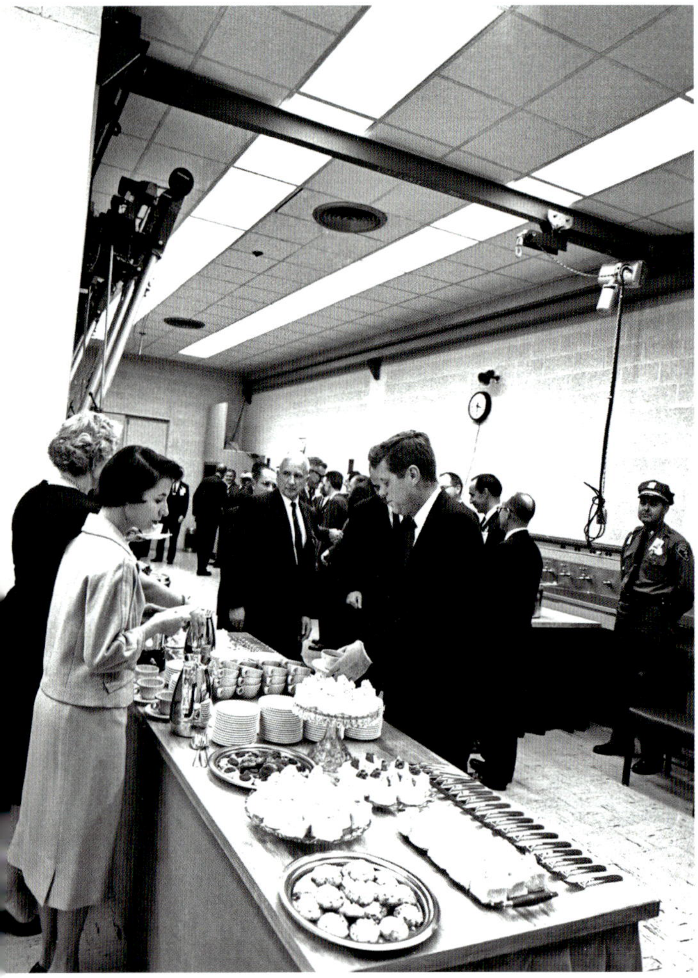

▲ The president helps himself to a cup of coffee at the reception. Observers say the president took his coffee with three teaspoons of sugar "and much too much cream." Bradbury is seen at center. (Courtesy of Los Alamos National Laboratory Archives.)

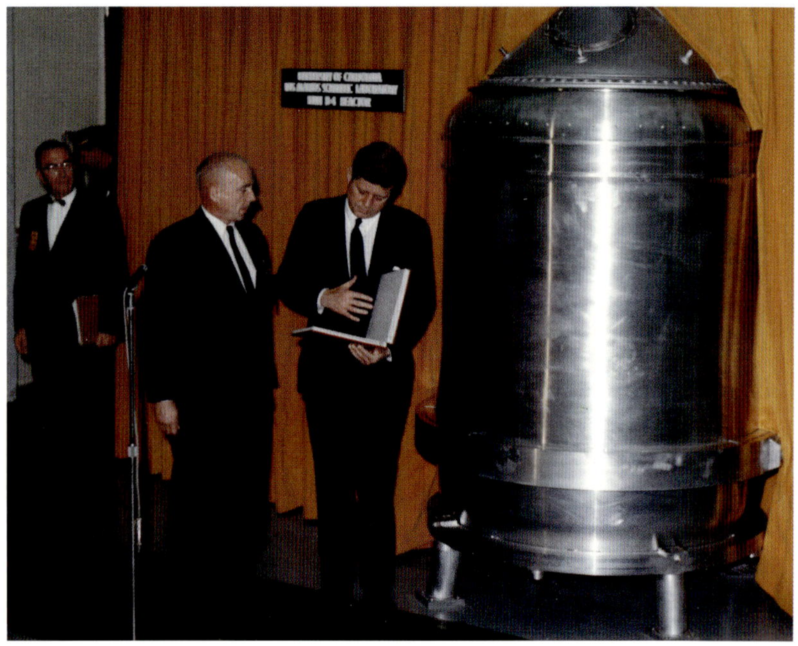

▲ About 3:40 p.m. the president receives a photo album from Bradbury near the Kiwi mockup just before he leaves. The classified aspects of the mockup are in a cutaway on the other side of the curtain. Rep. Albert Thomas is at left. (Courtesy of Los Alamos National Laboratory Archives.)

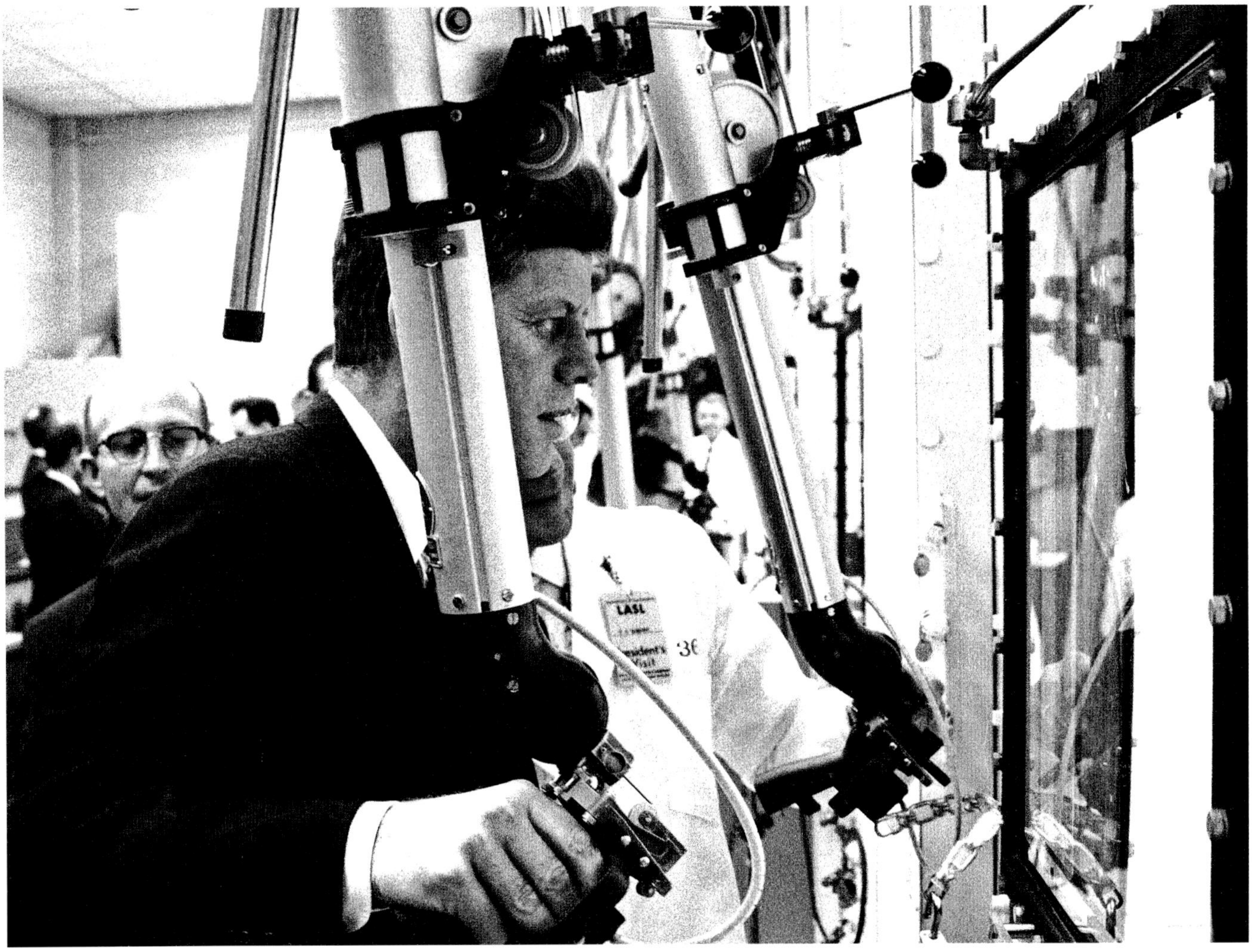

◥ Technician Hoyt Newbury shows the president how to operate a remote manipulator for a hot cell. The manipulator fingergrips and Kennedy's coffee cup and saucer were later displayed in the building and are now part of the Bradbury Science Museum collection in Los Alamos. (Courtesy of Los Alamos National Laboratory Archives.)

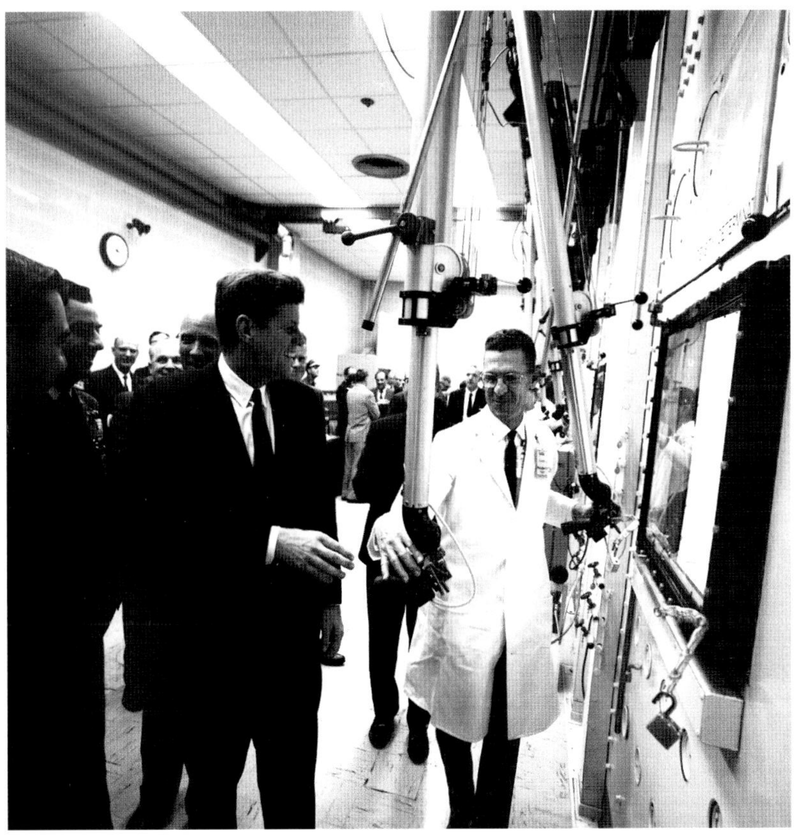

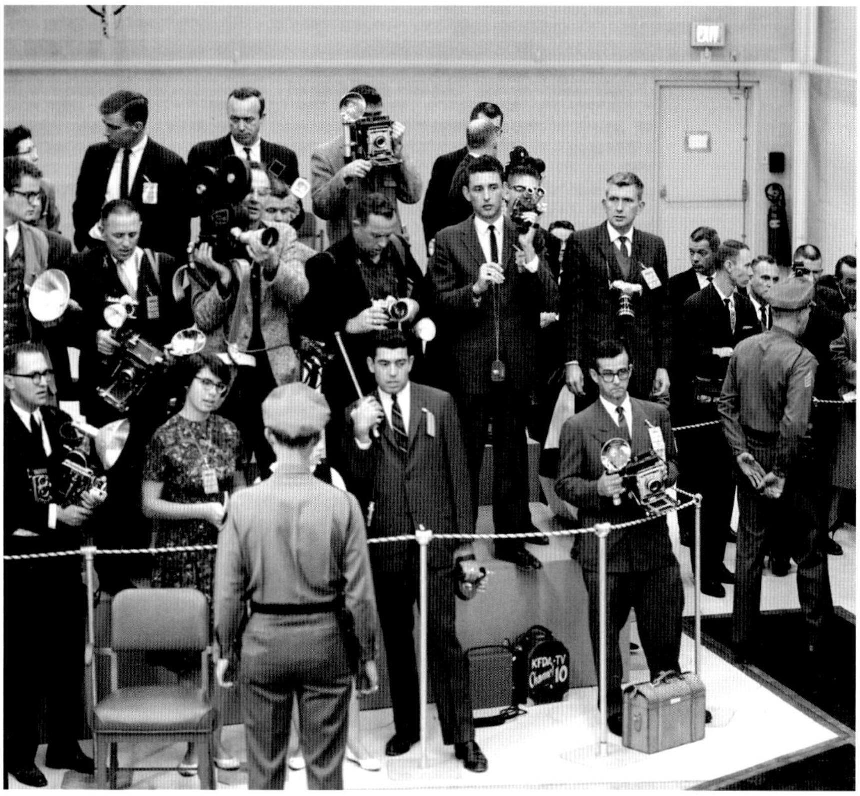

Reporters and photographers are admitted for a photo opportunity with the president in the CMR Building shortly before his departure. Newly named CBS News Southern Bureau Chief Dan Rather is third from left in the front row, holding a "shotgun" mic in his right hand, cabled to his cameraman with a 16mm Auricon camera in the second row, and holding a silent 16mm camera in his left. KFDA-TV (on the camera case) is the CBS affiliate in Amarillo, Texas.

The president's Lincoln departs LASL at about 3:45 p.m. on the way to a speech at Los Alamos High School, about a two-minute drive from the laboratory. Lincolns for the president's party are furnished by the Jones Motor Co. in Albuquerque. (Courtesy of Los Alamos National Laboratory Archives.)

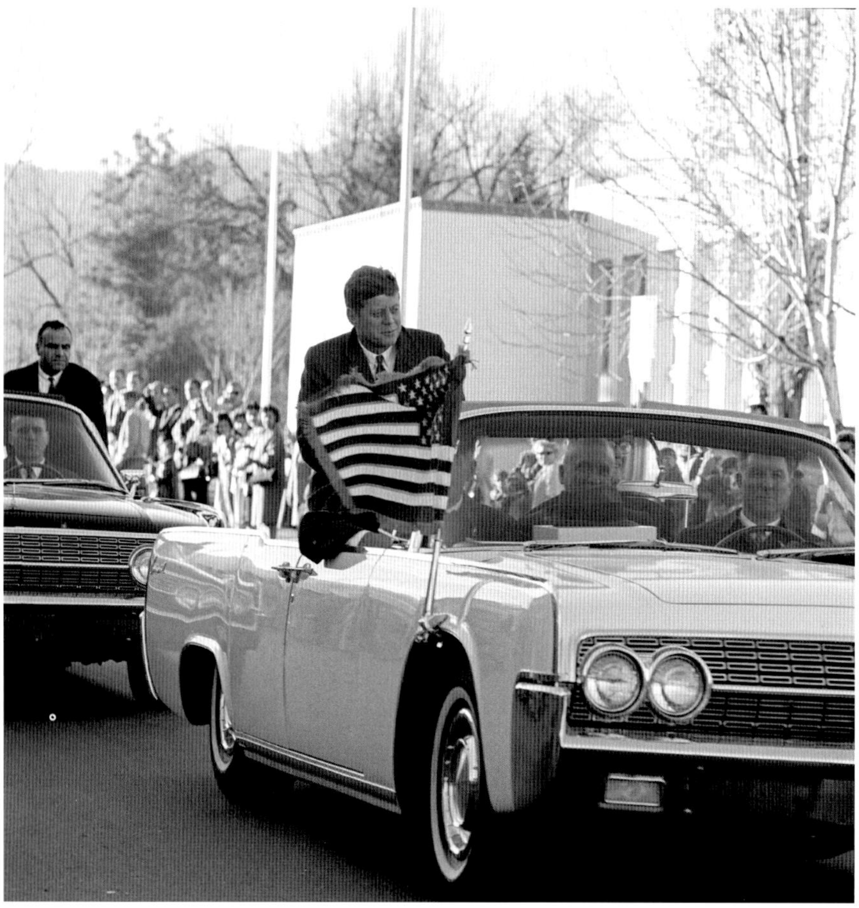

Residents along the motorcade route prepared a welcome display for the president at right.

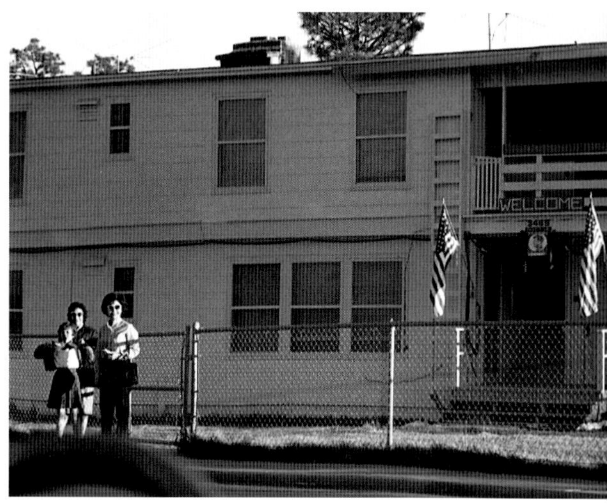

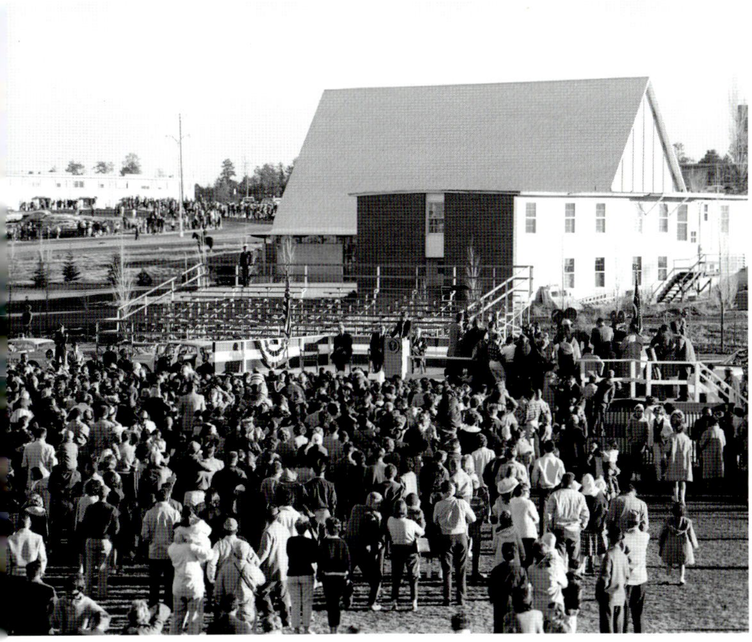

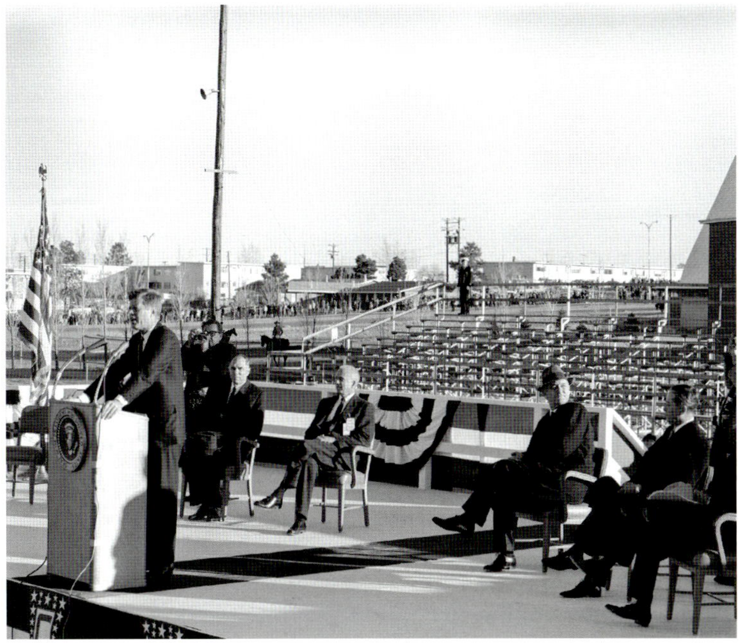

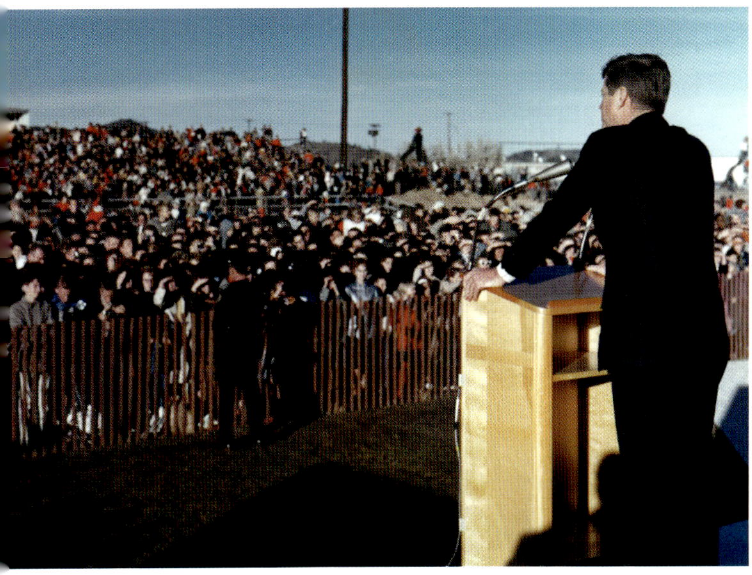

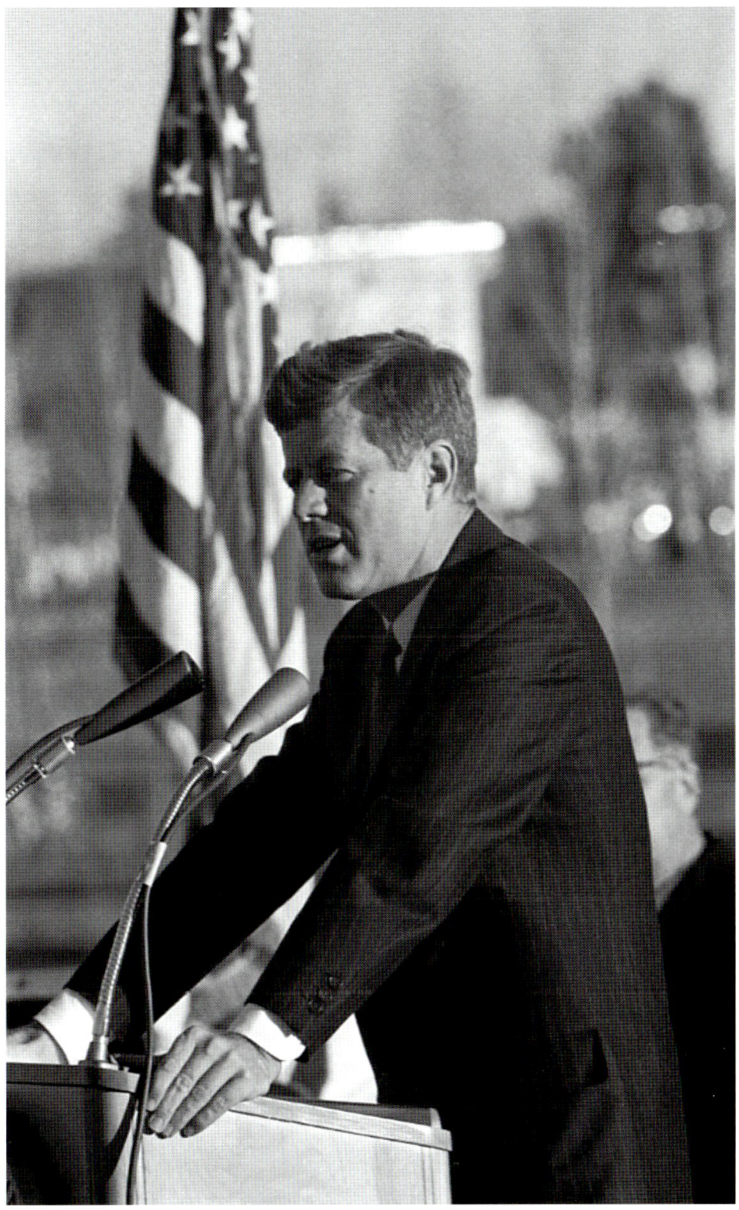

◥ The president addresses a crowd of about six thousand at the football field of Los Alamos High School at 3:51 p.m., speaking for six minutes. (Courtesy of Los Alamos National Laboratory Archives.)

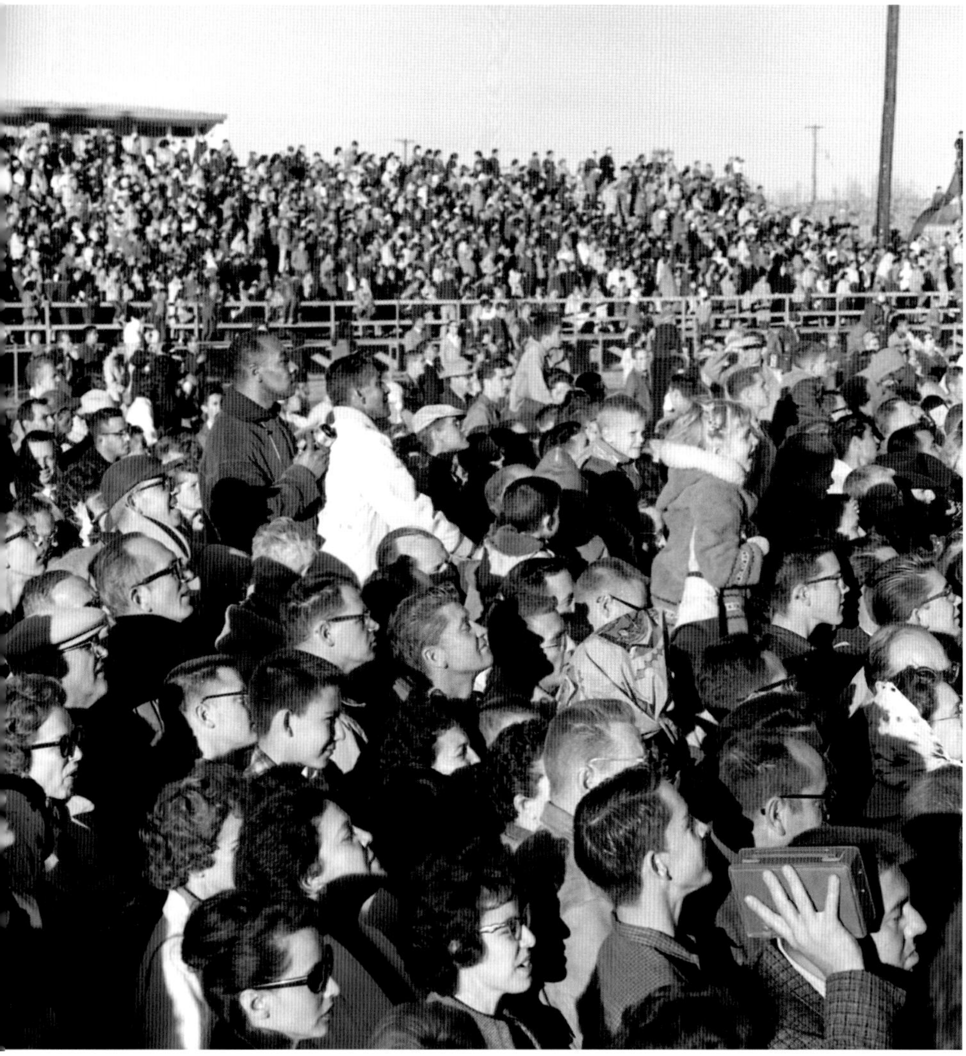

“The United States maintains the largest navy in the world,” the president says.

The United States maintains the largest strategic air force in the world. The United States today has hundreds of our sons and brothers in Vietnam and Thailand and all around the globe who in some cases are fighting and in some cases dying for the maintenance of other countries’ freedom as well as their own. . . . There is no group of people in this country whose record over the last 20 years has been more pre-eminent in the service of their country than all of you here in this small community in New Mexico.

We want to express our thanks to you. It’s not merely what was done during the days of the second war, but what has been done since then, not only in developing weapons of destruction which, by an irony of fate, help maintain the peace and freedom, but also in medicine and in space, and all the other related fields which can mean so much to mankind if we can maintain the peace and protect our freedom. (Courtesy of Los Alamos National Laboratory Archives.)

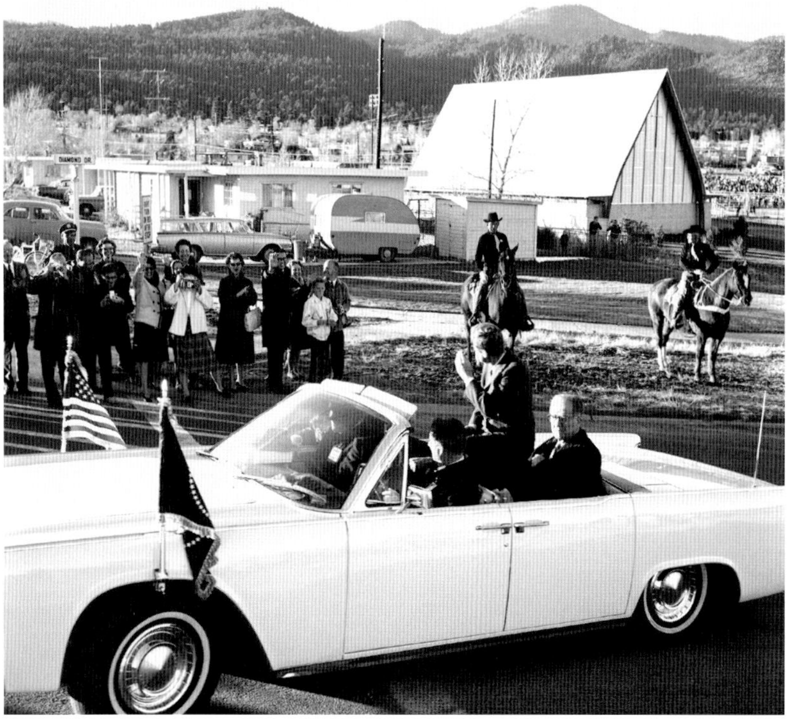

The president and Anderson pass two mounted deputies of the Los Alamos County Sheriff’s Office at right as the motorcade returns to Los Alamos Airport at 4:00 p.m., arriving eight minutes later. The airport was built in 1947 by the Atomic Energy Commission as part of LASL; today it is owned and operated by the county.

They next fly by helicopter to Kirtland AFB near Albuquerque, New Mexico. As New Mexico’s senior senator, Anderson is a major proponent of Project Rover. (Courtesy of Los Alamos National Laboratory Archives.)

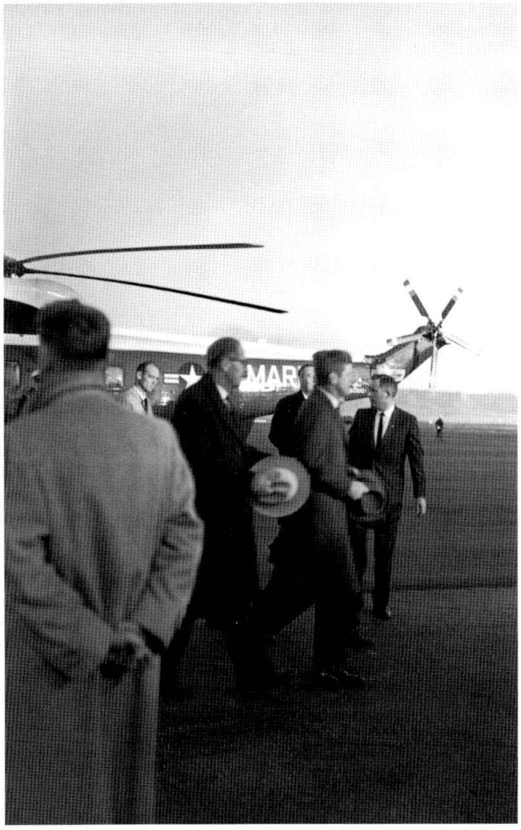

▲ Anderson and Kennedy arrive at Kirtland AFB, colocated with Albuquerque Sunport, at 4:30 p.m.

▼ After brief remarks the presidential party leaves at 4:56 p.m. on a thirty-minute motorcade to Sandia Laboratory, also located at Kirtland.

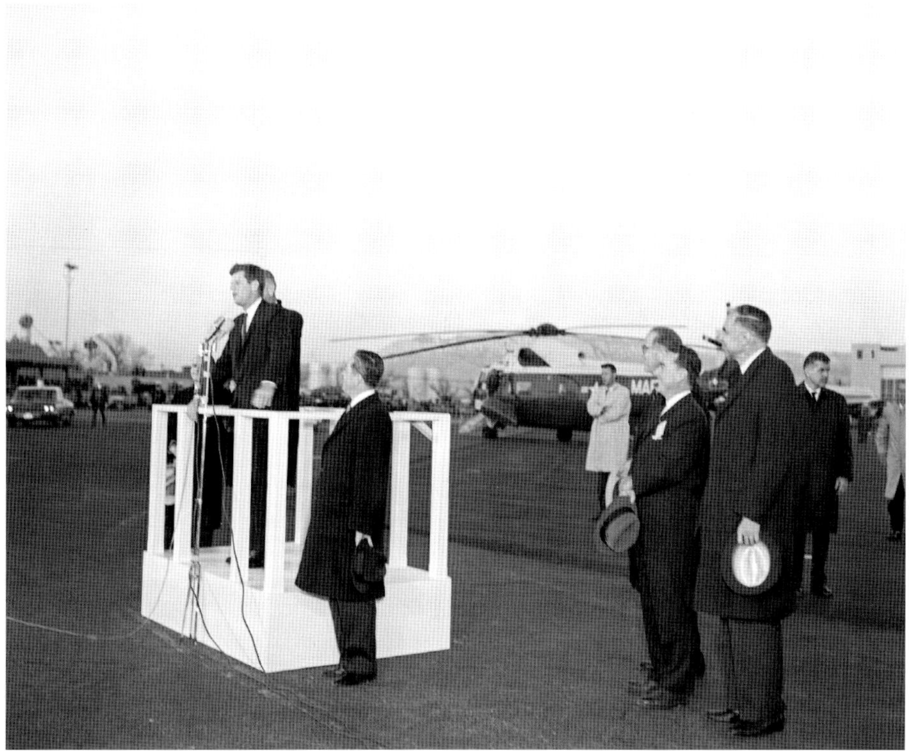

▶ Workers line the main road of Technical Area 1, which includes buildings devoted to Sandia's administration and the development of weapon systems components.

The nine-thousand-acre national laboratory was established in 1948 to develop, engineer, and test the nonnuclear components of nuclear weapons. It is managed and operated for the federal government at the time by Western Electric, an AT&T subsidiary.

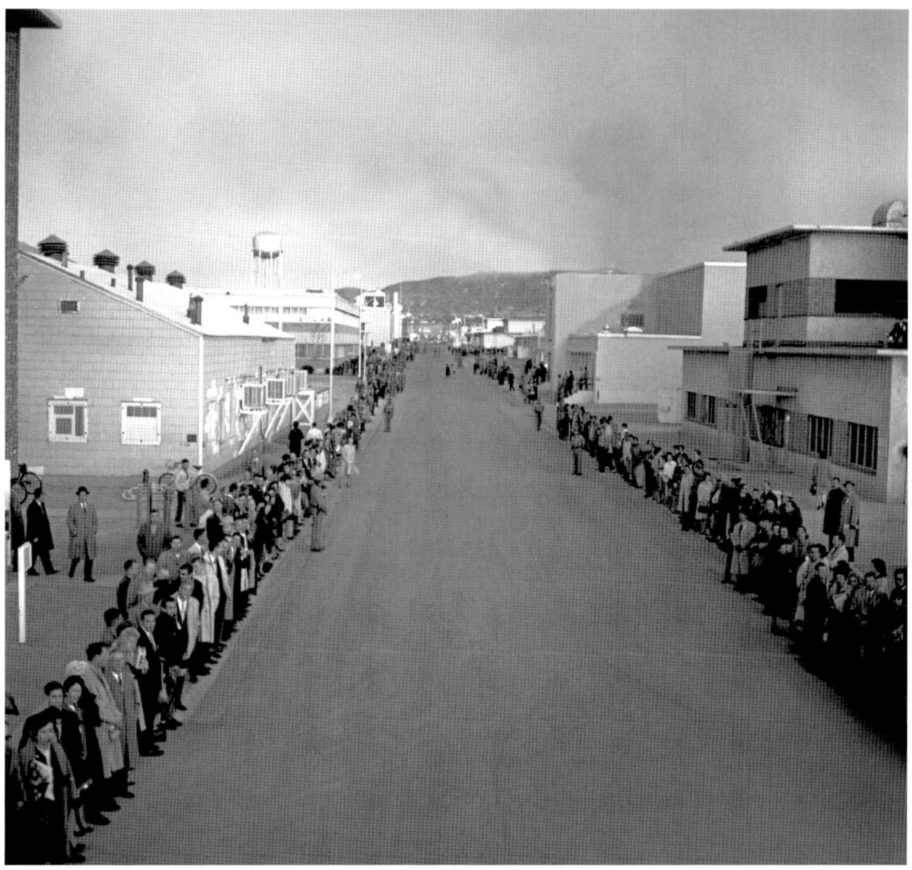

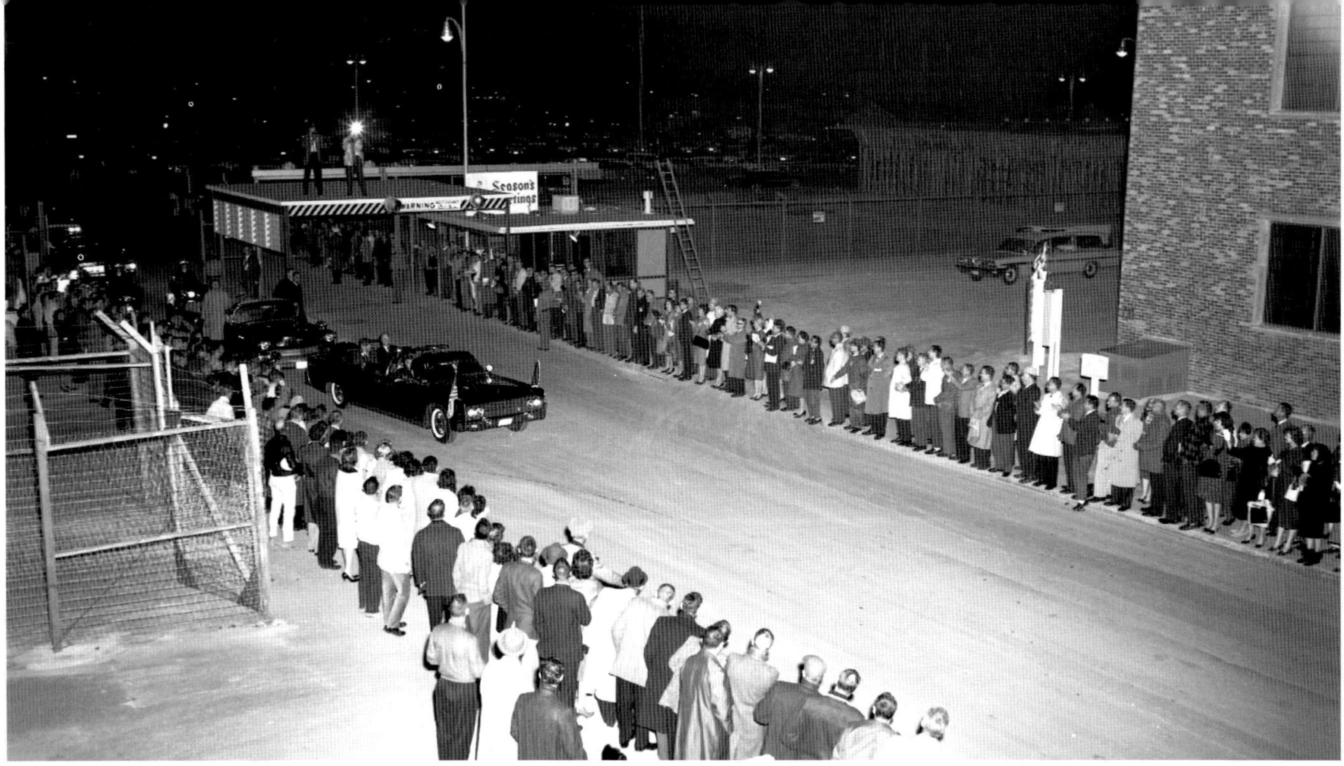

▲ The president arrives at Sandia Laboratory at 5:34 p.m.

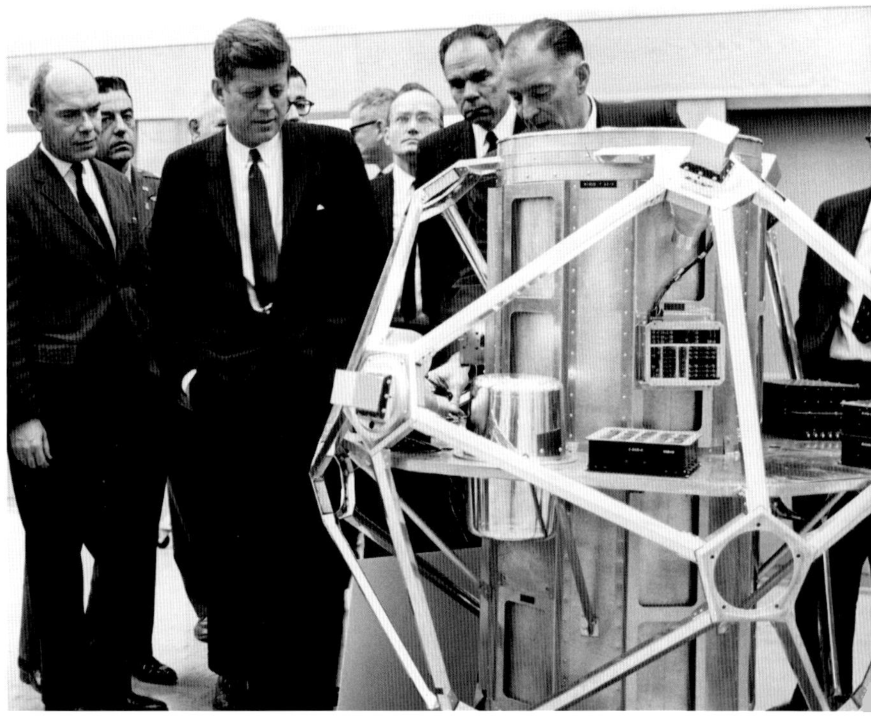

▶ Sandia President Siegmund Schwartz shows the president the sensors and interior components of a Vela nuclear detection satellite, with AEC Chairman Glenn Seaborg behind him and National Security Advisor McGeorge Bundy to his right. The Vela series is being developed by Sandia and LASL to verify compliance with the Limited Test Ban Treaty, which Kennedy would sign in 1963.

The president also receives a top secret briefing from AEC and Sandia managers. This is one of the few interior photos released, and most were altered to white out other displays and hardware.

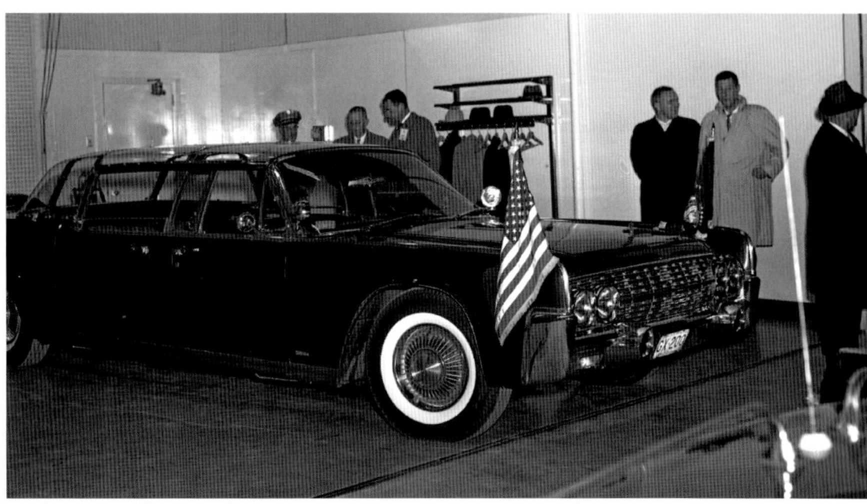

▶ SS-100-X is ready to depart from a loading dock in Building 892, a major weapons sub-assembly facility. The limo's six-piece Plexiglas bubble top, stored in the trunk, is installed for the trip to Albuquerque. The Plexiglas is not bullet-proof.

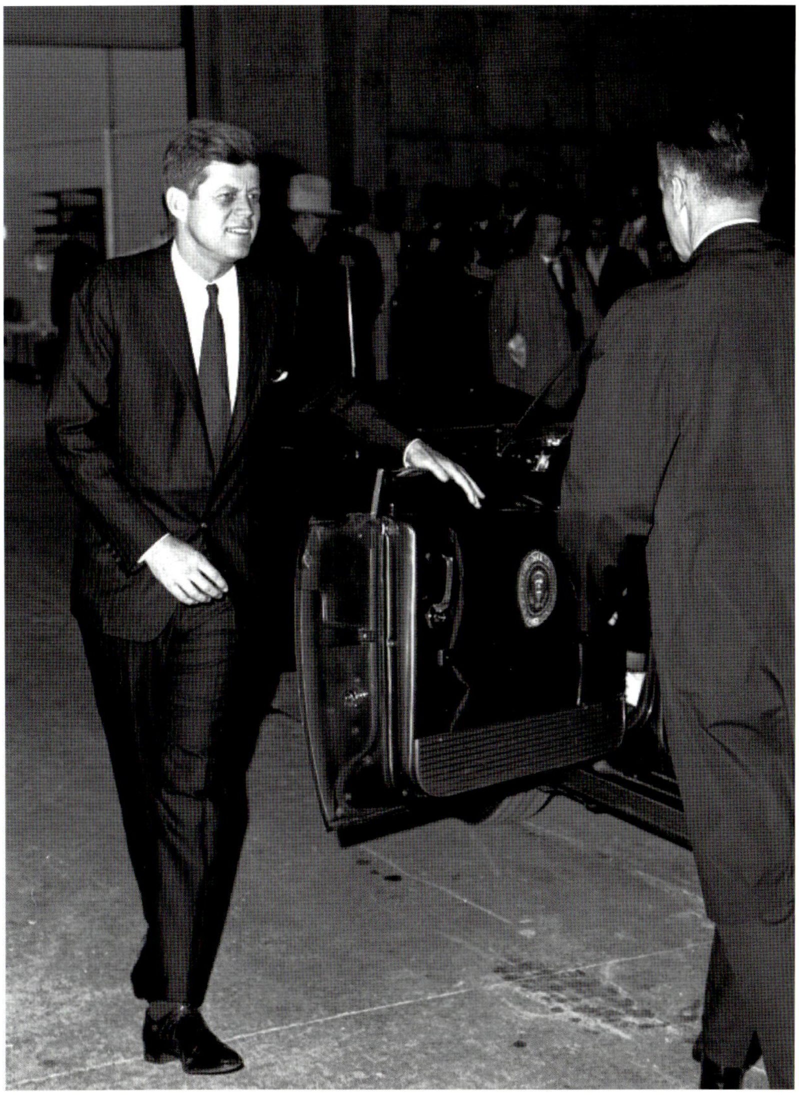

◀ The president enters SS-100-X as he departs for the Western Skies Motor Hotel, where he will spend the night. (Courtesy of Sandia National Laboratories.)

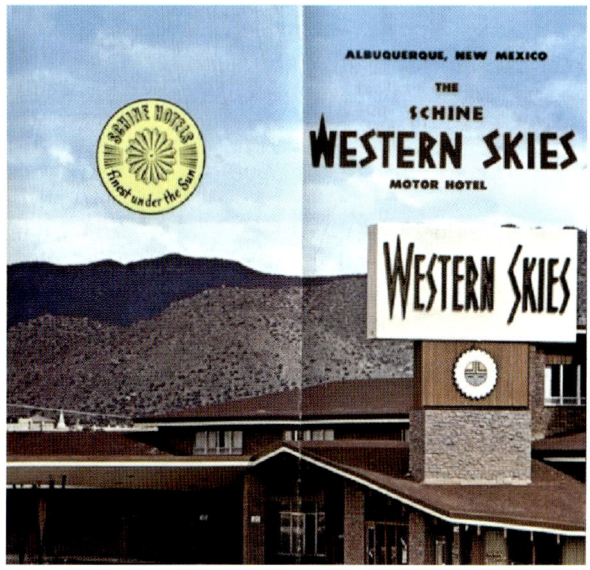

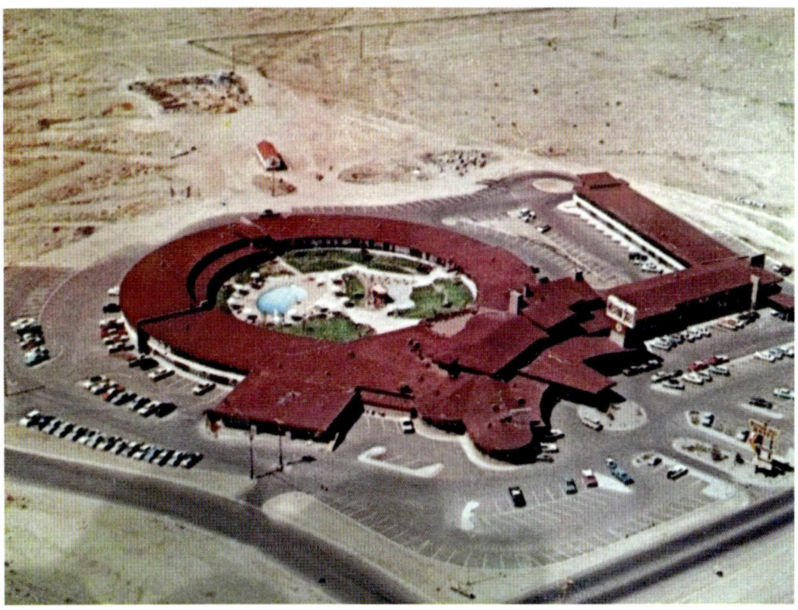

◀ The hotel manager's family gave up their room, subsequently known as the Presidential Suite, to accommodate Kennedy. "He was very cordial," the manager recalled, "and gave me a PT-109 pin." Robert Kennedy, Marilyn Monroe, Elvis Presley, Jordan's King Hussein, and other VIPs stayed at the hotel, which opened in 1959 and was demolished in 1988.

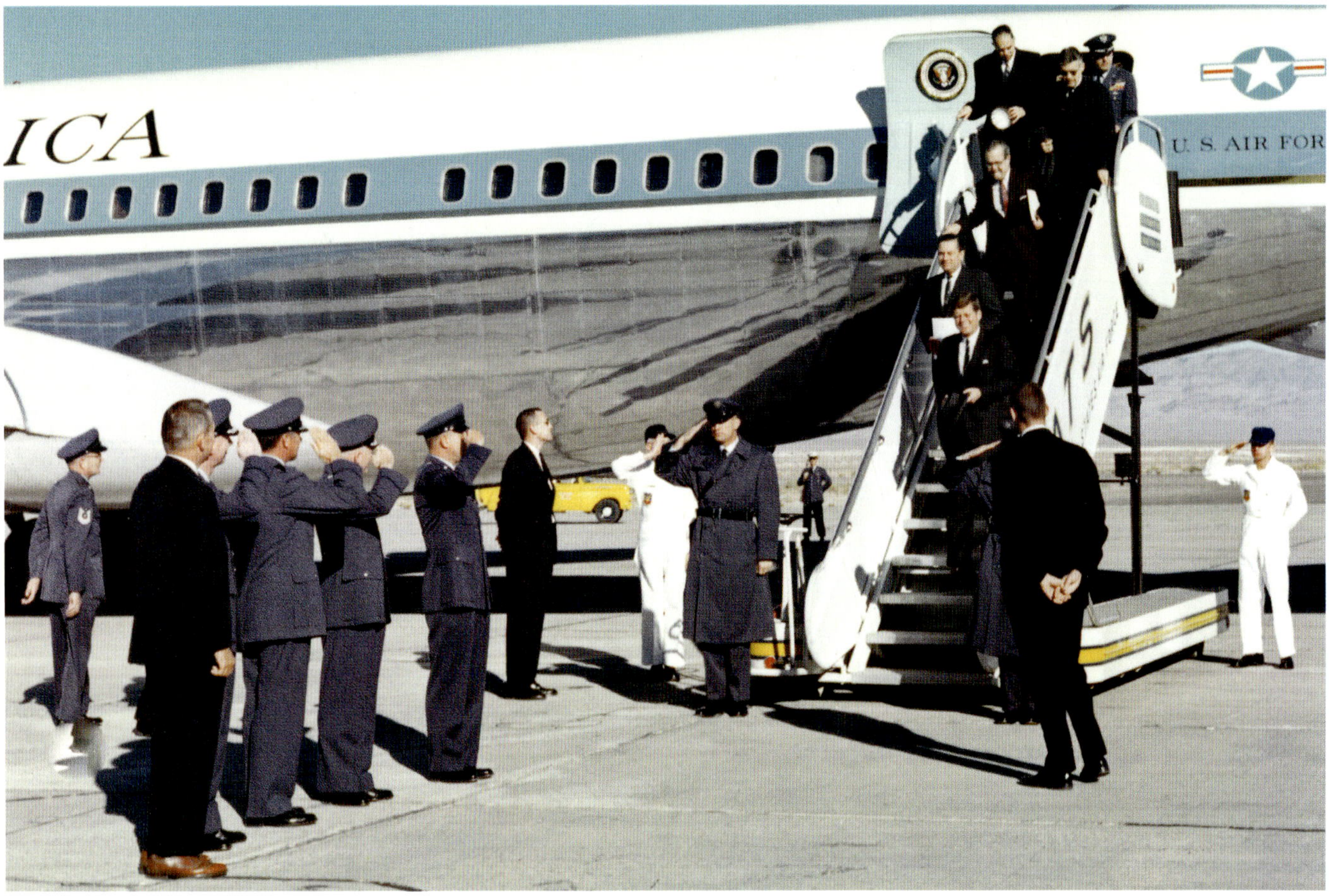

▲ On Saturday, December 8, after morning mass at the Kirtland AFB chapel, the president arrives at Indian Springs AFB, Nevada, at 9:12 a.m. PST (SAM 26000, call sign for Air Force One when the president is not aboard, had been moved from Santa Fe to Kirtland that morning for the flight to Indian Springs). His party next boards helicopters for Area 25 at the Nuclear Rocket Development Station.

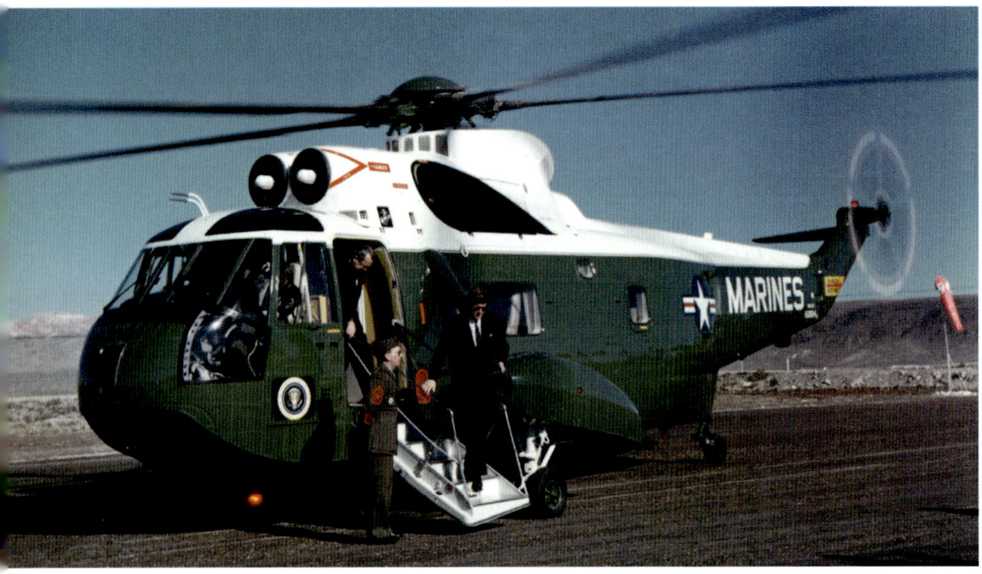

▲ Kennedy steps off Marine One at Area 25, arriving at 10:06 a.m. The station, at the Nevada Test Site, is in Jackass Flats on the northern edge of the Mojave Desert. This Sikorsky VH-3A Sea King helicopter had gone into presidential service in May.

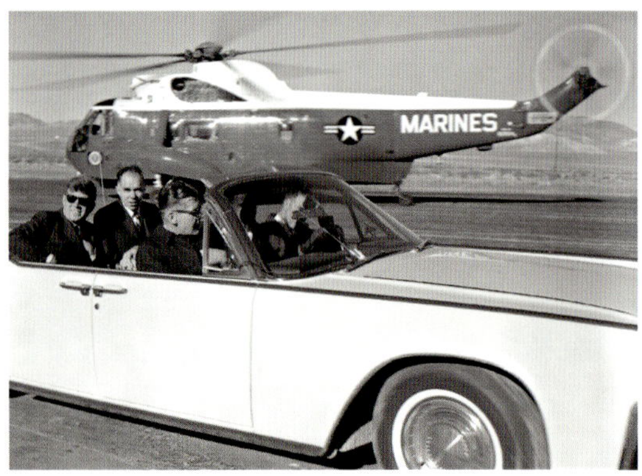

▲ Kennedy's motorcade departs for the Reactor Maintenance, Assembly & Disassembly (R-MAD) Building, with Seaborg riding with the president. Cars for this leg of the trip are supplied by Todkill Lincoln-Mercury in Las Vegas. (Courtesy of Los Alamos National Laboratory Archives.)

▶ The president enters an exhibit area set up for his visit in the R-MAD Building around 10:20 a.m., followed by Seaborg. Finger stands near the maps. Rover officials hope the president will support continued funding in next year's budget that he will send to Congress the following month; he had mentioned the project by name in his May 1961 speech to Congress.

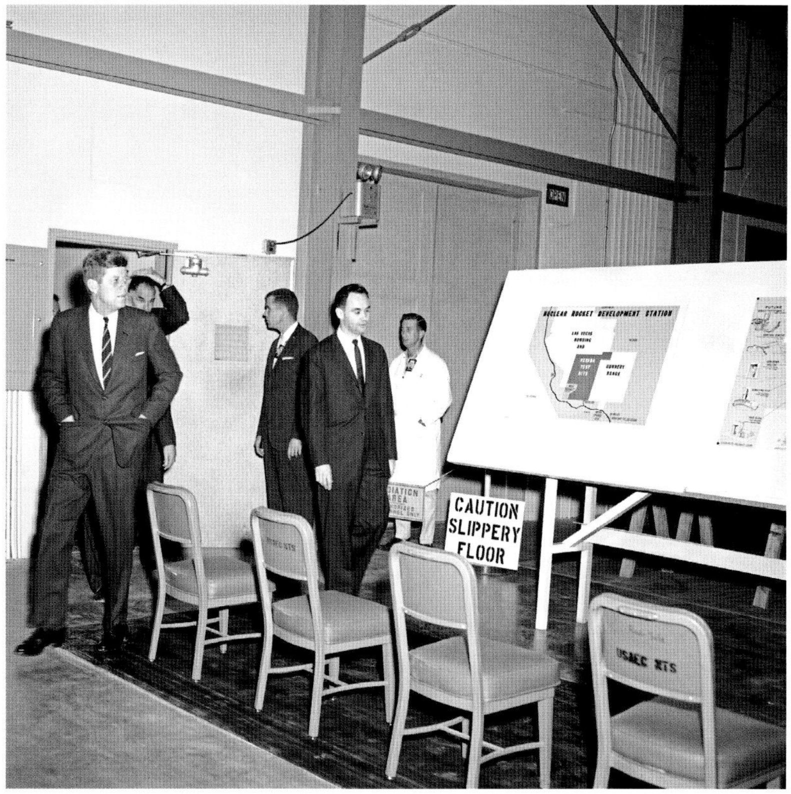

▼ A mockup of a NERVA nuclear propulsion rocket engine is at center in this photo taken prior to Kennedy's arrival. NERVA (Nuclear Engine for Rocket Vehicle Application) would be the next step, based on the Kiwi reactor. It demonstrates that nuclear thermal rocket engines could be feasible and reliable for space propulsion. The program would be cancelled in 1973, however, as funding for the US space program is further reduced by a Congress with little appetite for a manned Mars program.

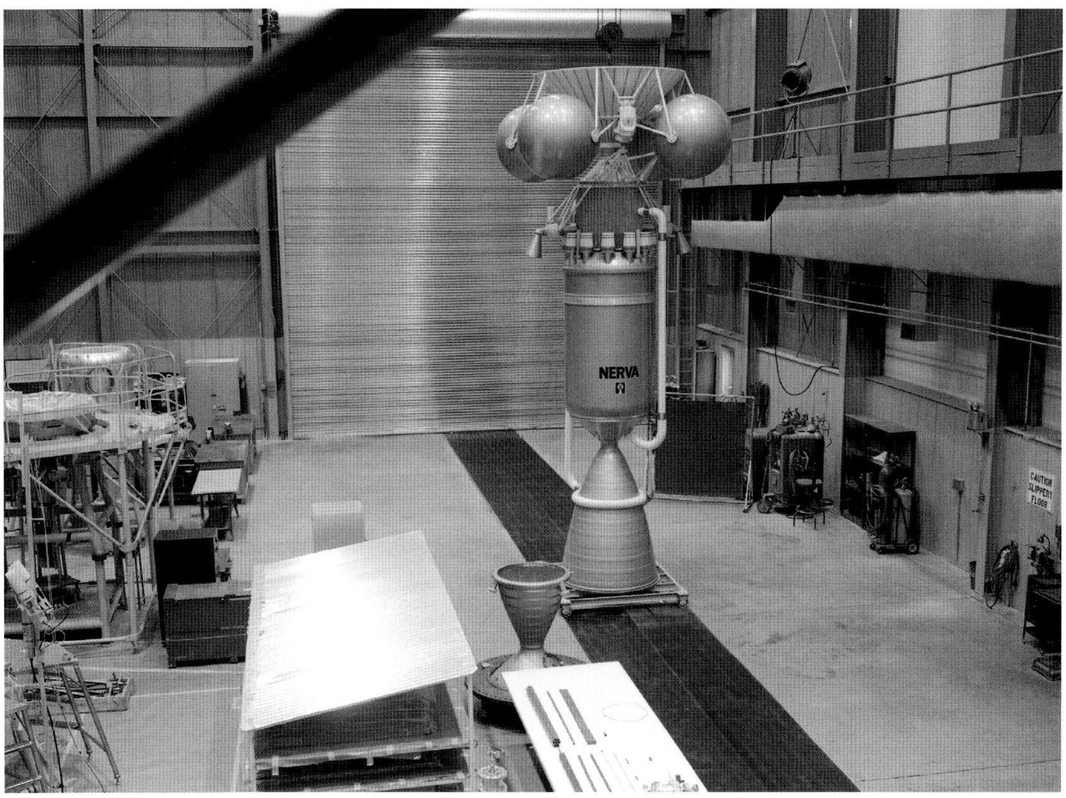

During his visit, Kennedy asks about a timetable for a Mars mission; he's told a one-year round-trip with astronauts spending forty days on the planet would be an option.

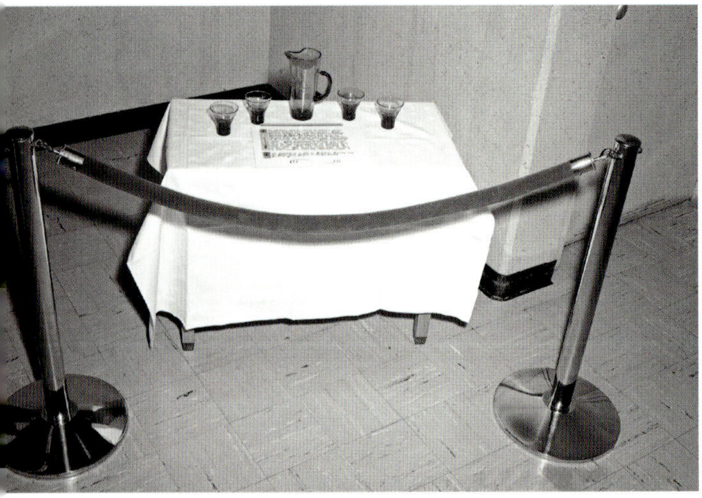

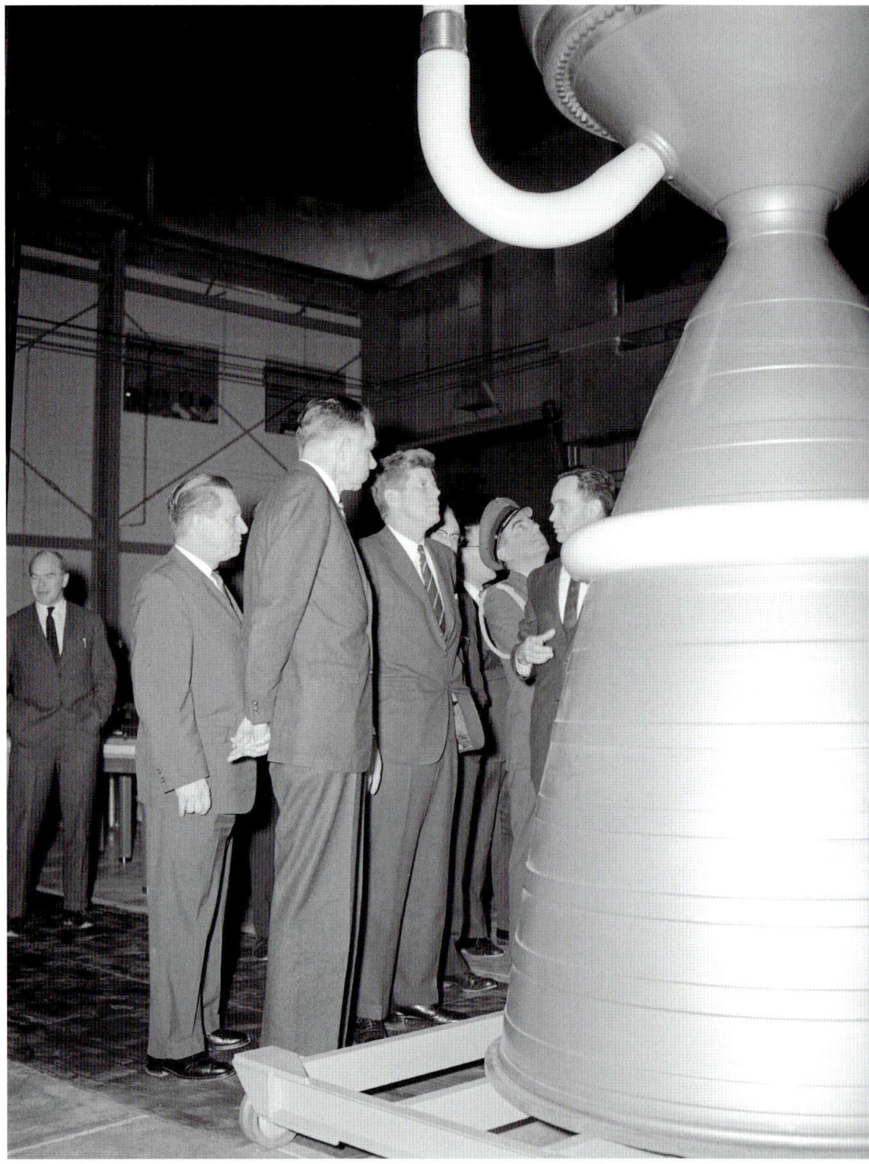

▶ Seaborg and the president are briefed on the NERVA mockup with Sen. Howard Cannon (D-Nev.) at left. (Courtesy of Los Alamos National Laboratory Archives.)

At a news conference five days later, the president is asked whether he'd seek more funding for Project Rover.

"We're going to let these tests go on, of the reactor," Kennedy says.

> These tests should be completed by July. If they are successful, then we will put more money into the program, which would involve the NERVA and RIFT [Reactor In Flight Test, a planned nuclear Saturn third stage], both the engine and the regular machine. We will wait until July, however, to see if these tests are successful.
>
> It should be understood that the nuclear rocket, even under the most favorable circumstances, would not play a role in any first lunar landing. This will not come into play until 1970 or '71. It would be useful for further trips to the moon or trips to Mars. But we have a good many areas competing for our available space dollars, and we have to try to channel it into those programs which will bring us a result, first, on our moon landing, and then to consider Mars.

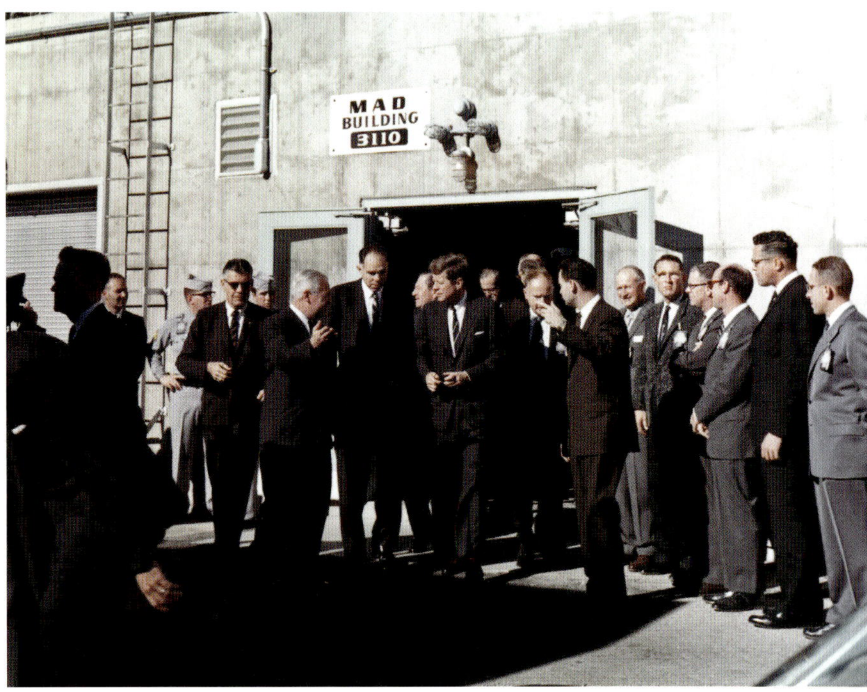

▶ Keith Boyer, Rover test director, speaks to the president following the briefing at the R-MAD Building. The group would next drive to the reactor and engine test areas.

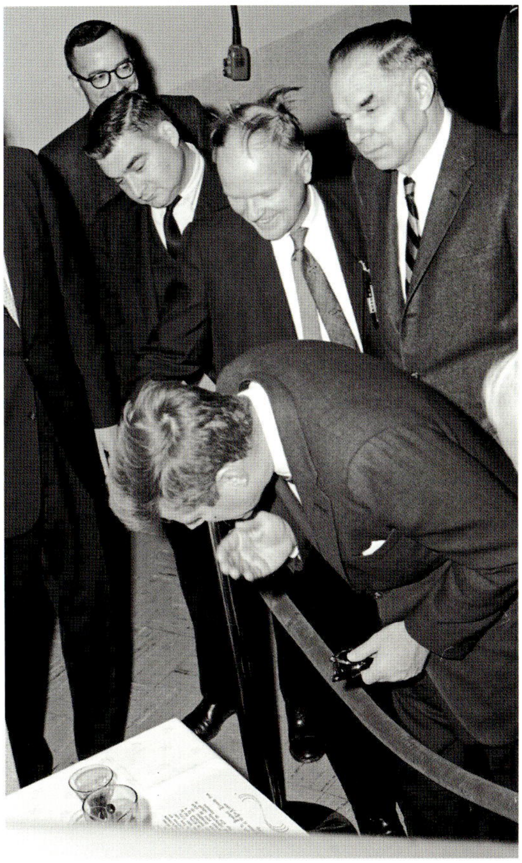

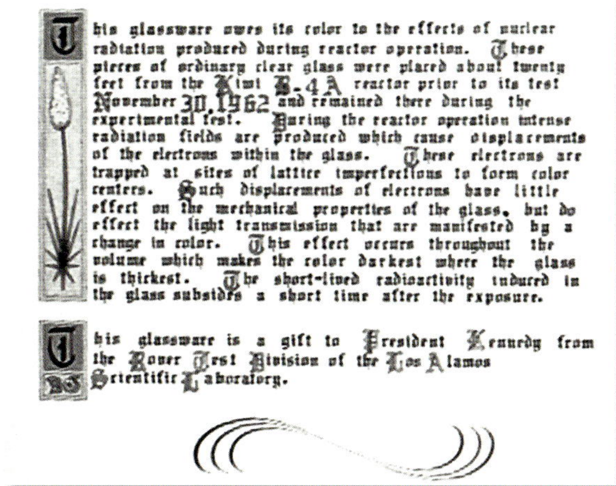

This glassware owes its color to the effects of nuclear radiation produced during reactor operation. These pieces of ordinary clear glass were placed about twenty feet from the Kiwi B-4A reactor prior to its test November 30, 1962 and remained there during the experimental test. During the reactor operation intense radiation fields are produced which cause displacements of the electrons within the glass. These electrons are trapped at sites of lattice imperfections to form color centers. Such displacements of electrons have little effect on the mechanical properties of the glass, but do effect the light transmission that are manifested by a change in color. This effect occurs throughout the volume which makes the color darkest where the glass is thickest. The short-lived radioactivity induced in the glass subsides a short time after the exposure.

This glassware is a gift to President Kennedy from the Rover Test Division of the Los Alamos Scientific Laboratory.

◤ The president inspects a set of glassware given to him as a gift, which had partially darkened when exposed to radiation at the November 30 Kiwi test. Such items are routinely presented to VIPs. Behind him are Salinger; Alvin Graves, director of test activities for the laboratory; and Seaborg. (Courtesy of Los Alamos National Laboratory Archives.)

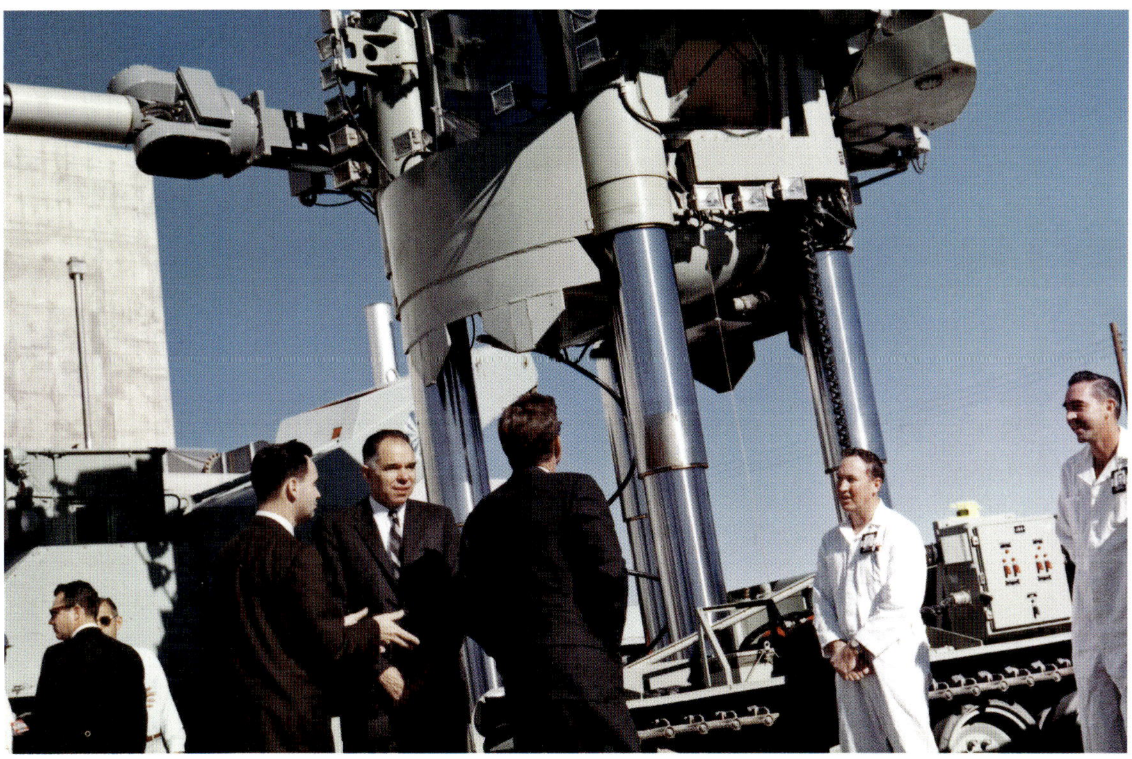

▲ The president stops to hear about the Beetle from Finger and Seaborg. It is a USAF manned robot built to service and maintain a planned fleet of atomic-powered bombers, a program Kennedy canceled in 1961. Left without a clear mission, the robot is undergoing testing for possible use with Project Rover. At right Randall "Tex" Scraper and another operator stand by in case Kennedy has questions.

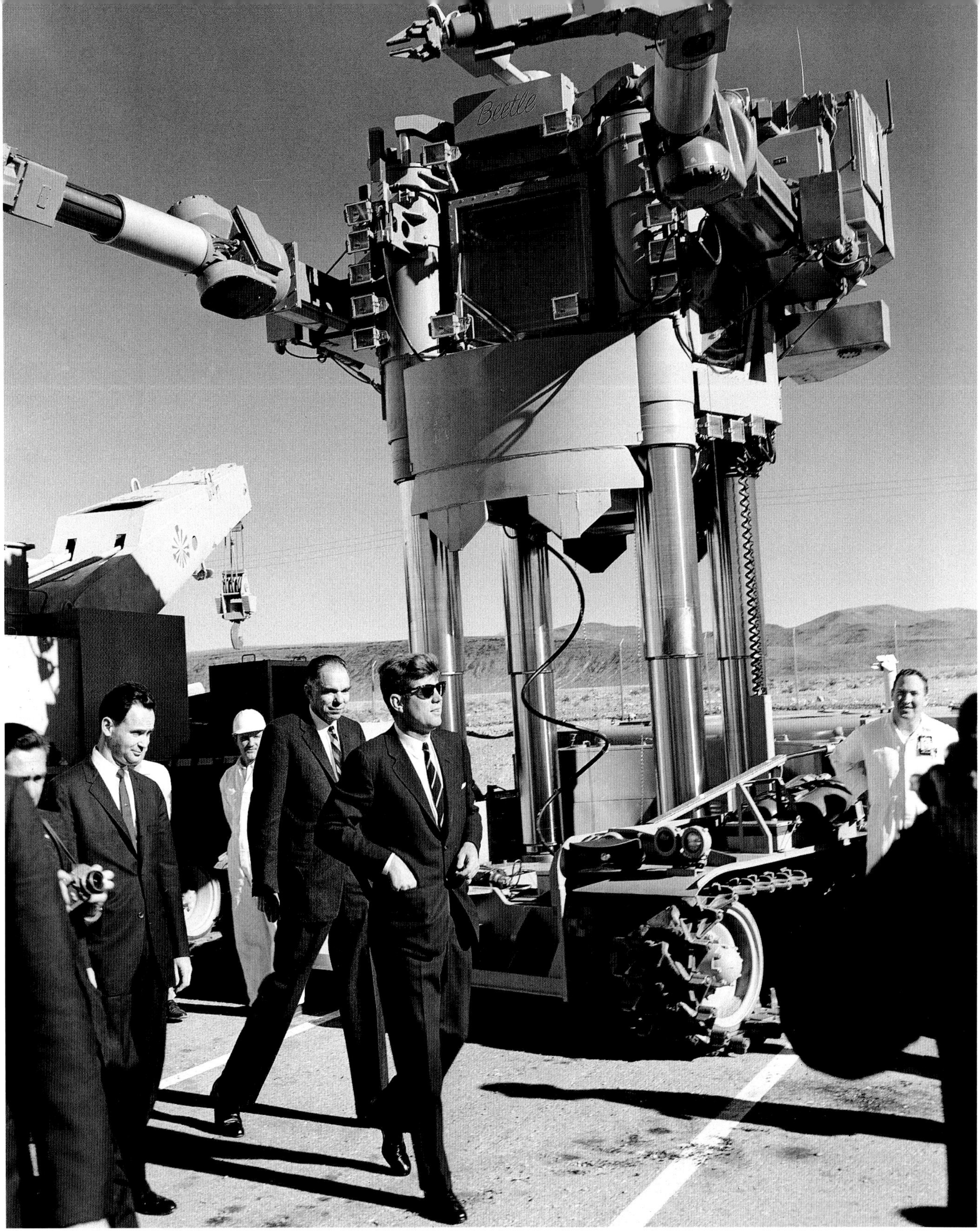

▲ Kennedy heads to his motorcade. The Beetle, built by Jered Industries in Detroit for General Electric's Nuclear Materials and Propulsion Operation Division, is a twenty-six-foot-tall, eighty-ton tracked vehicle. "The complexity of the Beetle requires a continuous preventive maintenance program to ensure its reliability," according to a 1963 USAF report. It is eventually scrapped.

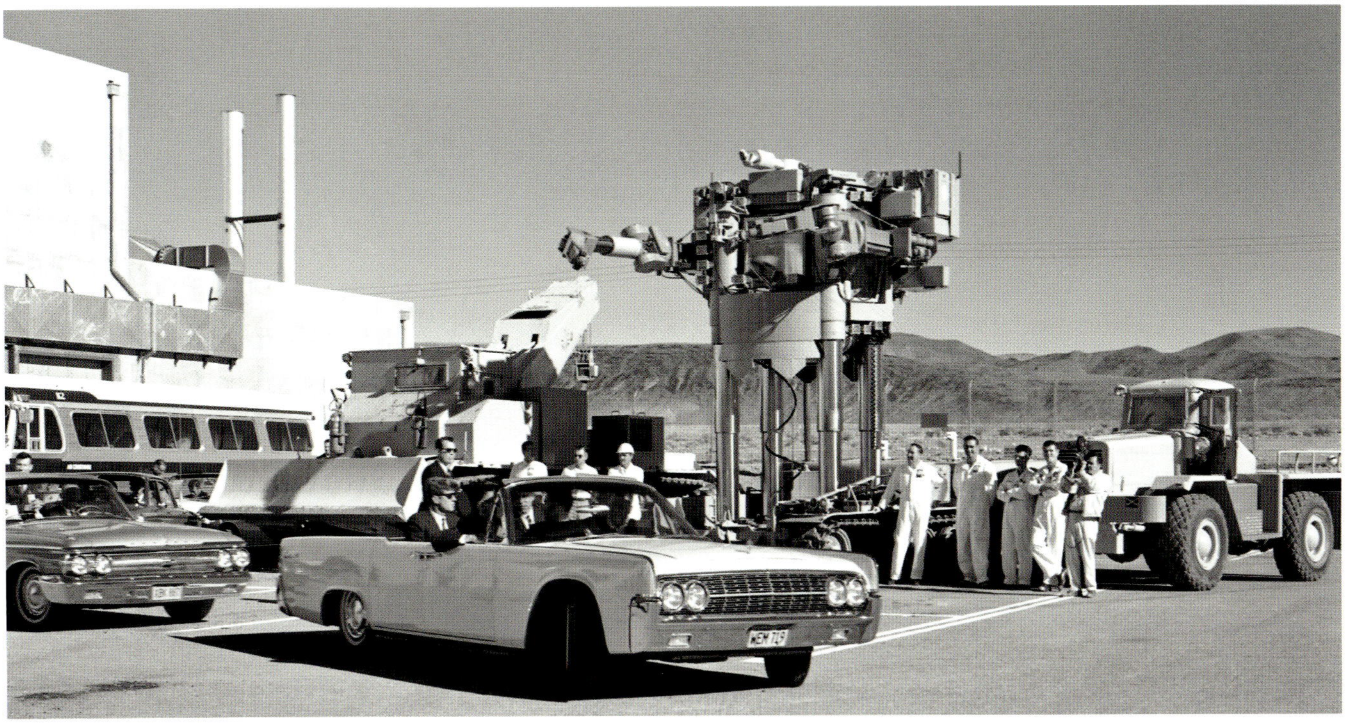

▲ The president's motorcade heads for Test Cell A (reactor testing), about 1.5 miles away, at 10:33 a.m. for a short loudspeaker briefing. The group would then drive about three miles to Engine Test Stand No. 1. En route, Kennedy stops to shake hands with Nevada Test Site employees. (Courtesy of Los Alamos National Laboratory Archives.)

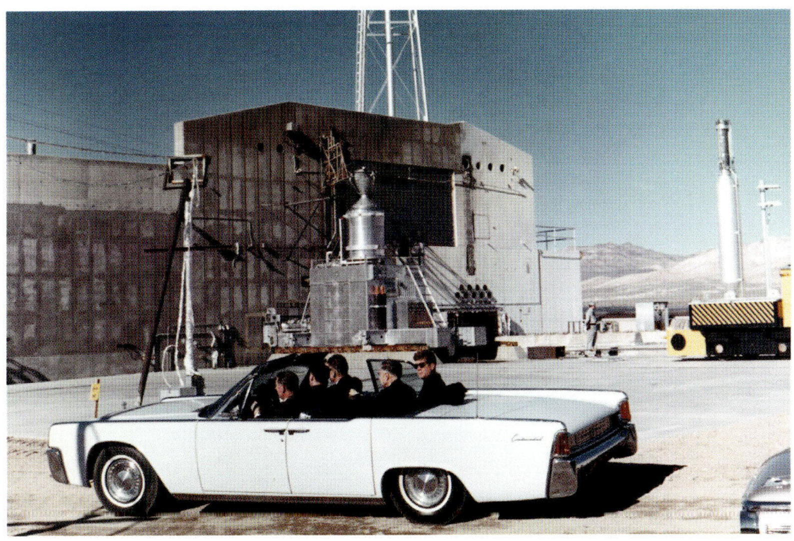

▶ Seaborg and the president arrive at Engine Test Stand No. 1 at 10:52 a.m., with the failed Kiwi B4A in place at center.

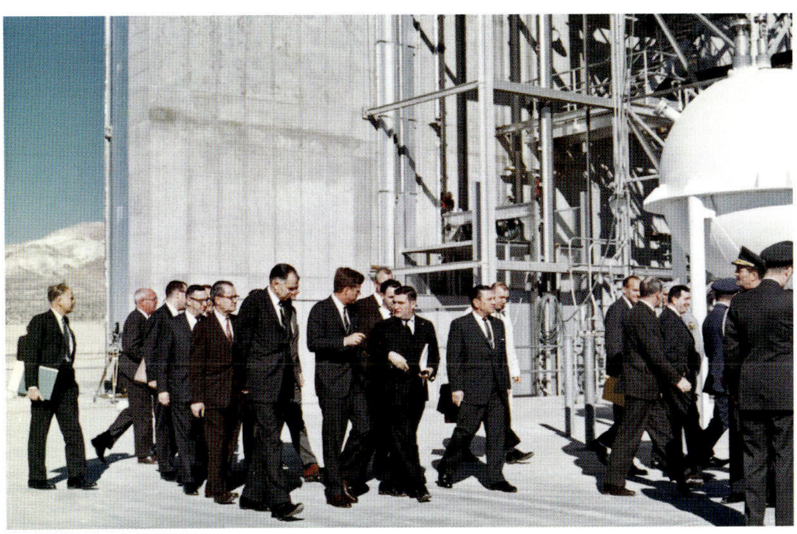

◀ The president chats with Pierre Salinger. Seaborg is at Kennedy's right; Sen. Cannon is right of Salinger. Science Advisor Jerome Wiesner is fourth from right. At far left is Graves.

▶ Seaborg and the president are briefed by Norvin Erickson of the Aerojet-General Corp. at 10:55 a.m. Sen. Cannon, Finger, McGeorge Bundy, Seamans, and Ink are also seen. Aerojet is the prime contractor for NERVA, with Westinghouse providing the reactor.

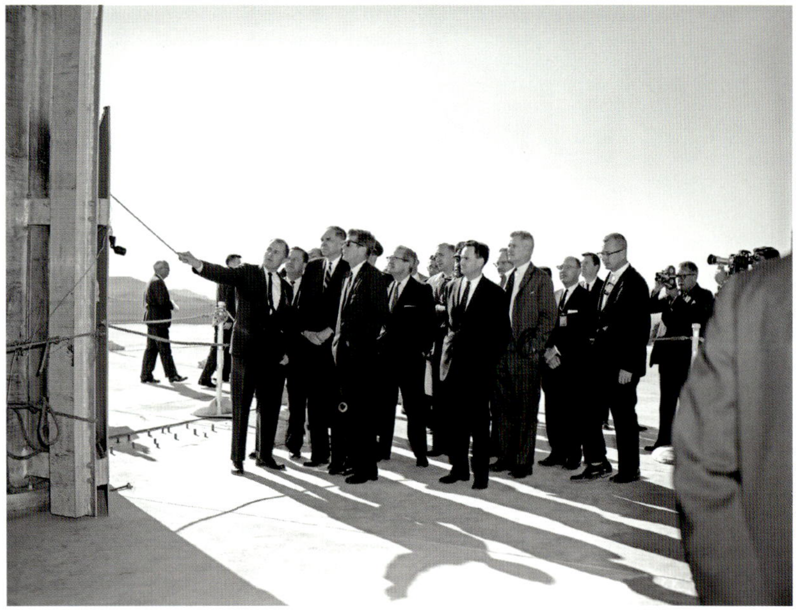

▼ Kennedy looks up into the test stand with Seaborg behind him. (Courtesy of Los Alamos National Laboratory Archives.)

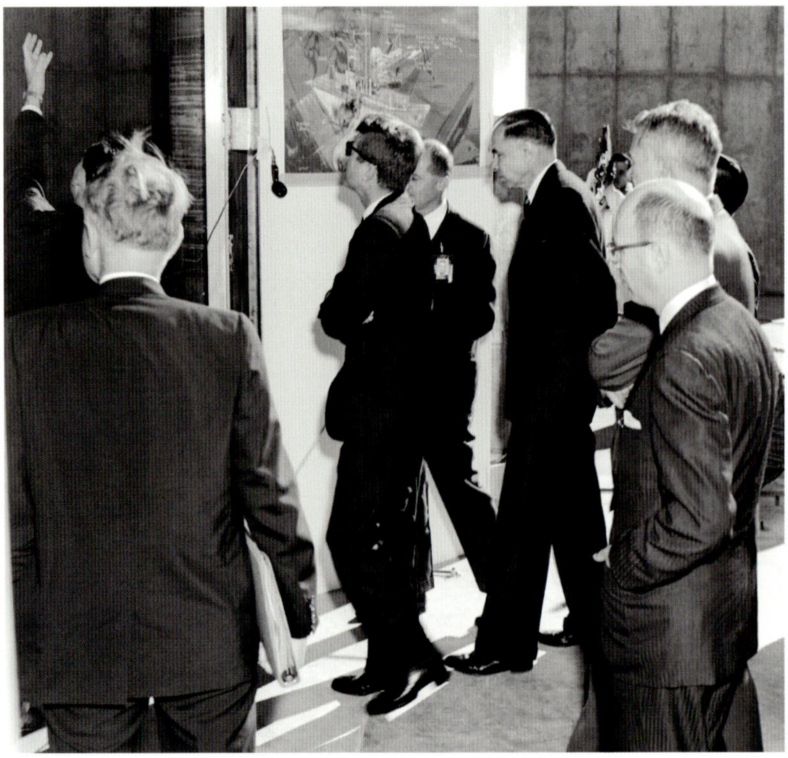

▼ L–R: Seaborg; Finger; Graves; Kennedy; Salinger (hidden); Sen. Cannon; Maj. Gen. Clifton; and Ink.

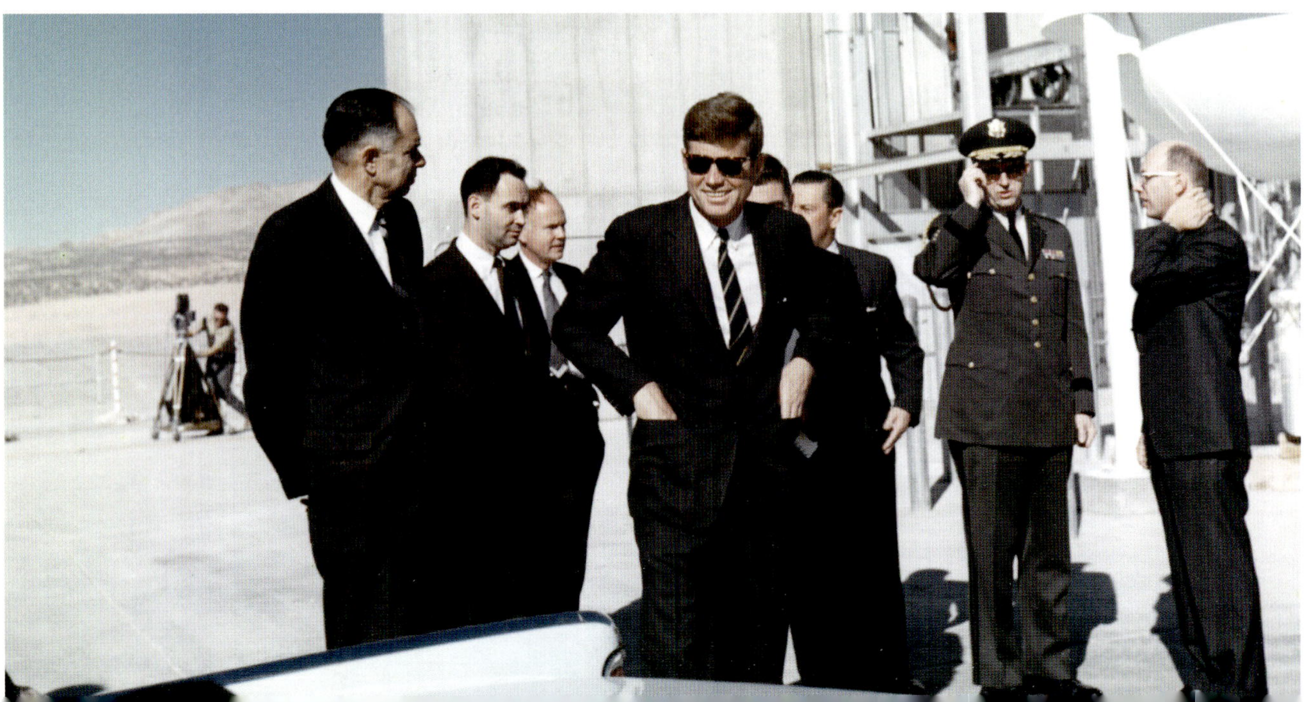

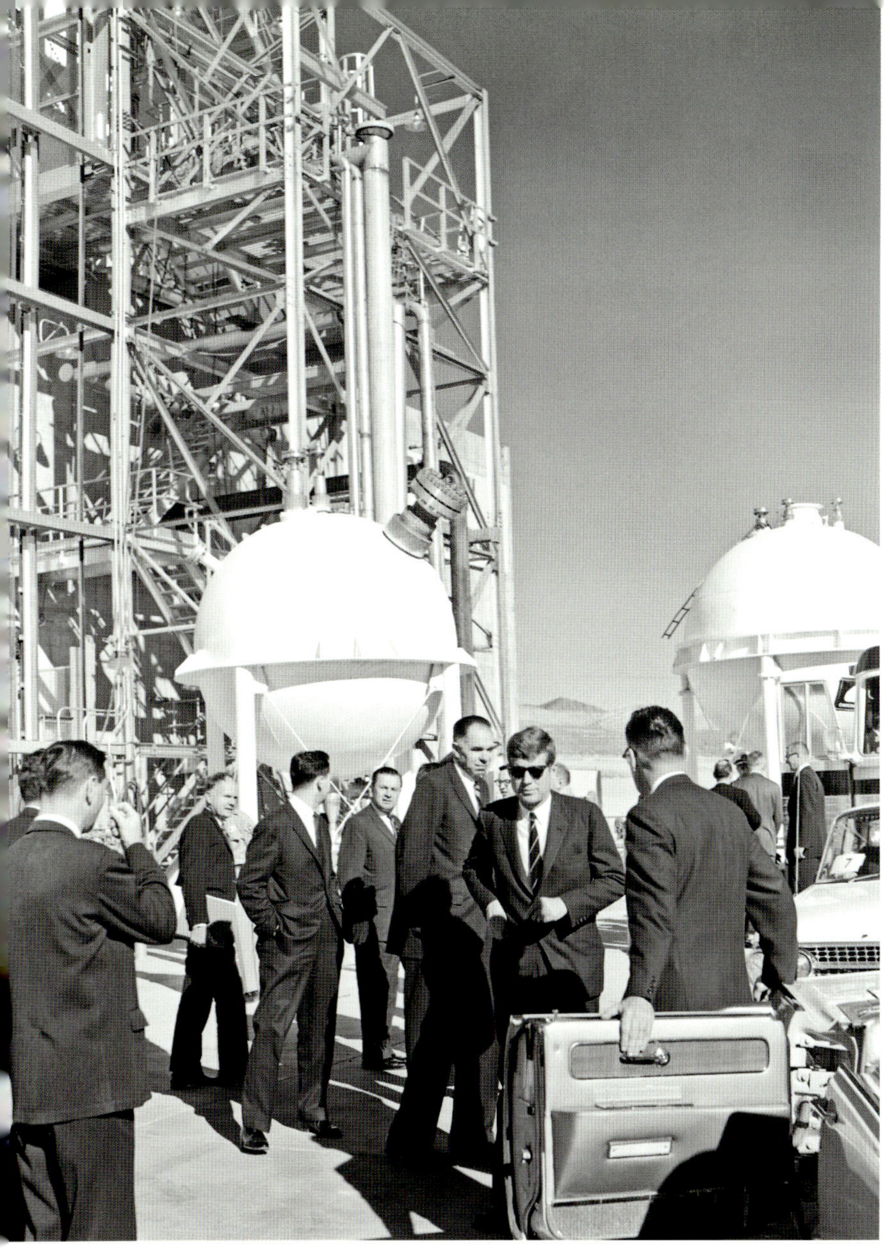

▼ Kennedy boards Marine One to return to Indian Springs AFB, where SAM 26000 is waiting.

During the flight, he sees Sedan Crater, created by a July underground thermonuclear test, the second in a series to investigate using nuclear explosions for peaceful excavation purposes called the Plowshare Program. At 1,280 feet in diameter, it is the largest man-made crater in the United States. In 1965 a group of future Apollo astronauts, including Neil Armstrong and Buzz Aldrin, would conduct lunar geology training at Sedan.

At 11:30 a.m. the president departs Indian Springs for Palm Springs Municipal Airport to spend the rest of the weekend at the California estate of entertainer Bing Crosby.

▲ The president departs Engine Test Stand No. 1 at 11:03 a.m. At Kennedy's right (R-L) are Seaborg, Cannon, Finger, and Graves. The two spherical tanks store liquid hydrogen to power the Kiwi engines. (Courtesy of Los Alamos National Laboratory Archives.)

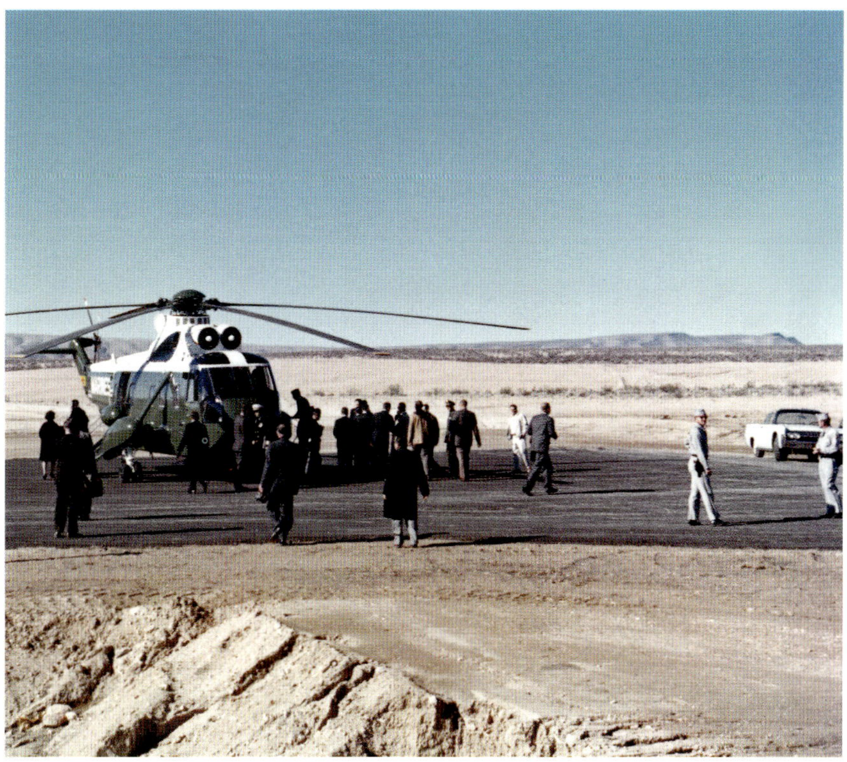

:07

JANUARY–AUGUST 1963

"There are great frontiers still to be crossed"

THE YEAR IN SPACE BEGINS quietly in 1963, but on March 28, the fourth and final Saturn I Block I (formerly called C-1), which President Kennedy had seen test-fired at Marshall the previous September, is launched in a successful suborbital test of the booster.

In May, the president hails the twenty-two-orbit final flight of Project Mercury during a White House ceremony with astronaut Gordon Cooper, the longest US manned mission yet; and he talks up Apollo.

Even so, critics, including former president Dwight Eisenhower and members of Congress in both parties, begin to argue that the manned space effort is too expensive. The House Appropriations Committee chairman calls it a "moondoggle" with the money better spent on social needs.

The Soviets, meantime, keep adding space firsts. On June 16, the first woman in space, cosmonaut Valentina Tereshkova, takes part in Russia's second joint flight, this time with Vostok 5, which also sets a five-day human spaceflight record. The same month, Kennedy attends an extensive Army missile demonstration in New Mexico.

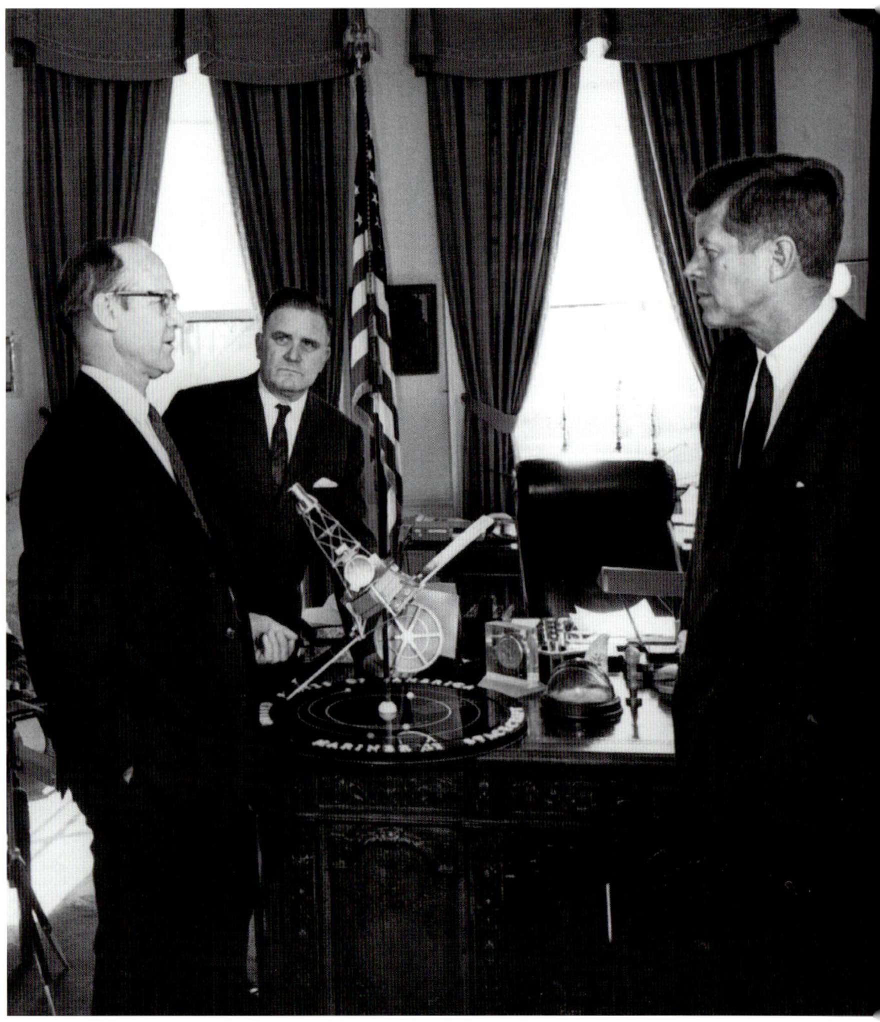

◥ Jet Propulsion Laboratory (JPL) Director William Picking and Webb present the president with a model of the Mariner II unmanned space probe at 12:30 p.m. on January 17, 1963, in the Oval Office. Launched from Cape Canaveral on August 27, 1962, the craft passed as close as 21,607 miles to Venus on December 14, 1962—and after five years of playing catch-up to the Soviet Union, the United States achieves its initial space first—the first successful flyby of another planet.

▶ L–R: Edgar Cortright, deputy director of NASA's Office of Space Sciences; Jack James, Mariner II project manager for JPL; Robert Seamans Jr., NASA associate administrator (in back); Robert Parks, JPL planetary programs director; Pickering; Webb; and Kennedy.

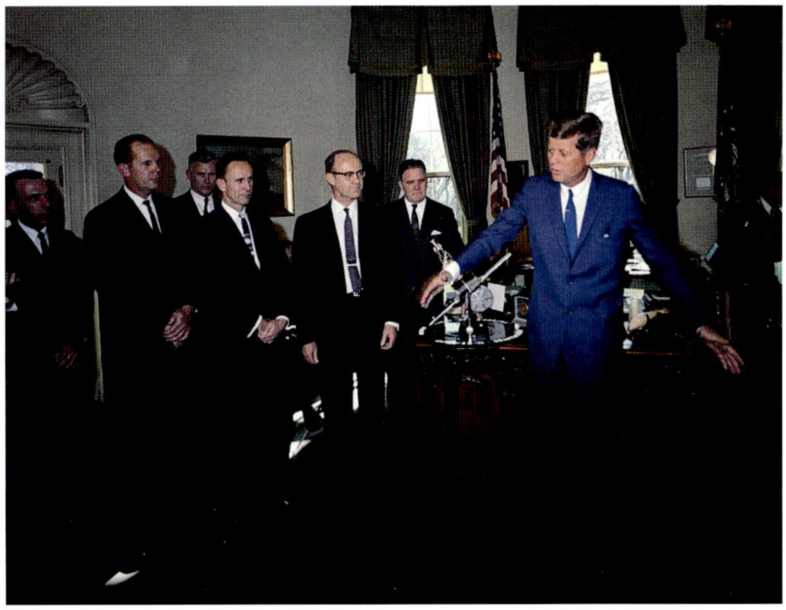

▼ Kennedy examines the Mariner model's microwave radiometer, which shows conclusively that the surface of Venus is sufficiently hot to cause the greenhouse effect in its atmosphere. The first successful spacecraft in NASA's Mariner program, the spacecraft is a simplified version of the Ranger lunar probe series. Its last transmission is received on January 3, 1963; it remains in orbit around the sun.

"This was an extraordinary technical accomplishment by the United States," Kennedy says, "and it indicates that there is a broad spectrum of mastery in the field of space, other than the effort of the human probe."

The president uses the Resolute desk, a gift from Queen Victoria to President Rutherford B. Hayes in 1880, built from timbers of the British Arctic exploration ship HMS Resolute. Kennedy was the first to have it in the Oval Office.

L–R: Seamans; Parks; Pickering; Webb; and Kennedy.

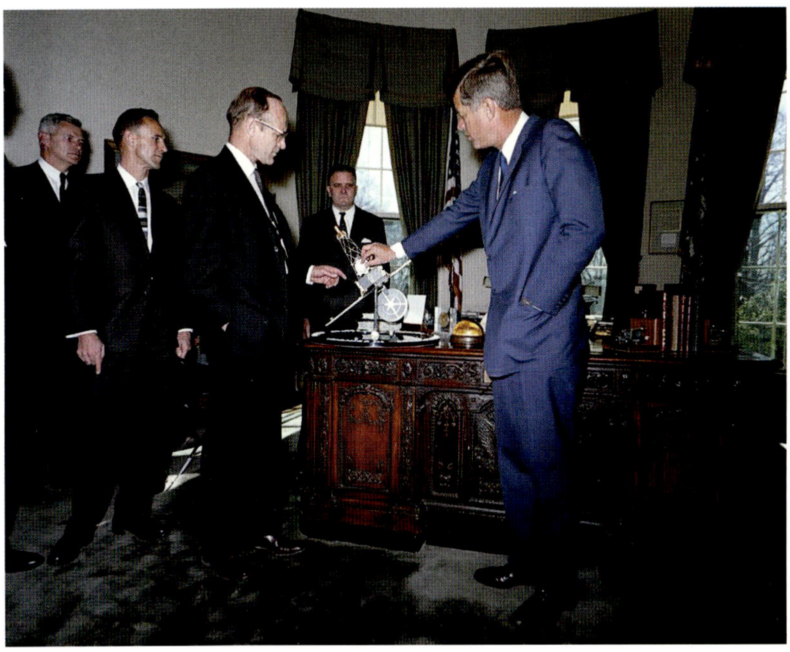

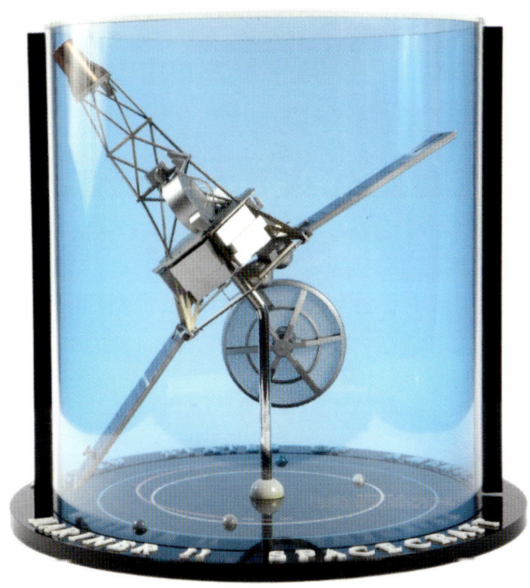

◥ Model in the John F. Kennedy Presidential Library and Museum collection.

▶ The president signs a letter to McDonnell Aircraft Chairman James McDonnell, thanking him for the one-eighth-scale model of a Gemini spacecraft as a Christmas gift from company personnel after his visit to the St. Louis plant the previous September. Two orange-tipped skids extend out, part of an alternative landing system abandoned in 1964.

USAF aide to the president, Brig. Gen. Godfrey McHugh, is at left in the Cabinet Room on January 30, 1963. (McHugh had dated future First Lady Jacqueline Bouvier in the early 1950s while serving in Paris as a USAF attaché.) Barely visible through the doorway are Army Maj. Gen. Chester Clifton, military aide to the president, and John F. Kennedy Jr. (sitting on the floor).

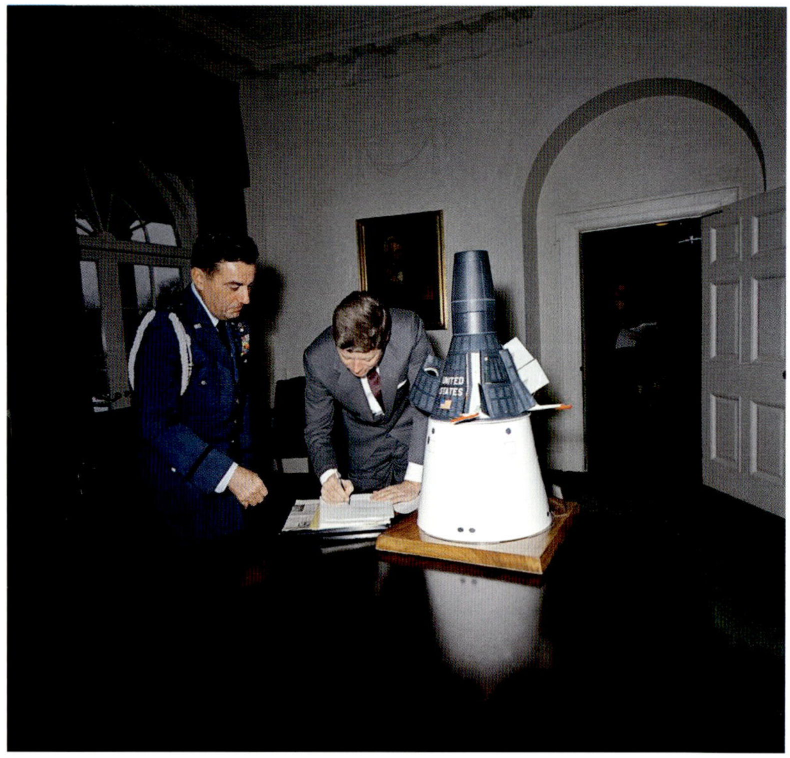

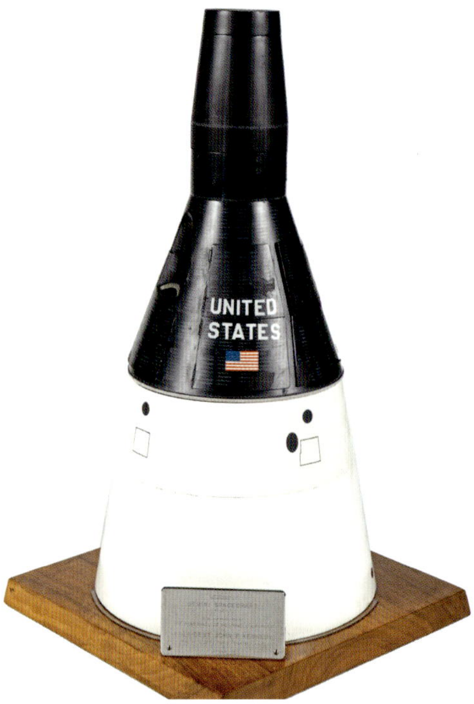

▲ The Gemini spacecraft model in the John F. Kennedy Presidential Library and Museum collection.

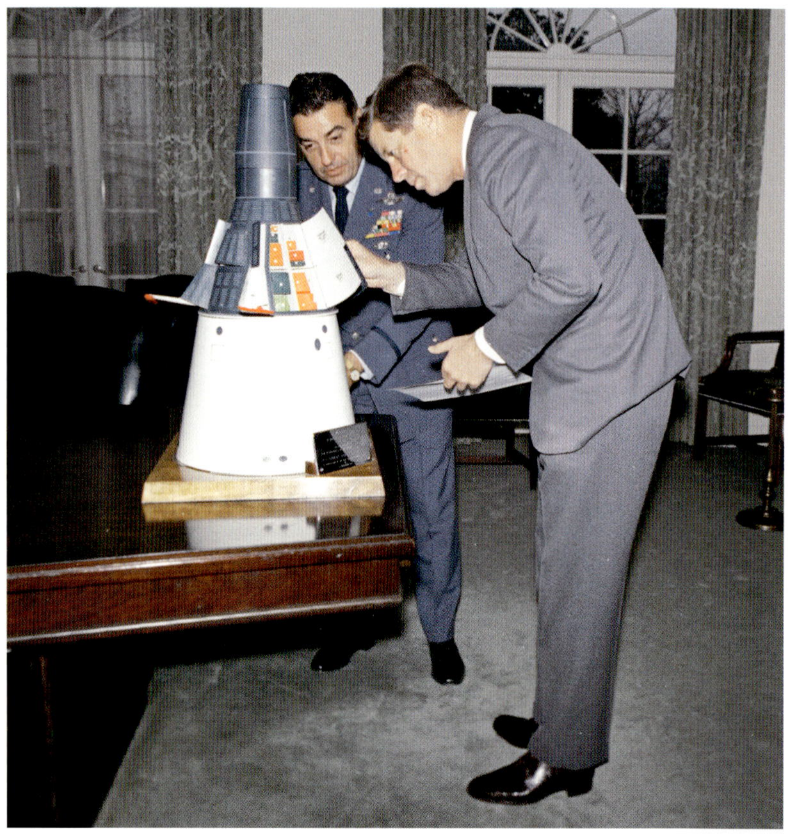

▲ The president examines the Gemini's components mounted behind access panels, intended to provide easier servicing than for Mercury spacecraft.

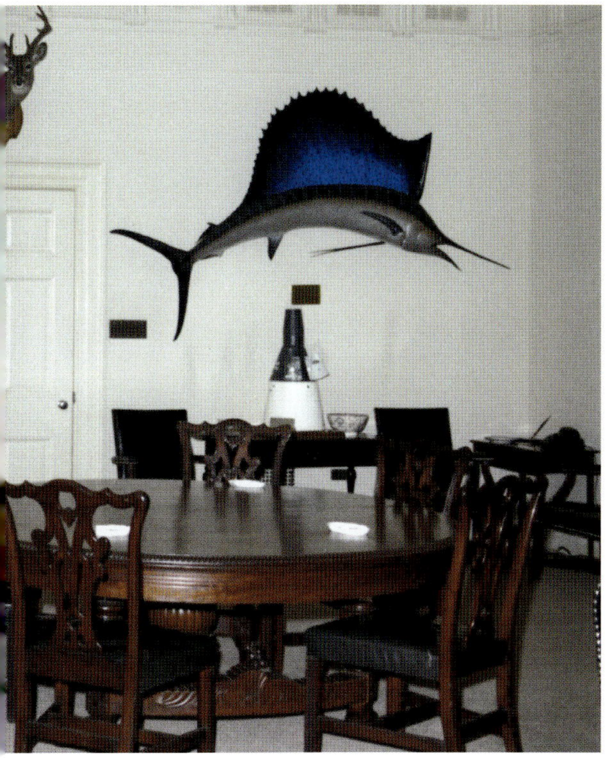

▲ The model finds a home in the Fish Room.

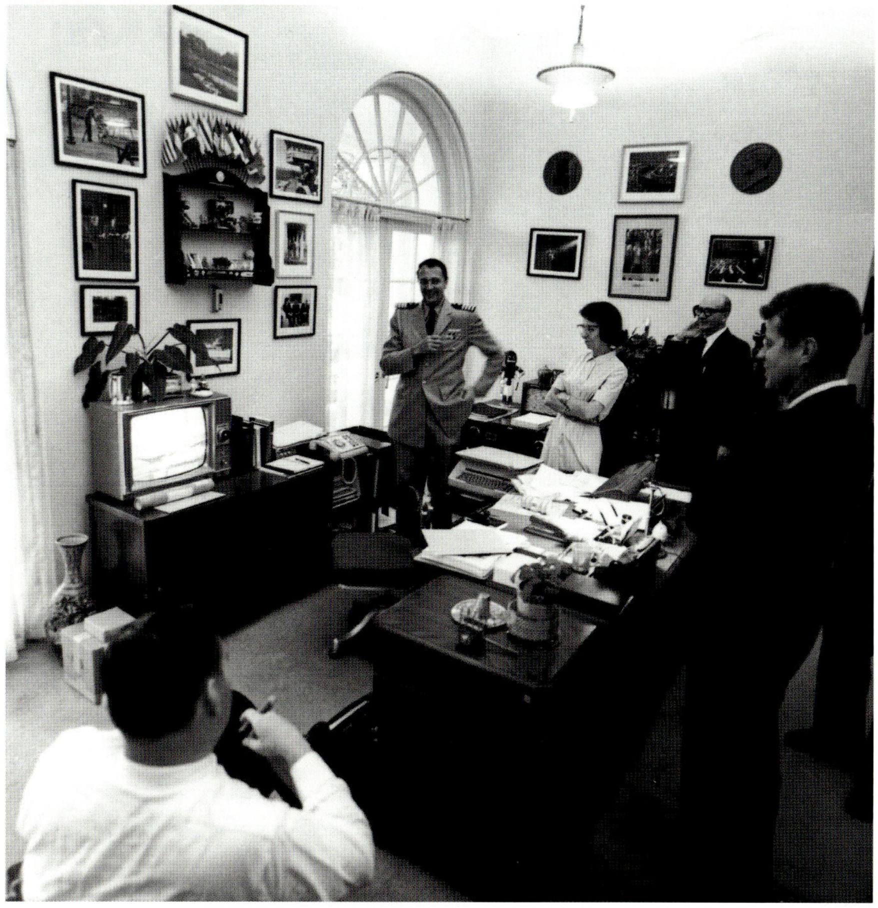

▲ At the White House the president watches the launch in the office of his secretary, Evelyn Lincoln (center). Capt. Tazewell Shepard Jr. is at left, with Secretary of State Dean Rusk next to Lincoln. Press Secretary Pierre Salinger enjoys a cigar at lower left.

▼ USAF Maj. Gordon Cooper, thirty-six, lifts off from LC-14 at 8:04 a.m. EDT on May 15, 1963, the final launch of the Mercury program. He spends thirty-four hours in orbit aboard *Faith 7*, the longest manned US space flight by far.

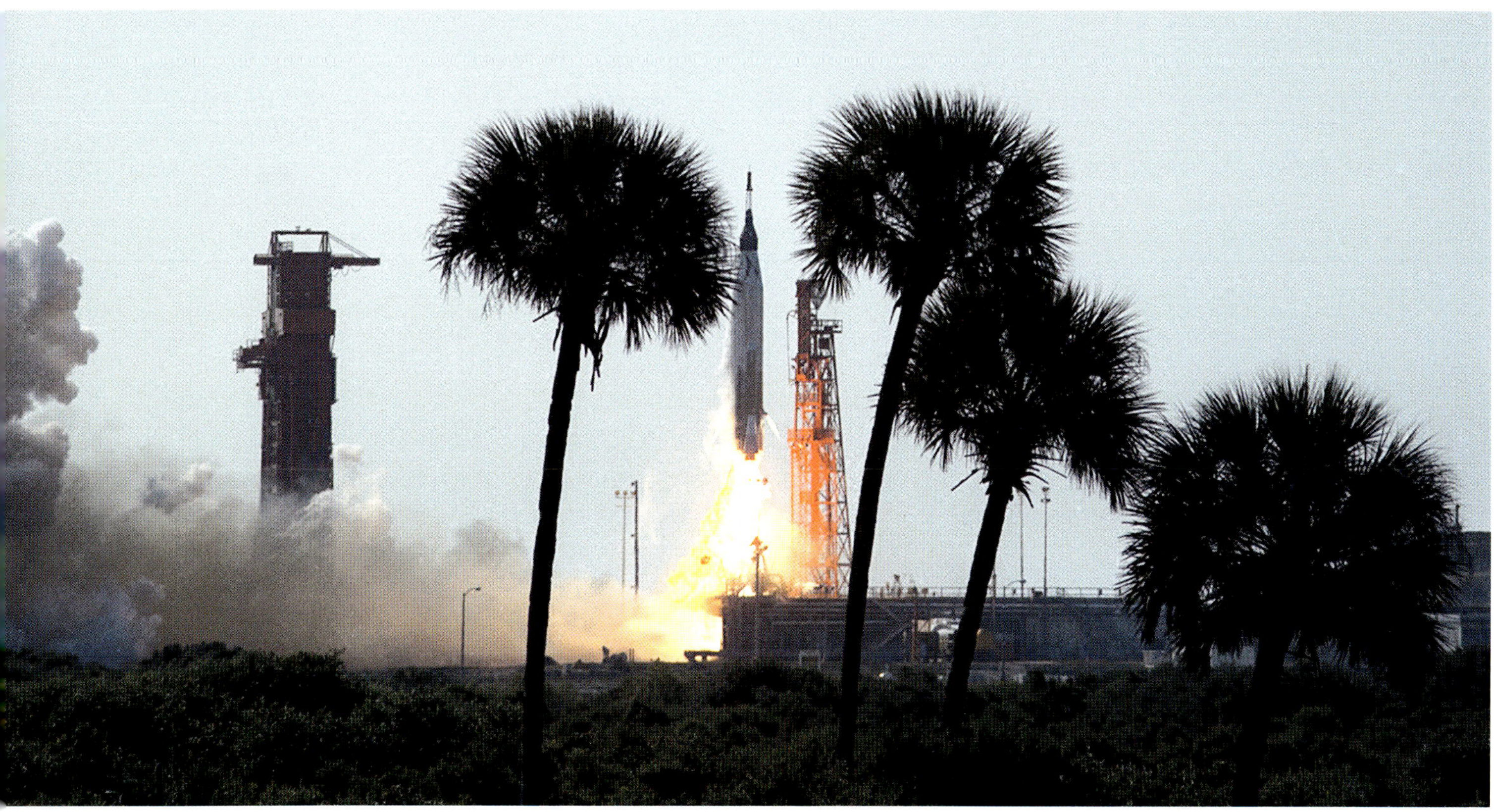

▶ Cooper's longer flight, comprising twenty-two orbits, means his spacecraft would pass over China six times, and once over North Vietnam and Cuba. In March, the Defense Department develops contingency recovery procedures—including the use of force if necessary—should Cooper (or upcoming Gemini astronauts) make an emergency landing in unfriendly waters. The State Department would work through British or Swiss diplomats.

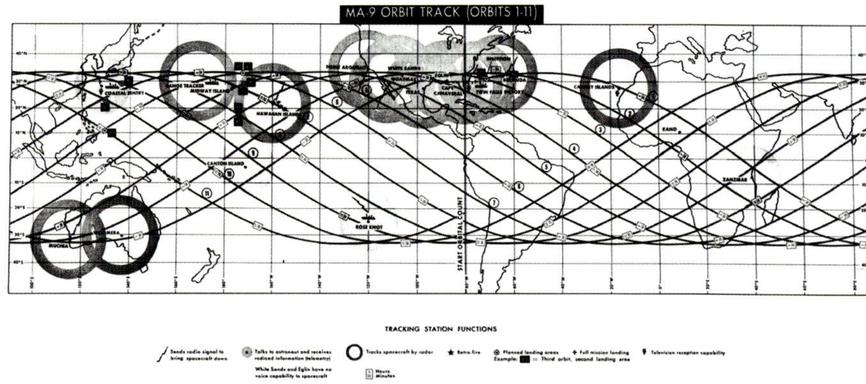

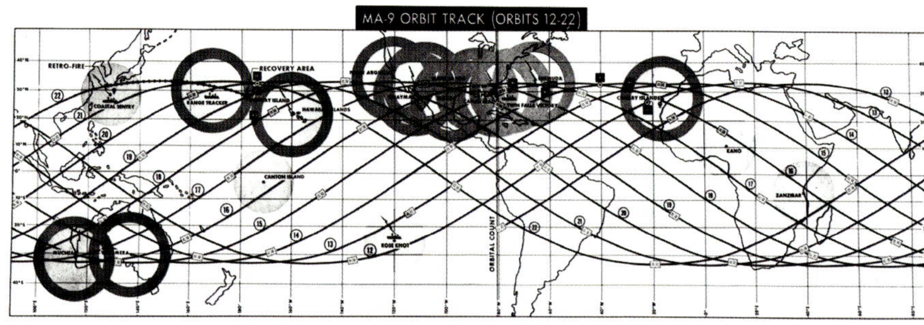

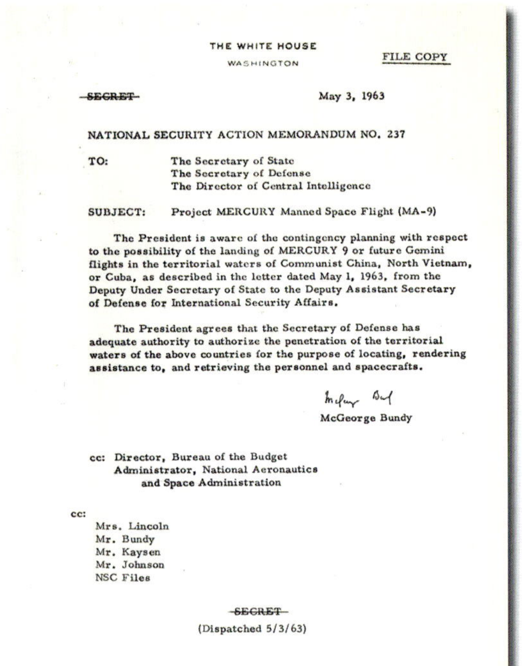

THE WHITE HOUSE
WASHINGTON

FILE COPY

~~SECRET~~ May 3, 1963

NATIONAL SECURITY ACTION MEMORANDUM NO. 237

TO: The Secretary of State
The Secretary of Defense
The Director of Central Intelligence

SUBJECT: Project MERCURY Manned Space Flight (MA-9)

The President is aware of the contingency planning with respect to the possibility of the landing of MERCURY 9 or future Gemini flights in the territorial waters of Communist China, North Vietnam, or Cuba, as described in the letter dated May 1, 1963, from the Deputy Under Secretary of State to the Deputy Assistant Secretary of Defense for International Security Affairs.

The President agrees that the Secretary of Defense has adequate authority to authorize the penetration of the territorial waters of the above countries for the purpose of locating, rendering assistance to, and retrieving the personnel and spacecrafts.

McGeorge Bundy

cc: Director, Bureau of the Budget
Administrator, National Aeronautics and Space Administration

cc:
Mrs. Lincoln
Mr. Bundy
Mr. Kaysen
Mr. Johnson
NSC Files

~~SECRET~~
(Dispatched 5/3/63)

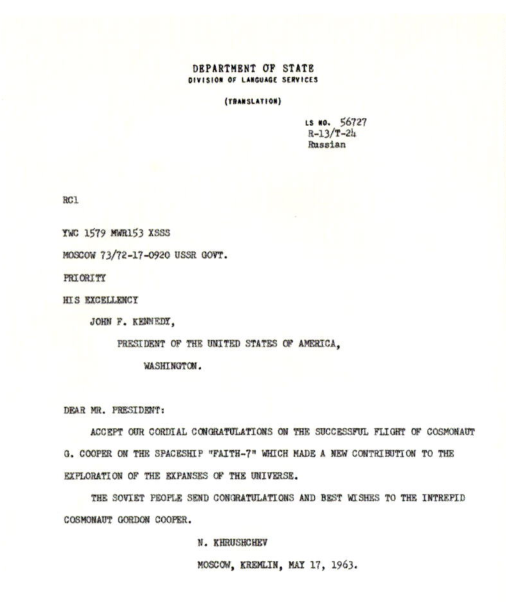

DEPARTMENT OF STATE
DIVISION OF LANGUAGE SERVICES

(TRANSLATION)

LS NO. 56727
R-13/T-24
Russian

RC1

YWC 1579 MWR153 XSSS
MOSCOW 73/72-17-0920 USSR GOVT.
PRIORITY
HIS EXCELLENCY
JOHN F. KENNEDY,
PRESIDENT OF THE UNITED STATES OF AMERICA,
WASHINGTON.

DEAR MR. PRESIDENT:

ACCEPT OUR CORDIAL CONGRATULATIONS ON THE SUCCESSFUL FLIGHT OF COSMONAUT G. COOPER ON THE SPACESHIP "FAITH-7" WHICH MADE A NEW CONTRIBUTION TO THE EXPLORATION OF THE EXPANSES OF THE UNIVERSE.

THE SOVIET PEOPLE SEND CONGRATULATIONS AND BEST WISHES TO THE INTREPID COSMONAUT GORDON COOPER.

N. KHRUSHCHEV
MOSCOW, KREMLIN, MAY 17, 1963.

▲ Less than two weeks before launch, the president signs off and the White House issues National Security Action Memorandum No. 237.

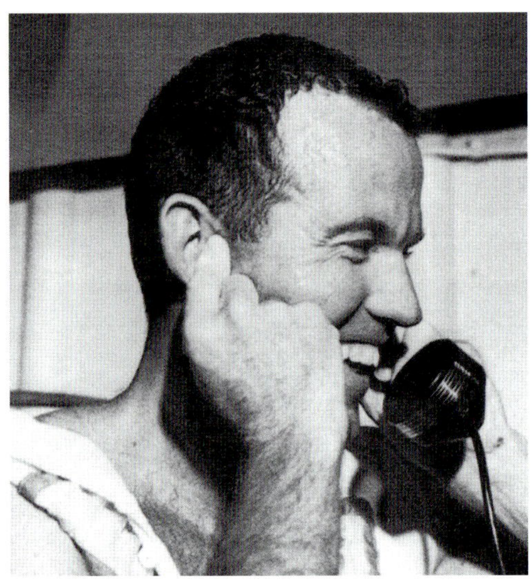

▲ Kennedy: "Major, I just want to congratulate you. That was a great flight."

Cooper: "Thank you very much, sir."

Kennedy: "We talked to your wife and she seemed to stand it very well." (He had called her in Houston to invite the family to the White House.)

Cooper: "Oh, very good."

Kennedy: "We're looking forward to seeing you up here Monday, but we are very proud of you, major."

Cooper: "Well thank you, sir. It was a good flight. I enjoyed it."

Kennedy: "Good, fine; I will look forward to seeing you Monday. Good luck."

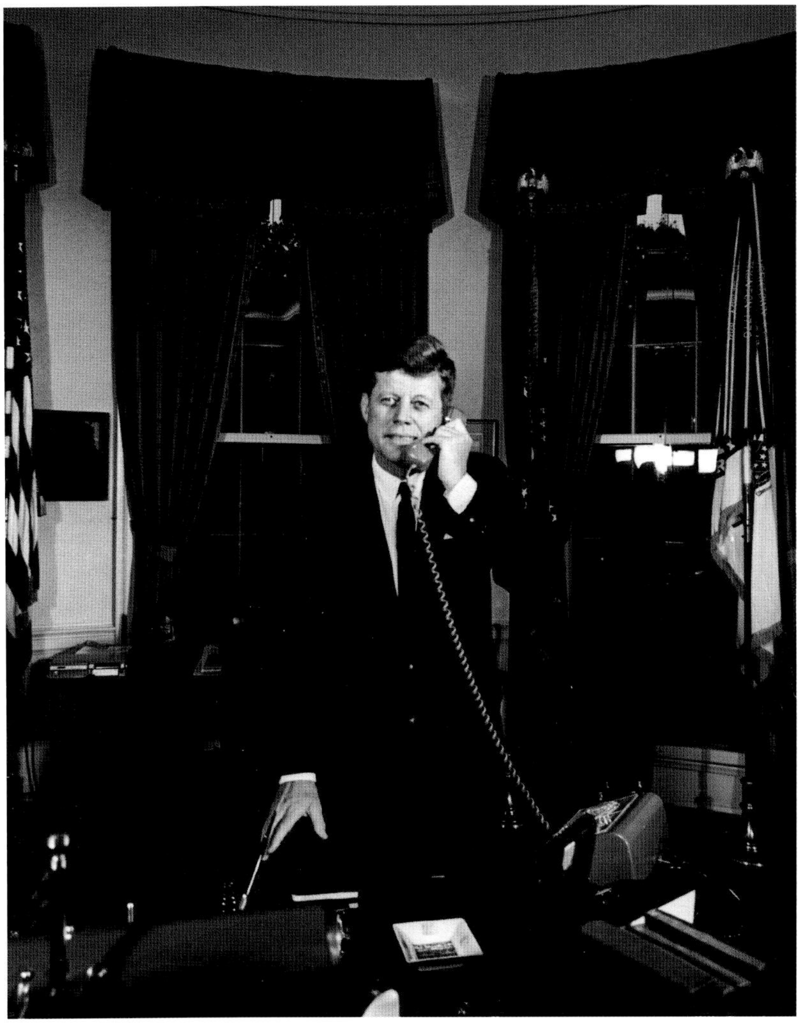

◀ Around 8:45 p.m. on May 16, Kennedy calls Cooper from the Oval Office aboard his recovery ship USS *Kearsarge.*

About an hour earlier, the president told a national broadcast audience from the Fish Room, "We're proud of Major Cooper, and we're proud of all those thousands of Americans who work with him to make this flight possible. And indeed, in a sense, all Americans were on this flight, because all of them have sustained this program in good times and in bad. And it represents a great achievement for our society and a great achievement for free men and women."

▶ On May 18, 1963, the president makes a return visit to Redstone Army Airfield in Huntsville, Alabama, to mark Armed Forces Day, but he did not visit Marshall.

Von Braun chats with Kennedy after the president's arrival by helicopter from Muscle Shoals, Alabama, where he had spoken at the thirtieth anniversary of the Tennessee Valley Authority. The president pulls Von Braun aside, telling him, "I have a lot of difficulties with Congress getting money for you people." Kennedy then asks how the space program is going and says he is pleased.

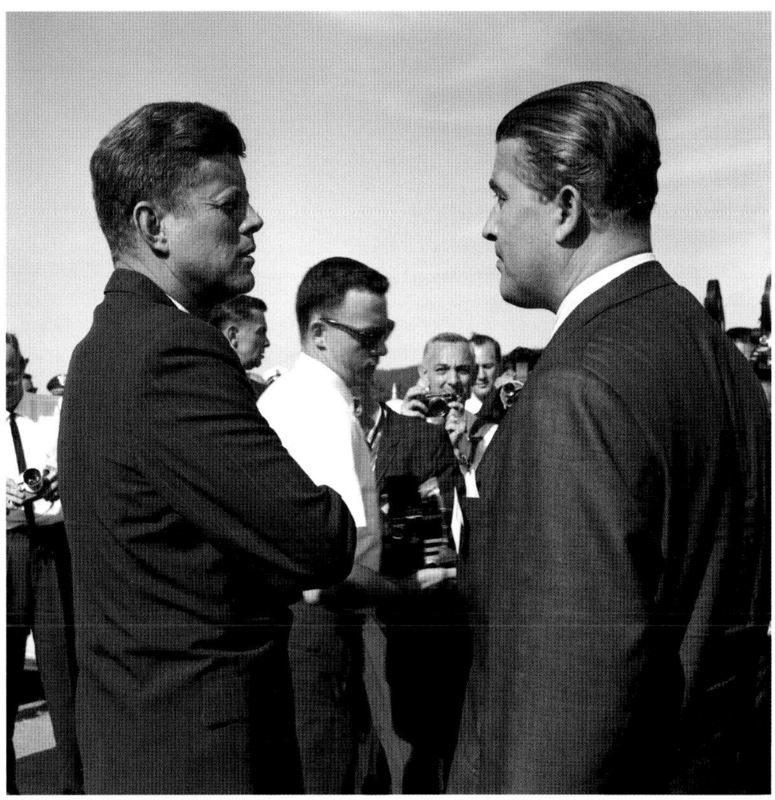

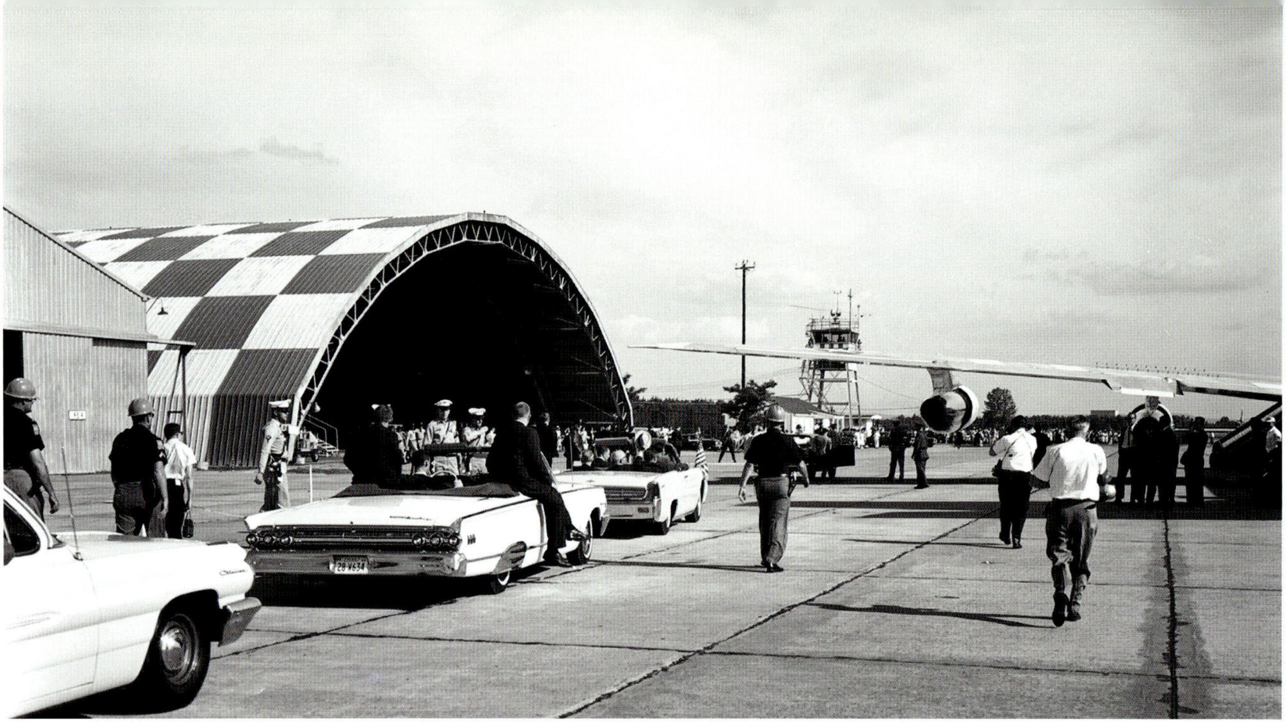

▲ The president and VIPs are taken by motorcade to a platform specially built for his appearance.

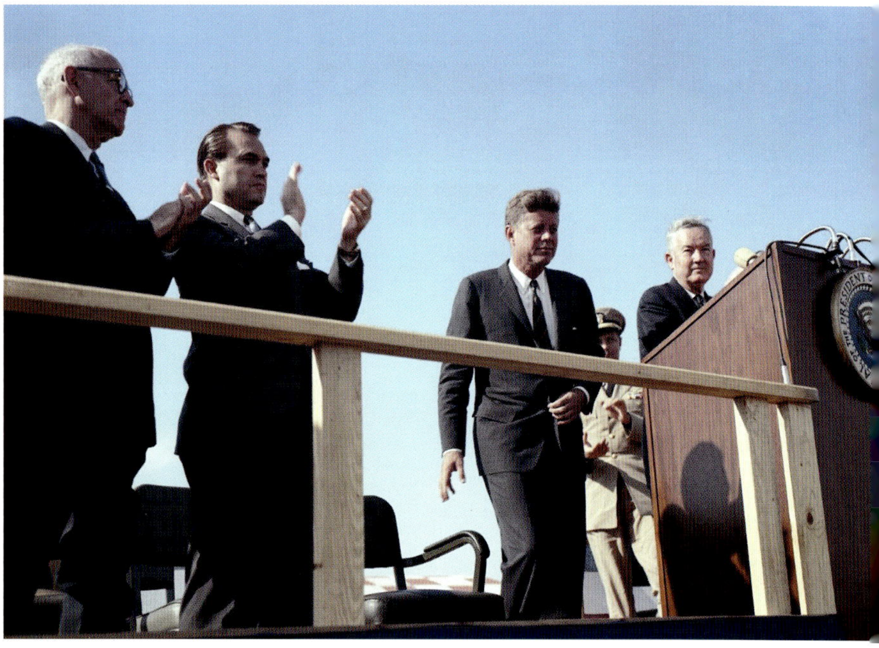

▶ Joining the president on the trip from Muscle Shoals is Gov. George Wallace (D-Ala.) (second from left), who, the following month, would lose in a showdown with the federal courts and the Kennedy administration over admitting black students to the University of Alabama. He would seek the Democratic party presidential nomination in 1964.

Sen. Lister Hill (D-Ala.) is at left; Sen. John Sparkman (D-Ala.) is at right. Some ten thousand Redstone workers and their families turn out for the event.

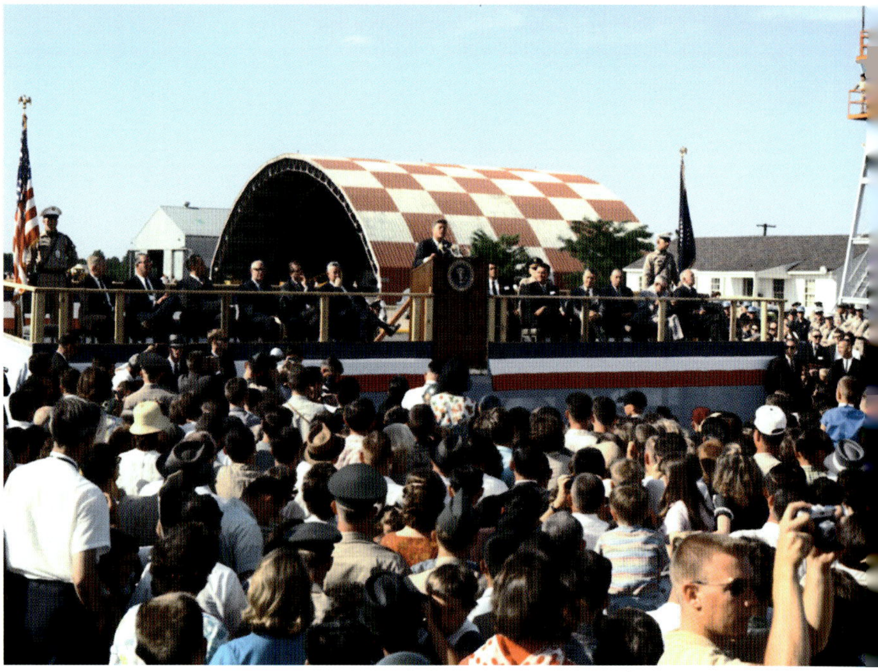

▶ The president's remarks at 3:50 p.m., lasting five minutes, note the Army's contributions to defense and NASA's responsibility to the space program. "So, ladies and gentlemen," he concludes, "we depend upon you, either you in the armed forces of the United States who help defend freedom, even here, of countries thousands of miles away, you who are building these missiles which not only raised an American into space, but raised the prestige and reputation of this country. I am proud to be here." Kennedy flies back to Andrews AFB at 4:15 p.m.

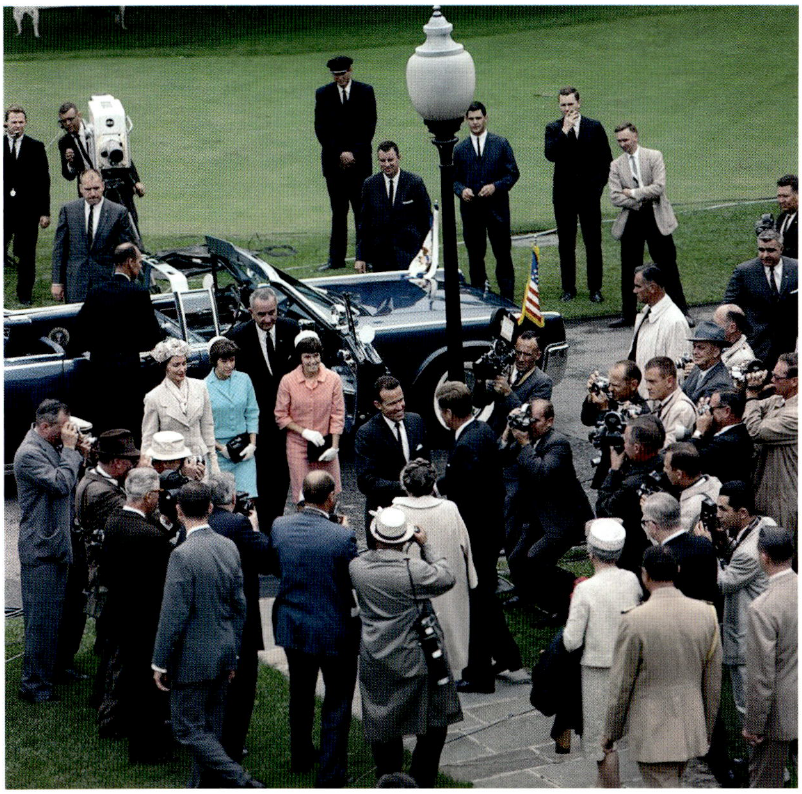

◀ The president greets Cooper and his family on a South Lawn walkway at the White House at 12:15 p.m. on May 21, 1963. The astronaut flew to Andrews that morning from Cape Canaveral. Cooper's wife, Trudy, and his daughters, Cam, fourteen, and Jan, thirteen, stand with Johnson behind the astronaut. Cooper's mother, Hattie, is next to Kennedy. It is the first time Cooper has seen her since his space flight. Cooper's aunt and uncle, Jewell and James Truscott, are at right behind the president.

Also pictured: Secret Service Agents Sam Kinney and Roy Kellerman, and United Press International photographer James K. Atherton (at right with crew cut and light jacket). An ABC-TV pool camera is at left.

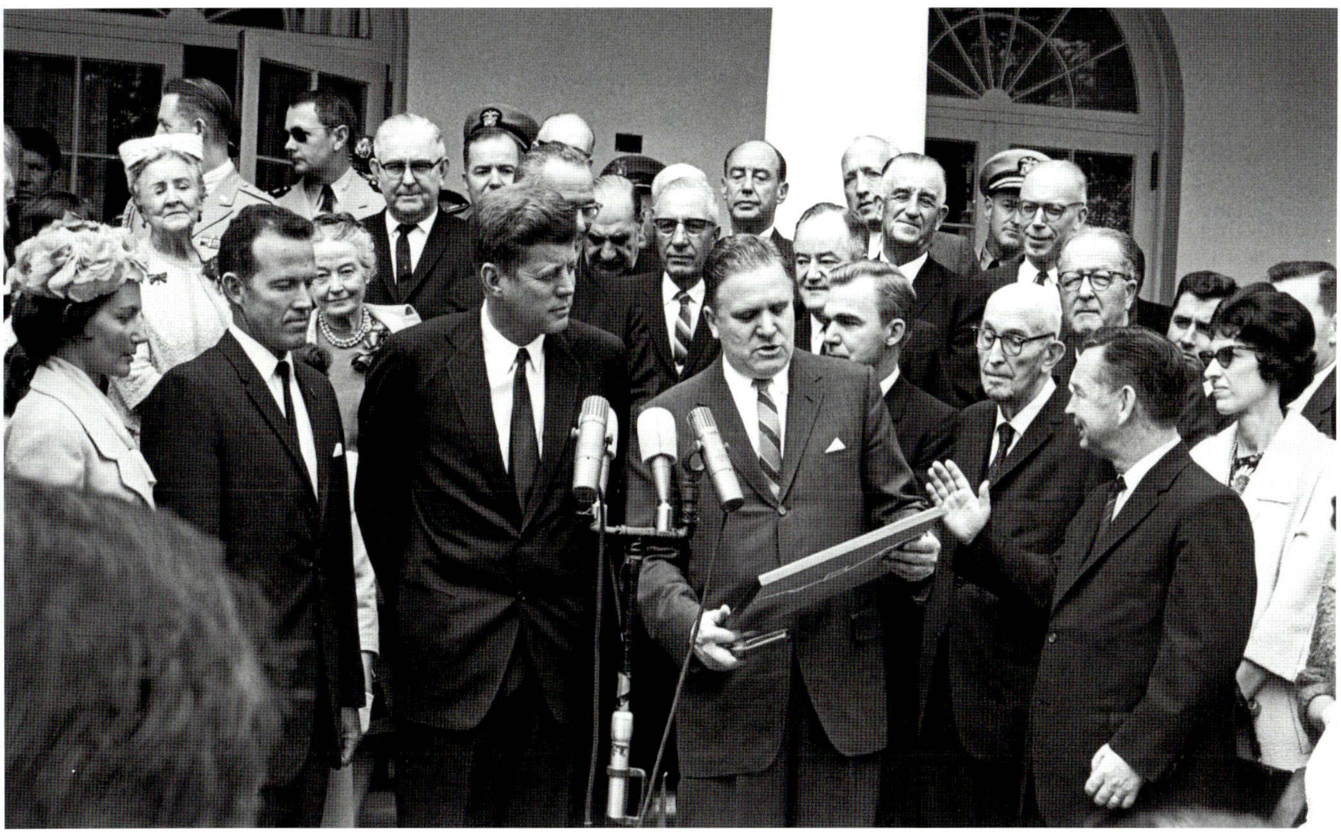

▲ In the Rose Garden, NASA Administrator James Webb first helps Kennedy present several NASA Outstanding Leadership Medals. To Webb's right are Sen. Carl Hayden (R-Ariz.), Sen. Anderson, House Majority Leader Rep. Carl Albert (D-Okla.). Also pictured behind Webb are United Nations Ambassador Adlai Stevenson and Senate Majority Whip Sen. Hubert Humphrey (D-Minn.).

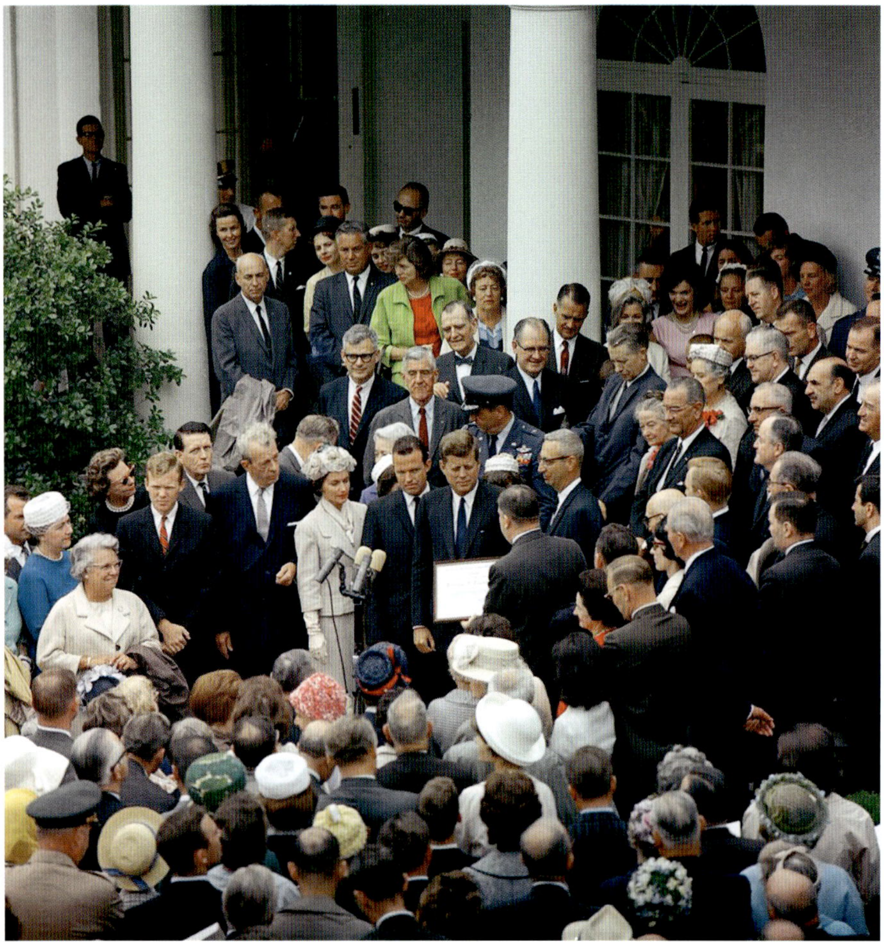

◀ Webb reads the Outstanding Leadership Medal citation for Mercury Project Office Manager Kenneth Kleinknecht, who stands to Kennedy's right. Others receiving the medal are G. Merritt Preston, MSC's top manager at Cape Canaveral; Mercury Flight Director Chris Kraft; Langley Research Director Floyd Thompson; and Maj. Gen. Leighton Davis, commander of the Air Force Missile Test Center. Vice President Johnson then presents NASA Group Achievement Awards to Rear Adm. Harold Bowen Jr., Mercury recovery operations commander; and Maj. Gen. Ben Funk, commander of the Space Systems Division of Air Force Systems Command, for their roles in developing the Atlas booster.

Others in the photo include astronauts Cooper and his wife, Shepard and his wife, Grissom and his wife, Mrs. Schirra, Slayton, Gilruth, Mrs. Kennedy, Mrs. Johnson, Sen. Humphrey, Senate Minority Leader Everett Dirksen (R-Ill.), Air Force Secretary Zuckert, Walter Williams, Rep. Albert Thomas (D-Tex.), Cooper's mother, aunt, and uncle, Sen. Smathers, Eunice Kennedy Shriver, Shepard's mother, Rep. James Fulton (R-Penn.), Sen. Clinton Anderson (D-N.Mex.).

◢ The president next asks the astronauts (John Glenn is visiting the prime minister of Japan in Tokyo) to join him for his remarks:

> First, perhaps we could have all the people here who have flown in space to come down here . . . this is a very small, exclusive group. We're delighted to welcome them and their wives. We've had a number of these ceremonies at the White House and at Cape Canaveral to pay tribute to a very distinguished group of Americans who have in our time, in this rather settled society, demonstrated that there are great frontiers still to be crossed; and in flying through space have carried with them the wishes, the prayers, the hopes and the pride of 180 million of their fellow countrymen.

An aide to Webb had suggested inviting aviator Charles Lindbergh, since it is the thirty-fifth anniversary of his solo transatlantic flight. Lindbergh is not present, but the president notes the anniversary in his remarks.

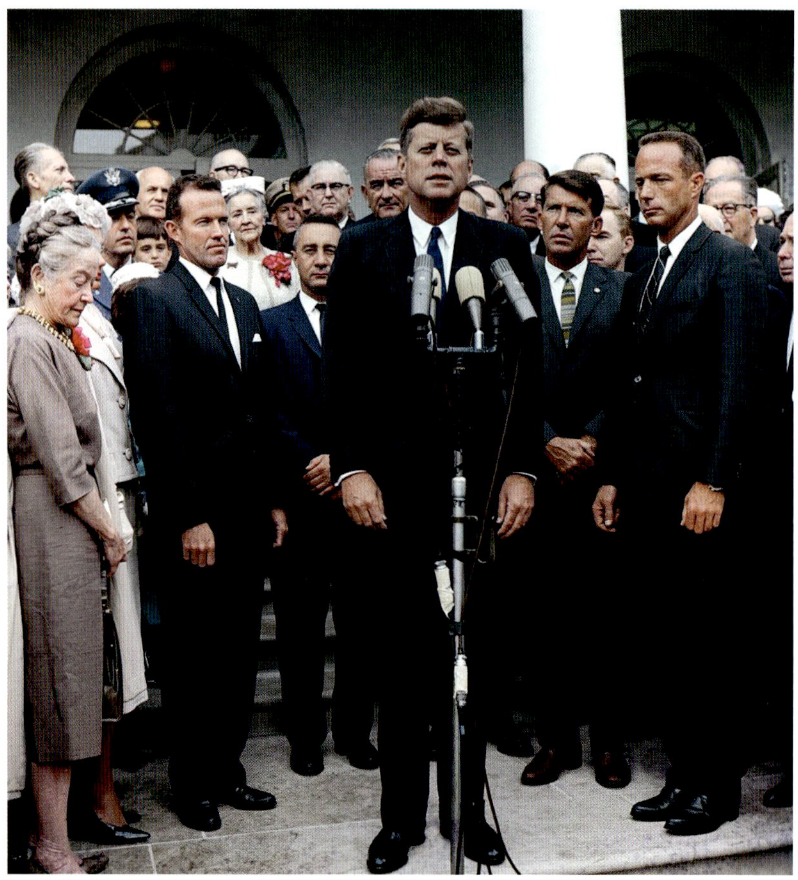

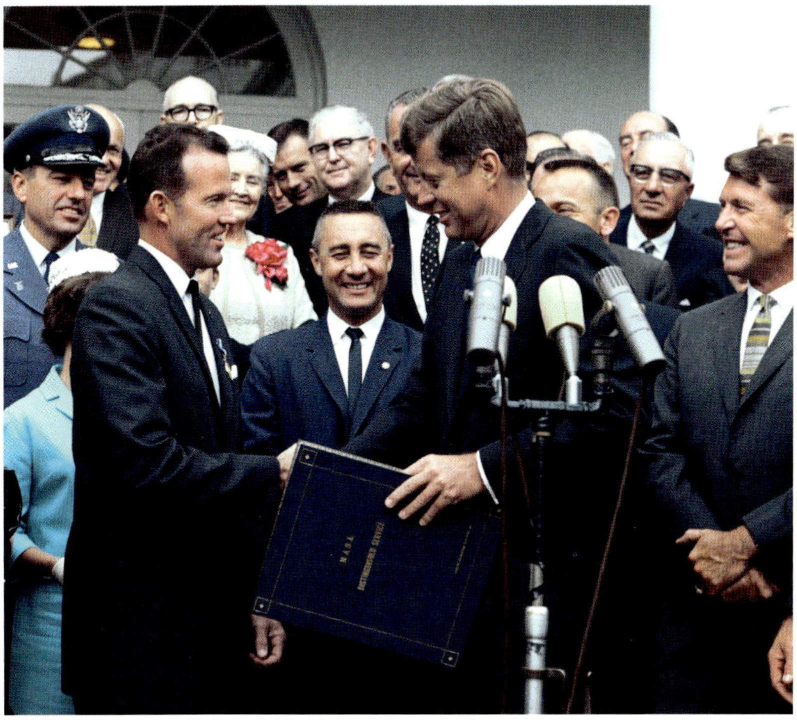

◀ "I think before the end of the '60s we will see a man on the moon," the president says, "an American, and I think in so doing, it's not merely that we're interested in making this particular journey, but we are interested in demonstrating a dominance of this new sea."

Referring to technical problems Cooper overcame during reentry, the president adds, "I think one of the things that warmed us the most during this flight was the realization that however extraordinary computers may be, that we are still ahead of them, and that man is still the most extraordinary computer of all."

Cooper simply says, "I didn't really have much to say after that. All I can say is it certainly is a great honor to be invited here to be presented this award. Thank you all very much."

▼ Following the ceremony, Cooper and Kennedy walk down the West Wing Colonnade toward the mansion.

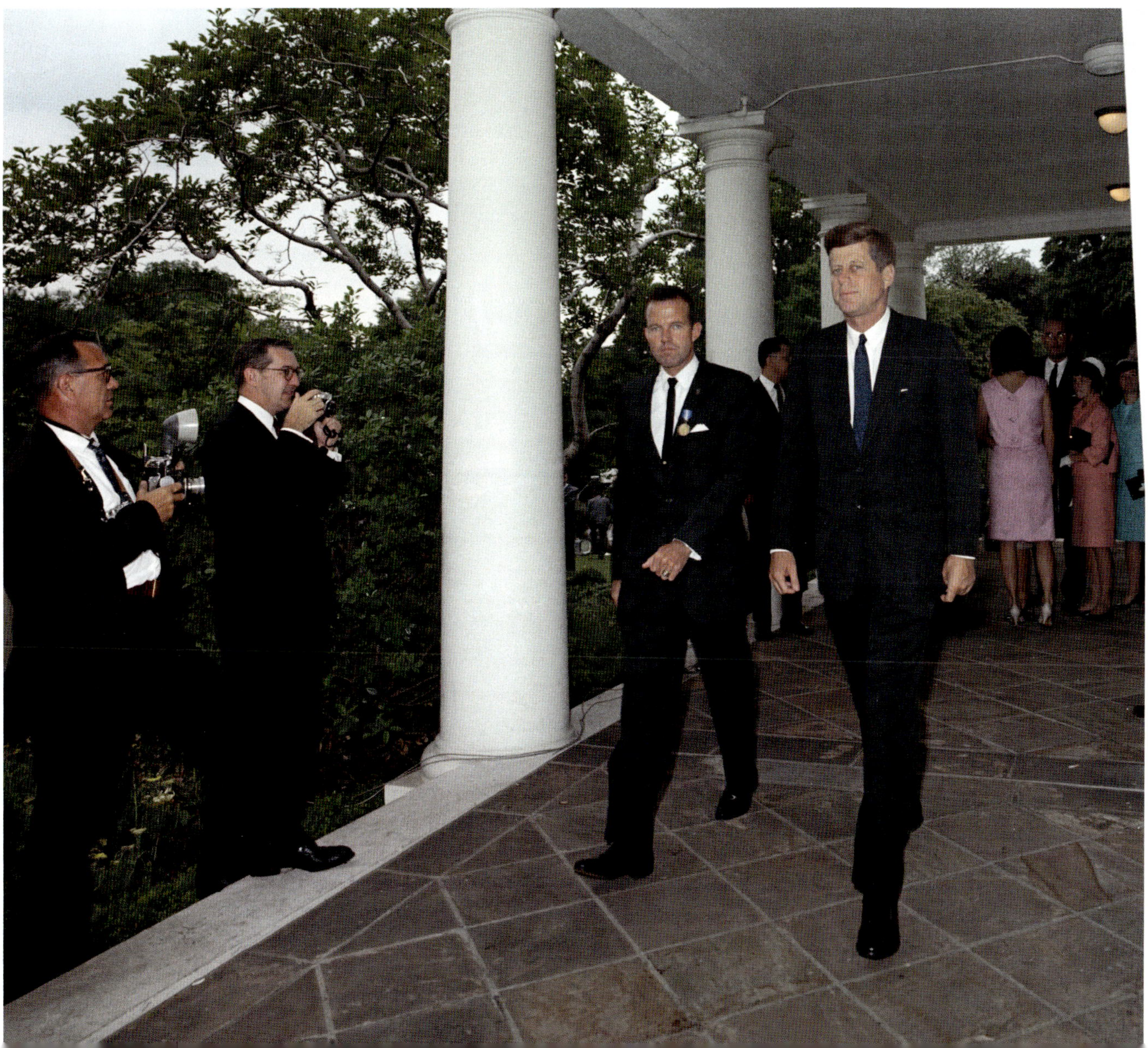

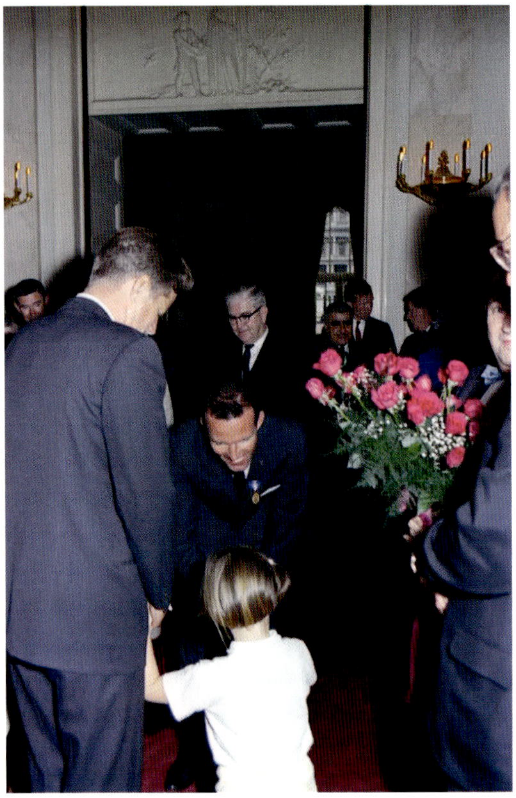

◀ Cooper meets Caroline Kennedy with the president in the Cross Hall. Rep. James Fulton (R-Pa.) is at far left; Cooper's uncle James Truscott is behind the astronaut.

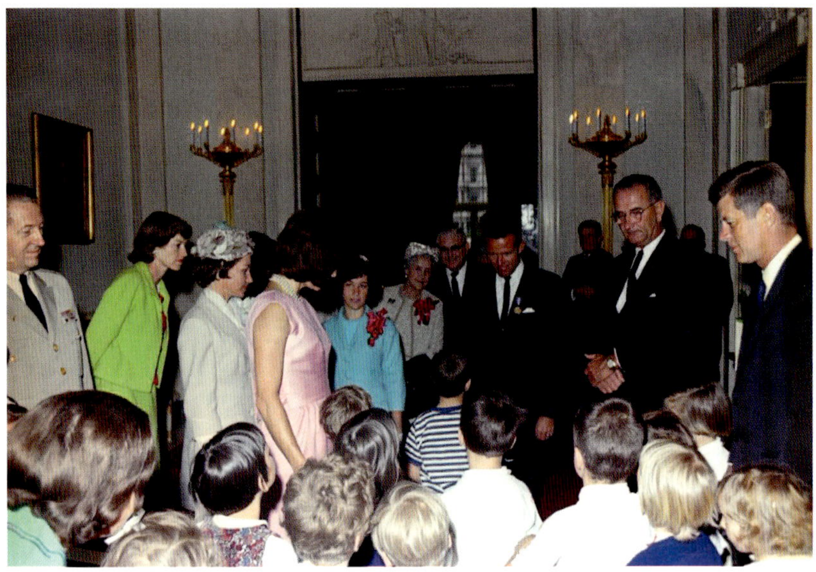

▶ Cooper speaks with a group of children. The State Dining Room is visible through the open door.

L–R: Maj. Gen. Chester Clifton; Eunice Kennedy Shriver; Cooper's wife, Trudy; Jacqueline Kennedy; Cooper daughter Cam; Cooper's aunt and uncle, Jewell and James Truscott; Cooper; Rep. Fulton (in background); Johnson; Caroline Kennedy (partially hidden); and the president.

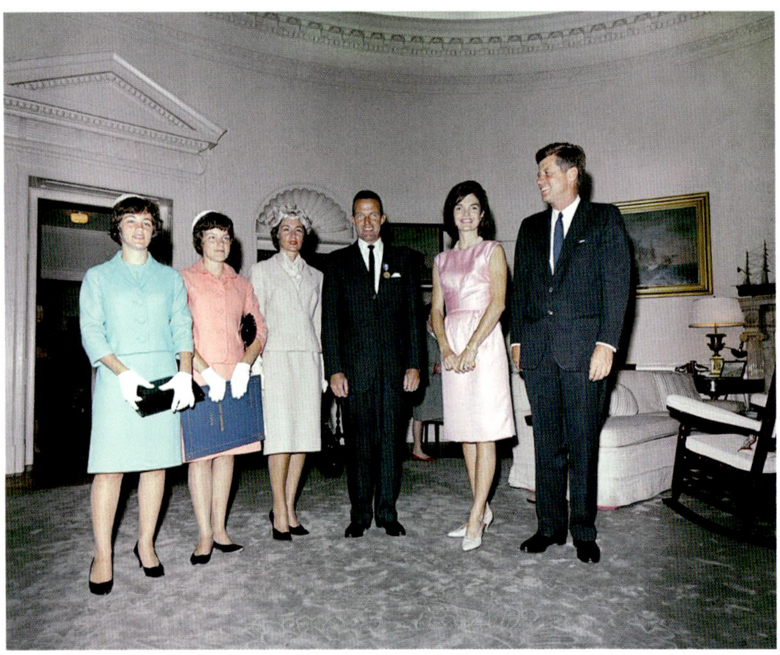

◀ The Coopers pose with the Kennedys in the Oval Office after the ceremony. Cam holds her father's medal case; Jan holds the medal citation. The First Lady's redecoration of the room, including red carpeting, will be completed just before the president's death in November.

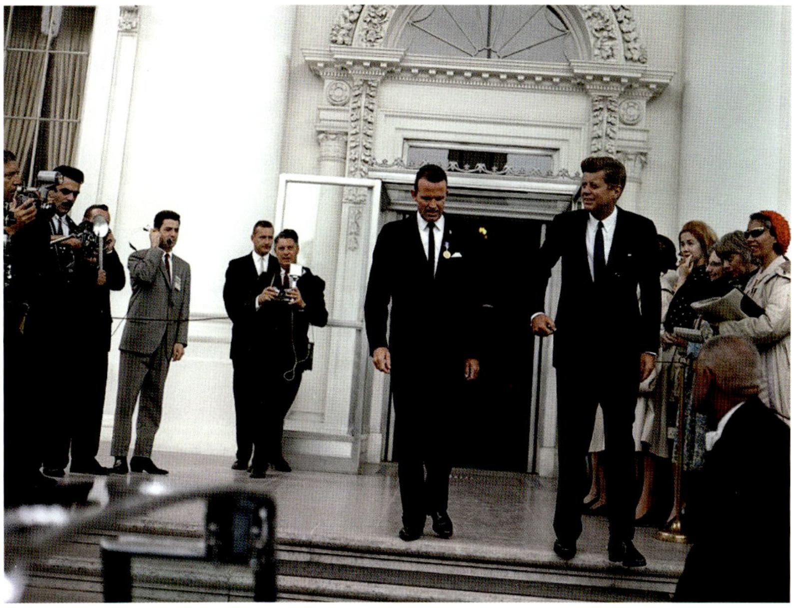

▲ Kennedy escorts Cooper to his waiting presidential limousine on the North Portico just before 1:00 p.m.

To Cooper's right are White House photographer Army Capt. Cecil Stoughton (left of doorway, holding camera) and Secret Service Agent Paul Burns (behind Stoughton). Stoughton, who took many of the photos in this book, also snapped the iconic photo of Lyndon Johnson taking the presidential oath of office aboard Air Force One in Dallas after Kennedy's death.

The astronaut and his family ride in a motorcade to the US Capitol, where Cooper, like Glenn in 1962, addresses a joint meeting of Congress. The crowd along the Pennsylvania Avenue parade route and at the Capitol is estimated to be 250,000.

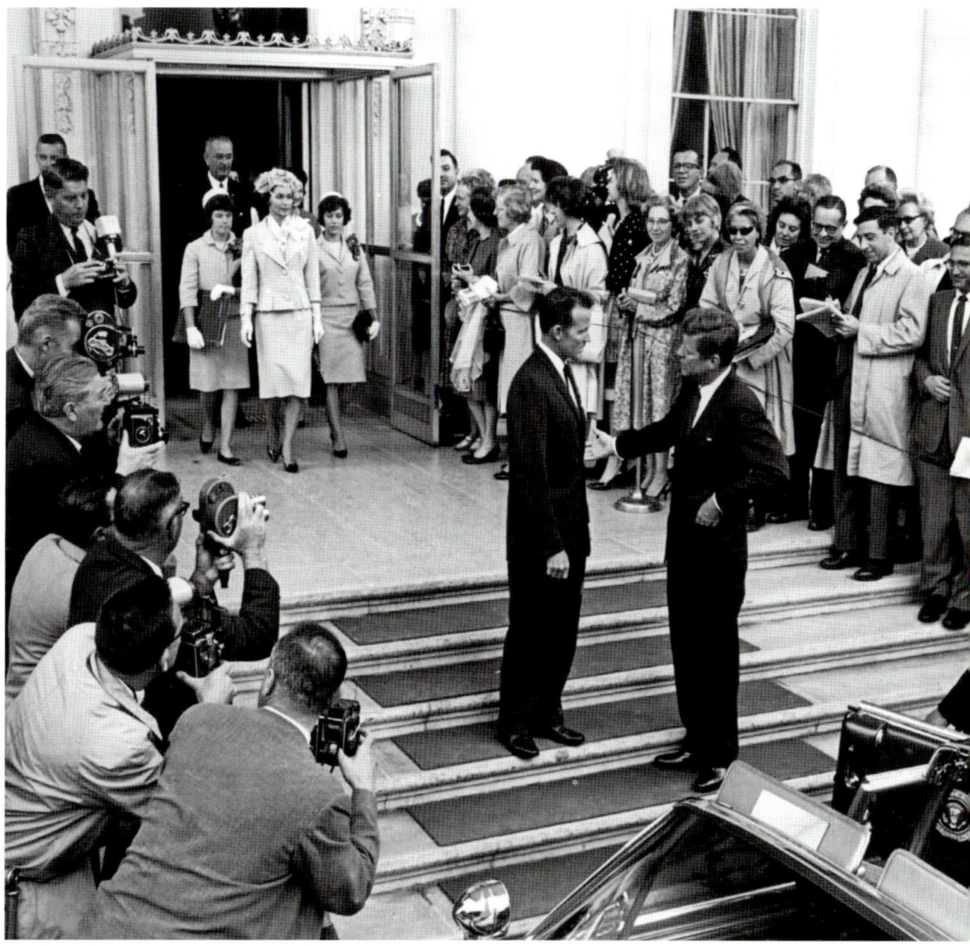

▶ Kennedy bids Cooper farewell.

On May 17, the president had called House Speaker John McCormack (D-Mass.) to discuss plans for Cooper's DC visit, recorded by Kennedy's secret taping system:

McCormack: "Are you gonna give him a big parade?"

Kennedy: "Well, wait just a second. He is coming here and I am going to decorate him, and then he would go up to the Capitol. I suppose that we would a . . . that they would parade him. What we are trying to do is get the most out of it for the space program."

McCormack agreed on the call to say Cooper's address to Congress is his idea rather than Kennedy's.

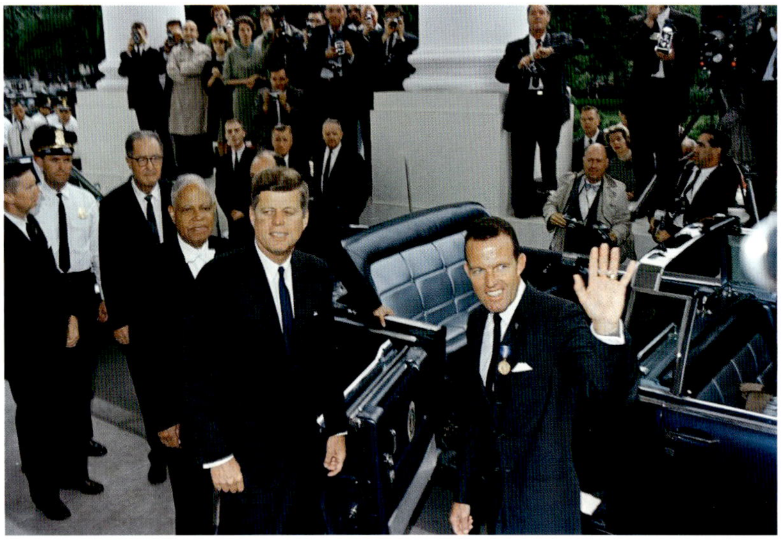

◀ Third from left is Sen. Anderson, who rides with Cooper and Johnson. As chairman of the Committee on Aeronautical and Space Sciences from 1963 to 1973, he is one of the most outspoken advocates of the space program. Also pictured: Secret Service Agents Win Lawson and John "Muggsy" O'Leary; *New York Times* photographer George Tames, and chief White House photographer Robert Knudsen, also responsible for many images in this book.

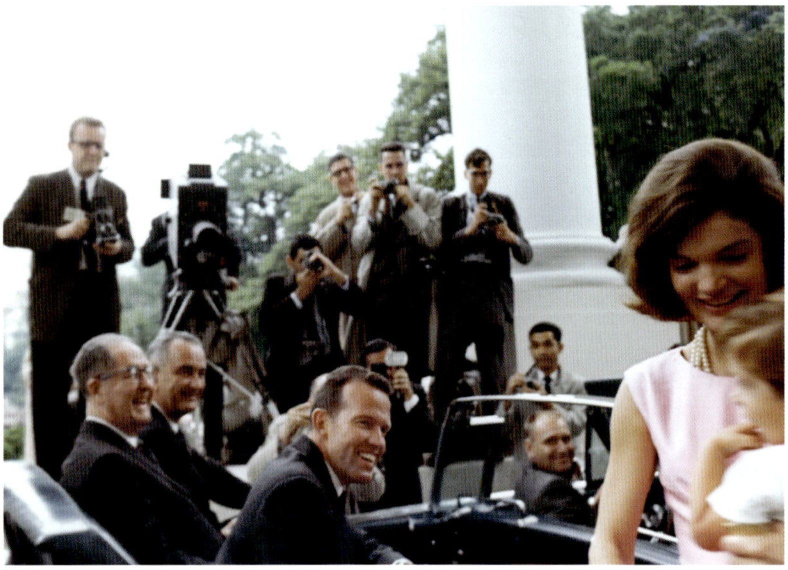

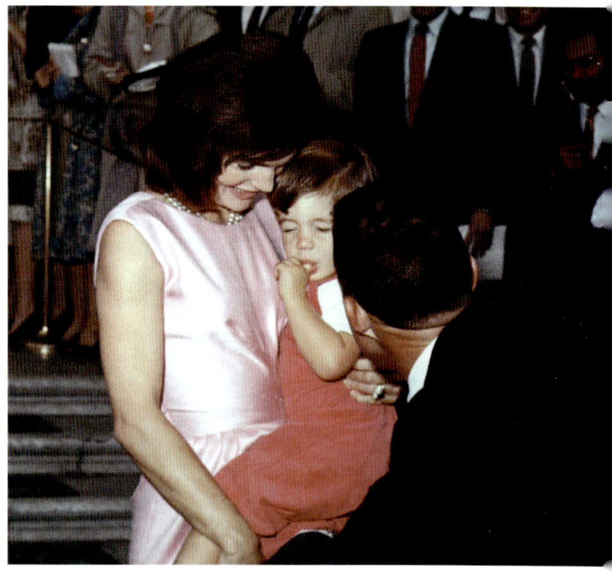

◥ The First Lady brings over her somewhat disinterested two-and-a-half-year-old son, John F. Kennedy Jr., to say good-bye to Cooper in the limousine. She is expecting her third child in August.

▶ In these still frames from a Defense Department film, the president arrives on Marine One at the White Sands Missile Range (WSMR) parade ground at 3:35 p.m. MST on June 5, 1963, after Air Force One had landed at Holloman Air Force Base, New Mexico.

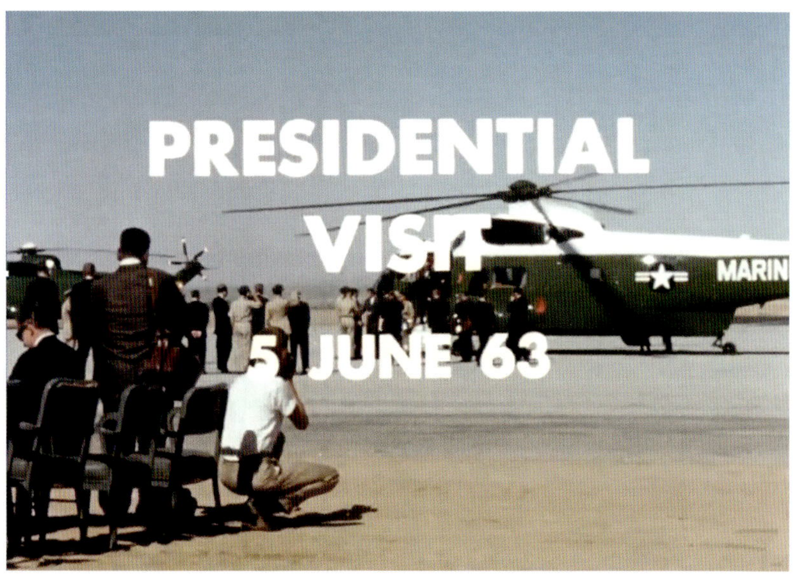

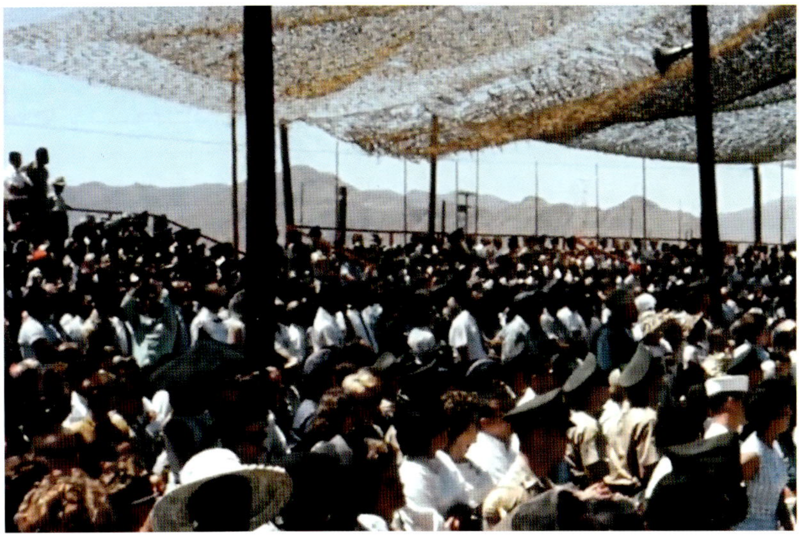

◀ Waiting are Army, Navy, and NASA personnel and dependents. Kennedy will witness seven Army and Navy missile demonstration launches over the next two hours.

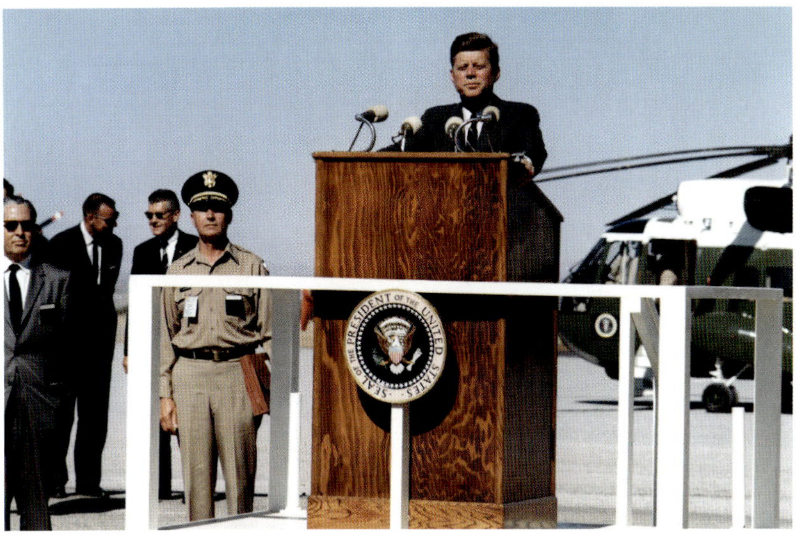

◀ Kennedy first speaks to the crowd of about thirty-five hundred just east of WSMR headquarters. "All of us who leave Washington, DC, with all of its complexities . . . get tremendously heartened by a visit to those of you who are working in the field and who can see, day-by-day, measurable progress which strengthens our country and those associated with it," he says. "This must give you the greatest satisfaction." WSMR commander Maj. Gen. J. Frederick Thorlin is at left, with Secret Service Agent Jerry Behn behind him.

▶ Kennedy greets guests along the rope line after his comments before heading to the first of two viewing sites five miles away for what is called Operation Missile Exercise White Sands. His visit is part of a five-day swing through five western states including Hawaii.

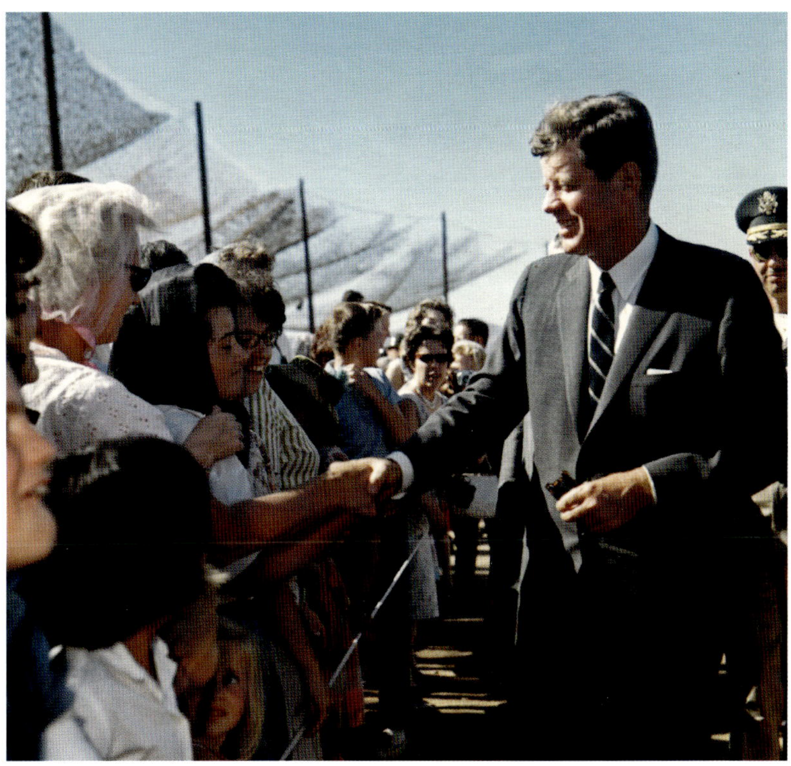

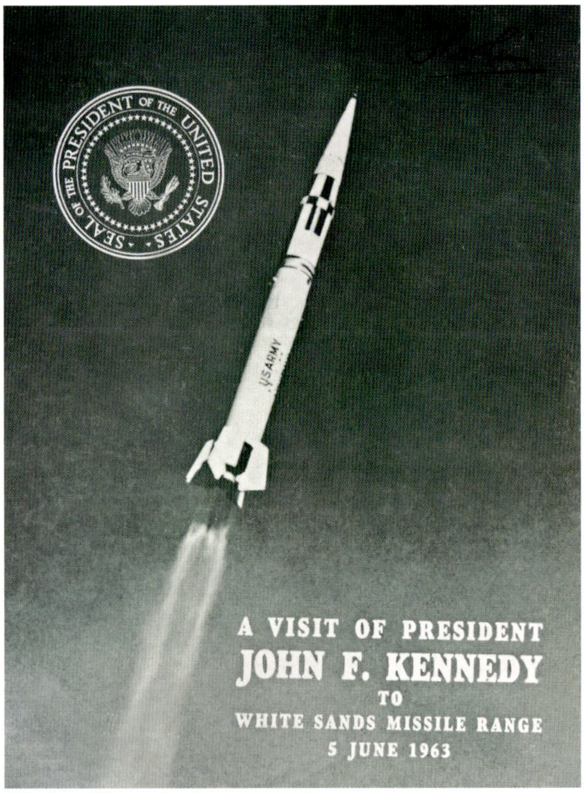

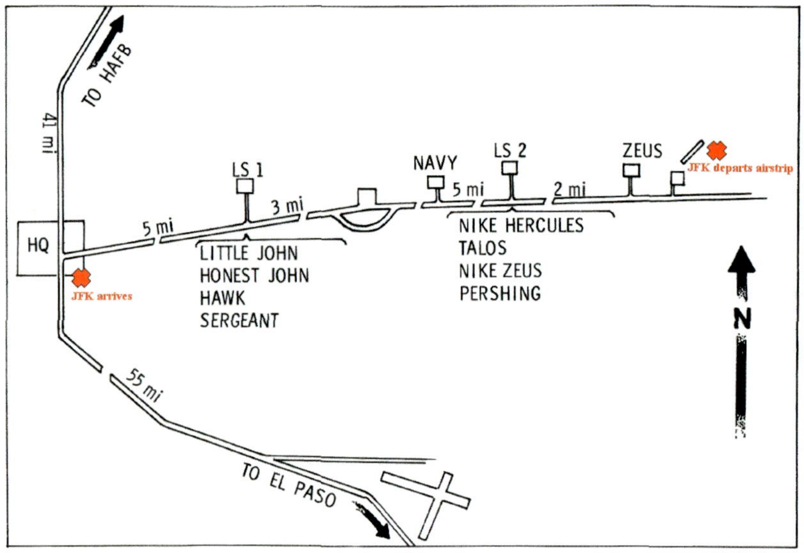

▲ Map for the president's visit from the official program (red text added).

▲ Maj. Gen. Thorlin's copy of the official program for the president's visit on June 5, 1963.

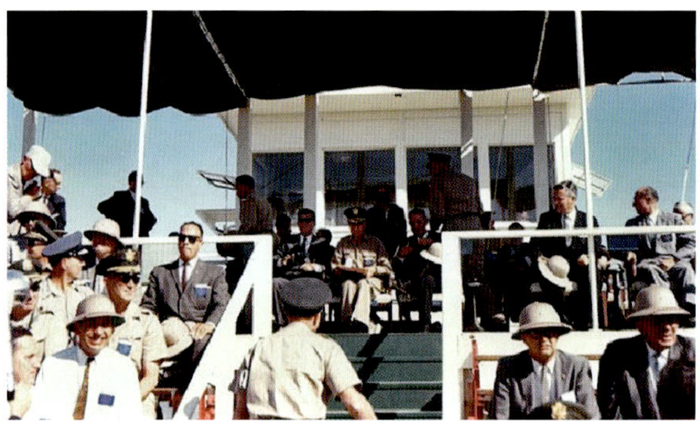

▶ The president settles in at LC-32, called Army Launch Site No. 1, as the exercise begins about 4:00 p.m. First up is an Honest John firing, the first unguided nuclear-capable surface-to-surface missile in the US arsenal.

Kennedy declines to wear a pith helmet, though Johnson does. Offering hats to reporters, Press Secretary Pierre Salinger asks, "Don't you want to be white hunters?"

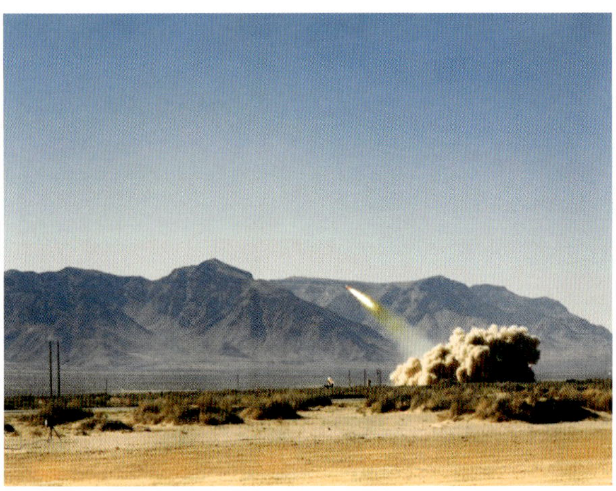

◀ The second launch, minutes later, is a Little John, a free flight artillery rocket system that carries either nuclear or conventional warheads. It is primarily intended for use in airborne assault operations and to complement the larger Honest John.

As with the Honest John, the missile is launched north toward a target ten miles away in the San Andreas Mountains; it was delivered by helicopter minutes before to demonstrate its mobility.

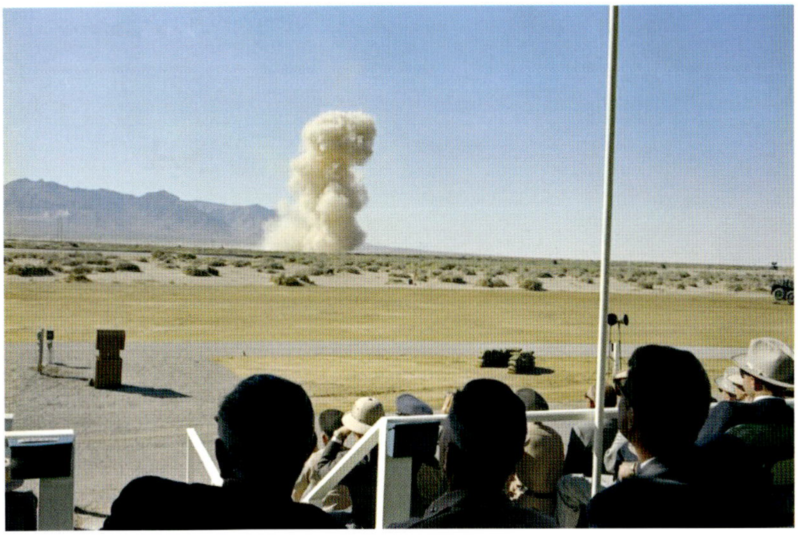

◀ Johnson, Maj. Gen. Thorlin, and the president see the smoke left by the Little John.

The dignitaries next see a Sergeant launch, a short-range surface-to-surface missile recently deployed in Europe and South Korea, also nuclear-capable.

The final launch at this site is a Hawk, which successfully intercepts a drone QF-80 fighter jet. Hawk is a medium-range surface-to-air missile designed to be a much more mobile counterpart to the Nike Hercules.

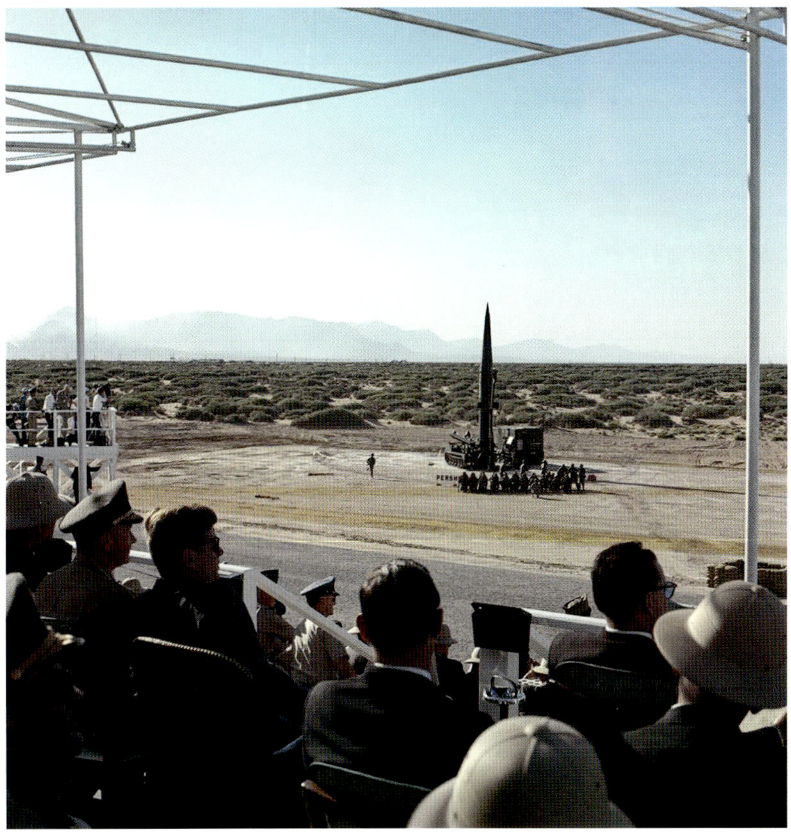

▶ The president arrives at LC-37 (Launch Site No. 2) eight miles away about 4:30 p.m., where the Army displays a Pershing, a two-stage field artillery ballistic missile system (its long range precludes a demonstration launch). It will replace the Redstone as the Army's primary nuclear-capable theater-level weapon in 1964.

The commander-in-chief first sees one Nike Hercules surface-to-air missile intercept another. Nuclear-armed Nike Hercules missiles are deployed at the time in the United States, Europe, Turkey, and South Korea.

Some three hundred members of the news media cover the exercise, including twenty from NATO countries that are customers for US weapons systems.

L–R: Army Chief of Staff Gen. Earle Wheeler; Johnson (pith helmet); Maj. Gen. Thorlin; Kennedy; and US Ambassador to Costa Rica Raymond Telles (center, back to camera), an El Paso native. Also in attendance are twenty-four members of Congress, including future president Rep. Gerald Ford of Michigan, the Joint Chiefs of Staff, three governors, and executives from defense contractors for the weapons systems.

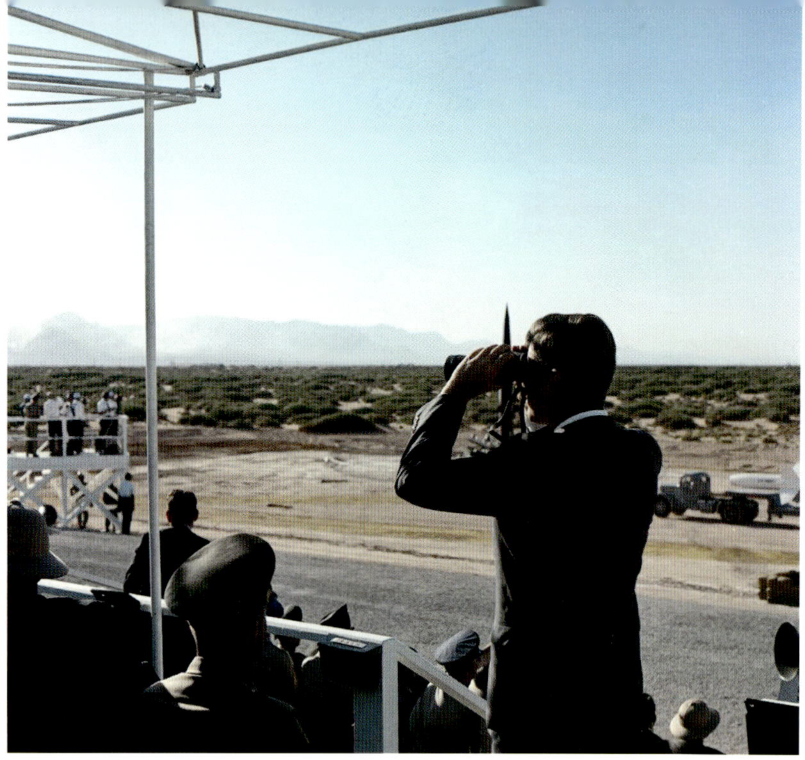

▶ Kennedy watches an attempt by a Navy Talos, a nuclear-capable, long-range ship-to-air missile, to intercept a drone QF-80 jet. It is the only failure of the day out of seven launches to the chagrin of Navy officials at the demonstration.

The Army modified the steps at both viewing stands two days before the visit to better accommodate the president's back problems.

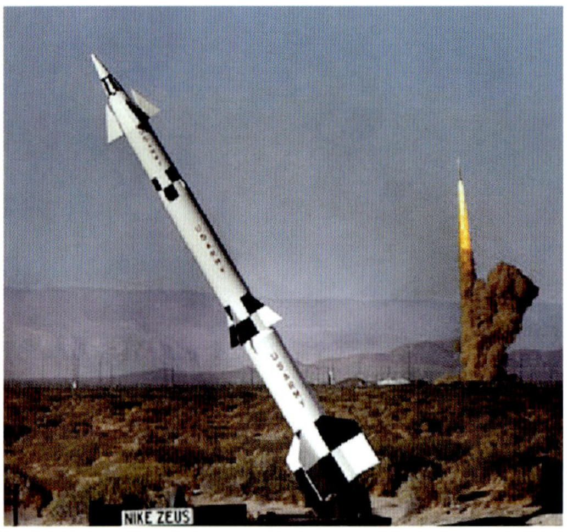

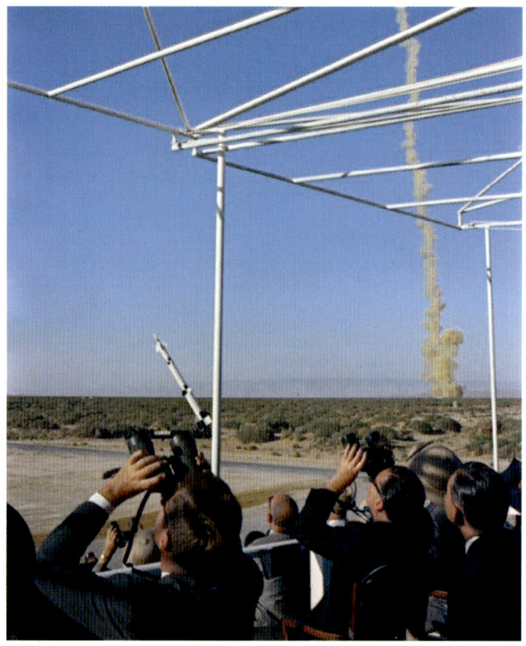

▶ The final test of the day is a Nike Zeus, developed to intercept incoming Soviet missiles. It is launched from an underground complex (another is in the foreground on display).

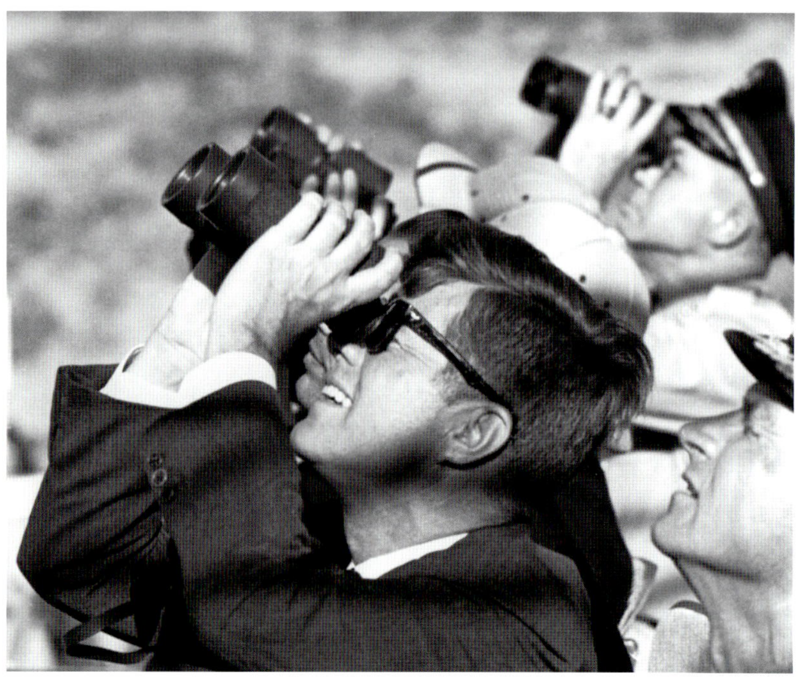

▶ The president watches as the missile climbs through the atmosphere. Kennedy had initially agreed to a large Nike Zeus deployment in 1961, but Science Advisor Jerome Wiesner cautioned him on the expense and the inherent complexities of the controversial system. Caught up in the debate over the system's effectiveness, Kennedy immersed himself in its details. The Pentagon had actually cancelled the Zeus program that January as ineffective but continued with a follow-on system dubbed Nike-X, a layered system with more than one type of missile and improved radar.

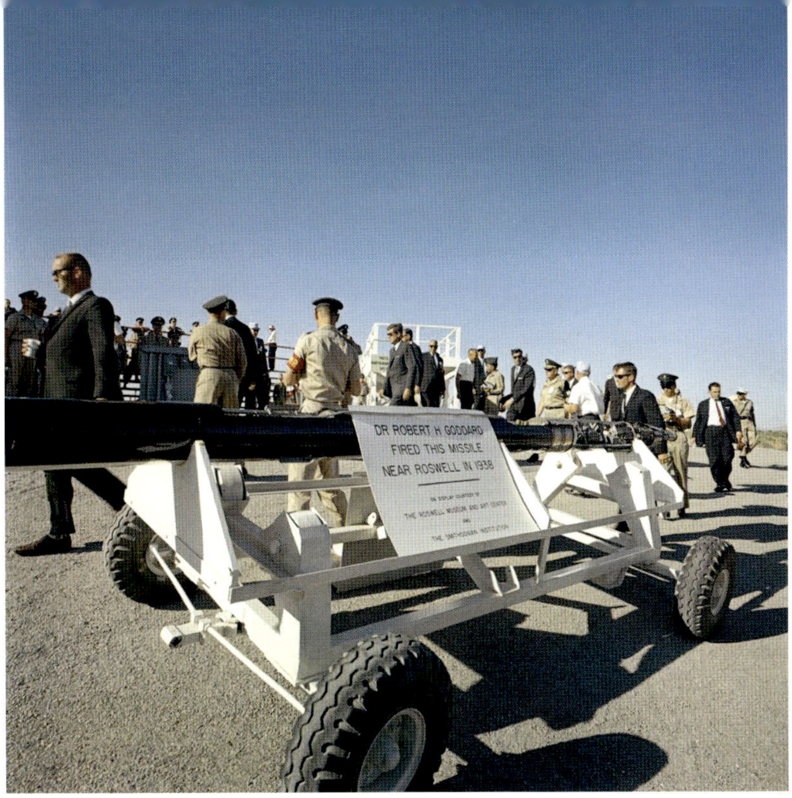

▶ Kennedy's party passes a display of a small rocket built by Robert Goddard and launched near Roswell, New Mexico, in 1938. Goddard had built and launched the world's first liquid-fueled rocket in 1926 in Massachusetts, but moved his operation to more isolated New Mexico in 1930.

▼ After more than two hours of weapons demonstrations, Kennedy and Johnson "troop the line" to inspect launch crews from the afternoon's exercise. (Courtesy of Warren C. Weaver.)

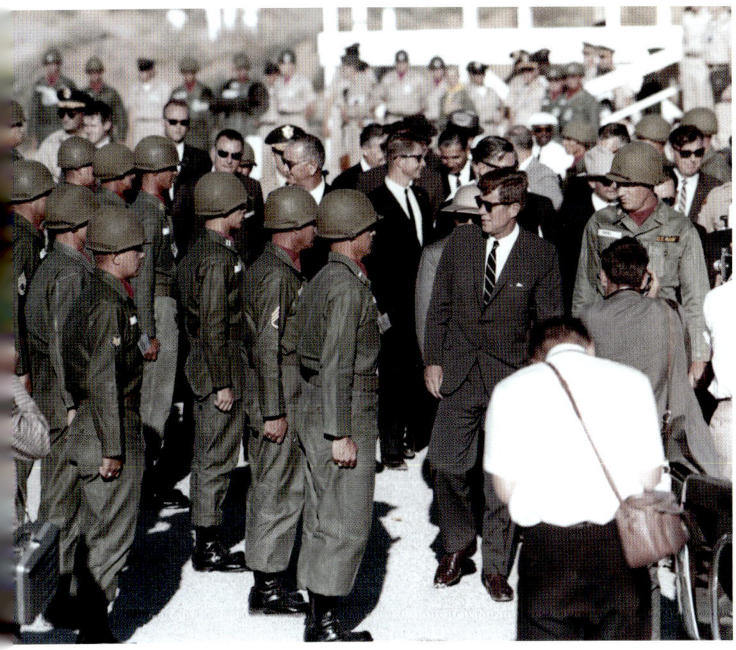

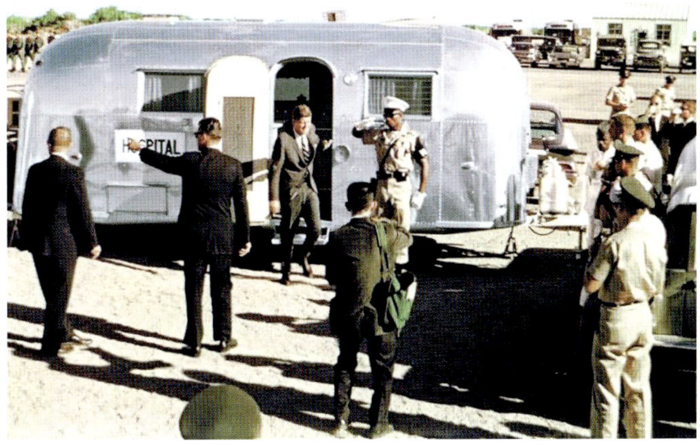

▲ The president briefly gives newsmen a start after he visits an Airstream trailer marked "HOSPITAL" to make a phone call.

▶ Kennedy accepts a scale model of the Sergeant missile from Sgt. 1st Class Harmon Swits of the 3rd Battalion, 38th Field Artillery. The Sergeant is already deployed in Europe and South Korea, carrying either a nuclear warhead or high explosives. Vice President Johnson (behind the president) receives a commemorative plaque from the 1st Pershing Battalion. Both the 1st and 3rd battalions are based at Ft. Sill, Oklahoma. Gen. Wheeler can be seen at center.

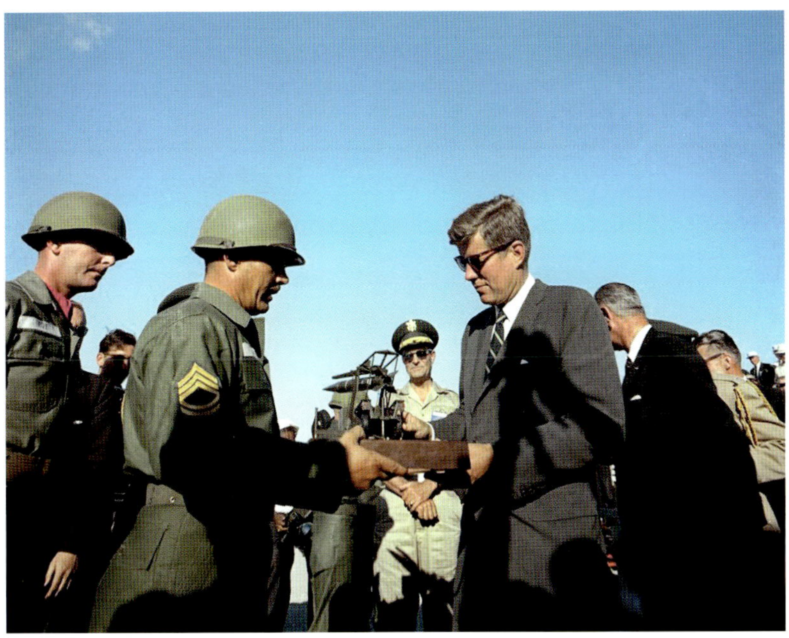

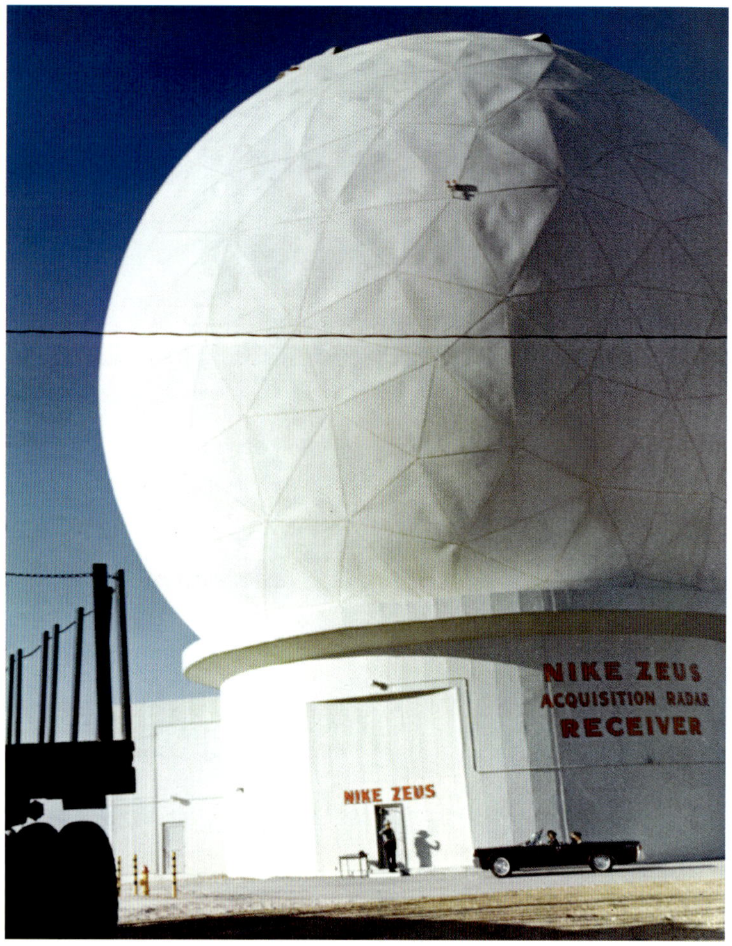

▶ About 5:00 p.m. at the Nike Zeus complex two miles away, the president next greets the launch crew, attends a short classified briefing on the missile system at the radar building, and sees the giant antenna inside revolve. His maroon Lincoln is provided by the Poole Motor Co. in Las Cruces. At 5:40 p.m. Kennedy leaves by helicopter for El Paso (Texas) International Airport (where SAM 26000 has been moved) to spend the night. He would fly to California and eventually on to Hawaii the next day.

▼ On the helicopter flight to El Paso after the WSMR exercise, New Mexico Gov. Jack Campbell hands the president a copy of this promotional report stressing the state's aerospace heritage and its desired role in the growing US space effort. Campbell and Sen. Clinton Anderson are enthusiastic advocates for the range to become a major space center. In August, NASA conducts the first of five Little Joe II launches from the range to test the Apollo spacecraft's Launch Escape System. WSMR is also the site for the first US test-launches of captured German V-2 missiles after World War II and for Redstone booster testing.

◢ The report argues that New Mexico is ideal for supporting space and defense programs, noting that "interracial problems are non-existent."

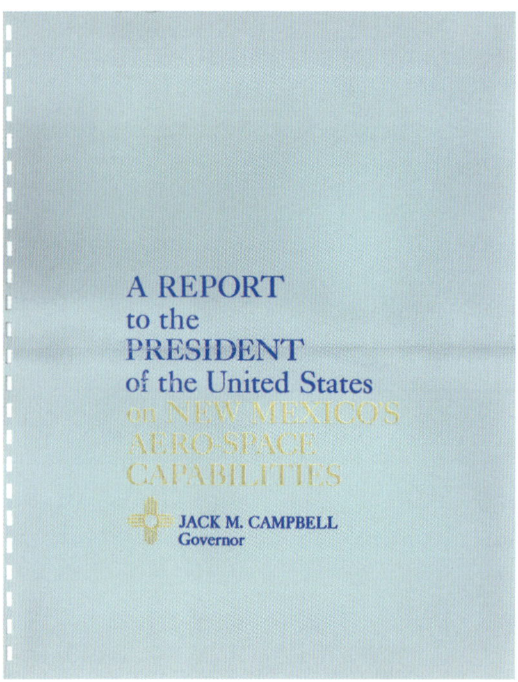

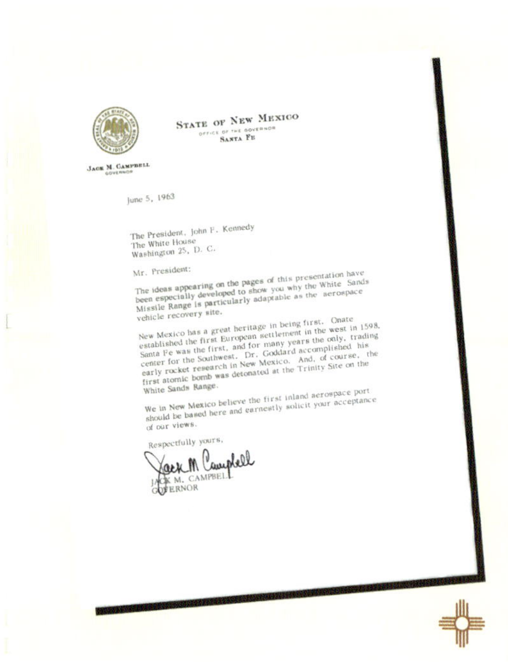

STATE OF NEW MEXICO
OFFICE OF THE GOVERNOR
SANTA FE

JACK M. CAMPBELL
GOVERNOR

June 5, 1963

The President, John F. Kennedy
The White House
Washington 25, D. C.

Mr. President:

The ideas appearing on the pages of this presentation have been especially developed to show you why the White Sands Missile Range is particularly adaptable as the aerospace vehicle recovery site.

New Mexico has a great heritage in being first. Onate established the first European settlement in the west in 1598. Santa Fe was the first, and for many years the only, trading center for the Southwest. Dr. Goddard accomplished his early rocket research in New Mexico. And, of course, the first atomic bomb was detonated at the Trinity Site on the White Sands Range.

We in New Mexico believe the first inland aerospace port should be based here and earnestly solicit your acceptance of our views.

Respectfully yours,

Jack M Campbell
JACK M. CAMPBELL
GOVERNOR

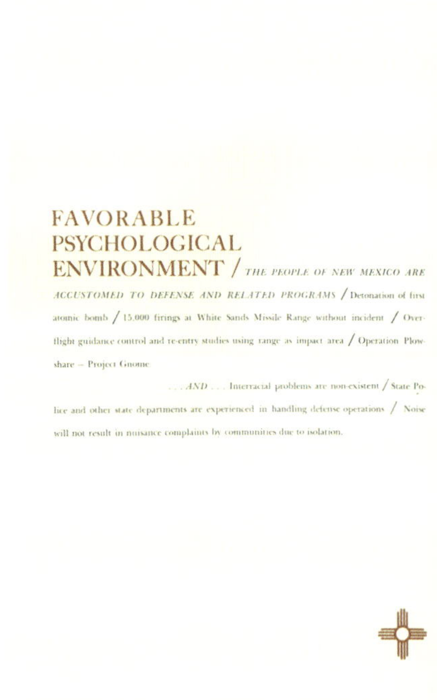

FAVORABLE PSYCHOLOGICAL ENVIRONMENT / *THE PEOPLE OF NEW MEXICO ARE ACCUSTOMED TO DEFENSE AND RELATED PROGRAMS* / Detonation of first atomic bomb / 15,000 firings at White Sands Missile Range without incident / Overflight guidance control and re-entry studies using range as impact area / Operation Plowshare – Project Gnome

. . . *AND* . . . Interracial problems are non-existent / State Police and other state departments are experienced in handling defense operations / Noise will not result in nuisance complaints by communities due to isolation.

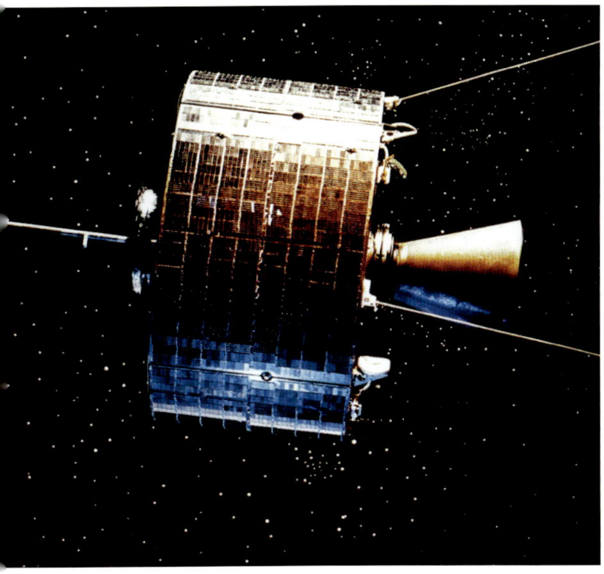

▲ Model of Syncom II.

▼ On August 23, 1963, Kennedy participates in the first live two-way conversation between heads of state via satellite. At 9:35 a.m. he speaks with Nigerian Prime Minister Abubakar Balewa from the Oval Office using two new US satellites: Syncom II, the world's first geosynchronous communications satellite launched the previous month, and Relay 1, in orbit since December. Balewa is aboard USNS *Kingsport*, temporarily stationed in Nigeria's Lagos Harbor. During the friendly but somewhat awkward two-minute conversation, the two men trade greetings but do not mention the significance of the transmission itself.

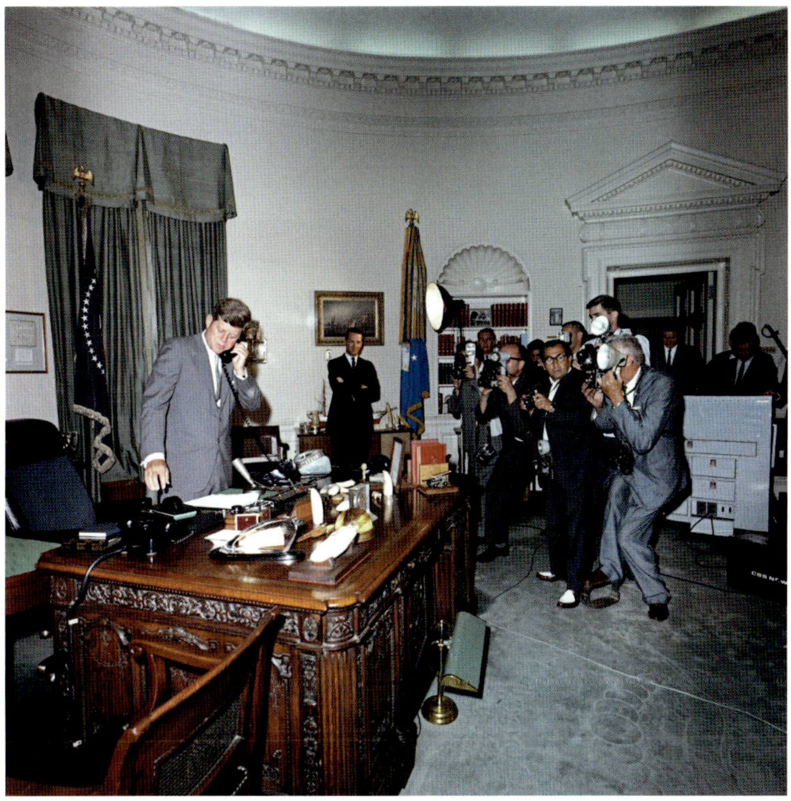

▼ Another page envisions WSMR as the landing site for future space flights. The installation is designated as a backup landing site during the Space Shuttle program, although only the third shuttle out of 133 landings touches down there in 1983 after heavy rains flood the prime site, a normally dry lake bed runway at Edwards AFB in California.

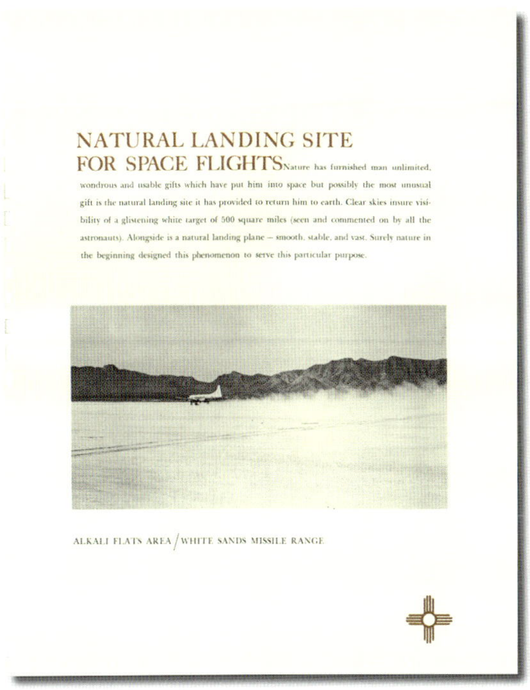

NATURAL LANDING SITE FOR SPACE FLIGHTS Nature has furnished man unlimited, wondrous and usable gifts which have put him into space but possibly the most unusual gift is the natural landing site it has provided to return him to earth. Clear skies insure visibility of a glistening white target of 500 square miles (seen and commented on by all the astronauts). Alongside is a natural landing plane – smooth, stable, and vast. Surely nature in the beginning designed this phenomenon to serve this particular purpose.

ALKALI FLATS AREA / WHITE SANDS MISSILE RANGE

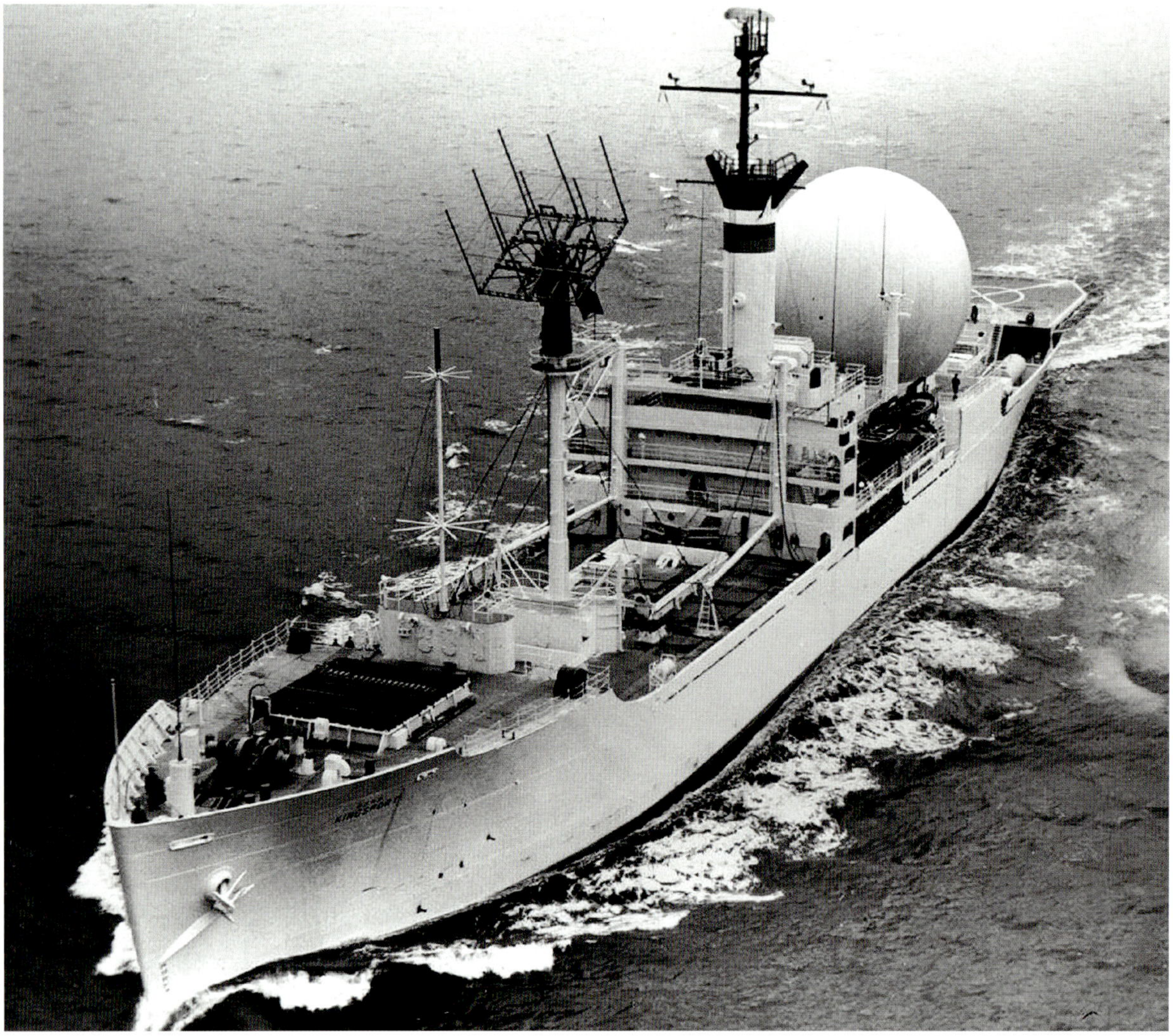

▲ USNS *Kingsport*, a former World War II victory ship, was converted in 1961 to become the first satellite communications ship, for use by the US Army Satellite Communications Agency. Modifications included a parabolic antenna on her afterdeck in a fifty-three-foot, plastic, air-pressurized radome. The antenna permits precision tracking of a satellite at any angle above the horizon. *Kingsport* serves as the terminal control station during testing and evaluation of Syncom II.

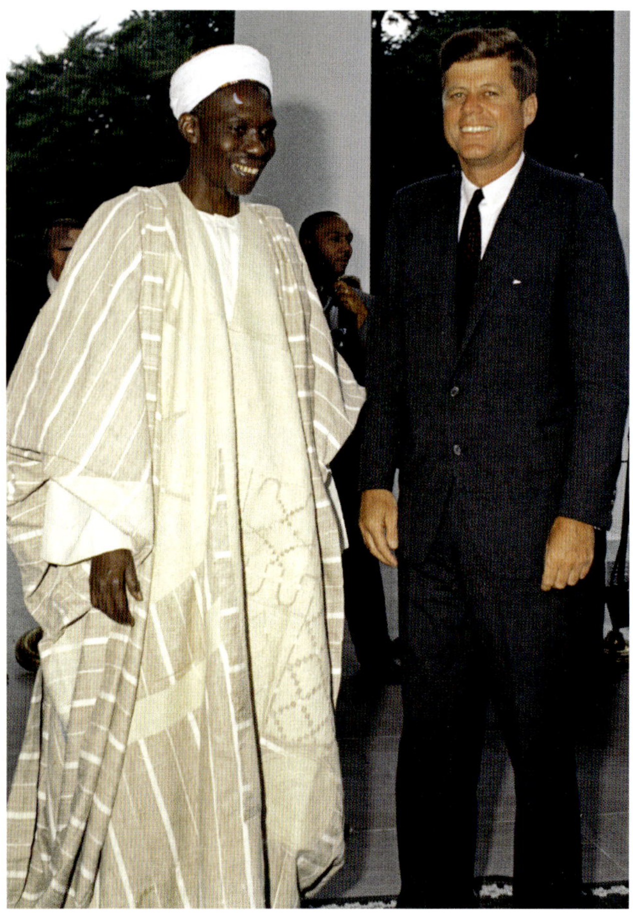

▶ Nigerian Prime Minister Abubakar Balewa with President Kennedy at the White House in 1961.

:08

SEPTEMBER–NOVEMBER 1963

"Space has lost a lot of its glamour"

IN THE FALL OF 1963, President Kennedy faces continuing concerns about the cost of the space race. The Congress trims his budget request for NASA for the coming year by eleven percent, and he expresses his qualms in a tape-recorded meeting with NASA chief Webb.

Publicly, the president stresses that the United States is catching up with the Soviets and would soon surpass them, at least in space lift capability. To underscore the point, he makes what would be his last visit to Cape Canaveral to see the record-breaking Saturn I on the pad. As a bonus, he watches from a ship as a submarine launches a nuclear-capable Polaris missile.

In his final speech addressing the United Nations in September, Kennedy again suggests a joint manned moon mission, but the initiative would die with him in November.

Kennedy meets with Webb in the Oval Office at 11:30 a.m. on September 18. Transcript excerpts are below:

Kennedy: "Well I talked the other day, about two weeks ago, to McNamara and [Deputy Defense Secretary Roswell] Gilpatric for a few minutes and said that I thought the space program, looking ahead, unless the Russians did something dramatic and we don't have anything dramatic coming up for the next twelve months, so it's going to be an

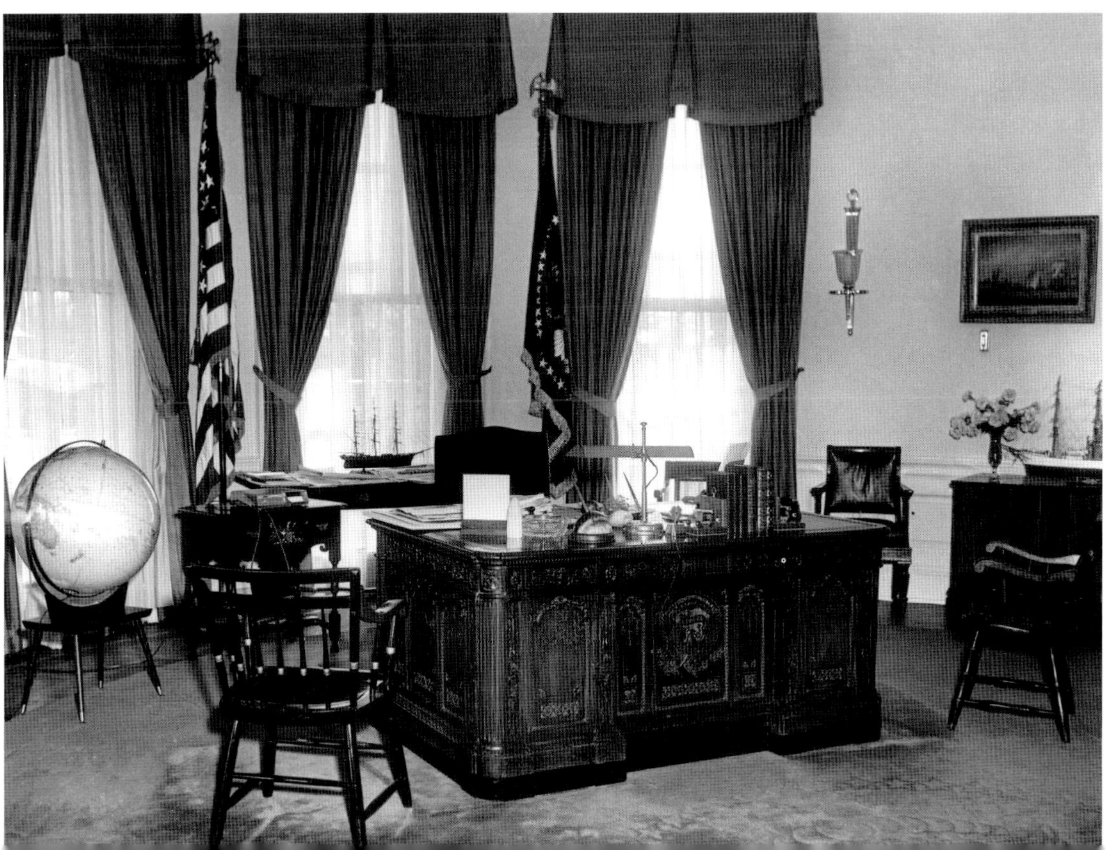

attack on the budget, but this looks like a hell of a lot of dough to go to the moon when you can go—you can learn most of that you want scientifically through instruments and putting a man on the moon really is a stunt and it isn't worth that many billions.

"Therefore the heat's going to go on unless we can say this has got some military justification and not just prestige. Otherwise Eisenhower is going to be kicking us around and we're going to look like he's probably right—they don't want to spend that kind of dough. Why should we spend that kind of dough to put a man on the moon?

"But it seems to me what we've got to try and do, is for the reasons you suggested: we've got to wrap around in this country, a military use for what we're doing and spending in space. If we don't, it does look like a stunt and too much money . . .

"I am concerned that I have a—I think this can be an asset, this program. I think in time, it's like a lot of things; this is mid-journey, and therefore everybody says, 'what the hell are we making this trip for,' but at the end of the thing they may be glad we made it. But we've got to defend ourselves now and I think that at least it's occurred to me that unless the Russians do something spectacular, the only way we can defend ourselves is if we put a national security rather than a prestige label on this.

"Obviously you want to present, like the thing you said, the kind of improvements in our national life which will come from this: the leadership of the United States and the national security we'll get from it—all those factors.

"The only thing that isn't, today particularly, a plus, in I think surveys a year ago our space program was a much bigger political—now it's not as much because this happens to be, as I said, a still period in it. [break] The difficulty is that I'm not sure how much, right now, I don't think the space program has much political positives."

Webb: "I agree, I think this is a real problem."

Kennedy: "I mean if the Russians do some tremendous feat, then it would stimulate interest again, but right now space has lost a lot of its glamour."

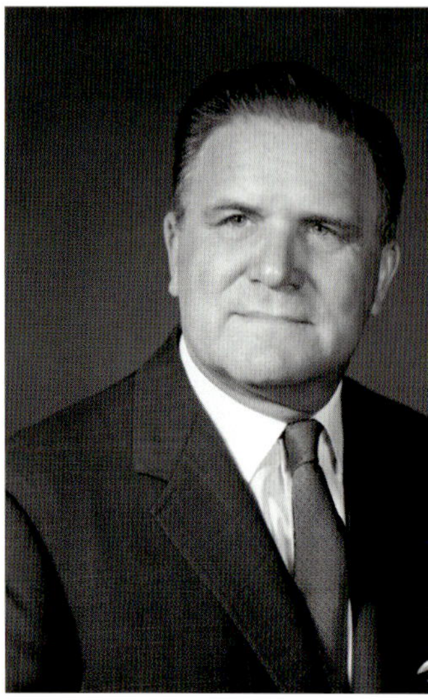

Webb

▼ On September 20, 1963, the president addresses the 18th United Nations General Assembly in New York at 11:15 a.m., delivering his second and final speech, again making a pitch for a cooperative manned moon program. (Photo by Teddy Chen.)

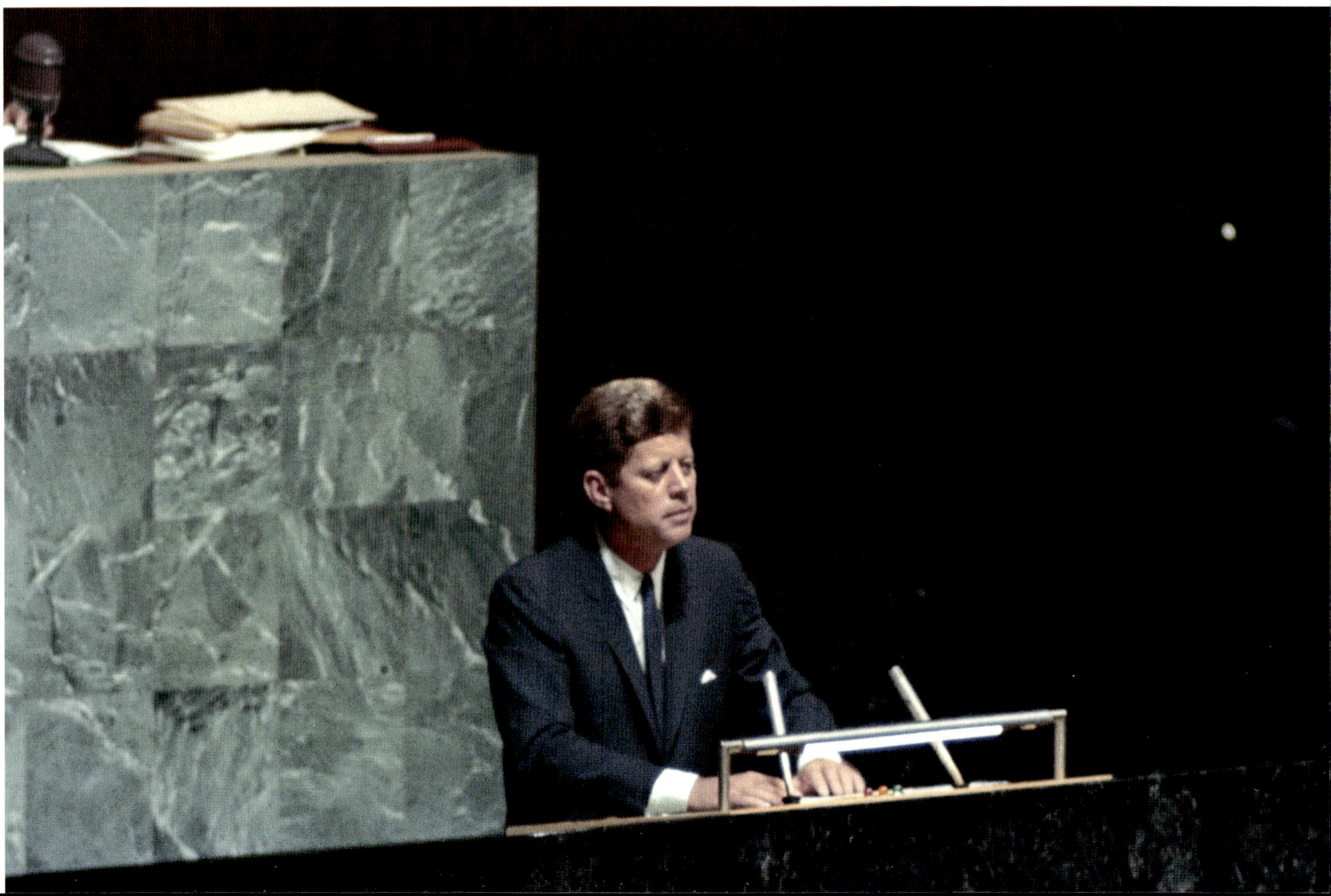

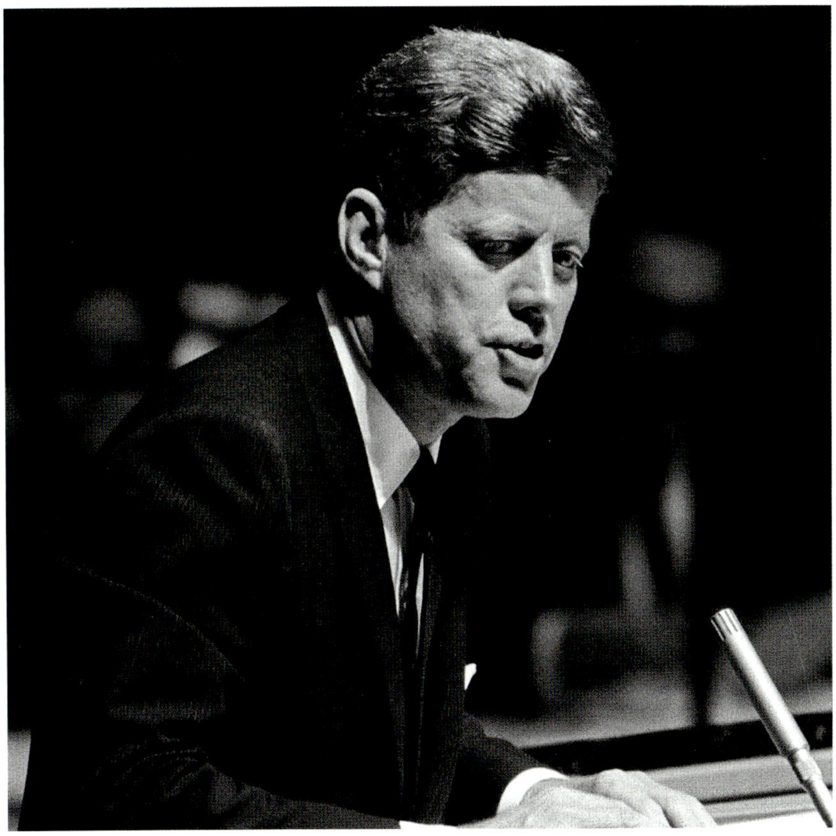

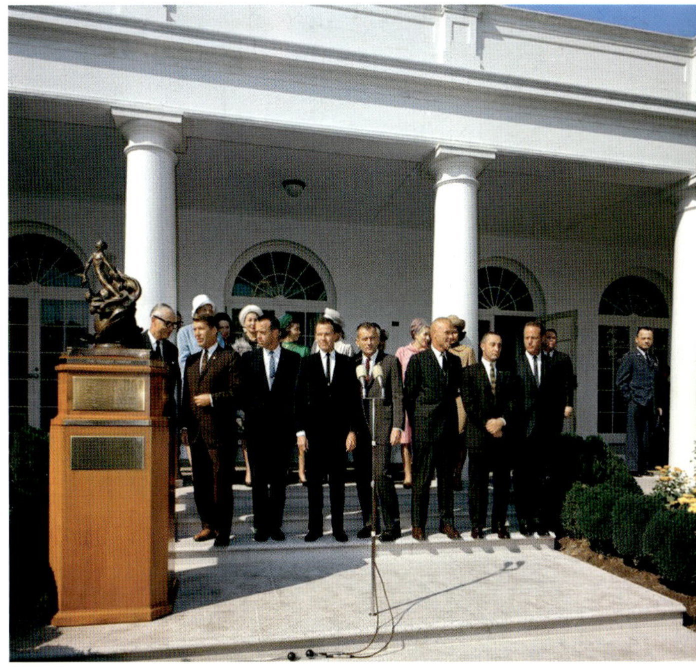

▲ "In a field where the United States and the Soviet Union have a special capacity—in the field of space—there is room for new cooperation, for further joint efforts in the regulation and exploration of space," the president tells the delegates.

> I include among these possibilities a joint expedition to the moon. Space offers no problems of sovereignty; by resolution of this Assembly, the members of the United Nations have forsworn any claim to territorial rights in outer space or on celestial bodies and declared that international law and the United Nations Charter will apply. Why, therefore, should man's first flight to the moon be a matter of national competition? Why should the United States and the Soviet Union, in preparing for such expeditions, become involved in immense duplications of research, construction, and expenditure? Surely we should explore whether the scientists and astronauts of our two countries—indeed of all the world—cannot work together in the conquest of space, sending some day in this decade to the moon not the representatives of a single nation, but the representatives of all of our countries.

◥ On October 10, 1963, the Mercury astronauts and their wives await the president's arrival to present the 1963 Collier Trophy, with the trophy at left.

The trophy has been presented since 1911 to those who have made "the greatest achievement in aeronautics or astronautics in America, with respect to improving the performance, efficiency, and safety of air or space vehicles, the value of which has been thoroughly demonstrated by actual use during the preceding year."

Front row L–R: Navy Secretary Fred Korth; Schirra; Shepard; Cooper; Slayton; Glenn; Grissom; and Carpenter. Back row L–R: Jo Schirra (partially hidden); Shepard's mother, Renza; Marjorie Slayton; Annie Glenn; Louise Shepard (face obscured); Rene Carpenter; Trudy Cooper (partially hidden); and Secret Service Agent Bill Payne (behind Carpenter).

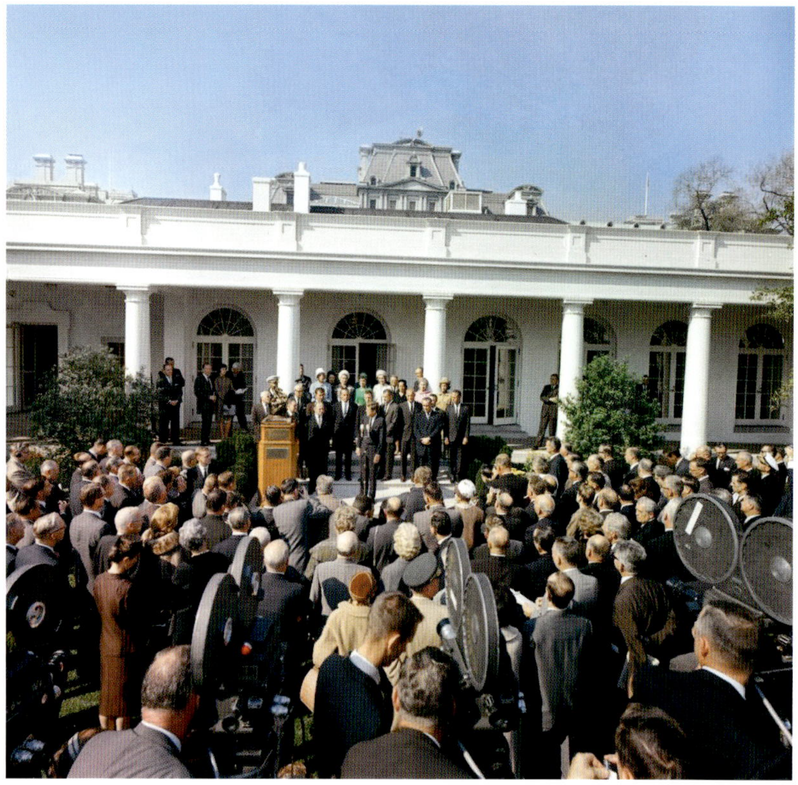

▶ With news film cameras in the foreground, Kennedy speaks at the 11:30 a.m. EST ceremony, the first time the Collier Trophy is given for a pure space achievement. Slayton, who would not make a space flight until 1975 due to health concerns, delivers brief remarks accepting the award. More than 150 guests fill the Rose Garden for the fifteen-minute event, including members of Congress and the president's cabinet, Supreme Court Chief Justice Earl Warren, and military and aerospace industry representatives. The president's father, Joseph P. Kennedy, watches the ceremony in his wheelchair from a window. The Old Executive Office Building can be seen above the West Wing.

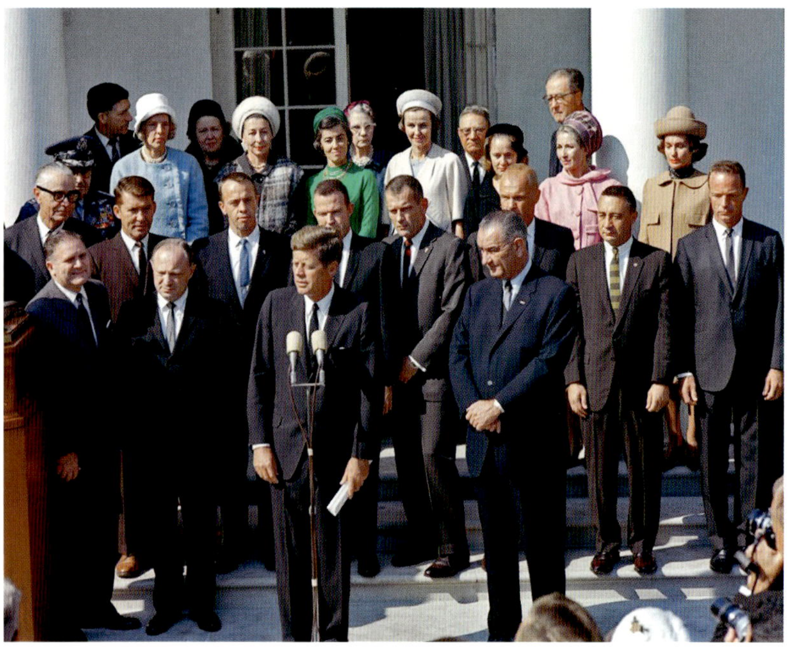

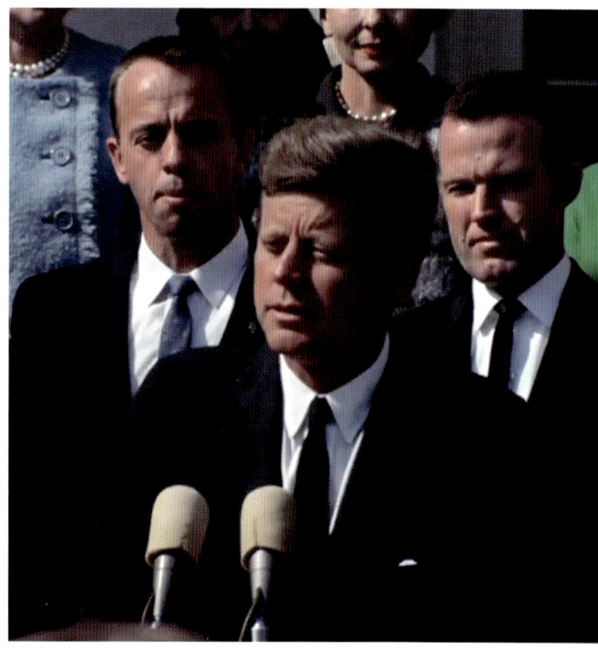

▲ Webb and National Aeronautic Association President Martin Decker stand next to Kennedy at left with the astronauts and their wives, and Johnson at right. Decker, whose aviation club has jurisdiction over the trophy, speaks briefly, as does Webb.

Others behind them, L–R: Korth; USAF Chief of Staff Gen. Curtis LeMay (partially hidden); FAA Administrator Najeeb Halaby; Grissom's mother and father, Cecile and Dennis Grissom; and Sen. Clinton Anderson. LeMay would receive the trophy in 1964; Webb would share it in 1966.

◥ The president is framed by the first and last Project Mercury astronauts, Shepard and Cooper, during his comments.

"I am particularly glad that the decision has been made," he says, "to award the trophy this year to [the astronauts]. I think it honors an extraordinary page in American history as well as in the history of flight, and I hope that this award, which in a sense closes out this particular phase of the space program, will be a stimulus to them and to other astronauts who will carry our flag to the moon and perhaps even someday beyond."

▶ Shepard (left), talks with naval aide to the president Capt. Tazewell Shepard Jr. (center) and FAA Administrator Halaby. Halaby, whose daughter would become Queen Noor of Jordan in 1978, later serves as chairman and CEO of Pan American World Airways.

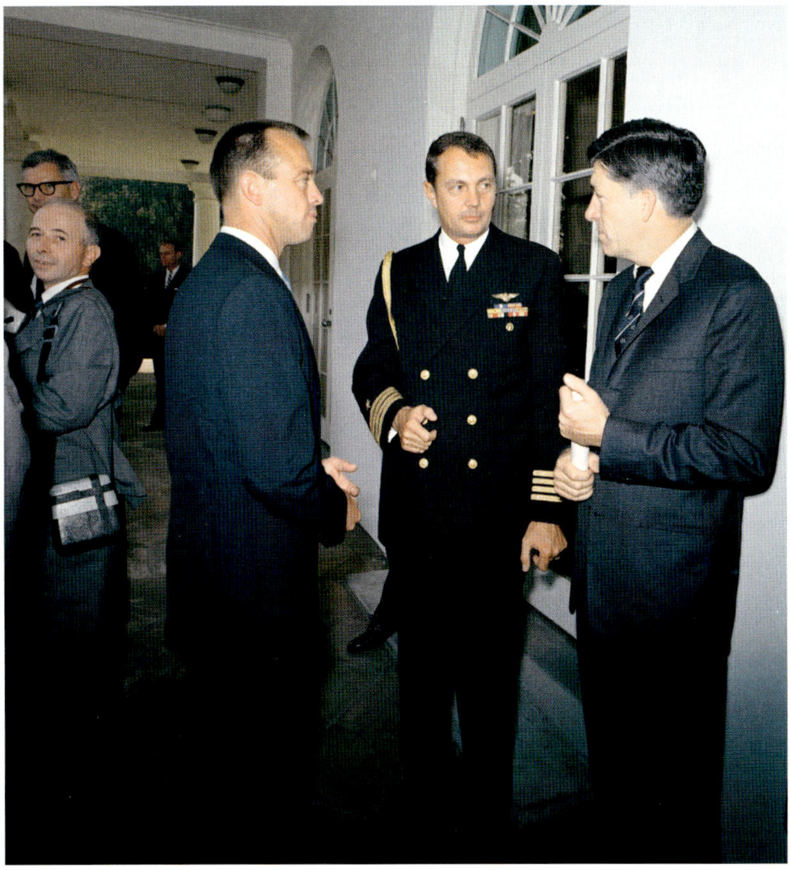

▼ Kennedy poses with the astronauts: Grissom (in front), Schirra, Carpenter, Cooper (in front), Glenn, Slayton, and Shepard. After the ceremony, Kennedy makes a point of asking Lt. Gen. Jimmy Doolittle to come forward to meet them. Doolittle led the surprise 1942 bombing run on Tokyo in retaliation for Japan's attack on Pearl Harbor. All seven astronauts had enlisted in the armed forces during the war; Shepard, Glenn, Schirra, and Slayton saw combat; Cooper served as a member of President Truman's Honor Guard as a Marine. It is the second and last time all seven astronauts would be together at the White House.

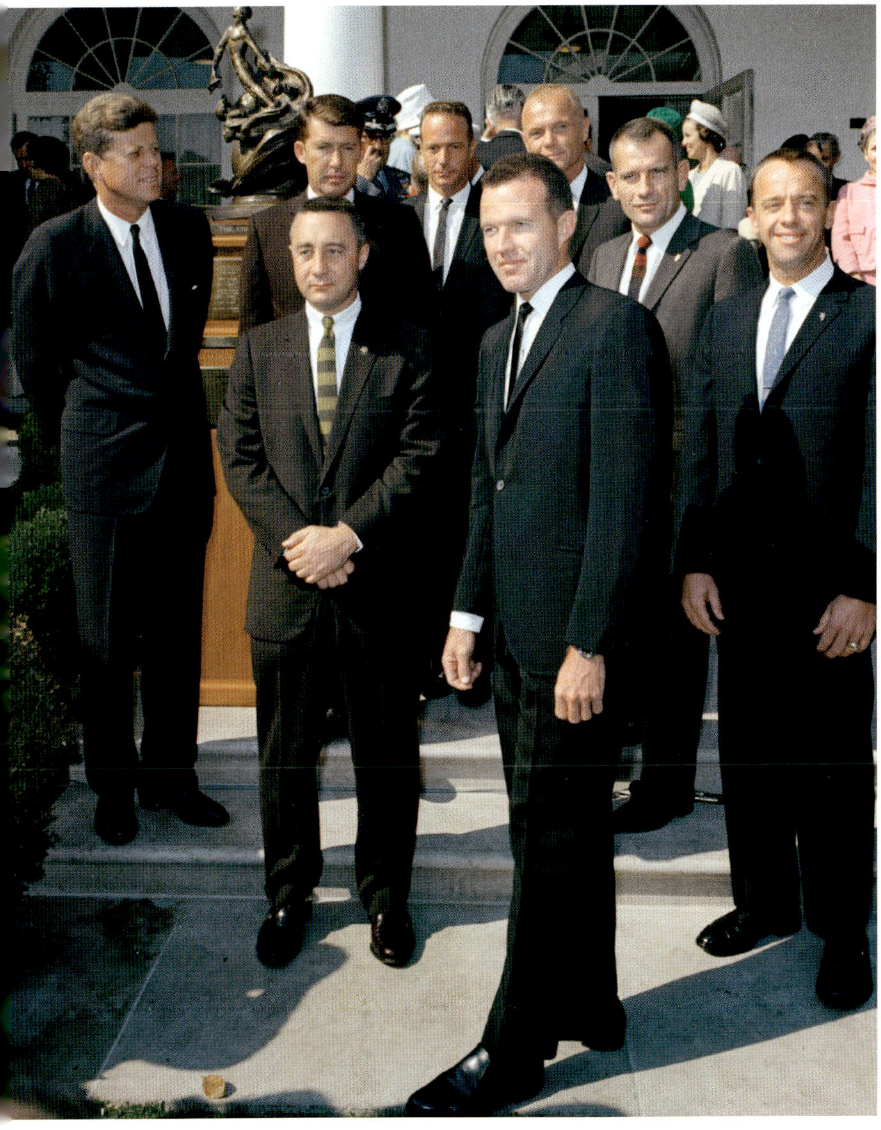

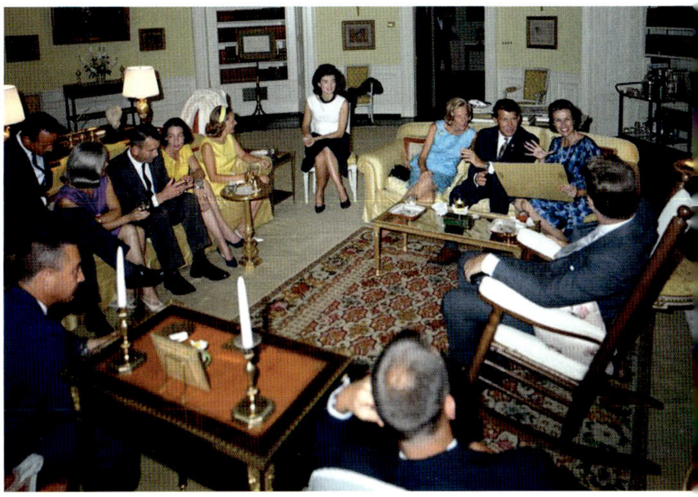

▲ The astronauts and their wives have drinks with the first couple that evening in the Yellow Oval Room on the second floor of the White House. Clockwise from right: Kennedy (in rocking chair), Shepard, Grissom, Carpenter, Rene Carpenter, Slayton, Marjorie Slayton, Betty Grissom, Mrs. Kennedy, Jo Schirra, Schirra, and Louise Shepard.

Earlier they attended a luncheon at the Statler Hilton given by *Look* magazine, sponsor of the Collier Trophy since 1957, where each man received a smaller replica of the award.

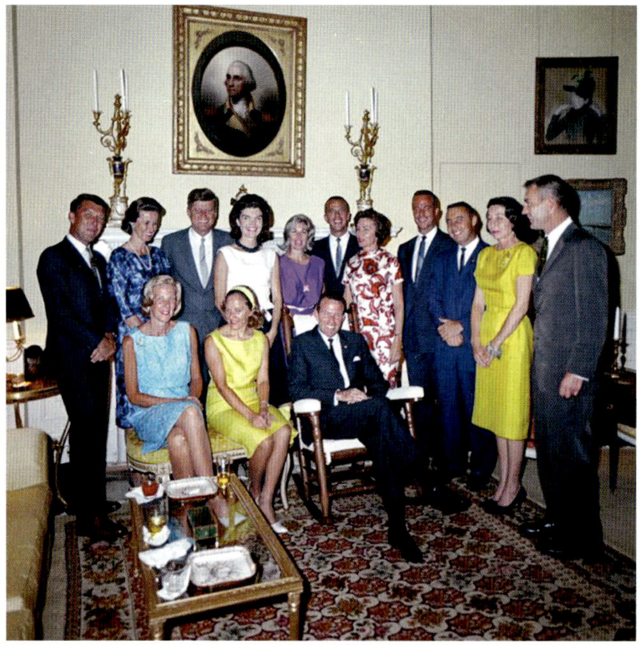

▶ It was "a small, warm, friendly gathering," Shepard later recalled. He used the opportunity to push for a seventh, multi-day Mercury flight he would pilot. "The president himself brought up the question—I had intended to, but he brought it up before I did—about my feelings on the flight. I expressed them, and I also expressed what I thought were the feelings of the people who opposed making the flight."

That afternoon, Shepard, Grissom, Glenn, and Carpenter watch from the US House visitors gallery as members approve $5.1 billion for NASA for 1964. The chamber, however, also narrowly votes to bar spending for "participating in a manned lunar landing to be carried out jointly by the United States and any communist controlled, or communist dominated, country." The vote is a reaction to the president's September 20 speech at the United Nations proposing joint lunar exploration with the Soviet Union.

Seated L–R: Jo Schirra; Betty Grissom; and Cooper. Standing L–R: Schirra; Louise Shepard; Kennedy; Mrs. Kennedy; Rene Carpenter; Shepard; Trudy Cooper; Carpenter; Marjorie Slayton; and Slayton.

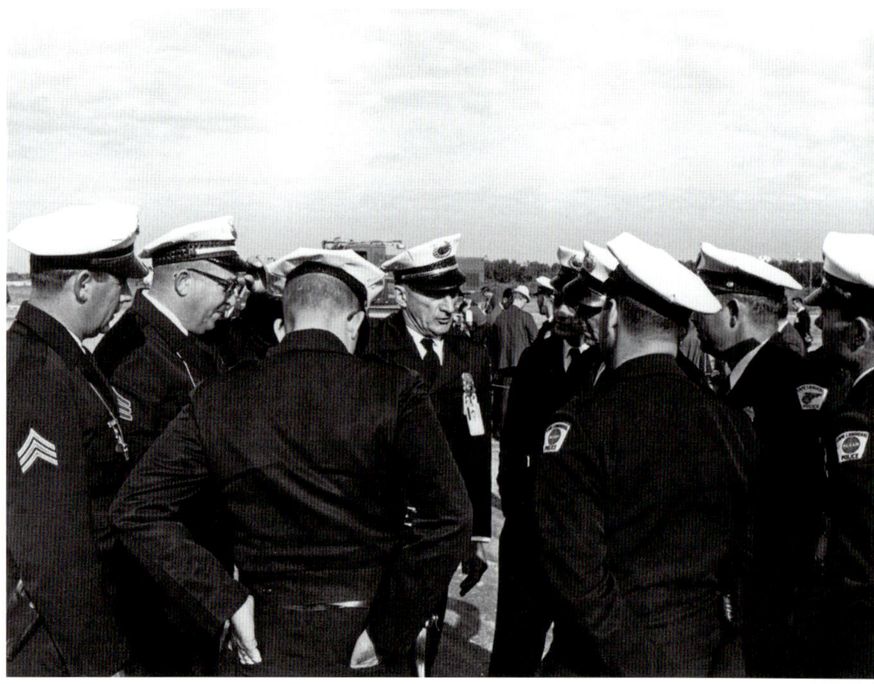

▶ Pan American Airways Security Police officers get a last-minute briefing at Cape Canaveral's Skid Strip on the morning of Saturday, November 16, 1963, before President Kennedy's final visit, a two-hour tour of launch facilities.

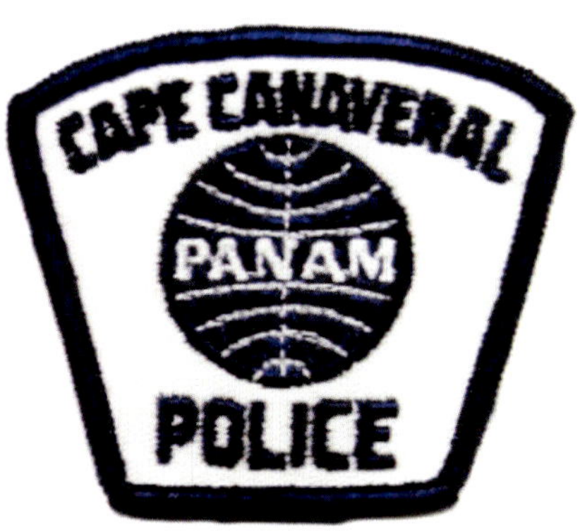

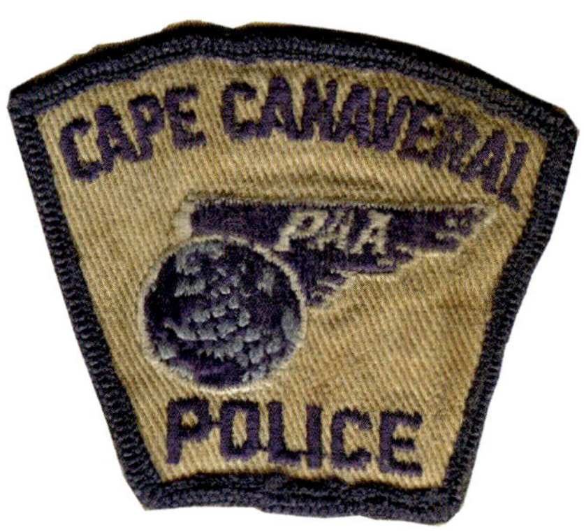

▼ The White House Communications Agency orders special "ring-down" phones be temporarily installed at each stop along the tour; picking up the receiver automatically calls the White House switchboard.

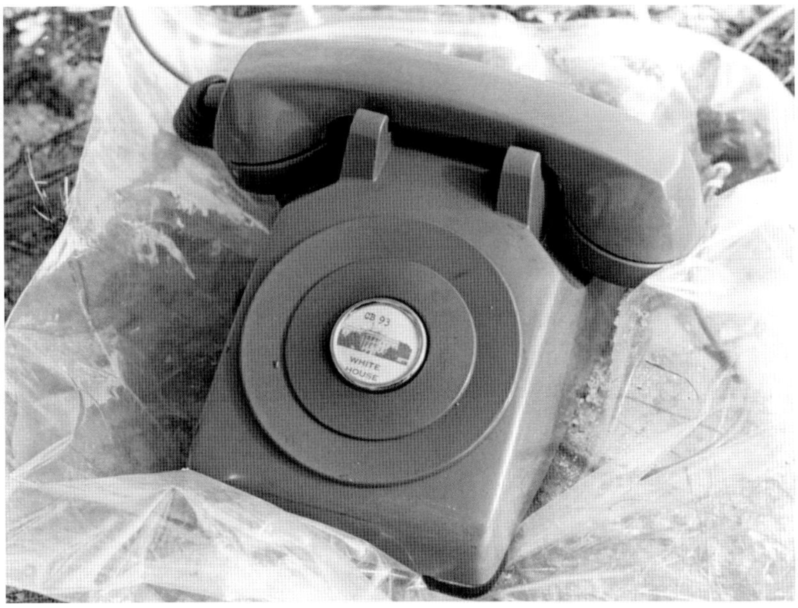

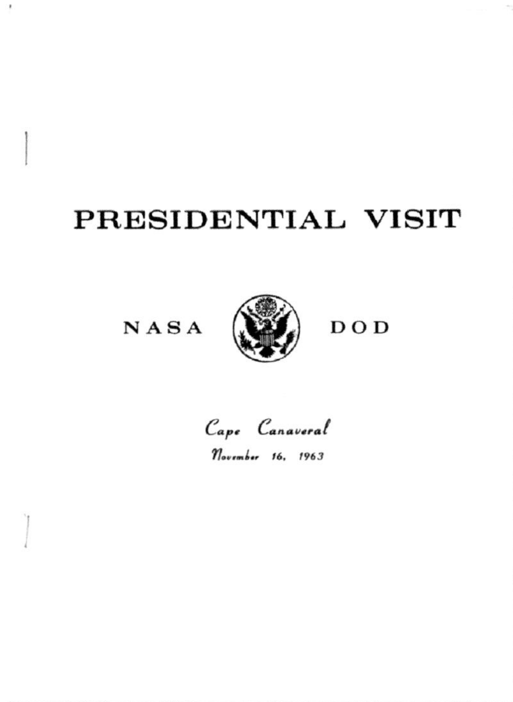

PRESIDENTIAL VISIT

NASA DOD

Cape Canaveral
November 16, 1963

▶ Members of the 536th Air Force Band, based at Patrick AFB, relax before the president arrives.

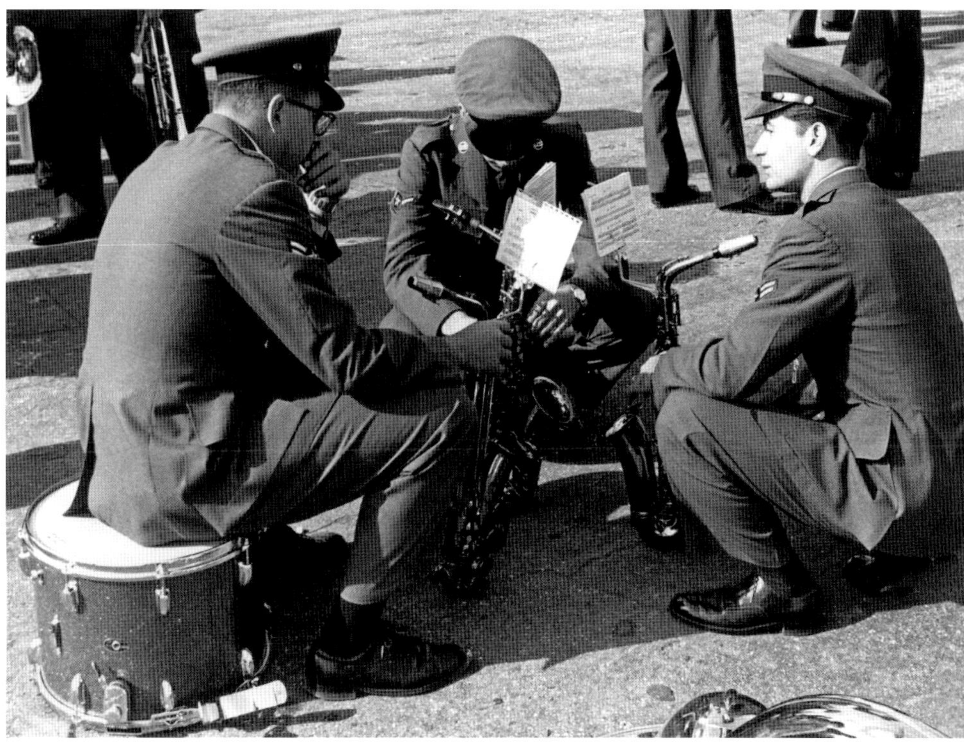

▼ The president arrives from Palm Beach AFB at 10:10 a.m. EST; behind him are Sen. George Smathers (D-Fla.) and aide Maj. Gen. Chester Clifton. Waiting to greet them are Maj. Gen. Leighton Davis and Launch Operations Center Director Kurt Debus. Kennedy's aircraft is SAM 26000, the new Boeing VC-137C (a modified 707) that had been delivered the previous October.

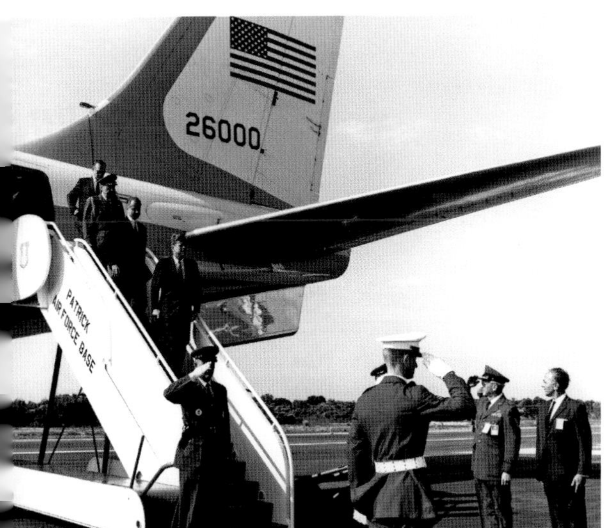

▶ The president is surrounded by Secret Service agents as he begins the tour, with Maj. Gen. Clifton at far right. The Air Force also proposes a tour of Minuteman missile test facilities, but it is dropped because Kennedy arrives about 30 minutes late.

The trip is intended to help bolster support for the Apollo program, which is coming under criticism from some in Congress over its cost; lawmakers have already made tentative cuts to NASA's 1964 budget.

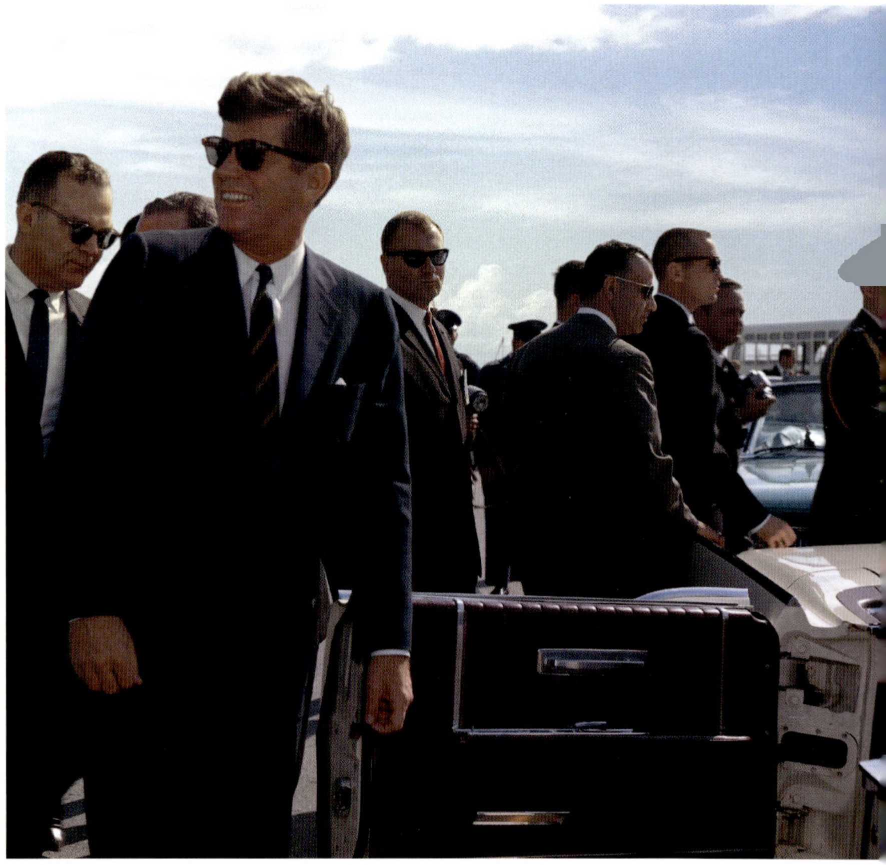

▼ First stop is LC-37, where the president receives a quick briefing at 10:32 a.m. near the blockhouse on the first Gemini spacecraft from astronauts Cooper and Grissom.

L–R: Jim Webb; George Lowe; Kennedy; Cooper; Grissom; and Mathews.

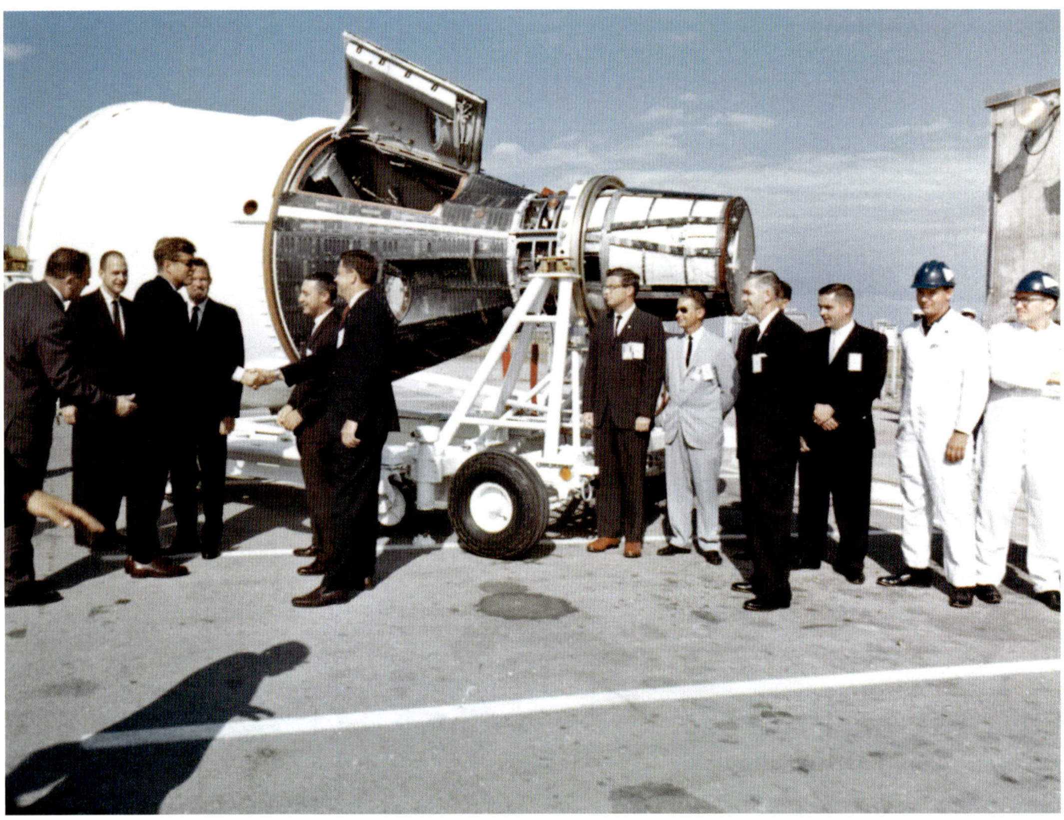

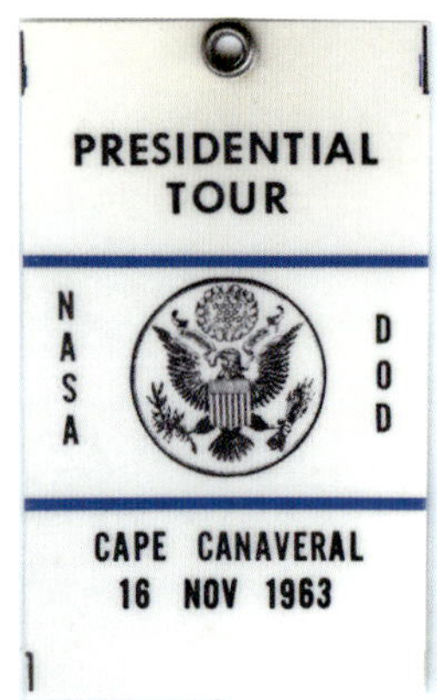

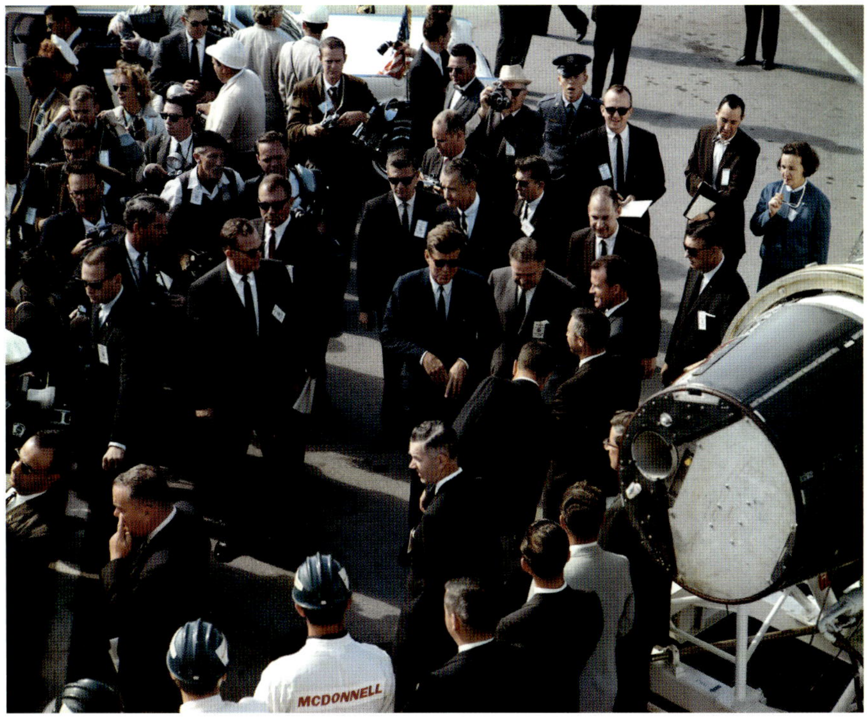

▶ Gemini I would be launched on an unmanned test flight April 8, 1964; Grissom would command the first manned flight in 1965. At upper right are Associated Press reporter Howard Benedict (bowtie) and Mary Bubb of Reuters.

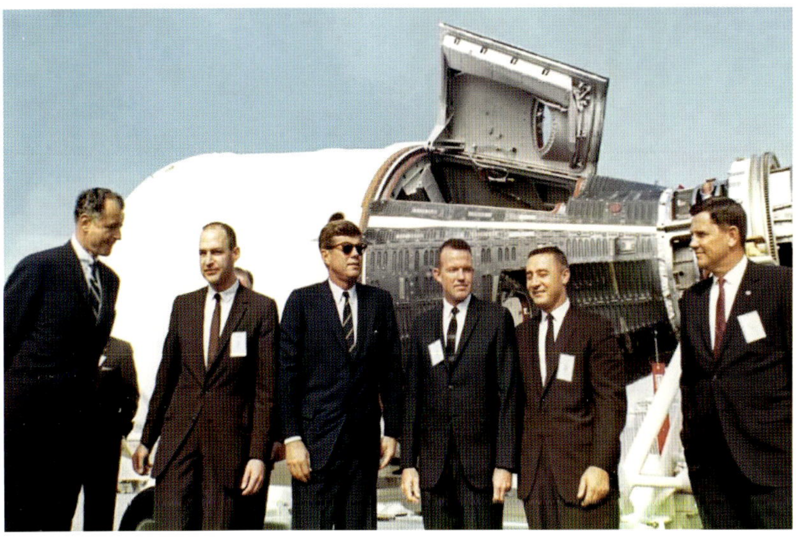

◀ L–R: Smathers; George Low, NASA's chief of Manned Space Flight at the time and also a NACA pioneer; Kennedy; Cooper; Grissom; and Mathews.

▶ L–R: Low; Cooper; Grissom; and Kennedy.

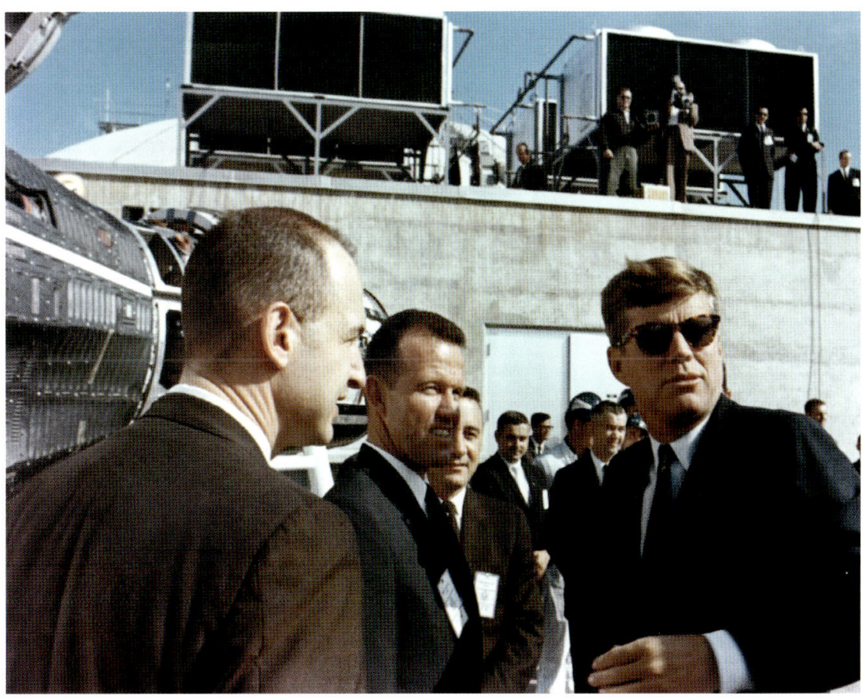

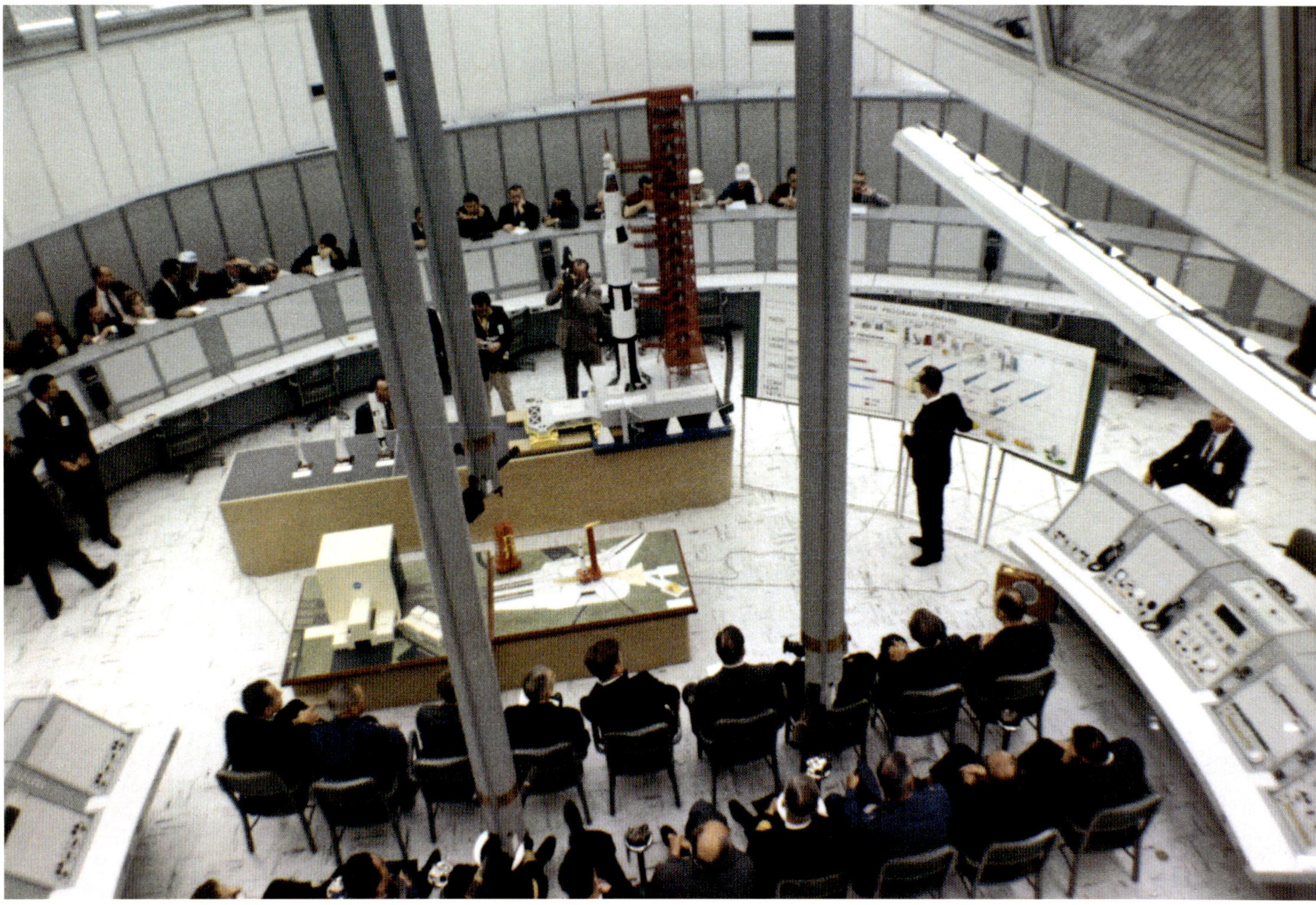

▲ Inside the LC-37 blockhouse the president and his party receive a twenty-minute briefing on the Apollo program starting at 10:35 a.m. Periscopes extend from the ceiling.

▶ L–R: Seamans; Webb; Kennedy; Dryden; von Braun; Davis; and Smathers.

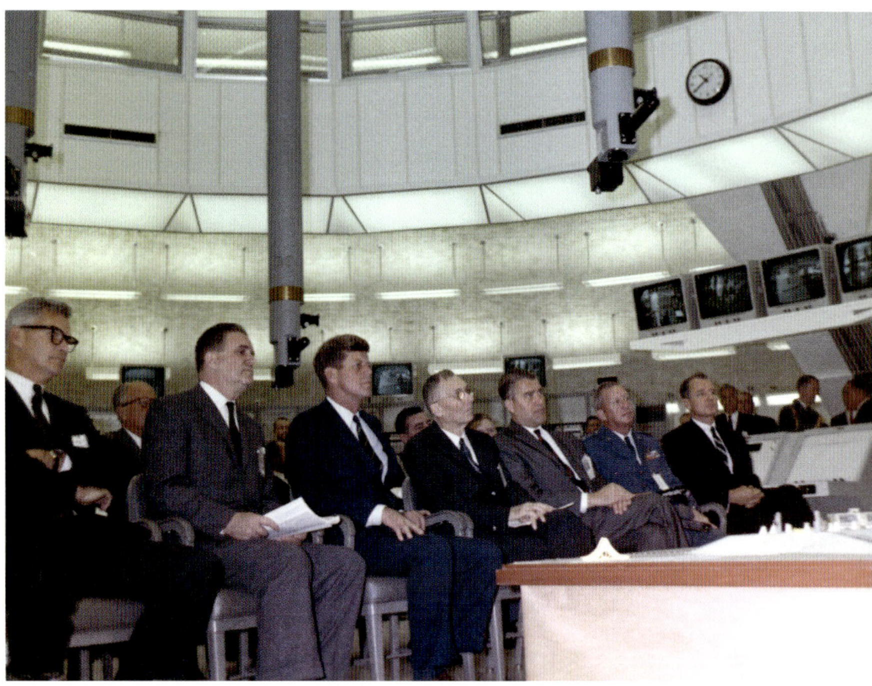

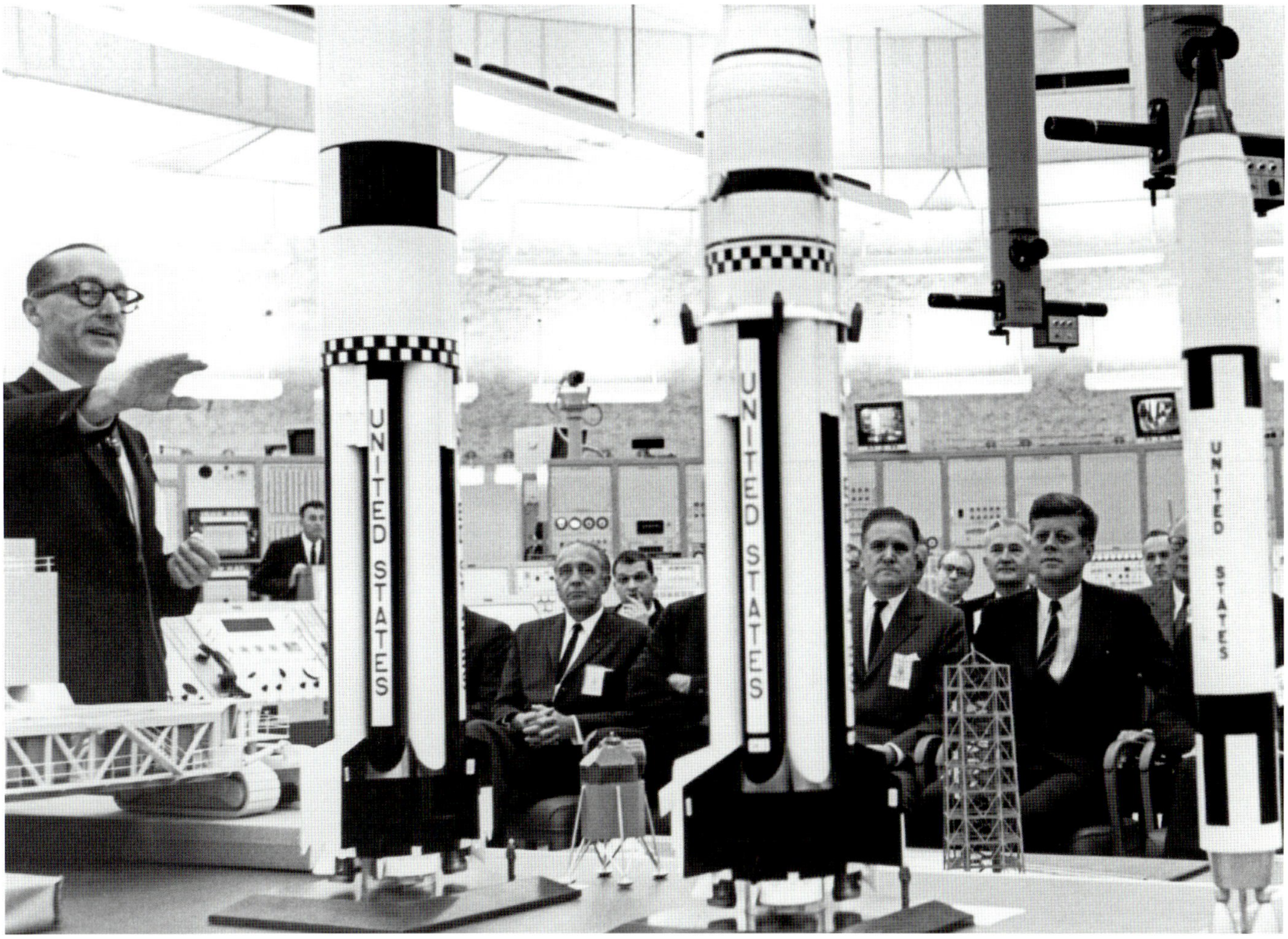

▲ Associate Administrator for Manned Space Flight George Mueller, who had joined NASA Headquarters in September from the private sector, leads the briefing. Known as one of NASA's most brilliant and fearless managers, he introduces the "all-up" philosophy of launching the Saturn V stages together, a key to Apollo's success. Mueller also champions a reusable space vehicle and plays a significant role in early Space Shuttle decisions.

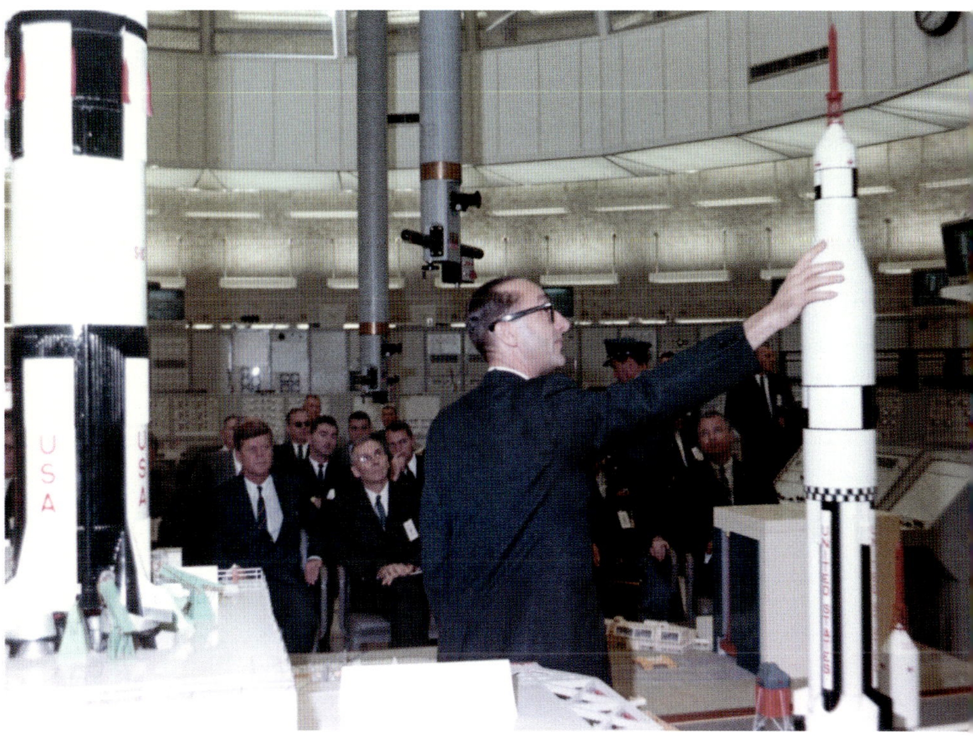

▶ Mueller with a model of a Saturn IB with a Saturn V at left. He succeeds Brainerd Holmes, who resigns under pressure in June after clashing with Webb.

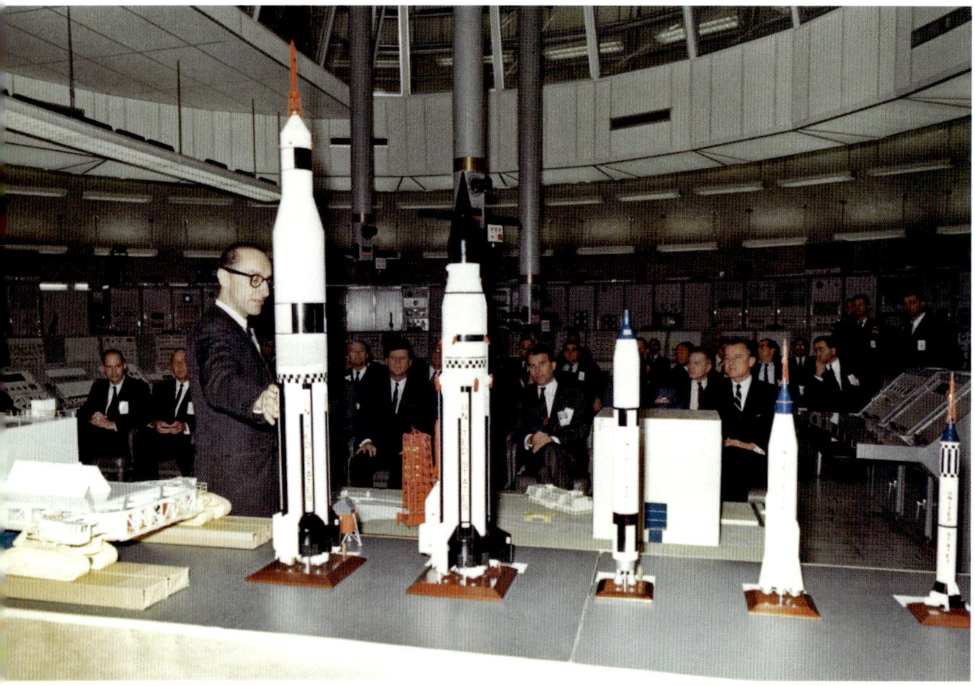

◀ Kennedy is impressed when told that the Saturn V model at center in photo below right is the same scale as the Redstone at far right in this photo. He replies with a smile, "Looks like we've come a long way!" A model of Saturn V's tracked transporter-crawler is at left in this photo.

▼ Webb and Kennedy listen, with a model of one of the three pads then planned for LC-39 (only two were built). A Saturn V on its mobile launcher is in place above the flame trench. R. Adm. I. J. "Pete" Galantin, director of special projects, is behind Webb.

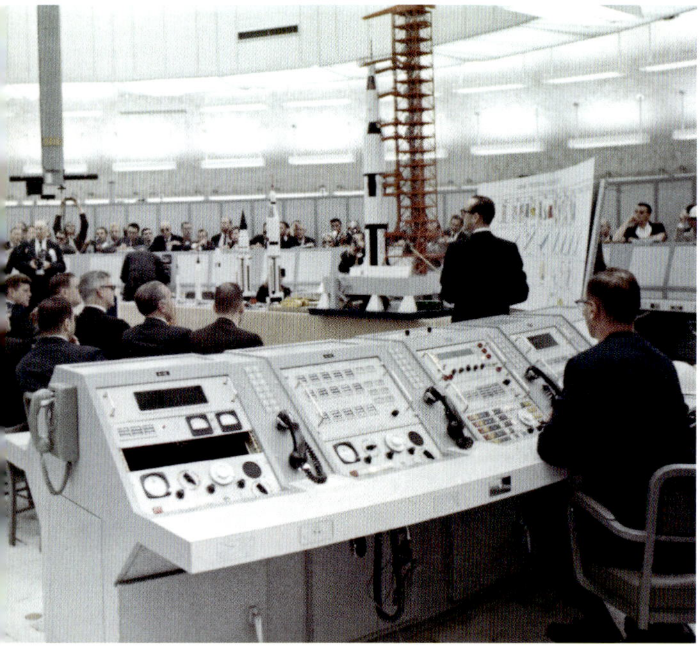

▲ Seated at far right is Bob Moser, chief test conductor. Moser's launch countdowns resembled an orchestral performance and earned him high praise as the launch test conductor for America's first satellite, *Explorer 1*, and Alan Shepard's Mercury flight.

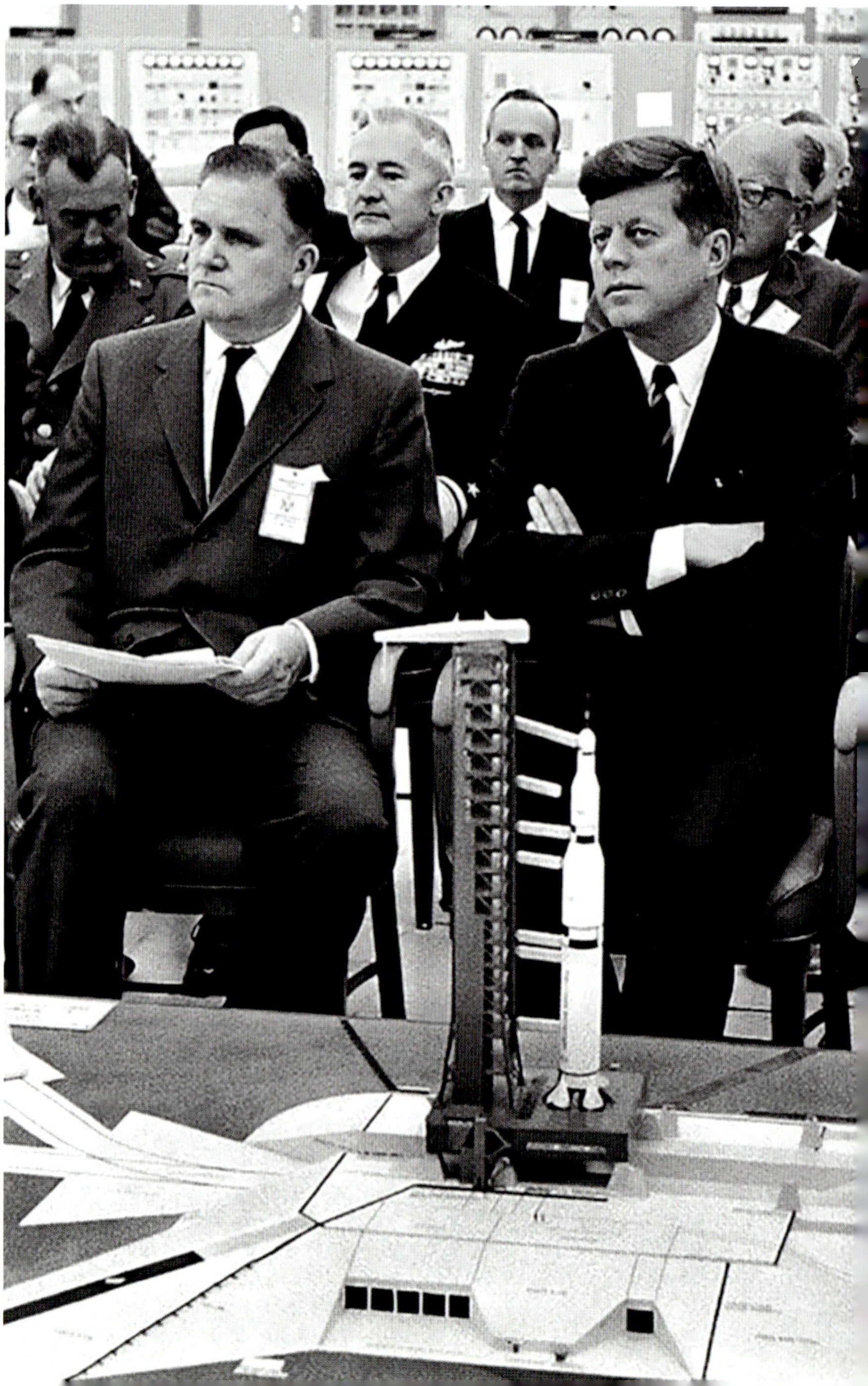

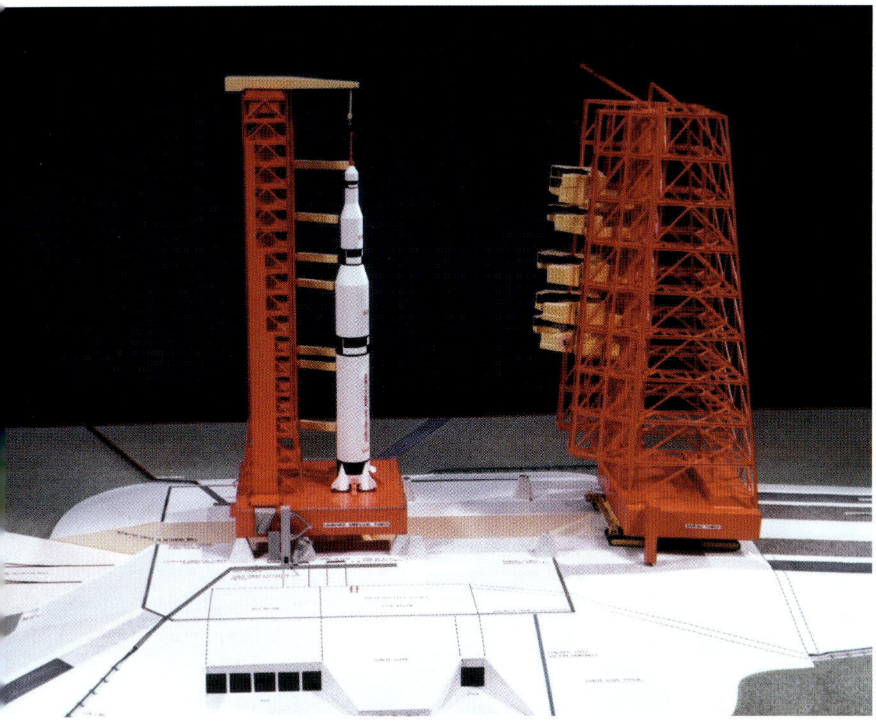

◀ 1963 NASA photo of LC-39 pad model with the MSS at right.

▼ Mueller holds the two stages of the Apollo lunar module model. At center are models of the Vehicle Assembly Building (VAB) and the MSS at LC-39.

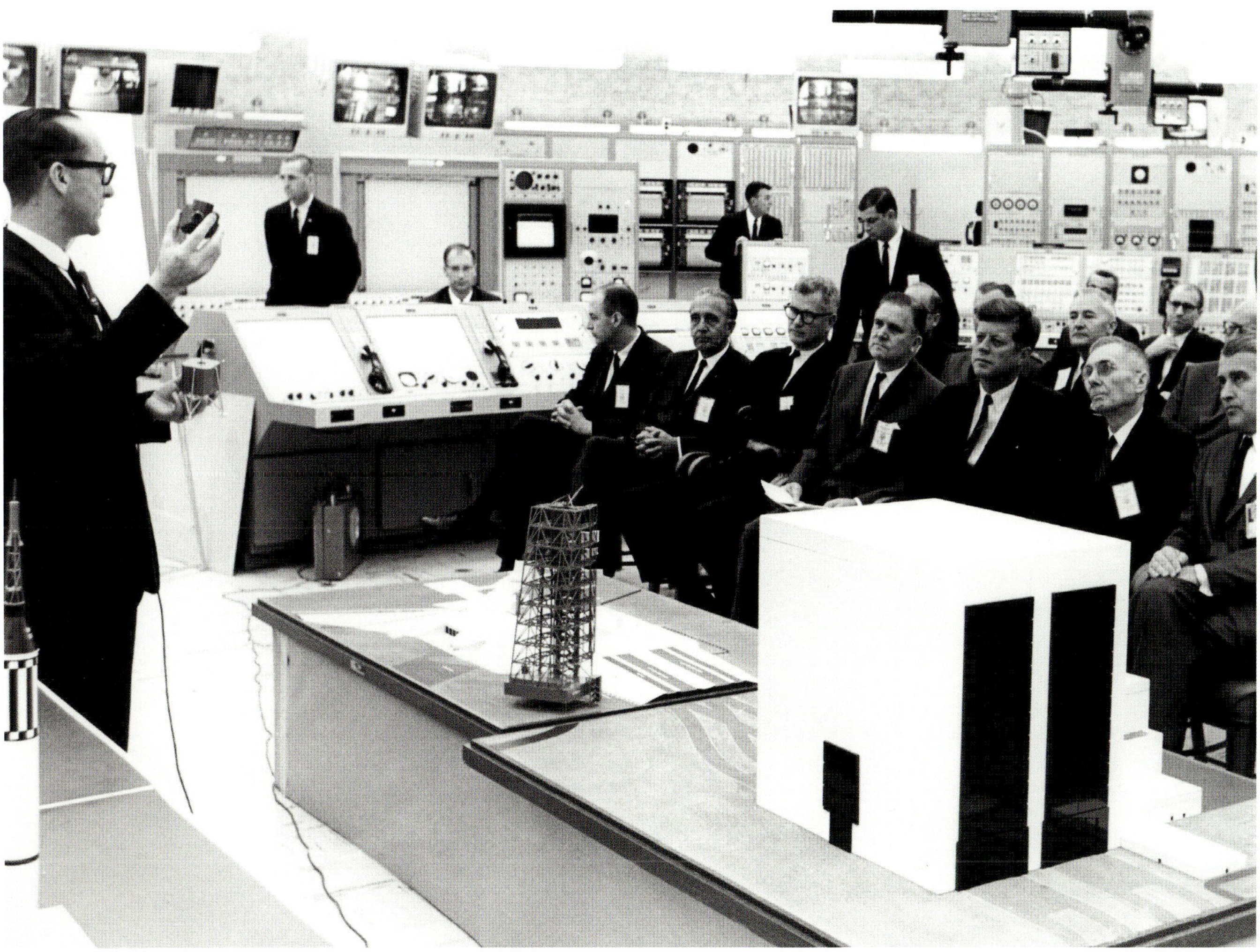

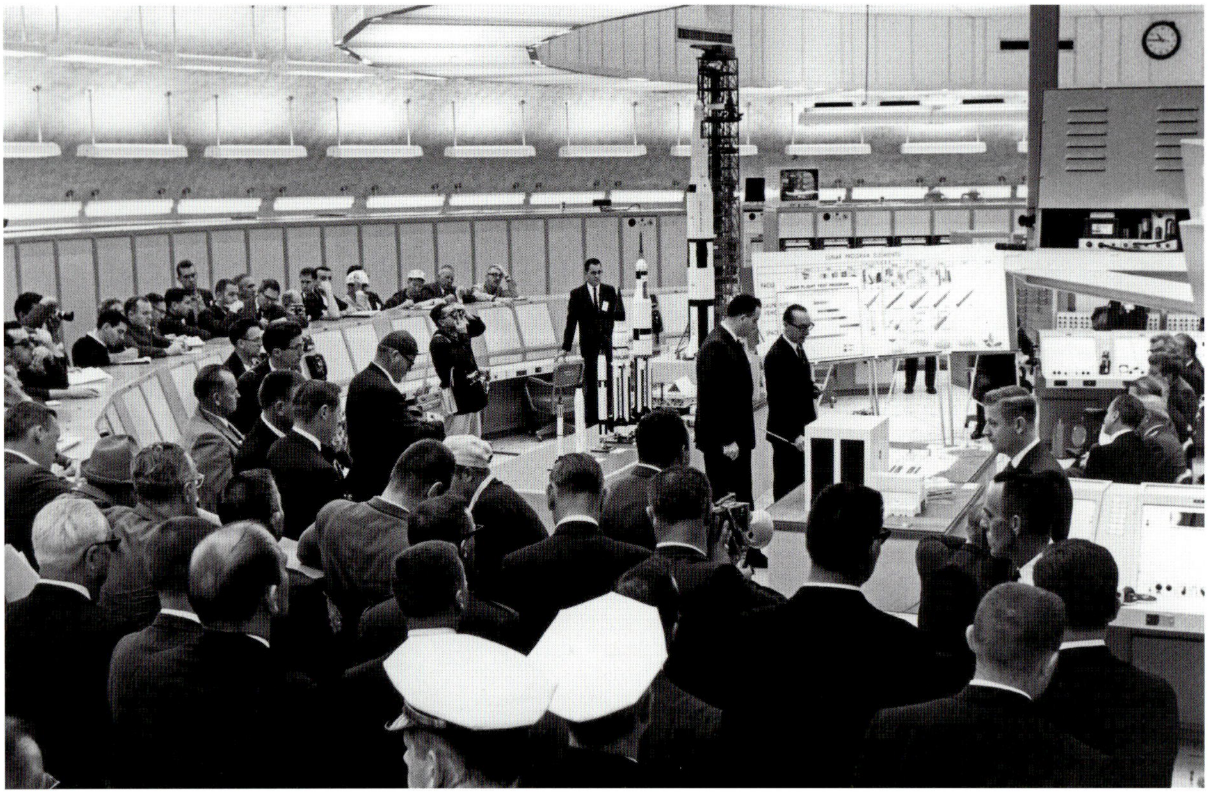

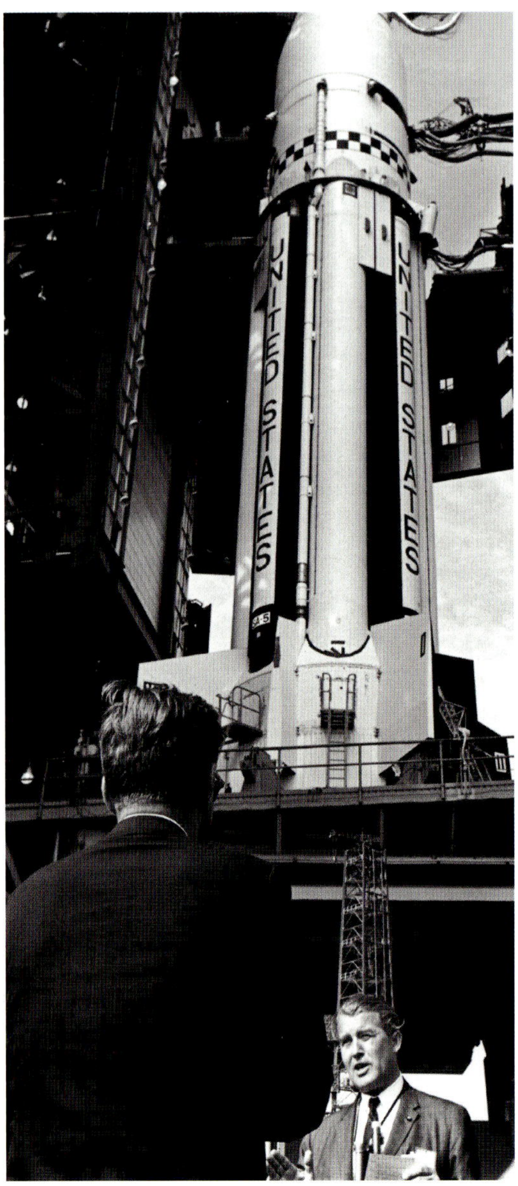

▲ Mueller is assisted by Saturn project officer Lt. Col. Rocco Petrone.

◀ At LC-37's Pad B at 11:00 a.m., von Braun briefs the president on launch preparations for the next Saturn I. The first of five "Block II" Saturns, its major difference is a second stage, the S-IV built by Douglas Aircraft Company. Combined with an improved first stage with thirty-one percent more lift capability, the United States finally has a more powerful space booster than the Soviets.

▶ S-IV model in the John F. Kennedy Presidential Library and Museum collection.

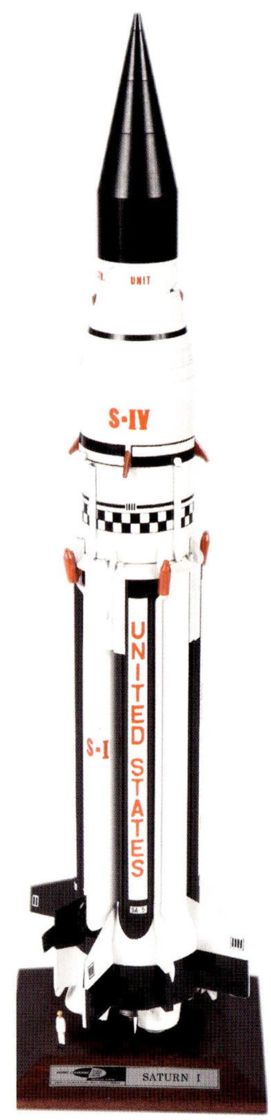

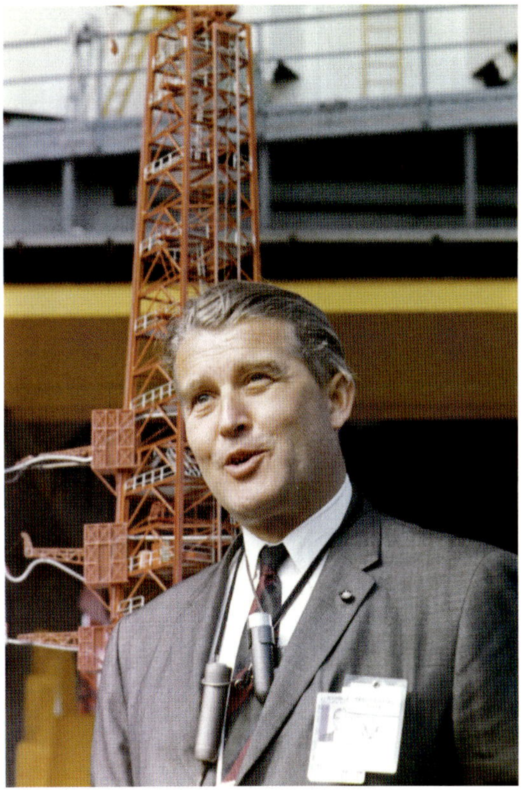

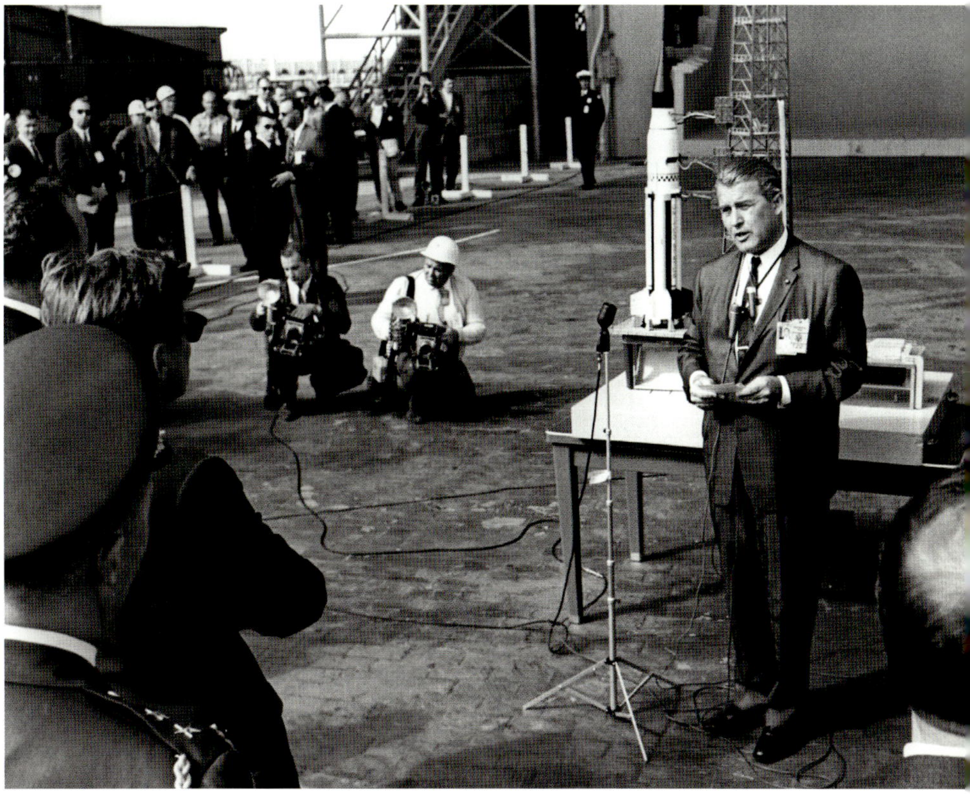

◥ It is the last time von Braun will see the president even though he and his wife had been invited to attend a planned White House dinner nine days later.

▼ Smathers, to Kennedy's left, had become a close friend of the president's when he was in the US Senate, serving as an usher at his wedding and managing Kennedy's 1960 campaign in the Southeast. "Together or singly, they were wolves on the prowl," recalled journalist Roger Mudd, "always able to find or attract gorgeous prey."

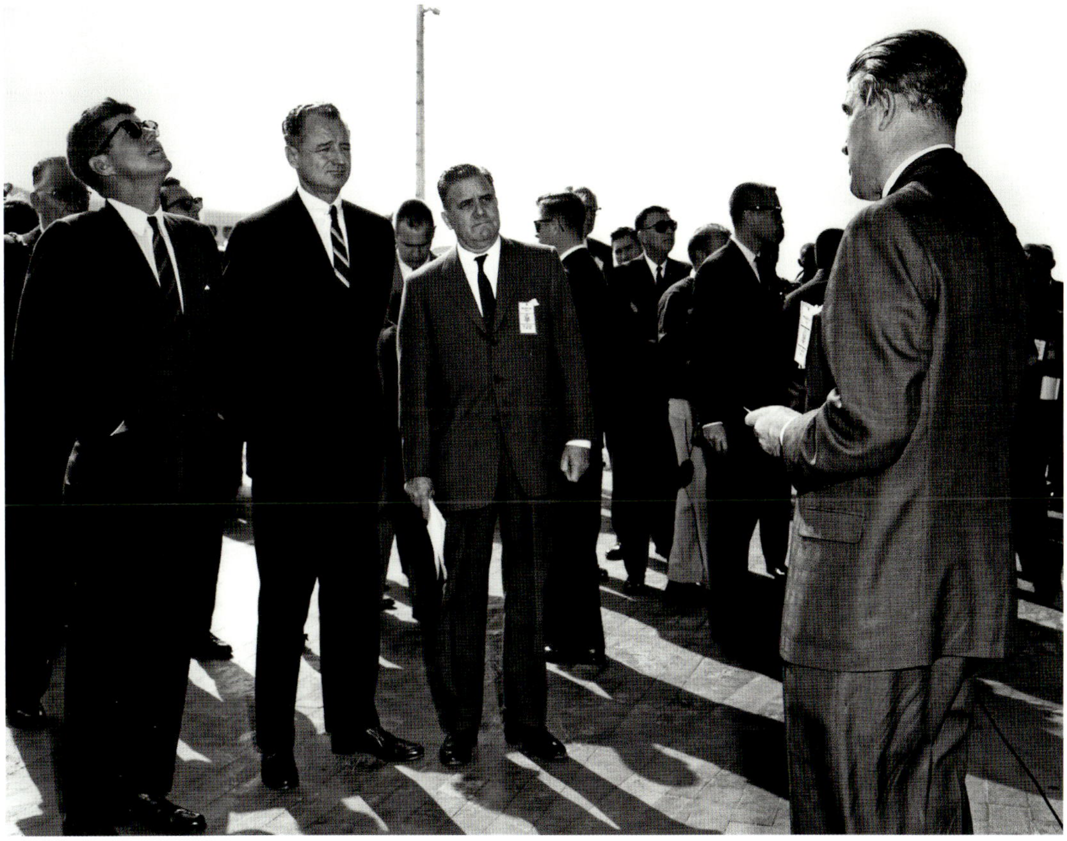

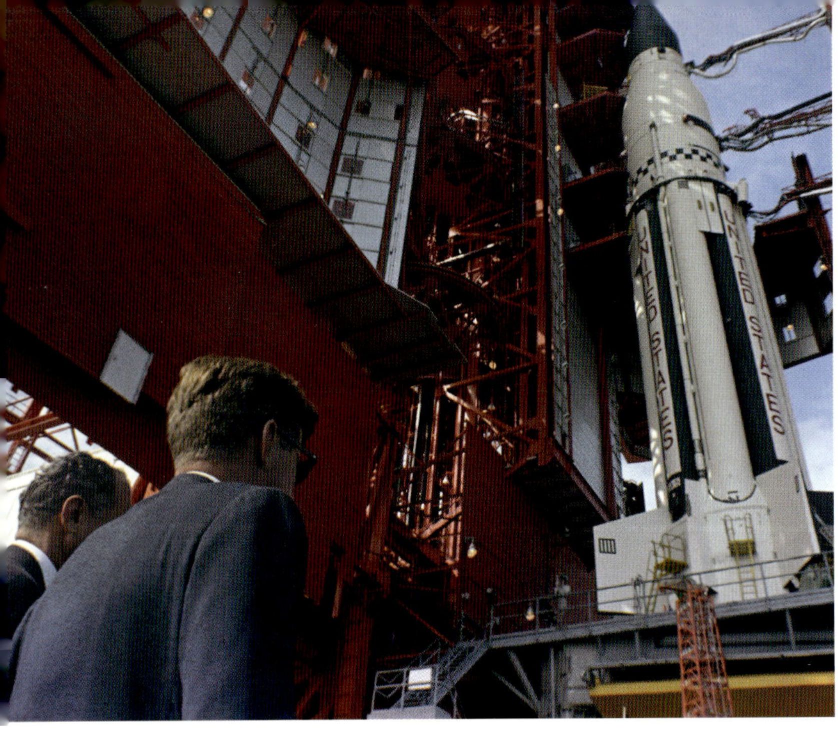

▲ The president would refer to this booster in a speech five days later at Brooks AFB in San Antonio, Texas: "While I do not regard our mastery of space as anywhere near complete, while I recognize that there are still areas where we are behind—at least in one area, the size of the booster, this year, I hope, the United States will be ahead."

▼ Von Braun points out features of SA-5 to the president. The black nose cone is from a Jupiter rocket; it replaces the version Kennedy saw the previous year at the Marshall Space Flight Center. The nose is filled with sand as ballast to simulate payload mass.

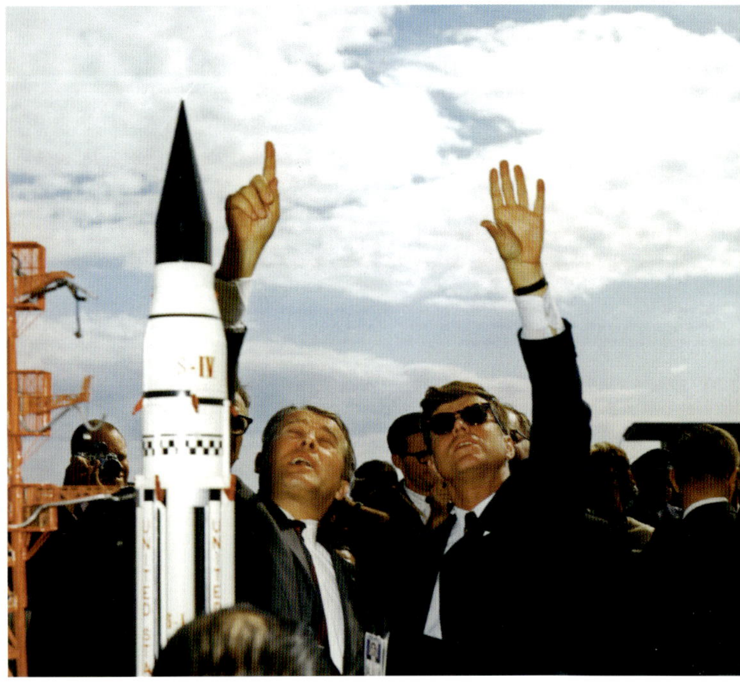

▼ Kennedy speaks with NASA officials with the orange flame deflector beneath the pad behind them, and the Saturn I's eight H-1 engines above. The Secret Service had wanted to keep Kennedy farther away from the unfueled booster.

L–R: Seamans; Smathers; Kennedy; Webb; von Braun (partially hidden); Deputy NASA Administrator Hugh Dryden; and Maj. Gen. Clifton.

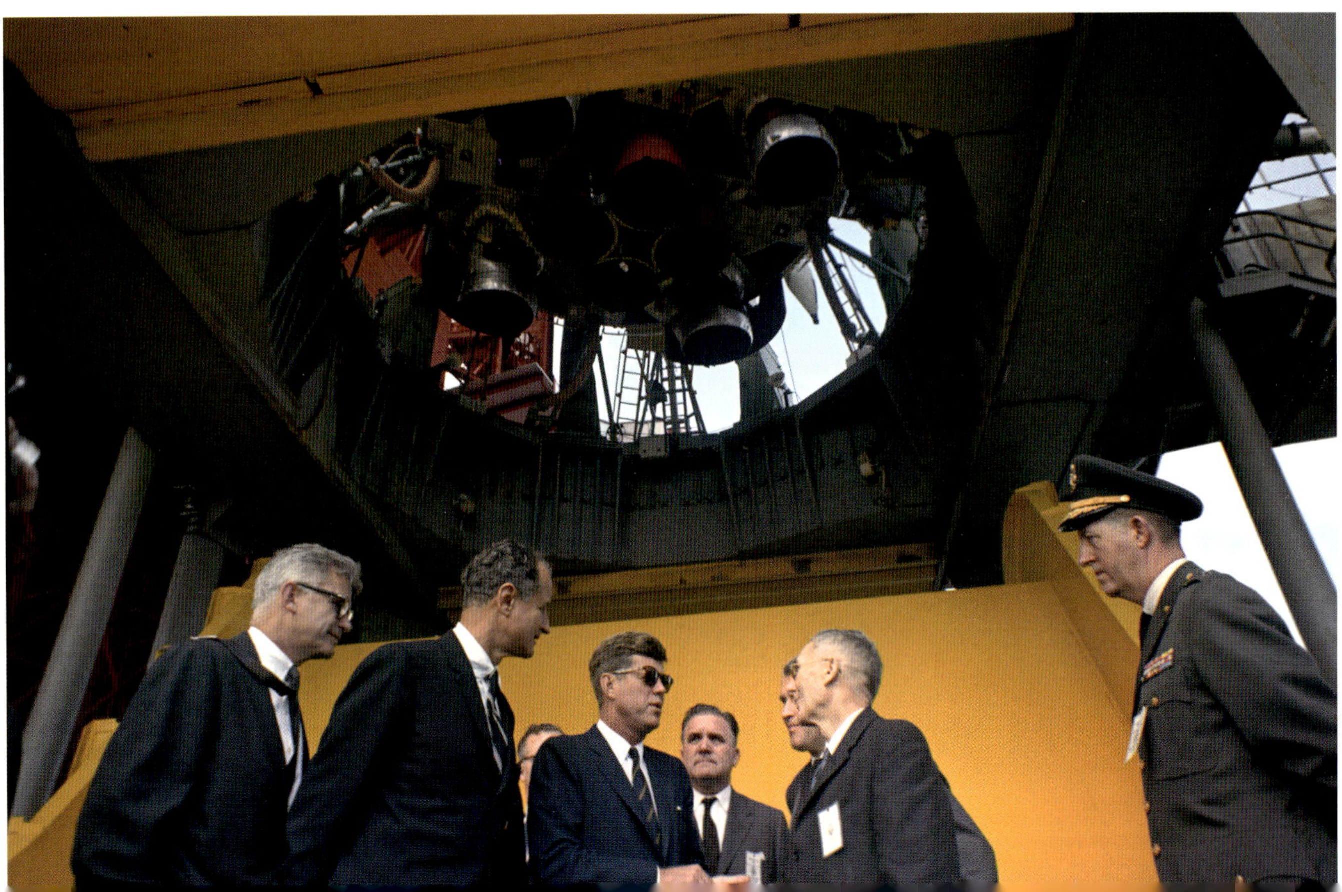

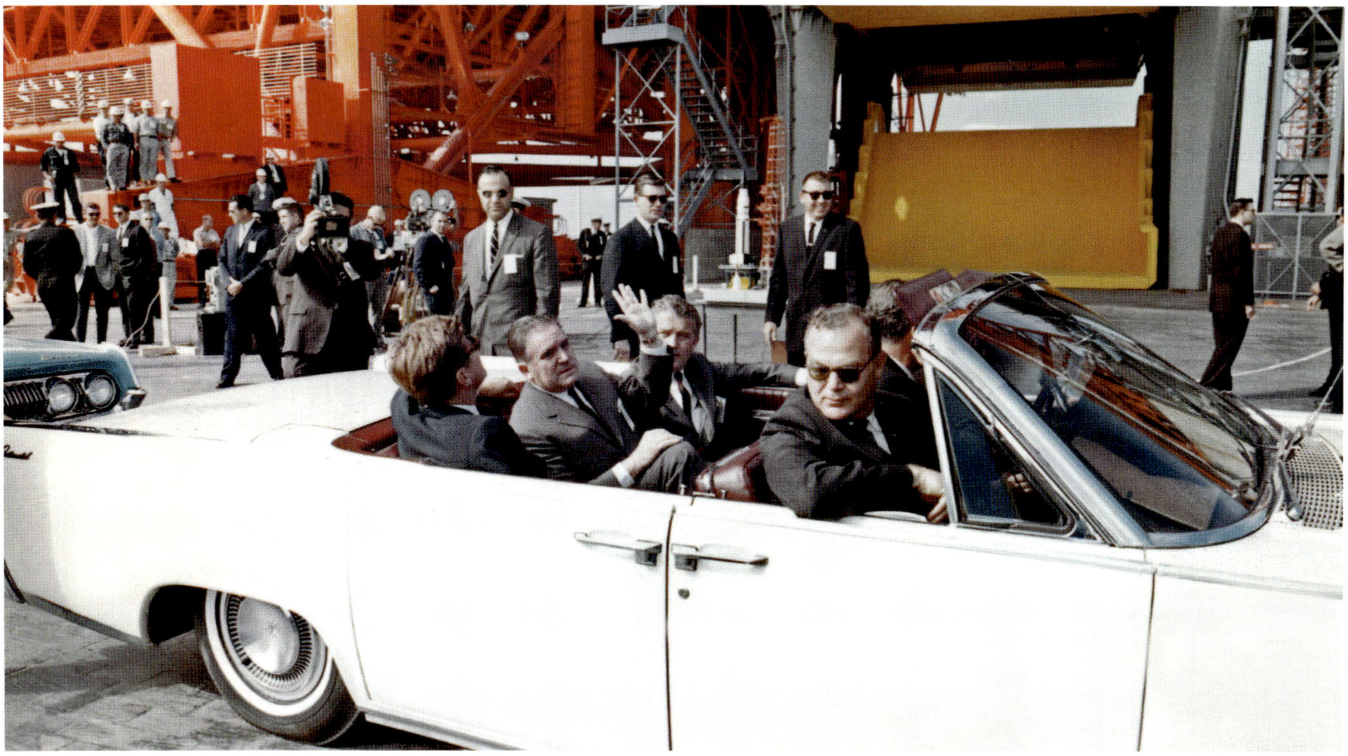

▲ The president takes a last look as Webb makes a final point. Kennedy intended to return to the Cape for the expected launch of the booster the following month.

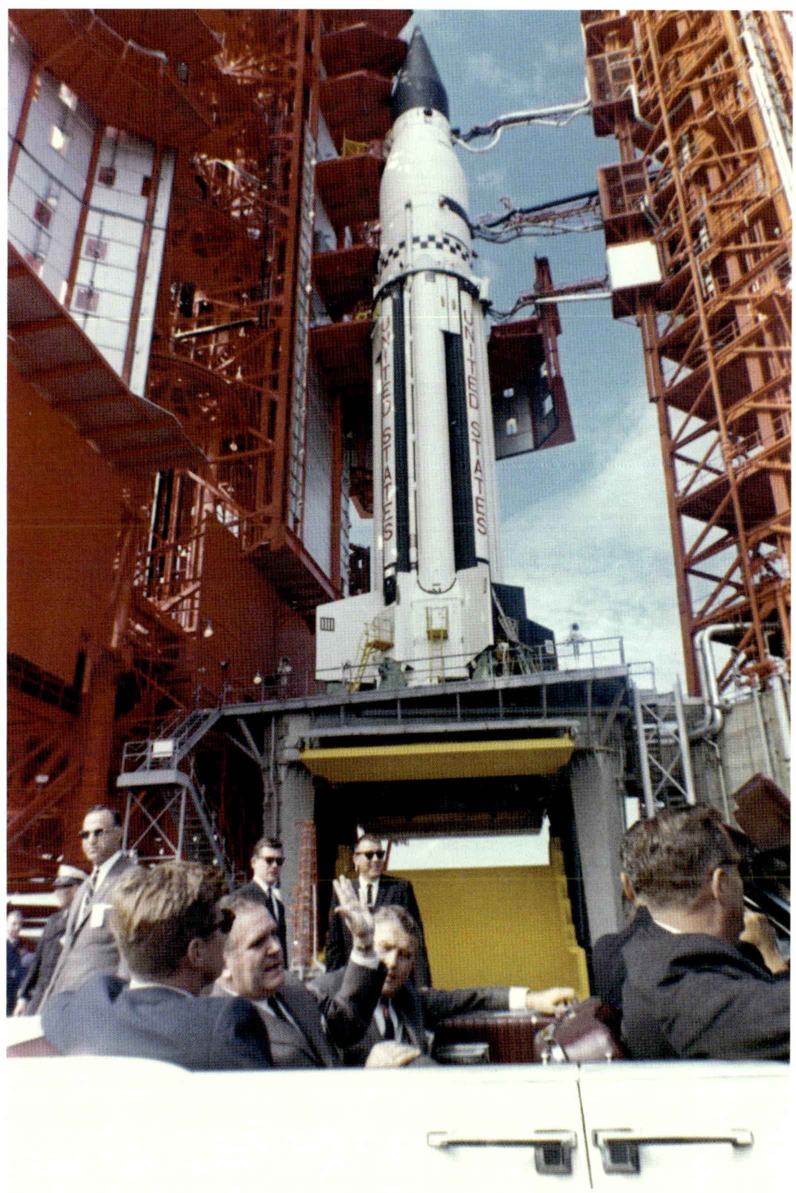

▶ SA-5 is the first Saturn to feature fins at the base; eight are added for additional aerodynamic stability. Standing behind von Braun is NASA Public Affairs Officer Gatha Cottee, serving as an escort for the news photographers. He had come to Cape Canaveral in 1954 as a still photographer for RCA and worked for NASA into the Space Shuttle program. The president next departs via helicopter from adjoining Pad A for an aerial tour of the area and a visit to USS *Observation Island* to witness a missile launch from a submarine.

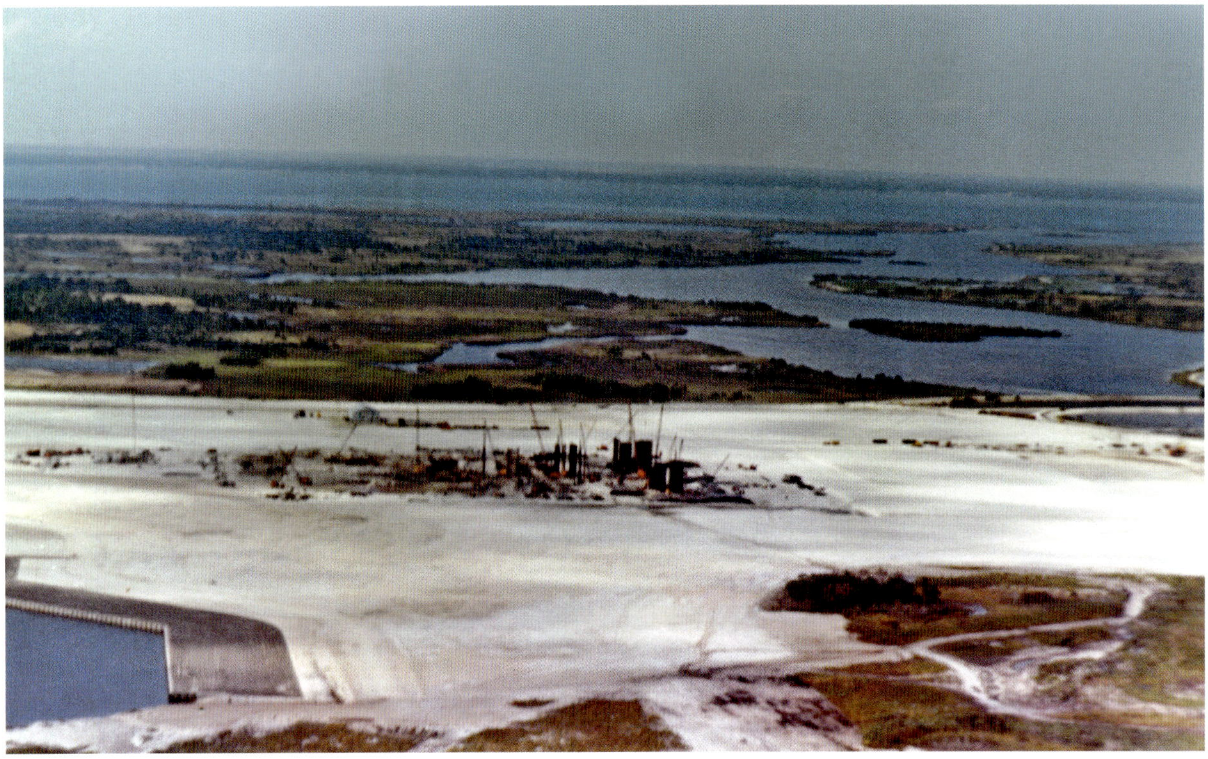

▲ After heading north past LC-40 and 41, Marine One circles over what would become LC-39, with the VAB beginning to rise on Merritt Island. This view looks west, with the Turning Basin, where Saturn V booster stages would arrive, at lower left and the Indian River in the distance. The president then flies over the KSC Industrial area before heading southeast, crossing the coast just north of Port Canaveral.

▼ Marine One prepares to land on USS *Observation Island*, a former merchant ship converted to supporting fleet ballistic missile development, about twenty-five miles off Cape Canaveral with a second VH-3A helicopter behind it.

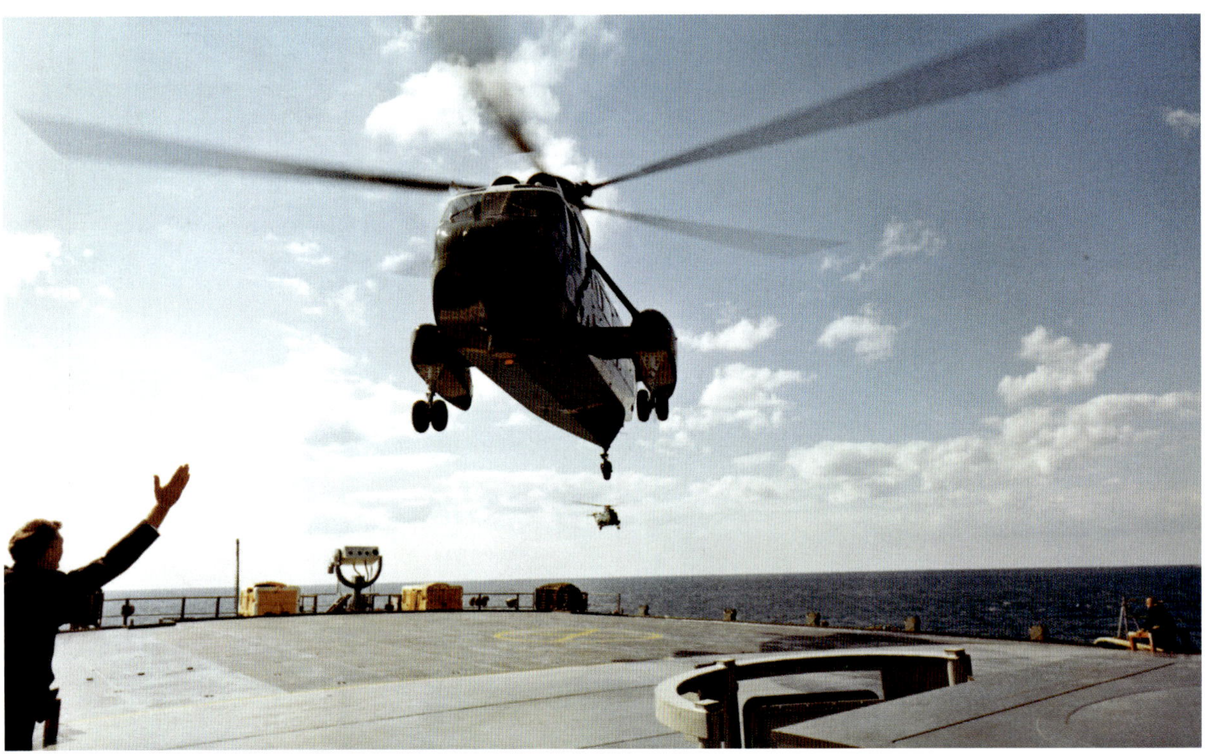

▶ Kennedy and Smathers (right) arrive at 11:45 a.m. At left are R. Adm. Galantin and Deputy Commander of the US Atlantic Fleet Submarine Force R. Adm. Vernon Lowrance.

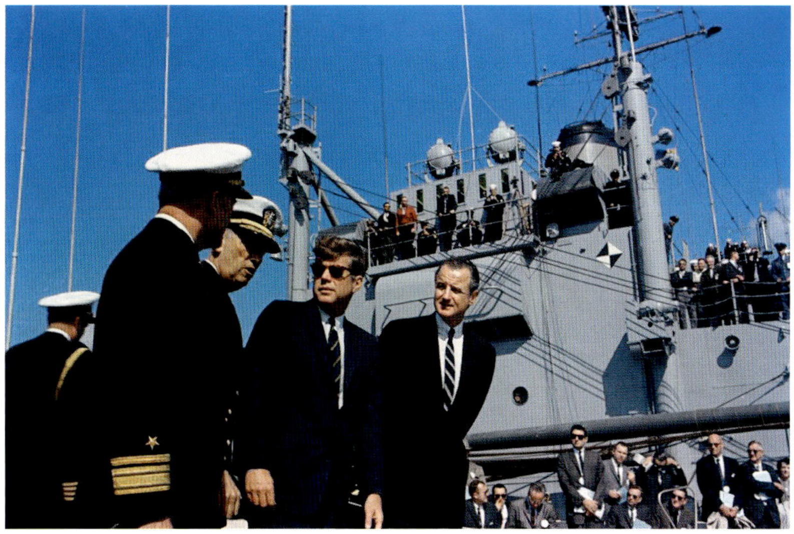

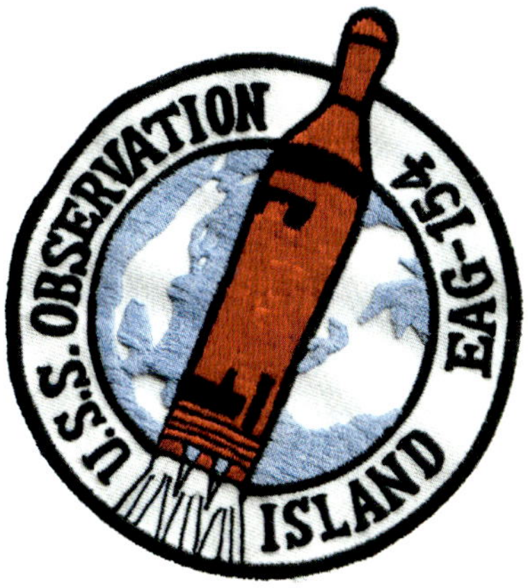

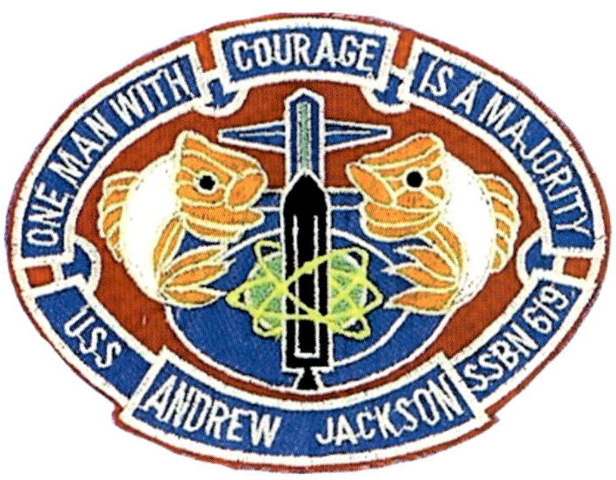

▶ The president dons a windbreaker with the insignias of the USS *Observation Island* and the submarine USS *Andrew Jackson*, a gift from the crews of both vessels.

L–R (in foreground): R. Adm. Lowrance; Sen. Smathers (back to camera); Kennedy, Maj. Gen. Clifton; and R. Adm. Galantin. Galantin had received the Navy Cross as a wartime submarine commander.

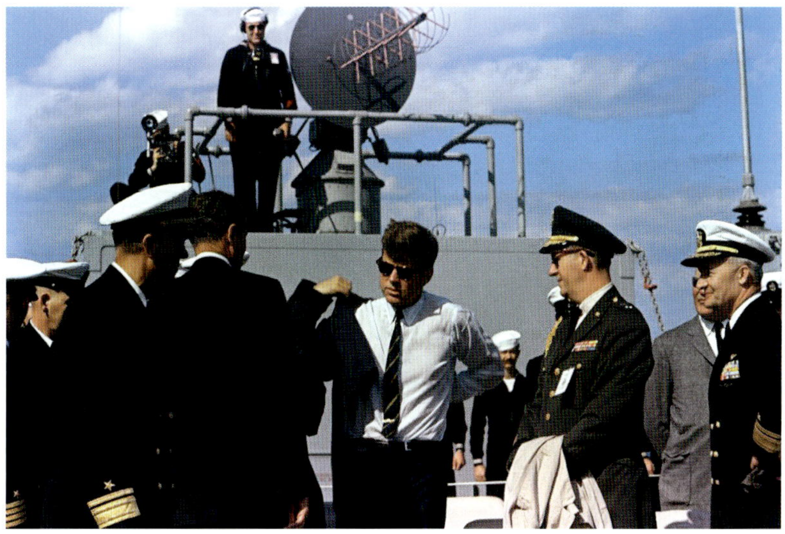

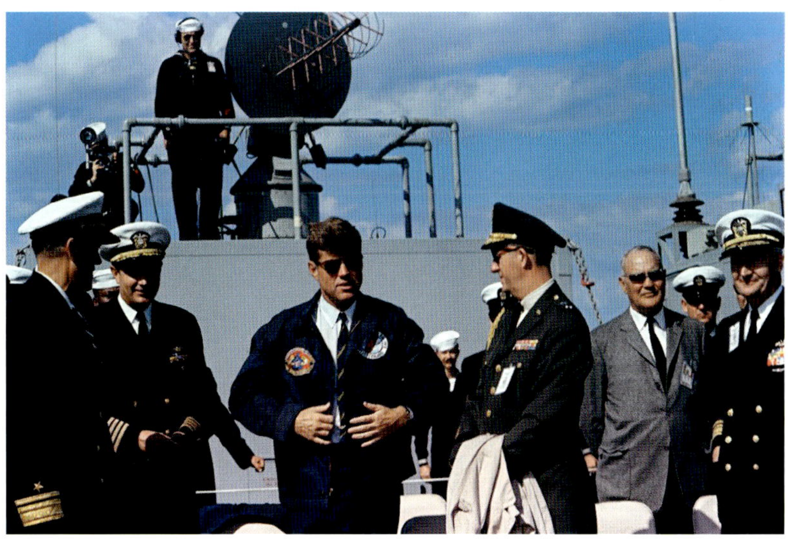

▲ Lowrance, a highly-decorated World War II submarine commander, served as director of the Office of Naval Intelligence from 1960 until June 1963, advising Kennedy during the Cuban Missile Crisis.

▶ Kennedy prepares for the launch of an unarmed Polaris A-2 submarine-launched ballistic missile (SLBM), a two-stage solid-fueled weapon with a range of seventeen hundred miles. SLBMs make up the third leg of the US nuclear triad, joining ICBMs and strategic bombers.

L–R: USS *Observation Island* Commanding Officer Capt. Roderick Middleton; R. Adm. Galantin; presidential naval aide Capt. Tazewell Shepard Jr.; Kennedy; Maj. Gen. Clifton (mostly hidden); Lowrance; and Sen. Smathers.

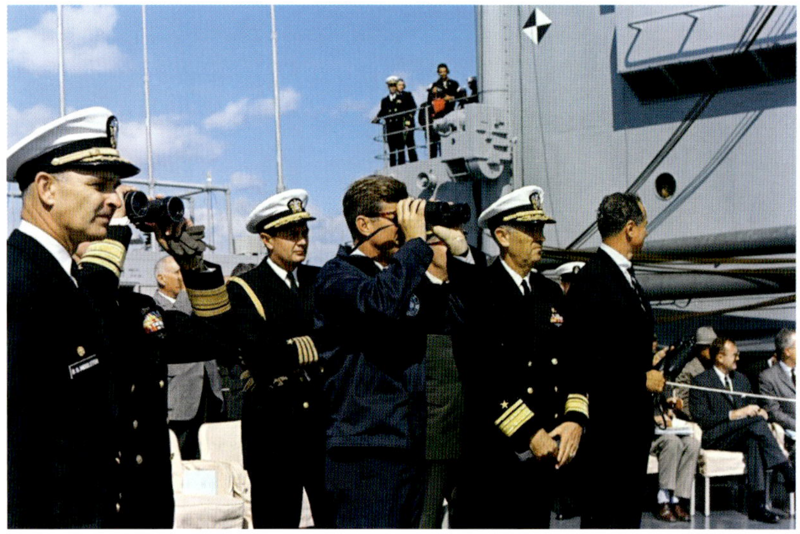

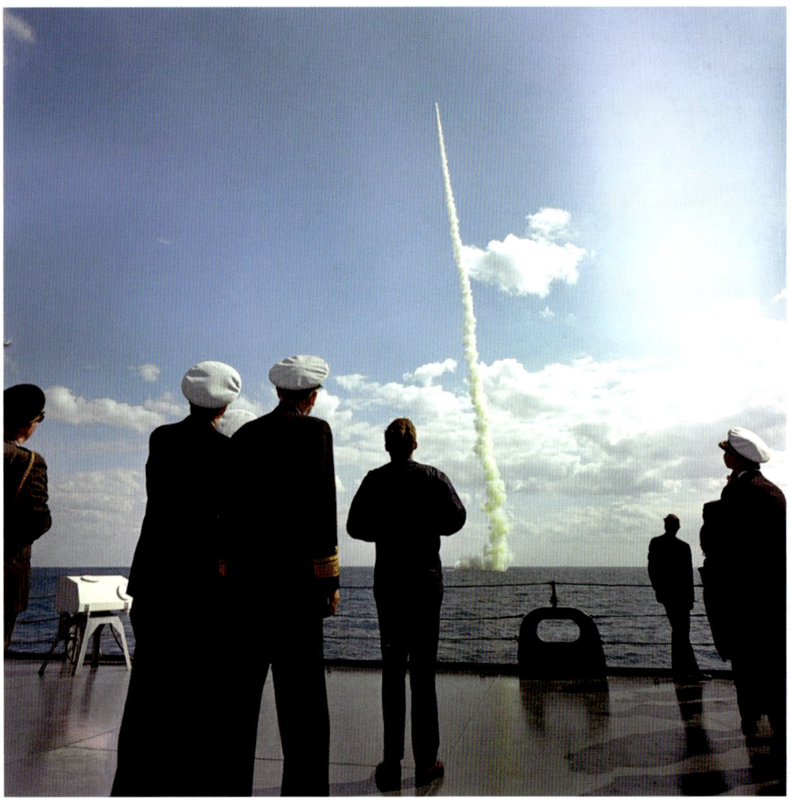

◀ The Polaris zooms skyward at 11:55 a.m., launched from the USS *Andrew Jackson*, a *Lafayette*-class nuclear-powered ballistic missile submarine fifty feet below the surface. It heads east down the Atlantic missile range to an ocean target near the British West Indies island of Antigua.

Three days later, the president writes in a letter to Galantin, "The Polaris firing I witnessed from the USS *Observation Island* on 16 November was a most satisfying and fascinating experience. It is still incredible to me that a missile can be successfully and accurately fired from beneath the sea. Once one has seen a Polaris firing, the efficacy of this weapon system as a deterrent is not debatable."

▶ The president speaks by radiotelephone to the submarine crew, congratulating Cmdr. James Wilson and his men for "impressive teamwork."

L–R: Lowrance; Middleton (partially hidden); Kennedy; and Shepard.

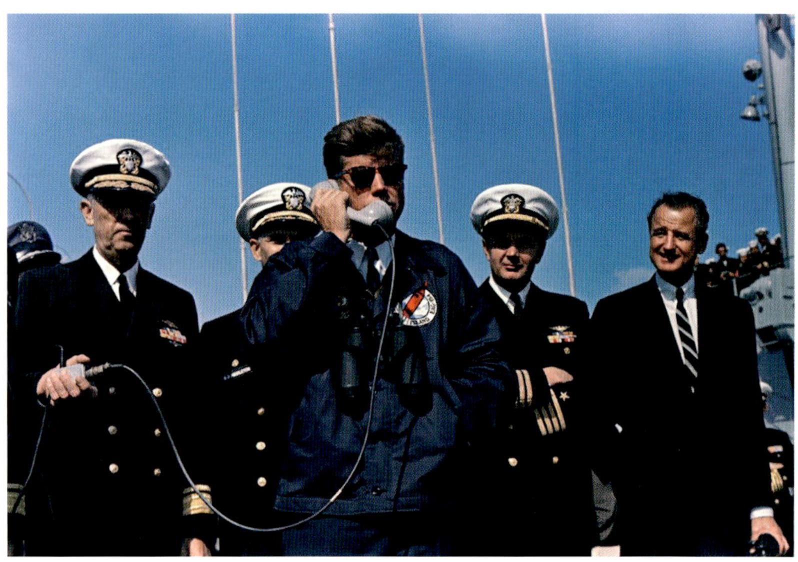

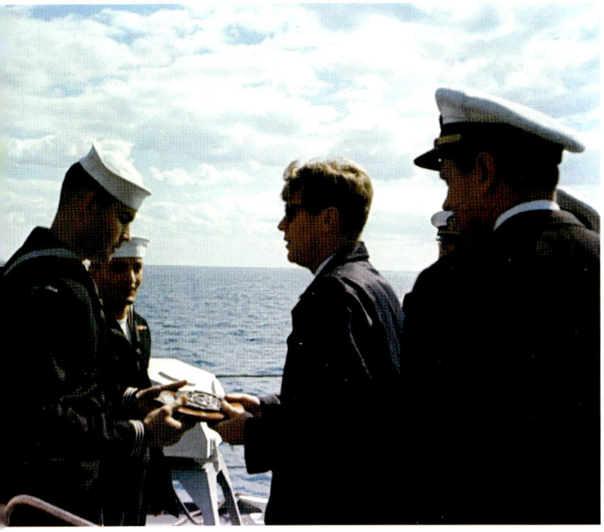

▲ Kennedy receives plaques from Torpedoman first class Joseph N. Roman of the *Observation Island* and Engineman first class Michael James Hoy of the *Andrew Jackson*. Shepard is at right.

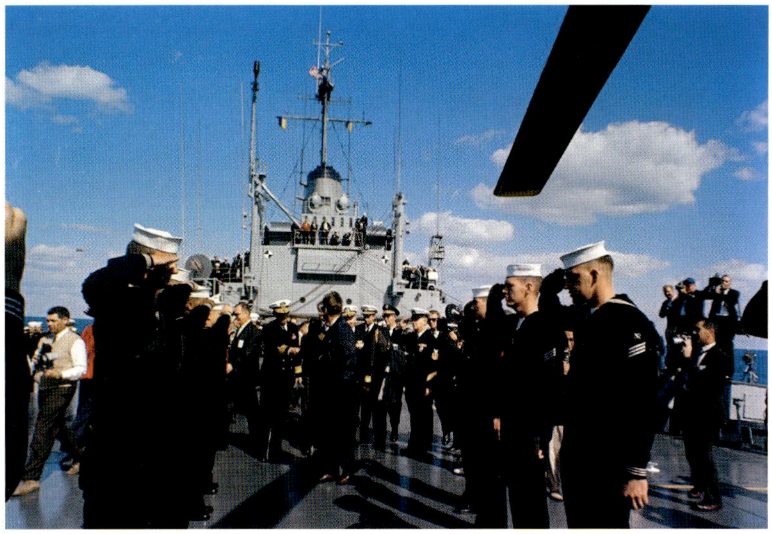

▲ Kennedy shakes hands with R. Adm. Lowrance. Sailors salute as he heads toward Marine One to return to Cape Canaveral.

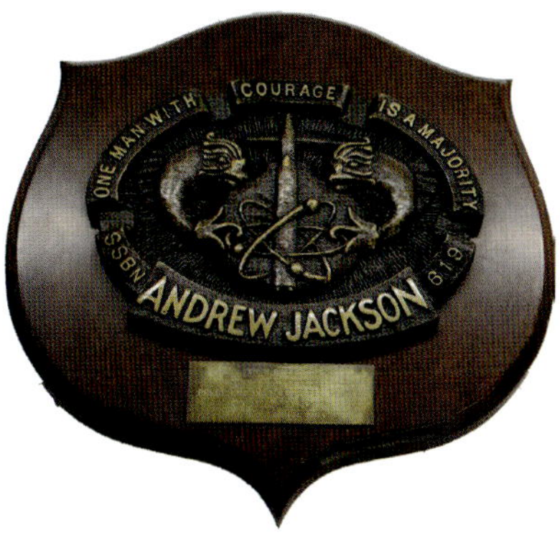

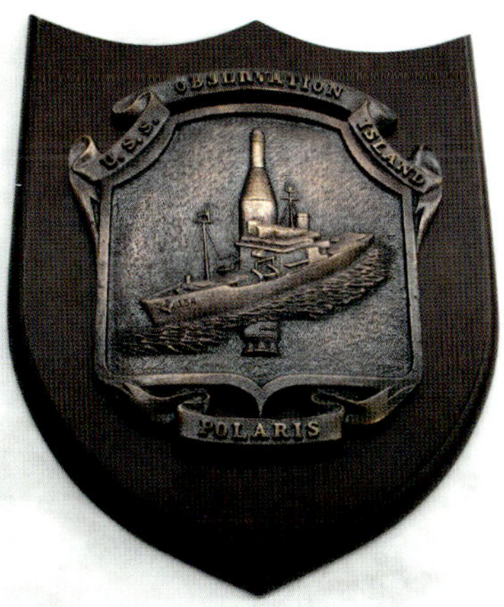

▲ Plaques from the John F. Kennedy Presidential Library and Museum collection.

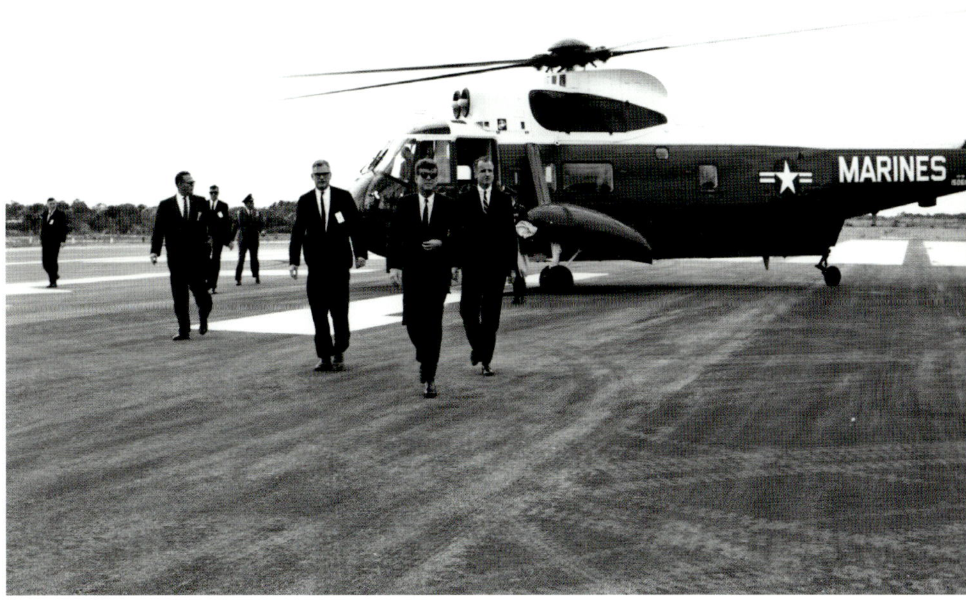

▲ Seamans, Kennedy, and Sen. Smathers approach SAM 26000 at the Skid Strip after returning from the Navy ship at 12:25 p.m.

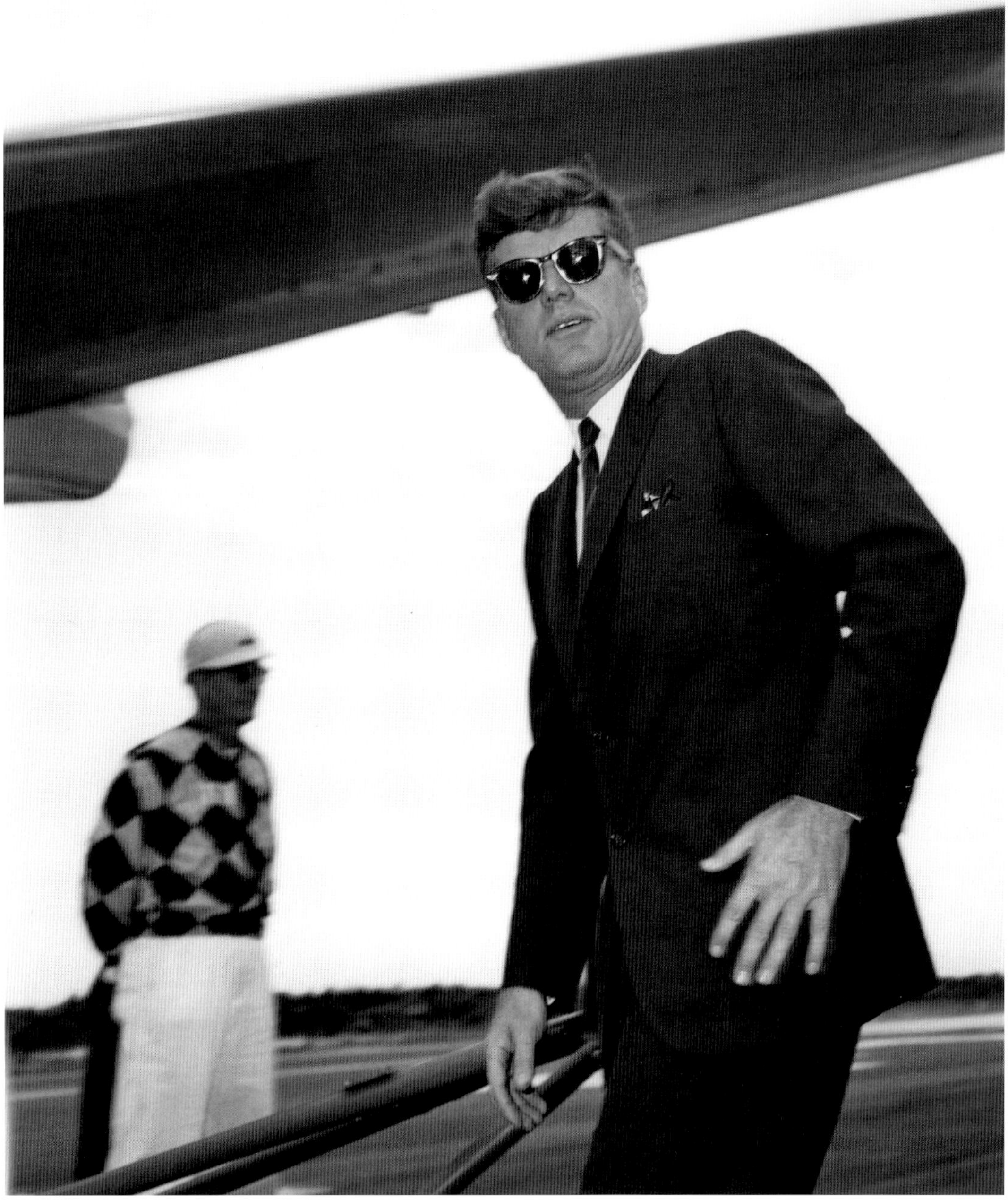

▲ The president prepares to board for the flight back to Palm Beach AFB at 12:30 p.m.

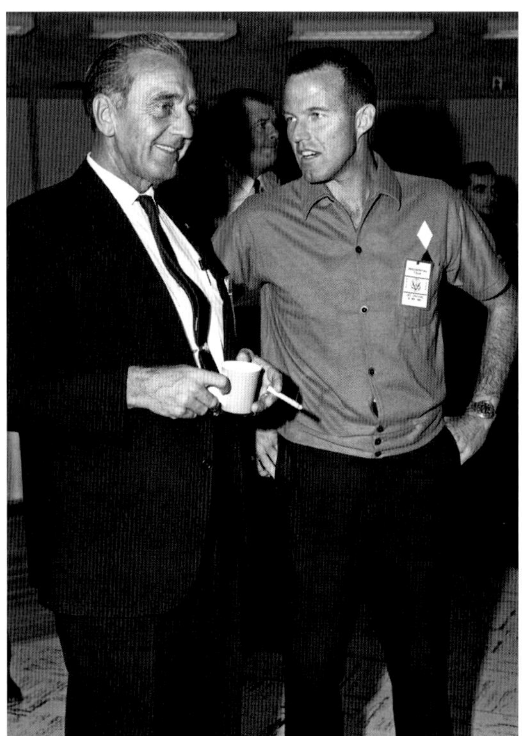

▶ That afternoon, with the presidential visit over, Debus and Cooper relax in the LC-37 blockhouse during a facilities tour for NASA Administrator Webb and his family.

:09

NOVEMBER 21, 1963

"This space effort must go on"

THE DAY BEFORE HIS DEATH, President Kennedy visits Brooks AFB, Texas, home to the nation's space medical research, and he again promotes the value of space exploration. Shortly before he leaves Washington, the Senate joins the House in cutting NASA's 1964 budget to $5.1 billion from $5.7 billion.

The administration is making fresh overtures to the Soviets about cooperation in space, after pondering a NASA report that the lunar landing alone would not guarantee US preeminence in space. But after Kennedy's assassination, the effort loses momentum, and President Lyndon Johnson would make continuing the Apollo program a memorial to his predecessor.

On November 22, 1963, the US communications satellite Relay 1 sends the first scheduled transpacific television transmission to Japan. It was to have been prerecorded greetings from Kennedy to the Japanese people but is instead the news that he was shot that day in Dallas.

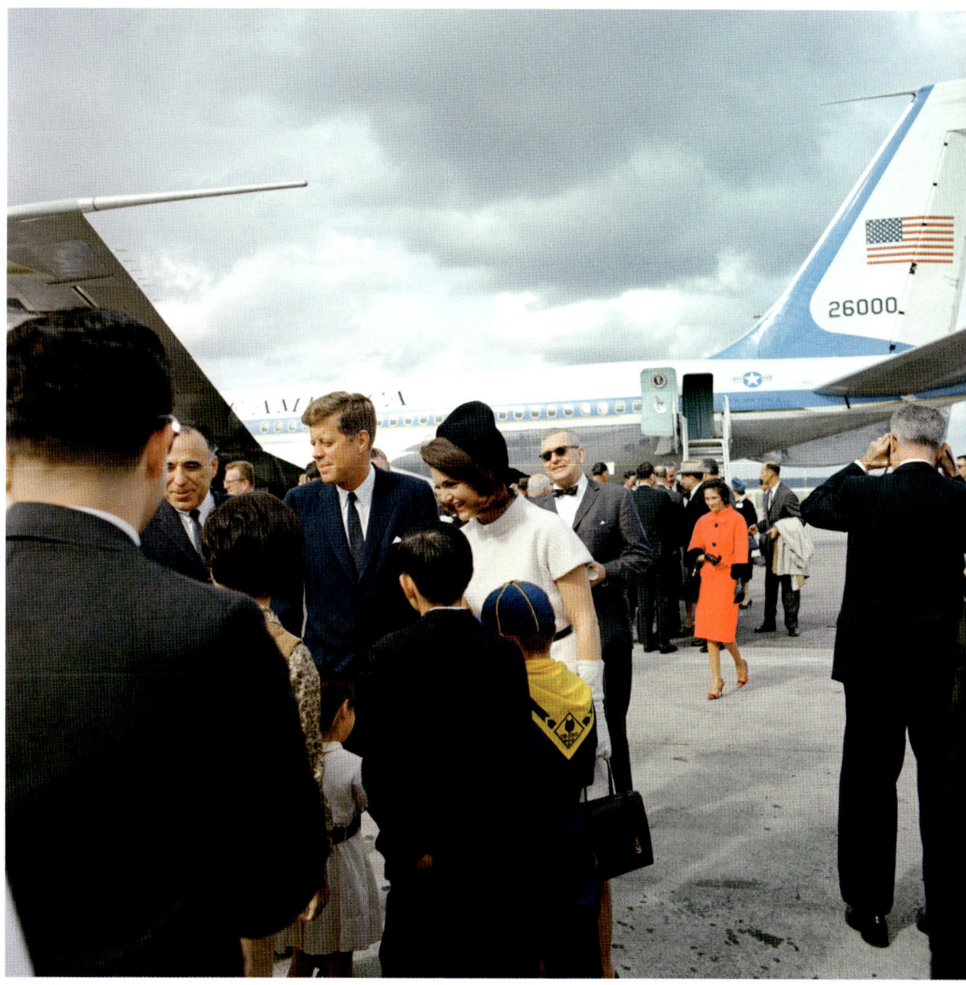

▲ On November 21, 1963, the president and First Lady arrive at San Antonio International Airport from Andrews AFB at 1:30 p.m. CST to start a two-day, five-city Texas tour aimed at promoting harmony among two factions of the state Democratic party.

▶ Rep. Henry B. Gonzalez, a Democrat who represented his native San Antonio in the US House from 1961–1999, is to Kennedy's right. He and his wife (red dress, previous page) also arrived aboard Air Force One. Gonzalez would ride in Kennedy's motorcade in Dallas the next day.

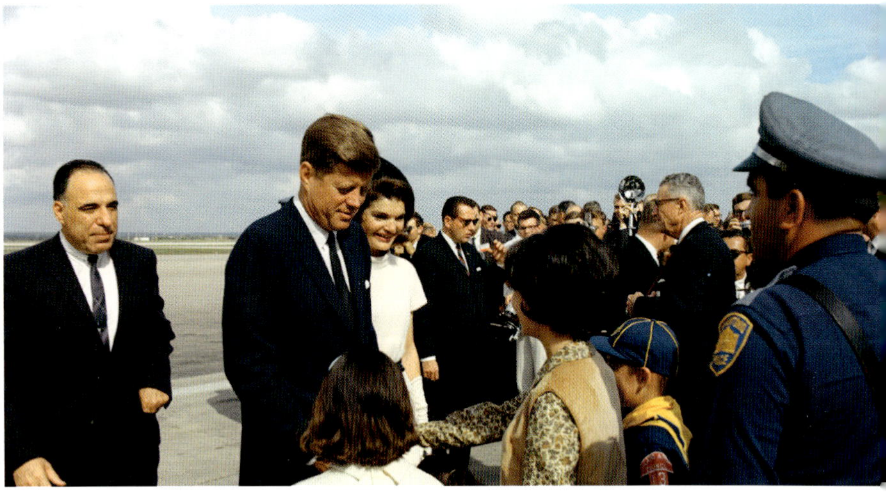

▶ The Kennedys head toward the motorcade. It is Jackie Kennedy's first official domestic trip as First Lady. A small group of African Americans pickets at the airport and at the president's local destination, Brooks AFB, charging segregation and discrimination in San Antonio.

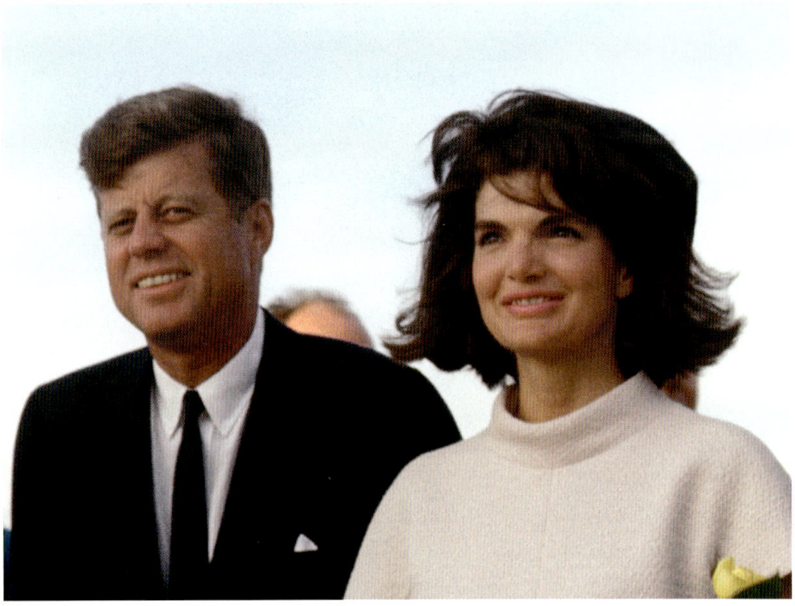

▼ Gov. John Connally (D-Tex.) and his wife, Nellie, ride with the first couple in SS-100-X to Brooks AFB, fifteen miles south of the city.

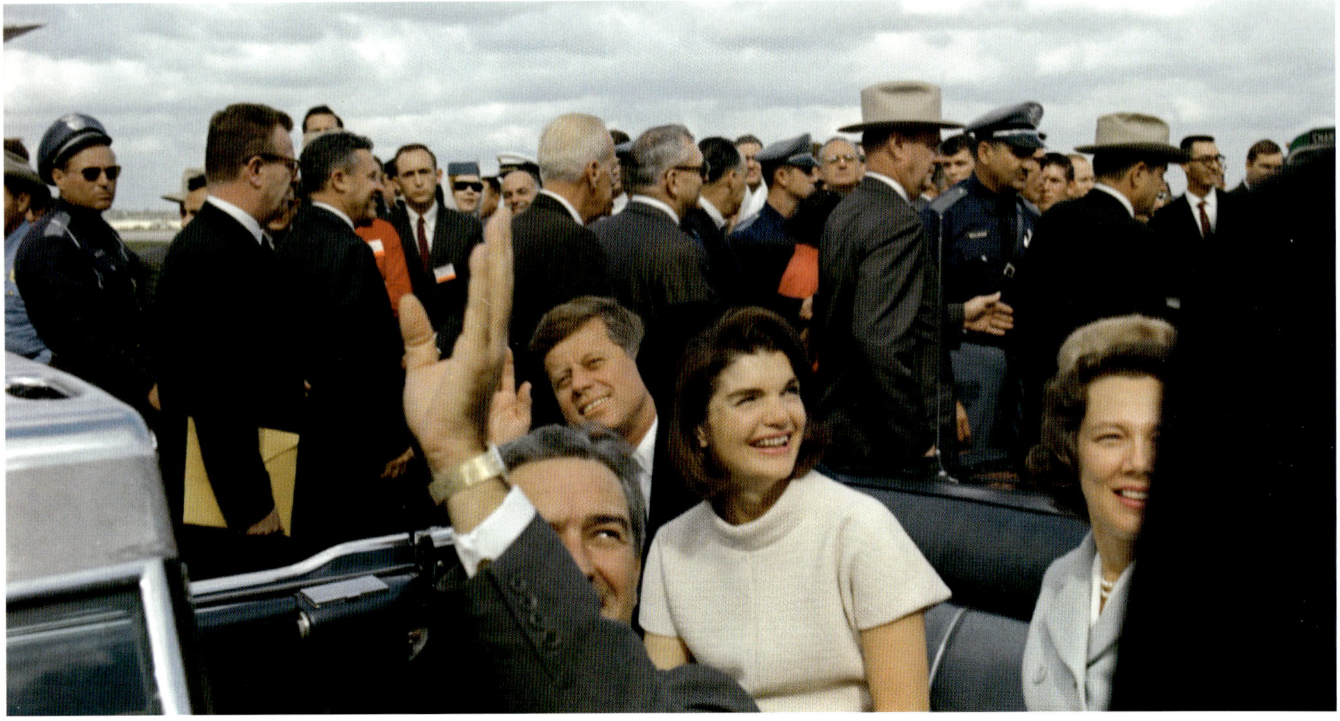

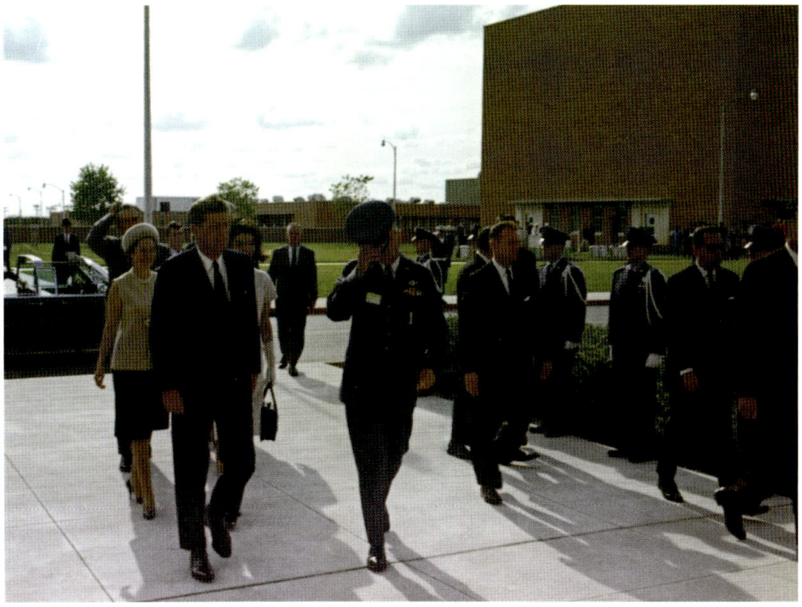

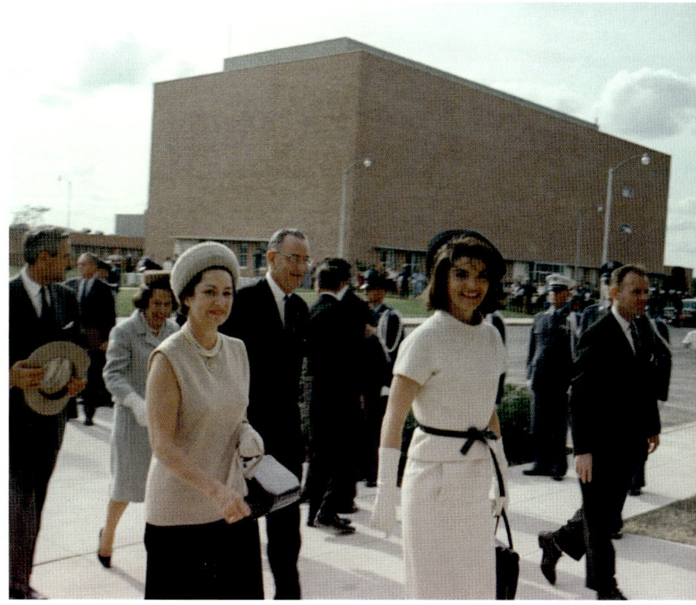

◥ Maj. Gen. Theodore Bedwell, commander of the Aerospace Medical Division, accompanies the president as he arrives at the rear of the Brooks headquarters building at 2:35 p.m. The First Lady, the Johnsons, and the Connallys follow. Bedwell served as SAC command surgeon at Offutt AFB, Nebraska, when appointed Aerospace Medical Center commander in early 1961. That November, when the center was transferred to the Air Force Systems Command as its Aerospace Medical Division at Brooks, he was retained as its commander.

Lt. Gen. George Schafer, Bedwell's operations deputy, later recalled the Kennedys being "very delightful"—not "overbearing" like Johnson.

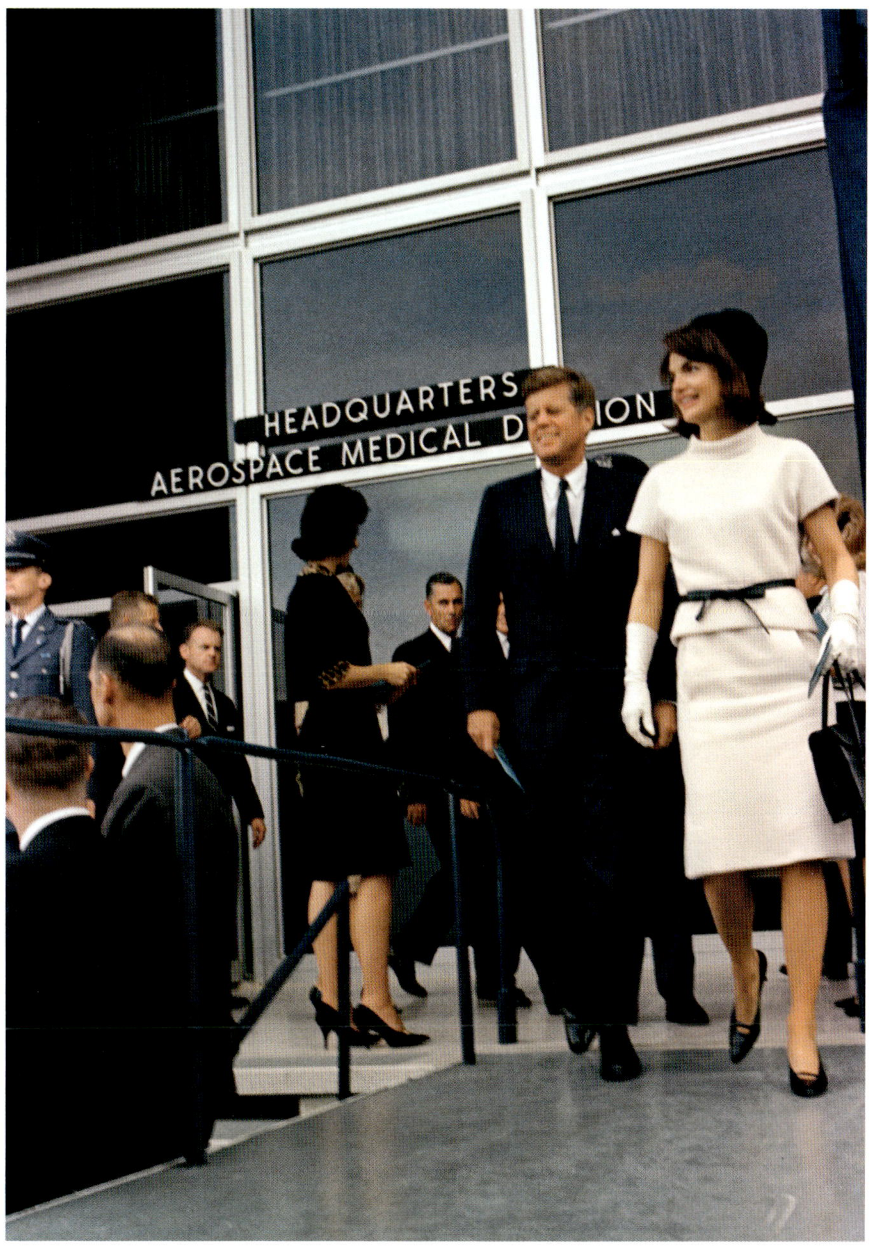

▶ The First Couple walk out of Building 150, which would be named for Bedwell, onto a temporary stage for the president's speech at the dedication of the Aerospace Medical Health Center. The event is part of a USAF reorganization and consolidation to create a national center for aerospace medicine, including teaching, clinical medicine, and research. Its mission is also expanded to support the US military and civilian space programs. Building 150 is today within the School of Aerospace Medicine Historic District and is part of the University of the Incarnate Word's School of Osteopathic Medicine.

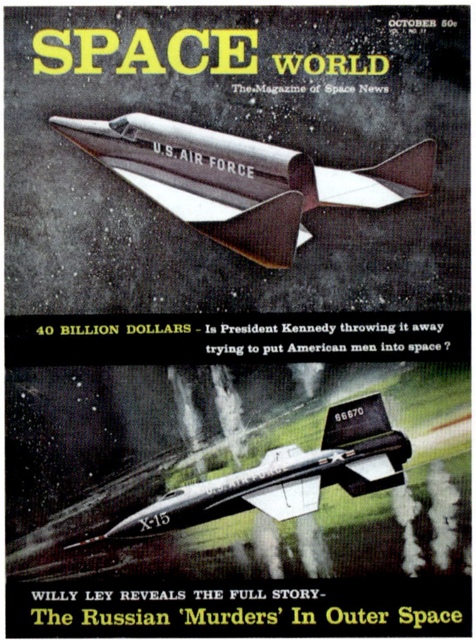

◀ The current issue of *Space World* magazine questions the president's priorities.

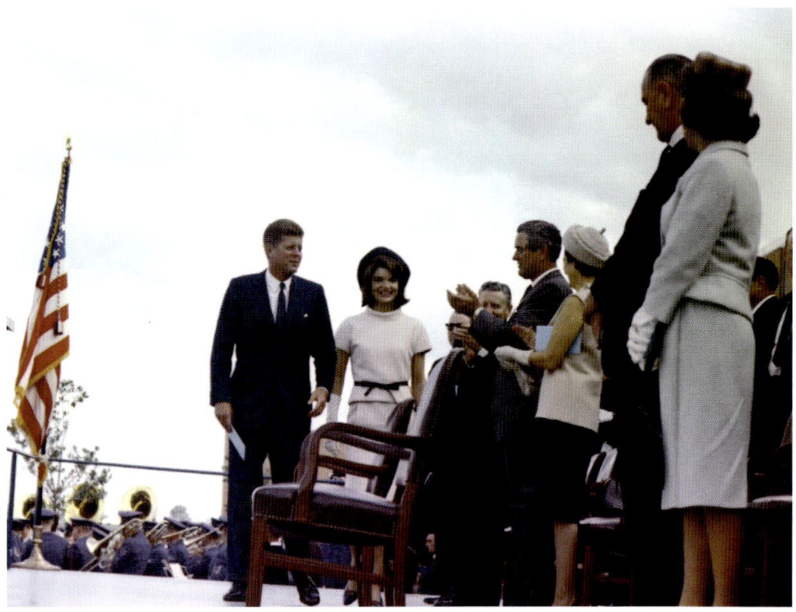

◢ The president speaks starting at 2:45 p.m. with a mockup of an X-20, part of the USAF's Dyna-Soar program to develop a space plane that could be used for a variety of military purposes. X-20 pilots go through medical testing at Brooks. Dyna-Soar, begun in 1957, will be cancelled in less than three weeks' time after Kennedy's visit over concerns about its cost and uncertain mission.

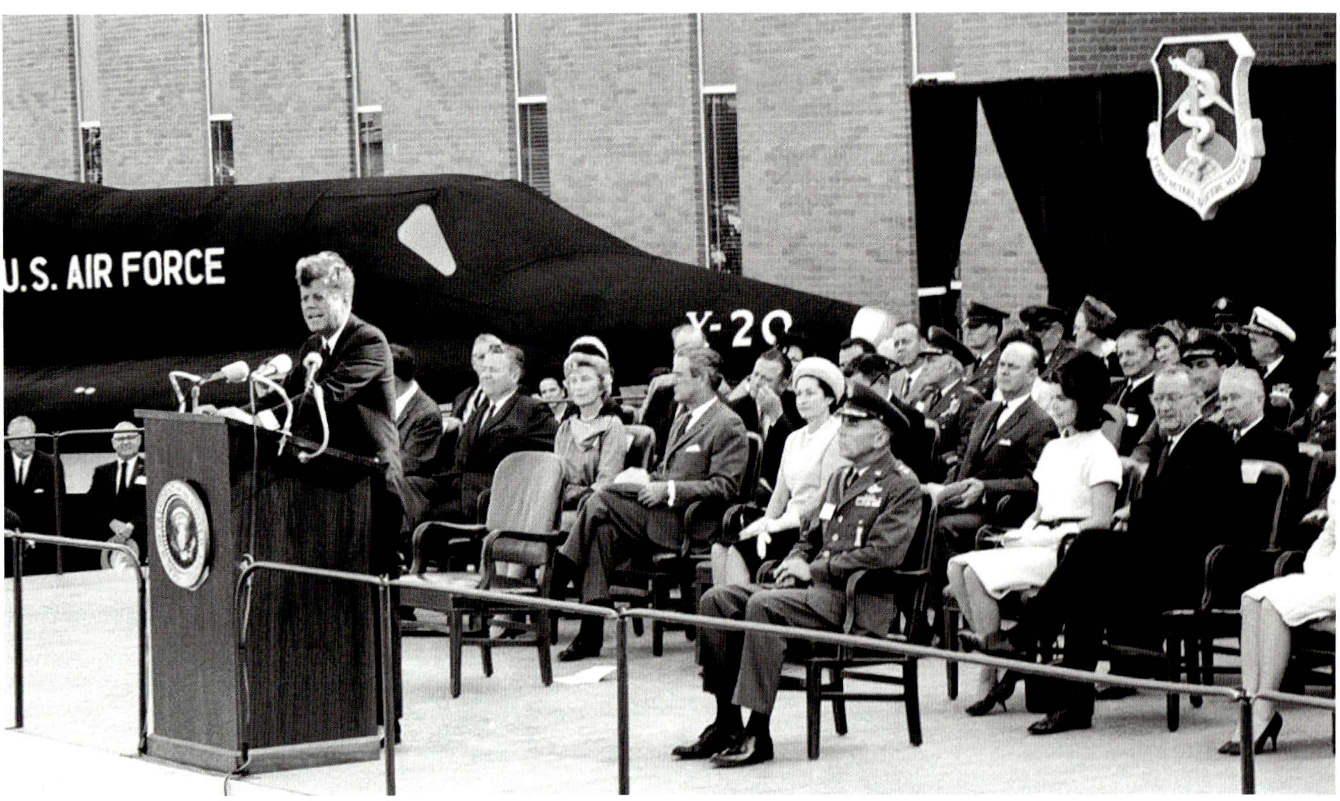

◢ Kennedy says,

Last Saturday, at Cape Canaveral, I saw our new Saturn C-1 rocket booster, which, with its payload, when it rises in December of this year, will be, for the first time, the largest booster in the world, carrying into space the largest payload that any country in the world has ever sent into space. . . . We have a long way to go. Many weeks and months and years of long, tedious work lie ahead. There will be setbacks and frustrations and disappointments. There will be, as there always are, pressures in this country to do less in this area as in so many others, and temptations to do something else that is perhaps easier. But this research here must go on. This space effort must go on. The conquest of space must and will go ahead. That much we know. That much we can say with confidence and conviction.

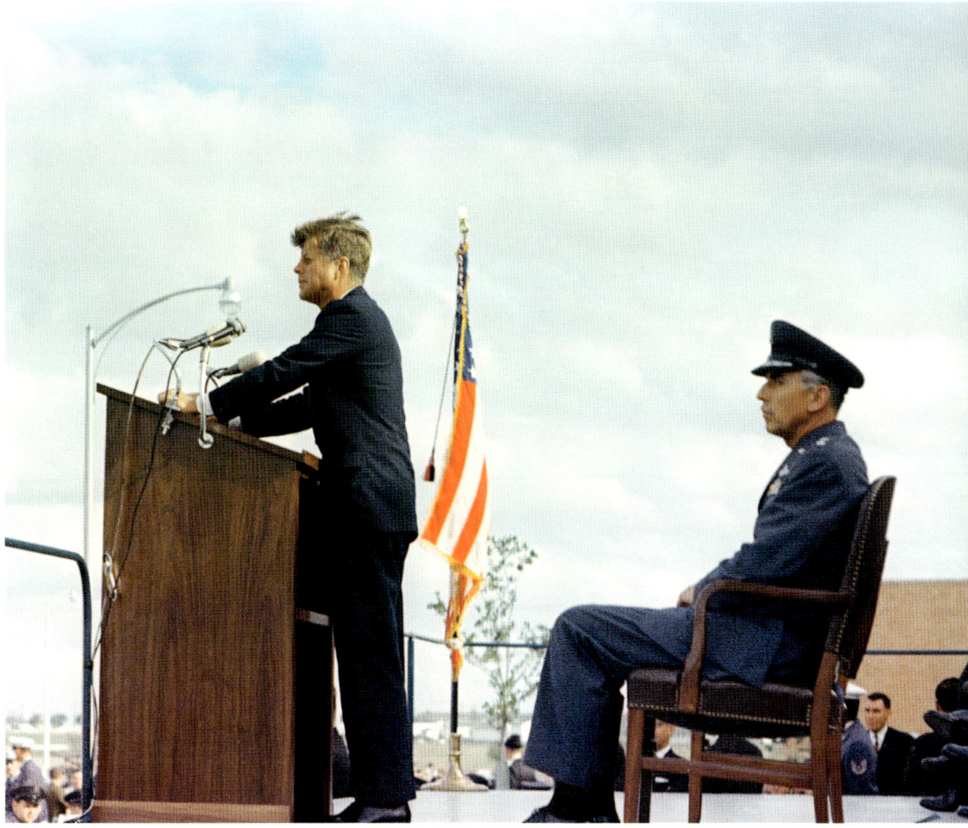

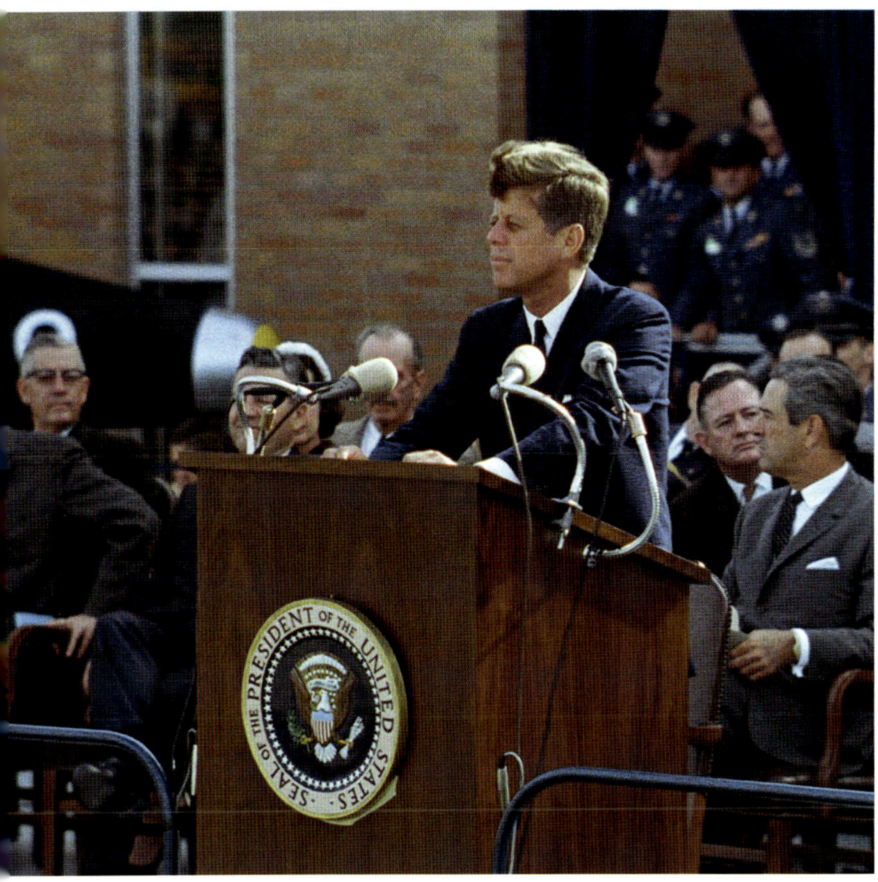

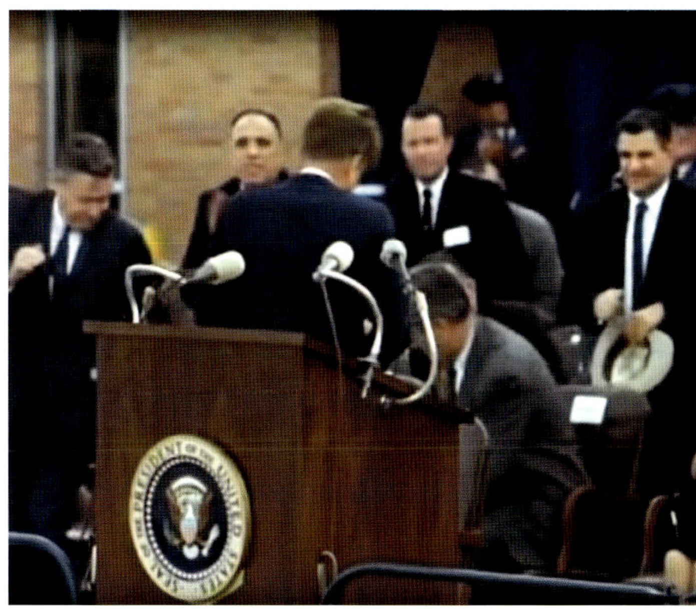

▲ Astronaut Gordon Cooper (center) was on stage with the president.

▶ "This nation has tossed its cap over the wall of space, and we have no choice but to follow it," the president concludes. "Whatever the difficulties, they will be overcome. Whatever the hazards, they must be guarded against. With the vital help of this Aerospace Medical Center, with the help of all those who labor in the space endeavor, with the help and support of all Americans, we will climb this wall with safety and with speed—and we shall then explore the wonders on the other side."

The crowd is estimated to be ten thousand. The Aerospace School holds an open house that morning with guided tours. "Visitors may expect to see such facilities as the high-altitude simulation chambers, space suits and the gravity-simulating centrifuge," reports the *San Antonio Express*. "At 1:00 p.m., the Air Force Band of the West, from Lackland [AFB], will begin a concert."

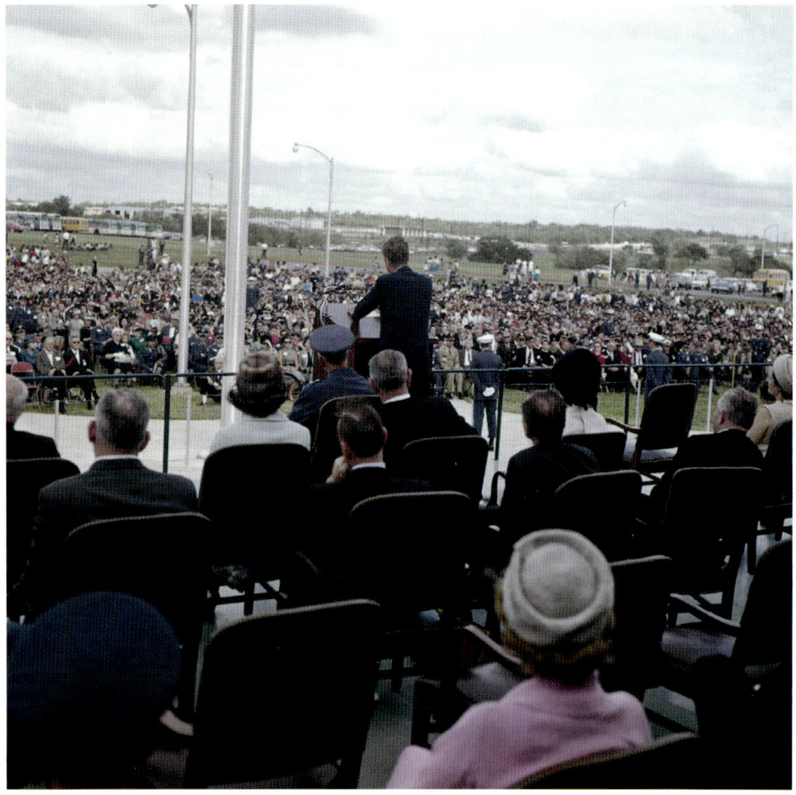

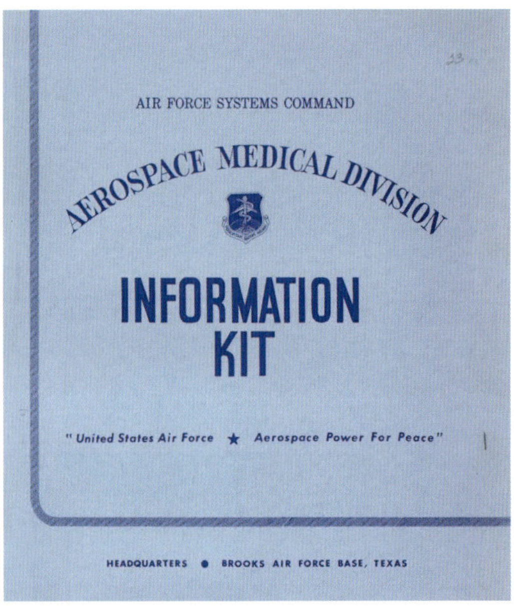

▲ Folder given to presidential guests at Brooks.

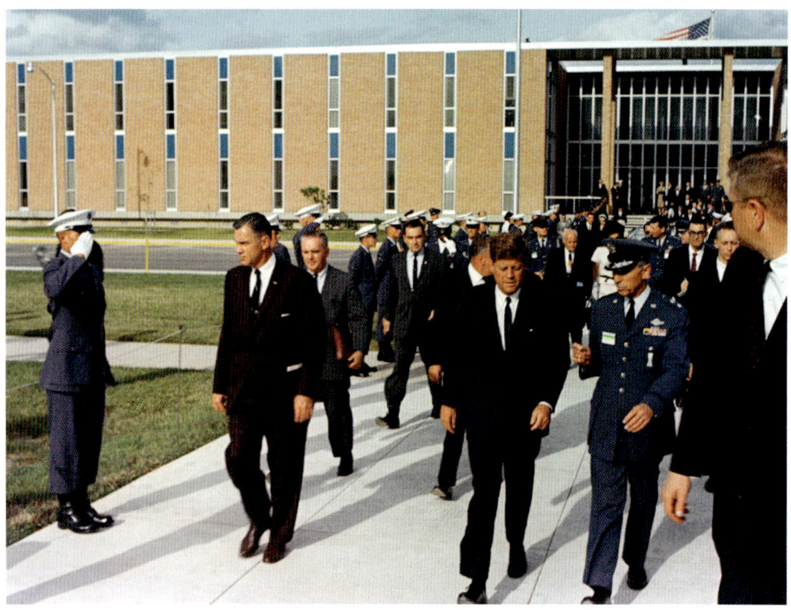

▲ At 3:05 p.m., Maj. Gen. Bedwell escorts the president to an unplanned tour of Building 170, the Bioastronautics-Biodynamics Laboratory, one of the six new buildings dedicated that day, to visit four volunteers sealed in an experiment. During the 1960s, acceleration studies utilizing human and animal centrifuges, space cabin simulations, and space nutritional studies were conducted at the facility, all of which were to contribute to the success of the Gemini and Apollo programs.

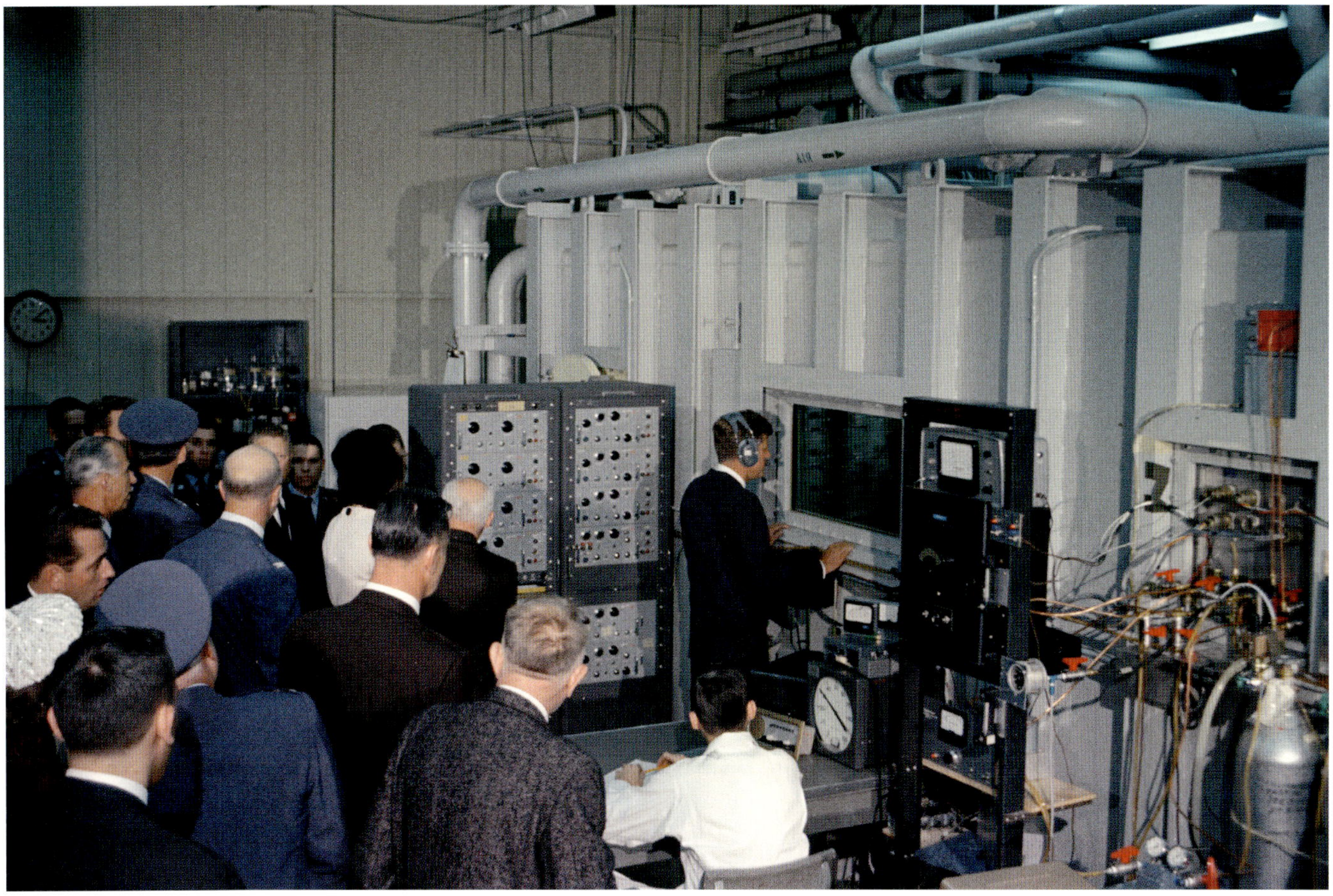

▲ Kennedy uses a headset to speak with four young airmen from an Aerospace Medical Division unit located at nearby Lackland AFB who are halfway through a 42-day stay in an altitude chamber with a hundred percent oxygen environment as a test for the Apollo spacecraft.

The president's son, Patrick Kennedy, had died in August, two days after a premature birth. He had been treated in a hyperbaric chamber. Kennedy privately asks the lead doctor whether the work at Brooks might lead to better treatment for premature infants.

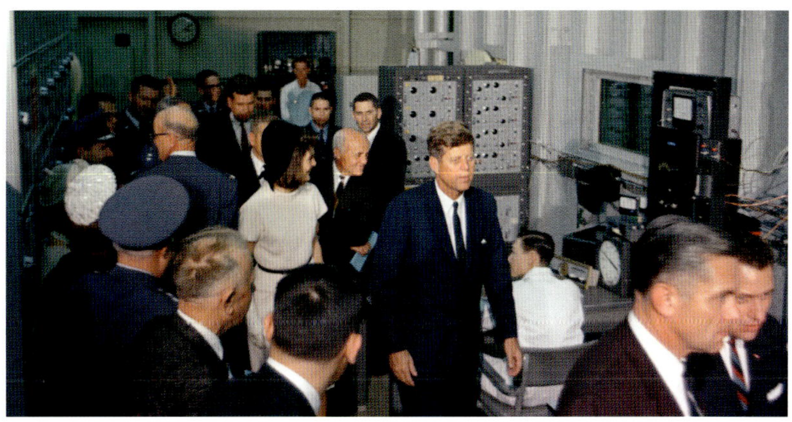

◥ The president's motorcade would depart for Kelly AFB at 3:25 p.m. (Although Brooks AFB closed in 2011, the chamber is still in use by Wyle Technologies at what is today known as Brooks, a mixed-use community.)

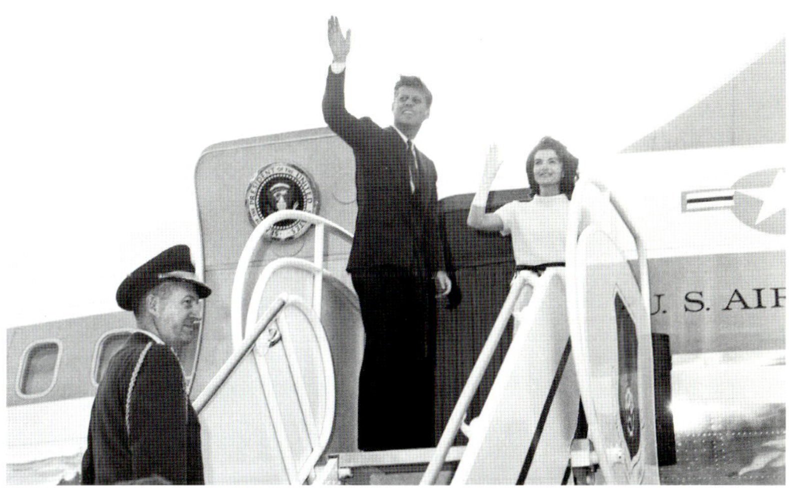

▶ The Kennedys wave good-bye at Kelly before their 3:52 p.m. departure for Houston International Airport.

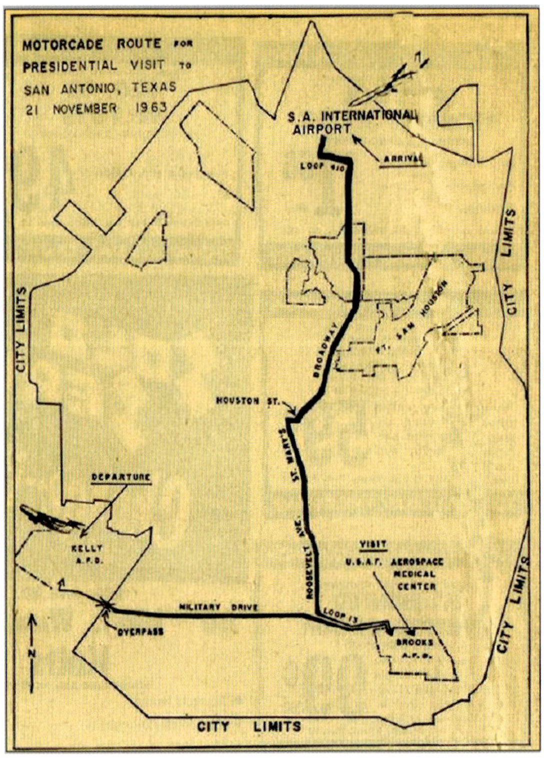

◀ SAM 26000 had been moved to Kelly from San Antonio.

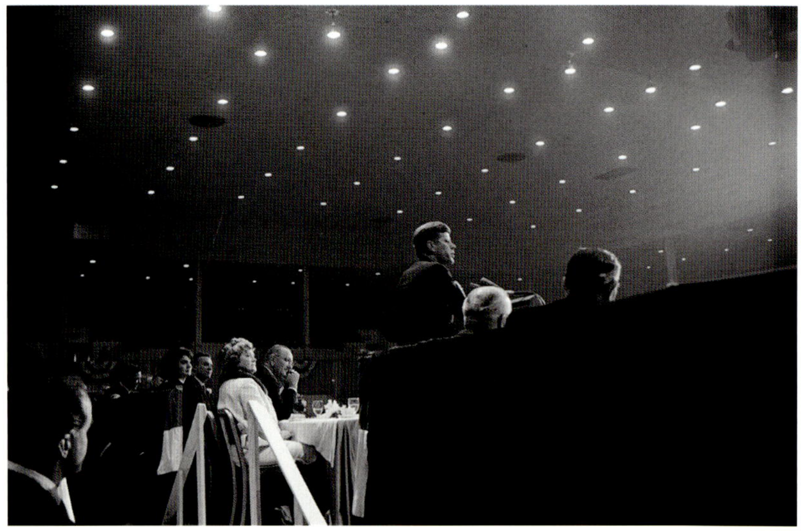

◥ At 9:00 p.m., the president attends a testimonial dinner for Rep. Albert Thomas at Sam Houston Coliseum in Houston. "He has helped steer this country to its present eminence in space," Kennedy says. "Next month when the United States of America fires the largest booster in the history of the world into space for the first time, giving us the lead, fires the largest payroll—payload—into space, giving us the lead . . ." Kennedy pauses and grins. "It will be the largest payroll, too," he quips, and the crowd roars. "And who should know that better than Houston. We put a little of it right in here. But in any case, the United States next month will have a leadership in space which it wouldn't have without Albert Thomas. And so will this city." The president would then spend the night in Ft. Worth before traveling to Dallas the next day.

Seated at the table on the left are Jacqueline Kennedy, Sen. Ralph Yarborough (D-Tex.), Mrs. Lera Thomas, and Johnson.

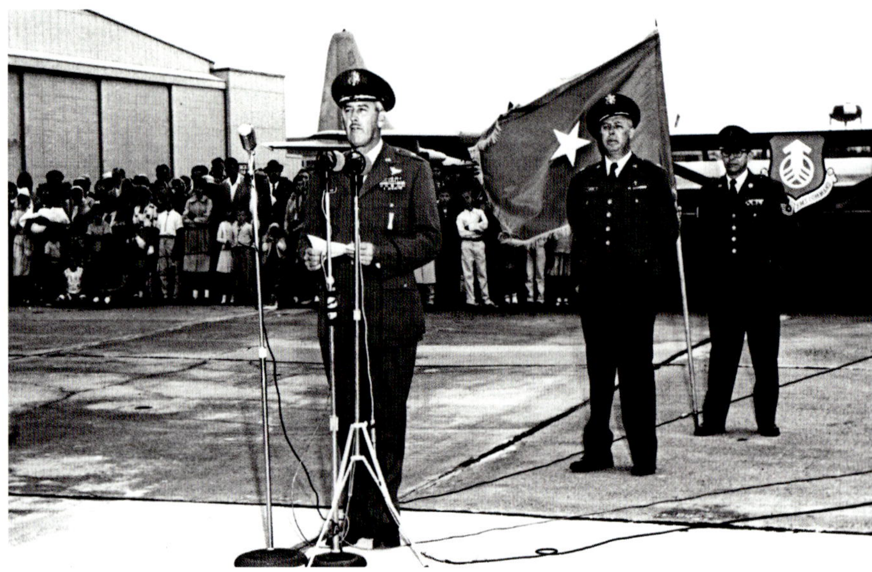

▲ Ceremonies to honor the president quickly follow his death on November 22, 1963. At Redstone Arsenal, some five thousand military and civilian personnel attend on November 23.

At Cape Canaveral, government facilities are closed on November 25. In this photograph, at Patrick AFB, base vice commander Brig. Gen. Harry Sands leads a memorial service that day.

Two days later, the USAF conducts two successful launches from the Cape: a Delta booster putting Explorer 18 into orbit; and an Atlas, lofting its Centaur second stage into orbit. The president had seen the Atlas at LC-36 during his final visit.

▶ SA-5 rises from the LC-34 at 11:25 a.m. EST on January 29, 1964. The three TV networks carry the launch live. The booster places the second stage into orbit; at 37,401 pounds, it is the largest and heaviest payload ever to go into orbit at that time. The achievement, however, long-promised by Kennedy, is not an objective of the mission but rather a bonus.

After the launch, Seamans said the blockhouse personnel wanted to call Mrs. Kennedy. "I suggested instead that I carry the sentiments of those involved in the launch back to her in person. When I returned to Washington, I contacted Walter Sohier, NASA's general counsel and a friend of the Kennedys. He didn't think Mrs. Kennedy would be interested in a visit, so imagine his surprise when he and I were invited for tea the following afternoon!"

The visit produces this exchange of letters:

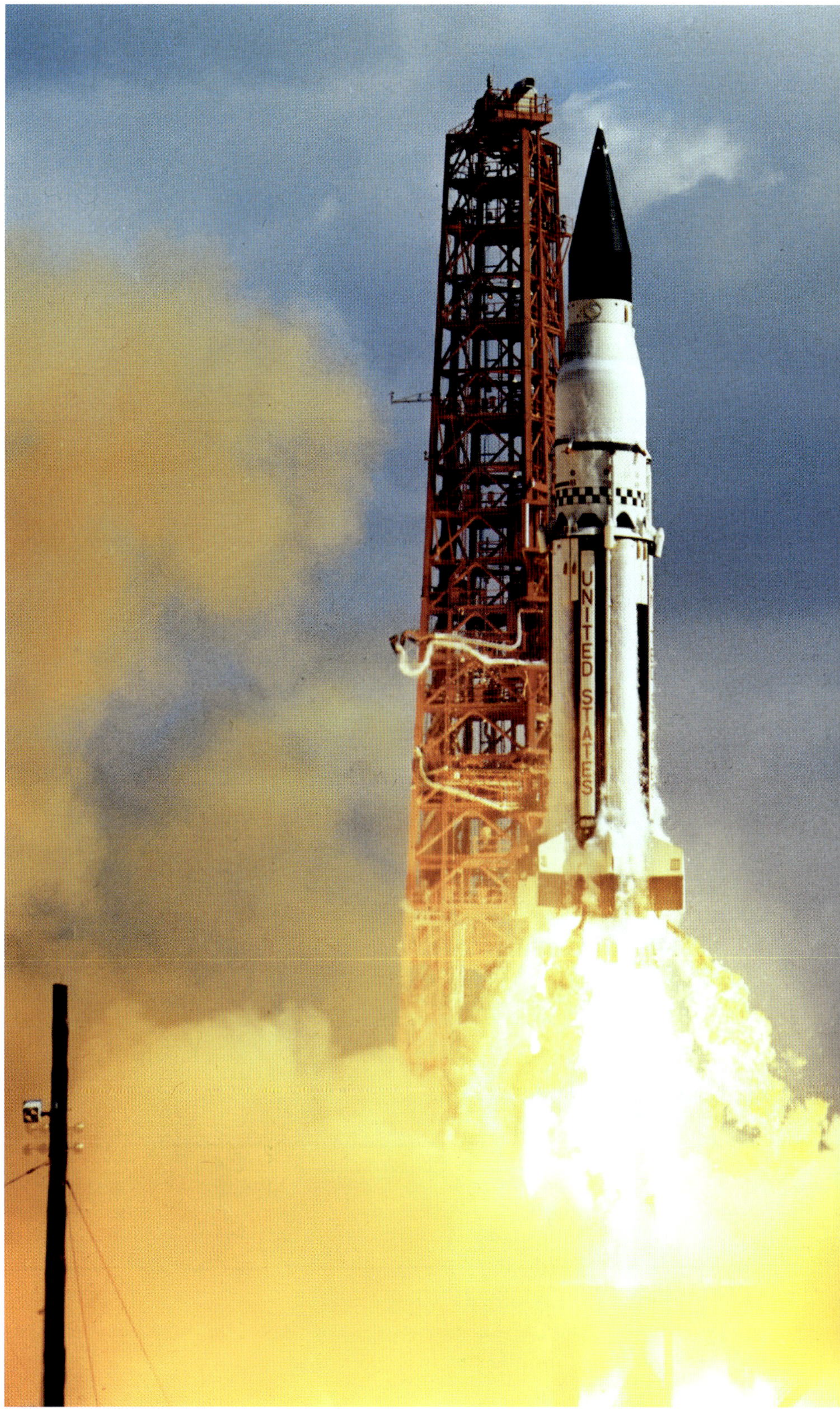

February 7, 1964

Dear Mrs. Kennedy:

Thank you for the pleasant visit you afforded us Monday evening. It meant a great deal to me to be able to tell you about the recent Saturn launch from the John F. Kennedy Space Center.

The accompanying detailed engineering model of the actual Saturn launched on January 29th is presented to you with appreciation from all of us. It was utilized by Dr. Wernher von Braun and the staff of the George C. Marshall Space Flight Center which has responsibility for the Saturn development.

Having seen young John's interest in space toys, and having barely escaped from your home with the other model that I brought, I am also sending some fairly sturdy launch vehicle models for his enjoyment.

Sincerely,

Robert C. Seamans, Jr.

March 14, 1964

Dear Dr. Seamans,

I do thank you for that most precious model of the Saturn—the one that Wernher von Braun and everyone worked on—(I could not believe my eyes when Walter Sohier brought it). John had a fleeting happy look at it—and then I sent it to Archives—to go in Jack's library.

Your thoughtfulness has touched me so much—that you would wish to come—and tell me about the Saturn booster—and think of calling me from the blockhouse when it was going off. All I care about is that people still remember what Jack did—and you were always thinking of him.

Then when you came and saw John—it was so kind of you to see how a little boy who had grown up so close to a father who always had exciting new plane and rocket models in his office to show him—who took him on his most cherished plane and helicopter rides—would still care so much about all those things—and feel so cut off now that they are no longer a part of his life.

Those "heavy duty" models that you sent him are his joy—taken apart and put together constantly—I do thank you more than I can say, for your thoughtfulness to him and to me.

Sincerely,
Jacqueline Kennedy

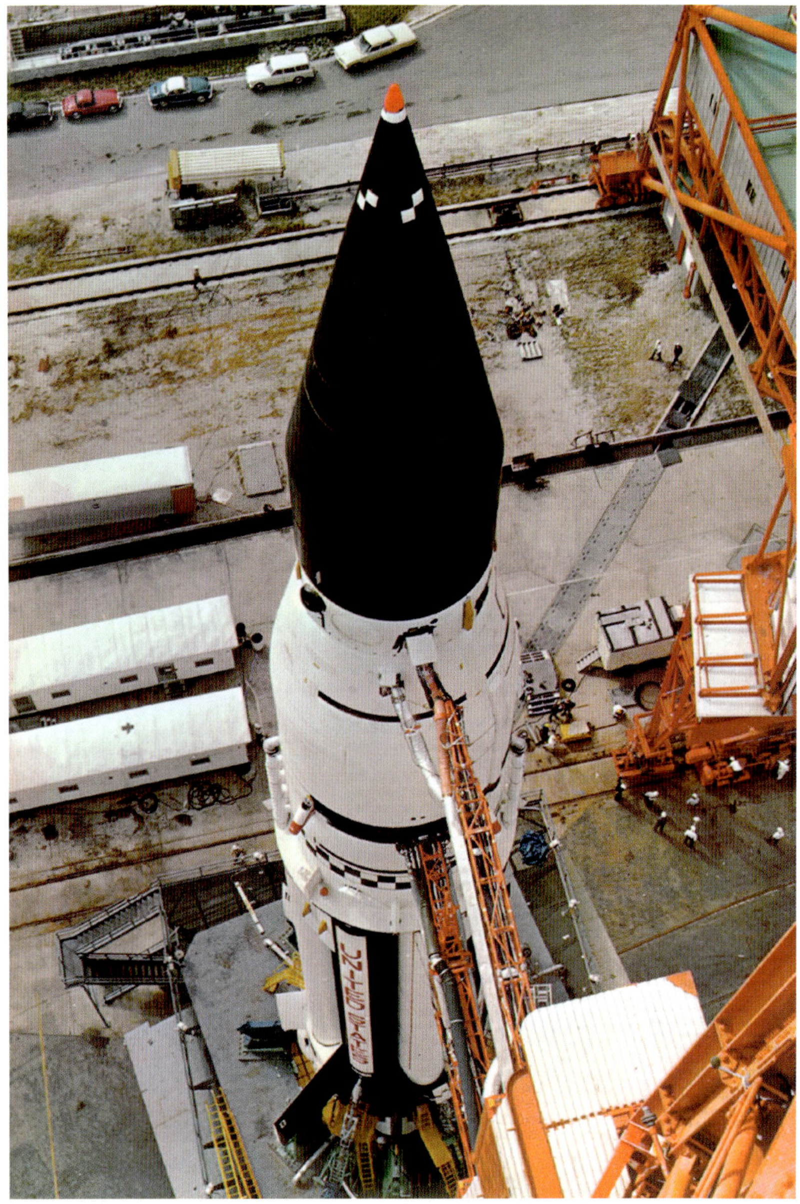

▶ In a November 29, 1963, interview (fully released by the John F. Kennedy Presidential Library after her death in 1994), Mrs. Kennedy tells author Theodore White she had hoped the SA-5 booster, which the president first saw at Marshall in 1962, then at Cape Canaveral earlier that month, would carry with it a small memorial to her late husband.

"Jack was so interested in the Saturn booster," she says. "All I wanted was Jack's name signed on the side of the nose of the booster somehow where no one would even notice. [Defense Secretary Robert] McNamara said that wasn't dignified. But then he changed the name of the Cape itself so that everything that goes to the sky, goes from there."

NASA had considered the request, as well as possibly having the payload section carry a tape of Kennedy's moon speech that would be played back from orbit. But worries about the symbolism of a launch accident stopped the plans. Rumors were so rampant that some special marking would be placed on the Saturn, recalled NASA Associate Administrator Robert Seamans, that special security precautions were implemented.

"I'm going to bring up my son. I want him to grow up to be a good boy," says Mrs. Kennedy in the interview. "I have no better dream for him. I want John-John to be a fine young man. He's so interested in planes; maybe he'll be an astronaut or just plain John Kennedy fixing planes on the ground."

:10

IN REMEMBRANCE

"For the eyes of the world now look into space"

ON NOVEMBER 29, 1963, President Lyndon Johnson issues an executive order renaming both the NASA and Air Force installations in Florida as the John F. Kennedy Space Center. NASA later clarifies this will only apply to its facilities on Merritt Island while the USAF renames the military launch site as Cape Kennedy Air Force Station.

The name change for the geographical feature, however, is not popular in Florida, especially in the bordering city of Cape Canaveral. In 1973, the Florida Legislature restores the former four-hundred-year-old name of the cape, which becomes official on October 9, 1973. The Kennedy family issues a letter stating they "understood the decision."

As president, Johnson continues to support funding for Apollo despite budget pressures from his Great Society social programs and the Vietnam War. Richard Nixon, defeated by Kennedy in 1960, would speak from the Oval Office to the two Americans who accomplish the late president's goal of landing on the moon just nine years later.

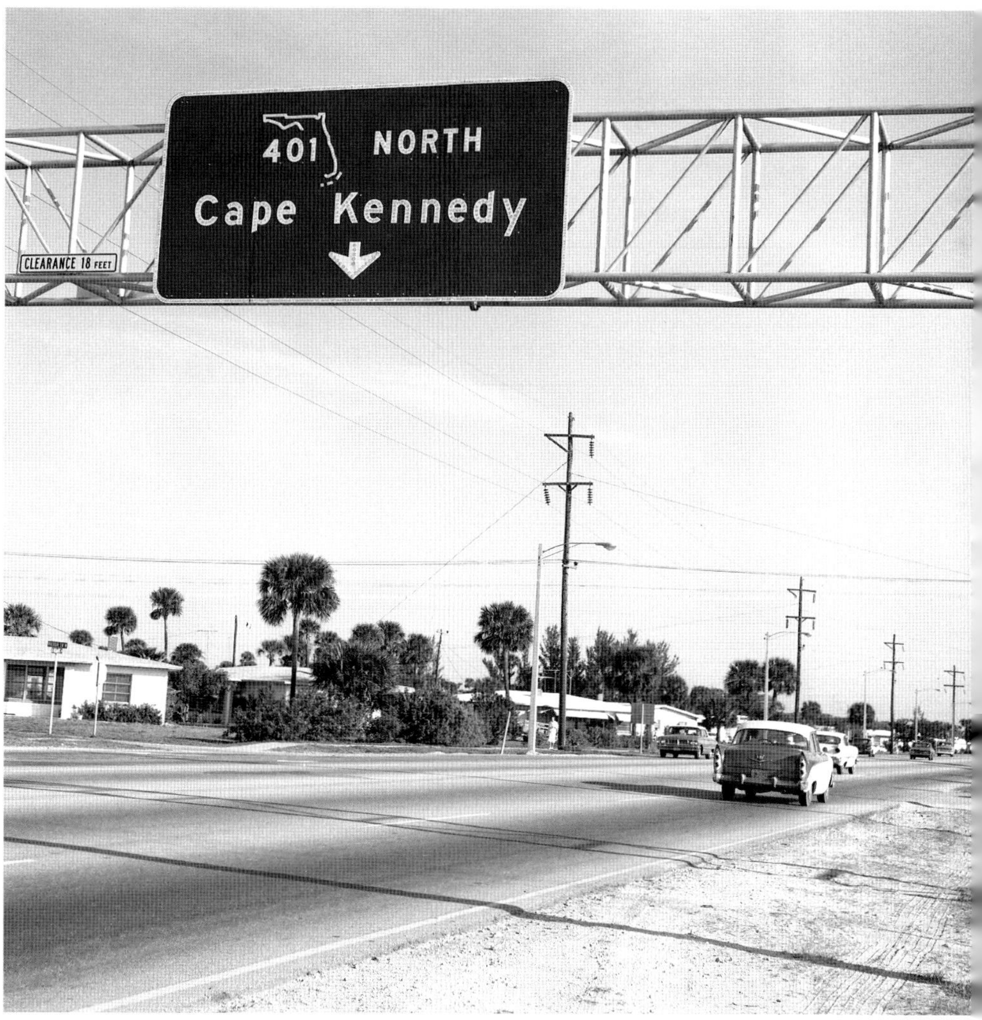

▶ A sign on North Atlantic Avenue in the city of Cape Canaveral points the way to Cape Kennedy in 1964.

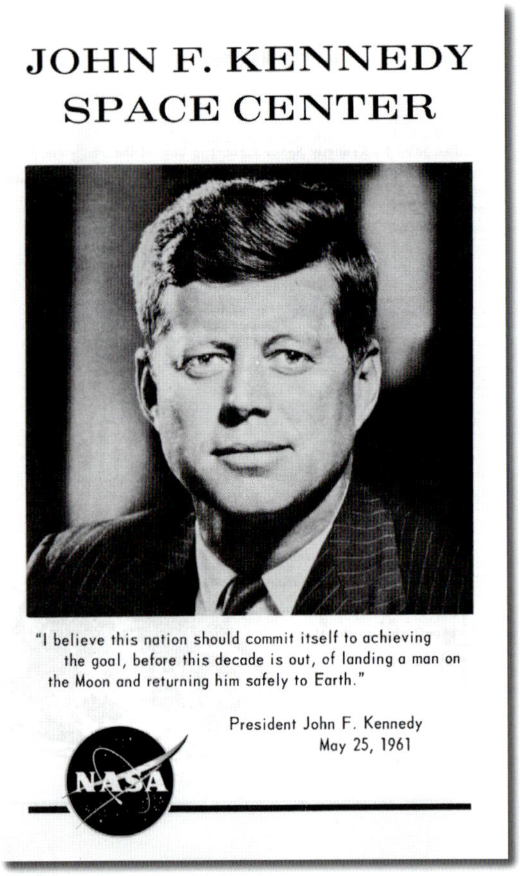

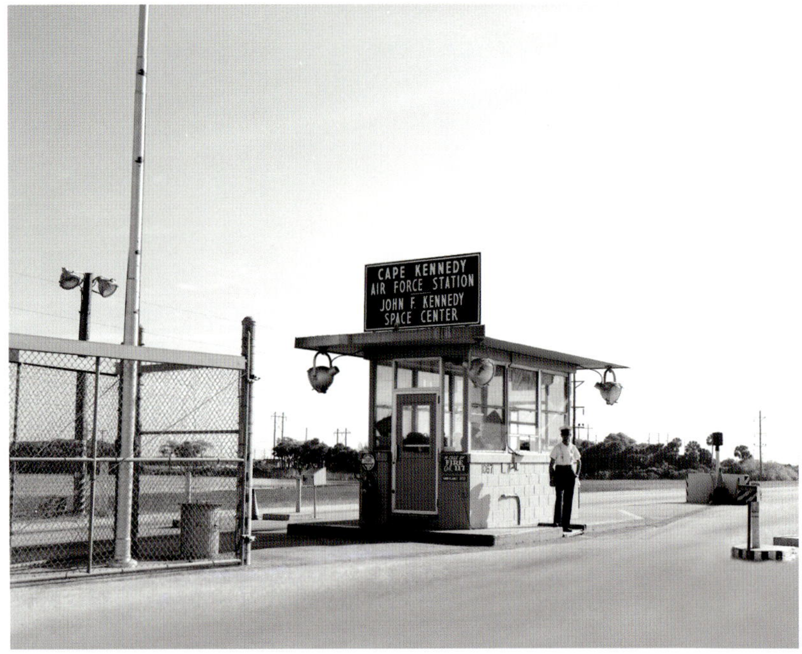

▲ The Gate 1 (south) entrance to the Air Force station on Florida State Road 401 in 1964.

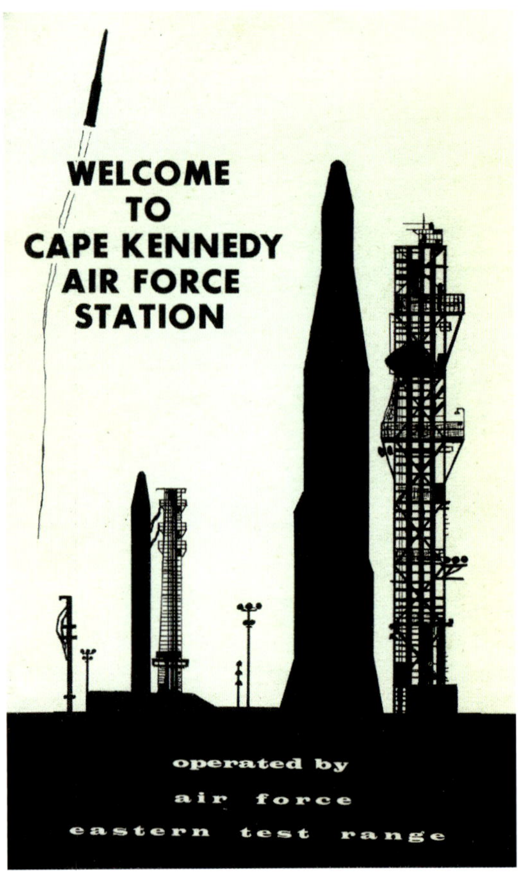

▲ Tour brochures from 1964.

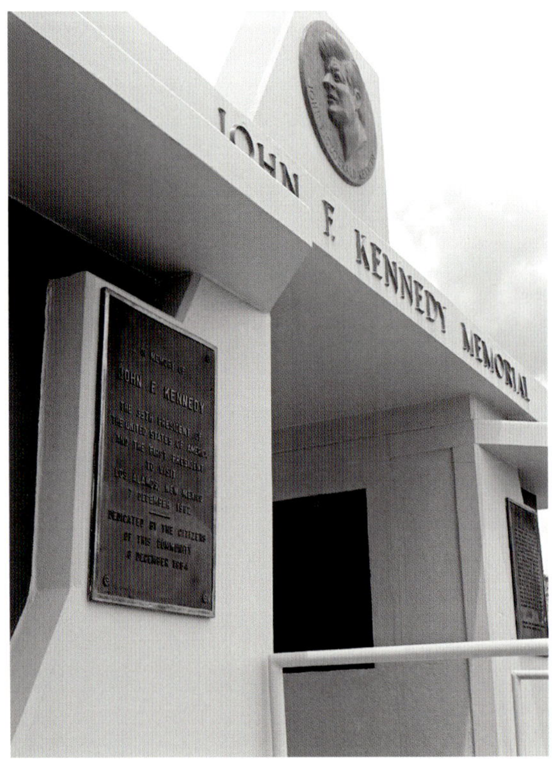

▲ In 1964, Los Alamos, New Mexico, citizens dedicate this memorial to Kennedy's visit just outside the Los Alamos High School football field, where he spoke in 1962.

This plaque marked the location of the president's lectern; the road in front of the building is renamed Kennedy Circle.

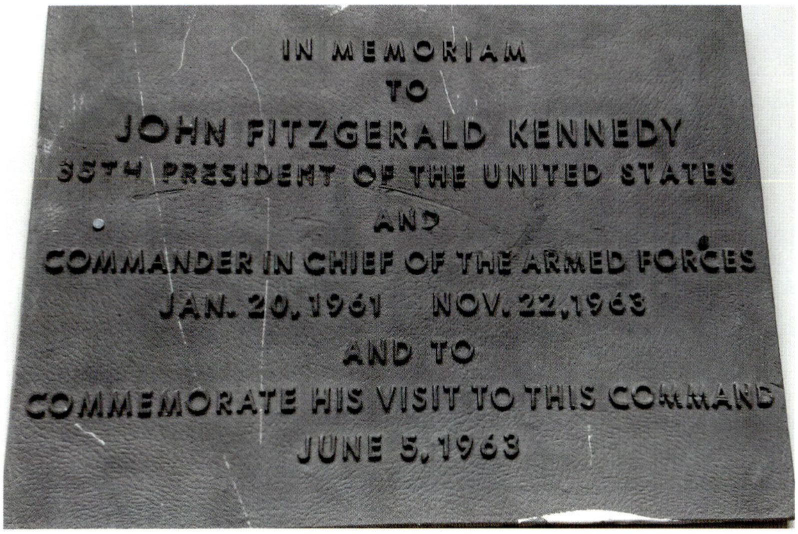

◀ Plaque at White Sands Missile Range, New Mexico.

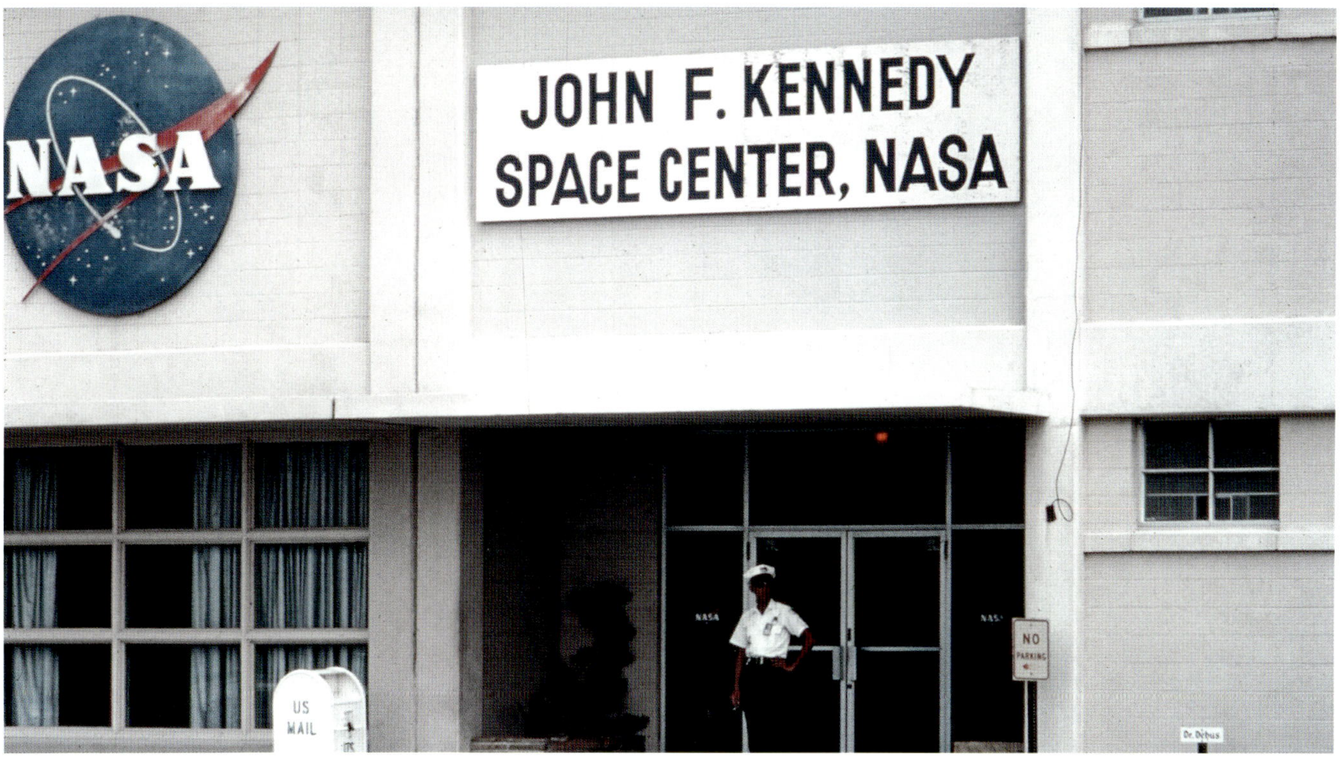

▲ KSC Headquarters, ca. 1964. (Courtesy of D. G. MacLean, *Entrance of the John F. Kennedy Space Center—Cape Canaveral, Florida.* Image no. PR19943, State Archives of Florida, Florida Memory.)

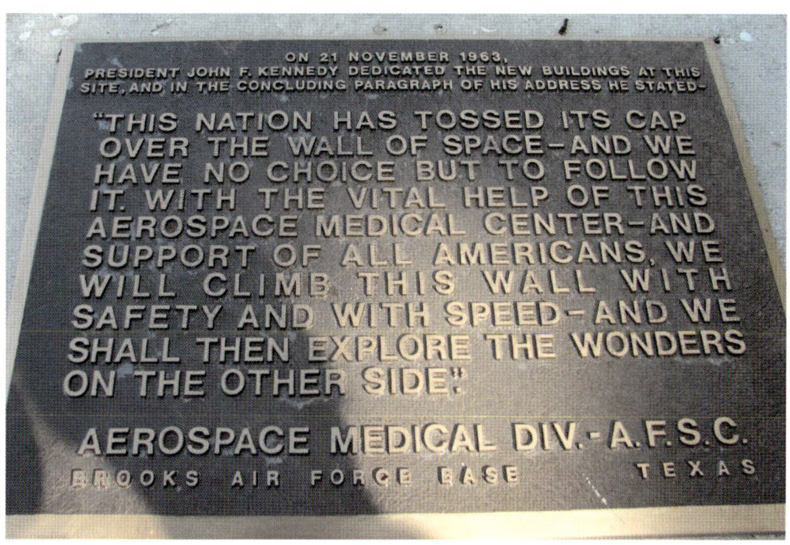

▶ Commemorative plaque at Brooks AFB in San Antonio.

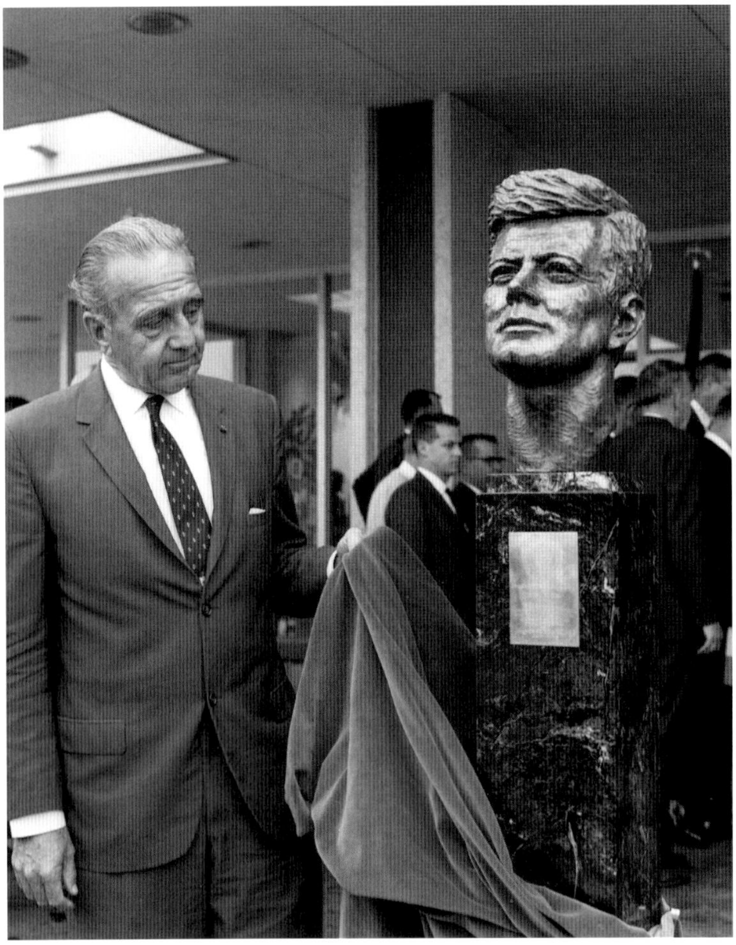

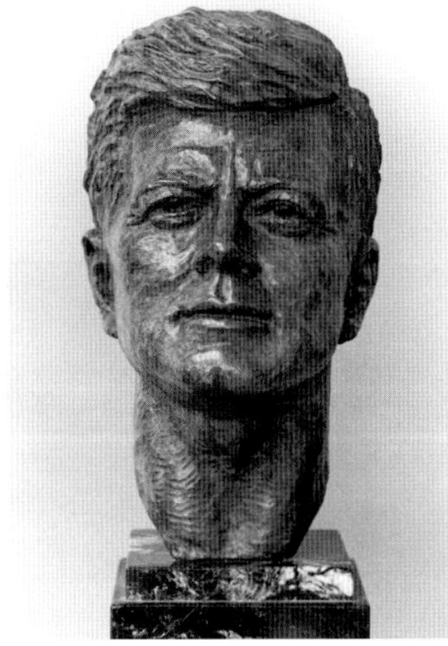

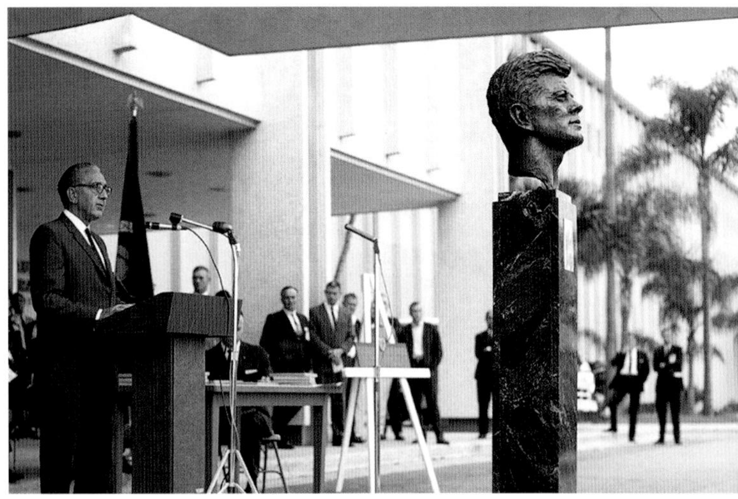

KSC Director Kurt Debus unveils a bronze bust of the late president outside the KSC Headquarters building on December 22, 1966. The bust is then moved inside to the first floor main elevator lobby.

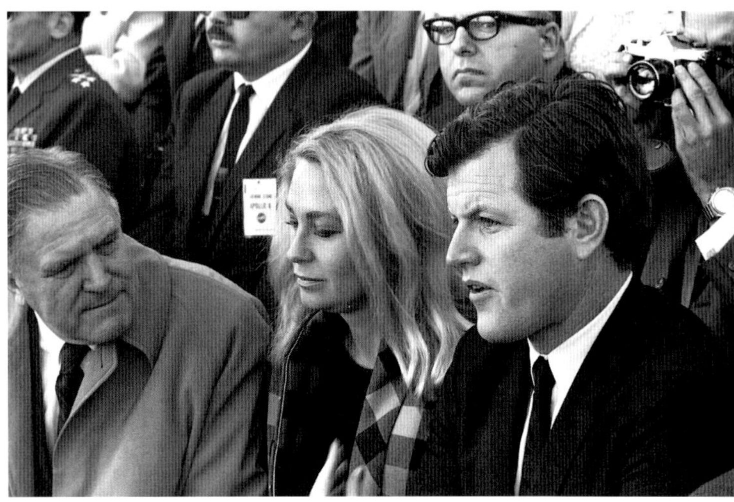

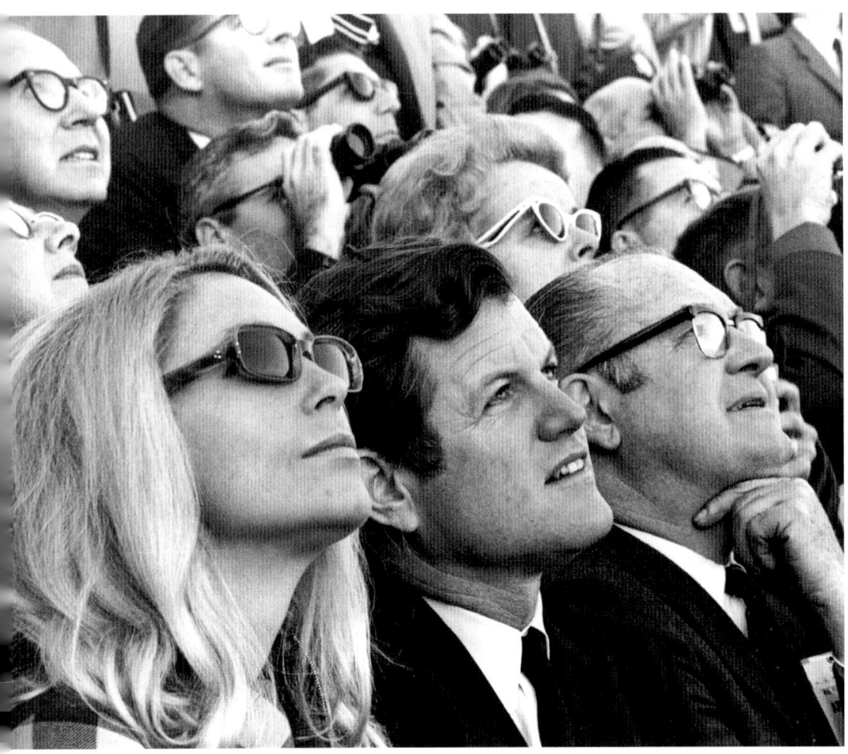

NASA's first two administrators flank the late president's brother, Sen. Edward Kennedy (D-Mass.), and his wife Joan at the launch of Apollo 8 on December 21, 1968, near the VAB at LC-39.

In the photo above, former NASA administrator Webb is on the left; in the photo at left, T. Keith Glennan, who served as administrator from 1958 to 1960, is on the right.

▶ In 1969, the Apollo 11 astronauts leave a small silicon disc on the moon, etched with statements from world leaders and four US presidents, including a quote from Kennedy's May 1961 address to Congress.

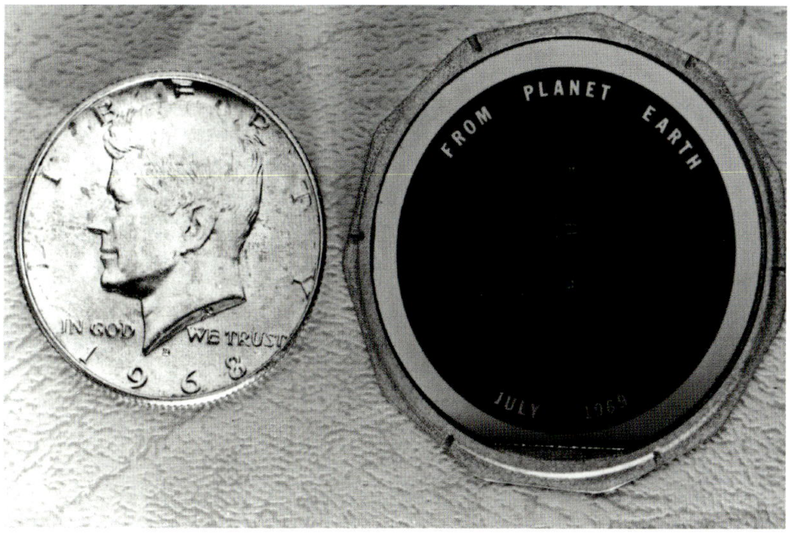

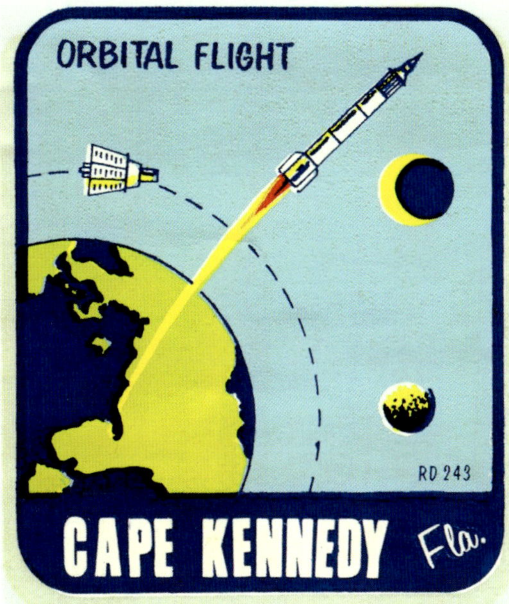

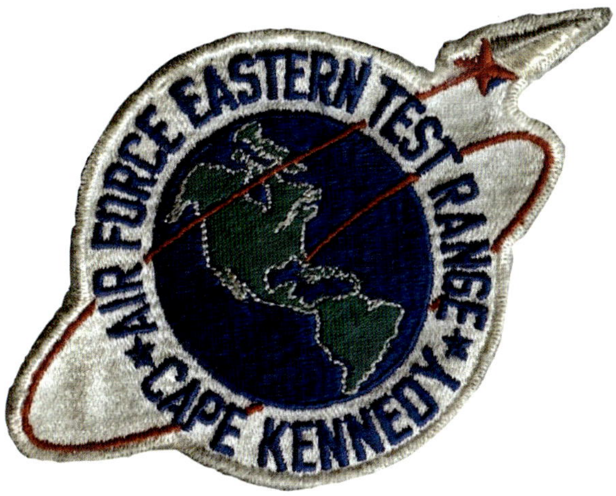

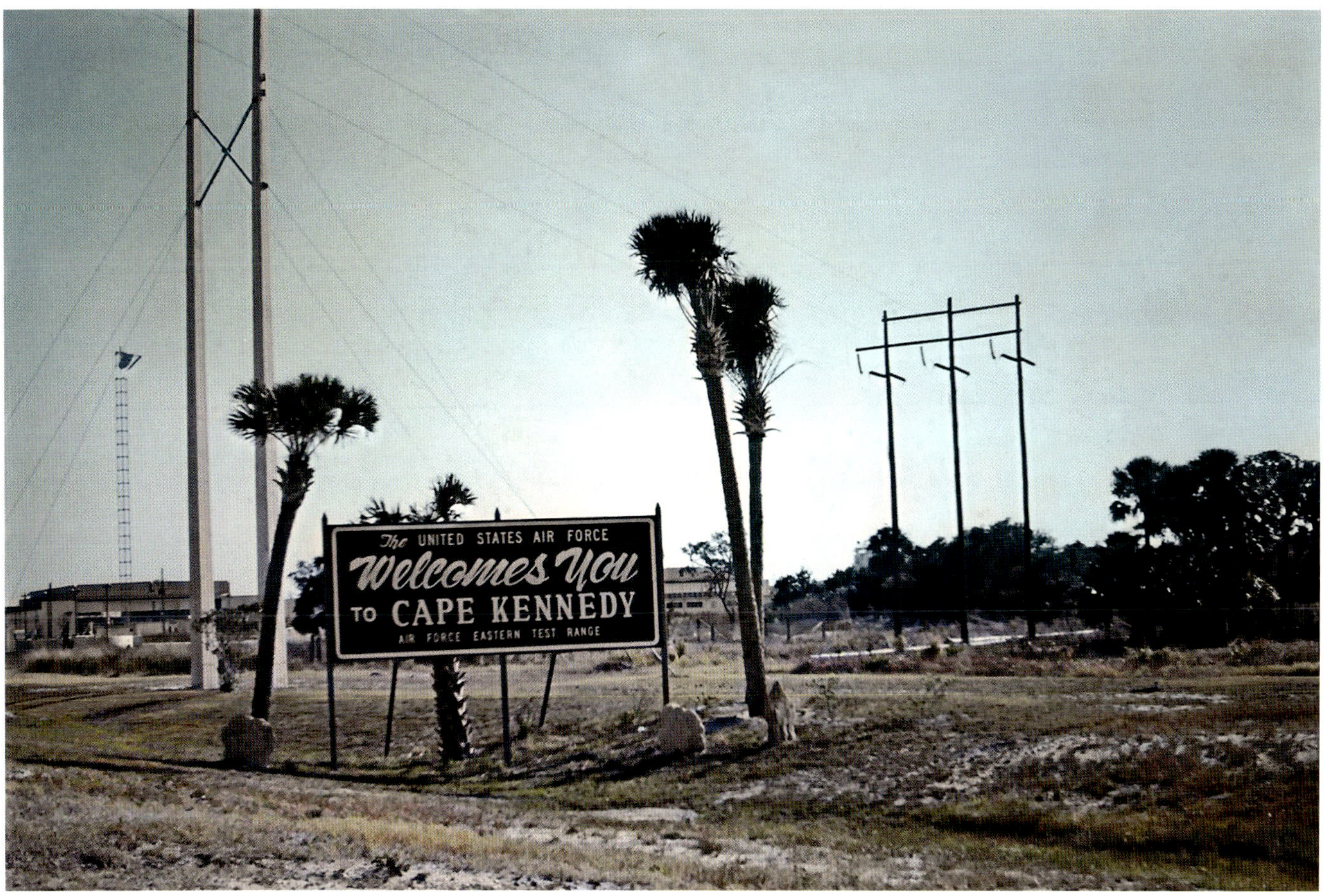

▶ The name change is shown in a variety of toys, records, pennants, games, ashtrays, and other items, reflecting the popularity of the late president and the excitement of the nation's launch center.

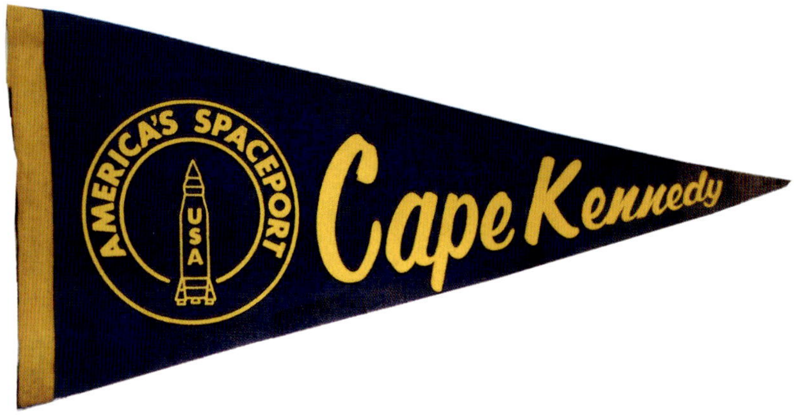

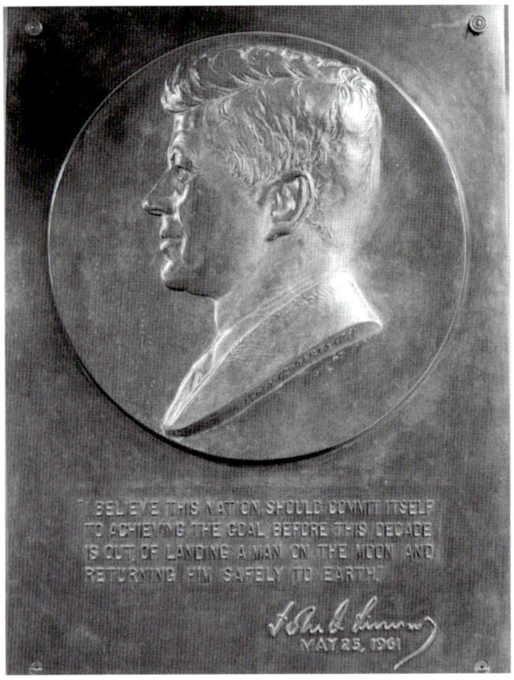

▲ A plaque at the KSC Visitor Complex.

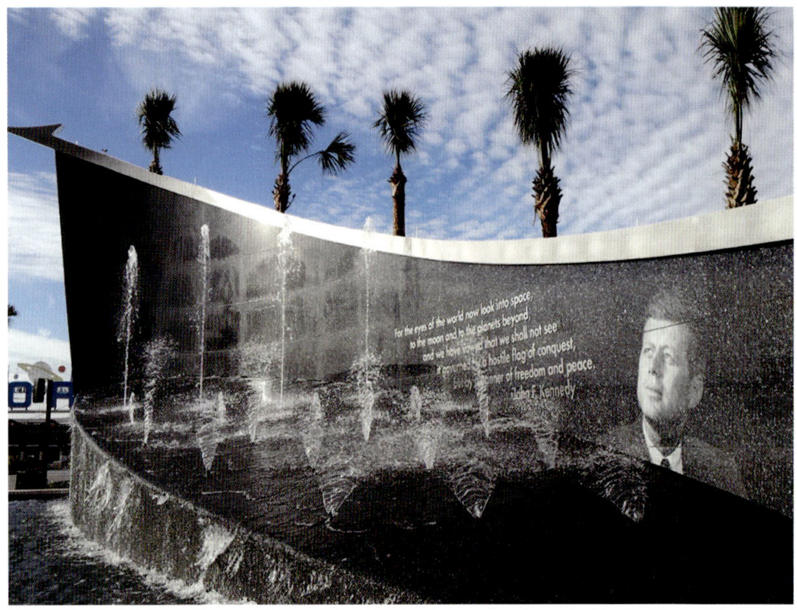

▲ In 2012, a seventy-five-foot-long granite wall and fountain are added to the main entrance plaza at the KSC Visitor Complex. The polished surface is laser etched with a portrait of Kennedy and a quote from his 1962 Rice University speech: "For the eyes of the world now look into space to the moon and to the planets beyond, and we have vowed that we shall not see it governed by a hostile flag of conquest, but by a banner of freedom and peace."

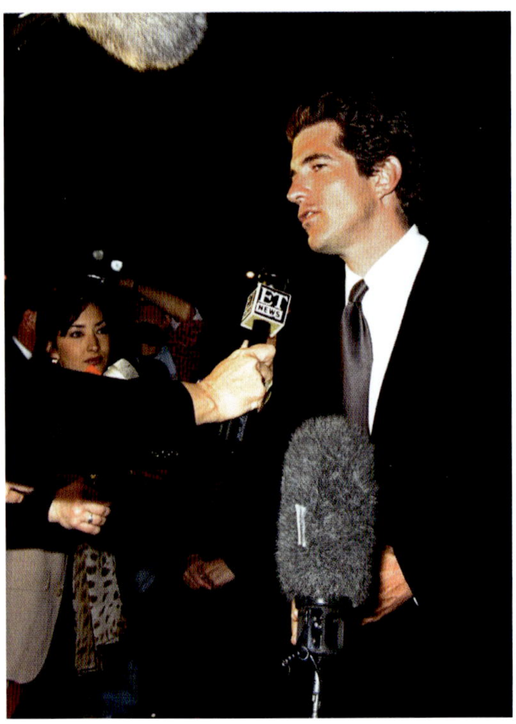

◀ John F. Kennedy Jr., editor-in-chief of *George* magazine, is among the speakers at the premier of an HBO miniseries, *From the Earth to the Moon*, at KSC on March 23, 1998. Kennedy will be at the controls when his private plane crashes into the Atlantic Ocean off Massachusetts in 1999 killing all onboard, with pilot error the probable cause.

THE PHOTOGRAPHERS

President Kennedy had the first official White House photographer, Cecil W. Stoughton. Born in Oskaloosa, Iowa, he enlisted in the Army before World War II and was assigned to a photographer training program. This included studying in New York under Alfred Eisenstadt and Margaret Bourke-White. Stoughton was next sent to Hollywood for training in motion picture photography with the First Motion Picture Unit. His commander, Ronald Reagan, later congratulated him on having beaten him to the White House. Stoughton served as combat photographer at Guadalcanal among other wartime assignments.

After the war, Stoughton was a photographer for the Army's Public Information Office. One of his photos was of the Army discharge of Elvis Presley in 1960. As a captain in the Army Signal Corps, he photographed Wernher von Braun.

On January 20, 1961, he was assigned to photograph President Kennedy's inauguration. His work so pleased the president that he was assigned to the White House full-time under the Office of the Military Aide to the President.

Stoughton's pictures of the Kennedys and their children helped shape the public's view of the First Family. He took more than eight thousand photos during thirty-four months, and as the only photographer aboard Air Force One immediately after the president's death, he took the iconic photo of Lyndon Johnson's swearing-in. He stayed with the Johnson administration until 1965. In 1967, after retiring from the Army as a major, Stoughton became the chief still photographer for the National Park Service. He died in 2008 at his home in Merritt Island, Florida, at age eighty-eight.

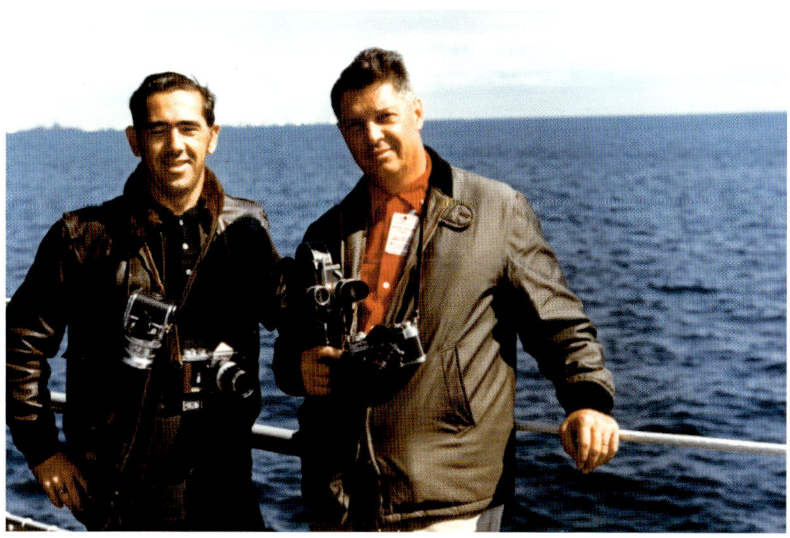

▲ White House photographers and Iowa natives Robert Knudsen (left) and Cecil Stoughton attend the fourth race of the 1962 America's Cup sailing yacht competition aboard USS Joseph P. Kennedy, Jr. off the coast of Newport, Rhodes Island, on September 22, 1962.

His colleague was Robert L. Knudsen, Navy chief photographer's mate, from 1946 until 1974 under the Office of the Naval Aide to the President. A native of Storm Lake, Iowa, he was first in his graduating class at the Naval Photographic School in Pensacola, Florida. Later that year he was transferred to Washington, DC, and assigned to the Office of the Secretary of the Navy.

Knudsen was detailed to the White House to provide photographs of President Truman's activities and then worked on the photography staff through the Nixon years. Among his most celebrated photos were pictures of President Kennedy's son, John Jr., in the Oval Office at eighteen months old. Most of the color photographs we selected from the John F. Kennedy Presidential Library are his, although both he and Stoughten almost always traveled with the president, and both men's work is represented in this book—with photos from the White House and from the field.

He photographed the president's autopsy in 1963, President Nixon's 1972 trips to China and the Soviet Union, his 1974 farewell in the wake of the Watergate scandal, and the White House weddings of presidential daughters Lynda and Luci Johnson and Tricia Nixon. Knudsen died in 1989 at age sixty-one in Bethesda, Maryland.

▼ President Kennedy with National Park Service (NPS) photographer Abbie Rowe outside the White House on May 3, 1962.

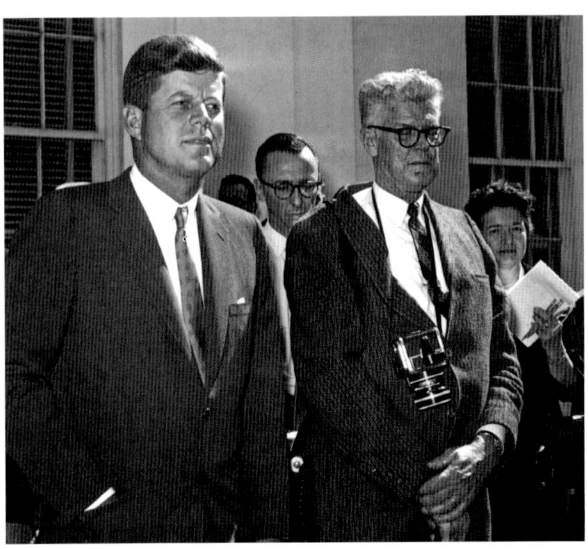

Abbie Rowe, born in Strasburg, Virginia, was hired in 1930 with the Bureau of Public Roads as a timekeeper on the Mount Vernon Memorial Highway project. When he photographed First Lady Eleanor Roosevelt riding on horseback along the highway in March 1938, she mentioned it in her newspaper column. Rowe's subsequent work at a waterfowl sanctuary led to his photographing birds, which so impressed the NPS that he became a photographer's apprentice.

As America entered World War II, the NPS assigned Rowe to provide photographic coverage of President Franklin Roosevelt's activities, particularly those away from the White House. Gradually, his duties were expanded to include documenting events inside the executive mansion as well. Rowe's work continued through the Johnson administrations prior to his death in 1967 at age sixty-one in Alexandria, Virginia. We used a number of his images showing activities in the Rose Garden and on the South Lawn.

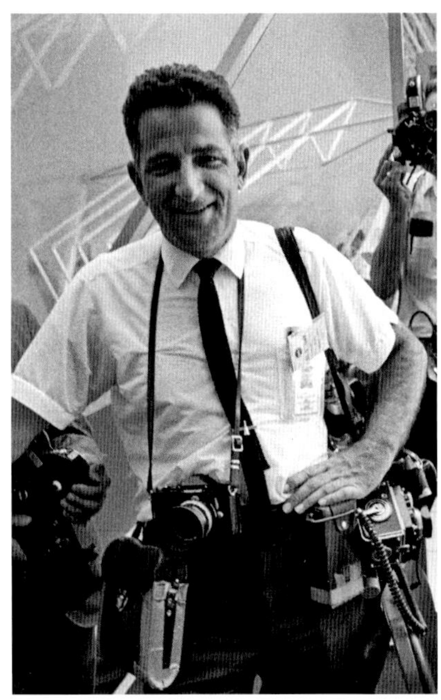

▶ We supplemented White House photos with images taken by a number of NASA photographers, but William P. "Bill" Taub, the agency's chief photographer at the time, took many of the pictures in this book involving the Mercury astronauts in the field. Born in Lorain, Ohio, he had worked at the National Advisory Committee for Aeronautics (NACA) before joining NASA in 1958, based in Washington, DC. From Mercury through the Apollo-Soyuz Test Program in 1975, he saw it all.

Taub, pictured here in 1971 at KSC, was also known for his tireless travel schedule that often required him to be at various NASA centers on short notice—a result of his talent and trust gained from agency officials. He died in Lanham, Maryland, in 2010 at age eighty-six.

BIBLIOGRAPHY

Baker, Deborah. "JFK: The Tragedy Still Resonates." *Albuquerque Journal*, November 17, 2013. https://www.abqjournal.com/302733/jfks-tragic-end-still-resonates-in-nm.html.

Benson, Charles D., and William Barnaby Faherty. *Moonport: A History of Apollo Launch Facilities and Operations*. Washington, DC: Scientific and Technical Information Office, NASA, 1978.

Bilstein, Roger E. *Stages to Saturn: A Technological History of the Apollo/Saturn Launch Vehicles*. Washington, DC: NASA History Office, 1980.

"Brooks Air Force Base, Building No. 160." Historic American Buildings Survey, HABS No. TX-3521-H. Santa Fe, NM: Southwest System Support Office. National Park Service, US Department of the Interior, 2003.

Brown, Harold. Interview by unidentified person. July 9, 1964. John F. Kennedy Presidential Library Oral History Collection. https://www.jfklibrary.org/Asset-Viewer/Archives/JFKOH-HAB-01.aspx.

Burd, Laurence. "Kennedy Hails Peace Gains." *Chicago Daily Tribune*, March 24, 1962, 1.

Campbell, Jack M. *Jack M. Campbell: The Autobiography of New Mexico's First Modern Governor*. Albuquerque: University of New Mexico Press, 2016.

Debus, Kurt. Interview by Walter D. Sohier and Eugene M. Emme. March 31, 1964. John F. Kennedy Presidential Library Oral History Collection, Boston, MA.

Duggan, Dan. "Duggan Recalls Kennedy Visit." *Hands across History* 5.1 (February 2009): 3, 6. Newsletter. White Sands, NM: White Sands Missile Range Historical Foundation and the White Sands Pioneer Group. http://www.wsmr-history.org/handsacrosshistory-02-09.pdf.

Finseth, J. L. "Rover Nuclear Rocket Engine Program: Overview of Rover Engine Tests Final Report." Huntsville, AL: Marshall Space Flight Center, Sverdrup Technology, 1991.

Geiger, Jeffrey E. *Camp Cooke and Vandenberg Air Force Base, 1941–1966: From Armor and Infantry Training to Space and Missile Launches*. Jefferson, NC: McFarland, 2014.

Gilruth, Robert R. Interview by Walter D. Sohier and James M. Grimwood. April 1, 1964. John F. Kennedy Presidential Library Oral History Collection, Boston, MA.

Glenn, John. Interview by Walter D. Sohier and Eugene M. Emme. June 12, 1964. John F. Kennedy Presidential Library Oral History Collection, Boston, MA.

Gore, Leada. "12 Things You Probably Didn't Know about John F. Kennedy's Visits to Redstone Arsenal" (blog). November 19, 2013; updated February 10, 2014. http://blog.al.com/breaking/2013/11/12_things_you_probably_didnt_k.html.

Greenwood, John T. *Space and Missile Systems Organization: A Chronology, 1954–1979*. Los Angeles AFB, CA: USAF Space Division, Chief of Staff, History Office, 1979.

Grimwood, James M. *Project Mercury: A Chronology*. Washington, DC: Office of Science and Technical Information, NASA, 1963.

Huddleston, Scott. "JFK Visit to S. A. Still Special to Many." *San Antonio Express-News*, November 20, 2013.

Kennedy, John F. Presidential Papers. July–November, 1963. President's Office Files. Departments and Agencies, Navy.

"Kennedy, Party Visit." *The Marshall Star*, September 12, 1962, 1. NASA weekly publication. Huntsville, AL: Public Information Office, MSFC.

"Kennedy Tour." Universal-International News, September 13, 1962. Newsreel.

Kolcum, Edward H. "Kennedy Stresses Peaceful Space Theme." *Aviation Week & Space Technology*, September 17, 1962, 27.

Kraft, Christopher C., with James L. Schefter. *Flight: My Life in Mission Control*. New York: Penguin Press, 2001.

La Follette, John P., and Joseph L. Dufour. "USAF Shielded Cab Vehicles Test and Evaluation." Kirtland AFB, NM: Development Directorate, Air Force Special Weapons Center, 1963. http://www.dtic.mil/dtic/tr/fulltext/u2/402748.pdf.

Logsdon, John M. *John F. Kennedy and the Race to the Moon*. New York: Palgrave Macmillan, 2010.

Low, George. Interview by Eugene M. Emme, Jay Holmes, and Addison M. Rothrock. May 1, 1964. John F. Kennedy Presidential Library Oral History Collection, Boston, MA.

Mack, Pamela E., ed. *From Engineering Science to Big Science—The NACA and NASA Collier Trophy Research Project Winners*. Washington, DC: Office of Policy and Plans, NASA History Office, 1998.

Martel, Claus. "Redstone Remembers President John F. Kennedy." *The Redstone Rocket*, Nov. 20, 2013. http://www.theredstonerocket.com/people_profile/article_a47a3428-51f3-11e3-baf5-001a4bcf887a.html.

Mathis, Don. "Countdown to Eternity: JFK's Last Good Day Spent in San Antonio." *San Antonio Rivard Report*, November 10, 2013. https://therivardreport.com/countdown-to-eternity-jfks-last-good-day-spent-in-san-antonio/.

McVicar, Jim. "President Kennedy Views Flawless White Sands Missile Shots." *El Paso Times*, June 6, 1963.

Minow, Newton. "Miracles in Space." *Chicago Tribune*, opinion page, July 23, 2013.

Morse, Mary Louise, and Jean Kemahan Bays. *The Apollo Spacecraft: A Chronology*, vol. 2. Washington, DC: NASA, 1973.

Mudd, Roger. *The Place to Be: Washington, CBS, and the Glory Days of Television News*. Philadelphia, PA: Perseus Books Group, 2009.

Navy Polaris Team. *November 16, 1963*. Booklet. Washington, DC: GPO: 1963. O-715–272.

Nuclear Rocket Development Station. Nevada National Security Site History. US Department of Energy, National Nuclear Security Administration, Nevada Field Office, August 2013 (Rev. 2).

O'Donnell, Kenneth P., and Dave Powers, with Joe McCarthy. *Johnny, We Hardly Knew Ye: Memories of John Fitzgerald Kennedy*. New York: Little, Brown, 1972.

Preble, C. A. "Who Ever Believed in the 'Missile Gap'?: John F. Kennedy and the Politics of National Security." *Presidential Studies Quarterly* 33 (2003): 801–26. doi:10.1046/j.0360-4918.2003.00085.x

Presidential Visit June 5, 1963 (M. F. 45 9524). Film. US Army Post Signal Division Pictorial Branch, New York, 1963.

"President Kennedy Presents Collier Trophy to Astronauts at White House, Washington, D.C., 10 October 1963." US Air Force. 1 film reel (color, silent, 35 mm, 819 feet, 9 minutes). John F. Kennedy Presidential Library and Museum. Digital identifier: USG-03-21. https://www.jfklibrary.org/Asset-Viewer/Archives/USG-03-21.aspx

"President Kennedy Presents Harmon Trophy to X-15 Pilots at Ceremony in Washington, D.C., 28 November 1961." Film (color, silent, 35mm, unedited, 566 feet). USAF Depository Basic: 35mm color original negative, USAF 31888, reels 1 and 2.

"President Sees an Atlas Firing." *New York Times*, March 24, 1962, 11.

Rosholt, Robert. *An Administrative History of NASA, 1958–1963*. Washington, DC: Scientific and Technical Information Office, NASA, 1966.

Seamans, Robert C., Jr. *Project Apollo: The Tough Decisions*. NASA's Monographs of Aerospace History No. 37 (SP-2005-4537). Washington, DC: NASA, 2007.

Shepard, Alan, and Deke Slayton, with Jay Barbree. *Moon Shot: The Inside Story of America's Apollo Moon Landings*. New York: Open Road Media, 2011.

Shepard, Alan B., Jr. Interview by Walter D. Sohier. June 12, 1964. John F. Kennedy Presidential Library Oral History Collection, Boston, MA.

Sidey, Hugh. "How the News Hit Washington." *LIFE*, April 21, 1961, 26.

Swanson, Glen E., ed. *Before This Decade Is Out: Personal Reflections on the Apollo Program*. Washington, DC: NASA History Series, NASA History Office, Office of Policy and Plans, 1999.

Swenson, Loyd S., James M. Grimwood, and Charles C. Alexander. *This New Ocean: A History of Project Mercury*. Washington, DC: NASA History Office, Office of Policy and Plans, 1966.

Talese, Gay. "Glenn Family Calm amid Cheers and Confetti." *New York Times*, February 24, 1962, 13.

Teague, Olin E. Letter to NASA Historian Eugene Emme. January 24, 1979. National Historical Records Collection, Folder 012499.

TRW Space Log: 1957–1982. Vol. 19. Edited by Madeline W. Sherman. Redondo Beach, CA: TRW, 1983.

"TV and Radio Coverage Planned for Reception to Glenn Today." *New York Times*, February 23, 1962, 12.

Von Braun, Wernher. Interview by Walter D. Sohier and Eugene M. Emme. March 31, 1964. John F. Kennedy Presidential Library Oral History Collection, Boston, MA.

Ward, Bob. *Dr. Space: The Life of Wernher von Braun*. Annapolis, MD: Naval Institute Press, 2005.

Webb, James E. Interview by unidentified person. April 29, 1969. Oral History Collection, Lyndon B. Johnson Presidential Library, Austin, TX.

Wells, Helen T., Susan H. Whiteley, and Carrie E. Karegeannes. *Origins of NASA Names*. Washington, DC: Scientific and Technical Information Office, NASA, 1976.

White, Theodore H. Personal Papers. THWPP-059–009. John F. Kennedy Presidential Library and Museum, Boston, MA.

White House Office of Appointments and Scheduling, The President's Daily Diary. John F. Kennedy Presidential Library and Museum, Boston, MA.

Wicker, Tom. "Glenn Gives Kennedy Account of His Most Anxious Moments." *New York Times*, February 24, 1962, 12.

Wiesner, Jerome B., The White House, Memorandum for Dr. Bundy. "Some Aspects of Project Mercury." March 9, 1961. Folder 18674, NASA Historical Reference Collection, NASA History Division, NASA Headquarters, Washington, DC.